10-
22-62
2- weeks lectre Eng tel.
3- who   "   "   Psyc.

Psychology

APPLIED TO

Life and Work

Psychology

APPLIED TO

Life and Work

Third Edition

Harry Walker Hepner

Professor of Psychology, Syracuse University

Management Consultant

Director of the National Panel of Consumer Opinion and the Onondaga
Consumer Research Panel—Division of Batten, Barton, Durstine & Osborn,
Inc.

Formerly in Charge of Personnel Research for
The Goodyear Tire & Rubber Company
The Philadelphia Company & Affiliated Corporations
Kaufmann's Department Store, Pittsburgh

PRENTICE-HALL, INC.

Englewood Cliffs, New Jersey

FIRST EDITION

First Printing	September 1941
Second Printing	March 1942
Third Printing	May 1942
Fourth Printing	January 1943
Fifth Printing	June 1944
Sixth Printing	February 1945
Seventh Printing	November 1945
Eighth Printing	May 1946
Ninth Printing	July 1946
Tenth Printing	January 1947
Eleventh Printing	May 1947
Twelfth Printing	September 1947
Thirteenth Printing	June 1948
Fourteenth Printing	September 1948
Fifteenth Printing	January 1949
Sixteenth Printing	July 1949
Seventeenth Printing	November 1949

SECOND EDITION

First Printing	May 1950
Second Printing	December 1950
Third Printing	June 1952
Fourth Printing	October 1953
Fifth Printing	December 1954
Sixth Printing	May 1956
Seventh Printing	January 1957

THIRD EDITION

First Printing	April 1957
Second Printing	July 1958
Third Printing	September 1959
Fourth Printing	September 1960
Fifth Printing	June 1961

LIBRARY OF CONGRESS CATALOG CARD NO.: 57–8790

PRINTED IN THE UNITED STATES OF AMERICA

73348 – C

Preface

We have now reached the stage in the development of the applications of psychology in industry where psychologists are working with men of industry and corporation psychologists are working with university psychologists. Psychology as a science that is being helpfully applied in modern life and work is stressed in the present treatment as in its predecessors, but the new subject-matter—group dynamics, communications, automation, and motivation research—especially benefits from this interfunctioning of those in industry and those who wear the academic robe. For example, the growing importance of psychological consultants has been given greater attention as they have earned professional recognition and as their role has become more important to the intended reader.

As the basic framework for the reader's thinking about the dynamics of the individual's behavior, the adjustment concept is still central; it is the "binding thread of theory" running through the work, albeit with interruptions, in a strong enough pattern, it is hoped, to provide integral unity rather than that fortuitous structure provided only by a book's covers. Recommendations arising from the widespread use of the second edition as a text have been liberally and gratefully incorporated in the revision.

The second concern, still manifest in this treatment, is the conviction that the reader should be offered help in dealing with his own personal problems and in becoming more effective in his social relations with others. Many a reader will not have opportunity to extend his formal acquaintance with psychology beyond the scope of this book, and I have therefore tried to present those psychological principles that are fundamental and significant in life and work. The reader should finish with a basis for better insight into psycho-dynamics as he lives and works with people. He will also have some foundation for a social philosophy that applies to our changing order, and so will be able to function more effectively in a position of industrial leadership.

Of course, a text such as this covers so wide a variety of topics that the reader should not imagine that he has been given final or conclusive information. Rather, he should feel that the present treatment of topics has opened the way toward further exploration on his own initiative.

No man can produce a text such as this on his own effort only. One of the functions of an author is that of obtaining from other teachers and researchers the fruits of their work and presenting them to students. Accordingly, I wrote to several hundred psychologists and asked them to be so considerate of the needs of students as to send me descriptions of any of their own or other studies which they might deem appropriate. Some of them were most generous in supplying suitable materials. When the contributed or suggested materials fitted into the established framework of the text, they were included. Students will gain benefit from these contributions. I am deeply grateful to these contributors.

Specific individuals to whom I am indebted in the preparation of the manuscript are Annette Klein Smith who abstracted hundreds of published articles in order that I might select the findings that update the book. Delia Anne Denslow and Gladys Kennedy typed and edited the manuscript. Additional acknowledgements for quotations are presented in appropriate manner.

HARRY WALKER HEPNER

Contents

---

* Special graphic or pictorial features are shown in heavy capital letters in the Contents.

26.   (*continued*)

SACRED OR SCARED? 517.   Will the mobility of labor continue to improve? 518.   SOCIAL AND POLITICAL TRENDS, 520.   The significance of the right to own property, 520.   Ideological conflict between democracy and totalitarianism, 520.   Why some persons turn to a totalitarian system, 521.   Frustration-motivated behavior in social revolution, 522.   Propaganda as a factor in individual insecurity, 523.   Are we entering a new era? 526.   Suggestions for the person who wants to be aware of the trends of our time, 527.   Security comes from within, not from without, 528.   **POSSIBLE ADJUSTMENTS TO OUR CHANGING ORDER,** 530–531.   Suggestions for the leader in industry, 530.

PART FIVE   *The Consumer*

27.   Markets: Psychological Factors
        and Techniques of Studying Consumers   534

Those who distribute goods work in the dynamic area of ideas, 535.   Identifying the market, 537.   METHODS OF OBTAINING CONSUMER RESEARCH DATA, 541.   The free-association or "open-end interview" approach to the consumer, 541.   The mailed questionnaire, 542.   Phrasing the questions, 544.   The personal interview as a source of consumer research data, 546.   MOTIVATION RESEARCH IN MARKETING, 547.   Need for motivation analysis, 548.   The depth interview, 550.   The special contribution of motivation research, 553.   Good consumer research is creative, 553.

28.   Advertising: The Appeal and Its Use;
        Measuring the Effectiveness of the Advertisement   557

THE APPEAL, 557.   How the appeal affects the reader, 558.   Appeals that have been found effective, 561.   THE USE OF THE APPEAL IN AN ADVERTISEMENT, 563.   The format or kind of advertisement, 563.   The illustration, 565.   Copy, 566.   MEASURING THE EFFECTIVENESS OF AN ADVERTISEMENT, 569.   The consumer jury or panel ratings, 570.   Prompted-recognition surveys of readership, 571.   Predicting effectiveness of advertisements previous to extensive use, 571.   **ONE SITUATIONAL TECHNIQUE,** 572.   Split-run tests, 572.   **WHICH AD PULLED THE BETTER?** 573.   Measurements of television and radio advertising, 574.   **COMPARATIVE PROVED NAME REGISTRATION,** 576–577.   Television commercials can be pretested, 578.   Gallup and Robinson, Inc., impact technique, 578.   Bodily reactions as indicators of responsiveness to advertisements, 579.

Psychology

APPLIED TO

Life and Work

"I like to study people" is a very common expression. Those who say it are apt to refer to unusual personalities. Furthermore, their interest in people is likely to be merely the entertainment variety. Actually, all people, including the everyday varieties of normal people, are interesting, too, but they should be given systematic study as in a course in psychology.

CHAPTER ONE

Reasons for studying psychology

People study psychology for various reasons. A few want to appreciate its influence in the big affairs of historical significance, but most people study it as an aid in dealing with their own problems of life and work. This chapter reviews some of these personal problems and indicates how psychologists deal with them.

We all like to study people. Psychology is surely among the most useful of all our sciences. Its importance is constantly impressed upon us by the delightful and the not-so-delightful behavior of our associates as well as of ourselves. Examples of pyschological influences are as numerous as people—ourselves, our friends, our work associates, and our leaders. Every human being, no matter how low or high his position on whatever scale of values we choose, is a living example of the subject-matter of psychology.

Somehow many people seem to think that psychology is more or less limited to the study of odd or atypical persons, such as the feebleminded, the neurotic, the insane, the genius, the problem child, or other deviates. They fail to appreciate that the so-called ordinary individual, the member of the great majority, is just as interesting as the most unusual personality. Furthermore, they are apt to assume that the outstanding leaders in business, political, and other affairs are motivated by logical, not by psychological, influences.

Actually, the leader is just as good (or poor) a subject for study as anyone else. Sometimes he deserves special study on our part because his behavior is likely to have wider effects on more people than that of the non-leader.

Recent events in world affairs have revealed to us some marked differences in the mental maturity and balance of leaders. The members of this generation are gradually learning about the close relation between the psychological characteristics of individual leaders and some effects those characteristics have on everyday human affairs. Many of us are beginning to realize that a leader may be so immature psychologically that he seeks to satisfy himself at the expense of other people, or he may be so mature as to promote the satisfactions of his people in such a way as to foster their personality development. Whenever we study the many historical influ-

3

ences in the shifting boundaries on maps of the world, we note how, in some instances, millions of lives have been affected by the impulsions of some maladjusted dictator to satisfy his complexes and those of his blind followers. The study of psychology shows us how we, as individuals, as well as our leaders, at times cling to immature and unintelligent patterns of behavior.

When a person trained in psychology listens to a business executive, labor union official, politician, preacher, or reformer, he says to himself: "Has this man analyzed the conditions of which he speaks and come to a sound objective solution, or is he merely giving vent to the impulsions or perhaps even the venom of his own mind?" The dictators and the tyrants in all human affairs, whether of nation, corporation, school, or home, will continue to blight the lives of others until people learn enough applied psychology to recognize the personality differences between tyrants and statesmen, between bosses and leaders, between schoolmasters and educators, and between neurotic females and well-adjusted women.

Most thinking persons look out upon a sorely troubled world. The problems of international relations are baffling, and the influences of leaders in international affairs are often discouraging. Furthermore, we can do little or nothing about many of the most discouraging problems at home or beyond our own shores. Even with the best of psychological training, we could not teach the people of a foreign nation to choose or direct their leaders more intelligently. However, through the aid of psychological insight, we, in our own nation and niche in life, can often interpret the most hopeless of situations; and this ability to interpret the mental factors helps to lift us to a more intelligent plane of living.

The ability to recognize psychological currents everywhere and to interpret them intelligently is a most desirable accomplishment. Young people, particularly those who seek to train themselves for the positions of leadership of today, want to see more clearly the human problems in our time. The complexities of our industrial civilization call for a wisdom which the members of this generation have not as yet fully attained. The psychological problems around us, in this country and in our own places, require the aid of all that psychological research can contribute. A review of some of these problems may stimulate us to study the helpful findings of psychological workers.

Outstanding problems that are partly of a psychological nature

One important kind of psychological problem arises from the fact that our magnificent industrial and technical development has not resulted in equally magnificent emotional satisfactions for many of our citizens. Engineers, scientists, and inventors have produced a technological age which is truly marvelous, but which has not always satisfied the hearts and minds of the men who operate its machines, nor of the customers who benefit from its products. We are like children playing with powerful but somewhat dangerous toys.

Economic insecurity, whether caused by political or other conditions, certainly has an important bearing on emotional insecurity. We must also recognize, however, that economic security does not imply emotional security.[1] Many persons with high incomes feel insecure because of psychological problems that wealth does not solve. Furthermore, unemployment is not entirely an economic problem; many unemployed people have a psychological immaturity which would cause them to be unemployed in any economic system.

The state of mind of any individual is often more important to him than his relationship to the state of the nation or the international situation. When a person no longer believes that individual ability determines individual success, he is apt to look to some stronger person or to some political system which promises to play the role of all-providing father.

When people lose faith in themselves and their ability to cope with life's problems, they are likely to turn to an untried system of government or leadership or to "escape" from the intolerable situation, as is exemplified by many of the 50,000 drug addicts in this country.[2] Or certain mental ailments may develop, as found among approximately 750,000 psychiatric patients in hospitals at the end of a recent year.

Problems of students who were not having academic difficulties

When we ask people about their own psychological problems, we find that almost all appear to be living with bothersome worries.

One of the best studies of personal problems of special interest to college students was made of 259 healthy, "normal" students, sophomores at Harvard from the classes entering in 1937–8–9–40. The problems reported were either raised by the students themselves or were recognized by the investigating staff. These students were selected for good health, satisfactory academic status, and overtly good social adjustment. They participated voluntarily in the research. With regard to such factors as socio-economic status and race or creed, these students were representative of a fair cross section of the college population. The investigations consisted of the coöperative observations of a physician, several psychiatrists, a physiologist, an anthropologist, a psychologist, and a social case-worker (who interviewed practically all the families as well as the young men themselves).

. . . In the first place, the students were made to feel that they were helping in the investigation by talking about themselves or asking questions, and that they were not encroaching on anyone's time. In the second place, each participant knew that he would be put through

certain routine examinations by different observers: the medical examination, the anthropological measurements, the psychometric tests, the psychiatric interviews, etc. In this way he became aware of different fields in the study of man, and his interest in his personal characteristics was aroused. We could observe a certain educational advantage in the system. Thirdly, he could voluntarily choose any one of the various examiners to discuss matters of concern to him.[3]

The report of the investigators omitted aspects of a boy's life which occurred before college or during postgraduate years and purely medical or other technical aspects that would not be in the sphere of a counselor. Problems resulting from military service, or that could be solved without too much trouble by the person concerned, were also omitted. Ninety per cent, 232 students, had problems they wanted to talk over. See Table 1–1. Twenty-seven men (10 per cent) seemingly had none.

The kinds of problems varied greatly according to individual situations. Most of them centered around social or family relationships. Many men revealed multiple interconnected problems, such as personality difficulties, adjustment to family and friends, college finances, and career. Others revealed only isolated problems in a setting of very sound personality.

The authors pointed out that in an unselected group of college students, more problems would be likely to occur than did in this study, as the selection of students eliminated obvious cases of poor adjustment.

Problems of students who were experiencing academic difficulties

The "Problem Check List (The College Form)," by Ross L. Mooney,[4] is probably the most widely used formal method of surveying students' problems. It lists 330 items that represent problems common to students. Students underline those that apply to them, and encircle the underlined

TABLE 1-1

KINDS OF PROBLEMS RAISED

(including both self-offered problems and those recognized by the Staff)

	Number of 259 Participants
1. *Social adjustment* (shyness, feelings of inferiority, social sensitivity, making friends, meeting and getting along with girls, immaturity *per se,* roommates, class dissatisfactions)	113
2. *Adjustments to family*	
a. Parental discord, separation, divorce, remarriage	14
b. Antagonism to parents, reaction to domination or discipline, family criticism, lack of understanding, family relations in general	69
c. Advice concerning physical or mental health of parent	18
d. Adjustment to death of parent	6
3. *Career and life work*	67
4. *Finances in college*	35
5. *Need for discussions centering around subject's personality*	
a. Emotional instability, tenseness, excitability, fears and concerns, "psychoneurotic" symptoms	50
b. Discussions of personality in general, integration of personality, handling of arrogance and egotism	47
c. Need for directions, objectives, purpose, and values	32
d. Mood swings	21
e. Rigidity, "just-so" personality	12
f. Possible mental illness	6
6. *Academic*	
a. Adjustment to Harvard, dissatisfactions with Harvard	20
b. Academic help needed, organization of time and work	14
c. Intellectual lacks for college or career	6
d. Field of concentration (majoring)	3
7. *Sex*	
a. Marriage, love affairs, sex relations	39
b. Problems arising from masturbation	17
c. Need for information concerning homosexuality	3
d. Information about venereal disease	2
8. *Others*	
a. Anti-Semitism, anti-Nazism	8
b. Religious conflict, search for religious belief	8
c. Alcohol	7
d. College scrapes	6
e. General advice needed	6
f. Help in getting job	5
g. Stammering, speech	4
h. Insomnia	3
i. Handwriting	2
j. Extracurricular activities	2
k. Revolt against New England	2
l. Extreme wealth	1

From Clark W. Heath and Lewise W. Gregory, "Problems of Normal College Students and Their Families," *School and Society,* Vol. 63 (1946), pp. 355–358.

problems that are especially troublesome. Students mark an average of 30 problems, but the range is from one to 106.

Items that were indicated as problems by 17 per cent or more of 430 Ohio State University students, tending to be selected for their academic difficulties, are shown in Table 1–2.

Short-term changes in student problems

The "Problem Check List (The College Form)," by Ross L. Mooney, also was given twice to a group of freshmen at Colorado State College of Education, in October and December of the same year (Table 1–3, 4).[5] The number of students who filled in the list both times was 190, and this study is based on the data furnished by those students.

Four items were checked by at least 25 per cent of the students both times

	Per Cent
Wanting a more pleasing personality	31
Worried by examinations	29
Slow in mathematics	26
Don't know how to study effectively	25

Classes had started only ten days before the October administration of the test, but the first quarter was nearing an end when it was administered again in December. In

TABLE 1-2

LISTINGS OF ITEMS MARKED BY SEVENTEEN PER CENT OR MORE OF THE CASES ARRANGED IN RANK ORDER

Per cent of Cases	*Items Marked*	*Per cent of Cases*	*Items Marked*
40	Getting low grades	22	Nervousness
38	Getting enough sleep	21	Failing to get ahead
37	Finding time for independent reading	21	In too few student activities
36	Tendency to worry	21	Inability to express self in words
	(All items above this line checked by *one-third* or more)	21	Poor memory for detail
31	Moodiness, having the "blues"	20	Tiring very easily
31	Concentrating	20	Too easily discouraged
30	Vocabulary too limited	20	Slow in mathematics
29	Finding where I belong in the world		(All items above this line checked by *one-fifth* or more)
27	Taking things too seriously	19	Inability to take good class notes
27	Fearing failure in college	18	Too little time for recreation
27	Slow in reading	18	Forgetfulness
27	Inefficient methods of study	18	Clarifying what I really want
26	Worry about examinations	18	Inferiority
25	Weak in spelling, grammar, punctuation	18	Needing to know my vocational strengths and weaknesses
	(All items above this line checked by *one-fourth* or more)	18	Sacrifices of parents
23	Getting a decent job after graduation	17	Forgetting past mistakes
22	Speaking up in class	17	Carrying on a conversation
22	Acquiring a more pleasing personality	17	Wanting security
		17	Feelings too easily hurt
		17	Inadequate high-school training
			(All items above checked by *one-sixth* or more)

From Ross L. Mooney, *Manual to Accompany the Problem Check List, College Form.* The Bureau of Educational Research, Ohio State University, Columbus, Ohio, September 15, 1942, pp. 41–42. Based on 430 students using second mimeographed edition, all from Ohio State University and tending to be selected for their academic difficulties. Later editions of the *Manual* have been published since 1942. Mildred Chapin Klohr, "Personal Problems of College Students," *Journal of Home Economics,* Vol. 40, No. 8 (October 1948) presents a survey of female college students.

December, there was a decrease of 24 per cent in the number of problems checked. The problems also changed somewhat—for example, "Curriculum and Teaching Procedures" problems, which were insignificant in October, jumped in December.

If the reader will examine the personal problems reported for the group of students who did not seem to have academic or common social problems (Table 1–1) as well as for those with academic difficulties (Table 1–2), he will find throughout a similar need

for the study and application of psychological knowledge.

Problems that led to discharge of employees

Personal problems that are related to personality also have considerable bearing on one's effectiveness and adjustment to work. In a study at a major oil company, character traits were said to represent 90 per cent of the causes for discharge and 76

TABLE 1-3

PROBLEMS WHICH OCCURRED FREQUENTLY IN DECEMBER AND SELDOM IN OCTOBER AMONG 190 STUDENTS

	October	December	Difference
Getting low grades	24	44	20
Tired of same meals all the time	7	23	16
Wanting to leave college	0	12	12
Not enough sleep	23	34	11
Not enough time for recreation	8	19	11
Too little chance to go to shows	4	15	11
Grades unfair as measure of ability	0	11	11
Purpose in going to college not clear	7	16	9
Dull classes	1	10	9
Too little time for sports	9	18	9
Too little chance to listen to the radio	10	19	9
Too little chance to read what I like	17	26	9
Not smart enough in scholastic ways	14	22	8
Not taking things seriously enough	11	18	7

TABLE 1-4

PROBLEMS WHICH OCCURRED FREQUENTLY IN OCTOBER AND SELDOM IN DECEMBER ARRANGED ACCORDING TO THE SIZE OF THE DIFFERENCES BETWEEN THESE FREQUENCIES

Item	October	December	Difference
Don't know how to study effectively	77	18	59
Trouble in using the library	53	4	49
Trouble in outlining or note-taking	51	4	47
Lacking self-confidence	62	27	35
Unskilled in conversation	61	29	32
Unable to concentrate well	56	25	31
Lacking in leadership ability	38	12	26
Afraid to speak up in classroom discussions	51	25	26
Slow in mathematics	61	36	25
Being ill at ease at social affairs	41	17	24
Afraid of making mistakes	48	24	24
Weak in spelling or grammar	45	22	23
Wanting a more pleasing personality	69	47	22
Wanting to learn how to entertain	28	9	19
Too easily led by other people	27	8	19

per cent of the reasons for which promotion was not granted.[6]

When Alanson H. Edgerton had spent over twelve years in an extensive study of vocational education, he too found that personality and character traits are often more important than skill or intelligence for success in employment. He and his colleagues examined 144,279 actual jobs in 2,630 fields and followed 15,824 youths through ten years of school and work.

Successful employees, he reported, must be versatile. Three-fourths of the employers he questionnaired wanted youths skilled in at least two kinds of work (such as lawyers who also knew banking, or stenographers who could keep books).

But more important than skill or intelligence, he found, is personality. In one sub-survey, studies were made of 3,607 men and women who had lost their jobs. It turned out that 77 per cent had been fired for tactlessness, unfairness, irritability, bad manners, etc. Again, Dr. Edgerton rated a group of job holders for (1) intelligence and (2) personality. The most intelligent 33 per cent earned only $139.44 more per year than the least intelligent; but the highest 33 per cent in personality earned $842.73 more than the lowest.

Specifically, well-liked employees are co-operative, loyal, polite, tactful, friendly, patient, alert, daring, confident, and cheerful.[7]

Psychological problems of businessmen

The employees of business are not the only workers who have psychological problems, some of which result in discharge. Executives, too, have their unique problems, both as individuals and as executives.

Business and industrial job failure due to psychological problems is not limited to the lower ranks of workers; many of their problems are shared by those in executive positions, although the greater responsibilities of such jobs create additional psychological hazards.

When we talk about businessmen and their psychological problems, we should recognize that the principles and problems of the mental life are common to all people of our civilized society. Students, business executives, employees, and customers have essentially the same emotions, feelings, and traits as individuals of other classifications. The psychological principles that apply to the person in the school and the home also apply to the same individual in the office and the factory. Basic principles are universal; only settings differ. As students of human behavior, we can be alert to the meanings in a person's behavior regardless of where he may be active.

When a man speaks to us he is always telling us two stories at once even though we commonly attend to but one of them. One is the tale he actually tells, and it may be about anything. The other is a story about himself—the story constituted by the fact that he, under the circumstances present, does tell us just that tale and tells it to us in just the way he does. The style and the matter of a man's speech or of his writings, it has been said, is a picture of what the man is—of his point of view, his character, his intellectual resources, his tastes, his temperament, et al. And all this is exhibited to us, if we but give it our attention, not only when a man expresses himself in language but equally where this mode of expression is of other sorts. How a man walks or sits, what sort of clothes he wears and how he wears them, what sort of house he builds, how he spends his leisure and his money, what he fights for and how he does it, the undertakings to which he devotes himself, the sort of gods he worships, which books he reads, the arts he cultivates and the sorts of products he makes them yield, the modes of conduct and the social institutions which he approves or disapproves—all these things provide us with a picture of the man and of his environment into which we can project ourselves in imagination as effectively as we can into the characters and situations represented in the stories he tells, the plays he acts, or the books he writes.[8]

The person who studies human behavior extensively wherever he finds it learns to see the patternful nature of the individual's activities, and how certain acts in behavior are related to other acts. The person's behavior becomes more meaningful as it fits into basic patterns that characterize the individual. For example, the executive who failed as a youth to learn how to compete in games with other boys is also apt to be unable to endure the presence of rivals in his business relations. Such an executive seldom hires subordinates or assistants who are as able as he. The department head who has ability but surrounds himself with weak personalities is harmful to the business concern and also is a problem to the college graduate who seeks to advance in that executive's department. The student, therefore, should seek to know psychological principles and patterns in behavior wherever he may find them in order that he may be able to use them when needed in business and other settings.

What psychology is not

In Greek mythology, Psyche was represented as a beautiful maiden having the wings of a butterfly. Psyche symbolized the soul. The butterfly symbolized human immortality. Originally psychology, from the root words *psyche*, soul, and *-logy*, a combining form meaning a science—the science of the soul—was a branch of philosophy.

A generation ago psychology severed its formal relations with philosophy and became a science in itself. It no longer studies the soul, nor is it interested in such problems as communication with the dead. Psychology and psychical research are two different fields, and the psychologist does not have very much hope of successful discoveries in *psychic* realms. Psychology has lost its mystical quality. It is not interested in cults or in magical influences on people who happen to be about us. It does not take the place of the witch doctor.

Psychologists are not interested in character analysis from observation of superficial physical signs, except to report that such methods of analyzing people are largely fallacious. Many sales managers mistakenly think that they are psychologists when they try to predict a man's selling ability from

the color of his hair or the shape of his chin.

Most psychologists are not interested in mind reading or in thought transference. They have not found that mental telepathy has sound foundations. Investigations of those incidents in the lives of their friends which indicated that mental telepathy might exist usually showed that such experiences were coincidences which occur in the life of everyone. When the psychologists have checked or examined phenomena of this sort, they have found that the apparently mystical should be treated in terms of natural laws.

Nor is psychology a short cut to success in business or in life. Many people who study psychology do so with the hope of finding a talisman for success. It will not make a mentally strong and powerful individual out of a weakling. It is of assistance, of course, in bringing out the latent possibilities of people and in enabling them to adjust themselves to one another; but we should look upon psychology as a science.

What psychology is

Psychology is method applied to mental phenomena, not magic. The outstanding approach to the problems of our modern age is our highly developed technique for gaining insight into all aspects of our experiences —namely, the scientific method. Steps in a scientific method are: (a) observation of a chosen phenomenon, (b) accumulation of the facts, (c) noting a pattern among the facts, (d) finding a plausible explanation of the pattern within these facts (hypothesis), (e) making a new prediction on the basis of the plausible explanation, and (f) checking the prediction experimentally—hence increasing or decreasing the belief in the plausible explanation, depending upon whether the new findings agree or disagree with the prediction. Albert Einstein once put it:

The scientific way of forming concepts differs from that which we use in our daily life, not basically, but merely in the more precise definition of concepts and conclusions; more painstaking and systematic choice of experimental material; and greater logical economy. By this last we mean the effort to reduce all concepts and correlations to as few as possible logically independent basic concepts and axioms.[9]

The use of the scientific method does not reveal absolute laws or ultimate truth. Rather, scientifically developed principles are descriptive statements of relationships observed between events. Each principle, though useful in describing relationships, is subject to further improvement. Scientists do not expect to discover final laws but they do seek progress toward continued enlightenment.

Delicate instruments have been invented to aid the observer in detecting and measuring variations of the phenomena under study. Involved statistical techniques have been developed for treatment of the data. The thousands of scientific studies being made by psychologists and other scientists are slowly modifying our daily work and living. They have already revealed possibilities for utilizing human and physical forces that were not dreamed of by our forefathers. The use of the scientific method for gaining insight has partially displaced unsound methods such as those of superstition and occultism.

Several organizations furnish those research and consulting services which bring various social sciences and management techniques to bear on problems of human relations. F. F. Bradshaw, president of one of these concerns—Richardson, Bellows, Henry & Company, Inc.—stated:

It has been said that chemistry is the result of the marriage of alchemy with mathematics. Whether or not that is true historically, it is true that the essence of science lies in measurement. Common sense told us that the world was flat, but measurement sent Columbus on his voyage of discovery. Painstakingly, piece by piece, patient scholars have taken man's experience and analyzed, defined, and measured. This is the history of science, and science is a foundation of modern civilization.

Sometimes people mistakenly assume that science is a body of fact. It is more than fact—it is measurement, prediction, and control. Sometimes ignorant people have insisted that science was fiction, especially wherein it was not fact. There is a vast difference, however, between fiction and theory—between simple prediction based on hunch and wish and scientific prediction based on measurement.[10]

We now define psychology as the "study of human behavior by scientific methods." *Behavior,* as used here, refers to more than conduct, deportment, or manner. It includes all normal and abnormal activities of the whole organism, even those of feeblemindedness and insanity. *The aims of applied psychology are the description, prediction, and control of human activities in order that we may understand and direct intelligently our own lives and influence the lives of others.*

Psychology is a most useful study because every man must live with himself and with others. Even though a person never studies it as a science, his every thought and act illustrate its principles. To live means to function, and behavior is the material of psychology. The unit of study is the individual.

Of course, a person may live a pleasant life and never study himself or his behavior. An angleworm and a cow are presumably content, but we have no evidence to indicate that they are intelligently happy. Happiness for the modern man demands more than mere organismic contentment. He wants to be physically comfortable, but he also wishes to know the laws of mental life, the principles of human behavior, so that he may utilize them for new satisfactions. Our present civilization rests upon the basis: "Let us study life and its conditions so that we may utilize our findings to rise to new and more intelligent levels of personal satisfactions and social relationships."

Every person is something of a psychologist. The roots of the subject are as old as the human species. However, modern scientific psychology is a relatively recent development. The first American laboratory was started in 1883 at Johns Hopkins University, and in 1889 the first title of "Professor of Psychology" was bestowed upon William James by Harvard University.[11]

Present-day psychologists pride themselves on their use of the scientific method. Formerly, it was not unheard of to set up a law after making a hypothesis. Now the accent is on objectivity and quantitative data. Statisticians and psychologists have collaborated to achieve scientific methodology. They have made possible the objective appraisal of facts with a minimum of subjectivity by devising methods of treating quantities of data to ascertain whether they have any real significance. A classic example is the concept of correlation, by which it is possible to compute what relationship one factor or group of factors bears to another factor or group of factors. The last chapter of this book presents a few of the more simple statistical techniques in use today.

Another method by which experiments are made more scientific and yield dependable conclusions is the use of control groups in experimental groups of subjects. Use of a control group with an experimental group makes it possible to learn which factors under investigation have a bearing on the findings. Animals are used frequently as subjects by some experimental psychologists because of the impracticability of running certain types of experiments on human beings. Through such experiments it has been possible to learn about important aspects of drives and motivations, effects of thwarting, and problem-solving behavior, for example. Caution must always be exercised, however, in generalizing that results obtained from animal experiments apply also to human beings.

In addition to the basic methodological tools already mentioned, such as statistics and experimental and control groups, there are secondary tools such as rating scales, morale and attitude surveys, readership surveys, the polling of selected samples or panels, and objective and projective tests.

Some psychologists who are particularly interested in personality and characteristic behavior have developed schools of thought or theories regarding it. Other psychologists are inclined to an eclectic view, and take some phase from each school or theory into their own thinking. There is much general agreement, however; as, for example, on the viewpoint that all types of personality deviate from the statistical "average" to a greater or lesser extent, and that all behavior is adjustive, although not necessarily successfully so.

Each person adjusts himself to his world in his own way. Average or so-called normal behavior is really only theoretical. There is no sharp division between normal and abnormal behavior. Behavior considered normal might be said to represent that of more than half of the people in a society. The other people differ more and more from the normal. Although such a definition would be but one of several possible and arbitrary ones, it should be understood that atypical behavior refers to the less common methods of adjustment in a particular culture.

When a person's behavior is so far removed from the norm of his society as to make him or society uncomfortable, psychotherapy is often indicated. This is a job for clinical psychologists, who utilize the work of experimental and other psychologists. To guide the process of therapy, clinical psychologists employ various diagnostic methods—tests to aid in ascertaining the dynamics underlying behavior, and devices that yield specific information, such as the encephalogram, a record of brain waves that reveals whether certain disorders are functional or due to epilepsy or brain tumors.

So much work has been done by psychologists that only certain major divisions can be treated in any course in applied psychology. The divisions chosen for consideration here, because of their probable value to the student as a student and as a potential leader, are the following:

Personality

[handwritten: people are both introvert & extravert, although neither pure ... behavior]

Students who are interested in improving their personalities—and most students are—are especially interested in principles that underlie personality development. Much serious work has been done in this field to ascertain relationships between environment, experience, natural endowments, the physical (organic) state of the individual, and his personality. As yet there are few final answers, although many hypotheses are being explored.

The oft-used terms "introvert" and "extravert" usually intrigue students. If they have come by some means to believe that they are either introverts or extraverts, they want to know whether it is possible for them to change. Here again they should be warned that extraversion and introversion represent positions on a continuum. Most people are neither one type nor the other; they have some introverted characteristics and some extraverted ones. It is the tendency to display more of one characteristic pattern of behavior than the other that makes a person introverted or extraverted. In view of this fact, is a person doomed to remain one personality type, or can he change? The answer is that he can change, provided he can acquire new insights that enable him to develop new behavior patterns.

Personal problems

MENTAL EFFICIENCY AND EFFECTIVE STUDY. Also of special interest to the student are his problems in mental efficiency and effective study habits. Since these are largely a function of the personality in action, a person with new insights can improve his habits in this area of activity. Experiments on the nature and methods of learning have revealed some helpful suggestions for every student.

VOCATIONAL ADJUSTMENT. The psychological problems of the student do not end with the completion of his college work. He must earn a living, as a professional worker or a businessman, most probably as an employee who has ambitions for himself as a supervisor, manager, or owner.

Vocational guidance has become more successful with the improvement of counseling techniques and the development of interest, aptitude, and achievement tests. Many schools require the student to take a battery of tests to ascertain wherein his abilities and interests lie and whether they are compatible with his educational record. Likewise, many employers test job applicants before hiring them to ascertain whether they are qualified for the job they desire and whether they meet the company's standards. Improved testing procedures to estimate the potentialities of applicants are becoming available.

Test-score profiles have been developed in an attempt to derive objective standards of interests, aptitudes, and abilities for various types of jobs. These profiles show certain characteristics that are typical of workers in the various types of occupations. Success in a vocation, however, cannot be guaranteed or predicted absolutely on the basis of test results alone. Again, success is a function of the whole personality.

Tests of ability and aptitude that are used in hiring are too numerous to mention here (see Chapter 16). The trend, however, is in the direction of trying to make sure that new employees will fit harmoniously into the organization from the personality standpoint as well as be able to do the work.

COURTSHIP AND MARRIAGE. Although a few psychologists have tried to develop criteria for ascertaining in advance whether a marriage will be successful, it has proved to be a difficult task. Some remarkably interesting studies have been made, however, and certain trends characteristic of successful and unsuccessful marriages have been found. Marriage is no different from any other social situation in which a person may find himself. <u>He must adjust himself, not depend on outside forces to do it for him.</u>

CHILD GUIDANCE. Most students, unless they are already parents, have little interest in child psychology. And yet <u>one of the best ways to understand the adult is to understand the child.</u> Research centers and individuals concentrating on the study of child psychology are responsible for many valuable contributions to the field of psychology as a whole. <u>Of primary importance is the growing appreciation of the importance of childhood experience because of its</u> effects on character and personality. Also highly important is the <u>conclusion</u> that no matter what the overt behavior pattern of the child, it is his way of adjusting to his world. This is as true of the "naughty" child as of the "good" child. Psychologists have also taught parents the importance of maturation in the child's learning and activities, so that children are now less likely to be pushed beyond their stage of development than they formerly were.

Dealing with employees

INTERVIEWING. Although applied industrial and business psychologists have done a great deal of work to determine the criteria of successful interviews and to ascertain how they can be made more diagnostic, <u>most interviews are still conducted in a casual manner and without a basic framework of thinking on the part of the</u> interviewer. Such unsystematic ways of interviewing permit <u>only subjective analyses</u>, whereas new interview procedures make the evaluation of interview findings more objective and significant. (See Chapter 15.)

MERIT RATINGS. Various methods of deriving appraisals of employees and of informing them about their work have been studied. Anyone who aspires to become a responsible executive should become acquainted with these findings.

<u>MOTIVATING EMPLOYEES.</u> To give management the "know-how" to motivate employees in the direction of improved efficiency and greater productivity, the American Management Association and other organizations are bringing to the attention of management the results of psychological investigations that deal with human motivations. By this means psychologists are giving managements the opportunity to make employees happier and more productive with improved results for both. Psychologists in collaboration with progressive managements have made time studies and <u>measured fatigue, effects of noise, lighting, and so forth.</u> They have studied <u>accident control, job evaluation, and values of different wage payment systems.</u> Training courses for supervisors have been developed by psychologists. *An employee should be motivated into doing a better jo*

<u>COMMUNICATIONS</u> AND <u>GROUP DYNAMICS.</u> Years ago when one man owned and managed a company, an employee could walk into his office and get a decision or the boss' point of view in a hurry. But that was before the days of mass production. Now the man at the roll-top desk is only a memory. <u>His counterpart today is the management chart—indicative of the many groups which participate in running a plant.</u> Decisions are influenced and made at many different points in the complex structure of <u>management, production, engineering, and sales. As a result, many members of the organization are uninformed or misinformed.</u> Unexpected dynamic forces arise within work groups. Supervisors and workers develop misunderstandings and frictions.

Methods of improving communication between modern managements and workers are becoming increasingly essential. <u>Group dynamics require special attention. The team approach to industrial relations has grown with mass production technology.</u> *Because of the Management chart many employers are misinformed about their employees.*

The American Psychological Association maintains an office in Washington, D.C. (Pictured above) which is the co-ordinating center for all APA activities. Journal subscriptions, membership applications, personnel placement requests and general APA business procedures are handled in this office. The staff is always glad to answer inquiries from individual members and from the public.

The APA, founded in 1892, is the major psychological organization in the United States. With approximately 14,500 members, it includes most of the qualified psychologists in the country. The purpose of the American Psychological Association is to advance psychology as a science, as a profession, and as a means of promoting human welfare. It attempts to further these objectives by holding annual meetings, publishing psychological journals, conducting a personnel placement service for psychologists who are members of the APA, and working toward improved standards of psychological training and service.

In order to give recognition to the specialized interests of different psychologists, the APA includes 17 Divisions. After becoming a member of the APA, any person may apply for membership in as many Divisions as he wishes. The Divisions are listed below with the number of psychologists in each Division:

Division of General Psychology—490; Division on the Teaching of Psychology—260; Division of Experimental Psychology—612; Division on Evaluation and Measurement—497; Division on Developmental Psychology—448; Division of Personality and Social Psychology—846; The Society for the Psychological Study of Social Issues—672; Division on Esthetics—75; Division of Clinical Psychology—1711; Division of Consulting Psychology—233; Division of Industrial and Business Psychology—514; Division of Educational Psychology—453; Division of School Psychologists—348; Division of Counseling Psychology—757; Division of Psychologists in Public Service—177; Division of Military Psychology—249; Division on Maturity and Old Age—204.

Dealing with consumers

Automation and related technological advances are increasing our production potentials to so high a level that it is becoming increasingly necessary for us to develop new and bigger markets. Psychologists are therefore being called upon to assist in finding markets through the discovery and stimulation of consumer wants. Consumers are being studied as never before by means of improved interviewing and other research techniques.

ADVERTISING AND SELLING. The most effective methods of advertising, from the standpoint of both the consumer and the advertiser, are being studied. Readership reports directed by such psychologists as Daniel Starch, and new mechanical methods such as eye cameras, have increased advertising effectiveness for each dollar spent.

These are a few examples of the kinds of positive contributions that psychologists have been making to daily life and work.

The very fact that more than one thousand psychologists were called upon to help solve wartime problems of a practical nature indicated that abstract knowledge of psychology and scientific methods is not a useless luxury in a desperately chaotic world. Rather, consulting psychologists in business are increasing in numbers and importance because of the contributions they can make toward the solutions of current problems.

The applied psychologist is a specialist who integrates the principles and other findings of psychologists who have special interests, such as those of experimental, social, and educational psychology.[12] He adapts and uses these principles and findings in practical situations. He applies them to personal problems of the individual and to the problems of other specialists, such as the executive in business.

Psychologists in business

Corporate hiring has not sought as intensively to fill the need for psychologists as it has to recruit its other professionals, such as engineers. In recent years, however, some business executives have called with increasing frequency upon psychologists and have invited them to assist in dealing with business problems, to act as consultants, and to work full-time in their organizations.

Gradually, managements are recognizing that they need more information on how people and groups in business interact. Businessmen today rely on data concerning cost-of-living, turnover, car loadings, retail sales and many other varieties of economic conditions. Eventually, business managements will also depend upon behavioral data concerning human conditions for guidance in making decisions.[13]

Accurate data on the number of psychologists who are now employed on a full-time

basis in business is not available. Finch and Odoroff made a study of the employment records in applied psychology, covering a twenty-two-year period, of all members and associates of the American Psychological Association.[14] They estimated that it is not improbable that one half of the total time of American psychologists is being devoted to applied psychology of all kinds, business and other.

The professional interests of American psychologists can be deduced to some extent from data on their memberships in the several divisions of the American Psychological Association. As shown by the data on page 15, the number of psychologists who are members of the Division of Industrial and Business Psychology is considerably smaller than the number who belong to the Division of Clinical Psychology.*

The several divisions of The Psychological Corporation's services are also indicative of the interests of psychologists and the areas of business in which they operate (see opposite page).

About one half of all Association members are employed by colleges and universities. Twelve per cent are federal employees, and nearly three fourths of this 12 per cent work for the Veterans Administration.[15] In comparison with a generation ago, the number of applied psychologists is growing but the number of professionally trained psychologists in business will continue to be a small percentage of the total number of trained workers.

It is obvious that very few college students will become *business psychologists.* Few psychology majors will ever wear the label, occupationally speaking, which they had as a major in their college studies. In this respect, psychology is similar to mathematics. Very few students who major in mathematics ever have the occupational

---

* Elizabeth Ogg, *Psychologists in Action*, Public Affairs Pamphlets, 22 East 38th St., New York, 1955, p. 5, presents a table: "Fields of Specialty for 11,069 Psychologists in the National Science Foundation Register." Those who reported as their specialty, "Industrial" or "Personnel," were 10.1 per cent of the total.

Aptitude tests help business and industry find the right person for the job and aid individuals in selecting the kinds of work in which they are most likely to be successful. Here, Dr. Harold Seashore, director of The Psychological Corporation's Test Division, goes over an aptitude profile drawn from the Corporation's widely used Differential Aptitude Tests.

Nearly 1,000 carefully trained field workers, supervised by some 250 psychologists in all parts of the country, enable The Psychological Corporation to carry out surveys of buying behavior, product preferences, opinions and attitudes. Most interviewers are students of psychology and have a keen, understanding interest in the scientific techniques employed in this work.

THE PSYCHOLOGICAL CORPORATION

The Psychological Corporation was founded in 1921 by 20 eminent psychologists under the leadership of Dr. J. McKeen Cattell, for "the advancement of psychology and the promotion of the useful applications of psychology." Today it is the largest professional organization in the world devoted to the service of business, industry, educational institutions, and individuals through applied psychology.

Its Test Division is best known but its main divisions and services are the following:

Test Division

Publication of Tests and Related Books and Pamphlets
Merchandising of Tests, including Distribution of Some Tests for Individuals and Other Publishers
Research in the Construction, Revision, Administration, and Validation of Tests
Advisory Service
Statistical Service and Statistical Research

Marketing and Social Research Division

Marketing Studies on Buyer and Consumer Behavior
Studies of Opinion on Economic, Social, and Political Questions
Surveys of Attitudes toward Individual Companies and toward Business in General
Training and Research in Techniques of Communicating Ideas
Measurement of Effectiveness of Advertising and Other Means of Communicating Ideas

Industrial Division

Surveys of Personnel and Industrial Relations Practices
Individual Evaluations and Personnel Audits

Management Development Programs
Personnel Selection Programs
Interviewer Training
Conference Leadership Training
Training Programs
Merit Rating, or Performance Review
Human Engineering, or Biomechanics
Employee Attitude and Morale Surveys

Professional Examinations Division

Testing for Colleges of Veterinary Medicine
Testing for Schools of Nursing
Testing for Schools of Practical Nursing
Administration of Achievement Examinations for Graduate Nurses
Scoring, Item Analysis, and Other Statistical Service for Schools, Colleges, and Other Organizations

The Psychological Service Center

Vocational and Educational Counseling
Personal Counseling—Work and Social Relationships
Home and School Adjustments of Children
Retirement Planning
Student Evaluation Services

The Psychological Corporation's offices are at 522 Fifth Avenue, New York 36, New York.

designation of *mathematician,* even though they use mathematics in their work. They are more likely to be called engineers, accountants, statisticians, or clerical workers; although they use mathematics constantly, they think of themselves, and their employers think of them, as trained in some business field, such as accounting, production, or selling. Similarly, students of psychology who go into business are likely to find many applications of their psychological knowledge even though they are not classified on a payroll as psychologists.

Very few students can ever hope to become expert psychologists who will solve psychological problems for business firms, but all who enter business should hope to improve their knowledge of psychological principles and techniques, to become more intelligent members of the business team. Human relations problems in industry are rarely solved by lone experts—they are solved by the members of a team. As one industrial psychiatrist has stated:

But how *do* you deal with people? Where and when do you deal with people? I want to nail down once and for all the fact that the problem of human relations in any industry, department store, government agency, educational institution or any other place where there is supervision of people, is solved by a team approach. Everybody in management is responsible at some time for the development of effective human relationships. . . .

The determining factor in what people feel and think is the kind of treatment they get on the daily job in millions of work places. Their satisfaction or dissatisfaction with the spiritual take-home as well as the financial take-home, will be their criteria for judging the worth of working.[16]

Each member of the team can, of course, improve his sensitivity to the ways people feel and think. He can improve his knowledge and skills as well as his awareness of psychological factors in daily situations. He can become acquainted with the findings of researches as reported in current texts and in journals such as *The Journal of Applied Psychology.*

Applied psychology has become so useful in modern industry that several organizations of consulting psychologists have offices in industrial centers. Rohrer, Hibler & Replogle, for example, occupies 3,050 square feet of floor space on one floor of the Field Building, Chicago. Similar offices are located in New York City; Hasbrouck Heights, N.J.; Cleveland; Los Angeles; Atlanta; Milwaukee; Dallas and Detroit. The professional staff of fifty-six is distributed among the nine offices. The doctorate is a prerequisite of employment for all staff members.

Psychology should contribute toward adjustment to change

Certainly, we cannot stop change any more than we can stop time. Almost every change which benefits some one person or industry brings new psychological problems to others. No one can prevent these changes which, in the long run, seem to spell progress. Nor would many care to turn back to the former modes of living, when life was simpler but everyone worked seventy hours a week and had to amuse himself by attending funerals and spelling bees. Every individual, stupid or intelligent, is jostled by the technological and social forces that surround him. What then can the intelligent individual do about it, if anything? What can he gain for this purpose from a study of psychology? A suggested major objective for the educated person of today is personal development in two important respects:

(a) To learn about the *modern techniques involved in dealing with people,* such as the clinical method of analyzing personalities, tests in hiring applicants, rating scales in promoting employees, recent developments in supervising employees, predicting consumers' wants, influencing groups of people, using clarifying statistics, and other factual methods. These are examples of knowledge that may be learned through college classroom approaches.

(b) To gain something more important than knowledge only, namely, the mental quality which we term *adaptability on the part of the individual himself.* This means that he must catch the spirit of the age in which he lives and become an intelligent participant in the changes taking place about him.

Of course, no man can foresee all the great changes that will occur in the later years of his life, but he can adapt himself to the changes occurring in his own time and place. His guiding attitude should be that of expecting changes and preparing to meet them. A fundamental psychological purpose for the intelligent individual, regardless of sex, vocation, or environment, is that of adjusting himself to the accelerated rates of change taking place about him.

Adaptability is far more than knowledge. It is a mental habit that can be acquired by anyone who really seeks it. *Adaptability is the habit of finding and using opportunities in the environment and following not the lines of least resistance but those of greatest opportunity.* The habit of acquiring new points of view, new skills, new facts, and new habits can be learned. Everyone can to some extent travel, attend classes, read books, see moving pictures, listen to the radio, talk with others, and learn new ideas from various other available sources. However, more besides travel,

education, and social contacts is necessary to bring about adaptability in one's self. Conscious recognition of one's mental habits or adjustments and intelligent direction of self-growth are most important. These principles will be treated in Chapters 2 to 8.

Once a person recognizes the importance of adaptability and then studies the principles of adjustment, he will discover how his psychological tendencies and habits can be modified in the direction of greater adaptability. The age-old laws of evolution are still with us. The struggle for existence is not new; only its form has changed. The machine has only accelerated the rate of change and accentuated the need for a certain kind of psychological development in order to capitalize the changes for individual benefit.

The individual who recognizes these rapidly changing conditions and their mental requirements may have two sustaining convictions. These are that the world still has many unsolved problems, and that determination to help solve an immediate problem always has been and always will be a worthwhile goal. Anyone can find self-expression in solving a near-by problem in his work through the three following channels of direct attack:

1. Improving the mechanical equipment.

2. Improving the methods of operating the equipment or of doing the work.

3. Improving the human relationships.

The fact that the worker in the past got much of his feeling of worthful participation from his craftsmanship does not mean that the present-day worker cannot achieve the same feeling. Anything now being done could be done better, more easily, more economically, or more pleasingly. For example, a stenographer cannot hope to improve the typewriter or office machine she uses, but she can always improve her methods of work.

Psychologists often work with industrial relations and other executives. Here is an example from the International Harvester Company plant. The members of the group include, left to right around the table: a division superintendent; works auditor; the company psychologist who is in charge of personnel research and testing; works manager; a consulting psychologist, Prof. C. H. Lawshe, of Purdue University; the plant training director; and another company psychologist on the extreme right of the table. The meeting dealt with an attitude survey and ways of gaining employee and company benefits from it.

The same situation applies to businessmen, teachers, and students. Many young people have not learned how to gain creative self-expression through the three general channels of improvement because the books they have read, the courses they have taken, and the diplomas they have earned do not require development of adaptability. Some of their studies have taught them to criticize life as it is. Few have learned to recognize the rapidly changing conditions under which we live, to feel in control of themselves, to tackle systematically the problems of the immediate job, and to become adaptable. Every man with a job and a steady income should assume that he may some day lose the job and his income. Every girl who marries should as-

sume that she may some day become a widow and have to earn her own living. No one can prevent catastrophe, but every intelligent person can prepare himself psychologically to deal with catastrophe.

Our ultimate dependence cannot be on systems of government or business, but on ourselves as individuals. Life and civilization always have been and always will be dangerous. Dangers change only their form. The entire history of civilization is one long series of crises. Some of the individuals who survived were only fortunate; others were intelligent. The spirited man is still master of his fate.

Some years ago when the *Titanic* sped across the Atlantic on her maiden voyage, she struck an iceberg and sank. One American newspaper cartoonist of unusual insight drew two contrasting illustrations of the tragedy. One drawing showed the ship broken and about to sink. Underneath that picture were the words: "The weakness of man—the supremacy of nature." The other drawing illustrated how a certain passenger stepped aside to give his place in the last lifeboat to a woman with a child. This picture had the words: "The weakness of nature—the supremacy of man."

Adaptability is far more than knowledge. It depends upon the ability to control one's habits and to change them intelligently. To do this, the individual needs the self-knowledge which psychology can often contribute. In the next few chapters we shall examine certain mental habits that inhibit and others that facilitate adaptability and thereby gain that insight which contributes to man's supremacy over himself as well as over nature.

Acknowledgments and References

1. H. Meltzer, "Economic Security and Children's Attitudes to Parents," *American Journal of Orthopsychiatry*, Vol. 6 (1936), pp. 590–608.

2. M. H. Seevers, "Drug Addiction Problems," *Sigma Xi Quarterly*, June 1939.

3. Clark W. Heath and Lewise W. Gregory, "Problems of Normal College Students and Their Families," *School and Society*, Vol. 63 (1946), pp. 355–358. This whole investigation was part of the Grant Study, 1938–1942.

4. Ross L. Mooney, *Manual to Accompany the Problem Check List, College Form.* The Bureau of Educational Research, Ohio State University, Columbus, Ohio, September 15, 1942, p. 39.

5. Nora A. Congdon, "The Perplexities of College Freshmen," *Educational and Psychological Measurement,* Vol. 3 (1943), pp. 367–375.

6. Karl A. and W. C. Menninger, *Business Week,* Nov. 5, 1955, p. 94.

7. *Newsweek,* April 1, 1940, p. 39.

8. C. J. Ducasse, "Are the Humanities Worth Their Keep?" *American Scholar,* Vol. 6, No. 4 (1937), pp. 467–468.

9. Albert Einstein, "The Fundaments of Theoretical Physics," *Science,* Vol. 91 (1940).

10. F. F. Bradshaw, "Management Science—Neither Fiction Nor Fact," *Advanced Management,* September, 1955, p. 4.

11. Emily S. Dexter and Katherine T. Omwake, *An Introduction to the Field of Psychology,* Prentice-Hall, Inc., Englewood Cliffs, N.J., 1938, p. 1.

12. Ralph Berdie, "The Field of Applied Psychology," *The Journal of Applied Psychology,* Vol. XXIV, No. 5 (October 1940), p. 556.

13. See statement by Mason Haire, *Business Week,* June 2, 1956, p. 126.

14. F. H. Finch and M. E. Odoroff, "Employment Trends in Applied Psychology," *Journal of Consulting Psychology,* Vol. 3, No. 4 (July–August 1939), pp. 118–122.

15. Dael Wolfle, "Annual Report of the Executive Secretary: 1948," *The American Psychologist,* American Psychological Association, Inc., Vol. 3 (November 1948), pp. 503–510. In 1949, the American Psychological Association, Inc., had 6,749 members.

16. Ralph T. Collins, M.D., Psychiatrist, Medical Dept., Eastman Kodak Company, "Psychiatry and Industry," *Mental Hygiene News,* New York State, November 1954, p. 4.

PROJECTS

1. No single textbook can possibly supply all the information now published in the field of applied psychology. Hence you should examine and note differences in the tables of contents of any of the following applied psychology textbooks that may be available in your library:

Bellows, Roger M., *Psychology of Personnel in Business and Industry,* second edition, Prentice-Hall, Inc., Englewood Cliffs, N.J., 1954.

Burtt, H. E., *Applied Psychology,* second edition, Prentice-Hall, Inc., Englewood Cliffs, N.J., 1957.

Ghiselli, Edwin E. and Clarence W. Brown, *Personnel and Industrial Psychology,* McGraw-Hill Book Company, Inc., New York, 1955.

Harrell, Thomas Willard, *Industrial Psychology,* Rinehart & Company, Inc., New York, 1949.

Maier, Norman R. F., *Psychology in Industry,* Houghton Mifflin Company, Boston, 1955.

Poffenberger, A. T., *Principles of Applied Psychology,* Appleton-Century-Crofts, Inc., New York, 1942.

Smith, Henry Clay, *Psychology of Industrial Behavior,* McGraw-Hill Book Company, Inc., New York, 1955.

2. Visit your library and examine the periodicals that might be of special value to the person who studies applied psychology. List the titles and content of several articles that appeal to you. Quote parts which you find interesting or of value to you. Be prepared to describe your findings to other students.

3. Do you know an adult who has been unemployed or irregularly employed for several years? Describe his psychological characteristics. Did unemployment cause his psychological problem, or did psychological problems cause his unemployment? Discuss.

4. Examine books and journals for descriptions of the work done by The Psychological Corporation. Perhaps you can read the *Encyclopedia of Psychology,* Philip L. Harriman, editor (Philosophical Library, New York, 1946), pp. 607–8.

5. Examine biographies and autobiographies of famous contemporary leaders. Point out any relationships between the leader's psychological characteristics and his policies or achievements. Read books such as E. S.

Bogardus, *Leaders and Leadership*, D. Appleton-Century Company, New York, 1934.

6. How does training to be a business technician differ from training to be a business leader?

7. A professor of astronomy in a large university frequently receives letters asking for astrological advice, such as: "My son was born under the sign of Taurus. He is contemplating joining the Navy. Will his life be safe?" Assume that you are the astronomer and compose a brief letter to the mother.

8. Many scientists believe that human nature and the social sciences have not kept pace with the physical and chemical sciences. Some have suggested that we should retard certain sciences until human beings catch up with them. What arguments can you present for or against the suggestion? Should we choose the goal of improving human adaptability to keep pace with developments in all fields?

COLLATERAL READINGS

Bellows, Roger M., *Psychology of Personnel in Business and Industry,* second edition, Prentice-Hall, Inc., Englewood Cliffs, N.J., 1954, Chapters 1 and 2.

Eysenck, Hans J., *The Scientific Study of Personality,* Macmillan Co., New York, 1952.

Haire, Mason, *Psychology in Management,* McGraw-Hill Book Co., Inc., New York, 1956, Chapter 1.

Ogg, Elizabeth, *Psychologists in Action,* Public Affairs Pamphlet No. 229, Public Affairs Committee, Inc., 1955.

Shaffer, Laurance F. and Edward J. Shoben, Jr., *The Psychology of Adjustment,* Houghton Mifflin Co., Boston, 1956, Chapter 1.

Smith, Henry Clay, *Psychology of Industrial Behavior,* McGraw-Hill Book Co., Inc., New York, 1955, Chapter 1.

CHAPTER TWO

The problem person is a person with a problem

The forms of behavior which we are apt to classify as inappropriate or abnormal really have important meanings for dealing with ourselves as well as others. The behavior of the problem person is not merely the effect of environment or the age in which he lives. It always has purpose for the individual. It is part of his pattern of adjustment to his problems. A first step in appreciating the real meaning of the behavior patterns that characterize an individual's personality is to become aware of the problems in his psychological development. When we recognize patterns of adjustment we can deal intelligently with the problem persons whom we meet in daily life and work.

The people of this nation have made some very great gains in bodily health and personal comforts in recent years. Material advantages, such as ownership of automobiles and indoor plumbing, have increased tremendously. The expectation of life at birth has steadily increased since the turn of the century, largely as a result of the control of infectious diseases, which formerly took a heavy toll of lives among infants, children, and young adults. For the first time in the history of the nation, the expectation of life at birth for white females is now 72.7 years, and that for white males is 66.6 years. Educational opportunities have improved for the boy and girl. In 1900, the average American youth's chances of going to high school were one in ten. In 1950, they were eight in ten. These and numerous other advancements might be cited as evidence of the progress of the American people. But what about their mental health?

Some figures on mental maladjustment

Currently more than six per cent of the population suffer from some sort of mental illness at any one time. One out of every ten persons will sooner or later need the help of a psychiatrist, and one out of every eighteen will spend some part of his life in a mental hospital. Almost as many people are admitted to mental institutions each year as are graduated from our colleges. Estimates by physicians indicate that as many as half of the people who go to doctors for physical complaints actually have mental or emotional disorders.

When the Rockefeller Brothers Foundation granted a fund for the establishment of a division of industrial mental health at the Menninger Foundation and Clinic, Topeka, Kansas, the announcement to businessmen included the following information about reasons for the grant:

. . . most people retain a sneaking suspicion that "mental health" or "maladjustment" is something involving only "crazy" people and perhaps "the slums," something far removed from their daily lives. Statistics provided by, say, the National Mental Health Committee ring no bell for them, although the chances are about one in four that they are one of the statistics. While "maladjustment" may not be the only cause, it's certainly a major factor in all of these situations:

For every four marriages a year, there is one divorce.

About 50,000 Americans are addicted to narcotics.

About 1,750,000 serious crimes are committed every year.

About 265,000 children between the ages of 7 and 17 are brought into juvenile courts each year.

About 12% of the 15 million men examined for induction into the armed forces during World War II were rejected for neuropsychotic disorders.

One out of every 18 persons now alive will spend some part of his life in a mental hospital.

In industry, more than in any other area of American life, we are constantly being reminded of the dissatisfactions, strife, and violence that occur between groups of our citizens.

In the words of Dr. W. C. Menninger: "Many jobs don't offer a very adequate outlet for some of the instinctive energy that is in all of us.

"True, there are some compensations. Sometimes we feel that our work is sufficiently worthwhile to make up for the fact that we don't have the outlet we need. Often we gain satisfaction from the very happy personal relationships we have on the job. One of the most advantageous aspects of any kind of job is the feeling that we 'belong.' Monetary gain, too, is often a source of satisfaction.

"In the opposite direction, we see, across the country, very many evidences of dissatisfaction with work. In management-labor difficulties, labor often appears to be fighting for material returns when it is actually striving for job satisfaction. The restrictive nature of work as we enforce it upon ourselves—the regimentation, the routine, and often the lack of opportunity for creativeness—adds, I think, to job dissatisfaction." . . .

In a study of 127 plants, a group of industrial psychologists found that the workers were galled by rules that assigned them to dining rooms and toilets inferior to those of their bosses and that left them to scramble for parking space in lots where stalls were reserved for executives. The worker, the research team said, was frustrated, made to feel like an "inferior creature, a number in a department." As a result, there was greater pressure through the union for more money to make up for an emotionally dissatisfying work atmosphere, and meantime the workers continued to exhibit all the hostility, sloppy production, inefficiency, and lack of motivation that resentment can produce.

Statistics on accidents indicate that some 30% of the workers become involved in 85% of the accidents, as a result of emotional troubles. Additional research has shown that the seriously troubled employee had three times as many safety violations, shop rule violations, and disciplinary contacts; two and one half times as many grievances and medical dispensary visits, and one and one half times as many minor surgical requirements, sick days, and absences for personal reasons as other employees.[1]

Many persons who read statistics about the increasing numbers of people who are confined in mental hospitals assume that the cause of mental illness stems from the faster tempo of modern life.

The idea that the hustle and bustle of modern life are responsible for the occurrence of mental diseases is not so convincing when explorers report that the natives of many primitive societies with more simple cultures suffer from the same mental diseases that are found among us. Besides the possibility that there is an increase in the incidence of mental disease, from what-

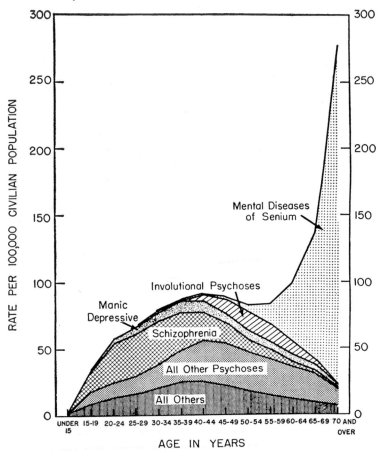

The relationship between a person's age when he is first admitted to a mental hospital and the kind of mental illness he is likely to have is shown in the graph on left. Different psychoses are associated with different ages. For example, schizophrenic and manic-depressive psychoses are most frequent among those in the age range of 15–44 years. There is a sharp rise in mental disease associated with aging, especially in the sixties. In 1949, the median age for all first admissions to State hospitals was 47.1 years.— R. H. Felix and Morton Kramer, "Extent of the Problem of Mental Disorders," **Annals, American Academy of Political and Social Science**, Vol. 286, March 1953, pp. 5–14.

Age specific first admission rates, per 100,000 civilian population, for selected diagnoses, to state hospitals for mental disease, United States, 1949.

ever causes, there are other likely reasons for the statistical changes: (1) our increased awareness of mental illness has led to the discovery of more cases; (2) a larger proportion of our population is now reaching the higher-age groups where the rates of admission are also highest (see the accompanying graph); and (3) more of those who need it can now be hospitalized because the space available has been increased.

Studies of the statistics on mental disease indicate that the highest incidence rates are not found among persons in the adolescent and adult years, the age-periods often regarded as of greatest psychological stress, but among those over 50 years of age.

Certainly, some of the increases in the incidence of mental disease can be attributed to our improved facilities for discovering persons having mental ailments, the increased number of mental hospitals, and decrease in the social stigma formerly, and to some extent still, attached to mental disease.

Obviously the costs of mental illness, whatever the causes may be, are very great, but current expenditures for overcoming this kind of illness are much smaller than for other diseases. We spend $100 a year for research for each case of poliomyelitis, but only twenty-five cents a year per case for mental disease. And for every dollar spent for research into the causes, treat-

END OF EACH YEAR

The number of resident mental patients increased from 150,000 in 1903 to 577,000 at the end of 1950. While an average of only 1.9 people in every 1,000 were long-term mental hospital residents in 1903, approximately 3.8 per 1,000 population were long-term patients in 1950. This figure represents a fourfold increase in the actual number of patients, and a doubling of the ratio of mentally ill patients to the general population.

"Although these figures indicate that psychiatric care is a very considerable element in the total picture of medical care, they do not imply the nation is rapidly becoming psychotic. The treatment of psychiatric patients requires, on the average, a much longer period of hospitalization than is required for general hospital patients." Of the 500,000 resident patients in state mental hospitals, one quarter have been hospitalized for more than 16 years, one half have been hospitalized for more than eight years, and three-quarters have been institutionalized for more

than 2.5 years. "Consequently, in any period of time, many more beds are required for treatment of a given number of psychiatric cases than are required for the care of an equal number of general patients. A complete turnover of patients in general hospitals occurs several times during the course of a year. . . . The relatively large number of hospital beds occupied by mental patients . . . represents the accumulation of patients with chronic mental disorders admitted in previous years, rather than a large number of patients admitted in the current year." The median length of stay for patients with mental diseases associated with aging—11 per cent of the resident population—is 2.4 years. On the other hand, schizophrenic patients, who make up 47 per cent of the hospitalized, stay for a median period of 10.5 years. For further information, see "Patients in Mental Institutions," 1946, U.S. Department of Commerce, Bureau of the Census, U.S. Government Printing Office, Washington, D.C., 1948, pp. 5–12.

For the source of this graph, and more details, see R. H. Felix and Morton Kramer, "Extent of the Problem of Mental Disorders," **The Annals, American Academy of Political and Social Science,** Vol. 286, March 1953, pp. 5–14.

ment, and prevention of mental illness, $100 is spent for hospital care of the mentally ill.[2]

In addition to the patients in hospitals for mental disorders, we have to consider the inmates of our prisons. About 700,000

short-term prisoners pass through prison gates each year. Long-term prisoners comprise another 150,000. Also, to the 1,750,-000 serious crimes committed each year should be added about 50,000 drug addicts if we wish to see the broad outline of the

TABLE 2-1

AGE DISTRIBUTION OF THE POPULATION IN THE UNITED STATES, 1850–1950; PROJECTED TO 1975

Age Group	1850	1920	1950	1975
Under 20 years	52.5%	40.8%	33.9%	36.5%
20–49 years	38.6	43.9	43.7	39.1
50 years and over	8.9	15.3	22.4	24.4
Total	100.0	100.0	100.0	100.0

Note: Includes population in the armed forces overseas; the projection for 1975 is based on the assumption that the 1950–53 level of fertility continues to 1965, and then declines to about the "prewar" level by 1975. Computed by the Statistical Bureau of the Metropolitan Life Insurance Company from various reports by the Bureau of the Census.

problem of major mental disorders and maladjustments.

The real challenge to the student

The figures cited above are impressive and give emphasis to the enormity of the problems of mental maladjustment that are on the institutional level. It is, however, the far greater numbers who suffer from minor mental or non-hospital varieties of maladjustment who offer the student of psychology his real challenge. Every student at times is confronted by classmates, relatives, and friends who are so unhappy or so poorly adjusted as to irritate or worry their colleagues. Some workers of the shop and office have sudden emotional outbursts that baffle their friends and supervisors. Husbands and wives sometimes are unable to meet the mental demands of married life. Sometimes, too, our own unhappiness or emotional disturbance may arouse us to our own need for a systematic approach to the study of adjustment and maladjustment.

We all meet peculiarly behaving people whom we should like to understand. Undoubtedly you have had some annoying experiences with friends, relatives, fellow employees, or students in college whom you consider queer, or sullen, overconscientious, over-suggestible, mentally twisted, disturbing, misfit, sexually perverted, and so on. How did their personalities become warped? What, if anything, might be done to help them?

What facts and points of view are needed by friends, parents, and executives to facilitate the development of strong personalities? How can you and I direct our own mental habits in order to facilitate our happiness and mental health? Perhaps we should begin our study of mental ailments by first noting their place among all human illnesses.

Human illnesses, maladjustments, and adjustment mechanisms cannot be classified into nonoverlapping or mutually exclusive categories, but the reader's background for further discussion may be aided by means of the following groupings:

A. Organic. The tissues have been impaired.

1. TRAUMATIC—Mechanical injuries or wounds, such as broken bones or cuts.
2. TOXIC—Poisons in the body, such as alcohol or drugs.
3. MICRO-ORGANIC—popularly called germ infections, these include illness caused by microscopic organisms such as protozoa, bacteria, and the viruses.
4. GLANDULAR—These may involve glands that pour their secretions into body cavities or the endocrines which pour their secretions into the blood stream.
5. TISSUE CHANGES—Cancer, tumor, arteriosclerosis, and so on.

6. PSYCHOSES, ORGANIC—So far as insanity is concerned, approximately 42 per cent of the cases are caused by organic conditions. These diseases with their percentages of total admissions are mainly senile dementia (8 per cent), cerebral arteriosclerosis (10 per cent), general paresis (7 per cent), and alcoholic psychoses (5 per cent). In these disorders a definite physical or organic basis is known to be present. In business, these organically caused disorders are seen in the occasional cases of brain tumor, epilepsy, sleeping sickness, strokes, general paresis or syphilis of the central nervous system, hardening of the arteries, and senile dementia.

B. Functional. These ailments do not involve any measurable impairment of the tissues. About 58 per cent of all psychopathic or mentally ill cases appear to have a functional origin.

1. PSYCHOSES, FUNCTIONAL—Pronounced mental disorders, which unfit the individual for adjustment to his usual environment, principally dementia praecox (23 per cent), manic-depressive psychoses (9 per cent), involutional melancholia (4 per cent), and others.*

2. PSYCHOPATHIC PERSONALITY—A general classification for persons who are neither psychotic nor neurotic. It is a convenient borderline term for social misfits that includes the pathological liars, sex perverts, vagrants, eccentrics, misanthropes, troublemakers, moral defectives, and criminals who commit crimes without extenuation. The psychopaths constitute about 2 per cent of first admissions to mental hospitals and 15 to 20 per cent of incarcerated criminals.

3. PSYCHONEUROSES—Mild mental disturbances or patterns of behavior which do not wholly unfit the individual for his usual environment. Often called "nervous cases" in the home and in business offices.

C. Common adjustment "mechanisms" or "dynamisms"—These are found among all normal persons and are not evidence of abnormality. They become maladjustments only when extremely inappropriate manifestations handicap the individual who uses them too frequently or too extensively. Examples of terms used for some of the more common adjustment mechanisms or behavior dynamisms are:

1. OVERCOMPENSATION—The behavior resulting from the extreme motivation is much greater than necessary for the situation. If expressed indirectly and to an appropriate degree, it may be a positive substitute activity.

2. DEFENSE MECHANISM—Maintaining a sense of personal worth by resorting to behavior that guards some aspect of the personality from scrutiny by others or by one's self.

3. IDENTIFICATION—A mental process which expresses itself in the form of an emotional tie with other persons (or situations) in which the individual behaves as if he were the person with whom he has this tie. "Before I do anything, I always ask myself what my 'hero' would want me to do." Also, basking in reflected glory.

4. REGRESSION—Reverting to the role of a child or living in an earlier, easier world as a means of escape from present situations of a frustrating or unsatisfying nature; returns to infantile types of behavior. "If I can't be a big businessman in the city, I can go back to the farm of my childhood."

5. RATIONALIZATION—Reasoning in regard to the problem is distorted to justify an act or

---

* The percentages of total admissions, given in parentheses above, should be differentiated from vital statistics of this kind which usually show first admissions, readmissions, and resident population in state mental hospitals. The percentages in parentheses do not total 100 per cent because of difficulty in classifying many patients who are placed under headings such as "other psychoses."

opinion which is actually based on other grounds, as in the "sour grapes" or "sweet lemon" or Pollyanna interpretations.

6. NEGATIVISM—Resisting suggestions from others, doing the opposite of what is expected, or, in some cases, doing nothing at all.

7. CONQUERING HERO MECHANISM—Role-playing, in imagination, in which the individual is superior or successful.

8. SUFFERING HERO MECHANISM—Role-playing, in imagination, in which the individual is inferior or attains superiority through his "superior" inferiorities.

9. PROJECTION—The tendency to ascribe to other persons or situations drives and complexes that belong to oneself. Ideas of reference and delusions of persecution are examples.

10. INTROJECTION—The tendency or act of absorbing the personality of others, or situations, into one's own mental life to the extent of reacting to external events as though they were internal ones. By some, this behavior is considered an extreme form of identification.

11. EGOCENTRISM—The observer is so tightly tied to his own personality that he is unable to share directly the experiences of others. The term is used also in regard to an act to overcome being ignored and to get attention, even if unfavorable, as a symbol of social approval.

12. HABIT SPASM—A convulsive involuntary contraction of a muscle or set of muscles that helps to reduce tension. An unconscious purpose may be attention-getting: "People will notice my twitches."

13. SEXUAL ANOMALIES, such as homosexuality, sadism, masochism, and exhibitionism.

14. INVALIDISM—Habitual ill health or exaggerated ailment resorted to as a means of dealing with one's problems. It offers the individual an apparently acceptable excuse in his failure to meet his own or others' expectations.

Most persons need not concern themselves about the organic psychoses—the severe breakdowns of the human machinery; or the functional psychoses—the extreme cases of mismanagement of oneself. The physician and psychiatrist must deal with these. In a brief survey of this kind, we must relegate cases which require hospital or institutional treatment to experts who specialize in those problems. Every person, however, has frequent dealings with the psychoneuroses and common adjustment mechanisms. At times every person exhibits symptoms of abnormality, in a mild degree, as 100 per cent management is not common among individuals any more than it is among businesses. "Qualitatively, we are all about the same; quantitatively, we differ widely." This old saying simply means that we all have the same behavior tendencies or traits, but we differ in the extent or degree to which we have them.

A study of the more common adjustment mechanisms—dynamisms—should enable us to recognize when we are using them, to avoid using them excessively, and to abandon inappropriate ones for more effective methods of dealing with our problems.

We need a basic pattern for our study of people

We want to learn to think of human behavior in its dynamic aspects—strivings, motivations and adjustments. These of course cannot be observed directly but they

The "bundle of nerves" person may need medical or psychological treatment, and should consult trained specialists in those fields; unfortunately, those who have to live with emotionally unstable, neurotic, or poorly adjusted persons do not have specialists from whom they can learn how to live comfortably in these relationships. The normally healthy and well-adjusted persons have to adapt themselves as best they can. To make the adaptation, a great deal of insight and patience must be acquired. Eventually, too, it often becomes necessary for the healthier individuals to develop a personal philosophy which recognizes that our associations with difficult personalities force us to strengthen our own personalities. We grow through positive adjustments to our problem friends and situations. The strengths we acquire through our relations with them enable us to attain satisfactions that would not come to us through ease. Furthermore, our insight into their adjustments helps us gain greater insight into our own, and we therefore evaluate our psychological kinships more intelligently and more highly.

can often be correctly inferred if we study behavior systematically.

The human being operates in as natural a manner as do other parts of the physical world. Every human act could be understood if we knew all the pertinent facts. True, we do not know all the important facts needed to understand each person, but we believe that a person's behavior can be understood on the basis of principles that can be learned. To understand an individual we need a pattern for our thinking. Furthermore, we need a pattern for our thinking which is far more meaningful than

a mere classification of the individual's behavior. Giving a person a label such as "introvert" does not indicate his other characteristics that are equally or more important. The label may even deter us from understanding him more completely. Nor does telling a person how we classify his behavior help him: it usually annoys him; furthermore, it sometimes harms him, because he may unconsciously accept the descriptive classification as a model from which to pattern his own behavior.

A classification of human maladjustments and common mechanisms such as the ones

"I simply can't stand being cooped up here any longer!"

The environment is incidental; the way the individual adjusts to the environment is most important. Reproduced by special permission from Ralph Fuller, the artist, and **The Saturday Evening Post** (November 25, 1933 issue), copyright 1933 by The Curtis Publishing Company.

we have listed is somewhat convenient for discussion purposes and record, but in handling people we need a scheme of thinking that is more meaningful. A human being is a living, responding organism and can be understood only when we visualize him as an active, adjusting personality that evolves over a period of years. This means specifically that we can gain little help from statements such as, "He has an inferiority complex," or, "That's a defense mechanism." Such terms should be used mainly as points of departure for our thinking about the individual's problems and the ways he characteristically deals with them.

Nor is a knowledge of hereditary factors of much value to anyone who deals with problem persons. We may know, for example, that if one parent has a certain mental disease, the expectancy rate of mental disease for the offspring is 16 per cent; if both parents are so afflicted, the expectancy rate for the children is 68 per cent. This knowledge does not help us in practical situations, because we are always dealing with a specific individual. For example: if we know that both parents of a person have a particular mental ailment, is the subject of our analysis a member of the 68 per cent group who become afflicted or the 32 per cent group who never do become afflicted? Such statistics are of little aid to the educational advisor or the employment man. Often a knowledge of them does much harm, because the man who guides his human relations by means of statistics only is apt to be unfair to the many people to whom the figures do not apply.

Furthermore, many vital statistics have a kind of fatalistic effect on the individual to whom they seem to apply in part. He assumes that, his ancestry being what it is, there is little that he can do about or for himself through his own intelligent effort. This is a most unfortunate notion, because everyone can direct his own psychological development to a surprisingly great extent.

A knowledge of environment has some value in dealing with people but only a very limited value when we deal with a person. The old arguments about heredity versus environment are usually beside the point, because the individual is not a sum of the two. He is the *product* of the two in interaction. The individual is not a rubber stamp of his background. Rather, he is more like a live rubber ball. He not only rolls in the grooves of his environment but he also bounces away from parts of it. And, like those of a football, his "bounces" are often unpredictable, though a knowledge of the field or area where the "bounce" takes place often enables the experienced observer to predict the direction of some of the "bounces."

Sometimes a football bounces just as one would expect; at other times it veers off in a wholly unexpected direction. On some few occasions, too, it scarcely bounces at all but comes to rest very quickly. This football analogy is somewhat helpful whenever we study a person's environment. To understand any individual in relation to his environment, we should ask three general questions:

1. *To what influences of the environment did he learn to react as expected?* That is, what influences has he adopted? Which ones does he now follow habitually in his life? For example, if he was reared on a farm, does he have a typical farmer's work habits and points of view? Or, if he was reared in the home of a Democrat, is he a Democrat? If he was reared in the slums, does he feel at home in the slums?

2. *To what influences of the environment did he learn to react in an unexpected or opposing manner?* For example, if he was reared on a farm, does he now despise farming and rural life? Similarly, does he dislike Democrats, and does he feel out of place in the slums?

3. *What influences of the environment might ordinarily be expected to affect the personality but have really had no effect?* Some people fail to react to certain influences in terms of acceptance or rejection; they react neither favorably nor unfavorably. Some farmers' sons grow up and neither like nor dislike the farm. The same principle can be noted when we study any person's background. His early environmental history may have had very little effect on many of his present habits.

These three concepts regarding the environment—*acceptance, rejection,* and *indifference*—compel us to seek for more than a knowledge of the peculiar person's environment.

The employment man who collects bulging files of data about his applicants should know how to organize and interpret the data. The college personnel man who has extensive card records of facts about each student needs a method of viewing the facts. The parent who learns the hundreds of incidents in the development of his children needs a pattern for his thinking in order to arrange the facts into psychological significance. Anyone who associates with people in business, in school, or in their homes should have a systematic approach to the interpretation of human personalities. The approach described here is known as the adjustment concept.

The adjustment concept

We can, if we wish, explain human behavior by many different systems of thinking, as shown by the several schools of thought in modern psychology. Each school makes its unique contributions by virtue of the fact that, when we study anything in terms of a given system of thinking, we often gain a new perspective of related matters. This particular system of thinking, the adjustment concept, is used by this writer because it is easily grasped and is most meaningful to persons who do not plan to become highly trained psychologists through years of graduate work in clinics and universities.*

To understand a person, we may first think of him as in a state of activity. He is always active, whether he is sleeping, thinking, daydreaming, resting, playing, or working. Even dying is an activity. Some ongoing activities are always present, because the motive of life is to function. For us to think of a living individual who is totally inactive would be impossible, for he would be frozen, mummified, or calcified. Basic to our thinking of human beings is the point of view of interaction, the adjustment concept. To say that an individual is always active

and that through his activity he develops may be trite, but to appreciate how a personality grows in the adjustment process is not always so simple as it sounds.

In his activities, the individual is always trying to achieve a satisfying state. In his functioning, his activity frequently is blocked or delayed by difficulties or barriers, and so he must learn how to overcome the difficulties or go around them.

A woodsman exploring in a forest exemplifies the adjustment idea. When he finds an obstruction in his path, he may use direct attack upon it, that is, remove it or go through it. Or he may go around it by means of a substitute or indirect route. Or he may decide to make a different kind of exploration, or even return to his home and do no more exploring at all.

Obviously, if the woodsman has once used a route, he will be apt to use it on the second and succeeding trips over the territory. He may use an old route even though he has found a better or easier one. An important part of the concept is that the woodsman does, at times, make new paths as a result of obstructions in his way. The barriers, often called frustrations, cause him to develop new mental habits and new urges to act.

Let us apply this barrier-adjustment idea to a few everyday situations. Assume that you are a student who is sitting comfortably in class and looking forward to a pleasant school experience. Suddenly the instructor announces an examination on some part of the course which you do not understand. You are annoyed by the barrier to your pleasant ongoing activity. You must make an adjustment. The adjustment you make will be one or more of the four general varieties:

---

* The treatment of the adjustment concept in this book must of necessity be limited to a few chapters as a background for dealing with certain selected aspects of the individual's life and work situation. Students who wish to read a comprehensive scholarly treatment of adjustment are referred to Laurance Frederic Shaffer and Edward Joseph Shoben, Jr., *The Psychology of Adjustment*, Houghton Mifflin Company, Boston, 1956.

DIRECT | ATTACK!!

Adjustment by direct attack upon the barrier or problem. The individual is in a state of ongoing activity, such as attending college. He finds that he must take a difficult examination. He studies diligently for the examination and overcomes the difficulty. If he fails in his first attempt, he persists until he succeeds. The original goal is kept and the successful adjustment tends to build up the ego—the individual's feeling of self-worth. His personality is strengthened and he is, to that extent, better prepared to meet future problems that involve volitional effort.

1. **Direct attack.** Examples:

   a. Study for the examination.
   b. Prepare for the examination by having someone quiz you on the accuracy of your present knowledge.
   c. Outline the subject matter, recite to yourself all parts which you understand, and learn the important parts which are not clear to you.

2. **Substitute act of possible positive value.** Examples:

   a. Change to another course.
   b. Transfer to another school.
   c. Decide to quit school and find a job in the business world.

3. **Substitute acts of negative value.** Examples:

   a. Arrange to sit near a good student who will help you during the examination.
   b. Prepare a "crib" for the examination.
   c. Feign illness at the time of the examination and thus postpone or avoid taking it at the designated time.
   d. Accuse the teacher of unfairness.
   e. Berate or ridicule the students who study for the examination.

4. **Advanced stages of negative value adjustment.** Examples:

   a. Imagine yourself the hero of fiction or motion picture adventures and ignore your problem.
   b. Contemplate suicide.

Of course, the student who deals with the examination barrier by *direct attack* also prepares himself to deal more effectively with new or later examinations in the same and other courses. He builds up efficient study habits. His ego or feeling of self-worth is increased in a sound way. He achieves a more satisfying state. His personality is stronger than it was previous to his dealing with the barrier. His behavior is integrative in the sense that it facilitates growth toward greater adequacy in the meeting of new and

Adjustment by substitute activities, positive and negative: Instead of taking the difficult examination, the student may develop a new goal, such as going into business. If he does this, his feeling of self-worth may or may not remain the same, depending upon the extent to which the original goal was associated with pleasant emotional patterns. The evasive substitute activity of negative value is represented by subterfuge. This type of adjustment tends to weaken the personality and to lessen the feeling of self-worth. The reacting person's ability to meet similar problems is decreased by the latter variety of adjustment.

POSITIVE SUBSTITUTE ACT | NEGATIVE SUB. ACT

more difficult problems. Accomplishments and satisfactions are increased.

A *substitute act* of positive value, at times, may be a more logical adjustment than direct attack. Although the decision to choose a substitute act may result in a feeling of failure with regard to the barrier thus avoided, it is likely to cause the individual to put extra energy into the substitute act. Not every student who fails in his school work and decides to go into business works harder in business than he did in school, but some do. A sense of failure in one field may stimulate the individual to put forth extra effort in another field.

The student who chooses to make an *evasive* adjustment weakens himself for the next problem. His ability has been lessened. The evasive experience has weakened his personality. In this sense, his behavior is nonintegrative.

Obviously, no person makes direct attack or intelligent substitute act adjustments in every situation. Everyone uses evasion and retreat at times, but the strong personality tends to use the first two habitually and the weak man ordinarily uses the latter two in dealing with life's problems.

If a given adjustment habit is once firmly established, it is easily repeated in dealing with the same or related barriers. Adjustments begin very early in life and are made every day until the end of life. Each time we deal with a problem, great or small, we contribute toward or detract from the effectiveness of our personalities. The employee

who has worked in an unsatisfactory position for a year, a day, or even an hour is no longer quite the same employee that he was when he first began to work. In the course of his employment he has developed new mental habits or tendencies toward new habits. In his reacting he may have acquired

Adjustment by retreat. A photograph of a state hospital patient whose emotional life has been turned wholly inward. He lives in a world of fantasy rather than of reality. His adjustment is of the retreat type.

either hatred or admiration for a department manager, or for certain kinds of work.

To repeat the adjustment concept, but to apply it to the worker who finds himself in an uncongenial job, the following outline elaborates the idea further:

The employee who finds his job uncongenial and wishes that he could get a new job can make any one or more of several types of adjustment. He can remain on the job he has, but utilize it for his personal growth. He may also make the adjustment by a substitute act of positive value such as seeking and obtaining another job. He may also remain on the job, but compensate for his dissatisfaction through a hobby, athletics, church work, art, etc. Substitute acts of negative value are of numerous kinds, such as finding fault with the world, criticizing others unnecessarily, acquiring functional illnesses, immersion in a cult, longing for death, etc. In this illustration, the negative substitute act is illustrated by the individual in the "gimme" response, getting unearned money from others.

1. Direct attack. Examples:

    a. Study the mechanical equipment used in the work, if any is used. Improve its design or invent new equipment.

    b. Study methods of doing the work. Practice the methods and improve them.

    c. Study the fellow workers and improve the human relationships. Influence the fellow employees and supervisors in order to have them like him as well as enjoy their work more fully.

2. Substitute acts of possible positive value. Examples:

    a. Obtain or continue to seek a transfer to another job.

    b. Obtain or continue to seek employment elsewhere.

    c. Compensate for dissatisfaction through a hobby, athletics, church work, art, etc.

3. Substitute acts of negative value. Examples:

    a. Criticise the job, the boss, the fellow workers, or industry as a whole.

    b. Feign illness or, as a result of subconscious maladjustment, become too ill to work.

    c. Adopt an air of superiority toward the job.

    d. Feel inferior in the job and avoid thoughts of the work as much as possible.

4. Advanced stages of negative value adjustment.

    a. Immerse himself in some mystical cult or pseudo-science such as a Hindu philosophy, astrology, palmistry, etc.

    b. Isolate himself and avoid any possible failure by making no attempts to change his status.

    c. Long for death and release from all life's problems.

The worker who habitually deals by direct attack with the problems of his job increases his ability to deal with more difficult jobs. He may never attain any famed expertness, but he tends to feel in control of himself in relation to the problems around him. He earns his own self-respect. He finds that life offers him many opportunities for growth and genuine happiness. He is confident about the future. Furthermore, in the process of adjusting himself to the barriers in his job, he acquires new behavior patterns, such as a dislike for certain types of supervision or a liking for certain kinds of work.

If, however, the individual's habitual methods of solving his problems fail to give him satisfaction, he feels frustrated. In *frustration,* continuing or recurrent strong motivation forces the individual to search for a solution to his problem. This searching, largely unconscious, results in highly emotionalized or unorganized behavior that lasts until some effective or seemingly effective solution is found. Frustrated persons are apt to be unusually forceful, persevering, and immune to appeals of logic and reason concerning the area of mental life colored by the frustration. As we shall see later, frustration-motivated individuals are a problem not only to themselves but also to those leaders who try to direct social movements rationally and objectively.

Predisposing and precipitating influences

Every person has many *predisposing tendencies* when confronted by a new problem. He may be young in years, but he is "old" psychologically. He is a member of a human race which is really millions of years old in terms of biological influences. Furthermore, his bodily equipment—sex, size, glands, muscular and other structures—all contribute predisposing influences in behavior. *Conditionings* (*a*) from a single intense emotional experience, such as a fright,

or (*b*) from repeated experiences of the same kind, such as customs, habits, beliefs, education, parental training, and the whole culture where he has lived, are additional predisposing influences. These have affected him over relatively long periods of time. They will be discussed further in Chapters 7 and 14.

Precipitating factors are influences which act over a short period of time. These are likely to be emotional or exciting states, such as a recent threat, thwarted habit, ridicule, failure, success, fatigue, or disappointment. Obviously, the child who has just been scolded is likely to react to frustration somewhat differently from the way he would react at another time.

No one can unravel all the strands in the web of human personality. Life is too complex. We can, however, collect available facts about ourselves or others and try to see how the known facts arrange themselves into patternful relationships. A knowledge of psychology and the ability to use intelligently such concepts as adjustment often contribute to the art of dealing with people. It is especially useful to those who have counseling, guidance, or executive responsibilities. A starting point in this kind of analysis of a person is the sources of frustration or barriers.

Barriers

When we note the peculiar behavior of a maladjusted individual, we observe his peculiarity and then try to think of the way it originated. We try to think of the person's problems.

The sources of frustration in the lives of different individuals vary greatly, but we can mention typical barriers that necessitate adjustment. The problems or difficulties that stimulate the individual to seek adjustment may be a part of the external environment or within the personality. The particular nature of the barrier is not especially important. Any environmental situation or charac-

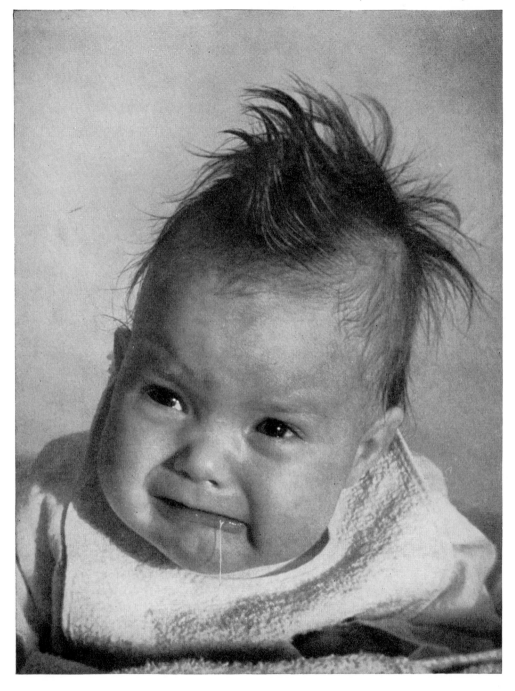

Frustration is as old as life. The picture was taken in the morning just before feeding time. The mother was standing at the side of the bassinet holding the bottle. The baby was annoyed at the delay and began to cry. There is only one time when the human being has no frustrations, and that is in the period before birth. Frustration begins at birth and ends at death. **(Photograph by Kenneth P. Marsh, Detroit, Michigan.)**

teristic of a person may constitute a barrier. The important factor is the meaning of the situation or characteristic to the individual who is adjusting. A feeling of resentment, inadequacy, or inferiority toward the situation often indicates the presence of a barrier.

The two broad classes of barriers are (*a*) those owing to lack of capacity, and (*b*) those owing to the necessity for abrupt changes in behavior (see Table 2–2). Obvious examples of capacity difficulties that demand adjustment are organic or physical conditions such as poor health or a crippled limb. Or there may be a chronic ailment or disability such as asthma, tuberculosis, heart murmur, epilepsy, color-blindness, or flat feet.

In the mental group may be found capacity problems such as low general intelligence, specific inaptitudes, emotional conflicts, bad habits, feelings of insecurity, lack of opportunity for training, and convictions of one's inferiority. Perhaps the most common personal difficulties are those which result from a lack of recognition for sincere efforts. This last type often occurs among children and students who think that they are doing well and then later find through comparisons with others that they appear to be inferior.

Bodily and mental punishment may accentuate the feelings of inadequacy. Many an introverted adult represents the effects of too many or too severe lashings of rod or tongue by the parent of the child. Any activity or situation may become a barrier if the individual is given punishment, neglect, or no approval in connection with it. Conversely, any activity may be satisfying if praise and prestige follow or accompany the activity.

Environmental barriers may be poverty, inhibiting customs or laws, and lack of opportunity for expression of the biological tendencies. However, the barrier objectively considered is not nearly so important as the interpretation that the person gives it. The same situation that is a barrier to one person may be a challenge or an opportunity to another. Among nations, a sterile soil and a harsh climate may result in the development of a virile nation, whereas a land of plentiful resources may have a race of fruitless people. Similarly, a poverty-stricken home may stimulate a child to achieve eminence while the son of the rich man on the hill becomes a weakling. It is significant that neither the poor boy nor the rich boy necessarily becomes strong or weak. The way each adjusts to his situation determines whether he will be strong or weak.

Nor can we hope to remove all difficulties from the life of anyone. To do so would only handicap him for life as it is. As Herbert Spencer said: "The ultimate result of shielding men from the effects of folly is to fill the world with fools."

Throughout infancy, childhood, youth, and adulthood, the individual is constantly bombarded by experiences in which he is shown his inferiorities and inadequacies. For many people, a few experiences of inadequacy cause them to develop habits, through their adjustments, which make ordinary activities, such as the study of certain school subjects, very difficult. Reasons for many inabilities and peculiarities can be traced to the early experiences of the child.

One girl could not be convinced that she was pretty enough to make a favorable impression on others. She had two sisters who were praised frequently for their beauty. One day a wealthy aunt visited the home and again praised the two sisters for their beauty. On one occasion, however, the aunt realized that she should make a favorable comment regarding the plain child and so she said to her: "And you, my dear, have a kind face." In spite of the fact that many people would rather have a kind face than mere beauty, this girl, who is now a woman, prefers work that isolates her from other people, especially those who are attractive in appearance. Any vocation that would require emphasis upon personal beauty or attractive attire is out of the question for her.

She has given up all hope of making herself attractive to others.

ANY SITUATION MAY BE A BARRIER TO ONE PERSON BUT A MEANS OF SATISFACTION TO ANOTHER. Personal appearance became a great barrier to the above-mentioned girl because her own appearance was associated with feelings of inferiority. However, to some women their personal appearance is an outstanding means of attaining satisfactions. Similarly, the study of music is a barrier to many children whose parents compel them to practice on the piano for hours. To other children, music is the one satisfying outlet for self-expression. Hundreds of school subjects, jobs, and activities are "meat for some and poison for others." The nature of the activity is incidental. What the activity means, represents, symbolizes, or is associated with in the mind of the individual is the important factor.

Tasks that are easy to perform tend to be satisfying but are not necessarily so. Tasks that are difficult to perform tend to be annoying but are not necessarily so. Many students can learn certain school subjects far more easily than their classmates but prefer to study other subjects that are more difficult for them. Many housewives can do their housework with ease but dislike it. Many employees can do the tasks in their jobs with ease but prefer to change their vocations. We should not assume that easily performed acts are always satisfying.

How executives contribute to the better adjustments of employees

Every executive can, and many do, facilitate the direct-attack adjustments of individual employees. The executive may apply the adjustment concept when he finds that a salesman's volume has fallen off suddenly in a territory where the business activity of other companies has increased.

The manner of the failing salesman may indicate that something is bothering him. The astute manager tends to make inquiries regarding the failing salesman's habits, health, home conditions, and so on. If he finds that the salesman's wife has learned to consider her husband's job a socially inferior one since her nagging mother moved into the home, the manager can discuss the situation sympathetically and prove that the husband's job is important. A few special assignments that include a title may be all that is necessary to build up the salesman's self-respect and social prestige with the wife and mother-in-law.

Psychological insight and skill are applied in business whenever an executive feels with, thinks with, and works with employees who have disturbing emotional problems. The executive may not be able to give a technical psychological name to the employee's variety of inappropriate adjustment, but if he discovers the bothersome problem, notes the kind of evasive adjustment being made, and then instills confidence in the employee by showing him the possible direct-attack methods, the employee's behavior is likely to improve.

The adjustment concept causes us to recognize that we should not think of an employee as *being* this or that—as, for example, being conceited or sarcastic when dealing with difficult customers. The individual is not conceited or sarcastic, but he *uses* conceit or sarcasm when dealing with another personality. He has acquired the habit of using certain evasive methods, "personality tools," when dealing with other personalities.

Similarly, when an executive's stenographer becomes irritable, the psychologically minded executive tries to discover her problem. Perhaps her father has lost his job and makes little attempt to find another because he assumes that his employed daughter will support him. Or the girl's boyfriend may have become interested in someone else. Or any one of thousands of other problems may have occurred, each of which might necessitate that the stenographer make an adjustment. During the process of adjustment, the insight and encouragement of the executive may be very helpful.

Of course, many men have attained the kind of growth characterized by the personality tools of direct attack and intelligent substitute acts even though they have never studied psychology. The psychologists have so clarified the process of adjustment that people who lack psychological insight may the more quickly acquire it.

The significance of the classification of problem-solving methods has been ably stated by Robert H. Seashore:

It has thus far been implied that in dealing with any maladjustment it is first essential to determine the nature of the problem being faced. The next step is to determine what the individual is doing about the problem, and if his efforts are not successful, to consider the other methods of problem solving that might be considered as desirable alternatives. The writer has employed this classification in several ways, the simplest being a discussion designed to assist students of elementary psychology in starting to plan a career. In this case they were asked to describe what they would like to achieve (either in general terms or by giving illustrations of other people's similar achievements) in each of five areas of endeavor: 1. educational, 2. vocational, 3. avocational, 4. leadership, 5. personal development. It was found that the students could do this fairly easily, particularly when they were urged to set goals which they would really be willing to work for if they thought there was some reasonable possibility of success. After listing the advantages and handicaps which they had for achieving each of the five goals they were then asked to describe what methods, if any, they had employed up to the present time to achieve each goal. If these did not appear productive of the desired results, they were then to examine the classification for alternative methods which might overcome the difficulties so far encountered. This procedure is based on the idea that the formulation of a problem is often more than half of the total process of solution, and that a systematic method of procedure may save both the student

and his advisors a great deal of time and wasted effort.

Perhaps the greatest importance of this classification for clinical psychology is that of attempting to analyze personality characteristics in terms of *habitual methods of responding to the principal types of situations which every person faces.*

. . . Furthermore, the classification in terms of problem solving behaviors is an operational one which tells what the person has been doing so far and lists the principal alternative things which he or his consultants could do in the future to provide a more satisfactory solution. The fact that such a classification is not a static one is perhaps one of its most hopeful features, in that it breaks down such large and vague concepts as social maladjustment into things which the person can do about particular problems in his social situation. In this it parallels the work of all individualized remedial education such as athletic coaching, time and motion studies on industrial operations, where it is already recognized that technical skill and guidance can often produce marked improvements in individual performance. From this point of view clinical psychology gets beyond the problem of diagnosis and endeavors to place a greater emphasis on the provision of technical facilities for assisting the individual to deal with his problems more accurately. Both the consultant and the client can contribute actively to such counseling, and if the method is made clear, there should be greater probability of the client's being able to develop skill in the methods of handling future problems himself, or at least recognizing when he needs expert assistance.[3]

Adjustments are more important than environment

From the standpoint of the incidence of mental disease, as discussed in the early part of this chapter, the adjustment concept means that the environment is often an incidental part in our important mental habits. The environment may be paced slowly or rapidly and be relatively simple or complex. The individual's adjustment to the pace, whatever it is, is what counts. In other words, it is just as easy to drive an automobile at fifty miles an hour as to drive a horse at twenty—once the driver has learned the art. The art of living is an individual matter and must be learned by the individual regardless of when or where he lives.

Whenever we compare the lives of those who succeeded in dealing with the conditions of life with those who have failed, we find that the strong persons developed good adjustment habits and the failures developed evasive and retreat habits. The same observation applies to the people of a nation. The strength of a nation does not wholly depend upon natural resources nor on geographical location but mainly upon the strength of personality of its people. We need only compare the resources and people of the various nations, as, for example, Switzerland versus Russia, to see ample evidence of this axiom. The leaders and citizens of the United States must recognize this basic truth or suffer through the lack of its application. If too many individuals learn to lean upon charity or other artificial aids rather than upon their own strong adjustment habits, this nation will become weaker and the eventual prey of the stronger. This means that everyone, regardless of race, culture, or age, can benefit from a thorough study of the adjustment process in order that he may guide his own adjustments intelligently.

Good adjustment means that the person to whom it is ascribed is one who usually uses the direct-attack and positive-value mechanisms in dealing with his problems. He deals effectively and satisfyingly with life and its problems without bringing about disturbing feelings of anxiety, hostility, or dependence on his own part or on the part of others. He feels that he has attained or is attaining goals that are satisfying to him and approved by society. When he helps to solve problems of value to society, he never exploits or injures other persons to attain his ends. He believes in and seeks to enhance those values which the race has found necessary for sur-

vival and for spiritual growth, such as truthfulness, altruism, and objective thinking. He feels that he "belongs" and that he is needed where he finds himself. He utilizes the immediate situation for further growth in his ability to deal with new and more difficult problems that befall him. He enjoys life intelligently and shares his enjoyments.

He is cooperative and an effective member of a team. He identifies with his immediate social groups: the work gang, office force, neighbors, and church, club, or association members.

He is master of himself. He does not unnecessarily upset the smooth tenor of his relations with others nor allow his own impulsive or ill considered acts to interfere with his plans or his social adjustments. He is consistent and stable without continuous bothersome tensions from conflicts and frustrations.

One purpose of education in general and of psychology in particular is to assist the individual in learning those adjustment habits which are of the direct-attack and positive variety. You and I, as laymen in the field of mental hygiene, can do very little to assist the psychotic, but we can do a great deal toward the development of sound mental habits in ourselves and our associates.

Tables 2–2 and 2–3 will enable the reader to see a general outline of the adjustment concept. This list of barriers and adjustments is not intended to be exhaustive, nor is the classification of any one item of behavior supposed to be fixed. The adjustment activities mentioned are not mutually exclusive kinds of reactions to barriers, but only frequently-met or modal varieties. As previously stated, any variety of behavior can be classified only in relation to its context or setting. However, a brief examination of these tables should help the reader in developing an alertness to the kinds of adjustment which he can observe in his everyday experiences.

TABLE 2-2

EXAMPLES OF BARRIERS TO WHICH THE INDIVIDUAL ADJUSTS

I. "Capacity" barriers:
   A. *Insufficient capacity* to perform satisfactorily the activities that others expect the individual to perform or that he himself expects to perform:
      1. Organic or physical:
         a. Poor health.
         b. Atypical body shape or size.
         c. Endocrine imbalance.
         d. Lack of athletic ability.
         e. Defective sensory equipment, such as deafness.
         f. Defective motor equipment, such as stiff joints.
         g. Unattractive personal appearance, real or fancied.
      2. Intellectual:
         a. Intelligence too low; for example, inability to do satisfactory school work or to handle jobs requiring brain work.
         b. Ability evaluated too high; for example, individual's parent expects him to be an honor student or an accomplished musician.
         c. Specific inabilities, such as lack of ability in mathematics.
      3. Social:
         a. Lack of friends and inability to make friends.
         b. Lack of ability to maintain ego in the face of bullying, ridicule, snubs, nicknames, and so forth.
         c. Competing with superiors; for example, an average student rooms with a bragging superior student.
   B. *Capacity too great* for required or present activities:
      1. Rating of individual's capacity by parent, teacher, mental examiner, or supervisor much lower than it actually is.
      2. Constant association with inferiors in education, health, or social development.
      3. Environment unstimulating, as among children of foreigners and among fellow workers who set poor examples; working hours too long for normal development, and so forth.
II. Barriers arising from a *change* in activities:
   A. Barriers arising because the individual is compelled to change his activities *abruptly:*
      1. Birth of another child in a family in which the individual was an only child and a transfer of affection from the older child to the newborn.
      2. Adoption into a strange family.
      3. Death of a loved person.
      4. Sex experiences that occurred too early in life and could not be continued satisfactorily.
      5. Disappointment in love; betrayal of confidence.
      6. Conflicts in love that require immediate adjustment.
      7. Sudden change from a higher to a lower standard of living.
      8. Sudden change from a lower to a higher standard of living.
      9. Loss of a job; new job not satisfactory.
   B. Barriers resulting from the individual's *lack of training or preparation* to meet his problems and his being thus compelled to accept new activities:
      1. Normal associations with other children forbidden by parents; consequently, child or adult now adapts himself to new environments or contacts with great difficulty.
      2. Puritanical, austere, or unsympathetic parents.
      3. Parents who have been too lenient and have not trained their child to solve adult problems, such as the wise spending of money, the acquisition of proper habits, freedom of choice, etc.
      4. Teachers who do not understand their pupils.
      5. Disinterest of parents in the child; broken home; mother who is employed or who is interested in other activities more than in the child's development.
      6. Compulsion to continue an unwanted education or to study subjects of no interest, such as music, languages, etc.
      7. Compulsion to take an unsatisfactory job.
      8. Association with superiors in studies or in work.
      9. Association with persons of greater wealth, refinement, ability, or charm, and a feeling of inferiority caused by the differences.
      10. Association with others of assumed superior race or nationality.

TABLE 2-2 (cont.)

C. Barriers arising from the *continuance of activities* that should have been superseded by other activities:
   1. Remaining in a social environment too long for personal development.
   2. Remaining in a job too long.
   3. Continuation into adulthood of inefficient or childish habits, such as poor study habits, lisping, temper tantrums, sullenness.
   4. Continuation into adulthood of childhood emotional tendencies, such as parent fixations: *Oedipus complex, Electra complex.*
   5. Clinging to outmoded religious creeds that appear to be out of harmony with new experiences—a condition found among some college students.

D. Frequent *interruptions* of ongoing activities:
   1. Frequent change of school.
   2. Frequent changes in the home.
   3. Frequent changes of home town.
   4. Frequent shiftings of tasks or of instructions in work.
   5. Reprimands by superiors.
   6. Naggings by mate.
   7. Frequent inhibition of desired acts that are not approved by society and the aroused energy of which is not directed into satisfying channels but accumulates from repeated thwartings.

TABLE 2-3

EXAMPLES OF ADJUSTMENT ACTIVITIES OF THE INDIVIDUAL

I. Adjustment by *direct attack* upon the problem:
   A. As applied to any problem:
      1. Repeated attempts to solve the problem.
      2. Stoicism.
      3. Enjoyment of difficulty.
      4. Refusal to accept defeat.
      5. Admission of the problem, recognition of its true nature, and treatment of it through intelligence and insight.

   B. As applied to an employee's situation when he wishes to grow through his work:
      1. Study and improve the equipment of the job.
      2. Study and improve the methods of work.
      3. Study the fellow workers and improve the human relationships.

II. *Positive substitute activities* that often enable the individual to go around a barrier or a problem:
   A. Activities in dealing with people:
      1. Doing favors for others.
      2. Taking positions of leadership.
      3. Being active in organizations, such as the church, a club, a lodge.
      4. Being socially popular.
      5. Speaking in public.
      6. Attending social functions.
      7. Debating.
      8. Making new acquaintances.
      9. "Playing politics."
      10. Playing games with people.
      11. Analyzing others.
      12. Supervising others.
      13. Associating with inferiors.
      14. Associating with superiors.
      15. Doing stunts or tricks.
      16. Persuading people.
      17. Selling things to people.
      18. Entertaining or amusing others.
      19. Improving or correcting others.
      20. Helping those who are weaker.
      21. Taking care of children.
      22. Impressing the opposite sex.
      23. Seeking the approval of others.
      24. Teaching others.
      25. Identification with another personality.

   B. Intellectual activities:
      1. Studying.
      2. Developing money-making schemes.
      3. Collecting stamps, books, and so forth.
      4. Creative writing.
      5. Creating mechanically.
      6. Inventing new systems, such as for production control.
      7. Studying and developing philosophies.

   C. Physical or manual activities:
      1. Mechanical work.
      2. Household work, such as sewing, cooking, etc.
      3. Physical labor.
      4. Outdoor work.
      5. Athletic activities.

TABLE 2-3 (cont.)

    D. Emotional activities:

1. Painting, or studying art.	4. Religious activities.
2. Studying music, vocal or instrumental.	5. Impersonating others, acting.
3. Writing or reading poetry.	6. Symbolical behavior.

III. *Negative substitute* or *evasive* activities:

    A. Handicaps to the individual:

1. Criticizing others.	6. Bluffing, conceit.
2. Annoying or teasing others.	7. Cynicism.
3. Rowdyism.	8. Sarcasm.
4. Bullying.	9. Argumentative responses.
5. Air of superiority.	10. Refusal to make decision.

    B. Mere annoyance to others, or not positively developmental when carried to extreme degree:

1. Distinctive mannerisms.	10. Fictionizing.
2. "Show-off" behavior.	11. Overagreeableness.
3. Doing tricks or stunts.	12. Travel in order to get away from difficulties.
4. Joining organizations merely "to belong."	13. Exaggerated attempts to impress the opposite sex.
5. Mimicry.	
6. Personal adornment.	14. Attending movies frequently.
7. Emphasis on clothing.	15. Excessive reading of fiction.
8. Talkativeness.	16. Ancestry worship.
9. Exaggeration.	

    C. Serious evasive habits indicating minor maladjustments.

1. Excessive daydreaming.	5. Invalidism.
2. Regression.	6. Sulkiness.
3. Projection.	7. Extreme introversion.
4. Introjection.	8. Alcoholism.

IV. *Retreat* adjustments:

    A. Solitude, stay-at-home habits to avoid ordinary problems.
    B. Mysticism.
    C. Living in another world—pronounced escape from reality.
    D. Death wish and suicidal tendencies.

Acknowledgments and References

1. "For These Personnel Problems—New Study May Give Answers," *Business Week*, Nov. 5, 1955, pp. 90 f. The article presents data by Drs. Karl A. and W. C. Menninger.

2. Thomas Parran, M.D. (Surgeon General, U.S. Public Health Service), "One Out of Ten," *This Week* Magazine, November 17, 1946. Approved by letter, dated June 14, 1948, from the Mental Hygiene Division, Federal Security Agency.

3. Robert H. Seashore, "Problem Solving Behavior in Conflict Situations," *The Training School Bulletin*, Vol. 44 (March 1947), pp. 202–210.

4. Leon J. Saul, M.D., *Emotional Maturity.* J. B. Lippincott Company, Philadelphia, 1947, pp. 16 and 17.

PROJECTS

1. Read Table 2–2 and check the barriers you have had in the course of your adjustment history. Select one of your barriers, preferably of the kind that would not embarrass you if a description of it were read by a friend or teacher.

    a. Write a brief description of the barrier or problem and the adjustment you made to it.

    b. State how the barrier and your adjustment to it have affected your own personality in dealing with others, in doing school work, or in earning your living.

    c. If you have a friend available for the purpose, ask him to read your description of your barrier and your adjustment. To what extent does he agree or disagree with your interpretation of your own psychological conclusions?

2. Hendrik Willem Van Loon was reported as having said:

"The purpose of education is to get a perspective of yourself so that you can understand yourself in relation to those around you. It enables you to have an active and pleasant life. It enables you to go through the world with the least amount of friction and a proper amount of understanding. That is all education is supposed to do. . . .

Let's look at our colleges and see what is going on. We find that they are doing little in the way of educating students. The colleges in the United States are simply big play pens where the incompetent can send their children for four years."

   a. Do you agree with Van Loon that colleges "are simply big play pens"?
   b. What evidence can you offer to refute his statement?

3. Magazine and newspaper articles often publish pictures of physically handicapped persons who achieve a high level of skill in some activity, such as the one-armed stenographer who turns in perfect copy in a typing contest or a one-legged swimmer who wins an aquatic contest. Can you describe examples of this kind from your own acquaintances?

4. In this book, the major criterion of good adjustment or psychological maturity is the degree to which the adjustment helps the individual in the development of his ability to deal adequately with new and more difficult problems. Leon J. Saul, in his book *Emotional Maturity* (J. B. Lippincott Company, Philadelphia, 1947), Chapter 1, offers additional criteria of emotional maturity. Stated very briefly, these are:

1. Does the child achieve the capacity to live independently of the parent organism?
2. Does the child enjoy the *giving* of himself in the activities of play, work, and social relations?
3. Is he relatively free from hampering feelings of inferiority, egotism, and competitiveness?
4. Do his standards and ideals of himself contribute toward growth as well as toward restraint?

5. Has he passed from the infantile stages of self-gratification to "object interest" in people and things outside himself to the levels of love and productivity?
6. Are his fears and angers controlled and directed toward creative rather than destructive ends?
7. Does he have a firm sense of reality?
8. Is he flexible and adaptable?

Saul then remarks (pp. 16 and 17):

"We have now mentioned eight of the major aspects of the emotional development of man and some of the characteristics of maturity to which each leads. This list is not exhaustive; these aspects are interrelated and are not all on the same level. But we have tried to discern some of the forces in the personality which are basic and from which the many other attributes of maturity are derived. We have seen that when the development is fulfilled the adult is predominantly independent and responsible, with little need to regress, and also is giving and productive, although still able to relax and to receive normally; he is co-operative rather than egotistical and competitive; he is in relative harmony with his conscience, which easily integrates with his mature feelings and behavior; his sexuality is free and integrated with mating and responsible productive activity, both sexual and social; his hostility toward others and toward himself is minimal but is freely available for defense and constructive use; his grasp of reality is clear and unimpaired by the emotional astigmatisms of childhood; and freed from childhood patterns, he is discriminating and highly adaptable. And among the many results of such development, his anxiety is at a minimum.

"It cannot be too strongly emphasized that maturity means not merely the *capacity* for such attitudes and functioning—but also the ability to *enjoy* them fully. It means that the individual now derives pleasure from the exercise of his adult powers and not only from his infantile demands. In the neuroses there is typically a protest against the adult productive, responsible activities and guilt and shame over the childish impulses; each vitiates the other. Normally, they are in such proportion and relationship that both are enjoyed."[4]

   a. Can you name an adult who has attained this high level of maturity?
   b. If the most mature persons whom you know have not attained this level of maturity in all its aspects, does that

mean that the individual should feel psychologically inferior? Which is the more important for the individual: to insist upon complete maturity for himself or to seek to gain a sense of growth for himself, a never-ending quest?

COLLATERAL READINGS

Dunlap, Knight, *Personal Adjustment*, McGraw-Hill Book Company, Inc., New York, 1946, Chapter 7.

Felix, R. H. and Morton Kramer, "Extent of the Problem of Mental Disorders." *Annals*, Vol. 286, March 1953, pp. 5–14.

Lehner, George F. J. and Ella Kube, *The Dynamics of Personal Adjustment*, Prentice-Hall, Inc., Englewood Cliffs, N.J., 1955.

Maslow, A. H., "Conflict, Frustration, and the Theory of Threat," *Journal of Abnormal and Social Psychology*, Vol. 38 (1943), pp. 81–86.

Patty, William L. and Louis S. Johnson, *Personality and Adjustment*, McGraw-Hill Book Company, New York, 1953.

Seashore, Robert H., "Problem Solving Behavior in Conflict Situations," *The Training School Bulletin*, Vol. 44 (March 1947), pp. 202–210.

Shaffer, Laurance F. and Edward Joseph Shoben, Jr., *The Psychology of Adjustment*, Houghton Mifflin Company, Boston, 1956, Chapters 1 and 2.

CHAPTER THREE

Adjustment by substitute activities that are often of some positive value

Frustrations and feelings of inadequacy often result in adjustments such as compensation, radicalism, or identification. Certain adjustments, though rather unusual, give the individual the motivation which enables him to apply himself to a life program or vocation. If the object of the motivation becomes a program that serves others, the motivated person is likely to become successful or even famous.

Whenever we study the lives of famous men and women, we are likely to find that their chief psychological assets were their adjustments to severe handicaps. The important point for us to keep in mind is not that a man has problems or failures but how he adjusts to his barriers, and whether his adjustments have value for other people as well as satisfaction for himself.

Beethoven was handicapped by deafness but wrote some of the world's best music. Byron's clubfoot and his poverty-stricken neurotic parents gave him a sense of inadequacy for which he compensated by writing poetry. Demosthenes and Moses are supposed to have been stutterers and yet both became famous leaders. Benjamin Disraeli suffered from ozena, a degenerative disease of the mucous membrane of the nose that produces a constant stench from the nostrils, but he became a prime minister of England. Arturo Toscanini, successively conductor of the Metropolitan Opera Company, the New York Philharmonic-Symphony Orchestra, the National Broadcasting Company Symphony Orchestra, compensated for his near-sightedness by developing a remarkable memory. Steinmetz, though deformed in body, left an imprint on our civilization by means of his genius for pure research.

The great men of the world have had all kinds of personal problems—some severe, some minor. Many factors entered into their success—too many for us to unravel clearly and completely. The nature of their handicaps is less important than the intensity of effort which resulted from adjustment to the handicaps. Certain it is that many of life's biggest prizes go to those with physical* or mental handicaps, real or imaginary. Perhaps if the progress of the world depended upon only the purely normal people (if such exist!) we would all still be living in primitive fashion.

Compensatory mechanisms

Many people of no great importance illustrate the compensatory mechanisms as well as do the famous. For example, many sculptors, musicians, speed typists, experts in fine needlework, men who write name cards with flourishes, and others whose work demands delicateness of touch developed their skills as the result of an effort to compensate for left-handedness. Many of these persons were potentially left-handed but were compelled to change to the right hand.† Of course, the right-handed person can achieve success in skilled movements just as readily as the left-hander, but the former often lacks the urge. Every individual has some psychological handicaps regardless of bodily health or high intelligence. Barriers to adjustment may or may not be related to intelligence.

The compensatory mechanism is easily recognized when we recall the example of anyone who, being little in stature or having physical defects, habitually assumes a haughty air, a cold gaze, a pompous manner, or a loud voice. Consider some of the military and political leaders of history who are known for their bombast as well as their short stature or physical defects.

Compensatory mechanisms are characterized by extra effort or aggressive conduct in order to defend the ego or feeling of self-worth. The individual's compensatory behavior enables him to reduce the tension caused by feelings of inadequacy. Confronted by a barrier to his ongoing activities, the individual naturally seeks to react in ways which appear to overcome the deficiency, decrease feelings of tension, and give increased feelings of self-worth.

Every person has some defects, and so we expect him to have the desire to feel superior in one or more respects. Each man wants to be worth while in his estimation of himself. If he is frustrated in the attainment of his goals so that he cannot meet his obstacles in a positive manner, he will do so in an indirect manner.‡ Inferiority cannot be endured. Superiority, or at least a sense of adequacy, must be achieved. A sense of failure, guilt, or shame is hard to accept. For example, the woman who feels inferior may ape the cultured or the rich and attend functions for which she does not care or lectures which she does not understand. Attendance at the opera may be imperative for her, because it puts her into the desired class of those who are admired.

When the individual is confronted with barriers to which he cannot make a direct adequate adjustment, he may seek satisfactions through substitute activities that have positive values. For example, pupils who cannot attain satisfaction in scholarship may do so on the athletic field. Girls who do not find their personal appearance attractive may become good students. High school students who find their studies very difficult are apt to quit school and seek jobs

---

* Alfred Adler has stressed the idea and given many examples of compensation brought about by some organ inferiority. See "A Study of Organ Inferiority and Its Psychical Compensation," *Nervous and Mental Disease Monograph,* 1917, for his early writing in this field.

† The child's stuttering which occasionally accompanies the shift from the use of the left hand to the use of the right hand is not caused by the inability of the brain to make the change but by a sense of inferiority brought about by the parent's or teacher's harsh treatment of left-handedness. When a person loses the use of his writing hand through accident and changes to use of the other hand, no speech defect arises; he has not been criticized for his awkwardness.

‡ An excellent treatment of frustration with examples of adjustments is presented in *Frustration and Aggression,* by Dollard, Doob, Miller, Mowrer, Sears, et al., published for The Institute of Human Relations, Yale University Press. 1939. See pages 12–17 for six good illustrations of the concept of frustration. Page 53 presents a summary of principles.

The employee who feels disgraced because his father has been convicted as a criminal may achieve satisfaction by taking up art, athletics, church work, stamp collecting, or by inventing new machinery.

When we study the lives of some labor leaders, we find that certain barriers confronted them in their earlier years of employment. They were not successful as workers themselves and so they dealt with their failure by helping the workers whom they believed to be as unhappy as themselves. Likewise, businessmen who cannot succeed in business often make an adjustment by entering another type of work, such as teaching. Teachers who cannot attain satisfactions in teaching may make an adjustment by going into business.

Compensations or substitute activities may be useless, even harmful, or they may be of great value to the individual and to society. The man who goes into the business world and finds that he is not a good businessman can substitute for that lack of attainment the satisfactions of church work and fraternal activities. Of course, the normal individual takes some interest in his community, his home, and other phases of good citizenship; but, if he remains in business and makes his outside activities a heavy sideline, he shows that he is not really well adjusted to his job. He is seeking compensation for some lack that he feels in his personality. It is usually well, therefore, that the general manager should frown upon outside activities of employees when those activities absorb very much time without bringing better adjustments to the man's job.

In this connection, we may ask whether every person goes into a chosen vocation in order to compensate for some inadequacy. Do not education and the examples of others have any influence in the choice of work? Of course they have some bearing with many individuals, as when a father tells his son about the money to be made in the legal profession and then has the son talk with some enthusiastic lawyer who convinces the lad that law is the most honorable and remunerative profession. Law, as a vocation, becomes associated with other desirable ideas of prestige, fame and wealth. However, it is also evident that many of the vocations we select are chosen as an avenue of expression for thwarted tendencies. If a boy is a poor athlete, he may take refuge in his books. If he cannot be worth while as a physical specimen, he may become a college professor, a scientist, a statistician, or an accountant.

Many positive or desirable substitute activities are compensations for inadequacies in social relations. The individual who meets barriers that make him feel inadequate may learn to obtain personal satisfactions from being kind to others, public speaking, playing politics, doing tricks, taking care of children, or teaching others. All these habits or tendencies are desirable and may be utilized vocationally. The understanding employer tries to give the employee the type of work that utilizes adjustment tendencies which are already well established.

To the counselor, adjustment by positive substitute activity is very important because evidence of such adjustment is likely to mean that the individual has a strong inner drive. When Daniel Starch studied the life histories of one hundred and fifty men by personal interview, analysis of their characteristics indicated that one important factor in the success of the ablest men was their inner drive. These men were divided into three groups: Fifty top executives, heads of America's leading enterprises, whose salaries ranged from $50,000 to over $200,-000; fifty second line, mid-level executives, whose salaries ranged from $7,000 to $20,-000; and fifty small businessmen, whose incomes ranged from $3,000 to $5,000.

. . . Of two men with equal intellect, of equal capacity to take on responsibility, or equal skill in handling people, the one with twice the drive will achieve twice as much, or six times as much.

Is it true that most men get to important positions because of wealth or luck?

I carefully searched the careers of our 150 men and found that 9 per cent of the men in the top groups went into their father's business; whereas, 20 per cent of the men in the low group did so.

Two facts are plain: Only one in eight men steps into his father's business, and actually twice as many do so in the low group as in the top group.

As to work, I have also diligently searched the careers of our executives and found that 78 per cent of the men in the top level worked hard and long; whereas, only 20 per cent of the men in the low group did so.

There are two powerful forces behind the inner drive in great men.

The first is their all consuming purpose—the goal from which there is no swerving—the preconceived destination which drives the locomotive on and on.

"Great souls have wills, feeble ones have only wishes" is an old Chinese saying.

The second force behind the inner drive of great men is not money or material reward. It is emotional—it is the anticipated satisfaction of achievement.[1]

The trained personnel man, vocational counselor, executive, and teacher are all interested in studying the individual in order that behavior tendencies may be utilized for greater self-expression. When a personnel man refuses to hire an applicant for a selling job and says to the applicant, "I will not hire you for the sales department because you really would not be happy there," the interviewer has recognized that the applicant's adjustments are not of the kind that would make him satisfied in sales work.

A man may be capable of selling and even have a good record in salesmanship work but still decide that he must do something else because his friends regard salesmanship as Babbitty and he feels inferior as a salesman. Hence, he wishes he were an artist or something respected by his friends. This principle is often important in labor problems.* Many dissatisfied employees are trying to find forms of self-expression whereby they may escape their feelings of social inferiority and appear superior in the estimation of their associates. The job or experience that causes one man to feel socially superior may cause another to feel inferior. A man's reactions to a job often depend upon how he is attempting to adjust his inner mental life rather than upon the job itself.

Many positive or desirable substitute activities are compensations for personal inadequacies, real or imagined. The person who has difficulty in admitting to others or himself some inadequacy in his personality may try to guard it from scrutiny by others. He develops some modes of behavior that shield or appear to shield him. He often protects himself from anxieties by such *defense mechanisms,* and his associates may learn to avoid any mention of his inadequacy. They know that any mention of his defect, real or imagined, is likely to result in exaggerated behavior or withdrawal from the social situation. Sometimes the individual's tendency to exaggerate some trait in order to draw attention away from a weakness and turn it in another direction results in *overcompensation.*

Usually, individuals who overcompensate are unable to accept defeat. Those who overcompensate work their way out of a difficulty by vigorous attacks. Sometimes the individual even accomplishes what appears to be impossible. One man, for example, was born with a very large clubfoot. Walking was difficult for him but he became an expert golfer who invariably walked faster than his teammates. When walking on the street with a friend, he always set a rapid pace in spite of obvious difficulty in walking at all.

When, however, an individual discovers

---

* Of course, a great deal of labor unrest comes from well-adjusted workers who believe they have a right to a larger share of the income from the business, better conditions of work. and so on. These desires may be no more evasive than those of a merchant who tries to get the highest possible price for his goods.

that it is impossible for him to attain success in the defeating activity, his overcompensation may take a substitute direction. The individual seeks success in some other activity. The new activity may be obviously related to the one in which defeat has been experienced. An unsuccessful concert violinist may, for example, resort to clowning by means of the violin. Similarly, an unsuccessful actor may become a teacher of public speaking.

Of course the substitute compensation may also lead to a different field. This is especially likely to happen when the frustration arises out of a lack of opportunity to exercise one's talent. A factory worker of high intelligence, for example, operates a machine that requires a great deal of manual skill. The worker lacks the muscular coordination necessary to develop a high level of skill. He therefore studies accounting in evening school until he overcomes his feelings of defeat.

Unfortunately, too, some persons overcome the reality of defeat by immersing themselves in projects. When the feeling of defeat is so unpleasant as to approach the painful, the individual may concentrate on some unusual project, preferably one that few people know much about. The project may have little real value. It may seem merely time-frittering to others, but to the individual it overcomes the painfulness of defeat in some other area. To observers, the individual is escaping *from* reality. If, however, the substitute activity opens up new emotional satisfactions as in the case of the fine arts, he may later find that he escaped *into* reality.

A sense of adequacy, however achieved, often enables a person to "endure" or adjust happily to numerous frustrations or problems that beset him as indicated by this example:

I once heard of a blind piano tuner whose disposition was so unfailingly even that the man whose piano he had come to tune set out intentionally to ruffle him, just to see if he could.

"What's that note you just struck?" he asked.
"That's C," said the blind man.
"Oh no, that isn't C," said the owner. "You must be slipping. Hit it again."
The piano tuner struck the note again.
"See?" said the man. "It's a little off."
"No," the blind man said with a smile, "that's C all right."
At this the owner gave up.
"Look here," he said, "I know that's C, right on the nose. I've just been trying to see if I could ruffle you. You know your business, and here I was, trying to tell you how to do it. Why didn't you get mad?"
"Why should I get mad?" asked the piano tuner mildly. "My wife loves me. Why should I get mad?"[2]

The Messiah complex

Any person who finds himself in a predicament because his life is unsatisfying is likely to try to solve his own problem by attempting to alleviate the predicaments of others. The student who plans to do college teaching and then later finds that he cannot do so may adjust himself by helping others who are in a difficulty similar to his. This type of adjustment is, perhaps, one of the most common psychological origins of the professional adviser. Teachers and executives who find their work unsatisfying or difficult often enter the advisory field as counselors, college deans, assistants to principals, welfare workers, or personnel men. Such counselors become engrossed in their work and are likely to be sympathetic toward those who seek their advice. This kind of adjustment is both psychologically sound and socially desirable. When people make comments about a clinical psychologist to the effect that he is trying to help others make better adjustments because he really is trying to help himself make better adjustments, the comments are complimentary. The adjustment is beneficial to both the advisees and the adviser. Personality development should be reciprocal rather than one-sided.

Identification with the underprivileged. Some persons make adjustments in the direction of identification with the misunderstood or unappreciated. Such individuals are apt to seek vocational expression through positions that enable them to be kind and helpful to the unsuccessful members of society. This kind of "uplift" tendency is often found among sons of very successful men, especially when the son feels that he has not met his father's expectations of him.

If the person who has made such an adjustment in the direction of helping others has had an intensely unpleasant experience in connection with his problem, he may develop an extreme form of the Messiah complex—the radical reformer's tendency. The radical wishes not only to help those toward whom he is sympathetic, but also to destroy all persons and features connected with the hated situation. He wants a new educational system, or a new economic order, or a new religion, or even an entirely new civilization. Back of those fanatics analyzed is an emotional history that explains the fanaticism. Most malcontents have had very unhappy childhoods which have a direct relation to their radical ideas.

Rowdies and radicals

The rowdy and the radical, who like to annoy or shock their associates, may have their desires to be noticed directed into worthy channels. Any skillful teacher knows that she can direct a rowdy pupil's impulses into better channels by assigning to him the task of controlling the other rowdies in the room. Or she may give him recognition by appointing him traffic patrol leader. Or he may be induced to protect the girls instead of teasing them. His rowdiness may be an attempt to gain the limelight, and any personal recognition accompanied with an assignment of responsibility is likely to be more satisfying to him than a continuation of his annoying conduct.

Similarly, the college student who has radical tendencies toward the economic order is likely to moderate his extreme points of view if he is assigned the job of helping some of the chronic down-and-outers. Few experiences are so likely to change the young industrial radical into a conservative as the task of hiring some of the industrial misfits, supervising their work, and then paying their wages out of his own money. When he goes into business for himself and observes many a worker's carelessness, tardiness, and irresponsibility toward the employer's needs, he is apt to decide that his former panacea for economic disorders is impracticable.

The college student who realizes that he is considered a radical by his acquaintances often has difficulty in getting a job. Many employers shy away from him. He imagines that they deny him employment because of his "advanced" ideas which clash with their interests. Actually many intelligent employers have little fear of so-called advanced ideas but they realize that the radical employee is rarely a good teamworker. He is likely to be either a free lance or, if in a group, a disturber of the group. Most employers like to feel that their employees like each other and function smoothly as a "team." Hence many avoid the radical as much for his lack of group integration as for his ideas as such.

Colleges are often accused of having nests of radicals among the student members. Some radicals can be found in any large group, but their numbers in the colleges are relatively small. For example, one study of 3,758 students of four state universities and fourteen church-affiliated colleges indicated that only 22 students made scores on a Conservatism-Radicalism "Opinionaire" that showed definite radicalism. The mean score of all students indicated, if anything, a slight tendency toward conservatism. There was a uniform tendency for seniors to be less conservative than freshmen. Women were uniformly more conservative than men. One college stood apart from the rest as definitely conservative.[3]

The small number of students who can be classified as radicals usually have problems in adjustment and are more in need of a clinical psychologist's services than a policeman's club.[4] Radicals reveal important personality changes in their histories, but the exact nature of the relationship between the changes and the radical political

activity can be revealed only through analysis of each individual's adjustments.[5]

When autobiographical material in one study of radicals and nonradicals was evaluated, it was found that radicals were more likely to consider themselves rejected by their parents, more pessimistic, more handicapped in social relations, more subject to inferiority, but that they had more special aptitudes than nonradicals. They did not show more undesirable adjustment mechanisms, however. These data should not be regarded as evaluations of radical theory or as implying neuroticism in radicals, but rather as an effort to establish the factors which sensitize certain individuals to, and prevent others from accepting, radical ideologies.[6] Another study of the characteristics of radicals and conservatives found no difference between the emotional stability of the two groups, but again the radicals had more inferiority feelings. Radicals were found to be brighter usually, better informed, slower in movement and decision, more introverted, self-sufficient, and dominant. Rarely were they products of small towns, but there was no distinction between the two groups in regard to size of family or of income.[7]

Radicals, rowdies, and reformers need the same constructive treatment which we should accord to others who are maladjusted. The business executive who finds that he has hired radicals should think of them as stimulating critics and decide whether the benefits from their criticism outweigh the annoyances they cause him. If their actions become a burdensome task for the executive, he should recognize that the normal employees also deserve attention. When the normal employees are neglected so that maladjusted radicals may be given more time and thought, the executive should refer the maladjusted employees to the specialists of a clinic and devote his best efforts to the more ordinary members of his organization.

The Oedipus and "secretarial" complex

Occasionally we meet the boy of seventeen who marries a forty-year-old woman. Such a marriage does not necessarily indicate that the boy has a mercenary motive. The woman may be a widow or spinster who has no money. Sometimes the widow has several children older than the bridegroom. Why does a young man marry a "girl" of that type?

In the Greek myth, Oedipus was led to kill his own father and to marry his mother, Jocasta. Freud and his followers have presented some evidence to indicate that sons become attracted toward the mother and daughters toward the father. The former fixation is called the *Oedipus complex* and the latter is called the *Electra complex.* Clinical psychologists have found that the boy who fixates his emotional life in the mother image may be jealous of his father, who is a great barrier to his love for his mother. When the boy grows up he may become rebellious toward the schoolteacher or the executive, because they are symbolic of the authority of the father. Some of the greatest men of history never married until after their mothers died. Others married but respected their mothers more than they did their wives.

The attempt to duplicate the mother or father image takes form even in the frequent marriage of near relations by neurotics. From this new relation, they seek and often find the comfort denied them by a reality which insisted upon leading them away from the pleasure and security of infantile life.

Many creative artists have married and been "comforted" by wives older than themselves. Yet in their work they betray conflict and turmoil, stained with their neurotic symptoms, buried in the inner layers of their conscious. Often the expedient does not succeed, and the artist hops from marriage to love affairs and then back to marriage, seeking relief from his psychic tension. The genius of Strindberg and Milton aches with the throb of unhappy sex lives;

Shakespeare derides his Ann Hathaway in his "Taming of the Shrew." Dr. Samuel Johnson, a notorious sufferer from hypochondria, finds his plain, ignorant wife the apotheosis of all womanly virtues because she ministers to his neurosis and gives him the infantile comfort he still seeks. Even Socrates had his Xanthippe!

The failure to relieve the pressure of an Oedipus fixation upon his mother is the key to the life and literary creations of D. H. Lawrence. This artist, aware of the truth of psychoanalysis, tried and failed to dissolve the complex which marred his sex and love life. His books shriek with the sex motif; all his life was dedicated to a war against the censorship of sex in literature. His personal as well as creative life was marked by a species of exhibitionism; all this represented a conscious attempt to free himself of the invisible cord that bound him to his mother. But with all his efforts, he was impotent to escape from his prison: all his protests, his invectives hurled against a "sex-as-sin-conscious" society, his attempts to find sex happiness with many women, represent a whistling in the dark. He remained unhappy and unfulfilled because of an Oedipus complex that never was solved.[8]

Edward A. Strecker, who has had extensive experience as a civilian and army psychiatrist, found considerable evidence to cause him to conclude that the high incidence of neuropsychiatric disorders (nearly 20 per cent of men of draft age, World War II) in the United States is largely the result of psychological immaturity. In the majority of cases, he believes this to be the fault of the mother (and occasionally the father) who consciously or unconsciously prevents the child from growing up. The mother who consciously or unconsciously but selfishly prevents the child's emotional emancipation is almost certain to have an adverse influence on the child's maturity.[9]

When a mother hugs and kisses her small boy far more than she does her husband, she may be conditioning her child for bachelorhood or for a troublesome married life. It is often quite natural for mothers to direct their starved affections upon their children because the fathers are too busy in the office and the shop to be companionable to their wives. For a while after marriage, the husband may have given his young wife all the loving companionship that she craved; but, as time went by and the children came, father had to get his nose closer to the grindstone. Consequently, he delegated all the care of the children to the mother.

The "secretarial" complex in business is one result of the over-affectionate mother. Some executives have a child-like dependence upon their secretaries. The executive who claims that he has the perfect secretary would be surprised to know that she is really average in comparison with good secretaries. His admiration is often based upon the fact that he unconsciously associates his secretary with his mother. In such a situation the secretary represents the mother image to the executive; she may be the most powerful member in the organization. His subordinates soon learn that they must not antagonize her. The secretarial complex is not wholly disadvantageous in its mild form. To some men it is a logical and helpful means of emotional adjustment. It becomes questionable, however, when the employer happens to be married and divorces his wife in order to marry his secretary.

The ability to recognize the Oedipus complex is also of importance to the businessman when employees will not leave the home town of their parents, even though their parents do not need them at home. Sometimes the individual is in a state of mental conflict, because he is torn between the normal desire for a mate and the old love of his parent; or, if married, between the love of the mate and that of the affectionate mother. Emotional conflicts of this type are taking place in the minds of employees at times, and in this way may unfit them for a whole-hearted application to business and life.

Identification

The person who, when at the theater, identifies himself with the hero, fights his battles, endures his hardships, conquers the villain, and finally marries the heroine, is not, for the time being, a mere observer or onlooker, but is the character in the picture or the play, psychologically speaking. Such a person makes many incipient movements that give reality to his imaginary acting. In like manner, the loyal college student attending the football game of his alma mater gives the player who is carrying the ball many a vigorous "shove" from the grandstands. For the moment the spectator carries the ball. He has identified himself with the team and is mentally doing the same things that the team is trying to do.

Every sport fan knows that the successful football team is the one in which the members identify themselves with the team as a whole. Each player does not play an individual game but integrates his playing with that of the entire team.

Through the achievements of other persons, groups of persons, and institutions, the individual may reduce tensions arising from his own inadequacies. Identification may be made with social and political organizations or reform movements as a compensation. An individual may also identify himself with his material possessions, as exemplified by the housewife who cleans and protects her home so well that it becomes uncomfortable to others. Possessions such as the house, clothing, automobile, office desk, or factory machine may be used to gain many subconscious satisfactions as well as obvious prestige values.

Positive identification is one of human nature's most valuable means of making wholesome adjustment. It is present in the life of every well-balanced personality; it is absent from the mental lives of certain patients in hospitals for the mentally ill. In other patients, the identifications are carried to an extreme degree. They identify themselves so completely that they become "Napoleons," "Hitlers," "Messiahs," and so on. The well-balanced person of any age

Identification with one's superiors. Some persons make adjustments in the direction of identification with the able, competent, and successful. Such individuals are apt to seek vocational expression through managerial positions.

is the one who has learned the art of identifying himself intelligently with the people and the tasks of his daily contacts. The factors of his personality are integrated into an effective working unit. He feels at home with his associates, his supervisors, his family. Unlike the cynic, he finds the age in which he lives reasonably admirable because he has identified himself with its admirable movements.

Identification is the important fundamental of a happy married life. Ideally and typically, two people marry, not mainly for sexual gratification but for more complete identification of their personalities. In the course of history, society has developed many institutions in order to enable its members to identify themselves with satisfying personalities. In addition to marriage, we have the church, which aims to have the individual identify himself with the cosmic power.

The good citizen identifies himself with his community and his nation. The well-adjusted pupil identifies himself with his school and his teacher. The great teacher first acquires a strong personality and then enables his students to live partially within his personality in order that they may thus develop their own personalities.

Teachers and business executives should try to assist their pupils and employees in identifying themselves with the age in which they live, the institutions of which they are a part, the social groups in which they are nurtured, and the employers or others who give them employment.

The true educator and builder of men instructs not by teaching subject matter only but by showing people their places in the scheme of things; by pointing out the trends of the past and the possible trends of the future; by discussing the problems of today that challenge us to excel our forefathers, and the beauties of the machines, of nature, and of man, in addition to their cruelties.

Identification is often brought about through personal sacrifice as in the case of soldiers who have been together in combat. Their shared hardships cause them to identify deeply with their combat group. In like manner, children reared in families where all members of the family share to the point of personal sacrifice for the family life often have deeper family loyalty than children of families where the parents do all sacrificing. In business, the executive who inspires employees to sacrifice their own comfort in order to make a contribution to the business develops far stronger identification of the employees with the company than the executive who thinks only in terms of what he or the company can do for the employees. The integrative adjustments of most persons are improved when they learn how to "give of themselves" to institutions and persons outside themselves.

The skillful executive who enables employees to identify themselves with his personality must also help them to transfer their identifications to other tasks, persons, and institutions. He may direct them so well that they wish to become a boss "like him." Later, the employees may find they are really interested not in the intrinsic values of their tasks but in the person who happened to supervise them. The able executive who has insight into the processes of identification among his employees is careful to see that they clearly differentiate between interest in him and interest in their work. Each worker should be led to find the intrinsic values of his work and to feel that he is a worth-while member of the institution to which he belongs. The same admonition applies to the teacher in relations with his pupils.

Children who are maladjusted may be induced to reveal the nature of the barriers in their adjustments by means of analysis of their identifications. Joseph C. Solomon, psychiatrist at the Baltimore Clinic of the Mental Hygiene Society of Baltimore, has reported how maladjusted children can be made to disclose "secrets that gnaw their minds."

The method consists in playing with dolls with the child. "Active play," according to Dr. Solomon, is a new method in which the children play a game about themselves without disclosing their own identities.

"By active play therapy," he said, "the psychiatrist is able to secure firsthand information from the mouth of the child as to how he or she is reacting to his or her environment."

The young patient identifies himself with the doll, and in his play is prone to make the doll express his own feelings.

"The mere putting his thoughts into words plays an important role in the child's mental catharsis," Dr. Solomon said. "It is generally accepted that the aeration of the child's mental conflicts has beneficial treatment value."

Children are also encouraged, he said, to express their animosities and to give physical expression to their hostilities, as well as to talk about them. After repeated demonstrations the patient no longer feels the need to express his hostility.

"It should be kept clearly in mind," Dr. Solomon warns, "that the method is partly a trick by which a child says things about himself that he ordinarily would not tell."

Resentment may result if the child feels he has been trapped. During the treatment the physician participates actively, and from time to time, as a suitable occasion arises, makes suggestions to direct the child's future thinking. Thus therapeutic suggestions are incorporated in the play.[10]

The alert executive recognizes adjustment tendencies and directs them into positive channels

Some executives are very sensitive to the feeling tones in the lives of their employees; others are unaware of them. The important action-channels of employees are not always those which are obvious to the observer. Such obvious emotions as the hysterical or angry expressions of the aroused worker are likely to be mere surface ripples. The really significant emotions are hidden beneath the surface—they are undercurrents in the inner basins of the individual personality. People suffer in silence for years. They brood over injustices. Their resentments are cumulative. Their reservoirs of emotional energy are recognized only by the executive who is alert to human emotions and their meanings. Once these reservoirs are revealed to the capable analyst, he may be able to direct the energies of the employee into channels of activity that lead to a more satisfactory and constructive life.

The executive who is alert to the barriers and adjustments in the lives of his employees is also likely to be alert to their strong qualities. If he notices that an office employee is especially skillful in persuading others but also has some show-off tendencies, the executive can direct the employee into salesmanship and train him properly for the work.

Another employee may not have the knack of persuading people but likes to entertain them by clowning, being the "life of the party," and by telling stories. Such an employee is likely to be invited to many social affairs where he amuses others but fails to achieve anything valuable for the employer or for himself. Accordingly, the employer may counsel him regarding training for public relations work that will build goodwill in the community for the company. The entertaining ability can be focused for a purpose which benefits both employer and employees.

The employee who is legally-minded may be given the responsibility of keeping in touch with governmental rulings that affect the business.

The employee who is fussy, meticulous, and overly careful can usually be placed in work which requires those habits, such as handling cash or performing an operation requiring manual skill.

Most employees are somewhat adaptable. Their adjustment tendencies, whatever they are, can often be directed for the advantage of both employer and employee. But to do so means that the executive must be alert to the potentialities within the individual, his deep-seated emotional tendencies, his adjustment history. Furthermore, the executive should have the manner of a leader who can, through a definite vocational program, inspire men by showing them visions of their better selves.

Acknowledgments and References

1. Daniel Starch, *How to Develop Your Executive Ability*, Harper & Brothers, New York, 1943.

2. Frederick G. Vosburgh, "If You Have Goodwill," *Phi Kappa Phi Journal*, March 1956.

3. Erland Nelson, "Radicalism-Conservatism in Student Attitudes," *Psychological Monographs*, Vol. 50, No. 4 (September 1938). The Lentz Conservatism-Radicalism "Opinionaire," Form K, was used.

4. Students of radicalism may wish to refer to Edward G. Benson, "Three Words," *Public Opinion Quarterly*, Vol. 2 (1938), pp. 130–134, and to E. S. Dexter, "Personality Traits Related to Conservatism and Radicalism," *Character and Personality*, Vol. 7 (1939), pp. 230–237.

5. Solomon Diamond, "A Study of the Influences of Political Radicalism on Personality Development," *Archives of Psychology*, Vol. 29, No. 203 (October 1936), p. 53.

6. M. H. Krout and Ross Stagner, "Personality Development in Radicals: A Comparative Study," *Sociometry*, Vol. 2 (1939), pp. 31–46.

7. E. S. Dexter, "Personality Traits Related to Conservatism and Radicalism," *Character and Personality*, Vol. 7 (1939), pp. 230–237.

8. Louis Berg, *The Human Personality*, Prentice-Hall, Inc., Englewood Cliffs, N.J., 1933.

9. Edward A. Strecker, *Their Mother's Sons; the Psychiatrist Examines an American Problem*, J. B. Lippincott Company, Philadelphia, 1946.

10. *Science News Letter*, March 12, 1938, p. 167.

PROJECTS

1. Terms applied to the adjustments described in this chapter are mainly the following:
   1. Substitute act having positive values.
   2. Compensatory mechanism.
   3. Defense mechanism.
   4. Messiah complex.
   5. Oedipus complex.
   6. Electra complex.
   7. Identification.

   How would you classify the adjustments present in the main characters described in the following paragraphs:

   a. Samuel is an office employee of a lumber company. He is intensely loyal to his employer, Mr. Brown. The town where they live is small, and Samuel and Mr. Brown have mutual acquaintances. Whenever Samuel can possibly do so, he praises his employer. Samuel's expressions of loyalty have become so extreme that Mr. Brown is often embarrassed.

   b. John is a college student of intelligence but he has many unpleasant mannerisms such as sensitiveness to any comments about him. When he is not angry, he is likely to give the impression that he dares anyone to insult him.

c. William is the son of a well-to-do widow. He had never been away from home overnight until this fall when he entered college. He soon became homesick and returned to his home because he felt that his mother needed any money which he might be able to earn.   *5*

d. Marylee says that she won't marry until she finds a man as nice as her daddy.   *6*

e. Robert Burns resented the repressions of the Scotch and wrote literature to express his own revolt.   *1*

f. An injury resulting from a hemorrhage at birth left Earl Carlson with a permanent scar on his brain, an area the nerve currents could not bridge. Hence, if Earl wished to eat his soup,   *4*

37 564

his brain would dispatch the message but the message would never arrive. Only a convulsive flood of energy with a series of haphazard muscular movements would result. The soup would never reach his mouth.

When Earl became an adult, he managed to go through college and became a physician. Later he became Director of the Department of Corrective Motor Education for the Birth-Injured and Allied Problems, the Neurological Institute, Columbia-Presbyterian Medical Center, New York, where he treated children with handicaps similar to his former handicap. (See Harry W. Hepner, *Finding Yourself in Your Work.* D. Appleton-Century Co., New York, 1939, Chapter III.)

COLLATERAL READINGS

Lehner, George F. J. and Ella Kube, *The Dynamics of Personal Adjustment,* Prentice-Hall, Inc., Englewood Cliffs, N.J., 1955, Chapters 4 and 5.

Patty, William L. and Louise Snyder Johnson, *Personality and Adjustment,* McGraw-Hill Book Company, New York, 1953, Chapter 10.

Shaffer, Laurance F. and Edward J. Shoben, Jr., *The Psychology of Adjustment,* Houghton Mifflin Company, Boston, 1956, Chapters 4 and 5.

Smith, Henry Clay, *Psychology of Industrial Behavior,* McGraw-Hill Book Company, Inc., New York, 1955, Chapter 7.

CHAPTER FOUR

Adjustment by substitute activities that are usually of negative value

"Do you enjoy novel reading, Miss Prim?"
"Oh, very much. One can associate with people in fiction that one wouldn't dare to speak to in real life."—Speed.

When happiness is difficult to attain and the individual lacks intelligent perspective of his barriers and adjustments, he is apt to seek happiness through fictions, psychological returns to childhood, blaming others for his situation; or to make some other form of evasive adjustment. These habits of evasion tend to weaken the individual for dealing with future problems.

A simple example of adjustment by evasion is the cashier who steals money from the cash register. Fundamentally, stealing is wrong; not because of the laws against it, but because it weakens the personality for dealing with future situations. This is a major criterion of the positive or negative values of an act of adjustment: Does it strengthen or weaken the individual for dealing with future problems?

Certain kinds of evasive adjustments are very common and so have been given names, such as regression, projection, and invalidism. Giving a type of adjustment a name has little value except as a convenience for discussion. However, the individual who knows the names of typical forms of evasion is likely to be more alert in recognizing and dealing with them.

Evasive and retreat forms of behavior have meaning; they indicate purpose and the use of poor habits in accomplishing the purpose. A discussion of typical evasive habits should increase our ability to appreciate what the maladjusted individual is trying to accomplish by means of his evasive behavior. Perhaps we can suggest or otherwise encourage the substitution of good habits for poor ones. The following discussion of evasions should also help us increase our psychological alertness in recognizing typical evasions on our part and possibly suggest methods of improving our own mental habits.

61

Adjustment by substitute activity of negative value may eventually lead to adjustment of positive value. The youth who has problems to which he first adjusts by escape into the "arty" or Bohemian aspects of the artist's life may thereby also find himself and eventually devote himself to art in its most meaningful and enduring forms. Similarly, the boy who escapes into the study of nature may thereby become interested in the best aspects of science. The adjustments of evasion do not always remain on the negative value level; many persons rise to positive levels from the negative value levels.

Defense mechanisms

The individual who has failed to develop adjustment habits that enable him to feel at home in his social situations may resort to excessively aggressive conduct and make himself a nuisance to others. More typically, however, he acquires habits of inferiority. He reacts with pronounced fear responses to most social situations. His mannerisms of inferiority enable him to avoid much competition and criticism. His habits of personality in social situations are poor because he chose poor adjustive techniques when confronted by barriers such as severe punishment by parents, criticisms by teachers, and the competitiveness of his playmates.

The pattern of convictions, attitudes, and overt behavior of social inferiority is indicated by symptoms which are described in the following inventory by Bagby:

1. *Sensitiveness to criticism.* The person with a pattern of social inferiority reacts poorly to criticism or ridicule, and suffers from it. Frequently he also shows "ideas of reference," that is, he is so sensitive about comments concerning him that he suspects strangers, sidewalk groups, and so on of criticizing him.

2. *Tendency to derogate others.* He belittles other people because by pointing out their faults he minimizes his own. Pointing out that others' accomplishments are "no good" builds up his own feelings of self-worth in a negative way.

3. *Poor reaction to criticism.* A person with strong inferiority feelings does not want an opponent who is his equal in strength or skill. He must win or have a rationalization for not doing so, therefore he does not want to compete with anyone who might surpass him. If he does and is beaten, he claims that his opponent had "all the luck," or that some minor physical condition handicapped him.

4. *Often preoccupied.* If he attends a social gathering that is mildly antagonistic or inattentive toward him, he is likely not to participate fully. He finds himself little jobs that will occupy him, or he attaches himself to a close

"American Gothic." How would you describe the probable adjustments of these two characters so excellently portrayed by Grant Wood? (**Courtesy of Grant Wood and the Art Institute of Chicago.**)

friend on whom he will shower all his attention.

5. *Rationalizes his inadequacies.* The person with strong inferiority feelings habitually creates socially-acceptable reasons for his inadequacies, so that he does not bear the onus of his failures. The student who explains away his low grade by declaring "the prof didn't like me," or "the grading system was unfair," is a typical example.

6. *Over-susceptibility to flattery.* He is so hungry for self-esteem that he gratefully and completely accepts flattering remarks made to him. Some persons with strong inferiority feelings flatter others to popularize themselves.

7. *Seclusiveness.* He does not develop normal social contacts because he fears disapproval. Frequently a person rationalizes that he has no time for them, that there are no congenial people around, etc., never realizing that the reason for his lack of social life is fear of disapproval.[1]

Of course other patterns of the symptoms of defensiveness in social situations occur. A common example is the very dignified gentleman who seems to wear an armor plating of dignity as a protection against criticism and social inadequacy. As one humorist said: "Don't mistake dignity. Lots of times it enables a man who says nothin', does nothin', and knows nothin' to command a lot of respect!"

Everyone is certain to meet this type of dignity. It is protective. The individual avoids risks of social failure by means of a manner which causes others to treat him with the kind of respect his manner demands. His associates sense his sensitiveness and tenseness. They defer to him when in his presence but they avoid his presence whenever possible. He is a lonely person and can be "reached" only when he is in circumstances where he feels sufficiently secure to be able to relax. In our modern American culture he is a poor leader when propitious circumstances place him in an executive position.

Anxiety

Anxiety is an emotional response to a situation such as a conflict or a problem that seems to have no acceptable solution. It evokes a sense of helplessness. All of us experience it at various times, and in different degrees of severity. It is, in fact, the most common form of personality disturbance. We have all experienced anxiety in some form: a sense of anticipatory dread, unfocused and not quite localizable; the cold, sweaty palms; the palpitation; the urgent and ill-timed call of nature; or the tense headache. Anxiety crops up most frequently among people attempting to make an adequate adjustment to the real world. It can be defined as an individual's fear-laden over-reaction to an adjustment situation. The threatening implications of the situation are felt because the individual already senses that he cannot cope with the situation. It becomes a threat to his self-esteem. Because anxiety is so prevalent, it is important to gain insight into the characteristic techniques of adjustment that anxious individuals adopt.

In an attempt to determine what these are, 50 high- and 50 low-anxiety students in an undergraduate course in education were given two tests: In one they were blindfolded and asked to trace a stylus through a maze. The other test was mirror tracing. Some from each group were given prior orientation to the tests. Others were not.

In those cases where there was no prior training given, the low-anxiety group was significantly superior to the high-anxiety group on the first trial of the maze. This superiority was not maintained over ten trials, however. The highly anxious subjects greatly benefited by successful repetitions of the maze. Because they had less intrinsic self-esteem they also clung to their initial goals more than did the low group after experiences of failure. Their need for high achievement made them less flexible in lowering their level of aspiration. They also performed better when they had received prior orientation to the test.

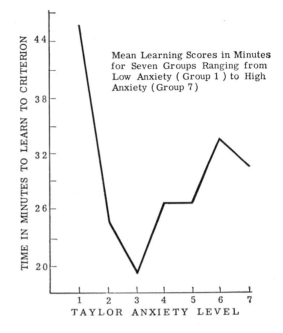

The student who wonders whether he should ever have any anxiety in regard to his work should study the above chart.

An anxious individual can learn to do a job, such as tracing a stylus maze, more easily than a person who exhibits little anxiety according to one series of experiments. Matarazzo grouped subjects into seven divisions based on the subject's level of anxiety according to the Taylor Manifest Anxiety Test. Those who were in Group 7 were the most anxious; those in Group 1, least anxious. The subjects who were midway—in Group 3—learned most efficiently. It took them only 19.33 minutes as compared with Group 1 who took almost 50 minutes. Those who were in Groups 6 and 7 took a long time to learn to perform the task efficiently. Still, they learned in a much shorter time than those who recorded very little anxiety. —From Matarazzo, Joseph, George Ulett and George Saslow, "Human Maze Performance as a Function of Increasing Levels of Anxiety," **Journal of General Psychology**, 1955, pp. 79–85.

There was no difference between the two groups in mirror tracing ability.

The results may mean that the reason the high-anxiety group reacted as they did was because they could not improvise readily in a novel learning situation. Tracing a stylus, while blindfolded, through a maze is unlike most other experiences an individual has. The highly anxious individuals tended to cling to stereotyped responses which had been useful in other learning situations. Only when it was apparent that these would not work were they discarded. Both practice and advance preparation produced better results, for they reduced novelty and unfamiliarity. Thus, the threat of failure and the danger of lowered self-esteem were mitigated. Anxiety was reduced, and performance improved when the elements of improvisation and newness were removed from the situation.[2] (See chart on opposite page for results of another experiment on relation of anxiety to maze learning.)

Students who feel anxious or worried sometimes think that their feelings will affect intelligence test and examination scores adversely. According to a recent study this does not appear to be true. Anxiety, in this test situation, did not affect intelligence levels. College sophomores, 101 in number, were tested using three criteria of intelligence. The subjects took intelligence tests while they were experiencing different levels of anxiety (as measured by the Taylor Scale of Manifest Anxiety). No relationship was found between the student's grade point average and his score on non-timed intelligence tests. Although anxiety levels affected scores on a timed intelligence test only slightly, the difference was large enough to be statistically significant. This may mean that efficiency, but not intelligence, is reduced when a certain level of anxiety is reached.[3]

Anxiety, though usually unpleasant, has considerable motivating value. A student, for example, thinks of low grades as incompatible with his self-esteem and becomes anxious about his grades. The resultant drive causes him to study. A positive adjustment has been made and tension is reduced.

Anxiety is also a frequent motivating factor in negative value adjustments. We see examples every day in the various forms of trial-and-error types of adjustive behavior. These may seem irrational to the observer, as in the example of the woman who feels anxious because of her imagined social inferiority and then treats sarcastically those whom she admires. Much of the so-called senseless behavior that we see, particularly the kind that obviously results in disadvantage for the individual, does have tension-reducing benefits.

Anxieties which are deep seated aspects of an individual employee's life style cannot, of course, be eliminated by counseling or supervisory skills on the part of the executive. Fears concerning situations outside the employee and anxieties within can, in some cases, be reduced by the executive. He can assure the employee of management's confidence in and respect for him, provide facts about the company's favorable business prospects, keep the employee busy at important tasks, and invite him to discuss his situation with other members of the organization.

Anxiety is one of the basic elements in some varieties of humor. The main themes in humor are sex and aggression because they are primary sources of most human conflicts and tensions. Anxiety often arises from inner conflicts over the inhibition of strong drives or impulses. Hence, a story or situation seems funny when it arouses anxiety and at the same time relieves it.

This interpretation of humor is Freud's. He found that humor gives pleasure by permitting the momentary gratification of some hidden and forbidden wish and at the same time reducing the anxiety that normally inhibits the fulfillment of the wish. A contemporary explanation of these views follows.

By making light of the forbidden impulse, treating it as trivial or universal, a joke or cartoon releases inner tension. The sudden release of tension comes as a pleasant surprise, while the unconscious source of the individual's tension is so disguised in the joke that it is usually not disturbing. . . .

From this theory we can derive a hypothesis that there are three types of reaction to a joke or humorous happening. If it evokes no anxiety at all in an individual, either because he has no conflict over the subject or because his conflict is too deeply repressed, he will be indifferent to the joke. If the situation calls forth anxiety and immediately dispels it, the individual will find it funny. But if it arouses anxiety without dissipating it, he will react to the ostensibly humorous situation with disgust, shame, embarrassment or horror. . . .

Psychotic patients tend to be either indifferent to cartoons or disturbed by them; when they do find one funny, they are likely to laugh uproariously at some totally irrelevant interpretation of their own. For example, a female schizophrenic was greatly amused by a cartoon of a fat man standing on a weighing machine with his back to the dial (his belly protruded too far to allow him to stand facing it). When asked why she found it funny, she explained: "The man is pregnant. . . ."

Mental patients and many relatively normal people resist laughter because it means a loss of self-control, which they fear. . . . The unfortunate individuals who cannot laugh (have "no sense of humor") are restrained, we believe, by a strong and vigilant guard against the release of unacceptable thoughts or wishes.

Play, according to psychoanalytic theory, is a way of mastering anxiety which most people develop very early in childhood. After a particularly frightening experience at the dentist's, a child is apt to go home and play dentist with a doll. The violent fantasies of the comics provide a release of aggressive impulses which the child can enjoy with impunity. . . .

It is no accident that comedians are often basically sad, depressed persons. For them, humor serves as a defense against anxieties arising from their relations with people. The wish to make people laugh becomes a pervasive and consuming drive; they must have laughter and applause as an expression of love. Alone or when not performing, they are apt to be withdrawn, melancholy, preoccupied. . . .

It is no easy matter to predict what cartoons will seem funny to a given person. But psychiatrists have found that they can predict pretty reliably which cartoons will disturb their patients. Undisguised sex, gruesome aggression, extreme prankishness and irreverence toward accepted authority are most often disturbing. However, persons whose sexual problems are close to the surface of awareness are apt to laugh boisterously—too readily and too loudly —at jokes about sex. . . .

Humor serves as a tension-releaser for most people. The more sorely troubled, who cannot relax in this way, may seek release in alchohol or pathological flights from reality. The capacity to laugh is a measure of one's adjustment to his environment. It follows that inability to appreciate humor, or deviant responses to it, can be regarded as a sensitive indicator of maladjustment and inner disturbance.[4]

These views are now applied in a psychological test which has proved to be a useful instrument for clinicians in bringing out emotional problems. Responses of the subject are studied in relation to what is known about his background and personality.

Regression

We occasionally meet the man who acts and dresses in the manner of several decades ago. We have also known the type of adult who talks of the "good old days when boys were gentlemanly and girls were virtuous." Such expressions may mean that he is simply giving evidence of having partly outlived his age. The problems of his present are too great for him to solve satisfactorily and he regresses mentally to a former happier state when life was more satisfying.

The employee who once had a good job but lost it may make an adjustment by living in that former happy state, or he may react to his present situation in an aggressive manner and look toward the future rather than the past. Psychologically, old age sets in just as soon as the past appears to be more pleasant than the present and the future. There is but one stage in the life of man when all his wants are satisfied just as soon as they occur, and that is when he is an embryo. As soon as he is born he begins to have wants which are not always satisfied when they occur. He must adjust himself to his world until death overtakes him and ends the process of adjustment.

The unmarried woman may regress to the days when she had a lover but lost him, or she may face the future with a zest for new loves and new adventures. Barriers such as a broken engagement, failure in studies, bankruptcy in business, or discharge from a good job should cause no tears, but should motivate the individual for a stronger attack upon new ventures. Failure to do this is illustrated when an older employee has failed in a hard job or a business for himself, and the remark is made: "The experience took the heart right out of him." In some forms of insanity, regression takes place to an extent that is almost unbelievable. The patient goes back to childhood in talk and conduct.

Regression, of the kind which is a form of relaxation that leads to possible later attack on one's problems, is found in childish hobbies and games. Toy trains are an example.

Children as well as adults regress. An older child, for example, who must adjust to the arrival of a new infant in the home may regress by losing previously well-established toilet habits or by crying a great deal. Parents who do not recognize the meaning of the regressions are apt to scold or punish the child. Instead, the understanding parents will show the child that he is wanted and loved.

Adults who regress are unhappy because they are no longer children. The world has moved on but they are left behind. In trying to adjust themselves to modern problems they take refuge, through their imaginations, in the mental life experienced when they were happy, carefree children. They find it satisfying to regress at times:

Backward, turn backward, O Time, in your flight!
Make me a child again, just for to-night!

The girl who longs for the ignorance and the innocence of pre-adolescence finds adjustment difficult. It would be better for her to prepare for motherhood or, if unmarried, to sublimate her sex energies into socially acceptable channels. Also, the middle-aged married woman who has not developed a deep-seated interest in her own family or in a career is apt to take an excessive interest in young men, especially if she was attractive when young. The poor adjustment to her increasing age and declining beauty cause her to regress to her youth when boys admired her. Many middle-aged women grow bitter when they can neither achieve an acceptable relationship with young men nor develop another interest that is intrinsically sound. Well-adjusted women grow old gracefully.

Regression to childish mannerisms, *infantilism,* is exceedingly common. The average grown-up frequently shows his infantilism by his temper tantrums, pouting, dawdling, weeping, clowning to attract attention, making grimaces, or noisy nasal and throat habits. These childish mannerisms are so common and meaningful that we can often recognize what a maladjusted person is trying to do if we say to ourselves: "What would the person's behavior signify if it were performed by a four-year-old child?"

Adjustment by regression or return to a former happier state is very common. Many of our nostalgic songs stress the scenes of childhood and youth.

The college student who suffers from "homesickness" demonstrates that he has a barrier in the form of being too closely attached to the members of his family and that he must turn to them to shield him and make his decisions for him. In the new college environment, he finds barriers in the form of strangers among faculty and student body who pay little attention to him, and so he develops fears and anxieties which result in physiological imbalances that lead to such physical symptoms as headaches, indigestion, or loss of appetite. His physical symptoms now "prove" to himself and to others that he should return home at once!

Regression is a serious problem to the new executive who has been hired to put a money-losing company back into the profit-making column. Many of the old employees have fixed habits which once were sound but are now inefficient in comparison with modern methods. The old employees may be pursuing methods the very opposite of those pursued by the man who is in tune with the new American tempo. What should be the attitude of the new executive toward an organization that is antiquated in methods and attitude? Should he "clean house" and "fire" most of the old employees and executives, replacing them with new blood? Or should he try to revitalize the old members? We must remember that adjustment habits cannot be erased and new ones formed at a moment's notice. The behavior patterns that are in the nervous systems of the old employees were put there by many thousands of repetitions, and new ones are difficult to produce. Shock is the only quick method, but this also does much harm. To rebuild an old organization may require so much time and effort on the part of the key executives that the end does not justify the means. However, this does not imply that all the old timber of the structure is bad. Certain employees bearing the scars of battle may be better because of having withstood the onslaughts of competition. The better policy may be to save the good material and scrap the outworn.

Fixed ideas

Every businessman has met the employee who was reprimanded for some slight infraction of the rules and who brooded over the reprimand for months—his feelings being wholly out of proportion to the seriousness of the affair; or the employee who had to be discharged and who returned again and again for a reconsideration of his case; or the old employee who demanded a pension even though the company has not given pensions to other employees and has never consciously given the impression that pensions were granted; or the executive who wants a decision in his favor, and, if it is not rendered wholly in his favor, reopens the case at each conference and insists upon discussing it, to the disgust of his fellows; or the person who loses a lawsuit and then carries the case to higher courts until the lawyers decide to neglect it or to postpone it indefinitely.

Why do these individuals persist in their fixed ideas? One reason may be that the ego of the complainant has been assailed. The concession demanded in his favor is desired, not for its intrinsic worth, but, as he calls it, "the principle of the thing." He wants the decision in his favor because he needs it to make himself appear worth while in his own estimation. The complaint often indicates that the individual is adjusting to a barrier of a failure type and he resents that his desired success cannot be achieved through normal channels. The really big man is willing to make concessions to others and does not feel that he has compromised his own integrity or worth. It is the little fellow who cannot accept anything less than complete surrender from others. The person who has some great achievement to his credit is not likely to feel the need of small concessions. It is well, therefore, to try to make the complainant feel satisfied by showing him that you admire him for certain other qualities and that he really does not need what he desires—you like him as he is.

Most of the persons who develop these fixed ideas lead so routine or narrow a life that they lack practice in making the daily little adjustments which we learn to make when we associate with many people. The employee who operates a semi-automatic machine for five days of the week and then goes home to a lonely room where he sleeps until the next day is a fit victim for fixed ideas.

Sometimes managers wonder whether they are supplying too many side activities and forms of recreation for their employees. The danger from these extra activities lies in the fact that they are often patronized by one group or clique, and the backward employees who need more contacts do not take an active part. To prevent this, it is well to see to it that each employee does take an active part in the company's recreational activities or in some other activities not sponsored by the employer. Employees should appoint committees to look after the retiring fellows who have no stimulating forms of recreation. Each and every employee should be encouraged to attend some company recreational affairs.

Executives themselves may lead too narrow lives. Of all the men whom the writer has ever met, the one most fixed in his ideas is an executive who lives only for his business, which he inherited. His two-year-old baby and his wife are merely incidental parts of the home, like the furniture. His mental and emotional life is too circumscribed, and, when he attends a conference where he can talk, his associates become angry and disgusted with his harping upon nonessentials that were considered settled long ago. To be normally adjusted, everyone needs many varied intellectual, emotional, and physical exercises.

Negativism

One of the greatest problems of the executive is that of securing the coöperation of his associates and subordinates. Whenever any program of action is suggested that involves some absent member of the organization, the question arises as to how to handle the absent but important individual. The point is raised as to how to sell the idea to him. Some member of the group may suggest: "Let's ask him to do the opposite of what we want, and then he'll want to do it." A few employees always seem to carry a negative attitude toward any ideas that are proposed to them. How did they acquire such reaction patterns?

Negativism is a defense. In many cases the habit pattern was established by the persons who reared the individual as a child. If we observe a mother rearing her child, we may find that she is constantly setting up barriers to the child by telling him what to do and what not to do. The commands flow in rapid succession: "Wash your face," "Say 'Thank you,'" "Give the toy to little brother," "Come here," "Stop that," and so on. Most of these demands from the adult come at times when the child is busily engaged in some absorbing activity, such as building a castle, flying an airship, or slaying a giant. Small wonder that he feels that adults are tyrants who spoil his fun and can be dealt with only by opposing them through breaking valuable articles or by other forms of naughtiness. Sometimes the repressions of childhood lead to later expressions of opposition to authority as in kleptomania or exhibitionism. These are simply adult varieties of "naughtiness" which the individual cannot explain.

Children who have the barrier of too much discipline from parents may withdraw into themselves and daydream rather than play active games, or they may voice their resistance in their dreams at night when they talk to themselves and say: "I don't have to," or "I won't do it." Boys who are reared by a mother and several older sisters who supervise every act of the child often acquire a negative attitude toward all women, and, if they marry, their wives are apt to say: "My husband loves me and I love him, but he does just the opposite of anything I tell him to do." Small wonder that he is negatively set toward any woman's requests, when women have "lorded" it over him for years!

Adjustment by negativism may be expressed passively, as in doing nothing when something is expected, or it may be active negativism—doing the opposite of what is expected. In some forms of insanity the individual may be so negative as to refuse to obey the normal promptings of the bodily processes, such as swallowing the saliva.

In industry, negativism may find an outlet when employees perform duties to the point ordered but no farther. The executive who finds that his employees are quarrelsome or do what is asked of them but no more may take stock of himself to learn whether he has hired a group of employees who were negative when hired or whether he has made them negative in attitude by the tone of his voice and the manner in which he gives orders. The dictatorial type of executive may get results by cowing his employees or by brilliant tactical strategy, but he seldom gets that teamwork which gives joy to the executive who knows that "the boys are with him to the utmost." The great leader of men has learned that it is best to explain the reasons for his requests in a straightforward but friendly tone and manner which convinces the employees that he believes in and likes them.

Fantasy, or daydreaming

The imaginary representation of satisfactions which the individual would like to attain but does not attain in everyday life is called *fantasy* or daydreaming. It is so easy an adjustment to make when a barrier arises that everyone daydreams to some extent.

In the *conquering hero* mechanism, the individual does not successfully face his situations in direct attacks, but pictures himself doing the deeds or possessing the things he desires. The boy who is thwarted in his attempts to do as he pleases at home can soar away in his imagination to wonderful lands of cannibals and kings, where he can conquer armies and achieve honor. As he becomes older, he daydreams of financial success, with several large automobiles, a magnificent estate, a yacht, plenty of money, and then, to cap the climax, he will become a member of the board of education and fire all the teachers whom he does not like! On other days he may picture himself as a great prize fighter, a football player, a bandit, or a preacher. The girl daydreams of the social approval of others about her, where she is a great singer, a social worker, a missionary, or a Joan of Arc.

A certain amount of daydreaming is normal and natural for all persons; but when it becomes a substitute for reality, it eliminates the necessity of actual achievement and causes the individual to live in a world of fantasy. In hospitals for the mentally ill, we find patients who are satisfied to live within their imaginations. Some of them imagine they are great men and women, such as Napoleon or Queen Victoria. As Kipling said, if one can dream and not make dreams his master, he is a successful man.

G. H. Green[5] has suggested four types of fantasy which are varieties of the conquering hero daydream. In the *display* fantasy, the dreamer gains social recognition for some act of ability or daring. In the *saving* daydream, the dreamer pictures himself performing some brave deed under extreme difficulties and thereby gaining the affection of the person rescued. In the fantasy of *grandeur*, the individual imagines himself a great person such as a king or even a god. In the *homage* daydream, the dreamer imagines himself performing a service for someone whose love he desires. Many other kinds of daydreams are used by individuals as a means of adjusting themselves to problems, such as the *destruction* daydream in which enemies may be put to death, injured, or destroyed in the fantasy.

The *suffering hero* or *martyr* type of escape is also common, as in the small boy who, because he is reprimanded, decides that he will be a very wicked bandit, rob trains, be put in jail, and eventually be hanged. His body will be brought home, and all his parents, relatives, friends, and teachers will be sorry that they mistreated him.

This type of behavior is also expressed on a milder level by the stenographer who becomes peevish and sullen. Usually she can be stimulated in several different ways. Her supervisor may approach the issue in a direct frontal attack and tell her to "snap out of it" because she is making the day unpleasant for everyone around her, or he may give her so much work to do and demand it so soon that she simply will not have time to think about herself. However, a very sensitive girl may be paralyzed by a severe scolding. It is well, therefore, to treat each employee as an individual rather than as one of a class. One rule should govern the executive: The employees must be stimulated to deal with situations as they are rather than as they would prefer them to be.

Important questions for the executive are: "What are my employees really thinking? What kinds of daydreams are they having? Are their minds filled with pleasant imagery?" The employees may apparently be busy at their tasks, but their minds may be filled with unvoiced curses for the boss and wishes that they were a thousand miles away from him and his picayune job.

Factory workers who perform repetitive jobs usually overcome boredom by means of daydreams. Mind-wandering of the fantasy variety is a protection against monotony.[6] It compensates for the deficiencies of life in general, and many a poorly adjusted person has sought a repetitive job so that he might enjoy his fantasies without the interruptions of the alert thinking which would be a part of a more varied job. Many machine tenders are very happy while at work—their minds are roaming about in delightful worlds of fantasy.

All persons like to get away from monotony and routine in order to enjoy vicarious adventures. When we go to the moving picture show and throw ourselves into the emotionality of the plot, we not only escape from our humdrum world but also "experience" worlds which we can never hope to enjoy in actuality. One reason why we do not care to see moving pictures or plays that describe life in its daily routine is that we want to escape our own realities and live in a new world rather than in the kind we have each day. Those of us who have routine jobs want to identify ourselves, for example, with the young man who was reared in the country but went to the city and there beat the captains of finance at their own game. We want to see beautiful women in the moving picture; women who are never troubled by boresome problems of taking care of crying babies and mending socks. We want the ideal pictured in the dramatizations to help us escape our problems. The happy ending is the only satisfying one, because we experience realistic living every day and do not find it sufficiently thrilling.

. . . the movie . . . notoriously furnishes an antisocial "escape" that takes mere murder in its stride and delightfully threatens maid, matron, and debutante with the fate that is worse than death. All this in a theater darkened just enough to enjoy the moral support of one's beshadowed neighbors without actually suffering their active chaperonage. Motion pictures thus become, in a milder degree, a recognized mechanism for multiple defrustration, like mixed bathing and the country club drink-and-dance.[7]

Projection

The process of ascribing to another person or institution the burden of our own repressions is commonly referred to as pro-

"He spends most of our vacations scolding his office help. He's getting even with a boss he used to have."

From "The Neighbors," by George Clark.

jection. The person who perceives in other people the traits and motives which he cannot admit in himself is probably using the mechanism of projection.

Occasionally we hear unjustified rumors of immorality as a result of projection. A woman accuses some reputable and important member of the community of gross immoralities. Such stories throw undeserved suspicion upon the accused individual. The suspicion should really be directed toward the accuser, for the accusing woman is merely projecting to someone else the impulses that she herself is trying so hard to combat. She could not bear to admit to herself her terrible impulses and so she built up pictures of others who did the things that shamed her self-respect. Many a reformer has retained the integrity of his selfhood by joining an organization to com-

bat the same tendencies that he had to fight in his moral life.

The fanatical reformer and chronic accuser are often unpopular among intelligent people, and the unpopularity is partly deserved. If one has a normal desire to improve the world, he will tend to do it in a quiet and tactful manner rather than by beating his chest and crying his aims from the housetops. The clinical psychologist who visits so-called liberal clubs is often amused by the large percentage of members who have not grown up emotionally and are projecting their own maladjustments upon a conjured monster, such as the economic or political system. Many of these club members are so maladjusted that they are unable to analyze modern problems objectively. Some prate glibly about coöperation and sharing with others when they themselves are rank individualists who emotionally could not coöperate even though they might intellectually wish to do so. We can rest assured that when our economic or political system does evolve into a better stage, its evolution will have been brought about by balanced personalities, and not by the self-styled projecting liberals. True, occasionally we all do some projecting, because admission of our own deficiencies is painful, but we cannot solve our personal problems by "jumping on somebody's neck." The well-adjusted personality does not condemn his environment; he analyzes it objectively and utilizes it in new ways.

The student who has the barrier of failure in an examination often projects the cause to the unfairness of the teacher. The man who slips in his marital relations tends to cover up his digressions by accusing others of infidelity. The man who fails in business does not, as a rule, blame himself, but imputes his losses to the "powerful forces of Wall Street" or governmental interference. The production foreman who falls down on his schedule may have sound reasons for so doing; but it is to be expected that he will suggest that the blame should be placed on some other executive. Forceful executives often develop the habit of asking their subordinates to perform certain jobs and of implying, when the orders are given, that excuses are not going to be even considered. This method has decided benefits, because it causes the subordinate executives to spend their mental efforts in working out schemes for the accomplishment of the desired end rather than in seeking excuses of the projectionist's kind. The executive who insists upon results and results only may develop the reputation of being hard-boiled, but his methods are sounder psychologically than those of the other man who accepts the excuses of poorly adjusted employees. Any organization that is made up of a large number of "projectors" is also a red ink organization.

The executive himself often projects his failures to factors other than himself. If the balance sheet figures are unsatisfactory, he can blame his employees, competitors, or government interferences; or he can calmly analyze the situation for the causes of failure and then busy himself on an improved plan of procedure for the next fiscal period. "Passing the buck" satisfies the "passer" but does not bring objective results.

Repression

An everyday example of repression arises when we have injured someone. We "forget" our shameful act toward him because we repress the memory. Some repressed memories, however, often produce an energy much stronger than those trivial experiences we forget because they are unimportant to us.

The energy developed by a repressed experience seeks an outlet. The repressed experience may appear in symbolical form in fantasy, dreams, or situations unconsciously related to the earlier shameful act. Irrational fears, dislikes, and strong emotions develop even though we are quite unaware of their origin. The person whom we injured becomes a scapegoat for our repressed memory. We find many apparently logical reasons for disliking him. We imagine that our dislike for him arises from his acts, not from our own. If, for example, we borrowed money from him years ago and felt ashamed because we never paid him back, we may eventually "discover" that he has become so despicable a character that he no longer deserves our friendship! The debt is forgotten and he is now so low a personality that we no longer want to associate with him.

A person represses something when he unconsciously denies that it exists, or when he fails to see its relevance to him. Although he may actually look at an object, or hear words, these make no impression upon his conscious mind. Or he may see the object or hear the words but fail to understand their real personal significance for him. This has been illustrated in many experiments, including one in which respondents were shown sentences describing sexual and aggressive feelings toward parents. They were asked to read these under varying degrees of illumination. The results: Different individuals found certain sentences more difficult to read, or distorted their meaning, although all were shown with the same degree of legibility. In general, this experiment showed that all subjects tend to repress aggressive and sexual material but women repress aggressive material to a greater extent than they do sexual and men repress sexual material to a greater extent than they do aggressive.[8]

The student who has cheated in past examinations and has a guilty reaction to it may be anxious lest he cheat again. He represses the memories of his past cheating and his impulsion to cheat again. He becomes scrupulously honest about cheating but projects the idea of cheating upon his fellow students. Even though his colleagues do not cheat, he believes that they do and he conjures up "evidence" to prove it. He may even head a reform movement for overcoming the evil of cheating in his college. This kind of common mechanism has given rise to the old adage, "There's no one so virtuous and anxious to impose upon others his idea of virtue as the reformed sinner!"

Scapegoating

All through history primitive peoples have transferred their own guilt and suffering to other living creatures. Civilized man continues to do the same today. Now, however, transfer is usually made to a person or a group of persons, whereas in ancient times an animal was often selected. Probably the most famous transfer ceremony on record is the one described in the Old Testament wherein the Hebrews, anxious to rid themselves of their feelings of guilt, transferred their sins to a live goat. (Leviticus 16:22.)

To rid themselves of feelings of guilt and suffering, people of today use similar methods. They find a scapegoat—an object, institution, person, or group of persons—on whom they can project their aggressions. These aggressions may be wholly undeserved. Although scapegoating is an ever-present phenomenon, it is particularly noticeable in times of social strain, such as during war, famine, revolution, or depression.

Aggression includes verbal and physical abuse, and the victim seldom retaliates because the scapegoat is invariably weaker than the persecutors. In eighteenth-century American history the Salem witches served as scapegoats, because to the accusers of that day the witches personified the devil whom the sin-ridden wished to attack.

There are other reasons for scapegoating. When people are deprived of what they want or what they have, they adjust by aggression, not necessarily against the source of their deprivation, but against any object, person, or group that is convenient. Although the chosen scapegoat may be partially blameworthy, the extent to which it is blamed is out of all proportion to its deserts. Usually, too, the scapegoat must take blame not only for immediate conditions, but for long-standing and deeply rooted frustrations.

The demagogue who seeks political power often encourages scapegoating. By pointing out a scapegoat, an unscrupulous person may achieve a unity among diverse elements who have only the scapegoat as a focal point.[9] Propagandists know that it is easier for most people to blame their own troubles on some persons or institutions, such as financiers, religionists, the educational system, foreign organizations, or any other popularly accepted "devil." The political opportunist finds out who the unpopular "devils" are at the moment and speaks for the projectionists in demanding reforms.

"Frankly, we need some one to act as a sort of goat around this office —think you can qualify?"

From "Grin and Bear It," by Lichty, courtesy of Chicago Sun-Times Syndicate. Reprinted by permission.

Experiments show that frustration such as a ruined evening may bring anger toward far-away people.

This was revealed when two psychologists learned that a group of young men at a camp was to be given a series of tests which would be boring to them and which were so difficult that everyone was bound to fail miserably. The time taken to give the tests forced the men to miss what they considered the most interesting event of the week, Bank Night at the local theater. The men, it was anticipated, would be frustrated and made angry by this situation.

Before the men knew the nature of the tests and the fact that they would miss Bank Night, their attitude toward the people of a far-away nation was measured by means of rating-scales.

After they had taken the tests and realized that they could not enjoy the evening at the theater, they were once again asked to rate this nation. It was found that their attitudes after the frustrating tests were reliably more hostile toward the nation than before.

Similar groups who were not frustrated by the tests and who rated the same nation twice revealed no such change. . . .

The psychologists who turned the test evening into an experiment were Dr. Neal E. Miller, of Yale University, and Richard Bugelski, of the University of Toledo. They see in the results an expression of the tendency to blame someone else for an individual's own misfortunes, known to psychologists as the scapegoat device. . . .

"In ordinary social living," Dr. Miller points out, "men and women suffer frustrations especially when they are unemployed or are compelled to accept a reduction in pay. Their anger can spread to scapegoats in the same way that the anger of the men in the camp spread to the people of a foreign country. It is one of the functions of propaganda to induce people to use as scapegoats innocent foreigners who, even though not necessarily responsible for the frustration, are made to serve as targets for aggression."[10]

Somewhat veiled hostility characterized men who were subjected to frustrating situations while being deprived of their night's sleep, Sears, Hovland and Miller found in an exploratory study. In order that the subjects, male college students, might not know the true nature of the experiment, they were told that the purpose was to study reflexes and motor activities of sleep-deprived men.

After attending classes during the day, the subjects reported to the laboratory at 7:30 P.M. where they were kept under close observation until eight o'clock the following morning. During the evening they studied and read. Games and cards were to be brought in about midnight to relieve the monotony, but the materials for these diversions never arrived. At 3 A.M. the experimenter who was to have brought them came in, but had "forgotten" the games. At midnight the subjects were suddenly told not to smoke any more, while the experimenters continued to smoke in their presence. A group discussion from which the men were getting some enjoyment was arbitrarily halted, and a period of silence was maintained. When the men became hungry in the late evening, they were told that a hot breakfast would be brought in at 5 A.M. At 6 A.M. the experimenter who had gone out to get the promised breakfast had failed to return, so the two remaining experimenters "decided" not to wait for him. They therefore tested the men's reflexes and motor activities to maintain the ostensible purpose of the experiment.

During all these frustrations an "in-group" was formed among the subjects, and the cleavage between it and the experimenters was obvious. Aggressive reactions to the frustrations were directed largely at the experimenters; however, they were almost entirely in the form of jocular references to the dullness of the experiment and wisecracks about the uncoöperativeness of the experimenters. The tone of voice and inflection the subjects used in making their "cracks" made their aggressiveness unmistakably clear. Typical of the remarks made by subjects are the following:

3:40 A.M. An experimenter ostentatiously lit a cigarette. Group of five subjects sitting together. "Where's this partial entertainment you offered us? How about some stories?" (É told dull joke; no laughter.) "We discussed cannibalism

THE JOYS OF AFFECTION

Spontaneous Drawings revealing the hostility aroused in a deprivation experiment situation. Note the sarcasm in the title!—From R. R. Sears, C. I. Hovland, and N. E. Miller, in the **Journal of Psychology**, Vol. 9 (1940), pp. 275–295.

earlier in the evening." (E: "Would you eat human flesh?") "We may yet tonight." (Meaningful look at one of the E's; much snickering among S's.)

3:50 A.M. "What would happen if we would walk out?" "I suppose you'd blackmail us." "I bet it would wreck your experiment if we did. Let's leave."

5:15 A.M. "Are all psychologists mad?" "They're all queer. I've been watching 'em for a couple of hours."[11]

One piece of aggression that was not a joke or wisecrack was done by the most outspokenly aggressive subject. The sheet of sketches which he drew to represent psychologists amused the other subjects highly. His sketches are reproduced in "The Joys of Affection."

It must be pointed out that hostility and aggression might have been expressed differently had the relationship between experimenters and subjects not been one of professors and students.[12]

Introjection

In projection, we shape the world to suit ourselves—to the satisfaction of the ego. In introjection, we do the opposite. The world shapes us in the images of itself. The introjectionist follows the surge of the crowd. In time of war, he believes all the propaganda that is put out by his side. In politics, he remains within the party lines and cheers without mental reservation for his candidate. He does not calmly analyze and then choose the better of two or more courses of action, but he adopts one course with all his emotional power. In business, he is the "carbon copy" man, the "yes" man. He tries to anticipate the slightest wishes and beliefs of his boss and then adopts those as his own. He likes to be dictated to and ordered about. He dwells within the shadow of his superior and scrapes and bows to the fiddling of those above him. His coöperation is as blind as it is devoted.

Many executives seem to prefer an organization of introjects. They are easy to handle. They satisfy the ego of the executive and he imagines that he is in full control of his employees, but his organization is one that neither thinks nor analyzes. It is too pliable. Too many companies are headed by men who like a pliable personnel. One business consultant claimed that he had one basic criterion for sizing up the strength or weakness of any business concern. His evaluation of the management was determined by comparing the top executive's ability with the ability of his associates. "If the top executive chooses associates, vice-presidents and department heads, who are as able as he, the whole organization is bound to be a strong one," according to this consultant.

The first grave charge against the one-man system (of business management) is that it creates an organization with only one thinker.

Eventually, the president who operates on the system will become the only thinker in his corporation. This does not mean that others in his organization will do no thinking about the business beyond their immediate concerns; but they will invalidate their constructive ideas by not freely expressing their thoughts. Either through fear or natural laziness, or a reluctance to feed another's vanity with the credit of their own ideas, they will lean more and more on the one-man head of the business for all decisions.

One of the greatest faults of the one-man system is that it stultifies creative desire, imagination, originality and ambition—all creators of ideas—by bringing together and training an organization of "yes" men. From my observation, we all have certain fundamental characteristics and we possess them from the cradle to the grave. Allow a child or a man to have his unopposed way long enough, and eventually he will be led to consider his own way as not only the best but the only way. His ego will encourage him to minimize or forget his mistakes and greatly exaggerate the importance of his successful decisions, and those around him who are dependent on him for their livelihood cannot be blamed for taking the easiest way and agreeing with their adversary quickly.

Throughout the plant and the office of a one-man business, men in high and low positions compete with each other, not on a basis of proved merit, but according to their standing with the "chief." And usually the most proficient "yesser" enjoys the highest standing. This is the greatest breeder of factory and office politics, of jealousy and ill-will. Disputes are not settled by the records or by other just means, but through front-office favoritism, and the organization is soon undermined by resentment and grosser emotions arising from the unfair competition.

In giving promotions and fixing wages and salaries, the system equally is at fault. Usually, advancement goes to the best factory or office politician. Loyalty and efficiency are seldom rewarded. That is why the morale of the personnel of any one-man business is often below par.[13]

What can the executive do when he finds that an otherwise good employee is too willing to imitate him? He can make at least one attempt to readjust him by explaining the situation very frankly and telling the "yes" man to agree less and to make more suggestions. The slavish employee may have been

Yes sir..Yes, Yes SIR!!

conditioned in that way by some other ex- ecutive who fired him for disagreeing with the boss. An executive cannot "jump" on employees for an honest questioning of his decisions and then expect them to be filled with helpful suggestions the next day. The fear of losing their jobs will give them intro- jective characteristics. Employees are not always to be blamed for "putty" minds. Cer- tain executives have so strong an inferiority complex that they cannot endure the pres- ence of subordinates who are their equals in ability.

Many introjectionists develop their intro- jective habits in their adjustments to cruel parents, stern teachers, or executives who resent suggestions. Through such experi- ences, the individual learns to cater to peo- ple at all times, rather than to cater to them some of the time and to oppose them when opposition is appropriate. An executive's study of the employee's past history will often reveal experiences which brought about the introjective behavior.

Compulsion neuroses and phobias

In the compulsion neurosis, the individ- ual cannot explain why he feels that he must perform a given act, but he dreads failure to follow the ritual which he has set up in his own mind. In its mild forms, it is found among normal people and is generally treated as an idiosyncrasy or a superstition, as in the individuals who tap wood in order to avoid a calamity which they have escaped thus far. Such compulsive acts are trivial and do not affect emotional health.

The more serious compulsions are known as *manias* and are given specific names to indicate their type as *kleptomania*, the im- pulse to steal things that are not needed; *pyromania*, the impulse to set fire to things; *onomatomania*, the impulse to say a word again and again or to hunt for it in the memory; *dipsomania*, the periodic uncon- trollable craving for alcoholic beverages; and *arithmomania*, the obsessive tendency to count everything, such as the stones in the sidewalk or the objects in a room. A mania is an exaggerated predilection to- ward a type of activity and is often con- trasted with extreme dread of some specific type of situation as in a phobia.

A *phobia* is a persistent and irrational fear of a harmless object or situation. The indi- vidual may know quite well that he has no logical reason to fear the thing that he fears. Examples are *claustrophobia*, fear of closed places; *acrophobia*, fear of high places, such as the tenth floor of an office building; *agora- phobia*, fear of open spaces, such as fields or wide streets; *pyrophobia*, fear of fire; *miso- phobia*, fear of dirt; and *aelurophobia*, the fear of cats, Napoleon's well-known fear. The phobia usually comes on very suddenly and overwhelms the patient, who is seized with trembling, sweating, pallor, and all the usual signs of extreme fear. All this, in spite of the fact that the patient knows quite well that his fears are merely morbid and under irrational control. Some persons having phobias are able to continue their daily work by avoiding the situations which stim- ulate the phobia responses. Others have phobias which unfit them for certain forms of economic life.

The woman who was afraid to look into a mirror for fear that she would find a hair on her face knew that the finding of a hair was no real cause for alarm; but still she became so fearful of seeing her reflection that she refused to handle silverware or to open her eyes in a room where there were windows. The executive who was seized with fear whenever he was in a building higher than the second floor knew that the building was perfectly safe; he simply could not go up to any height. The stenographer who spent most of her time washing her hands knew that her hands were reasonably clean, but still she feared they might be soiled. The bookkeeper who feared to make the figure five knew that figure was harmless, but still he feared it.

What are the barriers which give rise to such apparently irrational adjustments as manias and phobias?

Means studied the fears of a thousand college women and found that only 38 per cent of them indicated any knowledge of the origin of their fears.[14] About 70 per cent of the fears of known origin were due to some personal experience. The first five fears in their relative importance were: snakes, cancer, death of loved ones, death by burning, and bulls.

At least three of these fears are considered by psychoanalysts to be sexual in nature: snakes, burning, and bulls. If we accept the explanation of some psychoanalysts, we shall interpret these manifestations of abnormal fears and impulses as symbols of barriers which are inadmissible impulses. The woman who could not look into a mirror for fear she would see a hair on her face was unable to do so because hair symbolized some sexual wish that she refused consciously to admit to herself. The executive who could not go higher than the second floor of a building was fearful of a moral fall which might be brought about if he yielded to an immoral impulse. The stenographer's

fear of contamination was caused by the fear of repressed desires to yield to an immoral impulse such as the sexual entreaties of her lover. The figure five represented the five fingers of the bookkeeper's hand which were used in a sex perversion. And so on for other impulsions, such as the oversolicitude for the health of a wealthy aunt which disguised the wish for her death.

In most analyses of phobias, psychiatrists find that the origin of the fear is closely coupled with a sense of guilt or shame. That is why Freud and his disciples can find many illustrations of his theory that the phobia masks a repressed sex desire. Sex, to most people, is something terrible and unmentionable rather than a perfectly normal impulse.

An urge to do something considered reprehensible by the individual, with an anticipation of punishment, is especially frequent in the phobia. In many cases, too, the patient exhibits a history of early frustrations, aggressive impulses that were suppressed, and unappreciated fears of punishment. Many individuals whose behavior is restricted by a phobia are lonely and seek the security of being protected by adults.[15]

As soon as the phobia-bound individual understands the origin of his fear and is allowed to express the repressed impulse that it symbolizes, the phobia is likely to disappear. Scolding him will not banish the fear, but uncovering the origin of it may. If the fear persists, the cause has not been found or the process of readjustment is incomplete. A complete "cure" takes place only when the individual has achieved a readjustment to the anxiety-producing experience. Of course, this process of readjustment is one for the attention of the clinical psychologist.

Some phobias are more easily and logically thought of in terms of conditioned responses or as associative linkages. It is certain that some of the maladjustments of the individual are brought about through simultaneous associations, as in the case of th..

man who, during a heart attack, collapses in an open section of the city. He may then have an agoraphobia for certain areas.

Parents can do much to prevent abnormal fears. The main form of instruction given to children by some parents seems to be "Shame on you"; "Nobody will like you if you are so naughty"; "You know that you are a naughty little boy, don't you?"; and "God will punish little girls who tell lies." No wonder the children of oversolicitous parents often grow up to become fearful retiring nobodies while roughnecks of the slums develop into business and professional leaders. Fears do not dog the roughneck's every step. We must remember that the child fears in silence. Shame may be so strong that it is difficult to obtain admission. Cowardice may develop, and all because the father and mother and teacher have held up the bogey of shame. Every unnatural fear has a natural cause, and the attitude of the executive toward his employees and his children should be that of the analyst who sympathetically discovers the origin of the fear and aids the individual in gaining a better adjustment. A knowledge of what fears really mean is the first step in aiding the phobia-bound person.

Alcoholism

There are about four and a half million alcoholics in the United States today. Of these, approximately three-quarters of a million adults in this country have become alcoholics to such a degree that they have impaired their physical or mental health. These are the chronic alcoholics.

It is generally accepted that there is no alcoholic personality as such. Rather, numerous individuals cannot manage their lives in sobriety; they continue to resort to alcohol as a means of dealing with their psychological problems, such as feelings of insecurity and inferiority. Many are depressed because they labor under the unconscious fantasy that they were not loved sufficiently

by their mother in childhood.[16] The craving for alcohol is more a craving for the habit pattern that relieves tensions than for anticipated sensory enjoyment. The fact that when individuals take too much alcohol on a social occasion, certain ones become aggressive, elated, or "weepy"; indicates that the imbibing is related to the person's adjustment tensions.

Several intensive investigations of chronic alcoholics are now under way. One of these, at the Laboratory of Applied Physiology, Yale University, has found that alcoholics can be studied in terms of the following classifications of excessive drinkers:

1. The neurotic.
2. The psychotic.
3. The feebleminded.
4. Those who gravitate into drink as a means toward solving their problems.

Among 100 excessive drinkers, about 40 are neurotic, 10 are psychotic, and 10 are feebleminded. The personality patterns may be briefly described as follows:

The *neurotic* lacks patience with his world. He needs many props to support him. He will seek conditions under which the conflict between his wishes and reality are endurable. In order to escape from his world he resorts to daydreaming, but he fully realizes the difference between the real world and his imagined world. He may try, for instance, to obviate the conflict between his two worlds by adopting a job which permits seclusion, by a hobby, or by intoxication. His general conduct may be thought "peculiar" by others, but his overt conduct usually conforms to the standards of the real world. In other words, he is in touch with reality.

The *psychotic*, on the other hand, resolves the conflict between his dream world and the world of reality by retreating entirely into his dream world. He loses contact with the world of reality, and cannot distinguish between it and the dream world, or between right and wrong. For these reasons he is segregated from society.

In the incipient stage of the illness, some psychotics drink heavily to shut out such phenomena as auditory hallucinations. After a few months the psychosis becomes so fully recognizable as to necessitate hospitalization. Observers are apt to conclude that the psychosis was caused by the drinking, whereas actually the drinking was a symptom of the psychosis. Only over a period of years could heavy drinking in itself cause a psychosis.[17]

It has been noted that alcoholism is sometimes the symptom of a mental disorder. If drinking bouts occur periodically, perhaps at intervals of several months, there is a possibility that the patient is drinking during one or the other stages of a manic-depressive psychosis; if the drinking is steady and wild, there is a possibility of early schizophrenia or early general paresis. Other deep-seated maladies are sometimes the real cause of heavy drinking. In almost all such cases the patient needs hospitalization.

With the majority of alcoholics, however, the root of the trouble isn't so deep. It is the patient's inability to adjust himself to life as he finds it. Perhaps he has always been lonely; or dominated by the family; or tortured by fears—that he won't make good, that people don't like him, that he isn't manly. Or he may be a business and social success, yet hate his work and the people he goes around with. For a variety of reasons he may hate himself.[18]

On the whole, about 60 per cent of all inebriates come to their excessive habits through some "ailment," including feeble-mindedness as an ailment. This means that at least 40 per cent cannot attribute their inebriety to disease.

The fourth group of the 100 inebriates who are not in the neurotic, psychotic, or feebleminded categories are persons who have been drinking large amounts of alcoholic beverages as a form of social relaxation.

In the course of their drinking they have found, however, that intoxication will help them over situations which otherwise would take some effort to adjust to. Some minor misadventure may be a sufficient reason to "let themselves go" and to let intoxication "do the job"; they solve their troubles with drink. As they get "pampered" by intoxication, they may take recourse to it more and more frequently until they become as dependent upon alcohol as the neurotic, compulsive drinker. While they did not start from a disease, they become diseased. . . . Ultimately, then, all inebriates are diseased persons. But it is important to distinguish those who were brought to inebriety through disease and those whose inebriety brings about the disease. These latter excessive drinkers are usually gregarious persons, good mixers, and easygoing in contrast to the neurotic drinkers who, as a rule, are persons who never found their place among others, who always were lone travelers. When the "normal excessive drinker" becomes an habitual inebriate, he appears to be much like the neurotic drinker. By necessity he too becomes a "lone traveler," for he loses his friends and becomes isolated. Because of that he becomes as suspicious, sensitive, and selfish as the neurotic inebriate. But he can be helped. As he has arrived at his dependence through habituation, he can be trained away again from this habit. This can be done successfully if it is recognized that he is not of the neurotic type and that he, therefore, needs to be handled differently.[19]

The man who drinks for social relaxation should analyze his drinking habits as a precaution against becoming an alcohol dependent. Dr. Abraham Myerson, Boston psychiatrist, suggests seven test questions:

1. Can you enjoy a party only if there is liquor to release your social instincts?
2. Do you long for the time of day when you can drink without hurting your job?
3. Do you consider drink necessary to relaxation and enjoyment of life?
4. Do you turn reflexively to alcohol each day to overcome anxiety, disgust, fatigue or frustration?
5. Do you tend to drink to offset difficulties with your wife, your boss, your children or employees?
6. Is the goal of your drinking something other than the drink itself?
7. Do you *need* this drink?

If the answer to any of the questions is yes, the individual is in danger of becoming an alcohol dependent. The last question epitomizes the questionnaire. When a person feels that he *needs* a drink, he is drinking to escape. He craves the anesthesia which alcohol supplies.[20]

Alcoholics Anonymous, formed in 1934, is a nonprofit organization of former alcoholics who want to help other alcoholics stop drinking. Its purpose: To help the sick alcoholic recover if he wishes to do so. A drinker's honest desire to recover normal health and habits, and his belief in some form of Supreme Power, are the prerequisites for membership.

Members of Alcoholics Anonymous actively help the patient in his fight to regain normal health, and as his condition improves he in turn helps others in their fight. Some 24,000 former habitual drinkers, members of A.A., understand better than anyone else the problems of other alcoholics and ex-alcoholics, so a fellowship is thereby created which acts as a mainstay when regression threatens. The organization and its methods are endorsed by many physicians and clergymen.[21]

In view of the alcoholic's deep-seated inability to deal effectively with his problems, effective treatment is usually very difficult. The employer, wife, or friend of the alcoholic can seldom hope to overcome the victim's failures in adjustment. Psychiatric treatment is, however, likely to be far more effective than mere legislation. The businessman who finds that an employee or colleague is a chronic alcoholic must usually decide whether he should sever their business relationship or get along with the victim in spite of his annoying derelictions. Some alcoholic employees have qualities which compensate the employer for their recurring deficiencies; others can only be discharged, in the hope that they will find their way to an institution where positive treatment will be given them. Many will continue to drink until their adjustment problems have been removed and they have developed new mental habits.[22]

Some modern business leaders treat their alcoholic employees as sick people and give them the same consideration given to those who suffer from other diseases. Some companies work with Alcoholics Anonymous members, even taking them into their personnel departments.[23]

More recently several large companies such as Consolidated Edison, General Elec-

TABLE 4–1

DISCIPLINE IN CASES OF REPEATED INTOXICATION—PRACTICES IN AMERICAN INDUSTRIES

Disciplinary Action	For Salaried Employees COMPANIES	
	Number	Per Cent
Discharge	264	81.5
Send home	1	0.3
Refer to psychiatrist, or discharge	1	0.3
Refer to Alcoholics Anonymous, or discharge	1	0.3
Special handling after review with medical opinion	1	0.3
Discharge if rehabilitation fails ...	1	0.3
Place on probationary status	1	0.3
Depends on individual case	4	1.2
Fined	1	0.3
No problem	42	13.0
Not shown	7	2.2
Total	324	100.0

From a survey reported in "Personnel Practices in Factory and Office" (Revised), *Studies in Personnel Policy,* Number 88, National Industrial Conference Board, Inc. Copyright 1948. Data in this survey by the National Industrial Conference Board are based on information supplied to the Board by 2,479 companies with approximately five million employees. Because the whole investigation required so much data on so many different practices, inquiries were divided into six parts, and each part was sent to a different group of coöperating companies. The companies in each group were carefully selected to be representative to the same degree of different-sized companies and different types of industries. The smallest group comprised 360 companies, the largest 474, and the average 413. It is for this reason that "100 per cent" in the National Industrial Conference Board tables from this survey reprinted in this book represents in the neighborhood of 400 companies. Half of the coöperating companies reported on their practices with regard to hourly workers, and half with regard to salaried employees.

tric, and Allis-Chalmers have set up in-plant programs to salvage alcoholics in their concerns. A program of this type usually includes these interrelated phases: 1) recognition of the problem drinker and getting him to want to do something about his situation; 2) rehabilitation of the person through psychiatric, psychological, and counseling help; and 3) prevention of alcoholism—perhaps through education of the employees as to the nature and the cause of this illness. Some of these programs by industrial firms appear to have produced beneficial results but it is still too early to know just how beneficial or lasting the effects really are.

Habit spasms

Have you ever been in a railway station or some other public place and seen a woman stick out her tongue at intervals of every two minutes? Or have you seen the boy who recurrently pulls up one corner of his mouth until every passerby notices him and wonders, "What ails the kid?" Or the girl who rhythmically wrinkles her nose to the extent that she is called "Rabbit"? Have you heard of the man who was taken to the hospital because he would lie in bed, put his heels and the back of his head on the bed, and then give himself a toss up toward the ceiling? Or have you seen cases of chorea or St. Vitus' dance? The term "tic" is usually given to those muscular twitches which involve only a few muscles. Movements that involve a large number of muscles or the whole body are called "choreic movements." Habit spasms are found most frequently in children, but adults of this type come into an employment office, and the employment man is apt to say, "Did you see that fellow with the 'heebie-jeebies'?"

Why do some people act in so peculiar a manner? The origin of some cases of chorea is in the brain-stem, but most of the "tics" in children develop from some simple irritation of the clothing, such as a tight sleeve, tickling of woolen underclothing, or a sore pim-

ple. The child finds that the movement attracts attention to himself and continues to make the movement even after the cause has been removed. It acts as a sort of pacifier. The movement gives relief from the tension that comes with the urge to do an act when it is inhibited. The satisfaction gained is similar to that of the college girl who is anxious to be popular and, finding that the boys are not attracted to her in large numbers, then talks or acts in a loud manner; or an employee in business who has the ambition to be a big executive, but promotion is slow and he relieves the tension by adopting a distinctive mannerism. Recognition must be obtained in some manner, and it is natural for the habit spasm to continue after it has gained the ticquer much attention.

Does the tic indicate a dangerous adjustment so that the individual should not be hired? The answer is that he is no more dangerous than the individual who compensates in a less spectacular manner by taking up Sunday School teaching. Of course, if the individual attracts the attention of employees or customers to himself rather than to the work that the employees are to do or the goods that the customers should buy, then the ticquer is a nuisance. It is, however, inadvisable for the employment executive to hire the applicant having a tic with the thought that the habit spasm will soon pass away or that he can cure it. These habit movements are usually very resistant to curative treatment.

Sexual anomalies

The sex customs of modern civilization are the most remarkable illustration of the strength of the cortical control over the instinctive or animal nature of man. Bear in mind that throughout the millions of years of evolution of man's forebears, no males took part in that whole line of descent except those who had some sex impulse. Small wonder then that it is a strong force in the life of man. Freud and his followers have considerable evidence whereon to build their brand of psychology. With so strong a force, we need not wonder that perversions or anomalies take place in the sex lives of a significantly large percentage of the people. The occasions when it is necessary for the executive to deal with serious sex problems, such as perversions, are few in number. Many businessmen think that they can recognize a sex pervert when he applies for a job. This is not true. At least, no evidence has ever been obtained which indicates that it is possible to recognize the homosexual pervert. When someone meets a stranger and classifies him as a sex pervert merely on the basis of appearances, such as the gaze of the eyes, he is just guessing. The stranger may accidentally give him such an impression because of some characteristic of clothing or voice that unconsciously reminds him of a pervert whom he met previously.

In terms of Freud, the tendencies of the child are *polymorphous,* or many-form. The sexual sense has not developed in the young child. Later, as it develops, it tends to center its aim in some special direction, usually toward the opposite sex and normal conduct in sex life. However, the child's sex tendencies may be developed in any direction according to the influences that take place in the educational and adjustment process.

Nature has given man a strong sex impulse, but civilization has fenced in the impulse with dozens of taboos. It is only natural, therefore, that masturbation should be common. A passing addiction to it in infancy is considered normal by many psychologists. Contrary to popular interpretation, masturbation is not to be considered as a cause of insanity.

The best modern opinion has been well set forth by Malamud and Palmer whose conclusions we may briefly summarize. The frequency with which masturbation occurs bears no relation to the incidence of mental disorders. There is no evidence that the practice, per se, even when carried into adult life, is a cause of mental disorders, although it may be indirectly of importance because of the patient's attitude toward his act and of what he believes are possible sequelae. In this way masturbation may be a precipitating cause of disturbances of an inferiority and withdrawing type.[24]

When Malamud and Palmer found an abnormal mental state coupled with the masturbation habit, they found people who usually differed from the average in other ways too, e.g., by constitutional peculiarities, lack of proper sex knowledge, misinformation regarding masturbation, unsatisfactory environmental situation, and so on. In those cases where masturbation was believed to be of prime etiological importance, psychotherapy was highly satisfactory, indicating "that the disturbances were due to the conflict rather than the effects of the practice in itself."[25]

Pullias[26] made a study of the beliefs of seventy-five young men regarding masturbation and found that 87 per cent had heard of it as having a seriously damaging effect upon those who practice it. Huschka's[27] investigation disclosed that at least 128 of 320 problem children had been dealt with destructively concerning masturbation. Direct physical threats were employed and over half of these children had been threatened with actual genital injury, thus giving rise to what Freudians refer to as castration anxiety. Nearly all studies of masturbation have indicated that it is an important mental hygiene problem which often has serious effects on personality and should be handled by persons who have both intelligence and emotional balance regarding sex practices.

It is especially important to avoid giving the youth a feeling of guilt or inferiority in regard to sex. Such feelings are almost certain to give rise to defense mechanisms of the withdrawal-from-people variety. Or, in potentially more dangerous cases, mechanisms of aggression.

Sadism (the *a* pronounced as in *say*) refers to some few individuals who do not express their sexual tendencies in a normal direction but gratify sexual feelings by the infliction or sight of pain. The pain may be real or it may be simulated, in which case it is symbolic. This anomaly is found among men more often than among women, as we would naturally expect. An example is a famous American millionaire who raised rabbits and then tore them to pieces with his own hands. In any large organization, one is apt to find mild expressions of the sadistic variety in the form of persons who like to pinch others or stick pins into them.

Masochism is the opposite of sadism. The individual's sexual feelings are gratified when he suffers pain. The pain may be real or simulated. The latter is symbolic. The masochistic tendency is found among women more often than among men.

Exhibitionism is the gratification of sex by the exposure of the body, especially erogenous parts. It is the showing-off tendency in the extreme. Some analysts claim that the desire of some leaders in business and public affairs to be the "whole show" in the presence of others is merely substituting this type of exhibitionism for a more perverted and unacceptable variety of showing off.

Voyerism, a minor mental maladjustment which contrasts with exhibitionism, is the tendency to derive sexual satisfaction from looking at sexual objects and acts. The "Peeping Tom" who is occasionally caught by campus policemen is an extreme case of voyerism.[28] (The word comes from the French *voir*, to see.)

Less extreme are those people who show unusual interest in case histories from medical books, who insist upon knowing the intimate details of their friends' lives, and who are happy in listening to a particular kind of gossip about movie stars and other famous people. Some business concerns have "old maids" who are forever curious about what their associates do after working hours.

These employees can make an office rather unpleasant for other workers.

This unusual type of adjustment is used largely by people whose own lives are drab. They are more or less unable to make a satisfactory normal social adjustment, and so they devote time to watching and hearing about others whose activities are nearer normal.

Homosexuality, when used as signifying a perversion, is the term given to the desire for sexual relations with persons of the same sex. In this connection we must bear in mind that no man is wholly male, nor is any woman wholly female. Sexness is a relative trait. We are mixtures of physical and mental traits. Many women have the general bodily conformation and pilosity which is characteristic of the male, and many men have some typically female traits. It is rather to be expected, then, that some individuals would prefer members of their own sex. An exciting cause of homosexuality is that of isolation of the sexes as in penitentiaries, on shipboard, and in one-sex boarding schools. "Crushes" are likely to develop where the sex impulse has no normal outlets. Coeducational colleges are more in harmony with the mental life of human beings than one-sex schools. In the coeducational institutions the two sexes mingle with each other in a normal manner. The family type of social contacts is present. A boy is not some heroic sexless knight in armor to the girl who sees him each day in the classroom and notes his humanness when asked a question by the instructor. Boys and girls will continue to fall in love with each other until human nature changes, and the best preventive of sexual anomalies is to give the child and youth a sane and normal sex environment where parents are not shocked by sexual digressions but are intelligent in redirecting them.

Acknowledgments and References

1. English Bagby, *The Psychology of Personality*, Henry Holt and Company, New York, 1928, Chapters VII, VIII, IX. See also Laurance F. Shaffer, *The Psychology of Adjustment*, Houghton Mifflin Company, Boston, 1936, pp. 151–152.

2. See David P. Ausubel, Herbert M. Schiff, and Morton Goldman, "Qualitative Characteristics in the Learning Process Associated with Anxiety," *Journal of Abnormal and Social Psychology*, October 1953, pp. 537–547.

3. For further information see Joseph D. Matarazzo, et. al., "The Relationship between Anxiety Level and Several Measures of Intelligence," *Journal of Consulting Psychology*, June 1954, pp. 201–205.

4. Jacob Levine, "Responses to Humor," *Scientific American*, February 1956, pp. 31–35.

5. G. H. Green, *Psychoanalysis in the Classroom,* G. P. Putman's Sons, New York, 1922, Chapter II.

6. Morris S. Viteles, *Industrial Psychology*, W. W. Norton and Company, New York, 1932, Chapter XXIV presents an excellent summary of specific influences in monotonous work.

7. Kenneth M. Goode, *What About Radio?* Harper & Brothers, New York, 1937, p. 30.

8. For further information see Irwin M. Rosenstock, "Perceptual Aspects of Repression," *Journal of Abnormal and Social Psychology*, July 1951.

9. "ABC's of Scapegoating," Central Y.M.C.A. College, Chicago, Illinois, undated, presents a summary of the types of practices of scapegoating today.

10. This article is one of a series on the psychology of war and propaganda prepared by the Society for the Psychological Study of Social Issues especially for release through Science Service. *Science News Letter,* March 9, 1940, p. 157.

11. Robert R. Sears, Carl I. Hovland, and Neal E. Miller, "Minor Studies of Aggression: I, Measurement of Aggressive behavior," *Journal of Psychology*, Vol. 9 (1940), pp. 275–295.

12. Norman R. F. Maier, "The Role of Frustration in Social Movements," *Psychological Review*, American Psychological Association, Inc., Vol. 49 (1942), presents additional aspects of frustration in behavior.

13. Charles P. McCormick, *Multiple Management*, Harper & Brothers, New York, 1938, pp. 50–52.

14. M. H. Means, "Fears of One Thousand College Women," *Journal of Abnormal and Social Psychology*, Vol. 31 (1936), pp. 291–311.

15. O. Fenichel, "Remarks on the Common Phobias," *Psychoanalytical Quarterly,* Vol. 13 (1944), pp. 313–326.

16. E. Bergler, "Contributions to the Psychogenesis of Alcohol Addiction," *Quarterly Journal of Studies on Alcohol*, Vol. 5 (1944), pp. 434–449.

17. *The Drinker and the Drunkard,* Lay Supplement No. 10, pp. 11–12. *Quarterly Journal of Studies on Alcohol*, 1944.

18. Herbert Yahraes, *Alcoholism Is a Sickness*, Public Affairs Pamphlet No. 118, Public Affairs Committee, Inc., New York, 1946, p. 19.

19. *The Drinker and the Drunkard, op. cit.,* p. 15.

20. Charles Stevenson, "Rebellious Liquors in My Blood," *Nation's Business*, September, 1947, pp. 60–66.

21. *A. A.: An A. A. Publication,* The Alcoholic Foundation, Inc., P. O. Box 459, Grand Central Annex, New York 17, N.Y.

22. W. R. Miles, "Psychological Factors in Alcoholism," *Mental Hygiene*, Vol. 21 (1937), pp. 529–548.

23. A summary of the "Proceedings of the First Industrial Conference on Alcoholism" is published in *Business Week,* July 10, 1948, p. 25.

24. C. M. Louttit, *Clinical Psychology*, Harper & Brothers, New York, 1947, p. 355.

25. W. Malamud and G. Palmer, "The Role Played by Masturbation in the Causation of Mental Disturbances," *Journal of Nervous and Mental Diseases*, Vol. 76 (1932), pp. 220–233; 366–379.

26. E. V. Pullias, "Masturbation as a Mental Hygiene Problem," *Journal of Abnormal and Social Psychology*, Vol. 32 (1937), pp. 216–222.

27. M. Huschka, "The Incidence and Character of Masturbation Threats in a Group of Problem Children," *Psychoanalytic Quarterly,* Vol. 7 (1938), pp. 338–356.

28. "Night Club Patrons Cry 'Criminal' at 'Peeping Toms,'" *Science News Letter,* November 27, 1937.

PROJECTS

1. Study any tendencies you may have toward fantasy or daydreaming. Which of the following types seems to be dominant: Display fantasy; Saving daydream; Fantasy of grandeur; Homage daydream; Suffering hero daydream? Can you suggest possible causes for the direction the tendency takes?

2. Consider people whom you have known and list any examples of fixed ideas you may have noted. Can you discover ra-

tional relationships between the fixed ideas and their adjustment background?

3. Make a collection of newspaper clippings concerning persons whose peculiar behavior has gotten them mention in the newspapers. Compare any explanations given in the clippings with hypotheses of your own.

4. Read some recent articles on "Alcoholics Anonymous." Evaluate the benefits and limitations of the methods of this group.

5. Analyze, for his compensatory behavior, an acquaintance of middle age who has never married. To what extent has such activity resulted in satisfactory adjustment?

6. Draw up a list of beneficial and possibly harmful adjustment influences in coeducational and non-coeducational schools. Check those which you can substantiate from your own or your friends' experiences.

7. The following is taken from a book on gypsy life:

"Enraged at an insult to his race, Gabor gathered his Romani friends together and got uproariously drunk. Coming home penniless, he was so ashamed that, in order to rehabilitate himself in his own eyes, he beat his wife." From Irving Brown, *Gipsy Fires in America.* Harper & Brothers, New York, 1924, p. 207.

   a. Can you offer an instance of the same type of projective behavior from your own life?

   b. Or, from the behavior you have observed in some other person?

8. Read several reports of experiments on rat behavior to note some of the ways in which frustration seems to affect animals.

In an experiment made to ascertain the effects of irregular and insufficient feeding in infancy, it was found that rats that had been subjected to infantile feeding frustration in infancy hoarded more than two and one-half times as much as their freely fed litter-mate controls. Hunt concluded that the "results tend to substantiate the psychoanalytic claim that infantile experience is an effective determinant of adult behavior, and they are interpreted in terms of learning theory."

9. To realize how energy may be dammed up, conduct this experiment. Have a person time you for ten trials of thirty seconds each. During each trial make the figure 5 as rapidly as you can in the usual manner of making a 5. Then make the figure 5 in an inverted manner as rapidly as possible for the same number of trials and the same number of seconds to each trial. Then make the 5 right side up as rapidly as you can for about five trials of the usual thirty seconds each. Do not allow more than ten seconds rest between any of the trials. Plot a curve of the number of 5's made in each of the 25 trials. Note the waves of efficiency and the release of the dammed-up energy.

COLLATERAL READINGS

Fenichel, O., "Remarks on the Common Phobias," *Psychoanalytic Quarterly*, Vol. 13 (1944), pp. 313–326.

Franco, S. Charles, M.D., "Problem Drinker in Industry," *Personnel Series*, American Management Association, No. 163, 1955, pp. 25–26.

Josey, Charles C., *Psychology and Successful Living*, Charles Scribner's Sons, New York, 1948, pp. 63–74.

Kinsey, Alfred C., Wardell B. Pomeroy, Clyde E. Martin, *Sexual Behavior in the Human Male*, W. B. Saunders Company, Philadelphia, 1948, Parts Two and Three.

Lehner, George F. J. and Ella Kube, *The Dynamics of Personal Adjustment*, Prentice-Hall, Inc., New York, 1955, Chapter 6.

Maier, Norman R. F., *Psychology in Industry*, Houghton Mifflin Company, Cambridge, Mass., 1955, Chapter 4.

Shaffer, Laurance F. and Edward J. Shoben, Jr., *The Psychology of Adjustment*, Houghton Mifflin Company, Boston, 1956, Part Two.

Smith, Henry Clay, *Psychology of Industrial Behavior*, McGraw-Hill Book Company, Inc., New York, 1955.

CHAPTER FIVE

Adjustment by functional ailments

Patient: "Oh, doctor, I have the most awful pain somewhere in my shoulders."

Doctor: "And when did you first notice the pain, madam?"

Patient: "About two months ago, I think. Yes, it was two months ago. It was just about the time Mrs. Neighbor got her new fur coat; the snob."

A psychiatrist reported the case of a woman who claimed that she had stomach trouble because of a frog in her stomach. She "knew" she had swallowed a frog egg while on a picnic. Her physician ridiculed the idea but she was so insistent that he finally agreed to operate for the removal of the frog. Accordingly, he sent her to a hospital to be prepared for the operation and he, at the same time, hired a small boy to catch a frog for him. To give the woman the impression that she had really had an operation, an incision was made in her abdomen, and the doctor showed her the "frog," in a bottle of alcohol, which had presumably been removed from her stomach. The woman was delighted and at once recovered, but only temporarily. Three months after the psuedo-operation, she claimed that the first frog had laid some eggs and that she now had two frogs in her stomach!

This amusing example illustrates the uselessness of ordinary logical thinking in the consideration of the many ailments which are functional rather than organic.

When a surgeon is prevailed upon to operate for a functional disturbance, the operation does not, as a rule, result in permanent cure. A physician may occasionally give "placebos," pills which have no medicinal value, in order to satisfy a patient temporarily. However, physicians who treat the functionally ill realize that certain patients need an improved adjustment to their problems more than they need pills.

How illness often becomes a means of adjustment

Any form of invalidism is likely to be useful as a means of adjustment to problems. Almost every child learns that he can avoid unpleasant duties such as mowing the lawn, washing dishes, or studying his lessons, by feigning illness.

Jo is a boy of twelve who has been feeling very much out of the family picture. He is the youngest child. His sister is soon to be married and his brother has just started to work, but Jo is at an age when he is not particularly interesting to any member of the family. He has been doing only fairly well in his school work and he has definitely neglected his arithmetic.

One morning he went down to breakfast and ate rather heartily: he had oatmeal with cream, eggs, bacon, jam, and milk; and while he was eating he recalled that he was going to have an arithmetic test that morning. He had a queer, twitchy feeling of excitement in his stomach at the thought of the arithmetic test. He started walking slowly to school, thinking more about the test, and his stomach felt queerer and the oatmeal weighed very heavily on it. He had a vague feeling, which was hardly a thought, that if his breakfast were to come up he wouldn't have to go to school, and the arithmetic test came to mind again. Suddenly he found it hard to keep the breakfast down.

Shortly after his arrival at school, it did come up. He was sent home by the principal with a clear conscience to have a day in bed. The principal telephoned his mother, who immediately became concerned. She put Jo to bed in the guest room and made a fuss over him such as he had not experienced since he was quite a small boy. His sister came in and showed him her wedding presents; his brother stopped and had a talk with him before going out in the evening, an event which had not occurred for months; and his father spent the evening reading to him.

This upset stomach had a high value: no arithmetic test, and solicitude from all the people from whom he had been wishing attention for some time. The next time Jo was faced with a difficult situation and there was a queer feeling in his stomach, it was no longer necessary to go through all the preliminary steps. Now meals just come up without further consideration on his part.[1]

The child's convenient illness often brings about considerable sympathy and attention. Later the same child meets problems for which he lacks requisite skills or energies to solve. The poorly adjusted individual cannot admit to himself his own lack of courage to make direct attack upon his problems or duties. That would lower his sense of self-worth. However, the old habits of evasion through ailment take place subconsciously because the pattern for that kind of adjustment has been used in the past. His ego is sustained because he himself is not aware of the true cause of his ailment. He believes that he is ill. In fact he is ill, but the origin of the illness has been forgotten. He repressed the recognition of his inabilities or deficiencies.

We must not confuse *Repression* with *Suppression*. The latter is a conscious process; we use it when we force an idea out of our minds by deliberately attending to something else. A person gets a letter containing bad news on the morning of an important examination; he forces himself to put it aside and go through with the examination. In other words, he suppresses his tendency to grief or anxiety for the time being. If it were *repressed*, he would forget that he had ever had the letter. Such repression does occur, especially in certain neurotic types of personalities, but not out of a clear sky; that is, the matter repressed is connected with earlier conflicts which underwent repression. A young woman stenographer lost her job because she forgot to transcribe an important letter, and when she maintained that she had not taken it she was thought to be lying. The letter was addressed to a man whose name was that of a former sweetheart who had jilted her. The normal adult, apparently, does not make much use of repression; he handles his conflicts, his griefs and disappointments, in other ways.[2]

The executive whose office boy reports on the first day of the baseball season that he is too ill to work but at the same time winks knowingly to the boss, who himself enjoys baseball, has insight into the "illness." In contrast to the office boy, the stenographer, an introverted spinster, may have a splitting headache and find it necessary to go home and go to bed. She probably lacks insight into her adjustments because she fails to recognize that her illness is her subconscious method of avoiding a visit from a former classmate who always could capture more boy friends than she could.

Many ailments do have an organic basis, but some are wholly or partially functional. We must bear in mind that a pain is felt through the mechanisms of the brain rather than only at the point of injury. We say that the pain of the psychoneurotic is in his "head." Well, all pains are felt in the head. Surgeons tell us that, when they sever the foot of a soldier, the soldier can still "feel" the ache of his corns or the bed-clothes pressing on his "foot." The war veteran who had both feet cut off and yet predicted the weather from the aches of his corns was not merely "joshing" his hearers. Stimuli passed over certain nerve tracts which formerly conveyed impulses from his corns, and the response in his brain was quite the same as it had been before he had had his feet cut off. A psychological pain, therefore, is just as painful as an or-ganic pain. We do our friends an injustice when we tell them that they only imagine the pain and that, if they wanted to do so, they could forget it. They are not helped by scoldings. Rather, they become worse. But, on the other hand, we should not coddle the patient.

Some pains are conditioned responses, as we can readily see in many children. If father sits down to the table and tells moth-er that spinach gives him indigestion, the little members of the family tend to de-velop the same symptoms when required to eat their spinach. Mothers who suffer from painful menstruation condition their daughters to the same pains when they reach maturity. Epidemics of various sorts have been reported in schools, after one child had a real or a functional ailment that impressed the other children. For this reason, intelligent teachers and parents do not discuss their aches and pains in the presence of children.

Medical students often develop the symp-toms of the patients whom they study. When the writer arranges tours through state hospitals for the benefit of his stu-dents, he usually finds that one or two students develop enough symptoms to re-quire some form of treatment. In some cases the student must be sent to a psy-chiatrist for mental treatment before he

recovers. Suggestion, no doubt, plays an important part in many of our functional illnesses.

Functional illness enables the individual to evade barriers

In this discussion, we want to give emphasis to the part that illness plays as a means of escape from unpleasant prob-lems. The classic case of the girl who was engaged to the man she loved and became totally deaf when she realized that he no longer loved her is illustrative of a definite attempt to escape reality through illness. She became deaf on the evening when her sweetheart called with the express purpose of telling her that he no longer loved her and wished to be released from the engage-ment. Deafness enabled her to evade the problem.

Illness may be an escape from an un-pleasant situation even though such an ad-justment will not be admitted or recognized by the patient. One businessman of un-usual honesty borrowed money from his relatives and friends and earnestly expected to be able to pay it back from anticipated profits. Unfortunately, the business did not prosper and the money was lost. The debt-or could not face his creditors; nor could he commit suicide because he loved his wife and child. Suddenly he became total-ly blind and has remained blind for several years. The examining physicians are con-vinced that the blindness has no organic cause. Strange as it may seem, his blind-ness is not a barrier to him but is an accept-able mode of adjustment to an otherwise unbearable situation.

Sickness not only keeps fearful men out of battle but also enables new employees to seek to evade failure on the new job, as re-ported by one executive:

In this connection I might say that it has been a continual source of amazement to me how frequently men stay home during the first few weeks on a new position. One would imagine that nothing short of serious illness would prevent prompt and regular attendance on the job until it was thoroughly mastered and a competent understudy was on hand to keep things properly moving. But such is not the case.[3]

Thousands of employees are uncertain regarding their abilities and, being unable to admit their limitations, they may make an adjustment by becoming sickly. Sickness is often an acceptable excuse for vocational mediocrity or failure. Many executives, too, realize that they cannot achieve outstanding business success, and so their desk drawers are filled with pills and medicine bottles. Sickness, conscious and subconscious in nature, is an acceptable excuse for our inability to achieve the eminence we desire. People who evade their barriers by means of illness feel that employers, teachers, parents, friends, and relatives have no right to expect the "sick" to accomplish very much when they are "too ill" to work. At the same time, they have the satisfaction of knowing that they do drag through the day's work when others tell them that they really ought to be home in bed!

Most members of our American culture are sympathetic toward persons who are organically sick and toward those who use illness as a means of evading problems. Almost everyone is practically encouraged to use illness as an excuse for failure. This situation should lead us to be suspicious of the real reason for any illness which is not obviously caused by some organic condition. Furthermore, a knowledge of common adjustment patterns which include illness should enable us to choose more intelligently the person with whom we work or live, such as the employee or the mate.

The young man or woman in love as well as the executive should be able to recognize the more common patterns for maladjustment such as neurasthenia. A neurasthenic wife, for example, is the kind of spouse who keeps her mate busy propping up a partner who insists upon being hard to live with. The neurasthenic mate is a true psychological "ball and chain." For the lover, the time to recognize the neurasthenic is before marriage; not after. For the executive, the best time to deal with psychoneurotic employees is before they are hired. Of course, if the prospective neurasthenic mate or employee has compensating qualities, the marriage or employment may be satisfactory, but the one who must bear the effects of their maladjustments should be aware of the extra load he will have to carry. The person who knows the *syndrome* (pattern of symptoms) of the more common psychoneurotic ailments has an important advantage in human relations.

The psychoneuroses

Many experts refuse to classify the ineffective adjustment patterns that are commonly found in the behavior of psychoneurotic personalities. Their objection is that few cases of "perfect" patterns of symptoms are found among clinical patients. Combinations of certain symptoms are common, however, and our discussion will include the use of the more common terms in this division of psychological literature.

The terms *psychoneurosis* and *neurosis* are used interchangeably by many psychologists. In this book the term psychoneurosis is used the more often. It does not designate a specific disease. Rather, it indicates a level or degree of severity in maladjustment. It refers to a level between the psychosis, or insanity, and an inappropriate adjustment, such as a simple defense mechanism of little seriousness. A psychotic is incapacitated for his world. The neurotic is poorly adjusted to it. A humorous distinction between the psychotic and the neurotic is that "To the psychotic, 2 and 2 make 5. To the neurotic, 2 and 2 make 4, but he's unhappy about it!"

Some experts classify the psychoneuroses with organic ailments. Psychoneuroses often do involve many physical symptoms, such as headache, backache, indigestion, constipation, and dysmenorrhea. The extent to which these bodily symptoms are cause or effect or mere accompaniments of maladjustments is unknown. However, we shall describe these symptoms for the benefit of the psychological neophyte so that he can recognize them when he finds himself, his friends, or his employees having the reactions characteristic of the psychoneurotic.

Neurasthenia means literally *asthenia,* or exhaustion, of the nerves. It is often called nervous exhaustion or nervous breakdown. However, it is really not so much an exhaustion of nerve energy as a case of misplaced energy. It is more common among women than among men. The main symptoms in the syndrome are (a) chronic bodily fatigue, (b) irritability (occasionally the patient exhibits pronounced exhilaration, but this is soon followed by fatigue and irritability), (c) inability to concentrate attention on any one task, (d) bad temper, (e) moodiness, (f) self-analysis and self-pity and (g) *hypochondria,* or excessive attention to the functioning of the bodily organs, with continued functional pains, is a frequent accompaniment. As soon as the doctor shows the neurasthenic that she cannot have that kind of pain where she has located it, she then claims that the pain has moved to some other part of the body. The more attention the pain receives, the worse it becomes. Some people easily develop symptoms of various ailments when they read descriptions of the different maladies.

For this reason it is well to keep medical books in the physician's office and the public library. They should not be in most homes. If the housewife is tempted to buy medical books, let her buy, instead, a book on how to operate a tourist home or how to rear her children.

What are the causes? Some men attribute neurasthenia to heredity, but it is generally considered to be due very largely to an inability to face reality. It is an evasional device. As in most psychoneurotic ailments, the evading individual is likely to be in a state of conflict between his instinctive tendencies and his intelligent strivings. A housewife, for example, has instinctive urges to meet and enjoy the company of handsome men whom she likes, but she also knows that she must obey the rules of conduct of our culture. In her conflicts, physiological imbalances arise in her nervous system. Freud concluded that neurasthenia was nothing more nor less than the expression of suppressed sexual excitement.[4]

Neurasthenia may be accentuated by bad habits such as late hours, sexual excesses, and alcoholism. The endocrine glands may be a factor in the psychoneurosis, but that has not been demonstrated as yet. The strenuous life of the present age is supposed to be responsible in many cases. This is hardly correct. The stress of modern life for many people lies in the fact that they do not have enough important things to do. This applies particularly to the women of the middle and upper income classes. Labor-saving devices have eliminated most of the hard but beneficial labor of the American home. In addition to finding themselves more or less useless, many women have a kind of indefinable, unfulfilled longing to be something or to do something worth while. Many are out of the general scheme of things except as spectators or as they concoct something to do.

A device commonly chosen by an idle woman to escape neurasthenia and to make herself a part of the scheme of things is to "take up a cause." She hears that certain factory workers are underpaid and so starts a home for them; or she finds that some dogs do not have homes, so she starts a home for homeless dogs. Some of these "causes" are quite worthy and legitimate, but they are not a natural part of the lives of these women. As the term expresses it, "the cause is taken up."

Attaching one's self to a cause is better, however, than seeking relief in a continuous round of social pleasures. When a woman has a so-called nervous breakdown, because she has dashed from one meeting to the next meeting, then to a show, and then to a dance and supper at breakfast time, the breakdown is really caused by mental factors that caused her to dash around in circles. The rushing around to functions is merely the expression of a lack of adjustment to life, and the breakdown is just a nice name for a maladjustment. When effort is the result of conflict or disturbing anxiety and not a part of an integrative plan of living, then the effort becomes fatiguing and unsatisfying. The individual becomes irritable and moody. Life is futile.

What are the remedies? The usual method suggested by physicians is to take a rest cure at home or in a sanatorium. A rest cure of the right kind—a cure that builds up the integrative adjustments as well as the body—is desirable. Many cures, however, are more harmful than beneficial for neurasthenics. If the patient merely goes to a new environment where she sits down and does nothing, she is not helped to build a new philosophy of life that will revitalize her. Temporarily the rest is helpful if it removes the patient to an environment which does not have some of her old problems, and in so far as the maladjustment may be accentuated by a rundown physical state.

If the attention is directed to the bodily organs or functions, harm is done. Sensations of pain and discomfort are soon established even though the organic state is perfect. Detailed attention to the diet often makes the indigestion worse. The physician's questions regarding symptoms are interpreted to mean that the symptoms are present and suggestibility runs wild.

Pains and aches should be minimized by friends and associates, and the patient should be given mental pictures of health and strength rather than pity and sympathy. Make her feel that she is missing fun by her illness. Social contacts should be with those of dynamic, positive personalities. The mental imagery should be of a very happy sort. Autosuggestion is of value if the patient can

be trained to apply it with complete belief. If she can do so with conviction, it is well for her to renew her interest in some religion and to acquire a philosophy of her own.

The real problem is that of getting the patient to live outside herself rather than within her own feelings. She should acquire absorbing and satisfying work that fits into some plausible scheme for her own philosophy of life. Work which necessity forces her to do is the main help. Mental re-education is the best route to attain this end of a healthy outlook; but the whole scheme of treatment is more easily applied on paper than to the patient. Most of these patients are not ill enough for scientists to spend much time and effort on them, and so they are neglected and allowed to grow worse. Neurasthenia is exceedingly difficult to relieve for any great length of time, and it is much harder to cure. One lesson that the neurasthenics indicate to the parent is that his son and daughter should be required to work at some steady occupation which is worth while to society and to the individual. From the standpoint of sound mental adjustment, we should have many women going into business or some other kind of work, unless they are, of course, needed in the home. If business will not accept them, then we must expect to have more neurasthenic wives and daughters and to supply institutions and "causes" to take care of them.

It is difficult to secure data to prove that women are more afflicted with neurasthenia than are men, but many physicians judge this to be true. If so, it may be partly caused by the fact that we are more solicitous of girls than of boys. When Johnnie, aged six, comes into the house, crying because of a skinned nose, we tell him, "Be a man and stop crying." When his sister, aged eight, comes into the house crying because of a skinned knee we tell her, "Well now, that is too bad. Let's see that knee. Maybe we can put something on it to make it feel better." We still give women the impression that they are weaker than men and, therefore, that we must defer to them because they are women. Daughters should be required to work just as much as sons. The work may be different, but they should sense the joy of a positive productive life rather than the negative attitude of attention through illness.

Psychasthenia is a group term used for tendencies such as obsessions, manias, impulsions, and phobias.[5] In recent years the general term has been almost discontinued, because it is more accurate to treat these tendencies as specific forms of maladjustment. The individual with a mania may have a strong impulse to set fire to his home, to steal money, or to injure someone. Some psychoneurotics wonder whether they are alive and whether they are really themselves. Sometimes the world seems to be closing in about them and crushing them. They know that their fears and impulsions are without any real basis, but still they continue to fight them. We are not concerned here with the true or completely psychasthenic patient, but rather with the psychasthenic tendencies that are found among the members of the office, the school, and the home.

Many physicians consider the *anxiety syndrome* the most frequently observed form of the various functional illnesses. Typical symptoms are a constant feeling of tension and apprehension, headache, irritability, insomnia, desire to be alone, mental weariness, and feelings of unreality. Psychosomatic symptoms are dilated pupils, tremor of outstretched hands, increased pulse pressure, flushing, giddiness, perspiration, breathlessness, and feelings of suffocation. No one patient has all symptoms.[6] The presence of many of them, however, is recognized by those trained in psychosomatic medicine as a signal to treat the emotional as well as the organic causes.

In addition to psychoneurotic symptoms such as manias and phobias, we have other milder and more common negative-value tendencies.

Worry is the most common tendency un-

der this heading. In general, we consider worry an unpleasant mental state, and yet, like any other habit that is continued, it may become agreeable in its own way. A worry may hide a symbolic wish, as does the excessive worry regarding the health of a wealthy uncle whose money we hope to inherit, but we never discuss the wish with ourselves. A boy worries about the welfare of his mother when she goes away from home. Inasmuch as she has kept him tied to her apron string, he experiences a sense of relief and may secretly hope that the train will be wrecked in order that he may be completely free. A mother sends her children out to play, and when they do not come home at the usual time, she worries; partly because of the fact that some neighbor's child was lost or killed, but also because she will have a greater thrill when the children do come back. In many cases the worry is a kind of thrill or a preparation for a thrill. It relieves the monotony of housework. Worry may also be a kind of mental random movement which can be made for the solution of a problem when physical attention is impossible.

Temporary worry is not so great a problem as the persistent apprehensive variety of worry regarding one's financial status, health, or studies. In many cases there is just cause for worry on these subjects, but the psychasthenic does nothing about it. If a student is failing in his studies, he should not worry about it but get to work. If a person worries about his health, the answer is to have a thorough physical examination and then, if the worry is unjustified, stop it. But here comes the difficulty. When the chronic worrier is told all about the fact that he has no real reason to worry, he still continues to worry. For this reason, it is well to ask the expert in worry whether he really wants to stop worrying. Even if he answers, "Of course I do," he should have the idea emphasized most strongly that he must really want to stop worrying before he can reduce his worries. He must determine to picture in his mind positive, healthful, pleasant images rather than the expected unpleasant imagery. Furthermore, he must put into effect definite schedules of work and recreation which will help to develop new mental habits in dealing with his problems. He must achieve insight. If he cannot gain insight into the basic cause of his worry, such as the pressure of a conflict, he will need the assistance of a clinician.

Stage fright is a common negative-value tendency. Why should anyone be fearful when he speaks before others? If he has nothing worth saying, he can simply say so and sit down; but, if he has a message of any importance, he ought to be glad to give it to his fellows. Of course, a talk in public puts one in a position where the ego is liable to be assailed. The speaker knows that some members of the audience may know more about the subject than he does, and he fears their disapproval. This can be overcome by the speaker's frank acknowledgment that he is presenting his own experiences or views and that he would like others there to tell him wherein he is wrong. This does not mean that the speaker who is called upon for a five-minute report or discussion should then spend a half-hour in making apologies. Nor need his talk begin with an apology. But his attitude should be that of the student and learner rather than that of the polished expert. In fact, very many of our psychological difficulties, particularly our self-conscious feelings and fears, would vanish if we could only get ourselves into the mental state of the true student. The true student seeks truth and the facts. Whatever his searches may uncover, it will not jeopardize his ego, because his ego is not involved. The true scientist is interested in finding the things that fail as well as the things that succeed, because he wants to know all aspects of the problem—not just those that give him prestige.

If the speaker makes up his mind that speaking in public is an opportunity for him to exchange ideas with his fellows and at the same time an opportunity to learn more than he can give, he is likely to have little trouble in speaking anywhere, unless he has had a serious shock while speaking in public. If he has had a decidedly unpleasant experience while speaking in public, then he will have to regain his ease of speaking by gradual steps. He should begin on small and sympathetic audiences. He should practice on people who know much less than he does of the subject he talks about. He should get away from the idea that he is competing with anyone. He is just going to tell what he knows as clearly and as well as he can, and thereby he hopes to learn more himself.

Abulia or the *abulic obsession* is also a common negative-value tendency. This term is applied to the inability to get started on the job that awaits our action. We have a report to prepare or a call to make. We often find ourselves postponing it and procrastinating until we are too embarrassed to do it. This is one reason why operating a business according to a definite schedule is better than trusting to the initiative of the employees. A large part of the executive's work consists of setting schedules for his associates and then seeing that the schedules are followed. Almost everyone often finds himself unable to do the things that he wants to do but somehow never gets done. The answer is to make a schedule for his annoying hang-over tasks. The student, for example, should set a definite date when an assignment is to be completed, and at once start a small part of the task. He should not plan to complete the whole job or a large part of it at one sitting, but should make the outline, and then he will find that he can continue for a reasonable length of time.

Another help is "whenpecking." By this is meant enlisting the coöperation of one's colleagues. The businessman can, for example, tell his wife or secretary that he wants to finish a task by a certain date and request her to jog his memory occasionally. Some evening when he may have made up his mind to go to a stag party, his wife will say: "*When* are you going to finish that fourth lesson in business management?" He may be more or less offended at the insinuation, but he will know that she is right and probably will get busy on the important task.

When dangerous and irrational negative-value tendencies are persistent, such as the handicapping phobia, compulsion neurosis, impulsions to say indecent words in public, and the desire to injure some person who is loved and admired, then it is well to consult the psychiatrist. These impulsions are symbolic of patterns which have been connected with the adjustment of the individual to some unrecognizable and inadmissible impulse, such as the sex impulse.

Hysteria is a word used in many different ways by the psychiatrists, but it is most frequently applied to certain unstable emotional states that come and go without apparent cause. An example is that of a housewife who, while busily engaged in her housework, such as sweeping the kitchen floor, suddenly breaks forth into a fit of intense weeping. She may cry bitterly for a few minutes and then pick up her broom and resume her work. When she is asked why she cried she says that she did not cry. She is unable to recall the incident because of her mental dissociation. In many cases the individual also acquires a paralysis of a limb or an area of anesthesia, or has tics and tremors, or may be in a state of mental stupor and have strong delusions.

Hysteria is a mental disorder which is characterized not by hysterical behavior such as crying but by mental dissociation. One famous case of hysteria had a history of five different personalities.[7] Hysteria often includes pronounced disturbances in bodily and mental activity and may result in illnesses such as hysterical blindness, as in the case of the businessman who became blind after he was unable to pay back money borrowed for his failing business, mentioned on page 90.[8]

In some cases of hysteria the patient seems to acquire his functional ailment as an accompaniment of an emotional outburst. In the ordinary case of invalidism, the patient acquires the chronic ailing more slowly. Invalidism is more common among intelligent persons. Hysteria is more common among children and adults of low intelligence than among persons of high intelligence. The hysteria patients have a tendency toward simulation and delusions. Many of them have falsely accused those whom they love. Children have caused their parents to be brought into court, because they claimed that their parents had locked them in the attic or the cellar and had given them no food for days at a time.

The chief suggestion for all of us is the fact that disease may be truly organic, functional, or a combination of the two. If it is functional, it is just as serious as if it were organic, but it must be dealt with along psychological lines.

About one fourth of all adult patients consecutively admitted to Mayo Clinic during the course of a study received a diagnosis solely of some type of neurosis. Most of the neurotic patients were somewhat younger than the other members of their occupational groups, probably because people tend to become less emotional as they grow older. Figures also revealed a somewhat higher incidence of neurosis among women patients.

The lowest incidence of neurosis was found among railroad engineers, and the next lowest among farmers. Smith and Hightower believe that those who do manual work are less neurotically inclined than those who do other types of work. The highest incidence of neurosis was found among teachers, most of whom were females. Fifty-four per cent of the teachers examined had some type of functional disease. See Table 5-1 for comparisons of the incidence of functional disease among nine occupational groups.[9] Of course these findings apply only to the groups admitted to Mayo Clinic and may or may not be representative of other members of the same occupational groups.

TABLE 5-1

INCIDENCE BY OCCUPATIONAL GROUPS OF FUNCTIONAL AND ORGANIC DISORDERS
REPORTED FOR PATIENTS CONSECUTIVELY ADMITTED TO MAYO CLINIC

Occupation	Patients	Sex	Age, Years		Purely Functional Disease			Functional and Organic Disease			Some Functional Disease (Purely Functional Plus Functional and Organic)	
			Average	Range	Patients	Percentage	Average Age, Years	Patients	Percentage	Average Age, Years	Patients	Percentage
Clergymen	130	male	48	20–80	31	24	45	19	15	48	50	39
Dentists	128	male	45	25–77	31	24	43	7	6	50	38	30
Farmers	145	male	48	21–81	13	9	40	15	10	38	28	19
Housewives	116	female	44	21–74	31	27	40	11	9	44	42	36
Lawyers	166	male	48	23–79	31	19	44	28	17	47	59	36
Nuns	128	female	44	20–75	27	21	40	27	21	46	54	42
Physicians	129	male	47	22–68	13	10	48	9	7	52	22	17
Railroad engineers	100	male	57	33–66	4	4	50	5	5	50	9	9
School teachers	16	male	34	25–59	4	25	41	4	25	40	8	50
	106	female	38	18–63	36	34	39	22	21	43	58	55

The extent of neurosis in industry

The most carefully conducted studies to learn the extent of neurosis in industry were made during World War II by the Medical Research Council, Industrial Research Board, London. The sickness absences of some 3,000 workers of thirteen light and medium engineering factories were investigated for six months by a special staff of physicians and social workers. Judgment as to the existence or extent of neurosis was made as objectively as possible. Assess- ment of neurosis was made only after examination of each worker, after factory records had been consulted, after one and a half hours had been devoted to testing and examining each person, and after special examinations such as x-ray had been given where considered desirable. Neurosis was diagnosed "definite" only when it resulted in one or more days' absence from work, when the patient believed it to be illness, and when it was diagnosed by the medical examiner as being of neurotic origin.*

*Neurosis was the term used to describe any illness which was apparently of psychological origin. No cases of mental deficiency or organic nervous disease were included in the survey. A few abnormalities of personality were classified as minor neurosis when they seemed to indicate reduced mental health, but ordinarily they were not classified as neurosis. Only when mental inefficiency could be judged to be an illness or a deviation from the worker's usual mental efficiency was it classified as neurosis.

"Minor neurosis" also included a few cases of psychosomatic illness of doubtful origin, but did not include slight disabilities, such as occasional headaches or insomnia.

"Definite neurosis" was diagnosed when both doctor and patient agreed on the existence of disabling illness, usually causing absence from work.

The incidence of neurosis was found to be 10 per cent for all the workers; 9.1 per cent of the male and 13.0 per cent of the female workers suffered a disabling neurosis; and an additional 20 per cent consisting of 19.2 per cent of male and 23.0 per cent of female workers suffered minor neurosis during the six-months' period.

The study revealed that one fourth to one third of absences from work for reasons of illness were attributable to neurosis. Neurosis caused the loss of 1.09 per cent of the men's working days and of 2.40 per cent of those of the women.

The extent of the incidence of neurosis was revealed during the six-months' study period by the fact that 28.3 per cent of the men and 36.0 per cent of the women suffered from neurosis, and 9.1 per cent of the men and 13.0 per cent of the women suffered a definite neurosis.

Circumstances associated with less than the usual incidence of neurosis:

1. more than average normal domestic responsibilities, with under 75 hours of industrial duty per week;
2. more than average social contacts;
3. work found congenial.

Workers who had considerable domestic responsibility without excessive hours of duty at the factory or elsewhere (under 75 hours a week), experienced less than the average amount of neurosis; the same was true of those with a wide range of human contacts, and of those with a job that they liked. This is understandable since they were satisfying some common human aspirations and needs. Mere freedom from any source of worry appeared by comparison to be of little moment; though the small group with considerable sources of worry, such as those due to separation from close friends or to illness among relatives, had more neurosis than the rest.

Circumstances associated with more than the usual incidence of neurosis:

1. working over 75 hours of industrial duty per week;
2. taking the least adequate diets;
3. restricted social contacts, recreation, or leisure interests;

4. widowhood or separation, and, among the women, marriage with partial home duties;
5. considerable abnormal responsibilities;
6. work found boring, or disliked;
7. very light or sedentary work;
8. work requiring skill inappropriate to the worker's intelligence;
9. assembly, bench, inspection or toolroom work;
10. work requiring constant attention, especially if giving little scope for initiative or technical responsibility;
11. work programmes offering little variety;
12. tasks for which the lighting was unsatisfactory.

A decrease in social contacts was the circumstance most commonly associated with neurosis. Those whose leisure was usually spent alone, or only with their immediate family, suffered more than average neurosis, whether their contacts were reduced because of solitary interests, restrictions imposed by home duties, or other reasons. To a lesser degree, those with diminished recreation and leisure interests also suffered from a higher incidence of neurosis than the average. Neurosis was more frequent among groups whose domestic circumstances could be regarded as unsatisfactory, for example, those widowed or separated, and married women with partial home duties (i.e. with either housework or the care of children, but not both). This group of married women had poorer health, probably because it included most of those whose homes had been disrupted by the war. On the other hand, the married women with full home duties (both housework and the care of children) had experienced better health than the other married women and as good health as the single women, though they had been more frequently absent from work. Evidently wartime factory hours are unsuitable for married women with full home duties, but with shortened hours such women may be efficient and healthy factory workers.[10]

For supervisors in American industry, neuroticism among female workers has been reported as an especially difficult problem. Dr. Sylvia A. Sorkin in an address before a recent conference of the National Office Management Association gave results of a questionnaire sent to office managers. Approximately 900 responded. She told the conference delegates that from a listing of nine common office management "head-aches" mentioned in the survey, the problem of dealing with neurotic female workers was rated second only in importance to the problem of securing well-trained clerical workers.

Although a third of the executives who gave their opinions said that securing trained help was their biggest problem, nearly a quarter of them ranked the neurotic female as their most difficult problem. Neurotic male workers, on the other hand, got top billing as a problem by only 3 per cent of the executives.[11]

Malingering versus neurosis. The executive who supervises large numbers of factory employees sooner or later has the problem of deciding whether an employee who claims compensation is suffering from an organic ailment or is merely malingering. True malingering places a premium on fraud. Both malingering and neurosis may spring from maladjustments of personality, so that differentiation between the two is very difficult.[12]

An analysis of 1,000 consecutive disability insurance claims for psychoneurosis was made five years after disability had commenced. Almost 30 per cent of the cases had been incorrectly diagnosed. The mortality rate for these neurotics also showed that neurotics have a distinctly greater life expectancy than normal persons and that suicide is very rare among them.[13]

The fact that many neurotics, especially hysteria cases, do not have an organic ailment is often indicated by their ability to use muscles or limbs in certain situations but not when they are at work. One telegrapher, for example, could send messages perfectly when he knew that his key was connected to a testing machine, but he developed a cramp as soon as his key was attached to the main line. Many of these occupational neurotics can use their muscles very effectively at play but are unable to use them in work. The expert in diagnosis uses various tests to determine whether the claimant for com-pensation is malingering or neurotic. Important tests are willingness to take medicine regularly, to undergo surgical operations, to submit to repeated examinations, and the content of dreams and conversation.[14]

The occupational neurotic is usually very unhappy in his work or hates some part of it. Sometimes he merely associates some personal emotional problem with his work. Neuroses of this kind are more likely to occur when the worker is unable to quit his job because of his geographic isolation, requirements of a long-term contract, or enlistment in the army. An injury, fatigue of certain muscles, or an example of a fellow-worker may suggest the way in which the maladjustment can be made to disappear or how the patient's emotional problems can be corrected through systematic psychological treatment.

Allergies

Allergy may be defined as a special sensitivity to a substance that is harmless to most individuals. We all know persons who cannot eat certain foods without distress. Others cannot be in the presence of furry or hairy animals without developing asthma or skin eruptions. About 10 per cent of the people of the United States are allergic to a marked degree and another 40 per cent to a minor extent. Wheat foods, eggs, and milk are the most common causes of food allergies. The victims develop certain itches, aches, sneezes, and wheezes. In one community survey regarding allergies, it was found that 10 per cent of the people had hay fever, 3.6 per cent asthma, 2.9 per cent eczema, 3.7 per cent urticaria, and 3.3 per cent gastrointestinal allergy.[15]

Some allergies are undoubtedly of organic origin, but many appear to be psychological. For example, one woman always suffered from asthma when she went to a certain railroad station. Someone told her that the station dust was of an unusual chemical nature and that she could be cured by having an injection of the dust. Her doctor injected her with a solution of common salt. After that the attacks of asthma ceased.[16]

"Darling, this is our last night together. Tomorrow my hay fever starts." Courtesy of Crowell-Collier Publishing Co.

When 50 adult patients with bronchial asthma were taken from an allergy clinic and studied psychiatrically, 37 patients appeared to have an emotional component in their asthmatic attacks, 20 patients reported that the first attack was emotionally precipitated, and 30 patients showed neurotic traits usually of a compulsive nature.[17]

"Psychosomatic" illnesses

Every newspaper reader has become acquainted with the term "psychosomatic." To many people, unfortunately, it implies that the mind causes the ailment of the body. They imagine that psychological and physiological functions are separated. To overcome this erroneous dualistic assumption, the Army psychiatric classification system uses the term *somatization reactions.*

Reactions of this kind are brought about by interactions of nonseparable organic and psychological factors. Measurable damages are caused to the tissues and structures of the body. Peptic ulcers are an example.

There is still much question about the cause and effect relationship between the so-called psychologically induced ailments and emotional problems of people suffering from these afflictions. Does the emotional state of an individual precipitate his illness, or does the illness itself bring about personality changes? In one recent study, for example, results of projective psychological tests given to people suffering from asthma and ulcerative colitis were compared with a control group of patients suffering from malignant tumors—supposedly a non-psychologically based disease. The results of this study revealed no important differences between the groups on any of the tests in so far as their psychiatric implications are concerned. There were no important differences between the groups in mood, masculinity-femininity, aggressiveness-passivity, or responses to the Rorschach test. The author concluded that people with psychosomatic diseases do not appear to differ from other ill people in so far as these psychological indicators are concerned. While the etiology (origins) of the disease may differ, some of the diseases are not to be approached exclusively through treatment of the mind and others exclusively through treatment of the body. Ideally, all medicine should be psychosomatic, with the mind and body being treated as a unit.[18]

Other studies of patients having arthritis, colitis, and obesity indicate that many have deep-seated resentments or feelings of guilt.[19] Their resentments are likely to be directed against employers, members of the family, or teachers. When primitive men were aroused to anger against an enemy, they could expend their aroused energies against the enemy. Although civilized men are also aroused to anger, their heightened bodily activities cannot be promptly expressed, so they suffer a prolonged state of anxiety. When a man loses his job, he has the same fears experienced by his cave-man ancestors who needed food, but the stronger heartbeat and extra secretions are now superfluous. The biochemical changes which facilitate adjustive action must be suppressed, but suppression does not remove them. The aroused bodily resources find expression in protective and aggressive reactions of asthma, arthritis, duodenal ulcer, allergies, and hundreds of other apparently unrelated manifestations.[20]

Psychosomatic medicine and related researches are developing new and more effective approaches to the relations between emotions and bodily changes.[21] Modern medical practitioners now recognize that the energy of hate and resentment can cause (crippling) ailments, such as high blood pressure; that the constant wavering between desire for success and fear of failure may produce changes in stomach acids that in turn form stomach ulcers; and that certain skin eruptions may mask a confession of sin.

A famous physician, in an article, "Why Medicine Is Not a Science," has stressed the importance of understanding the mental life of the patient. Parts of his article are the following:

There are three states of ill health. The first is a functional impairment or misuse which is often impossible to detect and may not be noticed by the patient or his physician; the second brings definite symptoms of illness; the third brings structural changes. At present, patients are rarely seen before the second stage has been reached; more often, not before the third stage. To try to learn about an ailment under such circumstances is something like trying to learn about chess by watching only the last moves of a game between two experts, unaware that the outcome is frequently decided in the first moves. . . .

A study of the liver alone eventually becomes no study of the liver at all. Nor is this the only trouble with such specialization. It overlooks also the fact that the person as a whole is something different from a collection of viscera; the wholeness gives some extra, if indefinable, quality to the individual organs. Today we pay

for our knowledge of the parts in ignorance of the whole. . . .

In ancient Greece the doctor was primarily a philosopher and secondarily a physician. He was first a student of nature, and secondly a student of nature perverted by disease. Despite the great technical advances of our day, the future of medicine may well depend upon the training of physicians who will be once more humanists and biologists, as well as chemists and physicists. . . .[22]

To give these persons whose physiology of anxiety incapacitates them a label such as "psychoneurotic" or to accuse them of overworking their imagination does not help them. They merely drift from one doctor or faith healer to another. What each really needs is a reorganization of adjustment habits to know the true nature of his emotional problems, and to know how to develop new mental habits. For some, this may require the skills of the clinical psychologist. For other and milder cases, the friend or employer may be able to say to the psychoneurotic: "The problem that is really bothering you, young man, is the fact that you fear that the girl friend will tire of waiting for you and marry some other man. Face the issue. Talk it over with her. If you can't agree upon a practicable program of action, let her marry someone else and you do likewise. In the meantime, bear in mind that I'll give you my fellowship because I, too, once had the same problem."

An individual may make adjustments to his barriers quite differently from another because of differences in the weakness of certain organs, behavior habits, or constitution. As a result of frustration, one person may, for example, develop physiological imbalance which results in more colds. Another may have his repressed rages bring about physiological changes which result in high blood pressure or in doing more work. However, all persons need a recognition of the close relation between adjustment and health. For certain persons, poor health often means poor habits of thinking and of conduct. Almost any person who wants to feel faint can do so by saying to himself: "I am fainting. I want to faint." The neurotic achieves the same kind of end by subconscious wishes regarding his breathing, digestion, or circulation. An allergy, as well as other kinds of ailments, may simply be one effect of an evasion of some problem which he does not face consciously.

Remedies for invalidism

What should be done for those unfortunate psychoneurotics and others who try to make an adjustment to reality by the avenue of illness? Scolding will not help them; it only increases their problems. They need clinical analysis rather than censure.

A helpful suggestion is not the advice, "Use your will," but instead, "Understand the cause of your trouble," and, "What is the real purpose of your behavior?" If the physician makes exhaustive tests and can find no just cause for the illness, then he should ask the patient to analyze himself or to have himself analyzed for problems which he is evading. He should try to induce the patient to face the barrier which he dislikes to admit to himself. He must be convinced that the defect or the inability to accomplish his present aims should be used to achieve another end that is equally acceptable. The main remedy is the trite statement that the cause must be removed. To do this may require considerable assistance on the part of the psychiatrist or the clinical psychologist. Furthermore, in cases of serious maladjustment, the patient who is very intelligent and has read a number of books on abnormal psychology cannot analyze himself and make his readjustment alone. However, his special knowledge should make him more intelligently coöperative in developing better habits of adjustment.

Children are often told that they are "nervous" and should not study or work. This is a serious mistake. It is far better to allow them to learn the joys of strenuous work and play. If they are not reminded of illness,

but are encouraged to face life by direct attack habits, they will seldom develop the maladjustments which fond mothers call "nervousness."

Adults, too, are often told that they are "nervous" and should study or work less. This advice is usually a mistake. Work does not cause nervous breakdowns. Nervous breakdowns are the result of poor mental habits when adjustment problems, especially conflicts, appear. In the so-called mental breakdowns, the nature and the amount of work that the person does is largely irrelevant; the emotional reaction of the individual toward the work is all-important. If the worker's adjustment habits have enabled him to gain satisfactions from the work, the amounts and hours of work are incidental.

If the adjustment history has been essentially positive, the individual can recover quickly from strains of work or even "combat fatigue." Of World War II veterans whose afflictions had been diagnosed as "psychoneurosis," those who had combat experiences had more severe psychoneuroses than the noncombatants. But the combatants had more likelihood of improving after service than the noncombatants.[23]

Significant influences in some breakdowns in civilian life are precipitating factors, such as the boss's domineering manner toward the employee, the teacher's negligence of the pupil, the public's condemnation of a person, the husband's niggardliness, or the wife's nagging. When the poorly adjusted person is confronted by such barriers, his ongoing activities are blocked and a "breakdown" results. Such a person is not benefited by reminders of illness. He needs encouragement in performing his daily tasks and in becoming socially integrated.

Everyone should feel that he belongs in the social groups of his environment, but the maladjusted person has special need for being welcome in his groups. His associates should be friendly rather than critical toward him. Otherwise he will tend to withdraw into himself more than ever and will have more acute "pains." The attitude of the associates of the adult invalid should be one of encouraging him to carry on his work more intelligently rather than one of expressing mere sentimentality, or pampering.

As in practically all other maladjustments, the patient should be given work to do that requires complete attention. Of course, we should not ask others to work in order that they may be as wealthy or as important as someone else. Rather because, through work that is adapted to one's capacities, one can achieve the adjustment that comes from doing well work within these abilities. If work is reasonably satisfying, it may be carried on at all hours and for any number of years so long as the body is given a normal amount of exercise and care. If the well-adjusted individual works very hard, he simply gets tired and takes a rest. The well-adjusted individual uses direct attack in dealing with his illnesses, especially those of a functional nature. An unusual example of direct attack regarding a functional illness may be found in the way one organically sick man dealt with his ailment.

In 1920 Dr. A. L. Muirhead, a professor of pharmacology in one of the leading medical schools, found himself stricken with Addison's disease. Realizing that his affliction would end in death in a short time and being not only a physician but also an expert in the science of drugs, he determined to devote the remainder of his life to finding a cure. Instead of sitting back waiting for death in the Mayo Clinic, which he entered, he did all in his power to stave death off, chopped and dried adrenal gland substance which he put into capsules and took by mouth, and by rectum took preparations of the adrenal gland containing large quantities of adrenalin. In a short time he made a remarkable recovery, and for a while was apparently cured—the first instance in history of any such improvement in a sufferer from Addison's disease. The rejoicing, however, was premature, for Dr. Muirhead had not really been cured and had a relapse into his former condition. Although treatment was again instituted and although it did help a little, it did not prevent his death from this disease. But for several years the Muirhead treatment was the best that medicine could offer.[24]

Acknowledgments and References

1. Caroline B. Zachry, *Emotion and Conduct in Adolescence*, D. Appleton-Century Co., New York, 1940, pp. 69–70.

2. Winifred V. Richmond, *Personality—Its Development and Hygiene*, Farrar and Rhinehart, New York, 1937, p. 166.

3. Walter A. Lowen, in *Advertising and Selling*, July 1940, p. 31.

4. For an understandable discussion on this point of view, see John K. Winkler and Walter Bromberg, *Mind Explorers*, Reynal and Hitchcock, New York, 1939, Chapter XV.

5. J. C. McKinley and S. R. Hathaway, "Multiphasic Personality Schedule (Minnesota): IV. Psychasthenia," *Journal of Applied Psychology*, American Psychological Association, Inc., Vol. 26 (1942), pp. 614–624, reports a study of a scale for measuring psychasthenia.

6. K. Hazell, "The Anxiety Syndrome," *The Medical Press*, Vol. 216 (August 26, 1946), pp. 153–155.

7. Morton Prince, "Miss Beauchamp—The Theory and Psychogenesis of Multiple Personality," *Journal of Abnormal Psychology*, Vol. 15 (1920), pp. 82 ff.

8. Pierre Janet, *The Major Symptoms of Hysteria*, The Macmillan Company, New York, 1920, presents some classic examples of hysteria. A four-year case of functional blindness is described on page 168.

9. Harry L. Smith, M.D., and Nicholas C. Hightower, Jr., M.D., "Incidence of Functional Disease (Neurosis) Among Patients of Various Occupations," *Occupational Medicine*, Vol. 5 (February 1948), pp. 182–185.

10. Russell Fraser, "The Incidence of Neurosis Among Factory Workers," Medical Research Council, Industrial Health Research Board, *Report No. 90* (1947), pp. 8–10. Reprinted by permission of the Controller of His Britannic Majesty's Stationery Office.

11. Condensed from a release from the National Office Management Association, 132 W. Chelten Ave., Philadelphia 44, Pa., 1954.

12. E. Lewy, "Contribution to the Problem of Compensation Neuroses," *Bulletin of the Menninger Clinic*, Vol. 4 (1940), pp. 88–92.

13. P. G. Denker, "The Prognosis of Insured Neurotics," *New York State Journal of Medicine*, Vol. 39 (1939), pp. 238–247.

14. H. A. Davidson, "Neurosis and Malingering," *American Journal of Medical Jurisprudence*, Vol. 2 (1939), pp. 94–96.

15. W. C. Service, *Journal of the American Medical Association*, Vol. 113 (May 1939).

16. George W. Gray, "The Strange Ways of Allergy," *Harper's Magazine*, January 1939.

17. M. T. McDermott and S. Cobb, "A Psychiatric Survey of Fifty Cases of Bronchial Asthma," *Psychosomatic Medicine*, Vol. 1 (1939), pp. 203–244. A related study has been reported by J. L. Halliday, "Approach to Asthma," *British Journal of Medical Psychology*, Vol. 17 (1937), pp. 1–47.

18. Sheldon E. Waxenberg, "Psychosomatic Patients and Other Physically Ill Persons: A Comparative Study," *Journal of Consulting Psychology*, June 1955, pp. 163–169.

19. I. Bram, "Psychosomatic Obesity with Comments on 924 Cases," *Medical Record*, Vol. 157 (1944), pp. 673–676. This article describes results obtained by psychotherapy in cases of alimentary or psychosomatic obesity, caused by overeating for relief from tension. Psychotherapy was administered to 924 cases, and results in 59 per cent of the cases were excellent; in 20 per cent good; in 11 per cent fair; in 3 per cent poor. No results were obtained in 7 per cent of the cases because of poor cooperation.

20. S. Morrison and M. Fedman, "Psychosomatic Correlations of Duodenal Ulcer," *Journal of the American Medical Association*, Vol. 120 (1942), pp. 738–740.

21. Flanders Dunbar, *Mind and Body: Psychosomatic Medicine*, Random House, Inc., New York, 1947, presents an understandable treatment of this subject.

22. Ian Stevenson, M.D., "Why Medicine Is Not a Science," *Harper's Magazine*, Vol. 198 (April 1949), pp. 36–39.

23. Maurice H. Greenhill, "Clinical Features of the Psychoneuroses in World War II Veterans," *N. C. Medical Journal*, Vol. 7 (1946), pp. 585–590.

24. Edward Podolsky, M.D., "Gland Magic," *The American Scholar*, Vol. 3 (1934), p. 449.

25. Smith & Hightower, *op. cit.*

PROJECTS

1. Smith and Hightower studied the incidence of neurosis among consecutively admitted patients to the Mayo Clinic. They also studied neurosis among the Jewish male and female patients. A part of their summary follows:

   "We studied the group of Jews because, as has been said, some persons believe that Jewish patients are particularly emotional and neurotic. We were somewhat surprised at the results we obtained. Yet when the percentages which represent purely functional disease, or functional and organic disease, are compared, it is seen that the incidence of neurosis in this group is no higher than that in the controls.

   "We fully realize that a study of this type is not entirely accurate. Our results may not represent the actual incidence of neuroses in the population as a whole because the study was limited to persons who sought help from physicians. The least that it does, however, is to confirm the general impression that the incidence of neuroses among persons of various occupations differs greatly."[25]

   a. Interview some of your friends concerning the question of incidence of neurosis among Jews and non-Jews. Get your friends' opinions and discuss possible reasons for the assumption that Jews are particularly neurotic.

   b. Examine any published library articles on the same question to find whether other investigators agree with the Smith and Hightower findings.

2. Examine available textbooks that deal with public speaking and note how stage fright is treated. Which methods seem to you to be the most helpful?

3. List some of the "worthy causes" of your community which are likely to appeal to neurasthenics.

4. Recall some of your own abulic tendencies, such as those in writing to friends, checking your finances, seeing your dentist, and so on. Outline a definite procedure in each case whereby the necessary action may be taken at the proper time.

5. Women of today do not faint as much as women of a generation or two ago. What possible reasons can you suggest for this change of behavior?

6. Make a list of some of the things you have worried about during the past year or two. Check and analyze those cases in which your apprehension was a distinct handicap to the solution of the problem. Did worrying contribute to the solution in other cases?

7. Consider an acquaintance who says that certain common foods make him ill. What physical and psychological factors might be involved? Set up a procedure by which you might test objectively which factors are predominant.

8. Construct a hypothetical case in which the subject reacts through sick headaches or other form of invalidism. Have several friends suggest possible treatment and compare these suggestions with your own ideas.

COLLATERAL READINGS

Alexander, Franz, *Psychosomatic Medicine,* W. W. Norton and Company, Inc., New York, 1950.

Deutsch, F., and R. Nadell, "Psychosomatic Aspects of Dermatology with Special Consideration of Allergic Phenomena," *Nervous Child,* Vol. 5 (1946), pp. 339–364.

Dunbar, Flanders, *Mind and Body: Psychosomatic Medicine,* Random House, Inc., New York, 1947.

Dunlap, Knight, *Personal Adjustment,* McGraw-Hill Book Company, Inc., New York, 1946, Chapters 4 and 6.

Funkenstein, Daniel H., "The Physiology of Fear and Anger," *Scientific American,* May 1955, pp. 74–80.

Lehner, George F. J. and Ella Kube, *The Dynamics of Personal Adjustment,* Prentice-Hall, Inc., New York, 1955, Chapter 7.

Page, James D., *Abnormal Psychology,* McGraw-Hill Book Company, Inc., 1947, Chapters 5, 6, and 7.

Shaffer, Laurance F. and Edward J. Shoben, Jr., *The Psychology of Adjustment,* Houghton Mifflin Company, Boston, 1956, Chapters 9 and 10.

Weiss, Frederick A., Summary of Lecture No. 11 delivered before the Auxiliary Council of the Association for the Advancement of Psychoanalysis, "Physical Complaints of Neurotic Origin" in Hartley, Eugene L., Herbert G. Birch, Ruth E. Hartley, *Outside Readings in Psychology,* Thomas Y. Crowell Company, New York, 1950, pp. 494–503.

"What's a Nervous Breakdown, Anyhow?" *Changing Times,* May 1955, pp. 26–28.

CHAPTER SIX

Methods of treating the maladjusted

To bring on the triumph of intellect over mechanism, of responsible morality over irresponsible force, is our mission. If we think things cannot be different from what they are, we but add so much to the dead inertia of the world, which keeps them as they are; while if we will not succumb we may be part of the very forces that will help to make things different.[1]

The treatment of the seriously maladjusted or insane requires years of special training in universities, hospitals, and clinics. This work is done by psychiatrists, that is, physicians who have specialized in the investigation and treatment of mental disorders. Obviously, only experts should treat psychotics, those persons who have a pathological mental condition which tends to constitute a disease-entity. In this chapter, therefore, we shall differentiate between the serious and the minor maladjustments.

TREATMENT OF THE MAJOR OR SERIOUS MALADJUSTMENTS

The theories and methods that psychiatrists and clinical psychologists use are too complex for us to attempt a comprehensive discussion of them in this book. However, we as educated laymen can try to appreciate the importance of their work and coöperate intelligently with them.

FIRST, we should recognize our responsibility toward acquaintances who are suffering from serious mental ailments. One of the great lessons we have learned from our studies of the mentally ill is the need for realizing that a mentally sick person should be treated with the same consideration that we accord the physically ill. When a friend has a broken leg or has a fever, we take him to a hospital, sympathize with him, send him flowers, and visit him. Similarly, when a friend is sent to a hospital for mental treatment, we should treat him, not as a "nut," but as a person who is sick, for that is what he is. We should not attach a social stigma to the person who has been in an institution for the insane any more than to a person who has been in a general hospital for an organic illness. In many cases the former mental patient is not handicapped, but to some people he is stigmatized. The stigma is based on unintelligent popular misconceptions regarding the possible permanence of insanity. Many small employers still refuse to hire a former mental patient.

SECOND, employers should recognize that there are many kinds of mental disturbances and that each varies in the degree to which it incapacitates for work. The employer or personnel man should be acquainted with the five psychological terms for broad mental classification: the mental defective, the epileptic, the psychotic, the psychopathic personality, and the psychoneurotic.

The *mental defective* lacks some mental qualities or abilities which are present in the normal individual. The synonym for most mental defectives of the kind who visit employment offices is "feebleminded." These differ in their degree of mental limitation, and their intelligence can be measured by means of intelligence tests. Many of these people can and do learn to perform routine and repetitive jobs in industry.

The *epileptics* or, more correctly, those who are subject to convulsive states, can be employed in many cases. Some have convulsions only in their sleep. Others have them only at infrequent intervals. Many experience a preliminary signal before an attack, and some control their ailment by means of medicine. If each person who is subject to "fits" is considered in terms of the variety of his disorder and its control, certain types of employment which he can perform without danger will be found.

Some *psychotics* can be employed, at least during certain stages of the psychosis. In the case of the manic-depressive (having pronounced swings of elation and depression), the patient may have a disorder for one period of time only, or he may have it in recurrent cycles. There may be several years between attacks when the individual is normal and employable. Some psychotics are overactive during the early stage of an attack and work very industriously. Complete recovery from an attack is the rule rather than the exception.

Patients who are hospitalized for *schizophrenia* (literally, "splitting of the mind," formerly called dementia praecox) are incapable of work during the early stages of the disorder. After treatment, however, many can be discharged from hospitals and can work in a protected environment. About 30 per cent recover spontaneously or as the result of the newer methods of treatment, such as shock therapy.

Those who grow old and develop *senile psychosis* have defects of memory and judgment. If such old employees are allowed to work slowly at tasks that do not require new mental habits, they may fill certain jobs very well.

The *psychopathic personalities* include the pathological liars, swindlers, eccentrics, vagrants, sexual deviants, and certain types of criminals. They are deficient in moral values. Few are hospitalized and most are difficult to cure because they do not coöperate during therapy. Most have bad work records and get into conflict with the law. For most types of factory and office work they are useless, but many of them are members of our great army of transient and migratory labor.

The *psychoneurotics* are found everywhere. They are always in touch with reality and are not insane. Some have harmless obsessions, phobias, or forms of hysteria. Some are hypochondriacs who complain of functional ills and pains. They are often absent from work, complain about the employer, are easily fatigued, are irritable and have a bad effect on the morale of other workers. Many are merely childish, or make other evasive adjustments to their personal problems. Every large group of employees has some of these neurotics, and many are needed, in spite of their maladjustments, because of the good work they do in their specialties.[2]

Some persons, merely because they were known to be getting mental treatment, have lost their jobs and their friends. "So-and-so is going to a psychiatrist—he must be nuts" is still too common a verdict of employers and others. Much health education is needed to correct unfair attitudes toward the mentally ill.

THIRD, we should appreciate the chances for recovery or improvement of patients who enter a hospital for the mentally ill. The chance of discharge for the first-year patient in a mental hospital is better than 50–50. Of course, recovery rates vary, depending upon the age of the patient, the kind of mental disorder, and the treatment. For the senile and the arteriosclerotic the chances of recovery are very slight indeed, but for the younger people, those with schizophrenia and manic-depressive psychosis, the chances of getting out of the mental hospital fairly promptly are very good. Certainly the chances of recovery for many young and middle-aged patients are excellent. Especially important is the fact that current recovery rates are improving as the result of recent researches which are producing new and more helpful drugs and methods of treatment.

FOURTH, executives, parents, teachers, and personnel men should learn enough about the symptoms of mental disorders to know when it is advisable to refer employees, children, pupils, and acquaintances to experts for diagnosis. Psychiatrists and clinical psychologists are trained friends who may help increase our happiness. They are not mere classifiers of mental ailments and custodians of asylums; they are counselors to whom we may go for occasional check-ups of our mental habits just as we may go to the family physican for an annual check-up of our bodily condition.

FIFTH, we should learn some of the basic principles used in the treatment of the mentally ill so that we can coöperate intelligently with the psychotherapist. For example, some patients who voluntarily consult a psychiatrist report that they are not getting any help from the treatments.

These statements are often made because the patient's treatment has progressed to the point where he must either live on a new basis or else continue to "enjoy" his old inadequate mental habits. At such times of doubt we should encourage the patient to continue the treatments until he learns to live more satisfyingly in terms of the new mental regimen.

SIXTH, the investigations made by the specialists in mental disease have removed the fear of the direct inheritance of mental ills. Mental ills are not inherited like the color of eyes. Paradoxically, however, mental ills do run in families. Studies of sisters, brothers, uncles, aunts, parents, and grandparents of patients in mental hospitals have revealed no evidence of any exact theory of inheritance. There is no clear-cut case of Mendelian inheritance.[3] A mentally diseased parent cannot hand on this trait as he can hand on the color of his eyes.[4]

Mental disease does occur among the relatives of mental patients and among some racial groups[5] more often than it occurs in the general population. It is possible that a predisposition toward mental breakdown is inherited, but we are not certain because the parents of the mentally diseased also bequeath to the children a particular sort of family circle in which to grow up. Mental habits have a close relationship with mental disease or health, and this fact offers us much hope in the intelligent control of our mental well-being. We can do a great deal toward the development of sound mental habits in ourselves, regardless of who or what our parents were. The maladjusted person is not a poor helpless patient fatalistically sacrificed to his heredity or his environment. More powerful than the germ plasm or the parental pattern are courage and the desire to develop the adaptability necessary to deal adequately with one's barriers.

SEVENTH, we should appreciate the relation between bodily and mental health. A thorough physical examination should precede any psychotherapy, and the examination should be made by a physician who specializes in diagnosis rather than by an ordinary practitioner who is satisfied with taking the blood pressure and counting the pulse. An ailment such as arthritis is often treated as organic only. Yet family worry, grief, and other forms of emotional stress bear more than a chance relationship to the onset and flare-up of the chronic joint disease, rheumatoid arthritis, as indicated by a recent study of this ailment.[6]

On the other hand, hallucinations may be erroneously treated as purely psychological; yet voices heard by the mentally ill may have a basis in ear infections. Almost one out of every five patients examined at the Boston Psychopathic Hospital was found to have a toxic type of deafness.[7] Certain patients who were free from toxic deafness also suffered from auditory hallucinations but described them differently. This study indicated that an examination of the physical condition is so important in understanding many mental conditions that the diagnoses should be made with the utmost care.

Physicians and psychiatrists are giving many different kinds of treatments to the body, particularly the nervous system, as an aid in curing patients who were considered hopelessly insane. Some of these more recently developed treatments include electric shocks passed directly through the brain.

Electro-shock is a method of psychotherapy often used on patients who are not responding well to other therapies. A state of shock known as "coma" is induced in the patient by an electric shock passed directly through the brain in controlled amounts. Similar conditions are induced by means of insulin and metrazol. Electro-shock is particularly valuable in weakening those psychological defenses that keep the patient from facing his conflicts. It thus facilitates treatment by other therapeutic methods.[8] Electric shock seems to improve feeling tone and jar the patient out of his apathy and in-ertia. Rigidity of personality structure is decreased and the immediate release of hostility, especially in rigid personality and depressive cases, is striking. A more outgoing attitude is adopted which improves the patient's chances of benefiting from psychotherapy.[9]

Of 242 patients seen over a one-year period and treated with electric shock in a psychiatrist's office, only 21 per cent did not improve. The cause for lack of improvement in almost half of these cases was attributed to premature discontinuance of treatment. Sixty-three per cent of the 242 patients had affective disorders, 31.5 per cent had schizophrenia, and about 4 per cent had a neurosis. Of those whose conditions were improved by shock therapy, only fifteen patients (6 per cent) required subsequent hospitalization, and thirteen of these were considered unimproved. These data indicate that if electric shock is given in private treatments, the number of patients who will be committed to mental hospitals may be reduced.[10]

Insulin coma treatment has been reported as effective, too. One group of researchers in Vienna claim that in 85 per cent of the cases (of less than 6 months' duration) treated by this method there was a lessening of tension and alleviation of the condition. These favorable results were probably due to expert and intensive use of insulin, often in combination with electro-shock.[11]

No one knows what really happens as a result of these shock treatments. Perhaps some of the old nerve current pathways and synaptic junctions in the sick brains are so modified by the shock treatment that old neural patterns are lost. Metabolic activity is changed. Chemical and physiological activities are modified, but perhaps only future research will explain the reasons why shock and fever treatments are beneficial to some mental patients.

Psychosurgery, operation on the frontal lobes of the brain, has become accepted by some psychiatrists. Others, however, still doubt that the results justify this drastic operation. It is used in the treatment of what were formerly considered "incurable" cases of patients with an extreme degree of emotional tension and anxiety. The problem in surgery is to reduce the patient's self-awareness and sensitivity to limits he can tolerate —without making him apathetic and completely indifferent to events and people around him.

Reports from state hospitals in New Jersey, Texas, and West Virginia of the results of such operations on approximately 1500 patients reveal that 25 per cent to 40 per cent of these patients were able to go home. Otherwise they probably would have ended their days in a mental hospital. Some could even resume the type of professional activity which they had practiced before the mental illness.[12]

In one study, eight patients who received transorbital lobotomy were compared to a control group of eight who were continued on electro-shock. Rorschach tests indicated that the lobotomy resulted in a lessening of inner tension and reduction in self-awareness. The patients also lost their ardent enthusiasm and active interest. Severing the frontal lobes from the rest of the brain tends to have this effect because it apparently separates psychotic ideas from the usual accompanying emotions.[13]

Narco-analysis is a form of therapy during which the patient talks about or acts out the painful experiences which have caused an acute neurosis, anxiety state, or hysteria. It was used with good results during World War II for alleviating conditions caused by distressing combat experiences. The procedure is to administer to the patient a barbiturate drug which induces narcosis. Sometimes electrical treatment similar to that used in electro-shock but of lower intensity and longer duration is used to bring on this form of narcosis. While the patient is in this induced sleep, the therapist encourages him to talk about or act out his traumatic experiences, thereby bringing his repressed fears and anxieties to consciousness where they can be understood. With understanding comes release from the maladjustment expressed by the symptoms.

The "tranquilizing" drugs are now being used by psychiatrists with remarkable effects in treating psychotic patients. The more commonly used drugs are chlorpromazine (trade name: Thorazine), reserpine (Serpasil) and azacyclonol (Frenquel).

One of the psychiatrist's greatest problems in dealing with a psychotic individual is to make some kind of effective contact with the patient. This is especially true of the schizophrenic. The patient may be aloof and apathetic; he may fancy that the radio in the ward is directing insults to him personally.

The new tranquilizing drugs calm the patient without putting him to sleep. Their effects last longer than those of sedatives. Severely disturbed patients may be kept in an open ward instead of being locked up. Even "hopeless" patients become accessible to psychotherapy by reducing their anxieties and removing some of the barriers between the patient and the psychiatrist.[14]

One report indicated that, of 200 acutely disturbed psychotic female patients, 22 per cent had been discharged after six months of treatment with reserpine. This compared with a 4.7 per cent discharge rate from the same institution in the previous six months. About two-thirds of the group discharged had been able to maintain their improvement without any further medication. Of the remaining third who regressed, all responded to re-treatment and held their improvement on maintenance doses.[15]

At a conference on reserpine in the treatment of neuropsychiatric, neurological, and related clinical problems sponsored by the New York Academy of Sciences section of biology on February 3 and 4, 1955, New York City, 27 papers were presented.

Positive results with the new drug were reported in treating schizophrenia, manic-depressive psychosis, convulsive nervous disorders such as epilepsy, psychoses in the aged and disturbed adolescents. Other problems such as hyperactivity and irritability in infants, sickness caused by narcotic withdrawal, resistant headache patterns, asthma, bed wetting, and psychosomatic conditions marked by severe itching, also responded to the drug with varying degrees of success.

The consensus of the participants was decidedly in favor of the use of reserpine as a valuable aid in the treatment of a wide variety of psychiatric disorders found in state hospitals. Although some of the authors of papers reported complete remission of symptoms of some mentally ill persons, the drug was not called a "cure." Emphasis was placed on its role in making patients more amenable to other therapies, and less difficult to care for in hospital situations.[16]

Chlorpromazine, reserpine, and Frenquel are an important beginning in the treatment of mental ailments. Much remains to be done to solve the problem. None of the tranquilizing drugs helps all schizophrenics nor are the drugs effective in relieving melancholia (a profound, passive depression) or certain long-standing neuroses and psychosomatic troubles. There is also a tendency on the part of some therapists to prescribe these drugs for too many ailments and to allow neurotics to lean on the aid of drugs when they ought to learn to solve their problems themselves.

Recently, some researchers at Tulane University detected the presence of a twisted protein molecule in the blood stream of schizophrenic patients not found in normal persons.[17] This finding seems to confirm the conviction of many researchers who believe that the cure of many mental illnesses will eventually be found by the biochemists.

The drug LSD provides a remarkable new tool for the investigation of psychotic states.* When it is administered to apparently well-adjusted people, it produces the symptoms of psychosis. The subjects who took the drug felt confused, lethargic, and overcome by apathy. They felt that something strange had happened to them and things seemed different. Some also had the feeling that they did not exist or that parts of their body had altered form. Visual illusions appeared. The thought processes slowed down. Time lost meaning. The subjects' capacity to organize and verbalize was reduced. They couldn't put into words the unusual experiences they were having. They lost their usual ability to discriminate between themselves and others. They projected their feelings and attributed them to others.

The use of LSD gives doctors and researchers insight into the minds and feelings of persons afflicted by mental illness. The entire psychotic period can be telescoped into a period of six to twelve hours, and the emotional disintegration followed step by step. Too, by actually experiencing the psychotic state themselves, doctors can better understand the patient and communicate with and help him. Mental illness will no longer have to be so strange or mysterious; there will be fewer barriers between the sick and the well. When we know enough to be able to create a disease, we are closer to its cure. Various treatments can be tested on the experimentally induced psychosis.

Perhaps the most important result of the LSD experiments is that for the first time researchers can investigate experimentally the many relationships between the psychotic state and the body's chemistry and physiology. LSD shows that there is a definite link between physiological disturbances and mental changes. Evidently certain types of psychoses may be caused by chemical changes in the body.[18]

Many methods of treatment other than surgical, electrical, and chemical are being used experimentally. The therapeutic theater is an example. Here patients are encouraged to go on a stage and blow off steam through impromptu drama[19] while

* LSD stands for d-lysergic acid diethylamide tartrate. This is a derivative of ergot, a fungus which grows on rye.

psychiatrists listen and offer guidance. The psychodrama has been used in the treatment of marriage problems and for truancy on the part of maladjusted school boys.[20]

Generally, the philosophy underlying most forms of psychotherapy is that the sufferer must be treated as a personality and not merely as the bearer of a diagnosable disease.

Group therapy is an example of a method that helps the patient become better integrated through a special social group of fellow sufferers. The great number of acute psychopathological cases and the comparatively small number of therapists was the immediate cause for the adoption of group therapy on a large scale during World War II. In group therapy a number of psychoneurotic patients, usually not more than thirty, participate in group discussions of their difficulties, and thereby learn ways of adjustment more effective and satisfying than those they have adopted as manifested by their neurotic symptoms. Prior to being admitted to a group, each person is interviewed by a psychotherapist who ascertains the nature of each patient's troubles and familiarizes himself with the case. Usually this same therapist is present at the group discussions, held several times a week. He acts as discussion leader, urging patients to talk about their difficulties to the group, calling on them for comments on, reactions to, or interpretations of the troubles of the other members of the group, and encouraging progress reports. In the permissive atmosphere that prevails, patients discover that their difficulties are not unique; that other people have similar ones. As they learn more about the other persons in the group they develop a feeling of fellowship with them, and an identification with the group is built up. This identification furnishes the neurotic with a stabilizing influence and a support with which he can help himself. The situation simulates a small social community where he can find reassurance

and self-understanding, and thus adjust himself more adequately to the environment of his everyday life.[21]

The method of therapy most desirable in many cases can be decided upon by determining whether the maladjustment is a simple bad mental habit or of a deep-seated type. If it is of the latter variety, the patient is likely to resist assistance or be incapable of gaining insight and release without systematic professional counsel. Analytical rather than superficial procedures are essential. When strong feelings of guilt are predominant, a Freudian type of approach may be necessary. If feelings of inferiority are predominant, an Adlerian type of approach is likely to be effective.[22] But whatever approach is used by the therapist, the patient must be given a mental reëducation that enables him to live without old tensions and to participate in normal social relations.

Religion is believed by many people to have therapeutic value. The pastor can help those suffering from guilt through the healing effects of confession and forgiveness, those suffering from sorrow through mitigating their grief, those suffering from fear and anxiety through increasing their faith, those suffering from hostility through spreading the spirit of love. Mental health attitudes engendered or increased through religious experience include the sense of personal worth, trust in the ultimate victory of good over evil, membership in a communal fellowship, the support of invisible yet constant companionship, confession, and forgiveness, the urging and guiding of youth along approved paths, the aspiration and dedication of worship, and the discipline or way of life.[23]

So many different kinds of treatment are used that the layman is apt to wonder why chemical, physical, and psychological approaches are at times used for patients who have the same or similar disorders.

If one asks how could psychological medicine possibly cure an organic condition, the answer is obvious. It could not possibly cure an organic condition. If at the same time one asks, "How could chemicals possibly cure an organic condition," the answer must be the same. It could not possibly. We then perceive that the questions have arisen out of a misconception of the mechanism by which cures are achieved. Processes which go on in the body are of necessity some expression of metabolism. The chemicals which we take when we feel diseased could hardly be said to repair the damaged condition of the organism. Rather their sole purpose is so to change conditions in the organism as to bring about those functional conditions which will enable the organism more readily to cure itself. The organism must always cure itself through its metabolic activities. It will be seen from this analysis that the effects of chemical medicines are purely functional. Viewed from this angle, the situation is somewhat clearer and the question is now as to whether or not the psychological medicine can be of value in bringing about the conditions which will enable the organism to cure itself.[24]

Unfortunately, the bringing about of conditions which will enable the organism to cure itself is often very difficult in psychopathic cases. However, one helpful point of view for the student is that many psychopathic persons develop their mental disorders because they are confronted by problems for which they have no satisfactory answers. Many are in states of conflict.

Conflicts

A humorist described a tardy man and woman standing on a pier watching an ocean liner disappear down the bay. The disappointed woman turned on her husband and said: "Don't just stand there—*do* something!" Obviously, the poor husband could do nothing about it, but the wife's senseless demand for action illustrates how conflicts are likely to arise when no action is possible.

Many experiments have shown the possible effects of conflicts on mental well-being. Pavlov was one of the first experimenters to prove that abnormalities of behavior can be produced in an animal when the animal

has been trained to solve a problem by means of a specific act, and the conditions are changed so that the learned solution is no longer appropriate. Pavlov trained a dog by the conditioned-reflex method to discriminate between two visual patterns; the presentation of a circle of light was always followed by food, while the appearance of an ellipse whose axes had a ratio of 2:1 was not rewarded. The circle soon became a conditioned stimulus to salivation but the appearance of the ellipse inhibited salivation.

In the experiment, the conditions for the dog were changed. The ellipse was gradually changed to approach a circle and the dog continued to make perfect discriminations until the ratio of the axes had become 8:9, after which imperfect discriminations were made. Then the dog's behavior suddenly changed. He was unable to differentiate between the circle and the ellipse and became negative to all stimuli. As the training was continued, the formerly docile dog constantly struggled and howled. The dog had a "nervous breakdown." The confusion of the positive and negative stimuli was too much for him. The conflict could not be solved by any of his learned responses.[25]

Liddell,[26] Anderson, and other investigators have done considerable similar work with sheep. N. R. F. Maier and his associates have studied experimentally produced neurotic behavior in the rat.[27] Pigs, guinea pigs, and cats have been used in similar experiments on the effects of frustration.[28]

In Dr. Maier's experiments with rats, the rats were taught by reward and punishment to distinguish between two cards. Then, instead of being permitted a choice between a "reward" and a "punishment" card, an animal was shown only the "punishment" card while a blast of air was forcing him to jump. At the sight of the "punishment" card, the rat might resist action for as long as 15 minutes before he would jump. The rat was in a state of conflict.

He did not have a suitable mode of response for the problem situation. Neurotic symptoms developed in many rats. The "psychopathic" animal would tear out of the apparatus, run in circles on the floor, show intense tics, and then have varying degrees of coma. Maier found that an irritant which furnishes no release builds up tensions which the organism cannot handle, and these may resolve themselves in catastrophic reactions.[29]

As a result of his experiments, Dr. Maier believes that a cure for frustrated neurotic human patients is to find a way for the person to act. Dr. Maier's cure for neurotic rats is to encourage them to find something to do even though it fails to solve the conflict that confronts them. He calls this "abortive behavior." To cure them, he taught them to make just a halfway jump toward solving their dilemma. Possible human applications[30] of this principle might be:

A girl urged by her parents to marry might dislike both of two available suitors. Forced to marry, she would break down. If she engages herself to one but is cold to him, so that they drift apart, she is saved. A substitute activity, such as a career of nursing, would serve the same purpose.
Pregnancy [illegitimate] and the conflicts arising from sin contribute greatly to neurotic behavior by leaving no avenue for behavior and yet requiring that something be done. . . .
On the other hand, going to the electric chair, while it may produce tensions, does not produce neurosis because the individual knows just what he must do.[31]

These experiments with animals and the judgments of many specialists in mental disorders indicate that neurosis is often due to the fact that the individual patient is confronted by the conflicting character of difficulties imposed upon him, difficulties for which he has no direct attack or suitable substitute responses. The neurosis is a haven in his flight from reality. It is an escape from the facing of unpleasant facts, mostly in the form of impulsive attitudes that are irreconcilable to him. In the case

of the adult, some of the irreconcilable attitudes probably originated in childhood and are now in conflict with current drives. Inner peace can be developed when the individual finds an acceptable mode of action or makes a final choice in favor of one drive.[32] In some cases, willingness to accept an inevitable situation which the individual previously resented may resolve the conflict within him.

The experiments with animals have suggested some valuable concepts for the treatment of psychopathics. However, the most interesting and frequently used concepts in the use of psychological approaches to the treatment of psychopaths may be obtained from a review of the principles and methods of psychoanalysis.

What is psychoanalysis?

Sigmund Freud of Vienna was the originator of the technical method of psychoanalysis. He published his first investigations in 1895. Freud studied many cases of nervous disorders and was convinced that the main causes lay in repressed wishes or desires. The repressed desire or impulse was, he believed, of a sexual nature and had been repressed by the forces of education and social conventions. When the wish is repressed it remains alive and active in unconscious form. The theory, to many people, appears to be weird, while to others it holds a strong attraction for its interesting interpretations. Perhaps we should spend a moment reviewing the experiences which gave Freud his method of treating psychopathological maladies.

Before 1890, psychologists had already studied mental abnormalities. Hypnotism was known, and it was noted that, when patients were treated in certain ways, they developed multiple personalities. That is, they regarded themselves and acted as though they were different persons at different times. Sometimes one personality could not remember the other personality of the same individual. In other cases

One example of analysis of the unconscious as used in advertising. An insurance company advertisement contained headline and copy as follows:

Did you ever have a dream like this?

Most persons have had the dream of finding money scattered around, and picking it up hurriedly for fear some one would come along and take it away.

This dream, according to many psychologists, betrays a subconscious anxiety about the future, a fear of becoming suddenly poor. Is it any wonder that the dream is so common?

The copy further explains that those persons who are adequately insured need never experience the financial anxiety that this type of dream symbolizes. Courtesy of The Travelers Insurance Company, Hartford, Connecticut.

the various "personalities" might be more or less conscious of each other. This was then interpreted as indicating that nervous diseases were the result of a splitting-off of consciousness. One portion of the associations of the mental life broke off and formed a new or smaller "mind" of its own. Compulsions and obsessions were explained in this way, and the physicians of that time used hypnotism to reintegrate the dismembered personality or mind. In the hypnosis, the physician tried to bring the split-off part of the mind back to the main body of the personality. Freud was a physician and treated his patients in this manner.

In the early years of his experimenting, Freud noted that some patients remembered things when they were hypnotized that they could not recall when in the normal state of consciousness. Then, when these forgotten facts of a painful nature were presented to the patient in his normal state he showed very strong emotions. He seemed to respond to these unpleasant and forgotten facts in the same manner as though he were actually experiencing the painful situation that had been buried in the unconscious. In some cases the painful experience had occurred many years before and the patient had been unable to recall it. When, however, the painful experience was brought to the full attention of the patient and he reacted to the recalled situation with the same emotional responses that he should have had when the situation occurred years before, the patient became well. The conclusion was naturally reached that the abnormal mental states of the neurotics were caused by the fact that the neurotic had not made a complete and satisfying emotional response to some of his unpleasant impulses and experiences. The bringing-about of a belated emotional response in order to clear up a neurosis was called the "method of catharsis" and the new or belated emotional response was called the "abreaction."

Freud found that some of his patients could not be hypnotized, but he also discovered that the patients could themselves recall their forgotten experiences when they were encouraged to talk freely and at random. In these experiments, Freud found that the dreams of his patients were often related to the unpleasant things that they were trying to recall or uncover. He made studies of thousands of dreams and learned that the dream is symbolic of some repressed or hidden wish, that it may relate to infantile experiences, and that the repressed wish is one which, ordinarily, we do not admit that we would even entertain. In some dreams, certain symbolisms occurred again and again, such as snakes, knives, seeds, mountains, and wild animals. Freud interpreted these symbolisms to represent repressed desires that we refuse to recognize or carry through emotionally, and so they are stored in the unconscious and are allowed to come forth only in the dream life of the patient or in some abnormal manner during his waking hours.

Most of these desires were believed to be of a sexual nature, because sex is the one strong impulse that cannot be expressed freely in our civilization.[33]

The psychoanalyst considers the sex symbolisms as merely convenient means of reaching more certain conclusions, and he uses them in much the same manner that the mathematician uses the symbol x in algebra. The true psychoanalyst does not use these sex symbols as definite proof of the nature of the repression until he has further evidence from the past experiences of the patient. The faddist who dabbles in psychoanalysis is apt to jump to erroneous conclusions when he has learned some of the sex symbols but does not appreciate that the symbolisms merely provide working hypotheses until a verifiable conclusion is reached.[34] The psychoanalyst does not think of the sex impulse in quite the same way that the layman does. The former uses it in the genetic sense. Furthermore, the modern psychoanalyst does not sexualize all behavior. Rather, he more often points out to certain patients how preoccupation with sex interferes with a more mature relationship with people and work.

The "censor" (better, censorship) refers to the assumed group of influences which require the individual to repress his normal impulses. These influences are the social standards of our times, the reproofs given in childhood, and the many repressive influences of modern life. The reason why the individual patient's dreams express the repressed impulses more readily than the acts of his waking life is that these repressive forces are not parts of his conscious or intellectual life. When we are asleep, the conscious controls are weaker, the censorship is relaxed, and the impulses come into the dream consciousness in symbolic form.

Psychoanalysis is a special method of psychological observation

All scientists find it necessary to set up special concepts or formulas to explain the phenomena of their fields of study. Chemists have set up "atomic theories" to help them explain facts discovered by experiment. Astronomers, biologists, mathematicians, and others have deliberately set up theoretical constructs to give order to their data. Psychotherapists have found it helpful to follow the same procedure, employing a theoretical construct based on the "unconscious." PSYCHOANALYSIS IS A METHOD OF PSYCHOLOGICAL OBSERVATION IN WHICH DREAM ANALYSIS, FREE ASSOCIATION, AND STUDY OF TRANSFERENCE OF EARLY ATTITUDES TOWARD THE ANALYST ARE USED TO UNCOVER

COMMON PSYCHOANALYTICAL TERMS

The psychology student often meets terms used more often by psychoanalysts than by psychologists. For his information, definitions of the more common psychoanalytical terms are presented. If the reader wishes fully to understand these and related terms, he should read complete descriptions and cases that involve the use of the terms. Terms defined here are defined in the psychoanalytic sense rather than in the psychological sense. Often there is a great difference between the two.

catharsis: the expression of disturbing emotional experiences, particularly through relating them to a psychoanalyst; mental life is thereby purged of acute unpleasantness.

conscious: that part of mental life of which the individual is aware.

dynamisms: unconscious mechanisms by which the ego, charged with libido, deals with its three adversaries; the id, superego, and external world; through dynamisms the ego allows the id outlets and substitute satisfactions.

ego: the self, largely conscious but partly unconscious; mediates between id and external world in an attempt to satisfy both.

free association: an unrestricted and undirected association of thoughts and feelings that come to a patient's mind; gives psychoanalyst insight into dynamics of the patient's behavior and etiology of his disturbance.

id: the unconscious, amoral basis of mental life; aims at satisfaction of instinctive drives and motivations; ruled by "pleasure principle."

libido: sexual desire or energy that is attached to the ego or to outside objects or persons.

psychoanalysis: the psychological system originated by Freud; based on the theory that all behavior results from repressed material in the unconscious; also, the therapy based on this system.

resistance: during psychoanalysis a manifestation of client's desire to hold on to his old behavior and thought patterns because they satisfy a need; shown by refusal to accept analyst's interpretations.

subconscious: that part of mental life that is neither conscious nor unconscious, and of which the individual may be dimly aware.

superego: conscience; the moral aspect of personality; criticizes the ego when it permits impulses from the id to gain expression.

transference: displacement of an emotion (love or hate) from an infantile love-object to another person (the psychoanalyst during psychoanalysis).

unconscious: that part of mental life characterized by certain dynamic processes which cannot be brought to consciousness by effort of the will or by voluntary act of memory; the id rules it.

THE UNCONSCIOUS.[35] It uses a unique set of theoretical constructs to give order to its data and to apply effective methods of psychotherapy.

Its theoretical constructs are a great deal more abstruse and difficult to understand than the barrier-adjustment concept used in this text. One explanation for the use of a more abstruse set of concepts by the psychoanalysts is that the seriously maladjusted patient's behavior often requires a more involved system of thinking than is needed to explain the behavior of a normal or only slightly maladjusted person.

As previously stated, dream analysis is used. In addition to the study of the dream life of the patient, the psychoanalyst also uses "free association." In this method the psychoanalyst has the patient come to his office and makes him physically comfortable in an easy chair or on a couch. All possible distracting influences are removed. Perhaps monotonous noise is provided. The patient closes his eyes, and the psychoanalyst may ask him to think of some part of his personal history which the analyst wishes to investigate, and tells him to think aloud and to say everything that comes to his mind, no matter how trivial, how irrelevant, or how unpleasant it may seem to him. The object is to discover the repressed experience or submerged complex that had not been allowed full emotional expression when it occurred in the experience of the patient. The patient is asked to report his dreams and to express his thoughts freely. In this way the analyst tries to unravel the network of experiences that caused the disturbance.

The analyst may also use word associations. To do this he prepares a list of words that may have some relationship to the patient's history and asks the patient to give the first word that comes to mind when the words are spoken. The analyst records with a stop-watch the time required for each response to the stimulus word. After the list has been completed the patient is taken through the list again and differences in responses are noted. When a stimulus word touches upon the repressed experiences or complexes, certain disturbances are noted, such as the peculiarity of the kind of reaction, the increased length of time for the reaction, and the failure to repeat the former reaction. White[36] reported the associations of a patient who had made several attempts to commit suicide:

Stimulus Word	Reaction	Time	Reproduction
To harm	Self	6.6	Anyone
Stork	Large	4.4	Large
False	True	1.8	Not true

The average reaction time was about 1.6 seconds. In the above examples can be noted the lengthened time of reaction, inability to recall the reaction on repetition, and the irradiation of the disturbance to the next two reactions as shown by the lengthened time of the reaction. This patient had a brother who was arrested and brought into court, and she gave bond for him. She made the following responses: *Prison*—cell—4.2 seconds; *bond*—pay—4.2 seconds; and *judge* —to be judged—4 seconds.

The analyst seeks constantly to discover the tension-causing influences in the patient's life history and to guide the patient into and through the process of catharsis. He does more than encourage the patient to talk freely. He enables the patient to become aware of and to view in clearer perspective the significant phases of past experiences, especially those that gave him feelings of shame or painful unpleasantness. The patient understands more clearly the origins of his own attitudes and the fact that his reactions were, all factors considered, natural for him. In the course of the patient's self-revelation, the emotions that were inhibited at the time of the painful or shameful experience are allowed expression and he gains marked release from old tensions.

In addition to the method of catharsis, the analyst may use *transference*. This is an attempt to relieve the emotional tension by

"Hush! Father mustn't be disturbed," and similar highly emotionalized admonitions to the small child may permanently influence the child regarding parental authority. Fortunately, some children are not permanently conditioned by such situations—they react by negative adaptation. (**Courtesy of General Foods Corporation.**)

having the patient project upon the analyst all the emotional tensions that are uncovered in the analysis. Emotionally, the analyst takes the place of parent, lover, or enemy. It is apparent that transference requires a great deal of skill on the part of the analyst and many specialists neglect to use it intelligently:

If psychoanalysis had never made but one contribution to our thinking, it would have been fully justified for what it has had to offer regarding the mechanism and nature of the process it designates as transference. One of the reasons I have in mind for advocating a further study of hypnotic phenomena is that here is an opportunity for the experimental study of this process.

My own feeling is that the transference is the most powerful tool which the physician has at his service for therapeutic purposes, and when we consider that in the vast majority of cases he has not the slightest idea of the existence of this process of which he himself is a part I have perhaps said enough to indicate the importance of its adequate understanding. All forms of therapy, no matter what—surgical, drug, dietary advice—all of them have their component, great or small, of psychotherapy, and the power and efficacy of psychotherapy are bound up in the mechanism of the transference. In addition to this the transference, because it represents a great force, is capable, when used ignorantly, of doing much damage. Under these circumstances it becomes of the utmost importance for the physician to acquaint himself with its meanings.

significances, mechanisms, in order that he may make this force available at maximum efficiency for the welfare of his patient.[37]

To psychoanalyze a patient requires much time. Months and even years may be required to unearth the painful experiences and enable the patient to express the unpleasant emotions that were repressed years before. The personality of the psychoanalyst plays a very important part in the method. He offers not sympathy but understanding. The patient needs to realize that here is one person in the whole world who is able and willing to understand him. The psychoneurotic may have felt that he has been misunderstood and that he must hide his guilt and burden from his best friends. As proof of the fact that we are unwilling to express ourselves and tell all our emotional experiences, ask a group of persons to tell all the dreams that they can recall. Few indeed are the husbands who are willing to tell their wives all their dreams or the thoughts that have entered their minds. If maladjusted people could only realize that each and every impulse or idea that enters consciousness has a normal and natural cause, it would be easier for the mentally afflicted to deal with their own emotionally repressed impulsions.

In the various studies of the maladjusted, it has been found that some have tried to overcome their unpleasant experiences and impulsions by means of defense mechanisms. The boy who takes pride in being the worst roughneck of the neighborhood may be acting the part of the rowdy in order to make himself feel that he is virile. To tell him that he must be more gentle does not remove the cause of the rowdiness. The girl who takes refuge in invalidism to gain attention may not be helped by punishment or by being told to make up her mind to get well. The analyst tries to get at the cause of the maladjustment and then to enable the patient to *sublimate* the energies, that is, to direct them into substitute activities that are satisfying and socially acceptable. We can see examples of sublimation in daily life in the case of the man who loses his wife and then takes up golf and plays it strenuously, or the student who fails in his studies and then becomes a collector of stamps. It is probable that many of our strongest drives are attempts to sublimate energy and achieve a sense of worthwhileness because of failure to do so in some other activity.

Criticisms of psychoanalysis

Freud and his colleagues will go down in psychological history as pioneers and contributors in a field which needed them in their time. They opened new trails in the exploration of the human mind. Many of Freud's trails led to new discoveries of great value. Some of his earlier teachings have been modified by members of related schools of therapy, and they are now adding new contributions by their willingness to discard or correct some of the earlier concepts in his method:

1. A modification of the Freudian principles concerns the concept of the unconscious. Some critics claim that we are not motivated by suppressed wishes, but rather by a series of adjustments to our situations. These adjustments are not made by a part of the mind, but by the entire individual. The organism as a whole responds to the stimulus. By trial and accidental success we find that one kind of response results in failure and dissatisfaction whereas another response brings about success and satisfaction. The successful response is stamped into our neurological mechanisms and, therefore, is readily repeated. Repressed desires or suppressed wishes are not entities which have energy by themselves. They have no existence by themselves any more than my fingers have hidden peckings on a typewriter. It is only when I am stimulated as an integrated unit that my fingers peck on a typewriter. Therefore, it is often claimed, the "unconscious mind" is not subject to proof or observation but rather is an explanation

of phenomena that can be interpreted more adequately by objective means.

Freud himself did not use the concept of "the unconscious" in his last book even though he was the first man to develop it as a means of explaining unconscious learning. We now think of the word, "unconscious," as an inappropriate noun but a good adjective.

2. Phobias may arise because of a desire which has been stimulated and not allowed expression, recognition, or admission. However, critics claim that normal stimuli may become associated through action of the nervous system rather than through a subconscious mind, with abnormal responses as in the case described by Bagby:

A man suffered from a phobia of being grasped from behind, the disturbance appearing early in childhood and persisting to his fifty-fifth year. When walking on the street he was under a compulsion to look back over his shoulder at intervals to see if he was closely followed. In social gatherings he arranged to have his chair against the wall. It was impossible for him to enter crowded places or to attend the theater. In his fifty-fifth year he returned to the town in which he had spent his childhood. After inspecting his old home, he went to the corner grocery and found that his old boyhood friend was still behind the counter. He introduced himself and they began to reminisce. Finally the grocer said this, "I want to tell you something that occurred when you were a boy: You used to go by this store on errands, and when you passed you often took a handful of peanuts from the stand in front. One day I saw you coming and hid behind a barrel. Just as you put your hand in the pile of peanuts, I jumped out and grabbed you from behind. You screamed and fell fainting on the sidewalk." The episode was remembered and the phobia, after a period of readjustment, disappeared.[38]

3. Dreams are not always wish-fulfillments. A dream of falling may be stimulated by a sagging bed spring rather than by the fear of a moral fall; or a dream of being choked may be brought about by the tightness of the bed covers. Some dreams are the mere automatic and chance play of the cerebral associational mechanisms. One neural pathway happens to arouse another pathway and incongruous combinations of ideas result. Certainly many dreams are not related to the sex impulse. The child and the adult must suppress many impulses, such as those of self-assertion and gluttony. It is unfair to attribute all asocial impulses to sex energies which are not allowed expressions by our form of civilization.

It is true that the body is full of energy—energy which must be expressed in some form. The outlets for these energies may be socially acceptable or extremely harmful. For example, a man may become a butcher making his living by killing cattle and cutting up meat. This is a socially acceptable outlet for his energies. If these energies become perverted he may instead become a murderer of people.

4. The energy of the human organism may be thought of in many different ways. It may be called the *elan vital* or the *libido*, or we may accept it, as suggested by Jung, as a striving after larger experience. Adler, on the other hand, considered this striving as an attempt to achieve safety and power. Or we may designate energy with reference to its objectives and call it tendencies or impulses. It certainly may be analyzed without sex as a basis.

5. Conflicts between various impulses do give rise to behavior which may be thought of as resulting in a *complex*. However, the complex should not be considered bad in all cases. Lee Wilson Dodd has written a book[39] wherein he shows that certain complexes are not a stain but an advantage; not a leaden drag but a golden spur. The lame foot of Byron stimulated him to become a master horseman, a good shot, and the best swimmer in England. The assurance thus gained enabled him to become a great lover, poet, and patriot.

"Complex" is a Freudian term, but the inferiority concept comes from Adler. Whether a handicap produces a sense of inferiority and induces a complex, or results in a heroic resolve to achieve despite it, seems to depend largely upon the type of

The National Institutes of Health, Public Health Service, Department of Health, Education, and Welfare. Located in Bethesda, Maryland, it is one of the world's largest medical research centers.

One of the seven institutes for research is the National Institute of Mental Health. Fritz Redl, Ph.D., Chief, Laboratory for Child Research, and staff members' families posed to illustrate some of the settings used in behavior researches. Dr. Redl and the child of a staff member have the kind of private chat that would take place between a psychiatrist and an emotionally disturbed patient. Children under treatment at the Center are not separated from staff members even at mealtime. At least one staff member sits at each table. Meals are carefully planned under supervision of a nutritionist.

Examples of articles published are "Child Study in a New Setting," Fritz Redl; "Our Troubles with Defiant Youth;" and **Children**, a publication of the Children's Bureau, U.S. Department of Health, Education, and Welfare.

nervous constitution and earlier adjustment habits of the individual who has the handicap.

Contributions of psychoanalysis

1. Psychoanalysis has given us a method of treatment of the insane which has been of material help, even though the persons who use it sometimes do not believe all its published principles. In fact, some psychologists say that the bases of psychoanalysis are not true, but that it works anyhow. Since psychoanalysis has come into more or less common use in state hospitals, the per-

centage of cures, all factors considered, has probably increased. Whether these cures have been the result of psychoanalytical methods, chemical treatments, or both is open to debate.

2. Psychoanalysis has given us some valuable points of view. It has shown the importance of the emotions, the strength of childhood influences, and the ways in which we deal with our problems or evade them. It has shown us the dominating influence-shaping attitudes people have acquired about themselves, about others, and about their surroundings. Their adjustment habits have a great deal to do with their abilities, and the ways in which intellectual capacity is expressed. We now have some evidence to show that psychoanalysis has even made substantial changes in the intelligence quotients of certain individuals.[40]

3. For the businessman, psychoanalysis has a pointed suggestion in dealing with problem employees—namely, the importance of the art of listening. The executive of the old order took a keen delight in dominating his men. He knew how to put the "fear of God" into his workers. The new executive, like the psychoanalyst, tries to find out why the employee acts as he does. He wants to know what the peculiar behavior of a problem employee means, that is, what are the individual's problems and his adjustments?

The embezzler and the liar are extreme examples of employees who have problem habits and poor adjustments. Some of these people can be helped by specialists in mental disorders. The executive should learn from the specialists how to use intelligent methods in dealing with the problem employees in his organization. In the business world, when an executive insists upon remaining hardboiled rather than analytical and skillful in dealing with his employees, he must expect to have problem employees because he is a "problem executive."

Industry offers opportunity to contribute to integrative adjustments

Many a young person envies psychiatrists and clinical psychologists for their ability to serve humanity. He, too, would like to make a contribution to mental health but he does not want to acquire specialized professional training for that purpose. Such a person can, however, participate in the service toward better mental health, for emotional stresses arise in every walk of life.

One of the greatest opportunities today for the improvement of mental and emotional health is to be found in industry—not in psychiatric treatment, but in preventive maintenance. One need not be a psychiatrist or a clinical psychologist to sense symptoms of anxiety, fear, and "brainwashing boredom" in the people around him. He can contribute to the psychological health of his fellow workers, especially if they are under his supervision.

A company can survive and prosper only through the constructive cooperation of all of its members. Teamwork must be more than a slogan. It is a symptom of healthy minds and bodies; it is also a symptom of healthy management—the kind that considers what happens to people in the course of producing, as well as the ultimate product and profit.[41]

Dr. Molly Harrower, a consulting psychologist who has had much experience in industry, recently stated:

Human nature is not fixed and unchangeable. It is plastic, flexible, and has tremendous possibilities. But there is no such thing as suddenly changing an attitude.

If you want to change the direction in which a flower is growing, you must change the direction of the light, and you must do it gradually. The flower will die if you snap it off or force it in another direction. It's the same with an attitude. An attitude is a living thing that has grown up with a person. If it can be changed at all, it must be changed gradually. . . .

A suspicious person doesn't think of himself as being suspicious. He feels he is in a hostile world, surrounded by people—bosses, em-

Most students of psychology have read about Pavlov's conditioned-reflex experiments with dogs. Other scientists have used rats, pigs, cats and other animals in studies of conditioning. Here, for example, are pictures from studies being carried on currently at Michigan State University of Agriculture and Applied Science, Department of Psychology, using fish as subjects.

The fish prior to training are placed in raceways that are equipped with electrodes used in shocking (long metal bars running parallel with wall) and feeding apparatus (funnels). The electrodes are activated independently from a tower. The feeding apparatus is a hydraulic set-up that injects food into the raceway under pressure. It is controlled by a timing apparatus that permits automatic feeding for any length of time or time of day. Screens are used to disassociate the man—food approach response.

Left, the training and control raceways near the end of the training period (there are 2600 Brook trout in each section). The experimental animals have been conditioned to avoid specific trout predators, to feed appropriately (dawn and dusk and near the bottom) and to remain in cover during the bright daylight hours. Note that most of the tubular objects in the raceway are either metal or are covered with metal screens. These permit the animal to avoid the shock and, oddly enough, to establish preference for a dark place to feed.

Right, a close-up of a "cover spot" with shunt screen prior to the initiation of training.

Most laymen imagine that experiments such as these have no significance for psychology. Actually, these and related investigations contribute to the better understanding of certain principles involved in human behavior. Photos by courtesy of Prof. Donald Johnson and Michigan Department of Conservation.

ployees, friends—who are always doing irritating things which work out to his disadvantage. He sees himself in a threatening and unpleasant environment.

The problem is to get him to realize that he is carrying a hostile attitude into the world; that he is looking at things through black-colored glasses. How people see the world determines how they experience it. That, in turn, determines how they react to the world and, finally, how the world reacts to them.

Attitudes are formed way back in our lives. They become fixed by usage, emotionally engraved. It takes more than will power to change them.

If I had a suspicious attitude that had been formed in childhood because of repeated experiences which made me afraid of certain kinds of people, I couldn't change that attitude merely because I wanted to. And what's more, I would become suspicious of anyone who wanted me to change.

Few people realize that their emotional problems often result from the influence of old and inappropriate attitudes. Anyone with a stiff, inflexible attitude approaches a problem in terms of the past, instead of thinking about it against the background of the situation he is now facing. Trapped by his own attitude, he limits the freedom with which he can act.

It is the psychologist's job to discover to what extent those old erroneous ways of looking at the world prevent the patient from facing up to his problems constructively. He listens to the patient and attempts to give him some awareness of the forces that have been influencing his behavior. He tries to get him to see situations objectively by giving him some understanding of the facts as they are, without distortions or misinterpretations. There can be no change of attitude without a change in the way of looking at things.

Mentioning her work in industry, Dr. Harrower said that she has come across foremen who apply the psychologist's principles and techniques, and who do that without knowing it:

They seem to work miracles just by establishing a friendly atmosphere in their departments —an atmosphere of acceptance, warmth and affection. They are able to see things from the other person's point of view. They don't feel that they're being attacked personally when somebody differs with them.

They possess the ability to look at their employees objectively. They do not condemn; and instead of moralizing and judging, they try to understand. They are sensitive to the thoughts and feelings of the people around them. And they're aware of how their own actions affect other people. In short, these foremen are mentally healthy persons.

As to how foremen or anybody else can achieve the condition of mental health, Dr. Harrower gave us these comments:

Some people have grown up relatively unscarred by life. They hardly know what it means to have destructive, defensive or antisocial feelings. And neither are they burdened by feelings of anxiety.

Other people have achieved mental health the opposite way. They've had their share of troubles. But they've managed to work them through with the aid of a friend or relative, with someone they could trust and confide in, and who trusted and liked them.

Anyone who has never known someone who is reassuring, has missed something very important in life. Thus trust and affection, I am certain, are basic to the development of a healthy, wholesome personality.[42]

Acknowledgments and References

1. Felix Adler, *Creed and Deed*, G. P. Putnam's Sons, New York, 1877.

2. James M. Cunningham, Director, Bureau of Mental Hygiene, State of Connecticut Department of Health, has presented an excellent summary of mental illness and employability in *Trained Men*, No. 3 (1945), pp. 10–16.

3. T. A. Munro, "Consanguinity and Mental Disorder," *Journal of Mental Science*, Vol. 84 (1938), pp. 708–714, reports that 2.4 per cent of the 4,200 mental patients studied were of consanguineous parentage.

4. "Mental Ills Not Inherited Like the Color of Eyes," *Science News Letter*, May 20, 1939, p. 313. This article is a summary of a study by Drs. Horatio M. Pollock, Benjamin Malzberg, and Raymond G. Fuller in a book, *Hereditary and Environmental Factors in the Causation of Manic-Depressive Psychoses and Dementia Praecox*, State Hospitals Press, Utica, N.Y., 1939.

5. J. Slawson and M. Moss, "Mental Illness Among Jews," *Jewish Social Service Quarterly*, June 1936, pp. 343–350. Comparative rates per 100,000 population of first admissions to 17 mental-hygiene clinics, New York City, 1934, pointed to a relatively greater prevalence of psychoneuroses and related disorders among Jews, and of committed insane among non-Jews.

6. Stanley Cobb, Walter Bauer, and Isabel Whiting, *Journal of the American Medical Association*, August 19, 1939.

7. *Science News Letter*, November 26, 1938, p. 345. Findings reported by Dr. Alvin V. Semrad.

8. Donald M. Hamilton, "The Use of Electric Shock Therapy in Psychoneurosis," *American Journal of Psychiatry*, Vol. 103 (1947), pp. 665–668.

9. H. Selinski, "The Selective Use of Electro-shock Therapy as an Adjuvant to Psychotherapy" *Bulletin of the New York Academy of Medicine*, Vol. 19 (1943), pp. 245–252.

10. Edward F. Kerman, "The Efficacy of Electro-shock Therapy in Preventing or Shortening Hospitalization," *Journal of Nervous and Mental Diseases*, Vol. 106 (1947), pp. 1–10.

11. Joseph Wortis, "Physiological Treatment," *The American Journal of Psychiatry*, January 1955, pp. 515–517.

12. See Walter Freeman, "Psychosurgery," *American Journal of Psychiatry*, January 1955, pp. 518–520.

13. See Harry W. Allison and Sarah G. Allison, "Personality Changes Following Transorbital Lobotomy," *Journal of Abnormal and Social Psychology*. April 1954, pp. 219–223.

14. See Harold E. Himwich, "The New Psychiatric Drugs," *Scientific American*, October 1955, pp. 80–86.

15. Howard A. Rusk, "Aid for the Mentally Ill," *The New York Times*, June 26, 1955.

16. *Mental Hygiene News*, New York State Department of Mental Hygiene, March 1955, p. 1.

17. See *Business Week*, May 12, 1956, p. 29.

18. See "Experimental Psychosis" by Six Staff Members of Boston Psychopathic Hospital, *Scientific American*, June 1955, pp. 34–49.

19. J. L. Moreno, "Psychodramatic Treatment of Marriage Problems," *Sociometry*, Vol. 3, No. 1 (1940), pp. 1–23.
   R. Borden, "The Use of Psychodrama in an Institution for Delinquent Girls," *Sociometry*, Vol. 3, No. 1 (1940), pp. 81–90.

20. N. E. Shoobs, "Psychodrama in the Schools," *Sociometry*, Vol. 7 (1944), pp. 152–168.

21. For good summaries of various group therapies, see Martin Grotjahn, "Experience with Group Psychotherapy as a Method of Treatment for Veterans," *American Journal of Psychiatry*, Vol. 103 (1947), pp. 637–643; W. A. White, R. W. Hall, and others, "Group Psychotherapy; a Symposium," *Sociometry*, Vol. 8 (1945), pp. 243–561.

22. O. Kant, "Choice of Method in Psychotherapy," *Diseases of the Nervous System*, Vol. 5 (1944), pp. 325–329.

23. Paul E. Johnson, "Religious Psychology and Health," *Mental Hygiene*, Vol. 31 (1947), pp. 556–566.

24. M. N. Chappell, "Psychology and the Organic Disorders," *The Psychological Exchange*, 1931–32.

25. I. P. Pavlov, *Lectures on Conditioned Reflexes*, International Publishers, New York, 1928.

26. O. D. Anderson and H. S. Liddell, "Observations on Experimental Neurosis in Sheep," *Archives of Neurology and Psychiatry*, Vol. 34 (1935), pp. 330–354.
   H. S. Liddell, "The Experimental Neurosis and the Problem of Mental Disorder," *American Journal of Psychiatry*, Vol. 94 (1938), pp. 1035–1043.

27. N. R. F. Maier, *Studies of Abnormal Behavior in the Rat*, Harper & Brothers, New York, 1939. See also Maier, Glaser, and Klee in the *Journal of Experimental Psychology*, Vol. 26 (1940), pp. 521–546.

28. "Studious Laboratory Cat Breaks Down Emotionally," *Science News Letter*, March 18, 1939.

29. Norman R. F. Maier and Robert S. Feldman, "Studies of Abnormal Behavior in the Rat: XIV, Water Spray as a Means of Inducing Seizures," *The Journal of Comparative Psychology*, Vol. 39, No. 5 (October 1946), p. 286.

30. Possible limitations of animal experiments as applied to frustrated human beings have been analyzed by L. S. Kubie in "The Experimental Induction of Neurotic Reactions in Man," *Yale Journal of Biology and Medicine*, Vol. 11 (1939), pp. 541–545.

31. *Science News Letter*, December 31, 1938. See also, issue of January 13, 1940.

32. Frederick C. Thorne, "Directive Psychotherapy: Therapeutic Use of Conflict," *Journal of Clinical Psychology*, Vol. 3 (1947), pp. 168–179.

33. Many students of dreams of primitive peoples have indicated that the lack of sexual inhibition tends to reduce the number of disguised and symbolical sexual dreams. Among such savages, the most tormenting and easily remembered dreams are the nightmares of anxiety and hunger. See, for example, V. Elwin, "A Note on the Theory and Symbolism of Dreams Among the Baiga," *British Journal of Medical Psychology*, Vol. 16 (1937), pp. 237–254.

34. E. A. Gutheil, *The Language of the Dream*, The Macmillan Company, New York, 1939. This is a textbook of dream interpretation which presents dream symbols, analytical interpretations, and the uses of dream analysis in therapy.

35. J. F. Brown, "The Position of Psychoanalysis in the Science of Psychology," *Journal of Abnormal and Social Psychology*, Vol. 35 (1940), pp. 29–44.

36. William A. White, *Outline of Psychiatry*, Nervous and Mental Diseases Publishing Company, Washington, D.C., 1924, p. 338. For a later study of word associations, see Roy Schafer, "A Study of Thought Processes in a Word Association Test," *Character and Personality*, Vol. 13 (1945), pp. 217 ff.

37. William A. White, *Twentieth Century Psychiatry*, W. W. Norton and Company, New York, 1936, pp. 50–51.

38. E. Bagby, "The Etiology of Phobias," *Journal of Abnormal and Social Psychology*, Vol. 17 (1922), p. 17.

39. *The Golden Complex: A Defense of Inferiority*, John Day Co., 1927.

40. L. Chidester and K. A. Menninger, "The Application of Psychoanalytic Methods to the Study of

Mental Retardation," *American Journal of Orthopsychiatry*, Vol. 6 (1936), pp. 616–625. This article reports an increase in IQ from 62 to 90.

41. See *The Management Review*, American Management Association, October 1955, pp. 722–23.

42. These three passages taken from: "Dealing with Fears, Hostilities," an interview with Dr. Molly Harrower, carried in *The Foreman's Letter*, February 14, 1955. Published by The National Foremen's Institute, New London, Conn.

PROJECTS

1. Make a study of mental health clinics and published materials on mental hygiene that are available. The National Association for Mental Health, Inc., 1790 Broadway, New York City, is one of many organizations that can be helpful in furnishing objective information on the problem.
2. Study the behavior of a child or an adult who is considered to be dishonest or unreliable. Does this trait appear in all his behavior or only in certain kinds of situations?
3. Some businessmen have a "check-book complex." What experiences may cause them to evaluate abnormally many personal acts and plans in terms of cost and profit rather than in terms of happiness?
4. The assistant head of a department was asked to give a talk on an academic subject over the radio. He gave it without consulting the department head. When the latter learned that he had been denied this opportunity for publicity, he discharged his assistant. Analyze the possible reasons for discharging the assistant.
5. Analyze your behavior for evidence of inhibitions that are annoying and irrational. Can you think of experiences that caused them? Mention some things that your "censor" does not allow you to do.
6. Interview several persons regarding their attitudes toward persons who have or are now being treated by a psychiatrist. Do not try to educate them—just try to elicit their real opinions. How do your interviewees' attitudes differ in regard to the patient who is extremely depressed and has withdrawn from reality in comparison with, say, the sex offender such as the exhibitionist?

COLLATERAL READINGS

Bach, George R., *Intensive Group Psychotherapy*, The Ronald Press Company, New York, 1954.

Kant, O., "Choice of Method in Psychotherapy," *Diseases of the Nervous System*, Vol. 5 (1944), pp. 325–329.

Landis, Carney, and M. Marjorie Bolles, *Textbook of Abnormal Psychology*, The Macmillan Company, New York, 1947, Chapter 33.

Lehner, George F. J. and Ella Kube, *The Dynamics of Personal Adjustment*, Prentice-Hall, Inc., New York, 1955, Chapters 16 and 17.

Rogers, Carl R., *Counseling and Psychotherapy*, Houghton Mifflin Company, Boston, 1942.

Rusk, Howard A., "Aid for the Mentally Ill," *The New York Times*, June 26, 1955.

Shaffer Laurance F. and Edward J. Shoben, Jr., *The Psychology of Adjustment*, Houghton Mifflin Company, Boston, 1956, Chapters 14 to 17.

Smith, Henry Clay, *Psychology of Industrial Behavior*, McGraw-Hill Book Company, Inc., New York, 1955, Chapter 7.

Tallman, G., "The Psychologist in a Neurological Hospital," *Journal of Consulting Psychology*, Vol. 8 (1944), pp. 308–311.

"What You Should Know About Mental Illness," interview with Dr. Winfred Overholser, *U.S. News and World Report*, November 18, 1955, pp. 126–142.

CHAPTER SEVEN

Counseling: Predisposing influences and outline for study of the individual's adjustments—case problems

The distance runner is no sum of leg muscles, oxygen utilization, and "nerve," nor is the musician the sum of tone enjoyment, rhythm perception, and manual dexterity. Human traits, moreover, are responses not to outer stimulation alone; they are simultaneously responses to inner stimulation, which in turn depends upon an uninterrupted inner flow of energies, permitting an energy distribution that is unique for each organism.[1]

Anyone who counsels a person should be aware not only of the dynamics in the development of adjustment patterns but also of the predisposing influences. These underlie the thinking of the counselor and deserve our attention. As stated in Chapter 2, the environment is important from the standpoint of *acceptance, antagonism,* and *indifference* in adjustment. Every individual has many predisposing influences in the course of his adjustment history. Students of anthropology and sociology are especially aware of the cultural influences and differences.

Cultural and sociological factors

Man is a social being. Every child's ideas of what is right or wrong, what is to be done or not to be done, what is to be imitated or to be avoided are influenced by his cultural environment. The language, customs, and group ideas surrounding the child are significant factors in his growth.

Anthropologists have studied numerous cultures of primitive peoples and ethnic groups. Important differences and similarities to our own culture have been found. In some primitive groups, for example, each child is reared to distrust other members of the group. In others, the child is reared to give and expect coöperation and kindness. Similarly, discipline systems, sex taboos, rituals, folk tales, and attitudes toward objects vary from culture to culture. While celibacy, self-torture, and voluntary fasting are socially desirable in some groups, in others they are considered undesirable. The things the individual values, fears, seeks, or is ashamed of are conditioned by the family constellation and the culture to which the family belongs.

Despite similarities among members of the same group, wide individual differences are also found. Factors such as the sex of the child, the occupational status of the parents, education, and wealth may affect different children of the same culture in different manners. Changing conditions within the culture, such as war, plague, famine or economic depression may also modify the pattern of life for the individual of a given culture. Examples of these varieties of cultural influence can be observed from the study of first and second generations of foreign-born citizens of our own country. Certainly, many a child of foreign-born parents has had distinctive adjustment problems in the course of his emotional development in the United States. Sometimes the factors that enter into and modify reaction patterns can be appreciated more clearly by means of a study of anthropological and nationality influences. Such studies have their place in the training for greater insight into human personality. The psychologist would like to know about them whenever he deals with the problem personality or the person who has a problem.

In most cases, however, the analyst or counselor is more interested in knowing how the individual reacted to the factors in his early and later environment. The family constellation and how the child reacted to it, the adjustments made at the time and retained (or discarded), are usually of greater significance than a mere knowledge of the culture or of the family as such.

The early life history and work adjustment

Effects of a person's early life history and personality characteristics on his work adjustment were studied by the Family Society of Greater Boston between 1934 and 1943. This period covered the years of general unemployment as well as those during which the unemployment problem was mitigated. The people who were studied went to the society's offices for help in planning their work. Each one was counseled, some as few as six, and some as many as fifteen, times. All were seen over a period of from four to nine years. Through these years, background material was accumulated from the client himself and from other sources. A case history was written. Batteries of tests were administered. With this fund of information, the society explored the dynamics of the client's work adjustment.

After all the material collected by these methods had been studied, each client was rated on personality characteristics, including personal identifying facts, early life, current family life, early work history, response to counseling, general and specific work reactions, and general work adjustment and improvement.

On the basis of their composite ratings on these characteristics, some of the clients were selected as having made the best work adjustment and some as having made the poorest. Table 7-1 shows the characteristics that most clearly differentiated the two groups.

Summarizing the study, Friend and Haggard state:

We can see how tightly knit family relationships as a child carry over into good work morale as well as harmonious relations with fellow-workers, and how these relationships generate the worker's feeling that he has a place in the group as he did in his family. We can see how the worker "catches" from a good exemplar, from the leader in the home, a belief in himself and in his ability to cope with his work. These relationships and values are the keystones of a good work adjustment. On the other hand, a deep feeling of rejection as a child tends to result in a sense of worthlessness with regard to jobs. *For people, it seems, are able to endure the actual hardships of illness or poverty, the pressures from the outside, more easily than the inner emotional pressures—rejection and acute intrafamily antagonisms and self-doubt.*

. . . people clearly take their childhoods with them to their jobs, as they do their current family situations, their personality patterns and their ways of reacting to counseling. *One of the tightest links in our findings draws together the person's work and his personal adjustment.*

Similarly, the special values or demands which the worker makes of the job are often a later chapter of his experiences as a child. How much he prizes and accentuates special appreciation as a reward varies inversely with the degree of unity in his early family group and seems to be a means through which the individual strives to secure for himself a place with, and status in, the current work group. *The worker appears to compromise with life by going after the identical and specific satisfaction in work denied him years before.**

Persistent affect fixations

Of special significance in the study of later adjustment are the child's *persistent affect fixations.* This condition of mental development is one in which the individual remains attached to feelings which were characteristic of or dominant in an earlier phase of development. Everyone has some of these persistent infantile tendencies that color or form patterns of behavior in adulthood. The pattern of influence varies in degree and kind from person to person.

To understand an adult fully we must know how he reacted emotionally to his childhood situations and the extent to which

the childhood habits of adjustment persist. If we can appreciate how childhood emotional reactions color the later adult behavior, we may gain a clue from the unique adult behavior to the nature of the earlier childhood reactions. If our hypotheses about the adult and his childhood adjustments prove to be correct, we are in a position that enables us to evaluate and help direct his behavior more intelligently.

The child reacts to his environment in ways that affect his well-being in satisfying forms. Habitual or characteristic methods of attention-getting or problem-solving therefore develop, and as they prove to be effective in getting what he wants, they gradually become unconscious methods of meeting and interpreting many situations and obstacles. They become more deeply ingrained with time, and they also may become so adaptive that their original source and form frequently become obscured.

The reaction tendencies which these persistent affect fixations create in the child's personality help to mold his life style. They help to determine how others will judge him. These opinions are also important in the person's own evaluation of himself. They often influence the choice of his vocation. They steer him toward certain types of avocations, sometimes of the lone or seclusive type in which it is not necessary for him to adapt to or mix with others, and sometimes into group activities through which he may be able to express himself through dominance or through identification with the group. If we know the problems that an individual tried to solve or the difficulties under which he lived while a child,

---

* Jeannette G. Friend and Ernest A. Haggard, "Work Adjustment in Relation to Family Background," *Applied Psychology Monographs,* No. 16, Stanford University Press, Stanford, Calif., 1948, pp. 137–138.

Since the concept of work adjustment centered on the striking of a balance between the satisfactions which the individual was seeking from his work and the satisfactions which the job provided, the primary aim was to separate the groups on the basis of the individual's own feeling of self-respect about his work in terms of his particular qualifications and ambitions, be he executive or laborer. Basic to this concept are three cornerstone criterion items: the individual's over-all adjustment, the amount of satisfaction derived from his job, and his general capacity to use his job qualifications. Five more items which were judged to be indications of the caliber of the individual's occupational adjustment were added, giving a total of eight criterion items. The Highs or Best Adjusted were selected from those consistently rating "good" on the eight items; the Lows or Poorest Adjusted from those consistently rating "poor."

TABLE 7-1

SOME OF THE MOST OUTSTANDING CHARACTERISTICS OF THE BEST AND POOREST WORK
ADJUSTMENT GROUPS

Best Adjusted	*Poorest Adjusted*
Greater mutual affection in home.	Less mutual affection in home.
Early and current families closely knit and strongly unified. Greater familial loyalty.	Disorganization and lack of "togetherness" in family.
Less ambivalence toward current family and early homes.	Greater ambivalence toward current family and early homes.
Less resentment at family dependence or domination.	Greater resentment at family dependence or domination.
Greater capacity to counteract any early unfavorable family experiences.	Less capacity to counteract any early unfavorable family experiences.
Learned from parents a healthier way of dealing with life's problems.	Learned from parents a poorer way of dealing with life's problems.
Less antagonism toward parents.	Greater antagonism toward parents.
Less sibling rivalry.	Greater sibling rivalry.
Greater affection for father.	Less affection for father.
More satisfying school experience either social, athletic, or scholastic.	Less satisfying school experience.
Less sense of rejection.	Greater sense of rejection resulting in feeling of worthlessness.
Good sense of "give and take."	Poor sense of "give and take." Overly impulsive.
Better frustration-tolerance.	Poorer frustration-tolerance.
More self-reliant (make own decisions, reluctant to accept financial aid, etc.).	Less self-reliant.
Greater satisfaction from first jobs.	Less satisfaction from first jobs.
Greater insight into job needs or problems. Do more constructive and affirmative thinking about jobs.	Less insight into job needs or problems. Not apt to do constructive and affirmative thinking about jobs.
React objectively and positively to job counseling.	Tend not to benefit from job counseling.
Lesser tendency toward self-sabotage.	Stronger tendency to defeat themselves (as by drinking, quarreling, illness, marrying wrong person, etc.).
More optimistic and self-confident about jobs.	Not optimistic or self-confident about jobs.
Tend to blame themselves or business conditions for joblessness.	Tend to blame other people for joblessness. Tend to try to escape through drinking, etc.
Changing jobs usually means progress.	Changing jobs does not mean progress. More apt to switch from one kind of work to another.
Little delinquency or accident-proneness.	Delinquency or accident-proneness apt to be present.
Like competition in work, promotion on merit, group belongingness, responsibility, work geared to abilities.	Do not like competition in work, etc.
Like opportunity for new experience and to learn new skills.	Do not like to change work habits or learn new skills.

Adapted from Jeannette G. Friend and Ernest A. Haggard, "Work Adjustment in Relation to Family Background," *Applied Psychology Monographs,* No. 16, Stanford University Press, Stanford, Calif., 1948.

we often can understand his present behavior. The dynamics in his adult behavior are, in some cases, his interpretations of his childhood memories and his goals, conscious and unconscious.

If a person has retained persistent affect fixations that are not socially acceptable, he can change them at any time that he develops sufficient insight and determination to do so. Childhood misconceptions often can be corrected and better methods of dealing with life can be learned. But someone, usually a wise counselor, must be able to recognize from adult behavior the possible significance of cues to behavior patterns having a childhood origin. The ability to recognize cues in the adult's conduct and to see how they relate to childhood origins is one of the most important factors in psychological analysis.

If, for example, we meet an adult who obviously lacks self-confidence, has difficulty in coming into a social group and difficulty in leaving it, seldom completes sentences that he starts and repeats questions asked him, we wonder how his present emotional insecurity happened to develop. We have a right to wonder whether his present behavior stems from emotional insecurity in childhood. Were his parents incompatible? Was the status of his early home in danger of divorce or in danger of economic failure? If in danger of lack of income, is he presently motivated to deny himself normal comforts in order to save more money than he needs? Or is wealth so hopeless in attainment for him that money means little to him now?

If it is necessary for us to supervise him, to counsel him, or to live intimately with him, our relationship will be more intelligent and effective for both of us if we know how he defined himself as a child. If his convictions about himself were deeply emotionalized, his childhood self-evaluations are significant today. Table 7-2 presents a helpful list of common affect fixations of childhood, adjust-

ments in childhood, and later methods of adjustment.

Anyone who will carefully study the typical childhood affect fixations (Column A of Table 7-2), adjustments in childhood (Column B), and adult adjustments (Column C) will have a helpful list of cues toward understanding the person with a problem. Certain precautions are necessary, however. The child who had affect fixation number 2 may in adulthood make adjustment number 5. We cannot conclude that any one affect fixation or barrier *always* results in a corresponding adjustment tendency. We can recognize causal connections only when we have learned many pertinent facts about the individual and then see how the facts arrange themselves into a meaningful pattern. This fact makes necessary a wide knowledge of affect fixations and typical forms of adjustments. The lack of fixed or standard adjustments to specific barriers means that every individual must be comprehensively analyzed in order to be understood. Clinical psychology is a very complex study. The clinician knows, for example, that the adult cannot accurately recall childhood events. Nor can he describe how he felt as a child. The affect fixations of his childhood must be deduced from the case history.

From the standpoint of understanding the adult's personality, particularly his drives and his qualitative strengths and weaknesses, the persistent affect fixations are especially important. A good example with comments is the following, written by a psychiatrist:

Everyone's personality and behavior are colored and affected in a large degree by the childhood emotional constellations, but the *more* these interfere with adult behavior, the *more rigidly* they determine behavior, the more "neurotic" is the individual. Again it is a quantitative matter.

A simple example is a certain career woman, no longer young. Her father had been away a great deal while she was a child, and while at home he was partly very indulgent toward her but also partly irritable and neglectful. She reacted with longings for him but also with a deep resentment against him. This became a fixed pattern in her relations with men. She repeated it in her marriage and in position after position. She longed to be a favorite of the head of the firm but would never admit this. She would start off doing very well and making an excellent impression. But gradually her hostility to her employer would become so open and intense that it would only be a matter of time before some incident would precipitate her departure.

In one firm she became good friends with one of the junior members. He left later to go into business for himself and asked her to go with him. She was by this time openly hostile to the boss and gladly accepted the offer. Things went

well for a time, but then the old pattern reasserted itself. So long as this man was a junior partner, himself somewhat hostile and rebellious against their boss, she got on with him famously, for she unconsciously identified with him, as a child hostile to his father, like herself. But when this same man had his own firm and was in the father position himself, then she could no longer identify with him as a rebellious child, and she developed toward him the hostility she was destined by her inner reactions to have toward all men whom, for one reason or another, she looked to as fathers . . .

Such a tendency unconsciously to put certain men into a category is a failure to discriminate them from the original object, in this case the girl's own father. Often in this case, the men were in reality totally different personalities

TABLE 7-2

TYPICAL AFFECT FIXATIONS OF CHILDHOOD AND LATER ADJUSTMENT METHODS

A	B	C
As a child, did you feel that you were:	Which method of adjustment did you use?	In adulthood, which method of adjustment do you now use?
1. Small, helpless, of poor health, or defective in body?	1. Sickliness. "Nervousness" to prove need for special consideration.	1. Sickliness. "Nervousness." Pains that your family physician seems unable to cure.
2. The center of attention—a kind of toy or animated doll? Did games with others revolve mostly around you?	2. Unruliness in order to gain the limelight, sarcasm, bitter word-battles to deal with domineering parents.	2. Argumentativeness. Word-battles. Comedian knacks or witticisms to gain attention.
3. Disciplined severely, often punished for what you considered minor misdeeds? Suppressed?	3. Model behavior in order to deal with domineering parents, or hoping for affection by being a paragon of virtue. Self-righteousness.	3. Seek perfection for yourself. Self-righteousness. Consider yourself better than other people.
4. Rejected. Extra "human freight," unwanted, and given little affection?	4. Keeping to yourself to avoid failure. Seclusiveness in games and comradeships. Shut-in personality.	4. Seclusiveness. You avoid games and social affairs. Have very few friends. Or, you seek acceptance by others, want to be one of the group you admire.
5. Denied your rights, to be seen rather than heard, forced to be quiet and courteous? Domineered? Discriminated against?	5. Belligerence. Spoiling the fun of others to avoid games where you might fail.	5. Radical tendencies. Cynicism. You believe you could remodel the world.
6. Laughed at, frequently ridiculed?	6. Fear lest you might be ridiculed. Not taking school or work seriously.	6. Laugh off your obligations. Change interests without any real reason for the change.
7. Emotionally insecure because parents were incompatible, or food and shelter were uncertain or appeared to be uncertain?	7. Felt hysterical when parents argued or when sustenance was in doubt.	7. Lack self-confidence or are strongly motivated to make money or to win friends on whom you can depend.

from her father, and they were usually amazed at her reactions to them. But, because of her emotional pattern she saw them as a class and not as they really were. She must revenge herself on all men in superior positions for her father's treatment of her, instead of being angry only at him and treating other men as different individuals. This reaction against her father became a set pattern, carried with her years later after her father was long dead and she herself was a grandmother.

The constellation of desires and impulses always seeks and always finds ways in life of choosing individuals and situations in its efforts to be gratified. It is this complex of desires pressing for satisfaction which seems, more than anything else, to account for the persistence and the accuracy with which everyone repeats in adult life the emotional patterns of his childhood. And it is these patterns which cause one to fit other people into classes and categories formed by these desires. Perhaps mother was kind and sister a bitter rival—hence, an exaggerated tendency to look for love from older women and to fear and compete with women of one's own age. To put it another way, the person becomes "conditioned" to hating, loving, competing, and so on, in relation to certain individuals in childhood and then fails to discriminate between them and others but reacts to whole classes or categories of persons of his own making.

Some people do not emphasize whole categories of people so much as they select a few actual persons in life with whom to repeat their family relationships . . .

If a child has good relationships with most members of his family, then he has enough such models for later life so that he will probably get along well with people. But if most or all his childhood relationships are bad, then he lacks the models for good relationships and will almost certainly have serious difficulties with people in later life. Probably no one can live long without at least one good emotional relationship without developing serious neurotic symptoms of some kind.

We have focused upon the effects of external influences such as deprivation, spoiling, cruelty and domination in forming the patterns. In some cases, internal factors are also of importance, as when the development is impaired not so much by these environmental emotional influences as by long illnesses, severe shocks or congenital deficiencies, be these physical, intellectual or emotional. The end result always depends upon an interaction of the congenital and the environmental factors.[2]

Of course, everyone has many predisposing influences in his growth: early environmental conditions, his culture, race, sex, bodily physique, health, muscular structure, glandular functioning, and intelligence. Only one of these factors, intelligence, can be treated here.

Intelligence

Anyone who examines an individual's adjustments to life's problems is bound to note that his intelligence shows some direct relationships. People of higher intelligence can handle problems which are beyond the capacities of those of lower intelligence.

Intelligence has been defined in numerous ways. One recommended definition is, "The degree of availability of one's experiences for the solution of immediate problems and the anticipation of future ones."[3]

Some investigators think that the intelligence of an individual is probably fixed at birth, and certain ones believe that it is determined even before birth through heredity.* Whatever its basic origin may be, a person's intelligence quotient, as measured by various I.Q. tests, may vary over a span of years. In general, however, the range in

---

* Certain investigators who believe that intelligence is inherited often dismiss the low-intelligence person whom they have tried to aid but could not with the remark: "He was gypped by the genes." The mechanisms of genes and chromosomes are blamed for the level of mental ability. However, if intelligence is wholly inherited, we still have much to learn about influences and factors in inheritance.

"Stoddard has cleverly observed that, while California state institutions over the past thirty years have sterilized 13,000 insane and feeble-minded persons, the follow-up, sixteen years later, of Terman's gifted children reveals that about 40 per cent of the parents of gifted children report mental abnormality among their near relatives. As Stoddard observed, 'Very likely a genius is himself safe in California, but it seems reasonable to say his near relatives had better watch out.'" See *Addresses and Discussions Presenting the 39th Yearbook*, NSSE, "Intelligence: Its Nature and Nurture," 1940, p. 49. Last paragraph quoted from John T. Wahlquist, "Is the IQ Controversy Philosophical?" *School and Society*, November 30, 1940.

which an individual falls usually remains fairly constant. We would not expect a child whose I.Q. tests at 80 one time to have an I.Q. of 130 ten years later. We would not be too surprised, however to find that his I.Q. had gone up to 100.

$$IQ = \frac{\text{Mental Age} \times 100}{\text{Chronological Age}}$$

An individual may go through adjustment experiences which result in a raising or lowering of his intellectual capacity. In the case of some children, favorable educational influences tend to raise the I.Q. The child who is encouraged to think independently, to use his intellectual curiosity, to have his ability challenged, and to gain satisfaction from his intellectual endeavors may have an increase in his intelligence quotient.[4] The amount of the increase and the exact conditions under which it does occur is still largely a problem for future research.

In the clinical areas of child guidance, many cases of "pseudo-feeblemindedness" have been reported. The child is really intelligent, but acts as though he were feebleminded. He is afraid to undertake any activity, even play. The problem to which he is adjusting by a paralyzing fear may be a dislike of school because of the presence of other boys who "beat him up" and otherwise intimidate him.[5]

In the field of education, intelligence tests have been useful in estimating the learning capacities of pupils. For example, idiots (IQ under 25), imbeciles (IQ, 25 to 49), and morons (IQ, 50 to 69) have such limited learning abilities that special long-term instruction is necessary to teach them the simplest habits. Idiots cannot learn to dress themselves or to say more than a few simple words. Imbeciles can learn to talk to a limited extent and even do simple manual labor under close supervision, but they cannot learn the value of money. Morons can learn to read and write and perform routine factory tasks, but they cannot be expected to go beyond the fifth grade in school.

Differences in levels of intelligence are often summarized as indicated in the table on this page.

Morons have normal impulses but they cannot foresee consequences of their own acts and so often get into trouble with the law. They buy goods on credit but forget to pay for them. Among the girls, the percentage of illegitimate motherhood is very high. Many of the boys are likely to become professional toughs or petty thieves, or transients. One study of 504 transients indicated that feeblemindedness was an important background factor in transiency. The transient group studied contained twelve times the proportion of mental defectives as the general population.[6]

The records of gifted children have shown that, contrary to popular opinion, they do not become insane or die young. They do have some emotional problems, but they tend to achieve happier and more successful lives than their less gifted brothers. Of the 1,400 gifted children selected as being the

TABLE 7-3

Feebleminded:	IQ	Percentage Population
Idiot	below 25, M.A. 2 years or under	
Imbecile	25– 49, M.A. 2–7 years	1
Moron	50– 69, M.A. 7–11 years	
Borderline	70– 79	5
Dull	80– 89	14
Average	90–109	60
Superior	110–119	14
Very superior	120–140	
Genius	above 140	6

brightest among 250,000 Californians by Dr. Lewis M. Terman in 1922, one half of the boys have entered the professions and a fourth are in semi-professional occupations or business.[7]

College students in general are of superior intelligence. However, when the scores on the American Council Psychological Examination were converted into equivalent IQ's by Arthur E. Traxler, using the recommended procedure, wide differences between colleges were found. The quartile and median IQ's at 323 colleges varied greatly, as shown by Table 7-4.[8] For admission to college, there is no unqualified answer to the question as to what intelligence quotient is necessary. The IQ needed depends upon the college considered.

Usually, we do not use the term IQ for adults. When children near the age of sixteen, it is difficult to compute the relation between mental development and chronological age. For adults, we prefer to specify the Percentile Rank (P.R.),* that is, the percentage of the population or group that ranks lower than the person tested. If a test shows that an applicant has a P.R. of 75, it means that 75 per cent of the population (or group) rank lower in the test than the applicant and 25 per cent rank higher. Similarly, if an applicant has a P.R. of 50 on a test, he is higher in the trait tested than 50 per cent

of the population and lower than 50 per cent; hence, he is average for that trait.

Obviously, intelligence has a direct bearing on the individual's possibilities of succeeding in a vocation, most particularly the professional level of occupation. In regard to adjustment, the relationship is not so clear-cut. The psychoneurotic adjustment group, for example, compares favorably in intelligence with the general population.[9]

One extensive investigation was undertaken of Canadian soldiers to ascertain the frequency of emotional instability of the mentally retarded and nonretarded at different intelligence levels. The clinical findings in the examination of over 30,000 men revealed definitely a higher incidence of emotional instability in men diagnosed as mentally retarded than in those diagnosed as nonretarded. It was noted that as the intelligence scores advanced, the frequency of instability tended to diminish. The evidence suggested that the rate of incidence of psychoneuroses and other emotional disturbance declines as the degree of intelligence advances, although this relation becomes much less evident in the upper ranges of intelligence.[10]

A review of the findings concerning the relation between intelligence and personality inventories for members of the military services of the United States, World War

---

* The term *centile* is also used by many authors. Whenever we use either *percentile* or *centile*, we should recognize the specific group to which the term applies. For example, a given college student's intelligence test score may place him below the 20th centile on a specific test administered to college students only. When the same or another intelligence test is administered to members of the general population, the same student may fall above the 70th centile for that group. On the other hand, centiles are a convenient device for showing a person's score on different kinds of tests such as intelligence, dominance, musical aptitude, and so on. Many psychographs or mental profiles are constructed on the basis of the centile concept.

TABLE 7-4

OTIS EQUATED IQ'S CORRESPONDING TO MEDIANS AND QUARTILES OR PERCENTILES OF TOTAL SCORES IN THE HIGHEST AND LOWEST OF 323 COLLEGES AND UNIVERSITIES ADMINISTERING THE 1937 EDITION OF THE AMERICAN COUNCIL ON EDUCATION PSYCHOLOGICAL EXAMINATION

Institution	Q_1 or P.R. 25	Md.	Q_3 or P.R. 75
Number 1	118	123	126
Number 323	87	94	102

Gross scores of sixteen sample occupational groups on the Army General Classification Test. The large dot near the center of the line indicates the median score; the upright bars the 25th and 75th percentiles; and the ends of the line the 10th and 90th percentiles. Note that the intelligence test scores of the highest scoring persons of the semi-skilled and skilled occupations overlap the scores of the lowest scoring members of the professions. The members of any one occupation differ widely in their intelligence test scores. There is, however, considerable evidence for occupational hierarchies of intelligence. The highest classes are usually found to be the professional, next the managerial group, then skilled trade, semi-skilled, and finally unskilled.—From N. Stewart, "A. G. C. T. Scores of Army Personnel Grouped by Occupation," **Occupations,** October 1947.

II, revealed little evidence to support the idea of a common intelligence factor in personality inventory scores and adaptability to military life. There was some evidence, however, to indicate that the relation between adjustment to military life and intelligence is stronger in the lower reaches of intelligence than in the levels above.[11]

In a study of college freshmen in which the "Problem Check-List" by Ross L. Mooney was used, a very low negative relationship was found between the number of problems checked and both grades and intelligence test scores, indicating a slight tendency for poorer students to have more problems. "Correlations with grades show a tendency for those who make the low grades to have more problems in adjusting to college work."[12]

Certainly, we can conclude that neither high intelligence nor low intelligence guarantees either good or poor adjustment. The person of high intelligence has the advantage of capacity for greater insight into his problems and ways of dealing with them. How he uses his capacity depends on other factors, such as his childhood influences.

Dealing with problem persons

Everyone finds it necesary to deal with problem personalities, but we can deal with them more easily if we think of each problem person as a person with a problem. The adjustments he is making were affected by many predisposing influences in his environment and within himself, some of which we can recognize.

In our ordinary associations with an employee or other acquaintance, we collect many facts about him. These facts become useful in understanding him when we have a system such as the adjustment concept for our thinking.

Usually we begin our thinking about a problem person with his childhood. We want to learn how he felt as a child. We want to learn how he reacted to the childhood situations and whether the childhood habits of adjustment still persist. We can, by direct and indirect questioning or by talking with his friends, learn about his childhood barriers and adjustments.

To understand someone's problem personality, we can begin our collection of facts with his childhood situations and think from them toward his present habits. The difficulty of doing this is often so great that we should think of our knowledge of the person as a hypothesis for dealing with him rather than as a certain conclusion. However, at this point we have a *working hypothesis* and can use it experimentally. Furthermore, we must always use some assumptions in dealing with problem people in practical situations. The point is that our assumptions should be not mere random guesses but the results of intelligent thinking.

The person who wishes to learn the mode of thinking used by clinical psychologists may start to do so on a simpler level, through the adjustment concept.

The psychological findings about a human being cannot be satisfactorily arranged in terms of some algebraic formula, but the facts can be thought of in patternful relationships, as suggested by the Seven-Phase Outline of Table 7-5. Such an arrangement of information about a problem person enables us to appreciate wherein he is a person with a problem and how his psychological background influences some of his conduct.

We should try to learn enough psychology to be able to see the significant adjustments which occur in the lives of those around us. Of course, if we have a professional responsibility for the mental health of others, we should read many books on psychology and attend clinics in order to become alert to the subtle influences in the lives of our maladjusted associates as well as in our own mental development. To attain such a working

TABLE 7-5

SEVEN PHASE OUTLINE FOR STUDY OF PERSONS WITH ADJUSTMENT PROBLEMS

1. The Barrier: the problem or problems, ostensible or actual. See Section 1 of Table 2-2, page 43, for a list of barriers.

2. Predisposing Influences: long-term factors such as endocrine glands, bodily health, cultural environment, or personalities in the home. These may be known or have to be assumed.

3. Precipitating Influences: relatively recent factors such as a failure, insult, or loss. They may be known or have to be assumed.

4. Direct Attack Adjustments: these are adjustments which the individual should have made, or might make in the future. (See Section I of Table 2-3, page 44.)

5. Positive Substitute Activities: these vary with the problem, the individual, the total situation, and so on. These adjustments tend to strengthen the personality for future problems but not usually for the problem involved in the adjustment under consideration. (See Section II of Table 2-3.)

6. Evasive or Retreat Adjustments: these also vary with the situation but they tend to weaken the personality for dealing with the immediate and with future problems. (See Sections III and IV of Table 2-3.)

7. How Others Can Help Him: analyzing the adjustments of others has little value unless the analysis enables us to contribute to the positive adjustments and personality well-being of the person analyzed. Suggestions depend upon many factors, but especially upon the relation of the analyst to the person analyzed.

knowledge of psychology, the reading of biographies is helpful. Every person, famous, infamous, or ordinary, has some tendencies and purposes that have grown out of his own unique adjustments to his barriers rather than from intellectual reactions only to his environment. Every novel, for example, is both a narrative about imaginery characters and, to some degree, a treatise on its author's psychological experiences. We can never really appreciate a writer's novel, a philosopher's philosophy, a businessman's managerial systems, a politician's political program,* or a parent's methods of child training until we know enough about the individual's personal history to see how his present convictions are tied up with his psychological background.

Facilitating the mental well-being of others means that the executive, parent, teacher, or counselor shall enable the individual to deal effectively and satisfyingly with the frustrating problems before him. Mental health is not a matter of intelligence, education or income, but rather a reaction to the world and ourselves in terms of our feelings and the ways in which we learn to deal with life's problems. Appropriate adjustments can be taught to most people. Efficiency in adjustment depends very greatly on the ability of an individual to continue varying his responses until success is achieved. The mentally ill person is one who has lost this ability.[13] Intelligent supervisors and counselors often show persons with adjustment problems how to vary their responses.

Executives of the more progressive managements often help their inadequately adjusted employees make better adjustments. The executive may ask a consultant such as a physician to interview the problem employee. When the consultant makes his report, the executive does not ask "What is the case history of the employee?" or "What is the specific variety of maladjustment?" Instead, the executive asks "How can we help him?"

To the executive, "helping the employee" usually means "How can the company improve the employee's work situation so that he may be able to become better adjusted as a person?" In order to improve the work situation, the employee may be given new work, a new supervisor, different associates, a leave of absence, or a better interpretation of his work situation. Chiefly, however, the enlightened executive expresses his encouragement by means of the genuine warmth of his interest in the employee. In many cases, the executive does not discuss the employee's problem with him but he offers the kind of understanding that is supportive to the employee in his attempts to achieve an effective satisfying adjustment. The executive does not attempt therapy. That function belongs to trained specialists outside the company such as psychiatrists. If therapy seems to be appropriate, he may help the employee find a therapist, but the employee himself, not the executive or the company, has responsibility for the treatment. The main function of the executive is that of a friend who counsels, encourages, and interprets in a permissive manner. He does not solve the employee's problems for him; he wants the employee himself to solve them.

The main need of many people is ordinary friendly counsel and reassurance. Even animal experiments show the value of that. When dogs are purposely made neurotic by experiment, the presence of a human being or a friendly dog in a room reassures the nervous animal so that he does not always have a neurotic attack. Similarly, people need assurance that what they are doing, they are doing well. They can often be given sympathetic intelligent friendship in learning suitable modes of action.

Encouragement should be supported by a plan of action

This kind of friendly support becomes especially effective when the person-with-a-problem is given a feasible plan of action

---

* Some clinical psychologists believe that Thomas Jefferson and Alexander Hamilton differed in their ideas about government partially because of their different adjustment influences. Jefferson wanted a weak central government with a maximum of rights for the state and the individual. Jefferson had a dominant father who had oppressed him and so he believed in freedom for the individual and the state. Hamilton, on the other hand, wanted a strong central government with a minimum of rights for the individual and the state. Hamilton himself felt keenly his own fatherlessness. Many biographies and autobiographies point out similar relationships between early adjustments and later convictions. A good example of a book in this field is L. Pierce Clark, *Lincoln, A Psycho-Biography*, Charles Scribner's Sons, New York, 1933.

rather than friendly encouragement only. Ordinary encouragement to many people means the making of quieting remarks such as "Oh, that isn't important—don't worry about it" or "Forget it. It won't work out that way." A plan of action may be far more supportive as indicated by this example:

Henry, a major in psychology at college, had completed his junior year and was working in a factory office during his summer vacation. His supervisor was an old college graduate who liked to encourage students. One day Henry told the supervisor about the problem that was bothering him to a serious extent. While in college he had fallen in love with a girl who came from a home where the father held a high-income executive position. The girl had three older brothers who had graduated from engineering schools and were making substantial incomes. To Henry, who came from a low-income home, the girl friend's family was in an "entirely different league." He was worried, disturbed, anxious. He had been planning to work for a doctorate in psychology but that long-term program did not seem to fit his needs. He was also older than most students, 25 because of military service.

Fortunately for Henry, his supervisor did not say: "Forget it. You're just as good as anybody else. Eventually, you'll make just as much money as the girl friend's father or her brothers." Nor did the supervisor try to analyze Henry's early home life in order to have him realize why he had developed a tendency toward anxieties concerning difficult adjustment problems.

Instead, the supervisor discussed with Henry his scholastic record and his hopes for himself. He had done especially well in mathematics and liked the higher mathematics courses. He had been reading about automation and wanted to get into that field but he lacked the necessary engineering background to do so. He wanted to make enough money soon in order to get married and have a nice home.

The supervisor pointed out that one of the most rapidly growing phases of automation is data processing through the use of the new electronic computers. Men with mathematical training and some business background are needed in this field and can make rapid advancement. The supervisor gave Henry introductions to men and publications in the field. Henry followed through on the idea and soon lost his anxieties about his qualities in compari-

son with those of the girl friend's father and her brothers. He had been given understanding and encouragement by the supervisor but the encouragement was backed up with an appropriate plan of action.

Practically, then, helping the employee who has a minor maladjustment means helping him to learn to feel that his supervisors or counselors and associates like him and will encourage him while he puts into effect a plan of action which will displace the handicapping habits that we call evasion and retreat. The study of case problems, limited though such study must be, may be helpful to the student.

If students will present for discussion adjustment problems that they have observed or experienced, they can make vital applications of important psychological principles. The following problems are examples of the kind that students have presented for class discussion:

1. Rose Horn feels sorry for Mr. Ray, her employer. As his secretary, she cannot help being aware that he is under a terrific strain at home. He often comes to the office in a bad humor and is impatient and sharp with Rose; but he is always sorry for it afterwards and is very uncomfortable in her presence. Rose would like to help him if she could, but because of his extreme embarrassment in her presence, she is afraid that she would lose her job if she showed her sympathy. What should she do?

2. Donald Center is working during the summer vacation in a toy factory employing twenty people in all. Jack Horton, son of the owner, works with Donald. Jack is insolent to everyone and does not hesitate to countermand the supervisor's orders whenever he desires. He makes himself generally most disagreeable, the more so because Mr. Horton always upholds Jack in any disagreement that arises. What can Donald do?

3. Jerry Tompkins is a graduate of a good engineering school and now works for one of the Ford agencies in the Middle West. He is the only college man in the organization and has made fine progress in two years. In his opinion, he now knows the job well enough to be able to work on his own initiative, but his manager insists on giving him detailed instructions for each day, treating him as though he had not yet

proved his ability. What can Tompkins do?

4. Alice Jaynes is private secretary to Mr. Smiley, a self-made, headstrong, and uneducated man, who has a very limited vocabulary and uses poor and ungrammatical English. In dictating to Alice, he invariably makes serious mistakes, which irritate her and, more important, worry her, since she does not know how to handle the situation. She feels that she should not send out such letters, yet she is afraid to correct Mr. Smiley.

5. Frank White works for an old-fashioned employer who is making very little money. Frank himself is progressive and is anxious to improve the business by a dozen different methods that seem self-evident to him, but when he suggests any changes, his employer invariably refuses to consider them on the ground that they are too risky. Frank is not in a position to go into business for himself and fears that he will be worse off if he changes his job. He is, however, restless and dissatisfied. How can he make his employer more sympathetic with his ambitions?

The reader may gain some practice in the study of adjustments through reading and discussing the six case problems of the next pages. Discussion should lead to additional suggestions which may be written into the *"Other"* spaces of the cases partially analyzed for the reader. Phase 7, *"How Others Can Help Him,"* should, of course, include *what he can do to help himself* as well as suggest appropriate plans of action for his consideration.

Acknowledgments and References

1. Gardner Murphy, *Personality,* Harper & Brothers, New York, 1947, pp. 72 f.
2. Leon J. Saul, *Emotional Maturity,* J. B. Lippincott Company, Philadelphia, 1947, pp. 168–170.
3. H. H. Goddard, "What Is Intelligence?" *Journal of Social Psychology,* Vol. 24 (1946), pp. 51–69.
4. Beth L. Wellman, "Our Changing Concept of Intelligence," *Journal of Consulting Psychology,* Vol. II, No. 4 (July–August 1938).
5. Phyllis Blanchard, "The Interpretation of Psychological Tests in Clinical Work with Children," *Mental Hygiene,* Vol. 25 (1941), pp. 58–75, presents a discussion of this variety of so-called feeblemindedness.
6. D. Kaplun, "Feeblemindedness as a Factor in Transiency," *Mental Hygiene,* Vol. 21 (1937), pp. 96–100.
7. *Science News Letter,* March 11, 1939, p. 153.
8. Arthur E. Traxler, "What Is a Satisfactory I.Q. for Admission to College?" *School and Society,* April 6, 1940.
9. James D. Page, *Abnormal Psychology,* McGraw-Hill Book Company, Inc., New York, 1947, p. 96.
10. John G. Dewan, "Intelligence and Emotional Stability," *American Journal of Psychiatry,* Vol. 104 (1948), pp. 548–554.
11. Albert Ellis and Herbert S. Conrad, "The Validity of Personality Inventories in Military Practice," *Psychological Bulletin,* American Psychological Association, Inc., Vol. 45, No. 5 (September 1948), p. 404.
12. Nora A. Congdon, "The Perplexities of College Freshmen," *Educational and Psychological Measurement,* Vol. 3 (1943), pp. 367–376.
13. C. D. Norton, "The Psychology of Human Adjustment," *Mental Health Observer,* Vol. 6, (1939), pp. 1–6.

PROJECTS

1. Now that you have become acquainted with adjustment and some of its predisposing influences, make a list of important predisposing influences in your own development of which you are aware. Include factors such as health, physique, early childhood conditionings, and work experiences. Discuss the list with a parent or friend who knows you intimately. To what extent do you agree and disagree on the factors mentioned? Are you sufficiently objective and mature in your thinking about yourself to discuss your characteristics without emotional disturbances on your part? Are you aware of any topics that are too painful for you to discuss?

2. Read some of the recent literature on the stability of the IQ. Prepare a list of all the possible factors which might result in the raising or lowering of an individual's IQ.

3. Very few persons can describe their own persistent affect fixations. The counselor must deduce them from the case history. Read the life history of a famous man or woman who described his early life in detail, particularly his home life. Can you define the persistent affect fixations in his life? How did they appear to influence his career?

4. List some of the persons who showed a genuine warmth of interest in you. How did they express it? If you feel that few persons have ever expressed a genuine interest in you, why do you suppose that you feel that way? To overcome such a feeling on your part, plan a program of action that may help you overcome your feeling.

COLLATERAL READINGS

Bellows, Roger M., *Psychology of Personnel in Business and Industry,* Prentice-Hall, Inc., New York, 1954, Chapter 5.

Burtt, Harold E., *Applied Psychology,* Prentice-Hall, Inc., New York, 1948, Chapters 4 and 5.

Lehner, George F. J. and Ella Kube, *The Dynamics of Personal Adjustment,* Prentice-Hall, Inc., New York, 1955, Chapter 15.

Maier, Norman R. F., *Psychology in Industry,* Houghton-Mifflin Company, Boston, 1955, Chapter 20.

Employee refuses to accept an offer for advancement

Mr. Denison is one of your best and most intelligent workers. You find that you must promote a man to the position of foreman over thirty of Denison's fellow-workers, and Denison seems to be the logical man for the position. When you explain the work to Denison and offer him the foremanship, he says that he is not interested in becoming a foreman. He claims that he would be unable to direct the work of former associates because they know him too well. You, however, are convinced that he really would like to have the promotion.

1. The Barrier:

   a. Ostensibly, his lack of self-confidence.
   b. Actually, a fear of ridicule. (Assumed on analyst's part.)
   c. *Other assumption:*

2. Predisposing Influences:

   a. Has he developed a rut for himself in his present job?
   b. Has he failed in some previous position of leadership?
   c. *Other:*

3. Precipitating Influences:

   a. Has his wife recently discouraged him about his ability?
   b. Did any of his associates talk about his possible promotion?
   c. *Other:*

4. Direct Attack Adjustments:

   a. Take the job and try to develop self-confidence.
   b. Mingle more often with superiors.
   c. *Other:*

5. Positive Substitute Activities:

   a. Throw energy into lodge activities to gain satisfaction.
   b. Put energy into the present job, doing it exceptionally well.
   c. *Other:*

6. Evasive or Retreat Adjustments:

   a. Find satisfaction in solitude.
   b. *Other:*

7. How Others Can Help Him:

   a. Have him supervise only a few coöperative employees until confidence has been gained.
   b. *Other:*

The impractical dreamer

George is young and ambitious. He has been out of school for one year but has been unable to settle down to the routine position which he holds with a business firm. He is forever conceiving impracticable get-rich-quick schemes that would, he imagines, give him easy money quickly. His ideas are so impracticable, however, that he is missing opportunities to lay a foundation for his future in the firm where he is now employed.

1. The Barrier:

   a. Tendency to dream because of poor social adjustment.
   b. Does not realize what success really is.
   c. *Other assumption:*

2. Predisposing Influences:

   a. Is he still in the adolescent age of daydreams?
   b. Does he feel insecure because his father and mother are incompatible?
   c. *Other:*

3. Precipitating Influences:

   a. Does he find his present work very boresome?
   b. Does he see better-educated workers pass him in advancement?
   c. *Other:*

4. Direct Attack Adjustments:

   a. Increase his social participation.
   b. Enjoy small successes rather than dream of spectacular success.
   c. *Other:*

5. Positive Substitute Activities:

   a. Associate with inferiors whom he can impress.
   b. Develop a hobby of an unusual kind.
   c. *Other:*

6. Evasive or Retreat Adjustments:

   a. Adopt an air of superiority and tell others how clever he is.
   b. *Other:*

7. How Others Can Help Him:

   a. Build up his self-confidence through social activities.
   b. Explain to him the "romances" and "adventures" of his present job.
   c. *Other:*

Sex repressions

Richard is a young man who works in a large office and is troubled with sordid thoughts, especially about girls. He comes from a small town and has never been away from home before. The apparent freedom in social relations between the young men and women in his office keeps him emotionally upset because he is too self-conscious to make satisfying acquaintances of the girls. He therefore thinks of girls in a strange, abnormal way.

1. The Barrier:

  a. Ostensibly, an unhealthy mental attitude.
  b. Actually, lack of normal associations.
  c. *Other assumption:*

2. Predisposing Influences:

  a. Was he ridiculed in childhood for associating with girls?
  b. Was he too closely supervised or pampered when young?
  c. *Other:*

3. Precipitating Influences:

  a. Has he been talking with maladjusted men about lewd aspects of sex?
  b. Is he still really living in the country?
  c. *Other:*

4. Direct Attack Adjustments:

  a. Associate with normal and well-balanced girls.
  b. Join a club and learn to dance.
  c. *Other:*

5. Positive Substitute Activities:

  a. Become intensely interested in his work and avoid women.
  b. Get a job in his home town.
  c. *Other:*

6. Evasive or Retreat Adjustments:

  a. Criticize the freedom in social relationships.
  b. Gain satisfaction through daydreaming.
  c. *Other:*

7. How Others Can Help Him:

  a. Invite him to attend a mixed social affair.
  b. *Other:*

Symbolic activity

Mr. Amulet is a middle-aged man of higher than average intelligence who suddenly realizes that he has become superstitious. He finds himself doing things for good luck or to ward off evil omens—superstitious acts which he would have scorned a few years ago. He tells himself that he must stop these foolish tendencies, but he claims that he cannot.

1. The Barrier:

  a. Ostensibly, a desire to avoid injury.
  b. Actually, an unadmitted fear of harm because of some act of which he is ashamed.
  c. *Other assumption:*

2. Predisposing Influences:

  a. Many emotional experiences have given him a sense of guilt.
  b. Have friends impressed him with the efficacy of their pet charms?
  c. *Other:*

3. Precipitating Influences:

  a. Does he believe he escaped an accident because he obeyed a "premonition"?
  b. Has he recently committed an immoral act that has caused him to fear disgrace?
  c. *Other:*

4. Direct Attack Adjustments:

  a. Study superstitions and how they may be ways to compensate for unadmitted mistakes.
  b. Visit a psychiatrist.
  c. *Other:*

5. Positive Substitute Activities:

  a. Take part in religious activities as a means to adjustment.
  b. *Other:*

6. Evasive or Retreat Adjustments:

  a. Immerse himself in the mystical.
  b. Become intoxicated in order to forget his superstitions.
  c. *Other:*

7. How Others Can Help Him:

  a. Explain to him how one of your fears symbolized feeling of guilt.
  b. *Other:*

The self-conscious employee

Perkins is thirty years old and is a mechanic in a garage. He is sensitive and becomes easily confused when the foreman, Graves, comes into the room where he is working. Graves knows that Perkins is a good worker, but when Graves stops to watch Perkins, the latter becomes flustered and cannot work efficiently.

1. The Barrier:

 a. Habit of dealing with people by thinking of himself.
 b. *Other assumption:*

2. Predisposing Influences:

 a. Was he reared by parents who criticized forwardness?
 b. Was he disciplined severely and made to think of himself as unwanted?
 c. *Other:*

3. Precipitating Influences:

 a. Has Graves ridiculed him about his work?
 b. Was he recently ignored when he tried to be friendly?
 c. *Other:*

4. Direct Attack Adjustments:

 a. Become active in an organization to develop his self-confidence.
 b. Entertain the boss socially.
 c. *Other:*

5. Positive Substitute Activities:

 a. Find another job.
 b. Supervise his physical inferiors, such as children.
 c. *Other:*

6. Evasive or Retreat Adjustments:

 a. Criticize boss and firm.
 b. Daydream and picture himself a hero.
 c. *Other:*

7. How Others Can Help Him:

 a. Praise him for his "little" social successes.
 b. *Other:*

Behavior varies with the situation

Miss Palmer is considered a competent "complaint clerk" in the public utility office where she works. She is a pleasant and convincing talker. In the homes of her friends, however, she cannot carry on a conversation. She seems to have no opinion on any subject. When she is asked why she isn't more sociable, she says she just doesn't know what to say or talk about.

1. The Barrier:

 a. Early conditioning or a complex arising from an inferior social position.
 b. *Other assumption:*

2. Predisposing Influences:

 a. As a child, was she allowed to take part in family conversations?
 b. Were her parents socially inferior in the community?
 c. *Other:*

3. Precipitating Influences:

 a. Do her friends tell her that she is a wallflower?
 b. Has a confidence been betrayed by one of her "friends"?
 c. *Other:*

4. Direct Attack Adjustments:

 a. Tell her friends how she feels and ask them to help her gain confidence.
 b. Take an interest in other people and talk to them about themselves.
 c. *Other:*

5. Positive Substitute Activities:

 a. Lead a group of younger girls who will respect her.
 b. Express herself in activities that do not require conversation.
 c. *Other:*

6. Evasive or Retreat Adjustments:

 a. Talk about and criticize the girls whom she knows.
 b. Adopt an air of silent superiority.
 c. *Other:*

7. How Others Can Help Her:

 a. Do not give her advice—just show by your manner that you like her as she is.
 b. *Other:*

CHAPTER EIGHT

The counseling interview

Many persons assume that the guidance of human relationships can never become a science. They imagine that it can never be more than an art. Now, however, recent investigations by psychologists have shown that the scientific knowledge in this area can be enlarged. It is no longer necessary to assume that the facilitating of personality growth, as in the interview, must remain a wholly subjective field. It has been found possible to investigate experimentally the effectiveness of different counseling techniques. We have moved, to some extent, from the realm of opinion into the realm of science.

The extent to which ability in interviewing is needed in our modern civilization is indicated by the numbers of workers in the professions and businesses who do interviewing. It is estimated that there are about 2,500,000 persons occupying executive and supervisory positions in business and industry who spend from 50 to 90 per cent of their time in conferring with others. In addition to these, we have about 1,127,845 teachers and other school people, 403,793 nurses, 192,317 physicians, 181,226 lawyers, and 168,419 clergymen who discuss personal problems with counselees as a part of their daily work.[1]

The problems that employees bring to the counselor in industry vary widely, depending upon factors such as the responsibilities and reputation of the counselor. Most counseling done in industry deals with the work and the work situation. Counsel concerning personal problems is usually sought from persons outside the company. A few companies do provide counselors who deal with personal rather than work problems. As background for our thinking about employees' personal problems, let us take a look at the problems reported by Clifford H. Peace, Pastor-counselor, R. J. Reynolds Tobacco Company, Winston-Salem, North Carolina. During the month of January, 1955, a total of 33 employees with personal problems came to him as pastor-counselor for a total of 67 counseling sessions. He reported an average sampling to the American Management Association, in part, as follows:

146

A young lady came because, since her seventh year, she had not passed more than two consecutive nights without screaming in her sleep to the degree that she awakened her family. A man in his middle fifties came because he had been seized by a terrifying and unyielding anxiety that was interfering with his work. Another young lady in her twenties came because she felt uncomfortable socially and wanted to discuss her dating problems, and a middle-aged woman came whose estranged alcoholic husband kept making return visits while drunk, creating great emotional distress.

The next visitor was a woman in her middle thirties, the mother of two children, whose husband had fallen in love with another woman whom he refused to give up—and this wife deeply loved and wanted her husband. Then came a man in his late thirties, whose marriage to an emotionally immature woman had gone on the rocks and who was harassed by her incessant demands that he return, feeling that he could not and should not; a man in his early sixties who had been in a psychiatric hospital was trying to readjust to his job, and wanted the help of religion in doing so, and an attractive woman of 40 who felt trapped in a loveless marriage, who had developed a strange physical malady which her doctor believed was related in origin to her emotional anguish.

A woman in her sixties, a member of whose family was in a psychiatric hospital, felt that it might have been her fault. A middle-aged Negro woman felt an overwhelming sense of guilt, which was breaking her. A man in his early thirties, a budding alcoholic, was unhappy in his job and with his boss, while another of about the same age wanted to discuss the strange and dangerous conduct of a brother-in-law, who turned out to be in the early stages of a mental disease. . . .

One session was with a man whose supervisor had called to say that this employee was depressed to the degree that it was interfering with his work—because his wife and child had left him three months before. Again, a mother of three children wanted to get from a night to a day shift because she feared that her alcoholic husband was not taking proper care of the children while she was at work. A lawyer referred my next counselee, a young wife and mother considering a divorce because of her husband's immorality, and another wife in her twenties came because she could not wean her husband away from his possessive mother. . . .

A Negro woman of 42, in her seventeenth pregnancy, whose alcoholic and sadistic husband abused her and her children; a middle-aged white woman who was caught in the net of an illicit love affair from which she could not extricate herself; a middle-aged father, greatly concerned about the conduct of a daughter over whom he felt that he had lost all control; a rehabilitated alcoholic, who is making good but who came by for a little encouragement; and a man who wanted to discuss means by which our city could better meet juvenile needs. Finally, there was a wife whose thoughts of murdering her husband had become so fixed that she was on the verge of acting on them. . . .

These were not all of our 12,000 employees who had personal problems during the month. They were not the only ones who talked to personally interested supervisors or to members of the Personnel and Medical departments. These were the ones who came to the office of the pastor-counselor to talk about the things which troubled them. They have been listed just as they came. It was about an average month. During the last five and one-third years, 1,561 different persons have voluntarily come to my office for a total of 3,280 counseling sessions of an hour each. . . .

Does this mean that the employees of the R. J. Reynolds Tobacco Company are more emotionally unstable than other employees? The record tends to indicate that they are not. . . .

As this account of my counseling will indicate, we do have an awareness of the emotional problems of our employees and have established a facility whereby they may pursue a problem-solving approach to their emotional difficulties. There is a place where, through therapeutic listening, our people can communicate and drain off such tensions as anxiety, anger, grief, and guilt; where they may seek a clarification of their confusion in feeling and motivation; and where they can find ways of laying hold on a power by which they can live more adequately and creatively.[2]

Types of interviews

Many interviews are simple in nature and do not involve any special psychological insight or skill. Others are complex and require a high level of professional training. When interviews are classified in relation to the kind of individual problem involved, they are likely to fall into the four varieties.

information, judgment, skill, and *adjust-ment.* For example, some persons, who come to the counselor may need or seek a knowledge of facts. Such interviews are relatively simple to conduct. Other persons have all the facts they need but have difficulty in making a satisfactory judgment or decision about the facts. An example would be an employee who asks the personnel man whether it would be advisable for him to buy a home.[3]

In some cases, the interviewee has the essential facts and has reached a decision but feels that he lacks skill in putting the decision into effect. An example would be the employee who knows that he merits an increase in pay and has decided to ask for it but lacks skill in presenting his request. Again, many supervisors, although they know how they should treat employees, lack skill in dealing with them effectively. Role-playing, as explained in Chapter 21, may be helpful to them.

Adjustment problems are of course rather deep-seated in the personality structure and require considerable insight on the part of the interviewer. Counselors who deal with the more common adjustment problems such as those exemplified in vocational guidance, marriage counseling, discipline of the errant employee in industry, merit rating review of the employee, and other interviews that involve an understanding of the dynamics of behavior know that a knowledge of the fundamental principles in interviewing is essential.

One of the interviewer's major needs is a basic conceptual pattern of thinking that gives meaning to his observations and judgments concerning the counselee's behavior. The specific conceptual pattern recommended, that of adjustment, has been discussed in preceding chapters. In this chapter, we shall review some of the common types of human relations problems found in the world of work in order to emphasize certain helpful principles, especially for the counselor of employees.

Some counseling should be done indirectly without an interview

First of all, we must repeat that any act, as an act, has little significance. The *meaning* of the act in relation to the life and adjustment history of the "actor" is the important factor. If we can visualize the individual in his adjustment perspective we can often—but not always—improve our techniques in dealing with him or learn to accept him as he is. The several stages in the handling of problem personalities may be illustrated in the case of the typical supervisor who has a difficult employee.

Mr. Norton, a foreman, directly supervises John Teeter. Mr. Norton is a healthy, hard-working leader and tries to please his employees. John, an employee, is irritable and appears to be impossible to please when he is in his "moods," as other employees call his periods of unusual irritability. Mr. Norton is certain that John is an exceptionally good worker but he realizes that the other employees have difficulties with him. The employees believe that John's wife is very domineering and that John is trying to make himself feel better by "taking his poison out of himself and putting it on the hides" of his fellow employees. What can Mr. Norton, the foreman, do?

Theoretically, at least, attempted correction by systematic analysis is the best solution to any problem in dealing with our fellows. In some cases, however, it may be a very impractical course of action. Obviously Mr. Norton cannot go to Mr. Teeter and say: "John, we have decided that you mistreat us at times because you have marital troubles. We have therefore arranged for you and your wife to visit a psychiatrist regularly, and he will attempt to find the cause of your irritability in order that you may treat us decently!" John is not a psychotic. At worst he may be a psychoneurotic. His supervisor must decide whether he will attempt to help John make a better adjustment to his problem, or whether his disturbing conduct shall be ignored.

In John Teeter's case, Mr. Norton should

not initiate an interview with him in order to discuss his home problems. Rather, he might try to obtain more information regarding John's history, and then observe the ways in which he deals with his problems. He might recognize that John is very lonely and is without adequate ego-support. This knowledge and point of view might enable him to be friendly toward John, not in order to gain his favor, but in order to assist him in attaining feelings of self-worth in the work situation. If John's growth in the work situation strengthens his personality so that he feels able to deal with nonwork problems, he may be able to adjust more adequately to the home situation.

Mr. Norton might project himself into John's situation, the psychological process of *empathy* rather than *sympathy.* Such a method of procedure on the part of the supervisor would be better than for him to assume that he is a psychotherapist who can change an employee's adjustment pattern in one or two interviews.

Of course, when an employee's complaints and irritability are caused by tensions that are brought about by his resistance to some change or condition in the work situation, he should have an interview, or, at least, a chance to air his troubles in a permissive, non-threatening situation. Reducing his emotional tension may enable him to face the situation and adjust to it.

Psychological analysis of employees gives the supervisor insight into the behavior of employees who are irritable, who insist upon following red tape, who butt in, or who find fault only. Insight, good sportsmanship, and skill in handling troublesome men differentiates the supervisory leader from the supervisory boss. Of course, many supervisors and personnel men are too busy to use systematic, constructive effort to help the employee make better adjustments. The troublesome person is merely avoided. Many of our daily problems in human relations are dealt with in this manner.

An ordinary supervisor may avoid contacts with employees whom he does not like, or he may simply compel them to yield to his wishes. His power to discharge often enables him to deal with many disliked employees or unpleasant situations by compulsion rather than by skill. The method of compulsion by means of repeated threats of discharge is an old but declining method of supervision.

In some cases, negative adaptation through classification according to responsibility is necessary. Obviously, some peculiar people are not readjustable or improvable. They must be accepted. Sometimes the only feasible method of treatment is that of avoidance. Many such persons are not dangerous enough to be institutionalized, nor are they sufficiently sick to be treated by a physician, a psychiatrist, or a clinical psychologist. People who must deal with "cussed personalities" learn to tolerate them by classifying them as "patients" who are not responsible for their acts.

For example, if Mr. Norton were a member of a class in clinical psychology and were to visit a state hospital for the mentally ill, he would be likely to have a manic patient hurl epithets at him. The patient might curse him, call him wild names, and even spit at him. Yet Mr. Norton would not feel insulted, because he would know that the patient was irresponsible. He would call the patient insane, pity him, hope that he might be cured. A person who has some adequate knowledge of the dynamics of human behavior will make similar allowances for those maladjusted persons with whom he comes in contact.

We all have to learn to get along with irritable superiors, associates, friends, and relatives. Sometimes we do it by classifying them as not responsible for their conduct. Many married people react in this manner to mates who suffer from functional disorders. College students learn to react in the same way toward the unreasonable mother who is having difficulty in passing through the climacteric period. However, frequently repeated periods of irritability condition some persons against their loved ones to such an extent that an objective reaction is impossible. In some cases temporary separation may be necessary. Negative adaptation is the most natural and the easiest adjustment to the problem personality, although an insight-meaning adjustment is better. However, the insight-meaning approach to changes in human behavior is possible only in so far as one's reactions are controlled by the cortex of his brain, that is, in so far as intellect, rather than conditionings or strong emotions, governs the behavior. The correction of behavior may require reconditioning of a mental habit, the learning of a new mental habit, the analysis and redirection of subconscious influences, or the control of strong emotions, that govern the behavior. If the correction of behavior does require reconditioning of a mental habit, the analysis and redirection of subconscious influences, or the control of strong emotions, the assistance of the specialist in psychopathology is essential.

Fortunately, most everyday problems in human relations can be solved by the persons involved. Relatively few supervisors or employees need the services of the clinical psychologist. However, the trained personnel counselor should be able to assist and positively develop many persons who are sources of irritation in an organization for years before they grow to the point of needing to be institutionalized or die. It is important for us to realize that any psychological insight and skill acquired by executives, supervisors, and personnel men will be valuable in dealing with the employees who need counseling.

When the interviewee initiates the interview

The principles of the counseling interview vary somewhat with the type of interview and the extent to which the counselee seeks and needs the interview. In the personnel offices of industry, counseling interviews are of two broad classes: those conducted at the initiative of the counselee and those conducted at the initiative of the counselor. The former type is exemplified by the employee who comes to the personnel man and says that he would like to be transferred to another job, to arrange for a loan, to discuss a health problem, to ask the personnel man's advice in regard to chances for a promotion, or some other personal matter of direct or indirect importance to the employer. The latter type of interview, the counselor-initiated variety in industry, is exemplified by a disciplinary problem, as in the case of the employee who has violated a safety rule, the annual review of the employee's merit ratings, or an interview with a labor union steward concerning a union member's conduct. In this discussion, we shall treat chiefly the counselee-initiated type of interview, because it often calls for a knowledge of psychological dynamics. The counselee seeks help and, to some extent, is usually anxious to coöperate in the solution of his problem.

Although there are two principal methods of counseling, *directive* and *nondirective,* a vast number of adaptations of these methods can be made at the discretion of the counselor. It is his responsibility to employ as much or as little direction as he believes will be beneficial to a particular client. Even though some counselors use mainly one method of counseling, they adapt their technique to each situation. Neither method nor technique is peculiar to any one type of problem. Both main types are used today in business organizations,[4] psychological clinics, marriage clinics, and in vocational guidance.

Directive counseling is the older method. It assumes the counselor to be wise and understanding enough to control the interview from the time the client presents himself. The counselor takes the initiative throughout, asks leading questions, interprets the interviewee's answers and reactions to him, and offers advice or actual instructions for the solution of the problem.

Nondirective counseling as in psychotherapy, on the other hand, is interviewee- or client-centered. In psychotherapy, the therapist is not authoritarian in any respect. His function is not to interpret the interviewee's problem to him or to offer advice for the solution of the problem, but to create an atmosphere in which the client may talk through his difficulties and thereby get sufficient insight into his problems so that he may solve them for himself. To this end, good rapport and a permissive atmosphere are essential. Because the client has done the work of ascertaining the cause of his difficulties and has decided upon his own solution, it is claimed that he is far more likely to carry his self-chosen behavior through to a successful conclusion than under the older method.

The goal of nondirective counseling differs from that of directive in that it aims toward the greater independence and integration of the individual rather than hopes that such qualities will accrue if the counselor assists in solving the problem. The personality development of the individual and not the problem is the focus. The aim is not to solve one particular problem, but to assist the individual to *grow,* so that he can cope with the current problem and with later problems in a better-integrated fashion.[5]

One outstanding characteristic of the nondirective interview is the manner in which the counselor responds to feeling. He accepts without surprise or disapproval anything that the client tells him and replies noncommittally to the feeling behind the words in order to encourage the client to explore his problem more deeply. Often the reply is limited to "M-hm," or "Yes." Often it is simply a rewording of the idea which the client has expressed. Ideally this effects a crystallization of that specific facet of the problem in the client's mind, and after clarification of the various phases, self-understanding is ultimately attained.

"Effective counseling consists of a definitely structured, permissive relationship which allows the client to gain an understanding of himself to a degree which enables him to take positive steps in the light of his new orientation." The interview technique developed by Rogers and his students for bringing about such relationships, is most often described as "nondirective" for the reason that authoritarian and persuasive approaches have been discarded, and because no satisfactory positive designation has yet been found to express in a word what the counselor does and what the client experiences. In using the term, therefore, it is important to recognize its descriptive limitations and to emphasize that this counseling procedure implies more than passive listening and mere "not directing." Rogers defines the therapist's function as "not to pass judgment, but to clarify and objectify the client's basic attitudes." In order to do this, the counselor must work toward the skills involved in understanding what the client has tried to express, in verbal restatement or "recognition" of feeling in terms which the client can and will accept; and in control of the counselor's own impulse toward suggestion and premature interpretation. Even more fundamental is acceptance by the counselor of the client's right to self-determination, and belief in his capacity for constructive choice on the basis of insight rather than guidance.[6]

The wide acceptance by psychologists of nondirective interviewing, particularly in psychotherapy, as developed by Carl R. Rogers, is indicated by many books and articles published about the technique and its underlying principles. One recent issue of the *Journal of Consulting Psychology,* for example, is largely devoted to it. Some of the findings from the significant researches of a project of "parallel studies" are reported in the issue.

The ultimate aim of these "parallel studies" is to contribute toward the establishment of psychotherapy on a scientific basis. The investigators at the Counseling Center of the University of Chicago have sought to achieve this goal by formulating specific concepts of personality dynamics so that these concepts may be recognized and measured as to the degree of their presence as revealed in the interviews. Some of these concepts, for example, are self-regarding at-

SELF-REGARDING ATTITUDES ———   UNDERSTANDING AND INSIGHT —.—.—
ACCEPTANCE OF AND RESPECT ·········   MATURITY OF BEHAVIOR   — — —
FOR SELF   DEFENSIVENESS   —//—

Five objective measures applied to one successful counseling case. Note particularly how the curve for defensiveness declined as the curves for self-regarding attitudes and for acceptance of and respect for self improved.—From Nathaniel J. Raskin, "An Objective Approach to the Study of Psychotherapy," **American Scientist,** Vol. 37, No. 3 (July 1949), pp. 410–413.

titudes, acceptance of and respect for self, understanding and insight, maturity of behavior, and defensiveness. An individual is rated at each interview on all of these five aspects of his personality. Thus personality

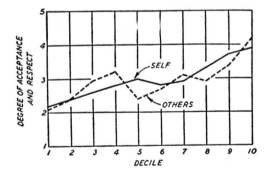

The relationship between the mean ratings on the "self" scale and on the "others" scale for ten cases combined. —From Elizabeth T. Sheerer, "The Relationship Between Acceptance of Self and Acceptance of Others," **Journal of Consulting Psychology,** American Psychological Association, Inc., Vol. 13, No. 3 (June 1949), pp. 174–175. Copyright, 1949, by the American Psychological Association, Inc.

changes in the series of interviews are more scientifically detected and measured; exact comparisons of the individual's reactions are made possible. Therapists, by employing the findings of these studies, will be able to control and evaluate more closely the progress of the individual through the psychotherapeutic process of counseling. Most important, the nature of successful psychotherapy can be more specifically and exactly defined.[7]

A diagram of five objective measures applied to one successful counseling case is shown in the figure on this page. The diagram shows that, at the beginning of therapy, defensiveness was great and acceptance of and respect for self was low, and that, at the end of the therapeutic sessions, acceptance of and respect for self had increased and defensiveness had diminished. Apparently as acceptance of and respect for self increases, there is less need for defensive behavior patterns.[8]

The researchers have quantified many aspects of the counseling interview never before analyzed in statistical terms. One study by Elizabeth T. Sheerer, for example, dealt with certain relations between the individual's concept of himself and his feeling toward others. Miss Sheerer found that when the individual's statements about himself were rated on a five-point scale, the average for the first interview was 2.2. The statements about other people rated 2.6. In the last interview the statement on self rated 3.9 while those statements reflecting on others had gone up to 3.8.

It was found to be possible to improve acceptance of and respect for the self by psychological treatment. There was also a closer relation between regard for self and regard for others after the finish of the treatment period.

Some of the implications of Miss Sheerer's findings were stated as follows:

The findings of this study appear to have implications that are at once commonplace and startling. The central conclusion is that one's attitudes toward others are related, to a decidedly significant degree, to the attitudes one holds towards one's self. In one sense, this is common knowledge. If we are to take it seriously, however, it might mean that change in attitudes of acceptance toward others can come about basically only through change in attitudes toward self. If we apply this to some of the problems of social psychology, it might mean that increased acceptance of minority groups, foreigners, and the like, could best be achieved by some type of group therapy which would tend to alter the individual's acceptance of and respect for himself. It might mean that in situations of industrial tension, or professional friction, the most effective means of approach would be through dealing with the attitudes of the person toward himself, rather than devoting our energies to the expressions of, and descriptions of, the external "causes" of the tension.

In any event the two central facts which emerge from this study promise to have considerable significance for social psychology as well as for our understanding of personality. That the individual's evaluation of himself and his worth as a person, can be significantly altered by the therapeutic process initiated by client-centered therapy is one of these facts; the other is that the individual's evaluation of others—the degree of acceptance and respect he feels for them—is significantly related to his attitude toward himself.[9]

Successful nondirective therapy demands that the client have intelligence above the borderline level, and that he be dissatisfied with his current adjustment.[10] Intelligence is necessary for the development of insight, a prerequisite to a better adjustment, and a certain amount of distress is necessary to impel the client to work earnestly for a better adjustment. Neurotic persons who have adjusted to their symptoms are poor prospects for improvements; and psychotics, because they are out of touch with reality, cannot be treated by this method. Most executives do not have the time or the training to use nondirective techniques, but many would benefit from a study of them.

Typical of sound nondirective counseling is the following excerpt from an actual case phonographically recorded and quoted in Rogers, *Counseling and Psychotherapy:*

S263. I find myself reacting quite strongly to the war situation. I have this very definite feeling—that if I were to be involved, that is, inducted into the army—

C263. M-hm.

S264. I feel it would not only be catastrophic to me in my present condition, but even if I were to have a cure in the meanwhile—my healthy ideals have always been that of—well, an abhorrence of regimentation, and I feel a love of individual initiative and private enterprise—that sort of thing, which seems to make a war situation very much intolerable to me. I had thought I would not be called (gives his reasons), but now I think I might be called, so it's had a very disturbing effect on me.

C264. You feel that would be just more than you could take.

S265. Even if I were up to my psychological ideal, I would find that such a life would be absolutely against my grain—the way I've been raised—the ideals that I've been taught to hold to, and the individual way of life that I have always pursued myself. (Pause.) So I'm reacting very much to that situation.

C265. M-hm. You've found it quite upsetting to you?[11]

An example of counseling by an executive who thinks in terms of adjustment

The personnel man or executive who has the adjustment point of view regarding the problem employee thinks of him as an employee with a problem. The psychologically sensitive executive does not usually lecture employees on their adjustments. He does not, as a rule, use any psychological jargon in dealing with them. He is likely to use a directive rather than the time-consuming nondirective technique. Occasionally, however, the trained executive may explain the adjustment idea to an exceptionally intelligent employee, such as a dissatisfied college graduate who needs counseling. Some of the principles set forth in preceding chapters are illustrated in the example shown on pages 159–163, typical of the college-educated employee who has a problem in adjustment and is being counseled by a trained personnel man.

A procedure such as this can be used successfully only by a high-grade executive who can explain mental habits and adjustments in an intelligent and sincere manner. He must be able to phrase his analyses in ways that the employee will understand and respect.

One important objective to be kept in mind by the executive is that his attempts to motivate the employee must be economically as well as psychologically sound. This means that the executive's function is not that of apologizing for the economic system, whatever it is, but to give the employee a sense of participation in the evolving economic scheme. Toward this end, the executive may point out unsolved problems of industry which the dissatisfied intelligent employee can help solve by his own direct attack adjustments involved in his own job.

The counselor-initiated interview

The disciplinary interview. The executive who has just cause for severely criticizing a subordinate often uses the old-fashioned method of threatening to discharge the man. However, the threat of discharge is not nearly so severe as some of the dramatic methods that are used by executives who have the knack of disciplining men. These experts in chastising men use dramatic situations, such as calling the errant employee into the boss's office and having him sit in the executive's chair. Then the executive plays the part of the employee who is to be disciplined. He makes a full confession, wherein he presents all the facts in the offense and asks the acting chief to make a decision and recommend the justified punishment or discipline. Such methods are forceful, but they do not strengthen the personality as in the counseling interview.

The counseling interview is often used in disciplinary problems, as illustrated in the sample problem on pages 164–166.*

Such a procedure requires an executive who tries to build employees by allowing them to build themselves. He must be normal in his adjustments, since the poorly adjusted executive will try to impress the errant employee with his authority—that is, he will make the employee feel inferior rather than a colleague of his. The educator type executive does not care to punish employees—he wants to enable them to use present situations to strengthen their personalities in order that they may be able to meet future problems more adequately. American businessmen are just beginning to study and practice skills in dealing with employees by methods that are more subtle than the older method of threat of discharge. Psychological approaches are more effective than force.

* The conversation presented in this example of the interview for motivation may sound unnatural to some readers. However, as previously stated, each interviewer must use techniques that are spontaneous. In real life, this example is not so unreal as it may sound.

The counseling interviewer sees human beings in terms of their ongoing activities and emotions. He has a dynamic concept of people. He visualizes them as making adjustments to their changing environments. He notes their resultant attitudes, emotions, drives, habits, and general behavior patterns. In his study of counselees, he sets up working hypotheses as to relationships between current behavior and past events. He checks these for himself by further questioning in the hope that the persons counseled will themselves discover the ways in which they have been dealing with their adjustive situations.

He tries to discover the factors that have influenced them in the past, and how their present ongoing activities may be directed into new channels that will give them a richer self-expression which will be of value to the group as well as to themselves. He does not want to remake human beings— he tries to help them to utilize their present tendencies for positive adjustment to life's problems.

Principles that often apply to the counseling interview

1. First of all, the specific problem volunteered by a counselee may be only a small part of the actual problem. Some interviewees find it very difficult to present their own problems, even though they seek an interview for that purpose. Complete frankness is often potentially embarrassing. The employee who calls on a personnel man to ask for a transfer to another job may like his present work, but he may dislike his supervisor or a fellow employee. To state the nature of his actual dislike might not be tactful. Similarly, the man who realizes that his poor health is partially caused by or related to his inability to live happily with his neurotic mother does not, as a rule, begin the interview with a statement to that effect. Such admissions are too painful to be handled in a casual manner. The good interviewer will sense such withholdings of facts and open an easy way for a gradual revealing of the significant facts. Sometimes the counselor can sense the counselee's unvoiced questions and discuss them without actually mentioning them.

2. The counselee's willingness to express his thoughts is influenced by the extent of his confidence in the counselor. Many counselees test the counselor by asking him questions the answers to which are not applicable to his immediate problem, but indicate to him the extent to which the counselor might be able to answer his personal question. Every counselor, when a counselee first appears for an interview, tends to get into the habit of asking himself: "What does this person think of me as a counselor?" "Does he have confidence in my ability to understand his problem and to view him objectively?" "Does he believe that I will keep his confidences?" "Is it easy for him to talk to me?" and similar questions. The wise counselor constantly seeks improvement of his techniques of establishing rapport with the counselee.

3. The outward manner and facial expression of the counselor should be friendly and relaxed. The counselor who has the art of getting repressed people to talk about personal matters has a rested, unhurried manner. He does not show surprise or shock at anything the counselee says or discloses. He evaluates most unpleasant facts objectively without any demonstration of annoyance or disgust. He sits in a relaxed manner and gives the impression that he has nothing to do other than to listen to the counselee. This relaxed manner during the interview also prepares the way for the counselor to end the interview whenever he desires. When he changes from a relaxed to a tense busy manner, the counselee usually realizes that the interview is over.

Some counselors improve their interviewing techniques by means of motion-picture studies of themselves in an actual or simulated interview. Every interviewer who sees and hears sound motion pictures of himself in action is certain to see how he can improve his techniques.

4. The trained counselor uses diagnostic instruments, such as psychological tests. He does not use them, however, in the mechanical manner of the psychometrician, whose use of tests is limited to the selection of applicants for jobs. Rather, he thinks of tests as opportunities to observe the counselee in a sample work situation—to note his grasp of instructions and his reaction to failure or success. The testee's scores are viewed as clues to possible strong points. Furthermore, demonstrations of the counselee's ability in action are more conclusive than mere test indications. Test findings are interpreted in relation to the individual's total situation.

5. During a counseling interview, the counselor listens for recurrent ideas, themes, or repeated statements in the counselee's conversation. Questions which the counselor asks himself are the following: Does the subject resent persons of authority, of higher education, of the opposite sex, or some other class of persons or institutions? What kinds of inadequacy or self-depreciation does he mention with strong emotionality? What topics, apparently incidental to the main problem, are repeated so often that, though apparently incidental, they obviously have a bearing on the crucial problem?

6. The aggressive counselee who has a disagreeable manner indicates that he has a problem which has advanced beyond his control. If he berates the counselor or ridicules his profession or business, the counselor should maintain his poise and look for the counselee's unexpressed problem. The counselor need not bother to defend himself if he has learned how to use a soft answer to turn away wrath.

The counselor does not blame the counselee for his past actions or present difficult situation. If the counselee is at fault, he should discover it for himself or be led to make the discovery. A good interviewer believes that all people have the right to make mistakes and that psychological growth often takes place most rapidly when we recognize and deal constructively with our own mistakes.

7. The counselor does not try to remake the personality of the counselee. To the counselor, most persons are pretty good as they are. Some persons, of course, can redirect into more effective channels their established tendencies, but the life style is so firmly established that a remaking of the fundamental personality pattern is impractical and usually undesirable. The advisee usually needs encouragement rather than criticism. The good counselor puts the emphasis on the counselee's strong points rather than his weaknesses.

8. The advisee needs a plan of action more than a mere review of what happened. The review of what happened is often a necessary step in the development of a plan of action, but a plan of action for the future is usually the main objective in the counselee's thinking.

9. Whatever plan of action is developed, the counselee should feel that it is *his* plan. If the counselor develops the plan for the counselee, it is too easy for the counselee to lean on the counselor for the execution of the plan.

A counselee will often cooperate very well in developing a plan but cooperation and acceptance do not insure that it will be put into effect. Putting a plan into action often arouses doubt, fear, and conflict. A plan usually requires changes in the life style of the counselee and he cannot easily put them into effect even though he wishes to do so. To aid the advisee who shies away from putting his own chosen plan into effect, the counselor can concentrate on analyzing the counselee's resistance and the reasons for it. Then, when the counselee can understand the reasons behind his resistance, he is better able to overcome his reluctance.

10. The counselor must be straightforward in his statements, avoid cleverness, subtlety, shrewd guesses, and astute hints. If the counselor wants to make a statement or communicate an idea, he should state it tactfully but clearly. The poor counselor often offers half-ideas in the form of subtle hints which are supposed to occur to the counselee after he has left the counselor. Good interviewers leave an effect of straightforward honesty. The counselee feels that he understands exactly what the counselor meant to tell him.

11. If the counseling is effective, a strong emotional relationship often develops between the counselee and the counselor. The counselor should be careful to avoid giving the impression that he has personally gained some special advantage over the counselee. Rather, the counselor should stress the idea that the counselee has really solved his own problem and that the counselor functioned as a convenient agent—not as an authority who developed the answer for the counselee. When the counselor and the counselee meet socially, after the counseling relation has passed, the counselor should respond in a friendly but matter-of-fact manner. Certainly, there should be nothing in the counselor's manner that suggests, "What I know about you!" or, "Why don't you act the way normal people do?"

If the counselor is also the employee's supervisor, the emotional tie developed should be that of the normal variety in which the two men identify themselves with each other. The employee should feel that his supervisor is a leader who believes in him and trusts him.

12. The good counseling interviewer makes frequent reviews mentally of the effectiveness of his techniques. At the end of the interview he asks himself questions such as the following:

a. Did I put the counselee at ease and enable him to talk freely?

b. Did I see his problem and his situation from his standpoint?

c. Did I find out his defenses, rationalizations, opinions, and attitudes?

d. Did I learn the various steps in the history or development of his problem and how his present situation became a natural one under the conditions involved?

e. Did I enable him to see his situation in its psychological settings, so that he now feels that he is in better control of himself in relation to his problem situation? Does he feel that he can make a better adjustment to his problem because he understands it more clearly?

f. Did I help him develop a plan of action which he recognizes as essentially his own plan?

Acknowledgments and References

1. *Statistical Abstract of the United States, 1954,* U.S. Dept. of Commerce.

2. Clifford H. Peace, "Pastoral Counseling with the Problem Employee," *Personnel Series,* No. 163, American Management Association, 1955, pp. 27–30.

3. Helen Baker, *Employee Counseling,* Industrial Relations Section, Princeton University, Princeton, New Jersey, 1944, presents the employee counseling programs of some sixty industrial concerns.

4. Douglas S. Arbucle, "Differences between Clinical and Industrial Non-Directive Counseling," *Personnel Journal,* Vol. 24 (1948), pp. 374–376. Also, John M. Butler, "On the Role of Directive and Non-Directive Techniques in the Counseling Process," *Educational and Psychological Measurement,* Vol. 8, No. 2 (1948), pp. 201–210.

5. Carl R. Rogers, *Counseling and Psychotherapy,* Houghton Mifflin Company, Boston, 1942, p. 28.

6. Helen Sargent, "Nondirective Counseling Applied to a Single Interview," *Journal of Consulting Psychology,* American Psychological Association, Inc., Vol. VII, No. 4, July–August, 1932, p. 183.

7. Nathaniel J. Raskin, "Development of the Parallel Studies Project," *Journal of Consulting Psychology,* American Psychological Association, Inc., Vol. 13, No. 3, June 1949, pp. 154–156.

8. ———, "An Objective Approach to the Study of Psychotherapy," *American Scientist,* Vol. 37, No. 3 (July 1949), pp. 410–413.

9. Elizabeth T. Sheerer, "The Relationship Between Acceptance of Self and Acceptance of Others," *Journal of Consulting Psychology,* American Psychological Association, Inc., Vol. 13, No. 3 (June 1949), pp. 174–175. Copyright 1949 by the American Psychological Association, Inc.

10. Carl R. Rogers, "The Processes of Therapy," *Journal of Consulting Psychology,* American Psychological Association, Inc., Vol. 4 (1940), pp. 161–164.

11. ———, *Counseling and Psychotherapy, op. cit.,* pp. 336–337.

PROJECTS

1. Assume that you are a college professor and one of your students has been found cheating in an important examination. The student has been called to your office. Write a dialogue of your conversation along the lines of the two cases presented earlier in this chapter.

2. *The back-number employee.* William Johnson, 38 years old, has been working for his present employer for fifteen years. Several years ago his work changed, but he was not able to adapt himself to the changed conditions. The firm progressed but Mr. Johnson did not. The personnel manager has been unable to transfer him to a vacancy with the same rate of pay that he now has, and he refuses a demotion with a lower rate of pay. He is married, has several children, and his character and general record are excellent. The management is confronted with the problem of either forcing him to accept a demotion or allowing him to draw a higher rate of pay than his work really merits. Assume that you are the personnel manager. What would you do about Mr. Johnson's case?

3. Assume that you are the head of a department having about thirty employees. One employee is a chronic faultfinder. He particularly belittles people having higher education. He takes no courses that might improve his own education, which ended in the third year of high school. He obviously tries to lift himself above others by "pushing them down." His constant defensiveness is having a bad effect on the morale of other employees and you decide that you must do something about it. What would you do?

COLLATERAL READINGS

Bellows, Roger M., *Psychology of Personnel in Business and Industry,* Prentice-Hall, Inc., New York, 1954, Chapter 5.

Blum, Milton L. and Benjamin Balinsky, *Counseling and Psychology,* Prentice-Hall, Inc., New York, 1951, Chapter 18.

Cantor, Nathaniel, *Employee Counseling,* McGraw-Hill Book Company, Inc., New York, 1945.

Gardner, Burleigh B. and David G. Moore, *Human Relations in Industry,* Richard D. Irwin, Inc., Chicago, 1950, Chapter 16.

Garrett, A. M., *Counseling Methods for Personnel Workers,* Family Welfare Association of America, 1945.

Maier, Norman R., *Principles of Human Relations,* John Wiley and Sons, Inc., New York, 1952, Chapter 13.

Rogers, Carl R., *Counseling and Psychotherapy,* Houghton Mifflin Company, Boston, 1942.

Shaffer, Laurance F. and Edward J. Shoben, Jr., *The Psychology of Adjustment,* Houghton Mifflin Company, Boston, 1946, Chapter 16.

Watson, Robert I., *Readings in the Clinical Method of Psychology,* Harper & Brothers, New York, 1949, pp. 528–637.

JOHN MILTON

John Milton graduated from college two years ago. After commencement he worked at several odd jobs for a year and then took a job as operator of a semi-automatic machine in the Burr Gear Company. He is the only college man in his department; most of the other men are illiterate. His production has been erratic, some months slightly above average, other months considerably below. He is paid on a piece-rate basis. He apparently dislikes his work, since he is absent frequently and seems to criticize the company and the industry in the presence of his fellow employees. The foreman has recommended him for discharge but suggests that one of the higher executives talk to him in order to have him realize where he stands. Fortunately, the employee initiates an interview by stating that he is disappointed with his job and the chances for advancement. The following conversation takes place (Early stages in the interview to establish rapport have been omitted from this report):

Principles of Interviewing Stated and Illustrated in the Executive's Thinking

The Conversation

"I'll have to get at the trouble from his point of view."

"He doesn't open up."

"Most of these foreigners in that department are good physical specimens. Only a giant could do more work than they do."

"The old story—college man expects a promotion just because he's a college man. He hasn't grasped the competitive nature of life."

Personnel Executive: "You say you are dissatisfied with your job. Perhaps we should have had a chat before this but we didn't, and now is your chance to open up and tell what you think of your work here. Let's be frank about it; we can make more headway than if either of us holds back his grievances. Besides, I want to assure you that you can be frank with me."

John Milton: "I don't think there is any need to be frank. I do my work and that seems to be all that is expected of me."

P. E.: "Your attendance and your production records show that you do not enjoy your work. Perhaps you expected something different when you finished college. What did you expect?"

J. M.: "In college, I was told that the world is waiting for hard-working, educated fellows, but I haven't found it so. I guess I was full of a lot of false enthusiasm. I'm working among a lot of dumb Bohunks who are stronger than I am. They work all day and don't mind it. When I work as fast as they do, I have to drag myself home at night. I used to think that if I got an education and worked hard I'd be promoted; but I haven't seen any promotion even when I did try for it. So far as I can see, a col-

JOHN MILTON (cont'd)

Principles of Interviewing Stated and Illustrated in the Executive's Thinking

The Conversation

"I'll have to build up his ego before I can help him."

"Let him get rid of all the poison in his system."

"The perennial alibi—drag. Perhaps that is a good starting point for us to get together."

"Ignore the 'barbs' that are not important."

"Ask him some questions to which he answers yes."

lege education doesn't mean a thing on that kind of work."

P. E.: "Thanks, Milton. I'm glad you are frank. I'm beginning to see your point of view. If only everyone would be as honest as you are, we could avoid a lot of unhappiness. College, or something, has made you more willing to state facts as you see them. Now that you have told me about some of the difficulty, tell me more. How about your relations with the foreman? Has he treated you squarely?"

J. M.: "Oh, yes, he's okay. I feel sorry for him. He's been here for fifteen or sixteen years, and he's still a foreman. He doesn't seem to have any drag either."

P. E.: "No. he doesn't have any drag and he doesn't want any. Neither do you. You wouldn't feel so proud of yourself if you gained a better job through unfair influence as you would if you won it on ability, would you?"

J. M.: "No, I wouldn't, but even that might be better than competing with the physical giants in my department."

P. E.: "Only as an escape from an unbearable situation. Now let's see whether we can get straightened out on the value of your college training. You spent four years in college and you enjoyed it while you were there; or didn't you?"

J. M.: "I enjoyed it very much."

P. E.: "Did you learn some things you didn't know before?"

J. M.: "Sure, lots of them. In the classroom and outside."

P. E.: "Think of your freshman year. Did you have some difficulty in getting adjusted to college? Was it different from high school?"

J. M.: "Sure. It took me several months to like it."

JOHN MILTON (cont'd)

Principles of Interviewing Stated and Illustrated in the Executive's Thinking	The Conversation

"We have to get together on one point even though it is a minor one."

> *P. E.:* "Would you agree that the step from college to industry is more difficult than the step from high school to college?"
>
> *J. M.:* "You bet. Much harder for anyone."
>
> *P. E.:* "It was for me, too. It took me a long time to realize that I had three choices: I could work *for* the company, I could '*work*' the company, or I could work *with* the company. Let me write them on this sheet of paper so that I can make them clear. (Writes them on paper.) In the past, you have been working for the company. You did what you had to do for the wages you received. You did not enjoy the work and you could not do so with your present point of view. To some extent, you worked the company when you held on to your job but did not work regularly. However, you might have tried to work us far more by catering to your foreman, tattling on the other fellows, or by restricting output through ostensible breakdowns of the machine you operate. You didn't do those things and I'm glad you are too much of a man to do them."

"Here's the crucial stage. I'll have to illustrate this so clearly that he will want to feel himself a part of the concern."

> *J. M.:* "No, sir. I've played straight there."

"Ignore the fact that he tried to upset the morale of his fellow workers because he won't do that if I can enable him to express himself through his job."

> *P. E.:* "Fine. However, you failed to work *with* us. That is, you did not consistently and wholeheartedly work just as though you gained self-expression from your job."

"His objection is evidence of interest."

> *J. M.:* "How could I gain self-expression from a job I don't like?"
>
> *P. E.:* "By recognizing the fact that the nature of any man's work is secondary to the meaning of the work to him. You will agree with me, I believe, when I say that almost any person would be glad to run the machine you operate if he believed that he was the only man in

JOHN MILTON (cont'd)

Principles of Interviewing Stated and Illustrated in the Executive's Thinking	The Conversation

"He can realize that any job may be satisfying if it has pleasant associations."

the world who could run it and if he were pointed out as the outstanding man in that work. Let me assure you that the nature of the work is incidental; the meaning of the work is most important. One can give his job meaning by one of three methods: First, he can do it better than anyone else. Second, he can improve the job by inventing a better machine or system to do the work. Third, he can improve the human relations in the job.

"Let's face the facts, pleasant or unpleasant."

"In your case, you cannot do the first because the other men are physically stronger than either one of us. You cannot do this second because you are not an engineer nor are you trained in production management. But you would do well to study the latter and see whether you could improve our production system.

"He has a real opportunity in his present situation, if he can utilize it."

"Your best chance is the third: namely, learn to understand how to influence the employees here. You may consider them Bohunks now, but the place and time to learn how to handle men is the place and time in which you happen to be. If you want to become an executive, you will have to conduct yourself in a manner which will cause those men to like and respect you."

J. M.: "That sounds all right. But how am I going to get them to admire me?"

"People learn to admire those who admire them."

P. E.: "By deserving their admiration. Study them and some of their customs. Realize their problems and you'll forget your own. Visit them in their homes. Let them give you some of their fine qualities. You, in turn, can give them some of your qualities."

J. M.: "What can I give them?"

P. E.: "Things you have that they

JOHN MILTON (concluded)

Principles of Interviewing Stated and Illustrated in the Executive's Thinking

The Conversation

do not have—your education. College should have given you some information in economics, psychology, sociology, and other fields. Find out what things interest them and contribute in simple language the things they want and need. Help them to learn to read and do simple arithmetic. Some of them came to America because they thought it the land of opportunity. Lose yourself in helping them and you will thereby find yourself in this company. There is the opportunity. Do you want to take it or to run away from it?"

"Every man has something to give other men if he can learn how to give it."

J. M.: "Can you explain the whole situation in more detail?"

P. E.: "I'll try. Perhaps we can both understand the problem and solution if we diagram it." (Draws the diagram in the accompanying figure and explains it according to the principles presented in Chapters 2–8. The evasive, substitute, and retreat activities of J. M.'s behavior are explained, and then direct attack is offered as the one sound form of adjustment. The adviser also presents any ideas that he believes to apply, such as those expressed in Chapter 7.)

"Let him make the decision."

BARRIER—ABRUPT CHANGE IN ACTIVITY REQUIRED

OLD GOAL

CRITICISM OF COMPANY AND EMPLOYEES

NEW GOAL

SUBSTITUTE ACTIVITY - NEW JOB

ON-GOING ACTIVITY— EXPECTING TO FIND SATISFACTION IN WORK

EVASIVE ADJUSTMENT

BARRIER—ABRUPT CHANGE IN ACTIVITY REQUIRED

SUFFERING HERO, DAYDREAMS

RETREAT

OLD GOAL

DIRECT ATTACK UPON BARRIER BY STUDY OF JOB

ON-GOING ACTIVITY— EXPECTING TO FIND SATISFACTION IN WORK

LEARNING HOW TO INFLUENCE FELLOW EMPLOYEES EGO IS RAISED

J. M.: "Sounds pretty good. I never thought of my job as having any opportunity in it. I'll try it."

P. E.: "Do it. I know you can if you will. You have the intelligence. All you need is the attitude and desire. You'll find ways of doing it. Tell me how you get along. Come to see me a month from now. In the meantime, I'll hear of your activities."

"Let him know that someone is following up his progress."

J. M.: "Thanks. I'll think it through and see what I can do."

P. E.: "Do so. Remember that when you help these other men, you also help yourself and this company."

"Any problem in industry may be integrated for the advantage of all parties."

J. M.: "Good-bye."

PRISCILLA PARKER

Priscilla Parker, a college graduate, has been working for the Blank Company for the past three years. She has never been tardy and has been absent only a few days. Her record, in general, is excellent. Some of her fellow employees have been tardy and absent more frequently than is necessary. The company decides to conduct a "Be-On-Time-Campaign." On the third morning of the campaign, Priscilla is caught in a traffic jam and is late. She records the correct time of her arrival. However, later in the day, she regrets her honesty and changes the record to show that she was on time. The timekeeper reports the falsification to her department manager, who calls her to his office for an interview.

The Department Manager's Thinking	The Conversation
	("D.M." is the department manager and "E." is the employee.)
"This girl has a good record and I must handle her in such a way that she will be strengthened by my treatment of her."	D. M.: "Good morning, Miss Parker. Won't you have a chair?"
	E.: "Thank you." (She drops into a chair, blushing and in an obvious state of nervousness.)
	D. M.: "The Timekeeping Department tells me that you ought to have a chat with me. Will you tell me your story?"
"I'll let her tell her side of the story."	E.: "Well, I left my home at the same time that I usually leave and I took the same trolley, but the car I was on had something wrong with it. It stopped several times and I realized that I might be late, so I decided to change to a Third Avenue car at Garden Street. I knew that I could walk the three blocks and make better time on the other line, but there was a fire at Garden Street and that detained me some more. When I finally got here I was late. I put down the right time when I came into the office. You know the rest, so there's no use my telling you."
"She ought to tell the whole story in her way."	D. M.: "I know part of the remainder but I'd like you to tell me, and give me your reasons."
	E.: "Well, I thought of the punctuality campaign, and I was sorry my tardiness would help spoil our department's chances for winning the departmental cup for having the best record. I haven't been late for three years and I was anxious to keep my own record perfect.

PRISCILLA PARKER (cont'd)

The Department Manager's Thinking	The Conversation
	That's why I changed the time slip later in the morning. But I know it was against the rules to do that."
"She must decide the significance of her act."	*D. M.:* "Why do you suppose we have the rule that office employees must be honest in recording their comings and goings?"
	E.: "Because we're paid according to the record; but I had intended to work overtime to make up for the tardiness."
"She ought to realize how her conduct affects others."	*D. M.:* "If you had worked overtime to compensate the company and no one had noticed your changing the record, would *you* have been satisfied with yourself? Would everything have been square for everybody?"
	E.: "The company would have been treated fairly, but I guess the people of the other departments would consider it unfair if our department should win the attendance prize. Wouldn't they?"
	D. M.: "Yes, they would consider it unfair and some might even assume that they would be justified in falsifying their records. How would that affect the Be-On-Time-Campaign?"
"Have the employee state the effects of her act on the company's efforts."	*E.:* "Well, the campaign and the prizes wouldn't mean anything if we didn't play the game fairly."
	D. M.: "Exactly. Changing the record was unfair to the other employees. But do you think that the falsifying of the record also had any effect upon you?"
"Have employee see the effect of her act upon her personality."	*E.:* "Yes, I guess it did. I didn't feel very easy about it after it was done."
"Find some redeeming feature in her act."	*D. M.:* "I'm glad to know that you were not trying to bluff yourself into feeling proud of an unfair act. Perhaps your feeling of dishonesty and regret will help you to meet such problems in the future in a straightforward manner. You know that your record with us is very good, but if you were to cause us to lose confidence in you, we should feel that we had to watch you constantly,

PRISCILLA PARKER (concluded)

The Department Manager's Thinking	The Conversation
	and that would be difficult for us."
	E.: "Yes, and it would be worse for me. I couldn't be happy if I worked in a place where people didn't trust me."
"Let the employee herself suggest the proper correction (punishment) of her mistake."	*D. M.:* "Of course not. But that is where you stand now. Neither your department head nor the Timekeeping Department can trust you in the future unless you square yourself with them and convince them that your misjudgment has improved you. What do you think that you ought to do in order to square yourself and deserve our continued confidence?"
	E.: "I suppose I ought to explain the whole matter to the personnel manager and the chief timekeeper and tell them how the experience has affected me. I also want to apologize to you."
"Arrange for employee to close the incident in her thinking so that she has no 'emotional hang-over' to disturb her morale."	*D. M.:* "Fine! You want to be square and we all want to forget about it. See the personnel man and the timekeeper. Convince them that you have benefited by this incident and I'm sure we can all forget about it. We want you to be happy here and have confidence in us and we want to have confidence in you."
	E.: "All right. I'll see them and come back and tell you about it. I'll be glad to get this off my mind. I want a clean slate."
"Allow the employee to think that she has solved her problem herself, but require a report of the completed correction."	*D. M.:* "Good. Come back and tell me when you've cleaned the slate. Thank you for your honesty and willingness to correct the situation yourself. That will be all."

CHAPTER NINE

Developing your own personality

The mere reading of a book on personality will not make you popular or skillful in handling people. It can only start you on the road to making yourself friendly and influential. It can suggest new ways to enjoy people and stimulate you to apply the methods that you already know but neglect to use. At times you may fail to achieve your ends. You may even be misunderstood. But failure should simply spur you on to improve your strategies.[1]

The number of different definitions of personality is about the same as the number of persons who have defined it.[2] Most psychologists restrict the term *personality* to nonintellectual traits, applying it particularly to the traits which determine a person's social effectiveness and happiness in life. However, most definitions tend to fall into two general classes: (a) those which define personality as the unique pattern or organization of the individual's adjustment habits, that is, the persistent tendencies in his mental life as developed through his capacities interacting with a complex social and physical world, and (b) definitions that give emphasis to the effect the individual has on other people with whom he comes in contact, his so-called social stimulus value.

What a man is

The first definition refers to what a man *is* psychologically, his fundamental character, rather than what he *does* in social situations. This idea has been expressed in the old adage: "Many a man would reach greater heights if he had more depth." A truly great personality, even though a famous person, impresses us more for what he is than for the achievements that have made him famous, as is explained by a scientist who had worked with Albert Einstein:

Material facts matter less in Einstein's life than in anyone else's. The world of his sense impressions, of cold, hunger, pain, is dulled by the great intensity of his internal life. The adventure of Einstein's life is that of his mind. . . .

167

As great as Einstein is as a physicist and a philosopher, he is still greater as a man.

I know that the last sentence sounds like a bad cliché. Yet it cannot be, because Einstein is the only great scientist of whom I could say it. When one comes in contact with him, one is not overwhelmed by his greatness as a scientist. This greatness is engulfed by the greatness and strangeness of his whole personality. Einstein is unlike anyone else. And perhaps this simple fact is the real clue to his fame. The real clue is not the spectacular discovery of the bending of light rays. If this were so, why should this fame persist in a quickly changing world that forgets today its idols of yesterday? It must rather be his inner greatness, which the people of the world somehow sense and need for their comfort. . . .

It is easy to say that Einstein is great as a scientist, but even more so as a man. But wherein does this greatness lie? And how is it reflected in the minds of the people? My answer may sound bombastic, but I believe it to be true. For me and for many others (some of them could not or would not care to formulate the answer explicitly), Einstein is the aloof conscience of the world. . . .

I do not know anyone as lonely and detached as Einstein. His extreme kindness, his absolute decency, his straightforwardness in dealing with men and social ideas is, in spite of all the appearances to the contrary, impersonal and aloof. His heart does not bleed, his eyes do not cry, yet his deeds are those of a man whose heart bleeds and whose eyes cry. Perhaps this aloofness and detachment make it possible for him to achieve the highest moral level any human being can achieve. The moral scale becomes unbalanced if the "I" is involved. It is sensitive and accurate for Einstein, because his "I" is little involved. . . .

A few weeks ago I received a letter signed by Einstein as the chairman of the Emergency Committee of Atomic Scientists. With it was a small pamphlet containing his article "Only Then Shall We Find Courage." Here he speaks with the insight and power of a prophet. Indeed, it is the conscience of the world that speaks to us—the wisest, simplest words ever spoken on a subject drowned in a flood of meaningless silly words formed into clichés by men who understand and learn nothing.

There was suffering in Einstein's writing, and strong indications that now the impact of a troubled world has invaded his aloofness. In his words there is a message for humanity. And it seems to me a thousand times more important that people should understand his simple words than that they should understand the Relativity Theory.

At the end of his article he writes:

When we are clear in heart and mind—only then shall we find the courage to surmount the fear which haunts the world.

These are the aims for which Einstein strove all his life: to be clear in mind and heart. He is one of the very few who have achieved this clarity.[3]

The truly educated man seeks more than knowledge; he searches for the basic principles by which men live. The learning of principles and the development of a philosophy of life are more important than the mere acquisition of facts. Facts change and disappear; principles remain. Basic principles are guides to judgment and provide a sense of values that lead to strength of personality. They enable a man to distinguish between cheapness or the conventional and grandeur of soul. The man who attains such maturity of personality has poise, power, and influence. He studies psychology, not to give him a feeling of superiority, but to enable him to enjoy all personalities. He does not pity the maladjusted nor does he identify himself with them. He enjoys them, because he understands and likes them in spite of their inappropriate adjustments. Insight into their adjustments increases his respect for all mankind. He loses his cynicism in constructive service to others.

The habit of using direct-attack methods of dealing with barriers is one of the goals of personality growth. The person who has achieved it has what people often describe in such terms as, "That man has good stuff in him," "He's made of good material," or, "There's a man who is a real man." Everyone has heard such statements about a few persons he has known.

Several years ago the author made a list of ten men and women who had been described in these or similar terms. In addition to those on his list, 160 others were chosen by a committee of acquaintances. The 170

The "Six burghers of Calais" were depicted in Auguste Rodin's statue as having attained a high level of maturity of personality. When the besieging English promised to spare the medieval city if six citizens would give their lives for Calais, six men had the courage to sacrifice themselves for their fellows. Rodin's statue of the historical event depicts no fear; only regret and awareness of the meaning of their act. Of course we do not know the actual psychological development of each of the six burghers, but we do know that Rodin's portrayal of their personalities was on the right psychological level of maturity. **(Courtesy of the Philadelphia Museum of Art, Philadelphia.)**

superior men and women were studied by means of many reaction questions. The answers of this superior group were compared with the answers of 200 persons chosen at random, 150 mentally sick patients of an institution, and a group of low-intelligence persons. The test that developed from this study, "Personality Maturity," is given in the Appendix.

Personality maturity means that the individual has developed a certain unification of the whole self, a dependable individuality. He is no longer a youth who seeks to try out all kinds of adjustments, all roads to experience, all ways to growth. He has learned that some modes of behavior lead only to new blockings or to deterioration. Past failures and successes have taught him what things are worth while for him. He knows his aims and the ways in which he will strive to attain them. His character is stable, and his scale of values has been established. When a man's maturity has become positive, he feels and believes that adjustments by evasion and retreat eventually result in a lowered ability to deal with the next barrier.

What a man does

As indicated above, the what-a-man-is aspect of personality growth resolves into the what-a-man-does concept. This is fortunate, because it means that every intelligent person who wishes to develop his personality to a high level of growth can do so by means of conscious effort. One of the most natural environmental situations in which he can work toward his own maturity is in those relations that involve people.

Most people who wish to improve their personalities think of them in terms of their social stimulus value or effectiveness in dealing with people. They realize that they are not alert to the handling of social situations. They are likely to be self-conscious.

The very term "self-consciousness" expresses their basic problem—they are conscious of the wrong person. The socialized person is conscious of others rather than himself. Fortunately, the art of dealing with people can be acquired:

The habit of becoming more aware of others than of yourself can be learned. For example, certain introverted college students asked me to conduct classes in personality development. In these classes I taught one basic principle or rule: *Watch the other person and do whatever appears to be appropriate.*

When the classes were begun, the students were unknowingly given a standardized interview where the interviewer asked six questions. Two of the answers were written incorrectly by the interviewer. The interviewer then tried to erase the error, using a wooden pencil with the eraser worn down to the metal. (Each student had been given a pencil with a good eraser.) The test of the student's habituated use of the above rule was observed and recorded. The poorly socialized students failed to offer their erasers to the interviewer.

After this first test, the students were trained in the practical application of the basic principle. The students themselves suggested extensions and applications of the rule, but pencils and erasers were never mentioned. After eight hours of training, they were again given the same test. Most students made a definite improvement as shown by the moving pictures which were taken without their knowledge. They had learned to objectify some of their

thinking; to lose their self-consciousness by becoming conscious of others. . . .

If you wish to have more friends or to be able to handle people happily, you, too, have to learn the art of forgetting yourself. You must lose self-consciousness by becoming more conscious of other people and by directing your thinking toward them. Personality, in this social sense, is not something that you have or are; *personality is what you do when you are with others. It is an activity, not a possession.* It is not a stagnant pool but a running brook.

This dynamic nature of personality is most fortunate. If you are seeking more friendships or wish to handle people more effectively, you can forget what you are. Simply concentrate upon others, and discover how to give them greater enjoyment. Think of each person as being a distinctive individual whom you try to understand and make a bit more happy. If you practise this fundamental principle, you will find, sooner or later, that you are popular and influential with others.

Your attainment of this social artistry is not so formidable a task as it may appear to be. You have already learned some knacks of handling people. If, on certain past occasions, you had not withdrawn into a shell of reserve when strangers or unkind persons were about, you would have learned more skills. Perhaps you were so wrapped up in your own feelings of doubt about your ability, imagined unattractiveness, or self-concern that you failed to watch the other person. Of course, if your thoughts and feelings were concentrated on yourself, you made a poor impression on him and you withdrew more quickly from contacts with the next stranger. . . .

Parents are at fault when they try to protect their children by isolating them from imperfect companions. Sooner or later the children may develop into first-class neurotics whose chief fault is the fact that in the game of life they "can't take it." Parents who constantly guard their children, not allowing them to play with other children for fear that they will learn the facts of life, are not fulfilling their parental responsibilities. Occasionally the children even run the risk of later becoming patients in hospitals for the mentally ill. The only way for a girl to learn how to handle men, or for a boy to learn how to get along with girls, is for both to go through a long practice period of training where each successful skill in getting along with people has been learned through hard experiences plus intelligent judgments. Socially speaking, every man is his own ancestor and his own

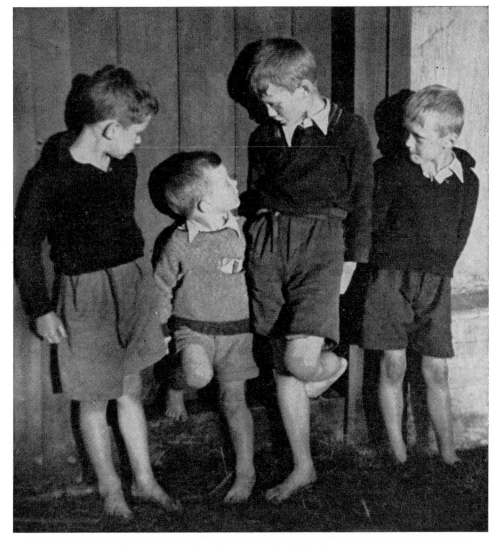

The arts of friendship begin in the early years. The child who must depend upon himself, unimpeded by excessive parental supervision, when making his own friends soon develops the knack of getting his companions to say: "He's young, but maybe it'd be okay for him to tag along this time." **(Photograph by Ward Hutchinson, Sharon, Connecticut.)**

heir—he makes his own future and he inherits his own past. What he does on a great occasion depends upon what he already is, and both depend upon the years of training acquired in the social arenas of life: the playground, the office, the shop, and the park bench on a moonlight night.[4]

The socialized personality and its resultant friendships must be earned. Many persons who find it difficult to earn friendships would like to improve their personalities, but they have the habits of the *introvert* rather than those of the *extravert*.

Introversion-extraversion

Introverts are characterized by their "shut-in" personality. They do not share their joys and sorrows with others, but keep them to themselves. They are largely self-sufficient for their emotional outlets. Anger, blushing, and laughter are examples of emotional outlets, and the introverts express them within themselves; that is, their emotions are introverted. Daydreaming is an example of an introverted emotional outlet. Introverts, in short, are vividly aware of their own inner lives.

Extraverts, in contrast, express their emotional outlets in action and in seeking the society of others. They do not sit alone with their thoughts, but depend upon others or upon activity for their happiness. Introverts are men of thought and extraverts are men of action. Scientists tend toward introversion and businessmen toward extraversion. Foremen and executives whose duties require the supervision of others are likely to be extraverts. The key executives of industry incline toward *ambiversion,* or a middle position on the scale of introversion-extraversian. Office workers, clerks, and stenographers incline toward introversion. Many accountants and research engineers are pronouncedly introverted.

It should not be assumed that all or most people are of either one type or the other. Rather, they tend to group themselves in the center of the scale. Each person has some qualities of each type, and his classification depends upon the degree to which he is introverted or extraverted rather than upon the absolute presence or absence of the characteristic traits. Furthermore introversion is expressed in several separate traits as in social and thinking areas. A person may be socially introverted but not thoughtful or moody.[5]

Laird devised a scale for the measure of introversion and extraversion.[6] The personality signs he listed are:

1. The introvert blushes easily; the extravert rarely blushes.
2. The extravert laughs more readily than the introvert.
3. The introvert is usually outspoken; the extravert is usually careful not to hurt the feelings of others.
4. The extravert is a fluent talker; the introvert can prepare a report in writing more easily than he can tell it in conversation.
5. The extravert lends money and possessions more readily than the introvert.
6. The extravert moves faster than the introvert in the routine actions of the day, such as walking, dressing, talking, etc.
7. The extravert does not take particular care of his personal property, such as watches, clothes, etc.; the introvert is found continually oiling, polishing, and tinkering.
8. Introverts are usually reluctant about making friends among those of opposite sex, while extraverts are attracted by them.
9. Introverts are easily embarrassed by having to be in front of a crowd.
10. The extravert is a more natural public speaker.
11. The introvert likes to argue.
12. The introvert is slow about making friends.
13. The introvert rewrites his letters, inserts interlineations, adds postscripts, and corrects every mistake of the typist.

Personality signs revealed in thinking and attitudes:

1. The introvert worries; the extravert has scarcely a care in the world.
2. The feelings of the introvert are easily hurt; the extravert is not bothered by what is said to him.
3. The introvert deliberates in great detail about everything—what to wear, where to eat, etc., and usually tells one why he decided to do what he did.
4. The introvert rebels when ordered to do a thing; the extravert accepts orders as a matter of course.
5. The introvert is urged to his best efforts by praise; the extravert is not affected by praise.
6. The introvert is suspicious of the motives of others.
7. The introvert is usually radical in religion and politics; the extravert—if he entertains any opinions—is usually conservative.
8. The introvert would rather struggle alone to solve a problem than to ask for help.
9. The introvert would rather work alone in a room than with others.
10. Extraverts follow athletics; introverts read books and "high brow" magazines.
11. The introvert is a poor loser.
12. The introvert daydreams a great deal.
13. The introvert prefers fine, delicate work (die making, accounting), while the extravert prefers work in which details do not bother.

14. The introvert is inclined to be moody at times.

15. The introvert is very conscientious.[7]

The study of personality traits or patterns of this kind has value to the supervisor, because those persons who are most introverted can be influenced by methods that are not successful with the extraverts. Praise, caution, and exactness appeal to introverts. Activity, speed, chance, and challenges appeal to the extraverts.

As salesmen are decidedly extraverted, it is hopeless to try to compel them to fill in and mail each day very detailed reports to the home office. Salesmen should have a minimum amount of clerical work to perform. Their paper work should be done by women, because women, as a group, are more introverted than men. Bank work usually attracts introverts. Bank workers who meet the public should be assisted by extraverted contact men and women in the lobby. Workmen who are to be promoted to supervisory positions should be extraverted rather than painstaking and retiring introverts.

In the forms of introversive adjustment which we call *retreat* the individual seeks solitude, prefers to stay at home, adopts cults of mysticism, studies his ancestry, or lives in a world of poetry, art, or fiction. Some religions have idealized this tendency by formalizing the retreat adjustment. Tibet, the center of religious fanaticism, has many old Buddhist monks who have kept themselves sealed up—except for small openings for food—in little huts since their early manhood. Some of them have not heard the voice, seen the face, nor touched the hand of a human being for more than forty years.

Many of our very studious college students are introverted, but college fraternities probably attract the extraverted and the introverted students in approximately equal numbers.[8] The differences between fraternities are likely to be greater than the differences between the fraternity and the non-fraternity groupings.

Some introverted students would like to become more extraverted but wonder whether it is possible to do so. The answer is a decided "Yes." On the other hand, many introverts say that they prefer to remain as they are because civilization needs introverts as well as extraverts. No one can argue with those who make this choice except in one important respect, namely, introverts are so very sensitive, their feelings are hurt so often, that they would be happier if they would learn greater skill in the social arts. Those who wish to acquire the social skills can do so by directing their thinking toward others and away from themselves.

Paradoxically, the socially skilled and interesting personality cannot be acquired if it is sought directly. It is a by-product, like happiness. "Happiness is a butterfly which, when pursued, is always just beyond your grasp, but which, if you will sit down quietly, may alight upon you." Or, as Hawthorne said: "Happiness in this world, when it comes, comes incidentally. Make it the object of pursuit, and it leads us a wild goose chase and is never attained."

As previously stated, self-consciousness on the part of the introvert means just what the term indicates—the individual is more conscious of himself than of others. Self-pity and similar ego-centered tendencies can be changed by looking out—not in. Extraversion can be attained by thinking more of external and social values, particularly how to deal with and handle people.

To socialize your personality, watch the other person and do whatever appears to be appropriate. In this social sense, personality is what you *do* with people; not something that you have.* Friendliness can be learned in the same way we learn arithmetic or French—by study and practice. The extent to which the college student, male or

---

* The second person is often used in this chapter for the greater interest of readers who wish to develop the social stimulus values of their personalities

female, has learned commonly used information about social relations can be measured by the "Social Knowledge Test" in the Appendix of this book. The students who score high in the knowledge of the Lower Social Strata and low in the Upper Social Strata questions should consider the desirability of increasing their study of social information. The college man or woman who has limited his associations to either class may be somewhat handicapped in certain occupations.

The adjustments made in early childhood are very important in the development of effective social skills. Many a child finds it difficult to adapt himself to others because he feels emotionally insecure. He may feel insecure because, for instance, he took too seriously the ordinary family quarrels of his parents. The frictions between his parents may have caused him to feel that they, and his world as well, were not dependable. He became emotionally insecure because the most important persons of his experience, his parents, did not seem to merit his belief in their dependability.

If the emotionally insecure child is also nagged a great deal, he is apt to grow up to be impulsive, self-centered, and unable to identify himself with his associates. He feels left out and, in awkward attempts to readjust himself, he behaves in ways that cause others to avoid him, thus increasing his feeling of not belonging. However, if he later comes to realize how his insecurity came about, recognizes that many parents show their affection for each other by their bickering, and he secures some dependable person as a friend, he is likely to develop adjustment habits that result in a feeling of belongingness. Practically, this means that the individual should frequently participate in group activities appropriate to his age and social status: sports, team or group games, dancing, committee meetings, and so on. In this respect, chess and archery are likely to be less developmental than baseball or amateur theatricals.

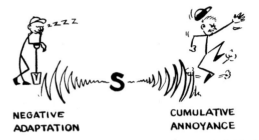

NEGATIVE ADAPTATION   CUMULATIVE ANNOYANCE

The adaptation-annoyance range. When an individual is stimulated by the repetition of any given situation, he may, on the one hand, completely adapt himself to the situation, so that it no longer elicits any reaction except one of boredom and dullness. On the other hand, each repetition of the stimulus may result in added annoyance. The effects of the stimulation are then summative. Each reaction adds to the accumulated annoyance of the previous sum. The worker who responds to his job in the latter way soon develops feelings of strong resentment that result in rebellion. If he cannot escape from the summative effect of the annoyance of his job, he will have to "explode" or "break" under the strain. The "explosion" may be expressed through the channel of fighting the boss, or through bitter antagonism toward industry or toward anything that symbolizes the annoying situation. The "break" may be in the form of the so-called nervous breakdown. Contrast this with insight-meaning response.

The feeling of belongingness can be achieved by anyone who consciously practices the best methods of doing whatever seems to be appropriate in dealing with people. This means that the intelligently socialized person not only accepts people but also thinks of them as sources of mutual enjoyment.

An important difference between the adjustment-minded person and the average layman is illustrated by the three ways in which we can deal with a problem person's annoying behavior: namely, (*a*) cumulative annoyance, (*b*) negative adaptation, and (*c*) insight-meaning.

Cumulative annoyance is exemplified by the employee who dislikes his boss and at the beginning of each day says to himself: "Another day of that man! Every time I see him I hate him more. When can I get away from him?" The individual who reacts to another person or situation in this manner soon develops intense feelings of resentment. Eventually he rebels, perhaps violently. If circumstances, such as the need

NEGATIVE ADAPTATION

CUMULATIVE ANNOYANCE

S

The insight-meaning response. When an individual is stimulated by the repetition of any given kind of situation, he need not adapt himself completely, nor need he be cumulatively annoyed. He may apply intelligence to the situation. He may seek insight. When he seeks insight, he makes observations. He notes annoying and satisfying factors. He looks for causes and effects. He discovers possible improvements. He utilizes the situation for self-expression. The situation acquires meanings for him, and these meanings radiate in all directions from the situation and result in the disappearance of feelings of dull acceptance or of resentment. The worker who reacts to his job in this manner becomes neither bored nor carpingly critical. He utilizes his job for creative self-expression.

for a job in order to support a family, do not allow him to quit, he must "explode" or "break" under the strain. He is the type of employee who is impelled to "tell the boss to go to Hell" and thereby lose the job he wanted to lose. This type of worker, if he does not explode, is apt to become a bitter critic toward industry, modern business, or something else that happens to symbolize his baleful situation. If he does not have an outlet for his pent-up emotions, he is likely to escape through the so-called "nervous breakdown."

Negative adaptation applies to many of our daily experiences with people. Some persons and situations are dealt with and forgotten. Examples of negative adaptation are the factory worker who has given up all hope of getting a better job and now does his work in a mechanical spiritless manner, the small child who does not react to his mother's constant scolding, or the husband who does not "hear" his wife's back-seat driving.

Insight-meaning is used by the worker who finds himself in an annoying situation, analyzes it, and discovers some interesting aspects of it. It is used by the boss who, when he is annoyed by the mannerisms of an employee, learns that the employee has a difficult home life and then tries to make the employee's life more interesting by giving him extra attention while at work. Insight-meaning is always more satisfying than either dull acceptance or cumulative annoyance. It can be used every day with our annoying associates, such as the back-seat driver, the teacher who scolds, the executive who threatens, the housewife who nags, the girl-friend who insists on having repeated personal attentions, and others.

A first step in the insight-meaning relationship to people is to become aware of their adjustments. Anyone who learns to apply the adjustment concept to the actions of people will soon develop a feeling of kinship* toward them. He will feel friendly toward them and they will sense that he understands and likes them. The psychologically intelligent person does not tell people how much he knows about them. Rather, he uses his insight into their personalities to help them make the adjustments and gain the satisfactions *they* seek. He never flaunts his knowledge of them but uses it as a background for friendly, mutually satisfying relationships. He learns how people feel and feels himself into their situations and problems.

Second, he notes what people do and like. He learns what topics of conversation interest them, what badges or insignia they wear, their hobbies, the brands of cigarettes they smoke, whether they are more deaf in one ear than another, the taut muscles which indicate tension, and subjects of conversation which are pleasant to them. He says "Goodbye" with his face toward the departing guest. When an old joke is told, the true

* "Empathy" is used by some psychologists to express the mental state wherein one person identifies or feels himself into the state of mind of another person. It is also used to mean mental projection of oneself into the elements of a work of art or into a natural object.

extravert does not show by his manner that he has heard it previously but laughs heartily. One of the tests of extraversion on the part of a listener is to look so interested when a story teller begins his story that the raconteur does not ask: "Or have you heard this before?"

This awareness of what people like does not mean that flattery can take the place of a sincere interest in others. Many misinformed persons fail to appreciate the importance of a genuine interest in work and people.

This principle is illustrated by the difference between flattery and a genuine interest in a person, as seen in the case of employees who imagine that flattery is necesary to gain promotion.

Should an employee use flattery in order to gain promotion if he believes that others are succeeding by this method? Mr. Edmunds is thirty-five years old, is married, and has been working for his present employer for ten years. He likes his work and, in general, he considers his employer fair. However, he believes that some of the younger men of the department who have been promoted gained their promotion through clever and tactful flattery toward his superior. Mr. Edmunds should:

1. Try to flatter his superior in order to gain promotion also.

2. Quit, and try to get a job where promotion depends upon ability rather than flattery.

3. Allow the others to do as they wish. He likes his work and he should be completely satisfied.

4. Discuss the situation as tactfully as possible with his superior.

5. Improve his ability by studying, taking an active part in technical associations, and contributing articles to trade journals. The future will take care of itself if he improves himself and builds a reputation for his ability.[9]

Third, the introvert who wishes to socialize himself should practice responding to others by means of his facial expressions. Typical introverts are surprised when they see moving pictures of themselves in conversation. They discover that they look as animated as the Statue of Liberty! If a person feels friendly, he should show it by lifting his eyebrows and smiling with his eyes as well as by grinning with his lips. Of course, friendliness is far more than facial expression. It is a sincere identification with others, but a sincere identification includes facial expressions which help to convey the feeling of friendship.

Fourth, the introvert should acquire the knack of asking questions in order to learn from others; not to argue with them. Usually, we can ask questions of a person about his occupation: what he does, who the leaders are in his field of work, changes since he has entered the field, and what successful experiences he himself has enjoyed.

Furthermore, the good conversationalist does not answer questions completely—he answers them only partially and then asks the questioner what he thinks about the unanswered aspect. He knows that when a person answers a question and then says, "Don't you think so, too?" the conversation is closed. The flow of conversation should not be shut off by requests for agreement but kept moving from topic to topic by requests for additional ideas.

Asking questions is an art which few introverts learn even though they argue frequently. They are so wrapped up in their own feelings about themselves that they cannot ask questions so as to enable the other person to expand. They are apt to ask questions to prove their own point, as found in this typical problem:

Who should take the initiative in correcting misunderstandings: the superior or the subordinate? A senior in a Liberal Arts College has had a reasonably good scholastic record. He is now in his last semester. In the first semester of his senior year, he failed a course under a certain professor, but continued the year course with this same professor. The student believes that he failed the first semester's work because he had a very heated argument with the professor. He also believes that he will fail this semester's work because he is sure that the professor does not like him. What should he do?

1. He should remain in the course, work hard, and say nothing to the professor.

2. He should request permission of his dean to change his course, explaining his reason.

3. He should discuss the matter with the professor and find out wherein he was wrong. He should then apologize, if necessary, and put himself on a friendly relationship with his professor.

4. He should tell the professor frankly what he thinks of his unfairness and demand that the professor treat him absolutely fairly.[10]

Fifth, the individual who seeks to make himself interesting to others usually finds it necessary to direct his thinking and working toward some definite end. He is apt to have a vocational program of some kind whereby he becomes a specialist or expert in some one field such as business, as exemplified by the mental habits of successful versus the nonsuccessful businessmen. The successful ones have chosen vocations which are appropriate for their behavior patterns.

Psychologists have found that no one or two traits cause a man to be a successful businessman. All human beings possess the same traits, but they differ in the degree or amount of possession of each trait. That is, if we were to list all the traits or qualities of the one hundred greatest men of the world and then list the qualities of one hundred unimportant men, the two lists of traits would be the same. However, the two groups would differ widely in the degree or extent of possession of each trait on the list. For example, the second group of men would have less intelligence and initiative than the first group; but high intelligence alone does not enable the youth to become a leader, nor does a high degree of initiative. Success depends upon a proper combination of essential elements.

The skilled housewife's batter is a correct combination of the proper ingredients, and, when it is given the favorable environment of the oven, delicious cake results. Similarly, the great leaders in business are those who have the effective "personality ingredients" or patterns of behavior.

Forty-one situations were described to 150 businessmen of five grades of income. Questions were asked and the answers were then treated quantitatively. The questions which gave differential values are shown in the "Executive Reaction Pattern" test in the Appendix. The results indicate that certain measurable differences do exist among the five classes. These differences have been statistically treated, and the questions can be used for employment purposes.

If the reader will check the appropriate items and then refer to the key in the Appendix of this book, he can score his answers and obtain an approximate estimate of the level of his own executive behavior pattern. The answers which have a plus value on the key are characteristic of the higher-salaried businessmen. The minus answers apply to the lower-salaried groups. The scorings of the answers to the 28 questions were not made during an "armchair" study, but were determined by a statistical analysis of differences in the behavior patterns. It would be difficult for a person to obtain the maximum rating by reasoning out the answers with the greatest plus values. For instance, in question 10, the highest plus value is given to the man who says that his family relations had a slight negative effect in stimulating him to do his best.

The student who wishes to develop the human relations skills of the executive must do far more than learn the correct answers to an executive reaction pattern test. Executive ability and skill in handling people are attained through daily practices in dealing with janitors, sales clerks, teachers, fellow employees, friends, and members of the family rather than through reading books. The following suggestions call attention to factors often neglected by those who wish to develop their personalities:

Ten suggestions for personality development

1. BE CONSCIOUS OF THE OTHER PERSON AND NOTE WHAT HE DOES. Talk about the subjects that interest him and he will think

of you as a person with an interesting personality. Forget yourself through an active interest in other people.

2. ASSUME THAT PEOPLE LIKE YOU. If you show that you want people to talk to you, they will respond warmly. On the other hand, if you act in a reserved, seclusive manner, people will assume that you wish to be let alone. If you show that you enjoy your own company more than the company of others, they will let you have yourself to yourself.

3. WHEN YOU GREET A PERSON, GREET HIM EMPHATICALLY. When you say "Good morning," say "GOOD MORNING"; don't say *"good morning."* Also wave your hand and smile. If you feel that you are faking when you first attempt to be cordial, just continue practicing cordiality until you do it naturally.

4. BUILD UP THE OTHER FELLOW'S FEELINGS OF SELF-WORTH. Note things about which he feels inferior. Offer him sincere compliments which prove that he has better qualities than he thought he had. Do not talk about him but compliment him on his intelligent acts. And remember that every woman likes to receive feminine compliments regarding her beauty and personal attractiveness. But phrase the compliment in an original way.

5. ADMIT YOUR OWN DEFECTS. You need not deliberately make an ass of yourself but, when you have acted as one, let others make humorous remarks at your expense. It makes them feel superior and keeps your personality more flexible. Accept yourself. People who can accept themselves as they are, view others as being accepting also. On the other hand, those who see others as rejecting tend to have a low opinion of themselves. When a person can accept himself fairly well, then it is possible for him to relate effectively to others, to understand them, and to regard them as persons of worth.[11]

6. PRACTICE USE OF THE WORD YOU AND AVOID I. One measure of your personality is the number of times you say *you, your, he, his, she* and *her* rather than *I, me, my,* or *mine.* The test of your socialization is not the ideas that you give others but the number of ideas that others give you.

7. ADMIRE YOUR FRIENDS. Perhaps you have already done many kindnesses for others which they repaid with meanness or infidelity. Perhaps you have lent money to some who never paid it back and, moreover, do not care to pay it back. These lapses of loyalty, goodness, and integrity should not sour one for the greater number of gifts received. In the totality of human relationships, human nature is remarkably good and fine.

8. LOVE SOMEONE INTENSELY. Man's normal state requires an outlet for his affections. If your wife is not of a lovable sort, love your child. If that is not feasible for you, assume responsibility for someone's happiness. A dog or a monkey may fill the gap, but a normal person can better look himself in the face if he gives his devotion to a human being instead of concentrating it on a dumb animal.

9. CHANGE YOUR ENVIRONMENT OCCASIONALLY. Take a vacation when it is due. Go to a new part of the country. Meet some new people. Leave your wife and children at home when you take a vacation and allow them to take a vacation without you. Sell your house and buy another. Change your office furniture. Of course, you should have a den of your own, where you can litter the floor with cigarette butts or cigar bands; a place where you can put your feet on the desk and feel at home, but even a den becomes monotonous and a new surrounding is needed.

10. ASSOCIATE WITH PEOPLE WHO ARE SUCCESSFUL AND HAPPY. Living within oneself alone is dangerous. We all need certain

contacts to give us new points of view, new thoughts, and new hopes. Attend at least one social affair each week. Call on your neighbors. Meet the fellows at the club. Go to church. Compel yourself to play cards, or dance, or sing, or tell stories, or play golf. When you do associate with others, do not consider your associates as either inferiors or superiors. Let your motto be: "All men are my equals, but no man is my superior." Try to learn from those who are experts in other fields, but do not envy them their money or position. Happiness does not lie in wealth, fame, or personal beauty. Rather, happiness is achieved through intelligent adjustment to what we have and are.

Acknowledgments and References

1. Harry Walker Hepner, *It's Nice to Know People Like You,* D. Appleton-Century Co., New York, 1939, p. 9.
2. Daniel Katz and Richard L. Schanck, *Social Psychology,* John Wiley and Sons, New York, 1938, Chapters 12–15, present a discussion of definitions of personality. See also, Gordon W. Allport, *Personality: A Psychological Interpretation,* Henry Holt and Company, New York, 1937, pp. 24–48.
3. Leopold Infeld, "Portrait . . . Einstein," *American Scholar,* Vol. 16, No. 3 (1947), pp. 339–341.
4. Harry Walker Hepner, *op. cit.,* pp. 5 ff.
5. J. P. Guilford, *Inventory of Factors* STDCR, Beverly Hills, Calif.: Sheridan Supply Co., 1940.
6. Donald A. Laird, "How Personalities Are Found in Industry," *Industrial Psychology,* October 1926, pp. 1, 2.
7. *Ibid.*
8. The 1939–40 scholastic averages of 2,081 independent and 911 fraternity men of one large eastern university revealed no significant difference.
9. Harry Walker Hepner, *Human Relations in Changing Industry,* Prentice-Hall, Inc., New York, 1934, p. 587.
10. *Ibid.,* p. 586.
11. Katharine T. Omwake, "The Relation Between Acceptance of Self and Acceptance of Others Shown by Three Personality Inventories," *Journal of Consulting Psychology,* December 1954, pp. 443–446.

PROJECTS

1. Obtain and study a copy of the Bernreuter Personality Inventory, obtainable from Stanford University Press (Stanford University, California)—or some other personality test. Study the items in relation to the traits they are presumed to measure.

2. Read descriptive material dealing with a number of personality tests. Suggest some ways in which such tests may be helpful to the individual and some situations in which they should be used with caution or not at all.

3. Culture has been defined as openness of mind, objectiveness of attitude, a sensitive appreciation of human values, an original point of view or philosophy of life, and a development of the potentialities of the human being. (*a*) Which courses in college have impressed you as being directed toward one or more of the five mentioned qualities? (*b*) Can you name any courses which are not directed toward one of these five qualities? (*c*) Can you name any work or recreation which could not be directed toward one or more of these five qualities if the individual so desired?

4. Make a point of complimenting several acquaintances on some good qualities they possess. Note the various reactions and analyze these effects.

5. A prospective borrower from a bank was advised by a friend to apply to the sour-mannered loan executive rather than to the jovial friendly one on the basis that the sour-mannered one could say "Yes" while the jovial executive was paid to say "No" charmingly. How would you evaluate this advice—what psychological principles are involved?

6. One of the most common methods of judging the personality of a person is his conversation. A number of individuals were

asked what words, phrases, and questions they disliked to hear from other people. The following list resulted. (It is not to be considered complete.)

ain't	loafer	shorty
brass	lousy	skinny
bum	mess	slob
Butch	nut	sloppy
cake-eater	piker	snob
crab	pill	stink
crumby	prune	stuff
cuckoo	punk	sucker
dumb-cluck	rotter	swell
highbrow	runt	yeah
huh?	shack	yellow
junk	simp	

Questions Disliked

D'ja eat?
How much did it cost?
Is that so?
What did I tell you?
What's it to you?
What's the big idea?
Why bring that up?
So what?
Haven't you finished yet?
How do you get that way?
How's every little thing?
Isn't that grand?
What did you do that for?
What makes you so sure?
What's on your mind?
What d'ya know?

Expressions Disliked

And how!
After me, you come first.
Bad egg.
Beautiful but dumb.
Believe me.
Cut it out.
Don't trouble yourself.
He means well.
Hello, old sock!
I done it.
I'll say so.
I'll tell the world.
Make it snappy.
Mind your own business.
No kiddin'!
None of your business.
Prove it to me.
Shut up.
That's just like you.
That's not true.
You flatter me.
You tell 'em.

a. Ask a number of your associates to check the items that they dislike to hear.

b. Check the items you use frequently. Then have a friend check those which he says you use. Compare the two lists.

c. Note the number of times you hear these terms used by low-salaried and by high-salaried businessmen. To what factors do you attribute any differences in their usage?

COLLATERAL READINGS

Burtt, Harold E., *Applied Psychology*, Prentice-Hall, Inc., New York, 1948, pp. 170–182.

Dichter, Ernest, *The Psychology of Everyday Living*, Barnes and Noble, Inc., New York, 1947.

Dunlap, Knight, *Personal Adjustment*, McGraw-Hill Book Company, Inc., New York, 1946, Chapter 14.

English, O. Spurgeon and Gerald Pearson, *Emotional Problems of Living*, W. W. Norton and Company, New York, 1945.

Evans, M. Catherine, "Social Adjustment and Interest Scores of Introverts and Extroverts," *Educational and Psychological Measurements*, 1947, Vol. 7, pp. 157–167.

Lehner, George F. J. and Ella Kube, *The Dynamics of Personal Adjustment*, Prentice-Hall, Inc., New York, 1955, Chapter 16.

Morgan, John J. B., *How to Keep a Sound Mind*, The Macmillan Company, New York, 1946.

Patty, William L. and Louise S. Johnson, *Personality and Adjustment*, McGraw-Hill Book Company, Inc., New York, 1953, Chapter 10.

Shaffer, Laurance F. and Edward J. Shoben, Jr., *The Psychology of Adjustment*, Houghton Mifflin Company, Boston, 1956, Chapter 11.

CHAPTER TEN

Improving efficiency in mental work—effective methods of study

A person's own convictions regarding his abilities are powerful factors in his mental efficiency. His convictions about himself can be changed and his methods of work improved, but his methods of work will not improve until such time as he himself determines to improve them and persists in learning the new and better habits.

What is a good student? College students have various definitions of the "good" student, most of them not very complimentary to the student who makes superior marks. Psychologists who have devoted years to the development of study techniques and to reading clinics for students with scholastic difficulties offer definitions somewhat more meaningful than the students' typical definitions.

Stromswold and Wrenn,[1] for example, recommend five diagnostic constructs of possible hypotheses of need on the part of the student:

1. *Misclassification.* Students in this category lack the aptitudes, interests, or other personality qualifications needed for the curriculum being pursued.

2. *Inadequate educational background.* Students with this handicap are performing work at a level below their potentialities because of inadequate preparation in one or several areas.

3. *Inadequate use of time.* This may be mainly a symptom of some other disorder.

4. *Interference with study by problems outside of the scholastic realm.*

5. *Inadequate command of study habits and skills.*

The counselors who have studied and assisted failing students know that effective counseling cannot be confined to study habits only. Instruction in study habits, time scheduling, and reading clinics have proved to be of little value unless the personality development has been appropriate for effective study. The mental habits and attitudes of the student, his convictions about himself, his modes of adjustment to his problems, are determining factors in his record as a student.

The student who is in emotional turmoil because of personal problems, such as conflict with parents, poor social contacts, or financial difficulties, may or may not be a good student. Some students adjust to these problems by overcompensation and become scholastic "overachievers." These students are found in every college. They are among the top-ranking students scholastically, but they are not "good" students in the best psychological sense. Truly good students enjoy life in many areas, have a stable emotional life, can concentrate on their tasks, recognize their own aptitudes and limitations, and have a high degree of interest in the subject matter they study.

In Chapters 2 to 7 we saw how habits and attitudes growing out of adjustments tend to result in outstanding achievements. The motives developed in the processes of adjustment on the part of the individual are exceedingly important, not only in setting up and striving toward vocational and other goals, but also in setting up psychological resistances which handicap the individual in learning common school subjects. The normal person's nervous system will perform the functions involved in learning one subject just as easily as it will those involved in learning any other subject. Only the conditionings and habits growing out of adjustments result in inabilities to learn certain kinds of subject matter, such as mathematics or languages. The individual's own definitions and convictions regarding himself are the potent factors in his talent and skills, or lack of them, as is proved by the results from drills in spelling. Experiments show that when drills are given to a poor speller, he improves his spelling only when he himself really determines to improve it. Mere repetitious drill has almost no value—the individual's attitude toward the drill is all-important. Sometimes the individual's convictions regarding his inabilities are so deep-seated

in his personality that a clinical approach is necessary to make the later exercises in spelling worth while.

The following statement by a psychologist who spoke at an annual meeting of the American College Personnel Association explains more fully the need for a clinical technique in dealing with certain inabilities:

The clinical technique which follows from the theoretical conception of the problem must therefore aim to bring about in the subject a re-examination of those ideas which block his development. Academic difficulties and social maladjustments are both conceived of as due to resistances arising from the subject's* idea of himself. Obviously, the method must rely upon inducing the subject to observe the system of contradictions in which he has become involved.

Let us take the case of an intelligent student who is deficient, for example, in spelling. In almost every instance, poor spellers have been tutored and practiced in spelling over long periods without improvement. For some reason such a student has a special handicap in learning how to spell, though not in learning the other subjects which are usually considered more difficult. This deficiency is not due to a lack of ability, but rather to an active resistance which prevents him from learning how to spell in spite of the extra instruction. The resistance arises from the fact that at some time in the past the suggestion that he is a poor speller was accepted and incorporated into his definition of himself, and is now an integral part of his total personality. His difficulty is thus explained as a special instance of the general principle that a person can only be true to himself. If he defined himself as a poor speller, the misspelling of a certain proportion of the words which he uses becomes for him a moral issue. He misspells words for the same reason that he refuses to be a thief. That is, he must endeavor to behave in a manner consistent with his idea of himself.

In these cases, we find that this self-definition as a poor speller, and consequently the resistance to learning how to spell correctly, can usually be removed in from one to five interviews. The majority become average or better than average spellers within the space of two or three months.

A study of the spelling behavior of these stu-

---

* The reader will note that the word "subject" as used in this context refers to "the person experimented upon": not to a course of study.

dents shows that each individual seems to have a definite standard of poor spelling which he unconsciously endeavors to maintain. If his spelling test is cut in two, it will be found that each half contains approximately the same number of misspelled words. If we study his letters or written theses, there is likewise a striking consistency in the number of misspelled words per page. Strange to say, the spelling of foreign languages seems to be impaired very little if at all, showing clearly that the difficulty cannot be attributed to eye movements, left-handedness, or other mechanical interferences. Evidently the conception of one's self as a poor speller usually has reference to one's native language only.

The clinical technique consists in first finding several strong values apparently unrelated to the value in question which can be used as levers, so to speak, and then demonstrating the inconsistency between these values and the one responsible for the deficiency. Almost every student considers himself independent and self-reliant, for example. On the other hand, it can readily be shown that the poor speller expects his defect to be condoned and treated sympathetically; that, in effect, he has his hand out begging for indulgence. If the contradiction can be demonstrated from his own viewpoint, a reorganization becomes compulsory. His definition of himself as a poor speller is vigorously rejected and a determined effort made to establish the opposite definition. The result obtained is out of all proportion to the effort exerted to bring it about. Spelling assumes such interest that it is studied at every opportunity, even from the advertisements on street cars and subway trains. An elaborate analysis to convince the subject that his difficulty really is due to a fixed idea of himself does not seem to be necessary in the remedial treatment of spelling. He should, however, be asked to recall when he first accepted the role of a poor speller, ceased to worry about it, and dismissed the question as closed.

It is significant that not only poor spellers, but stammerers and others with similar defects, freely admit as a rule that they accept themselves as they are and make no effort to change. This is an excellent defense, of course, for they feel no inconsistency once the definition has been accepted. And they often attempt to avoid the effort of maintaining a more useful definition by referring the defect to heredity or neuromuscular maladjustment.

Our experience also shows that unless a person has an unusually optimistic view of the future he would not be likely to anticipate a lenient attitude on the part of others in regard to errors in spelling. This optimism also appears in the fact that poor spellers seem almost universally to count on the services of stenographers who are good spellers, and many are able to quote the names of several people who became famous in spite of a deficiency in spelling.

Those who claim that they "do not have a mathematical mind" are likewise victims of their own resistance. Such a student may have defined himself in childhood as the exact opposite of some unassimilable companion who had been held up as a shining example of mathematical proficiency. In other cases, remarks by parents or teachers that the child was lacking in aptitude for mathematics seem to be the explanation. The suggestion was accepted and is now a part of the student's conception of himself. In one instance, a student who despised mathematics in high school, during his freshman year acquired a sudden attachment for the subject and is now a professional statistician. This boy's older brother was proficient in mathematics, and the two had been in conflict for years.[2]

The clinical technique is helpful in those cases where individuals have proved that they can learn many subjects but claim they are unable to learn one or two specific subjects. The individual is apt either to continue to assume that somehow he is incapable of learning the "difficult" subject or to use evasion, such as searching for some magical or quick means of attaining his ends. He may, for example, read the biographies of great men, study success books, or books on "how to have power of will." Such epigrammatic books, articles, and lectures are inspiring; but if adjustments to environment have already given him an urge, he can accomplish more by the practice of prosaic acts, such as outlining meaningful material, plotting graphic charts, and learning the cold facts of his courses and tasks.

Concentration

Informal polls among college students indicate that lack of concentration or poor concentration is the most common of poor study habits.

"The passing of the disestablishment act in 1867 did not satisfy the nationalists under . . . The passing of the disestablishment . . . The passing of the disestablishment act in 1867 did not satisfy the nationalists . . . passing of the disestablishment act in 1867 did not . . . the passing . . ."
—"Vic the Vet," by Gabe, Syracuse University, **Daily Orange.**

The much-voiced complaint, "Every time I start to study, I all at once just seem to find myself daydreaming!" needs analysis. What causes these daydreams? It may be run-of-the-mill emotional problems, the current girl or boy friend, financial difficulties, or breaking away from home ties. All of these can be a hindrance to concentration.

However, *knowing* your particular problems is to be on the way to solving them. Find out what it is that is taking your interest from studies and guiding it into daydreaming sessions. If you do not wish to consult a clinical psychologist in order to find out, try the system of studying for a week with a paper and pencil always at hand. Each time that you catch yourself daydreaming, write down what it is you had been thinking about. At the end of a week, you should be aware of some of your major problems. Some students find this technique an aid to sticking to a subject.

Concentration is so closely allied with interest that in order to be able to concentrate, interest must first be developed. Poor concentration may stem, too, from a spotty background in a subject area. Failure to think ahead so that you know what is coming and the reason for it may leave wide gaps in your thinking. Inexperience or careless observation may have left you with a weak perceptual background. An inadequate vocabulary of either general or technical terms could prevent you from maintaining a continuous thought pattern. This in turn contributes to a lack of interest.[3]

It is profitable to recognize that the big problem in studying lies in creating interest. There is such a thing as achieving a

CONVENIENT FORM FOR WEEKLY WORK SCHEDULE FOR STUDENT

Work Schedule of _____

"forced" interest in a subject. Many students have not only created this forced interest, but have gone ahead and achieved a "real" interest through the study of formerly disliked subjects.

There are helpful methods by which enthusiasm for subjects can be developed. One technique that works at times is for the student to study exceptionally hard for the first examination in a course. If the student is successful in getting a high grade, the high grade helps to develop interest in the subject: success generates interest.

Another technique is reading ahead of lectures. This practice will help to eliminate much of the disinterest students have toward especially difficult subjects. For example, in an economics course, the instructor may announce that the subject of the next lecture will be the "Law of Supply and Demand." The student, by reading this material in the text before the lecture and, if time permits, in the library texts and periodicals, facilitates his own understand-ing of the subject and, hence, increases his interest in it.

Scheduling

Scheduling study time is the most controversial of the study techniques. "Why schedule—I just have so much time," or, "I just work until I'm through," is a typical reaction. If you are receiving grades commensurate with or beyond your mental ability, or if you have time for sufficient relaxation to make for enthusiasm in your work, you probably do not need scheduling. If, on the other hand, you constantly worry because you are "not on top" of your work, then scheduling is a prerequisite for your study.

Students differ widely in their desire for and ability to follow a schedule. A student should plan a schedule for his first week in school, realizing that this schedule will probably be changed by conflicting class meetings, unavailable courses, or inability to get the teachers he desires. However, by the second or third week of school, as he becomes oriented to the semester's work, he can plan another study schedule, knowing that this one is to serve as a guide throughout the term.

A college student usually takes from fifteen to twenty-one class hours per semester, and his professors advise that about two study hours be given to preparation for each hour spent in class. With this simple yardstick of study-time requirement, and with fixed class hours each day, the student can arrange his individual schedule either to increase or decrease his study time, according to his scholastic needs. Some students and instructors think in terms of a weekly schedule. A series of twenty-four hour schedules is likely to be more effective for most students. At the end of each day, the student sets up a feasible, rather than an ideal, schedule for the next twenty-four hours.

It is a good idea to arrange studying time as soon after lectures as possible. Researches indicate that study immediately, or within a reasonable time, after a class is far superior to the same amount of study the day or the night before a class. In this program, good students often allow for a short period of review just prior to the lecture.

Another important point to remember is that spreading the learning period over the semester is far more effective than cramming in all the subject material at the end of the semester.[4] This means that reviewing must be a constant practice. It is imperative to "keep on top" of your work throughout the semester, and this can be achieved only by wise scheduling.

The evidence from Frederiksen and Schrader's study of how students spend their time shows that the student who gets high marks relative to his ability tends to be a pretty serious sort of fellow with definite academic interests. He is likely to take more courses, study more than the average student, and attend evening lectures. He indulges less in frivolous activities such as going to parties or movies. He does engage in bull sessions, but in moderation.

In general, women in college spend more time than men in extracurricular activities—other than athletics. They attend lectures or concerts, and indulge in social activities—dates, parties, movies, and the like. They spend less time in athletics, physical recreation and in voluntary course reading. They attend fewer classes (presumably because they tend to take fewer laboratory courses) and are less likely to have a part-time job.[5]

Physical setting

It is highly important that the college student study in the right setting. A good desk lamp is desirable. Soft, diffused light should illuminate the rest of the room to eliminate contrast and strain. His desk should be so situated as to facilitate the maximum of efficient concentration. Generally, it is a good idea to have it away from windows affording campus views. If the room is shared by another student, it is a good idea to arrange the desks so that the two students are back to back while studying. Nor should the student, when at work at his desk, be able to see his bed or an inviting easy chair. The chair for study should be of the hard straight-backed variety. This will enable the student to maintain a reasonable state of muscular tenseness during study, a state that greatly aids effectiveness of study.

Keep a specific desk and chair for study only. Lounging and recreational reading should be done in another chair. Eventually, if the particular place of study is consistently used for study only, it will cause the student to settle down to intensive work almost immediately. In order to build up sustained attention habits, the student should begin work as soon as he sits down. Oftentimes it is difficult to get started. Hence, routine tasks such as reorganizing notes or recopying a theme might be tackled first as a "warming up" for the real work.

Reading as a study tool

The increasing awareness of reading ability as an aid to successful study is readily seen in the development of reading clinics as an integral part of college and university programs. The importance of reading in the entire program of education can hardly be exaggerated.[6]

Reports from reading clinics emphasize two facts: (1) the average student reads unnecessarily slowly and inefficiently, and (2) after a period of intensive training, such a reader can increase his speed, improve his comprehension, and increase his overall efficiency.[7]

Comprehension is the first objective in reading. Improving comprehension is an aid to speed also. Increasing the speed means that the time spent in study can be reduced. From 85 to 90 per cent of all studying done in high school and college is concerned with some form of reading. With adequate training in reading a student who has been spending four hours per night in study can do the same amount with better comprehension in two hours.

The poor reader reads slowly, generally about 100 to 150 words a minute, comprehends poorly; makes many "regressions" (backward movements of the eyes over material already read); reads word by word or phrase by phrase; must move his eyes six or seven times to cover an average line of print; reads with his tongue, throat, and vocal chords; and tires easily.

The student reads for different purposes on different occasions, and his methods on each occasion should fit the purpose for which he is then reading. The more intelligently he reads, the more inclined he will be to vary his rate of reading and his method of attack.

Most persons can make their easiest and quickest improvement by varying the rate of reading. Various rates of reading may be used for different types of reading material. The light novel and the tabloid newspaper can be skimmed or scanned and comprehended easily, but more complex novels and the more difficult magazine articles must be read more slowly and carefully. The physics test, the economics book, and the philosophy pamphlet must be read even more slowly. Reading clinics have found that the rate can vary from some 40 to 1,000 words a minute for the same individual, reading different types of material.

An understanding of the reading process has helped many students to improve their reading skills. During reading, the eyes are in a constant state of movement. In the actual process of perceiving words, however, the eyes are fixated or stopped. It is during these stops that words are read. How many stops do you make per line? It is a simple procedure to find out. Have someone sit across from you and count them. The number of stops varies from two to six or seven per line according to the skill of the reader and the difficulty of material being read.

The skillful reader reads fast, comprehends exactly, has few regressions, reads phrases and sentences—rarely single words —can absorb an average line of print with one or two eye movements, does not move his lips, reads actively, thinks with the author, has superior concentration, and remembers what he reads.

The student should make certain that his reading procedure is correct before he begins to read. Many students find that a graph representing reading speed serves as a stimulus to practice. Another device is to have constantly on hand a book which is enjoyable and which can be read rapidly—this can be a light novel or a book of short stories. When one book is finished, another can be started immediately. A definite reading program of 15 to 20 minutes a day can be set up, and the chosen reading material will thus be consistently read. Such consistency brings about results. With these books, too, occasional pages can be timed as a check on speed.

Speed of reading and comprehension are closely correlated. Often students show surprise that comprehension can increase along with speed, until they realize that single words do not make pictures or ideas. It is only when several words or phrases are comprehended that a visual picture or idea ensues.

A simple device for improving reading comprehension is *written recall*. The student should take a meaningful paragraph, page, or section from a textbook, read it, close the book, write a summary of the important points, and then check his writing with the text. Some students prefer to write

At Temple University, Department of Psychology, guidance in various types of reading activities is given in class. One adult is working independently on o pacer, another on an individual tachistoscope. Two are being timed by the instructor to improve their rate and comprehension of reading through organizational skills.

Perceiving units of material, controlled for difficulty and speed, improves with practice. At Temple University such work on a tachistoscope is continued as part of the instructional program until the functioning eye-span and speed of perception is close to the probable potential level of efficiency.

Southern State College student is receiving instruction in the use of the reading accelerator. This machine is designed to help the pupil increase her speed of reading. A careful diagnosis of reading difficulties is made through the use of diagnostic reading tests. Vocabulary drills, reading accelerators, reading films, slides, tachistoscope, and reading material at the student's level and in his field of interest are utilized in improving reading skills. If a student's difficulty centers around emotional adjustment the counseling center is used as a referral source where a coordinated effort is made to assist the student.

Students at Washington University participating in training for rapid reading by means of the PerseptoScope, a new instrument produced by Perceptual Development Laboratories, Inc., of St. Louis, Missouri. It combines in one 16 mm film projector three major forms of projection— still, flash (or tachistoscopic), and animation. It will project one frame at a time, with an indefinite exposure time, flash an image at various fractions of a second, and project at various speeds ranging from 1 to 8 and 24 frames per second.

Tachistoscopic training is emphasized early in the training program to develop a one-look seeing habit of reading. A typical lesson contains tachistoscopic training, controlled reading of articles on film, with tests, and printed practice reading articles, with tests. By keeping a daily record of their progress, students can watch their own improvement.

Reading skills and comprehension are so important in learning that psychologists are giving them increasing attention. Pictured here are programs at three colleges which exemplify the many investigations and services currently being undertaken in this area. Temple University photographs by courtesy of Prof. C. H. Smeltzer; Southern State College, by Dolph Camp.

a rough outline, which usually brings about the same result. Vocabulary-building, as an integral part of reading ability, should always be in the developing stage.

An extensive knowledge of the exact meanings of English words accompanies outstanding success in this country more than any other single characteristic. To keep your vocabulary developing requires constant and continuous surveillance. Many systems are in use for this purpose. The most common one uses 3″ x 5″ card indexes, generally set up with a word on the front of each card and its meaning on the back. Thus, in odd moments, the cards can be shuffled and a private word game can be played. When words have been mastered, the cards are usually filed and then occasionally reviewed. Some students prefer to keep a section in their notebooks for vocabulary improvement; others like a small notebook devoted entirely to new words. The particular system by which you improve your vocabulary is not significant; that you do have some system is important. Without one, your vocabulary either levels off or declines. It is imperative to keep your vocabulary developing.

The importance of increasing over-all reading ability is evident today in many places. To cite just one example, thousands of Air Force officers will in the future be able to read their way down through their mountains of "paperwork" with much greater speed and ease. The reading rate of officers in the Air University, Maxwell Air Force Base, Montgomery, Alabama, was speeded up by special training from an average of 250 words a minute to approximately 600 words a minute.[8]

The following rules or practices will help the student improve his reading methods:

1. Prepare your mind before beginning to read. Ask yourself how this book or article fits your plan of development. What questions should the author answer for you? Recall other articles on the same subject and ask yourself how this article relates to your previous studies.

2. Make a preliminary survey. Note the exact title, the author's position and his other writings, the year the book was written, the publisher, and the preface. The intelligent student reads the preface to learn why the author wrote the book and the treatment or points of view which he believed to be of value to the reader.

After reading the preface, read the table of contents and page rapidly through the book to note other main headings and the illustrations. Get the outline of the book in your mind. Note the parts in italics or capital letters or ideas which the author wants to impress upon the reader. Reading a book twice may seem unnecessary and a waste of time—but it is not, because double reading aids the formation of stronger and more lasting powers of recall.

3. Read rapidly. Beware of "dozing" study. Don't think that you are studying when you merely hold a book in your hand and look at words. If you cannot throw yourself into your study and work at high pressure, stop entirely and stand before an open window, or take a few exercises.

Force yourself to read rapidly.[9] Urge yourself to speed up. Begin at once to read rapidly. At first this may interfere with the clarity of comprehension but if you persist, you will soon find that you can learn ten times as much by speeding up. Spending a lot of time in study is far less important than a small amount of time well spent at consistent intervals. Don't dawdle. Go to it full steam ahead. Whenever you find yourself gliding off into daydreams or irrelevant meditations, bring yourself back sharply. Let each digression act as a reminder to get back to the job at hand.

4. Vary the rate of your reading. Read the simple or already known parts rapidly, or skip them entirely. Concentrate upon the important and difficult parts. If you do not understand the meaning of a word, look it up in the dictionary. If you find it difficult to grasp a principle, try to draw a diagram illustrating it or make an outline of the author's own statements. Make it a rule never to do straightaway reading at a regular rate unless you read for entertainment.

5. Make marginal notes or underscore the main ideas. Try to summarize the author's ideas in your own words by writing a sentence in the margin. A good plan is to underscore important items or draw a vertical line in the margin for important paragraphs or sentences. Always read with a pencil or pen in your hand so that you can indicate important passages. A book well-read has many penciled passages.

6. Use "active self-recitation." Think while you read. Spend a large part of your study in thinking over what you have read. Do not accept the author's statements blindly. Consider his views in the light of your own ideas or those of others. Be open-minded and willing to learn, but do not accept without some analysis of statements. Ask yourself whether the author is stating the results of impartial investigations or merely his own opinions. Do his conclusions follow from his statements? Is he trying to sell you some pet idea?

Notemaking

The notebook is the badge of the student, the engineer, the explorer. The standard 8½″ x 11″ looseleaf notebook with a stiff cover is recommended. One well-organized notebook, in addition to class and book notes, can also be used for material passed out by instructors. The obvious advantage of one notebook is that work materials are always at hand. With actual notemaking, a system of abbreviations is necessary. Much time can be saved if this system is a consistent one. Many students, especially in the first months of college, before the abbreviations have become automatic, have found that a page set aside in the notebook for abbreviations is an aid to the mastery of a system.

In actual college work three kinds of notemaking are found: notes on lectures, notes on borrowed books, and notes in a book. Making lecture notes makes you an active rather than a passive participant. It is an aid to learning, for it requires you to evaluate ideas, to organize thoughts, and then to jot down the meaningful items. Good lecture notes are brief, but good lecture notes have complete sentences and are organized under meaningful headings. Making notes on radio programs, a sermon, or a talk can give added practice. In class lectures, being ready for the lecture is essential. Notes from the previous lecture should have been reviewed. Reading ahead

of lectures, in textbook and reference books, is valuable here also.

The question whether notes should be rewritten will depend on how expert a notemaker you are. If your original lecture notes are ready for use in review, then rewriting is not necessary. Otherwise, it is.

Notemaking from library books is essentially the same as lecture notemaking. You must sort out the salient points of a chapter or a portion of a book or magazine article. This task is made easier by reading the entire assignment to get an over-all picture or framework. Then go back and actually write out the points or facts of this framework.

Making notes in your own books is essential to active learning. A consistent set of symbols is necessary to indicate important facts, points of disagreement, connection of key words or phrases, and numbering or a series of ideas. Important points can be underlined or can be marked by vertical lines in the margin. A soft lead pencil or a red lead pencil will mark so as to show up plainly. Brief markings will serve the student best—key words, important phrases, and, of course, ideas that need clarification. Through notemaking on an assignment, the important points stand out so that skim reading will serve as a review.

Using the library

In student life, knowledge of efficient library usage is essential. The librarian is always there to aid research and investigation, but time can be saved by one's own ability to dig out necessary information. In a new college situation, you should spend every available minute during the first weeks in becoming familiar with your college libraries.

Three types of card catalogs are in use in libraries: (a) *Dictionary*—alphabetically arranged by author, title, and subject; all cards are in terms of one alphabet; (b) *Divided-*

catalog—divided into two parts: subject catalog and author and title catalog, (c) *Classified* (mostly in technical libraries)—arranged by broad subject or some practical scheme related to the type of material. The dictionary type of catalog is the one in general use and the one you would expect to find in most libraries.

The catalog serves as an index to the library. It contains author, title, and subject cards for the books in the library. These cards are important in that on each the call number of the book concerned is given. The author, title, place and date of publication, and publisher are also given. For most books in the library there are three cards in the card catalog: one, the author card; one, the title card; and one, the subject card. Some books, particularly fiction, have only two cards, and some (autobiography) only one. More cards may result from dual authorship. Also, if the book deals with more than one subject, each subject will be represented by a card in the catalog. On subject cards, the subject is always typed in red at the top of the catalog card so that it can be readily distinguished from an author or title card. In order to get a book from closed stacks, you must copy the author, title, and call number of the specific book wanted on a call slip. It is important to be extremely accurate in copying the call number, making sure that no letter or number is omitted, since an omission may result in having the wrong book delivered. Also, sign your name legibly. Then give the call slip to a staff member at the circulation desk.

Fiction is usually found in a separate section or room. It is arranged alphabetically by last name of the author and under each author alphabetically by title. All the books by Somerset Maugham, for example, will be together. Books other than fiction are arranged according to a special system of classification. The Dewey Decimal Classification is widely used.

Besides learning from books, the industrious student will learn from periodicals. The newest ideas in any field are in the magazines. Using periodicals beyond the limit of assignments imposed by instructors can give you a richer background and a knowledge of current material. As has been mentioned, periodical reading in the field of a new course or an unfamiliar topic can give you extensive information.

To find pertinent information in magazines, you must use periodical guides. The card catalog is an index to books; the *Reader's Guide to Periodical Literature* and similar periodical indexes are indexes to contents of selected magazines. In the front of each issue of an index are lists of the magazines indexed, the abbreviations used, and an explanation on how to use the index. Entries are alphabetized under author, title, and subject. Libraries often have special call slips, and to obtain a desired issue of a periodical, it is necessary to copy the following from the index—name of the author and the title of the article, the name of the periodical, the volume number, the date, and page number. Large libraries usually have a call number for each different magazine to be found in the card catalog. The *Reader's Guide* indexes general periodicals, but for special fields the following indexes are invaluable. The titles indicate generally specific areas covered:

Agricultural Index
Annual Magazine Subject Index
Art Index
Book Review Digest
Dramatic Index
Education Index
Engineering Index
Industrial Arts Index
International Index to Periodicals
Monthly Catalog, U.S. Public Documents
The New York Times Index
Public Affairs Information Service

The achieving student becomes quickly familiar with the indexes that will be useful in obtaining articles in his particular fields of special interest. Business administration students, for example, will find a wealth of material on applied science, business finance, and technology in the *Industrial Arts Index*.

In addition, a library has many reference books, such as dictionaries, *Roget's Thesaurus of English Words and Phrases* and *Webster's Dictionary of Synonyms*. Encyclopedias, as a beginning tool in research, save much time; in them information on every subject of importance is given in alphabetical order. However, a paper based on encyclopedia reading only is not enough to satisfy a professor's assignment such as a term paper.

How to write

Many college courses consist primarily of a sort of correspondence between professor and student. In such courses it is imperative for you to be able to write. If you can express your ideas in writing, the assignment of a theme, a book review, or even a term paper will present few insurmountable barriers.

First, be sure that you have something to say. Secondly, no matter how small or large the assignment may be, always make sure that the facts supporting your ideas are correct. Third, make a rough outline.

And then—write.

In this initial setting down, it is getting the ideas on paper that is important. If this is very difficult to do, you may not have enough material on the subject. More reading in books or periodicals may be necessary. Definite ideas to express, accompanied by interest, make writing easy.

In reading, the garnering of background material is the objective, it is not the "lifting" of whole sentences or paragraphs for your paper. Ideas are not formed in a vacuum; hence the necessity of wide knowledge. With patience and practice in writing, you can put your ideas across to other persons.

Writing is a skill that requires consistent practice. If you find it difficult to write, do not confine your writing to assignments. Do other kinds of writing for practice. Write friendly letters. See how well you can get across a mood, an event, a day-to-day routine to family or friends. Make summaries of radio talks or the Sunday sermon. Keep a journal.

In writing it is not enough to say a fact once if you really want to put it across. Rather, the point must be made in more than one way. Approach it from different angles or enlarge your original premise.

Many students lose credit on written assignments through neglect. They fail to read what they have written in order to polish and correct the finished product. At the college level, misspelled words, incomplete sentences, grammatical errors often affect one's grade.

An important written assignment should be done in the rough as soon as possible. After the rough outline or plan has been developed, let your ideas "simmer." Keep notes on any new ideas and on hints for the rephrasing of particular sentences. The day before the assignment is due, make the final revision.

All college assignments should be typed.

Professors may be traditionally thought of as absentminded, but they are quick to pick out the theme written at the last minute, perhaps while the writer was being bored in the preceding class. Effective writing of any kind, from class assignments to best-seller novels, is hard work. If you will work diligently at writing, aiming for accuracy and clarity, you can achieve the desired qualities.

How to remember

Many people dislike the idea of memorizing because memory is thought of only as a mechanical process of "learning by heart." Thinking and memorizing are usually considered as alternatives. Actually they are a part of the same process and go together. Material which has been thought through is remembered without much effort. Memory is a by-product of study, and the general principles of study apply to memorizing.

Most students want to be able to recall studied material for one of the two more common kinds of examinations: the essay test and the objective test. In studying for an essay examination, the understanding and organizing of major ideas are especially important. The making of outlines should be a part of the study for recall.

Objective examinations cover the study content extensively. Underlining of many factual items is important so that reviews can be made easily and frequently.

Good students also do studying that is "instructor-oriented." That is, they are alert to note the ideas stressed by the instructor, and they make extra effort to understand and memorize them.

The main way to improve memory is to improve the methods of learning. However, the following rules may aid in improving the ability to remember:

1. Get the meaning of the material to be remembered. Be sure that you clearly understand the material you want to recall. Think of the new ideas from every angle and try to apply them to practical situations. Do this not only when you are reading but also when you are at leisure. When you are walking or riding to and from your home, do not waste the time in idle reverie. Utilize your spare time. Perhaps you may think it dangerous to keep active mentally so large a part of your time. Have no fear. No man ever went insane or had a breakdown from mental overwork, but a lot have gone insane or broken down from overworry or other inadequate mental habits. Most of the talk about breakdowns from mental overwork is rationalization. The idle and the ignorant are the ones who suffer most from neuroses; not those who are exceedingly busy.

2. Always study with the intent to remember. Herein lies the cause for much forgetfulness. Occasionally a teacher repeats certain outlines of lectures to his students and asks them to memorize the outlines. Later on he finds that he himself cannot repeat the outline because he simply dictated the material from his lecture notes. Whenever you study, do so with a determination to remember the things

studied, and you will be surprised how easy it is to recall your past mental efforts.

3. Stop frequently during your studying and check up what you have learned. Compel yourself to recall what you are learning. Spend about 40 per cent of your time reciting to yourself. If you cannot recall what you have read, turn back and read it again. By a little practice along this line you will treble your ability to remember what you have covered. Imagine you are teaching the material and see whether you know it so well that you can explain it clearly to someone else. If you are unable to explain the meaning to someone else, you do not understand or know it. Go over it again and study each sentence and paragraph until you are able to tell what it does mean.

4. Use repetition. Don't expect to recall everything that you study unless you repeat the difficult parts over and over. In the case of definitions of technical terms, formulas, dates, and outlines, where the material has few natural clues for recall, don't hesitate to commit to memory verbatim. Of course, parrotlike recitation is wasteful, but don't consider yourself above mechanical repetition of certain material.

5. In committing to memory it is better to read aloud than to read silently and it is better to read to someone else than to yourself. Attention is better sustained in this way, because an appeal is made to the ear as well as to the eye and some help is gotten from the "feel" of the words in the throat and mouth. The value of reading to another person is that it promotes accuracy of thinking and insures proper emphasis of the several ideas.

6. Attempt to remember only the important material. Confine your efforts to the essential and relegate the nonessential to references to the dictionary, encyclopedia, and textbooks.

Mark with a red pencil items you have to learn verbatim. Then study each item with the intent to understand, and the material will practically be memorized. The index to a book is a useful key to the most important facts, references, and key words. If you cannot identify an item listed in the index, even though you know you have studied it, review it.

7. Carry the learning of important items beyond the point necessary for immediate recall. Experiments show that we forget about 60 per cent of material barely learned within one day after learning. This means that information necessary in your life work must be studied more than is sufficient barely to recall it the next day. The fading of impressions must be

met by overlearning. Superficial learning of the spelling of a word may satisfy the immediate need, but it will not satisfy the needs of correct spelling a year later.

8. Space your study. Experiments have shown that it is better to memorize a certain amount of material at intervals than to try to complete the job at one sitting. Don't try to do seven hours of studying in one evening of each week, but study one hour on seven evenings of each week. This allows the individual to organize new material in relation to past experience.

9. If necessary, invent some artificial scheme for learning and recalling material which lacks rational associations. This is seldom necessary, but may be helpful in recalling material, such as the height of the volcano of Fujiyama, which was reported as 12,365 feet. Simply remember that we have 12 months and 365 days in the year.

Or you can use acrostics. As one man said: "In my public school days we had a speaker give us a talk once a month. Of the fifty or more talks which I heard I recall the subject of but one. In that case the speaker's subject was 'Grow' and the method of growth which he suggested was 'Go right on working.' The first letter of each word forms the word 'Grow.'" Acrostics can be used to advantage in remembering lists of words or names.

For temporary recall, it may be very helpful to try to visualize facts or principles. Try to picture them in unusual lights, colors, positions, and so on. However, it is best to depend upon logical connections by understanding the relationships of the material to be remembered.

Techniques of creative thinking

Many persons who do original thinking seem to want the public to believe that they do their thinking with the efficiency of firmly disciplined methods. Actually, studies of creative thinkers indicate that they make many false starts, waste time in random and exploratory movements, have desultory periods, and waver between unmanageable fantasies and systematic attack.

Investigations indicate that some creative thinkers realize that they are driven by a kind of demon or creative urge. A student

of creative thought has reported one man's consuming purpose and commented on such drives as follows:

Eden Phillpotts, the Devonshire novelist and dramatist, writes: "For my own part the creative urge is a demon that drives, and will doubtless continue to drive, while my intellect, such as it is, functions normally and does not begin to wither with age. As a boy at school there was a longing to make things. I was always drawing. Then I longed to be an actor and create character; then I found these mediums beyond my power and turned to writing."

Perhaps such a drive is instinctive, reaching down into the very foundations of the personality. Perhaps it is conditioned and due to education, perhaps to abundant and overflowing energy. There are a dozen theories to explain it. In some it is not always persistent. It may lie dormant for years and then, when aroused by an inexplicable circumstance, drive the mind with a lashing hand. Whatever its source, we are certain that the immediate occasion for creative activity is the adjustment to some inner and controlling purpose, the resolution of some dissatisfaction with the world as it is, the ambition to idealize reality.[10]

The several stages in the process of creative thinking have been designated by Graham Wallas[11] essentially as follows:

1. *Preparation.* This stage refers to the study of the problem, its essential aspects, and the consideration of similar problems and their solutions.

2. *Incubation.* When the thinker has made the first step, preparation, he often takes a walk, a drive, or carries on some other activities wholly unrelated to the main problem. During incubation, the unconscious mental activities may be applied to the problem while the individual is engaged in easy physical exercise or routine tasks. However, close attention to some other problem, or intense emotional reactions from thrilling motion pictures, seem to be less beneficial than the kind of mind wandering which we experience during a train ride or in easy reading for one's entertainment. Time spent in just "sitting still" is likely to facilitate incubation far more than

vigorous continuous search for an answer. Idleness and relaxation are often more helpful than an attempt to stuff one's self with "good reading."

3. *Illumination.* This refers to the appearance of the "good idea," coming seemingly from nowhere. The thinker usually has an intimation of the coming of the sought answer. He is conscious of the "dawning" for which he has searched.

Sometimes the thinker may recognize that he has experienced a great discovery but decide to postpone its consideration. Later he may find that he cannot revive the great idea whose birth he throttled. Failure to record the "flash" or to follow through may result in tragic inability to do so later, as reported regarding an artistic composition:

Berlioz struggled against the creative impulse and eventually killed it. He suffered from poverty while at the same time his wife's health was causing him anxiety. One night there came to him the inspiration for a symphony. It ran in his head, an allegro of two-four time in A-minor. He rose from his bed and began to write. But he thought: "If I begin this bit, I shall have to write the whole symphony. It will be a big thing and I shall have to spend three or four months over it. That means I shall write no more articles and earn no more money. And when the symphony is finished, I shall not be able to resist the temptation to have it copied (which will mean an expense of a thousand or twelve-hundred francs) and then of having it played. I shall have a concert, and the receipts will barely cover the cost. I shall lose what I have not got. The poor invalid will lack necessities, and I shall be able to pay neither my personal expenses nor my son's fees when he goes on board ship. These thoughts made me shudder and I threw down my pen saying, 'Bah! Tomorrow I shall have forgotten the symphony.' But the next night I heard the allegro clearly and seemed to see it written down. I was filled with feverish agitation. I sang the theme. I was going to get up, but the reflections of the day before restrained me. I steeled myself against the temptation and clung to the thoughts of forgetting it. At last I went to sleep; the next day upon waking all remembrance of it had indeed gone forever."[12]

What restless energy to create, disturbing even sleep! What fatal adjustment to inner reality! Such artistic immolation and the death of such an idea sears the mind. The blocking of a creative purpose either by circumstance or lack of technique not only smothers inspiration; it leaves the personality hobbled, unable longer to vault the fences to creative freedom. And it makes one shudder, but perhaps also admire an artist who was heroic enough—or was it mad enough?—to substitute duty for genius.[13]

Hutchinson investigated the frequency of "scientific hunch" as recognized by chemists, mathematicians, physicists, biologists, and men of similar standing. Answers to a questionnaire sent out by the Educational Department of the American Chemical Society yielded the report that 83 per cent of the 232 directors of research laboratories and "American Men of Science" replied affirmatively to the question: "Have you ever received assistance from the scientific revelation or 'hunch' in the solution of an important problem?"

Hutchinson has reported several examples of illuminations from the many sent him:

Bertrand Russell remarks, and in this his experience parallels that of a large number of scientists: "In all the creative work that I have done, what has come first is a problem, a puzzle, involving discomfort. Then comes concentrated voluntary application involving great effort. After this, a period without conscious thought; and finally a solution. This last stage is usually sudden."

Sir James Flinders Petrie, Egyptologist, illustrates the same points. "My work is mainly historical. I never try to settle a difficult problem off-hand. I first assemble the material, state the problem as definitely as possible, and then if no solution is evident, leave it alone. From time to time I look over it to refresh my memory, but never to force a solution. After waiting days or years I suddenly feel a wish to go over it again, and then everything runs smoothly and I can write without effort. . . ."

A physicist writes: "For two years I had been thinking about solid solutions or mixed crystals. There is a good bit known and some regularity has been discovered, summarized as Vegard's Law. (The law states that the crystal cell dimension is a linear function of composition in molar percentages.) One morning on going to look up something in the *American Mineralogist*, I came across a paper which denied this law in regard to mixed crystals. Its denial was based on the measurement of crystal spacing and not on the cell dimension to which Vegard's Law is said to apply. This wrong application amazed and disgusted me. Being out of mood for further work, I went to meet a friend who was going to town and was vaguely glad of the relief. I returned to the laboratory for my hat and arrived at the car before my friend. I was slightly annoyed at his delay. But suddenly, without warning, the idea flashed upon me that I could start with Vegard's Law and deduce a law for the variation in spacing which these men had measured, and could use all their measured data to check it."[14]

4. *Verification.* When the "good idea" or important solution has appeared to the thinker, he tests it in the light of known facts and reason. Perhaps he also explains it to colleagues in the same field of thought.

Creative thinking for most great thinkers has a pattern which may be described as drive, problem, conscious effort to solve it, passivity, repeated periods of conscious efforts and passivity, sudden illumination, and verification.*

The doctrine of transfer of training

Years ago, particularly during the days of the phrenologists, people thought that our minds were divided into faculties. It was believed that the faculties or "departments of the mind" could be trained as we train individual muscles. The curricula of the day required students to study certain subjects for their so-called mental discipline. Indeed, many people still erroneously believe that dead languages, mathematics, logic, and sciences should be studied, not because of any usefulness of the subjects themselves but because of the mental discipline which

is supposed to be acquired for other subjects that are useful.

Numerous investigations of these old claims have been made and we now know that we do not have such general powers or faculties. For example, there is no power of memory, but many memories. One may have an excellent memory for certain kinds of facts such as baseball statistics and a very poor memory for historical dates. To him, the baseball statistics are important, whereas the historical dates are needed only to pass an examination. The learner's attitudes toward the materials to be learned are far more potent in his abilities to recall them than any previous drills in unrelated subjects such as history, geometry, or Latin. The recall of a past experience or bit of information is not at all like the playing over of a wax record which has been traced by study of unrelated subjects. Remembering is a creative process.[15]

A simple example of the need for creative remembering, and the transfer when training is rigid and extensive but not creative, has been aptly phrased by Thorndike: "Soldiers trained to unquestioning and immediate obedience to their superiors are not characterized by notable obedience to law, conscience, or the civil authorities."[16]

This is not to say, however, that there is no such thing as transfer of training. If there were not, each new task we undertake would have to be learned through specific instruction or trial and error. Judd[17] proved how first teaching the principle involved in a task promotes faster learning, because the principle is generalized by the learner and applied to other situations. In his experiment, two groups of boys shot at a target submerged in water. One of the groups was

---

* These stages in creative thinking have been studied in the work of artists. See the study by C. Patrick, "Creative Thought in Artists," *Journal of Psychology,* Vol. 4 (1937), pp. 35–73. The process of creative thought in sketching pictures was studied by having artists sketch pictures while expressing their thoughts aloud, and by having them answer questions concerning their usual practices. Fifty professional artists and 50 unpracticed sketchers served as subjects. The reports revealed the four stages of creative thought: namely, preparation, incubation, illumination, and verification, already revealed in other studies of creation. The course of thought in artists and nonartists is similar. Nonartists draw more objects and more different kinds of objects than do artists.

first taught the principle of light refraction; the other was not. Although both groups made similar errors at first and corrected them through trial and error, the value of knowing the underlying principle was proved when the depth of the target was changed. This time the instructed group did much better than the uninstructed group. In another similar experiment, results showed even more clearly the value of theoretical background in solving a problem. Hendrickson and Schroeder's instructed subjects did better than uninstructed ones even in initial aims at the target.[18]

Knowledge of facts or principles in itself does not insure a transfer of learning to a new situation, however. There must be a basic understanding of the knowledge so that the possibility of its application to other situations may be realized.

Transfer of training depends upon the conscious acceptance by the learner of methods, procedures, principles, sentiments, and ideals which are common to the past subject and present interest. We make transfers whenever and wherever we sense a later experience as being similar to a previous one. This sensing of similarities or relationships may be vague or it may reach the level of fully conscious understanding. The more clearly or fully the relationships are sensed or recognized, the greater is the likelihood of transfer.[19]

Of course, this fact does not mean that no one should ever study Latin, logic, geometry, or zoology. Good reasons for the study of such subjects may be found in direct needs for the subjects themselves or in the cultural backgrounds which they supply. A student should study these subjects when the subjects contribute something directly to the student's needs or interests.

Furthermore, almost any subject has so many intrinsic values and relationships to one's contacts with life that any subject, when well taught and thoroughly learned, can contribute to one's intellectual growth.

Suggestions for the office and professional worker

Most people find that on certain days they get things done more speedily than on others. Is the increased speed and productivity merely psychological or actual? The fact is, each person has not only better and worse days, but also better and worse hours. While these are often psychological, there is also a very definite physical basis for our improved ability at certain times and lessened drive at other times.

The rise and fall of our working efficiency coincides with temperature variations in our body. Even when we are perfectly well, our temperature varies as much as three degrees in a single day. These temperature changes reflect our basal metabolism, that complicated process by which our body burns oxygen and keeps us going. Certain studies indicate that most people fall into one of three types:

a. *The Morning Type:* He wakes ready to go full blast. Packed with drive, he reaches his peak around noon, then cools off gradually. By evening he is pretty well burned out.

b. *The Evening Type:* He hates to get up and goes through the morning listless, lethargic, even surly. But soon after noon, he begins glowing. By late afternoon he is a fireball. His energy lasts into late evening.

c. *The Half-and-Half:* This happy man has the virtues of the other two. His personal thermostat gets him off to an early start. It cools him down at midday and fires him up again for the afternoon.

A person's cycle is not permanent. It is fixed by habit and habits can be changed. A few weeks' effort may do it. To raise your body heat in the morning, take a long, hot shower or bath, or up to a half hour of calisthenics. If you can change your temperature, you can alter the whole cycle.

The common tendency is to delay mental

work until the afternoon. This is often a mistake. Try yourself on these questions:

—Are you using your best hours doing secondary tasks which you might handle just as easily later?
—Do you do a lot of desk work or other straightening up when this routine could be done later or at day's end so as to start you off with a zip?
—Do you insist on handling routine correspondence to "get it out of the way" and leave your mind free for bigger things? Actually, you'd do better hitting those bigger things first. . . ."
—Have you made a conscientious effort to advance your cycle? Bear in mind that even if you're the evening type, you'll suffer a loss of efficiency later in the day. This is because, in most cases, you will already have been at work for a certain number of hours—and thus have used up a portion of the energy not otherwise restored.[20]

For most of us, an attractive surrounding increases our efficiency. Eliminating the clutter on a desk helps to get things done more quickly and seems to help straighten out the clutter in the mind.

UTILIZING TIME EFFICIENTLY. It is obviously impossible to specify how much time any office or professional worker should spend on each operation in the day's work. However, the places and occasions where one's time is wasted or misused are not in the performance of his regular duties but in the attention given to the bothersome trivialities adequately described by James Gordon Gilkey in his "Secrets of Effective Living":

Once I read about a man who was tied down and the ants ate him.
His fingers, his ears, his eyes, everything.
At last they even devoured his brain,
Emptying his skull bit by bit.
I am tied down, too, and little things are eating me—
The friend who calls me on the phone and talks and talks,
The agent who is determined to sell me a new mop,
The children who quarrel and will not do their lessons,
The letters that must be answered before night somehow,

The ice man's short weight, the butcher's carelessness,
All these little things are devouring me alive.

The time-consumers that "eat" us are social obligations, "being a good fellow," eating too much, and chasing ephemeral ideas that appear promising but end in rainbows without any pots of gold.

Our social obligations—receptions, playing bridge, golf, driving just for a drive, formal dinners, fraternal meetings, conventions, and community drives all appear essential to the development of a balanced personality and vocational advancement. In many cases, wives insist upon them. Some of these affairs do bring us in touch with people whom we ought to know. Some do bring in business later, but it is a waste of time in the long run to cultivate people merely for the sake of getting business rather than as the result of a natural liking for them. All these side lines become dangerous when they control us. Selling tickets for charity affairs, putting up decorations, buying theater tickets, lending money, giving talks before Sunday schools, writing letters of introduction, and so on, all have their place, but they tend to devour time and effort and end nowhere. It is seldom that people trust their fortunes or important problems to the accommodating man. When we are seriously ill we go to the doctor who is so busy professionally that he has no time to give to little things. We prefer to deposit our money in the bank whose president is noted for his ability and stability rather than in the bank whose president is a public beast of burden. To achieve things worthy of the respect of our fellows, we must respect the obligations of our own work to the extent that we fulfill them before we oblige others.

The ambitious individual need not confuse the performance of his own duties with an abrupt disregard for the needs and feelings of others. To refuse to take time to be accommodating to others does not necessitate coldness of manner. The daily acts of the worthwhile life can be invested with cordiality and friendliness. Our social relations should be more than mechanically reciprocal. They can be made delightfully pleasing. If a person lends us a book, we can do more than just thank him. We can prove to him that we read and enjoyed it. If we dine in a restaurant on a fifty-fifty basis, we should not forget the tips. We need not say to a person, "I see you do not remember me," but can state our own name without reminding him of his failure. When we win a big score in a bridge game, we need not go into a detailed recital of how it was done. When we greet the stenographer and the elevator operator, we can make the greeting just as friendly as the one we bestow upon our best customers. These little daily acts do not consume much time, but they do bring greater returns in human happiness and popularity than years of trifling services.

MEMORIZING NAMES AND FACES. Remembering the names of people whom we meet is not a mysterious gift that is given to politicians and denied to others. The politician finds it necessary to know people's names when he meets them and he consciously practices learning them. He seriously wants to know their names. Students in laboratory courses in psychology have taken part in an experiment where they repeated the colors in a color-naming test. The colors were only five in number and were irregularly arranged in one hundred bits, each of the five colors appearing twenty times. After the colors had been named over as often as two hundred times by each student, not one student could repeat the colors from memory in correct sequential order. Their efforts had been concentrated upon naming the bits of color as seen and not in connecting them in a series that could be remembered. Similarly, when we meet strangers, our attention is concentrated upon the impression that we make on the stranger and not upon knowing his name. We are too conscious of ourselves to grasp the name

of the stranger. Our self-consciousness will tend to disappear if we determine to know and remember the names of those whom we meet.

Quite frequently, when we meet strangers and are formally introduced to them, we do not hear the name, or, if we do hear it, we get it incorrectly. To insure clarity, we should spell the name and ask its owner whether it is correctly spelled and pronounced. The chairman at businessmen's luncheon clubs frequently ask each member to stand up and state his business affiliation. After this ceremony is over, few, if any, have learned the names. Most of the names are mumbled, and repeated too rapidly to make any neural impression. If members of clubs wish to become acquainted, the leader should ask the secretary to write each name on a blackboard or have each person write his own name on the board. Each of the other members should then write, on a piece of paper, the name of each stranger and try to connect the name and person in his own mind. Before the meeting ends, each person should try to recall the name of each member and verify his recollection.

A similar method can be used at bridge parties, dances, and banquets. Here the formal introduction must be hurried by the hosts and a request for enough time to write down each name and verify it would break into the smoothness of the occasion. However, when the guests are seated or participating in the activities, then the names of strangers can be requested from a near-by associate. Effort should be made to meet the strangers and learn something about their personalities.

Some memory-training systems advise the student to connect the name of the stranger in a grotesque or irrelevant way, as, Mr. Pitts might remind us of the fiery pit—Hell. Or, Mr. Long may be very short and the contrast seems to enable us to associate the name with his height. However, such irrational associations are not nearly so effective as a logical connection of facts regarding the personality of each stranger. The time and effort expended in making such incongruous connections can be spent more profitably in making logical connections of correct facts about the person.

The feeling tone in names must also be recognized. Persons whom we like, we remember. The name of the girl at the dance who is most attractive to the youth will be remembered for years. He puts forth effort to learn her name, telephone number, and other items of information. Conversely, we tend to forget those whom we dislike or do not care for. If a number of older men are asked to state the number of times they were engaged to girls before they were married, one is likely to find that those who were engaged to three or more girls cannot recall their names. They cannot recall them simply because some unpleasant experiences are associated with their memories. The true politician likes people, and his pleasant feeling toward them assists him in recalling their names.

When the name of the person is to be fixed so that it can be recalled, it should be repeated during the conversation as often as politeness permits. The average individual is able to recall about one-third more names when he has spoken the name once than when he has remained silent.[21] The salesman should get into the habit of prefacing many of his statements with "Mr. Prospect," and ending some of them with "Do you agree, Mr. Prospect?" After the stranger has left one's presence, it is well to think of him—not as "that fellow in the blue suit" but by name. And he should be thought of in terms of a clear visual image.

FREQUENCY OF USE AND ERROR. Frequency of Use and Error is a principle worked out and successfully applied by Dr. John A. Stevenson, President of the Penn Mutual Life Insurance Co. This principle works, as proved by Mr. Stevenson himself, for he has had a remarkably successful career. He has been a salesman, a sales manager, and a college professor, and at the age of thirty-four he attained a high executive position in the business world.

This principle can be applied by anyone anywhere. It is so simple that one is likely to say that it has always been known in a general way. But, since it is simple, it can be applied with profit to many jobs. It can be applied to an employee's tasks as follows:

Frequency of Use means that you:

1. Make a list of the things which you use or do in your daily work.
2. Find out how to improve these things which you use or do.
3. Perform your daily work according to the improved methods which you have discovered or found advisable.

Frequency of Error means that you:

1. Make a list of mistakes which you often make in your daily work.
2. Find out how to eliminate these errors.
3. Eliminate the errors in your daily work.

Let me illustrate. Suppose you are a shoe salesman and are selling shoes of various kinds of leather and prices. Make a list of the things you do each day, such as meeting customers, finding out the kind of shoes they want, measuring their feet, finding shoes from stock which they might want, making sales, giving change, and so on. Then find out how to improve each of the things you constantly do and apply your improved methods.

Now make a list of the errors you make, such as saying the wrong things to customers, grammatical errors, misjudging the size of shoe needed, and so on. Learn how to correct these errors. Then eliminate them from your daily work.

It all sounds very trite, but it is more easily said than done. Just to find how interesting and practical it is, let the reader take two sheets of paper and on the one make a list of the "Frequencies of Use" and on the other "Frequencies of Error" of his own vocation. It is well for the individual to work out the principle for his particular work and try it. The results may be surprisingly effective.

Acknowledgments and References

1. S. A. Stromswold and C. Gilbert Wrenn, "Counseling Students toward Scholastic Adjustment," *Educational and Psychological Measurement*, Vol. 8, No. 1 (Spring 1948).

2. Prescott Lecky, "Personal Counseling; The Theory of Self-Consistency in Personnel Problems," *Report* of the Annual Meeting of the American College Personnel Association, 1935.

3. For further information see Stadtlander, Elizabeth Louise, *Planning to Study Efficiently*, Educational Publishers, St. Louis, 1950, pp. 22–23.

4. Robert W. Frederick, Paul C. Kitchen, and Agness R. McElwee, *A Guide to College Study*, Appleton-Century-Crofts, Inc., New York, 1947.

5. Norman Frederiksen and W. B. Schrader, *Adjustment to College*, Educational Testing Service, Princeton, N.J., 1951.

6. C. W. Hunnicutt, "A Functional Program in Reading Instruction," *School and Society*, Vol. 67 (May 22, 1948), pp. 377–81.

7. Norman Lewis, *How to Read Better and Faster*, Thomas Y. Crowell Co., New York, 1944, p. 10.

8. *Science News Letter*, September 18, 1948, p. 178.

9. Luella W. Pressey, *A Manual of Reading Exercises for College Freshmen*, Ohio State University Press, Columbus, Ohio, 1928, presents some helpful exercises for students who read very slowly.

10. Eliot D. Hutchinson, "The Technique of Creative Thought," *The American Scholar*, May 1932.

11. Graham Wallas, *The Art of Thought*, Harcourt, Brace and Company, New York, 1926.

12. Romain Rolland, *Musicians of Today*, translated by Mary Blaiklock, Henry Holt and Company, New York, 1908.

13. Eliot D. Hutchinson, *op. cit.*

14. *Ibid.*

15. Numerous experiments which indicate that remembering is a creative process are reported by F. C. Bartlett in *Remembering*, The Macmillan Company, New York, 1932.

16. E. L. Thorndike, *Human Nature and the Social Order*, The Macmillan Company, New York, 1940, p. 307.

17. Charles H. Judd, "The Relation of Special Training to General Intelligence," *Educational Review*, Vol. 36 (1908), pp. 28–42.

18. Gordon Hendrickson and William H. Schroeder, "Transfer of Training in Learning to Hit a Submerged Target," *Journal of Educational Psychology*, Vol. 32 (1941), pp. 205–213.

19. E. E. Bayles, "An Unemphasized Factor in Current Theories Regarding the Transfer of Training," *Journal of Educational Psychology*, Vol. 27 (1936), pp. 425–430. H. R. Hamley, "Formal Training: a Critical Survey of Experimental Work," *British Journal of Educational Psychology*, Vol. 6 (1936), pp. 233–249.

20. Ray Josephs, "Gaining a Golden Hour Every Day," *American Business*, February 1956, p. 12. From a book *How to Gain an Extra Hour Every Day* by the same author, E. P. Dutton and Co., New York, 1955.

21. Harold E. Burtt and A. C. Beck, "Remembering Names Connected with Faces," *Journal of Industrial Psychology*, January 1928, pp. 34–38.

PROJECTS

1. Keep a careful record of all your activities for one week. Is your time being used efficiently? If not, make a study schedule and then follow a definite time schedule, suggested by the form on page 185.

2. Below is a list of "do" study habits. Post a similar list over your desk and check each night on your study habits:

    a. Had eight hours sleep.
    b. Followed a definite time schedule.
    c. Prepared the next assignment immediately after class.
    d. Reviewed assignment and preceding lecture notes before class.
    e. Checked written assignments.
    f. Added words to my vocabulary.
    g. Took a brief scanning view over before reading.
    h. Took part in class discussion.
    i. Discussed a lesson with another student.
    j. Read a book or journal in the library for collateral reading.

3. Do you find it difficult to concentrate? For one week study always with an extra sheet of paper at hand. Each time that you find

your attention wanders from your studying, list the subject of distraction.

4. Write a set of rules for remembering people whom you meet.

5. Devise a written form of recording new words being added to your vocabulary. Some students use a page in their notebooks, others use a separate notebook, still others keep small card files.

6. What is a card catalog? What information is found on most cards? How are the cards arranged?

7. What indexes does your college library have? Explain each item of one magazine entry in a periodical index.

8. After reading an assignment, develop questions that your instructor might use on the next quiz.

9. When an executive requests a subordinate to give him a report, the executive usually wants it as soon as possible. After the report has been submitted, the executive may neglect to read it for several days or weeks. What is the cause of this habit on the part of the executive? How can the subordinate adjust himself to such wishes of his superior?

10. To what extent does playing the stock market decrease the efficiency of businessmen who do it? Should the ambitious businessman determine not to bother with speculation?

11. Where can the businessman obtain his best ideas or do his most effective thinking—in the office, at home, in the club, on the golf course, or other places?

12. Is a clean desk indicative of personal efficiency? Make a study of this problem by preparing a list of the best executives whom you know and then observing the tops of their desks.

13. What are the psychological reasons for the fact that some executives find it difficult to delegate routine tasks to subordinates?

14. Experiments indicate that muscular tension and thinking go together. In one experiment, when the muscles of the arms were tensed, the learning time was reduced 13 per cent, and arithmetical problems were solved 10 per cent more rapidly and 6 per cent more accurately. Should a man attempt to keep his muscles in a state of tension when he is on the job?

15. Analyze a definite job according to the principle of Frequency of Use and Error.

COLLATERAL READINGS

Bird, Charles and Dorothy M., *Learning More by Effective Study*, Appleton-Century-Crofts, Inc., New York, 1945.

Burtt, Harold E., *Applied Psychology*, Prentice-Hall, Inc., Englewood Cliffs, N.J., 1948, pp. 151–170 and 184–186.

Cole, Luella and Jessie M. Ferguson, *Student's Guide to Efficient Study*, Rinehart and Company, Inc., New York, 1946.

Frederick, R. W., P. C. Kitchen, and Agnes R. McClure, *A Guide to College Study*, Appleton-Century-Crofts, Inc., New York, 1947.

Gerken, C. d'A., *Study Your Way Through School*, Science Research Associates, Chicago, 1953.

Hultin, Greta L., *Studying in the Twentieth Century*, Division of Student Personnel at Wayne University, Detroit, Mich., 1945.

Prouty, Helen, "Personality Factors Related to Over and Underachievement of College Students," *The American Psychologist*, August 1955, p. 364.

Robinson, F. P., *Effective Study*, Harper & Brothers, New York, 1946.

Rust, Ralph M., and Francis J. Ryan, "Personality Factors Associated With Academic Achievement in College," *The American Psychologist*, August 1955, p. 382.

Stadtlander, Elizabeth L., *Planning to Study Efficiently*, Educational Publishers, St. Louis, 1950.

Stromswold, Stanley A., and C. Gilbert Wrenn, "Counseling Students toward Scholastic Adjustment," *Educational and Psychological Measurement*, Vol. 8, No. 1 (Spring 1948), pp. 57–63.

Weigand, George and Walter S. Blake, Jr., *A Study Skills Manual in College Orientation*, Prentice-Hall, Inc., Englewood Cliffs, N.J., 1955, pp. 57–64.

CHAPTER ELEVEN

Choosing a vocation

Many people think of choosing a vocation as wholly a problem in prediction of the person's future vocational abilities, successes, or failures. Psychologists, too, are interested in facilitating the individual's choice by means of valid prediction devices, but they are even more interested in improving his adjustments to the possibilities within himself and his environment. The psychologically well-adjusted person is likely to be a vocationally happy person.

One of the pioneers in the field of vocational guidance became interested in the work because he met a boy who worked in a bird store during the day and studied architectural drawing at night, but had an ambition to become a sea captain! We all know of similar persons who are confused about their vocational objectives, many others who accept their daily grind because they do not know what else to do, and a few who are really enthusiastic about their work.

Vocational decisions must be made continuously

Studies of college students' abilities to make lasting vocational choices indicate that permanence of choice varies with the kind of professional training. Law and medical college students are more likely to enter and remain in their chosen professions or areas of work than business students.

Some changes in occupations are probably beneficial and natural. A physician in the private practice of medicine who concerns himself with health problems in the community can make a logical and easy step to politics. The university teacher of chemistry may pass on to chemical research in a corporation. Our available evidence indicates that such shifting about in occupations does take place among the successful members of society. For example, a study of the persons listed in "Who's Who in America" indicated that occupational changes were made after the age of 35 by one-third of these successful persons.[1] Perhaps a great deal of the vocational shifting which constantly takes place signifies one way in which individuals are making adjustments to the psychological problems within

203

themselves as well as to the problems of making a living.

Many persons who have had to choose a way to make a living thought that the choice was determined by chance. But *chance* here, as elsewhere, is simply another name for the influence of a large number of unknown factors. Chance, in the determination of vocational choice, simply refers to the influences of many factors, such as those of adjustment. These psychological influences are now being unraveled in some cases. However, chance will have to continue to play the major role for some generations to come, because science must make many discoveries before we can foretell the future of a youth. We shall probably never reach "that day when men's biographies can be written in advance." However, the man who is dissatisfied with his vocation, or who is at the threshold of his economic life and must choose an occupation, can be given some helpful suggestions.

Several important basic facts should first be fixed in the mind of the person who is seeking vocational guidance for himself or is trying to counsel others who are misfits. One of these basic facts is that "the square peg and the round hole" idea is an erroneous simile. This expression implies that the human being is vocationally fixed and unchangeable in his nature. It also implies that the occupation is rigid in its requirements. On the contrary, human beings are very adaptable. Consider the record of man's progress through the ages and note the many adaptations he has had to make. Few of us would choose the life of the cave man, and yet, if conditions demanded it, many men could meet the demands of primitive life in a highly successful manner. Few of us would choose the trade of the skilled artisan; but, if a sudden industrial upheaval demanded it, we could become blacksmiths and carpenters just as readily as we become salesmen, teachers, and lawyers. Each man

---

How do people feel about their jobs?

Ever wonder what most people think about their jobs? Science Research Associates of Chicago asked half a million workers—from the president on down—in 850 companies how they felt about pay, company efficiency, personal goals, etc. Here are some of the results.

Pay. Only one third felt they were paid enough to live comfortably.

Hours. Ninety percent said their working hours were okay.

Pensions, insurance, etc. Seventy-three percent found "fringe benefits" satisfactory.

Company pride. Eighty-six percent were proud of their firms.

Company efficiency. Sixty percent thought their companies could operate more efficiently.

Self-importance. Eighty-one percent felt their jobs were important.

Personal goals. Only thirty-six percent knew where they stood and where they were headed.

From *Changing Times,* the Kiplinger Magazine, October 1954. The results referred to are from surveys in many companies. The questionnaire form used is the SRA Employee Inventory, published and serviced by Science Research Associates, 57 West Grand Avenue, Chicago 10, Illinois. Further information may be had by writing to SRA's Management and Personnel Research Division.

who goes into any vocation must adapt himself to some extent; and he, in turn, also modifies the job to fit himself.

We are not fitted by nature for one occupation and one only. It is probable that most persons who are now successful in one field could also become equally successful in some other occupation. No one is perfectly fitted for any occupation. The choosing of a vocation means that we must choose the one that requires the least amount of adjustment and gives us the greatest amount of personal satisfaction. Very few individuals are "born" to any vocation. A person of high intelligence who has had a favorable previous environment could succeed in at least a dozen fields, unless one of those fields required some special organic quality, such as the ability to hear a wide range of musical notes or to distinguish sharply between shades of colors. However, limitations of the sense organs or motor equipment are exceptional in modern vocational adjustments.

So far as we know, the brain does not at birth have certain neural patterns for specific vocational functions. Nor do such patterns develop in the brain except as the adjustments bring them about. Of course, we exclude such native endowments as exceptional qualities or limitations of the sensory apparatus. Insofar as neural capacity is involved, a great majority of persons who are in doubt as to the vocation to be chosen could pick any one of several and succeed equally well in any of the several.

Vocational decisions must be made continuously. An individual cannot make a single decision that will settle his vocational future. Rather, he must make a series of decisions, not only as to the kind of work he shall do, but also as to the kind of training he shall acquire, the place of training, the job he shall seek, and the manner in which he shall advance in his chosen field. As he develops ability in a given occupation, he must choose the phase in which he shall specialize. And, later in life, he must decide upon the kind of activities that will give him

the greatest amount of self-expression. Occasionally he must decide upon the factor that shall be construed as success or failure for him; whether his objective shall be happy associations with his children, opportunities to influence the lives of others, fame, or wealth. The selection of this objective cannot be made at the beginning of life but must be decided as time brings about new situations and conditions. Not only does the individual change, but society, business, and occupations change. The occupations which are important in one decade may be of little consequence in the next decade. The progress in aviation and the automobile industry could not be foreseen forty years ago.

No one is born for a particular occupation. Nor should we think that, if an individual fails to find his one niche in life, he will be doomed to a life of failure or mediocrity. No one should be continually looking for a "niche." If he is, it is quite probable that he never will find it, because each man must make his own.

Nor should we seek to follow the vocational pathways that some other successful individual traveled. Much as we admire Lincoln, none of us can be just like him or do what he did. We can hope only to make a place in life for ourselves which we can fill as well, proportionately, as he filled his. The man who hears of how some relative, classmate, neighbor, or friend has become wealthy or happy and then attempts to follow in the same footsteps is apt to find that his feet do not fit those footprints. We cannot take the personality and conditions of some other individual and superimpose them upon ourselves. Each man must establish his own career for himself and in his own way rather than by imitating a predecessor. He cannot even imitate, as a rule, his own father, unless the successful father gives the son so great a head start that it is difficult for the youth to fail. This rule also implies that the boy who goes to "dad's alma mater" just because his father happened to go there should realize that times have changed, and that his needs may not be the same as those of his father when he was young.

The vocational advice of parents and friends

The vocational advice of relatives and friends is likely to be defective in many respects.

Parents who attempt to influence the choice of vocation for their children often do so as a compensation for their own deficiencies. The parent may say it is for the child's good. Actually, it may be a form of display for the parent. When parents find that they can no longer hope to become famous or to achieve their adolescent dreams, they project their hopes for glory into the brightest or favorite child of the family and compel the child to enter the profession which, in their opinion, offers the desired prestige or wealth. When a boy fails in college and the personnel adviser suggests to the parent that his son should become a mechanic or a businessman rather than a surgeon, the parent is likely to answer disgustedly: "Why, that's no profession at all. I want my son to amount to something." Such an answer indicates that the parent is the one who really wants to amount to something.

The vocational guidance given by many teachers, employment managers, preachers, and lecturers is in the same class as the home remedy of the friend who never studied medicine or the human body. The physician, with all his years of training and experience, makes many errors in diagnosing our bodily ills, but the untrained friend who tries to do so makes many more.

If a person is in need of vocational guidance and asks some of his friends for suggestions, he may be surprised to find that each person's advice differs from that of all the others. Many friends can give only general and trivial suggestions which have but slight value. For example, a case study was made of each of a number of adults who voluntarily sought vocational guidance. To assist in the analyses, each one of the subjects gave personality rating blanks to several persons, six or less, who knew him well. These six friends were to check on the rating blank the items that applied to the person being rated and to offer any helpful vocational suggestions. An analysis of the rating blanks for 36 ratees as filled in by the 191 raters resulted in the following table:

TABLE 11-1

Traits	Percentage of 191 Raters Who Listed the Trait in Their Ratings
Learn to do things that you dislike	26
Control your temper	21
Be more patient	17
Be less nervous	17
Smile more often	16
Think less about your own troubles	16
Do not sulk when things go wrong	16
Be more tactful	15
Be more enthusiastic	14
Improve your vocabulary	13
Learn to talk to all kinds of people	13
Be more aggressive	13
Learn more about human nature	13
Be less sensitive	13
Shave more frequently	9
Improve your table manners	6
Don't tell shady stories	5
Prevent your halitosis	2

In addition to the above, many other characteristics were mentioned by the friends of the advisees; but this table will be sufficient to illustrate the nature of the suggestions of the friends who rated the individuals. Some helpful suggestions were given, and the ratings gave a composite picture of how the person rated appeared to the raters. The ratings were a group estimate of the individual, and, in some cases, suggested avenues for further psychological exploration. The main deficiency in the ratings of these persons who sought vocational guidance lay in the poverty of helpful suggestions regarding any specific occupations which the ratees should enter. Many of the traits listed are really suggestions for better adjustment habits.

Vocational guidance in the sense of showing a person what he should do is very difficult. It is very difficult even for the trained vocational psychologists. Most modern vocational psychologists do not try to study a youth in order to tell him what he should do but to help him improve his adjustments to life by means of a vocation. Perhaps the psychologist also points out what the youth is likely to do. A boy may have certain adjustment tendencies which can be pointed out to him and suggestions may be given him for the utilization of his established tendencies. However, the boy's choice cannot be controlled. The individual himself must make his own adjustments and his own choice. Guidance cannot play the part of a benevolent parent who adjusts conditions for the child; guidance can only prepare the youth to meet his own difficulties.

The logical question arises: When the psychologist analyzes a person for the purpose of vocational guidance, how does his analysis differ from that of the acquaintances who know the individual? Chiefly, in two ways. First, the experienced psychologist who has had some clinical training knows much about adjustment patterns of individuals. He can recognize tendencies which can be utilized in a vocation in order to bring about better adjustment and more satisfying fruits from the advisee's efforts.

Second, the modern vocational psychologist supplements his clinical and other subjective estimates with objective tests. The tests which he uses have been standardized on thousands of individuals and are fairly accurate; so, if two psychologists test the same person, their findings tend to be the same. The psychologist also tries to find the specific channels through which the intelligence expresses itself, as in mathematics, music, mechanics, social contacts, and so forth.

An example of the value of the testing services of the psychologist may be shown in the case of a boy in a western New York high school who was sent to the commercial teacher by the principal. The principal told the teacher that the boy was of low intelligence and could not do good school work. The quality of the boy's work in all his courses was of such a low grade that the teachers had given up all hopes of teaching him. Because the other teachers were tired of the boy, he was sent to the new commercial teacher of the school. This teacher also found that the boy's reputation for poor work was correct so far as commercial subjects were concerned. He was the poorest student that this teacher had met in that school.

Fortunately, the commercial teacher had had courses in mental testing, and he gave the boy several intelligence tests just to find out whether his intelligence was as low as it appeared to be. To the teacher's surprise, the boy scored slightly above normal in all the tests. The teacher then gained the boy's confidence and found that he had a serious inferiority complex. One of his teachers whom he had had four years previously had convinced him that he was a "dub and a dumb-bell." After that he made no effort to do good work, but rather tried to live down to the kind of reputation he was given. The commercial teacher changed the boy's attitude and he then did good work in all his courses, because all his teachers knew that he could do good work and required him to do it.

In this example we see that the counselor used tests as an aid in his diagnosis of the boy, but he supplemented the test results with his own subjective insight into the boy's adjustment habits and helped the boy readjust himself to his barriers.

Methods of choosing a vocation

Some of the current methods whereby the individual can predict or tries to predict his own behavior for vocational adjustment have been mentioned, but we shall list the more common ones:

1. Pseudo-scientific schemes such as phrenology, character analysis, astrology, etc. These have no value and need not be discussed further.
2. Choose a problem to the solution of which you can devote your life.
3. Analyze yourself according to some systematic plan and make a decision.
4. Have yourself tested with the few valid psychological tests now available.
5. By means of a systematic analysis of your adjustments, recognize the conscious and unconscious drives in your own personality.
6. Allow yourself to be made a case study by a vocational psychologist.

One of the best ways for the intelligent person to choose a vocation is to select a problem that needs solution. The modern scientific student often does this and develops his interest in a problem into a new vocation. For example, a girl who was a student in a college of home economics found that the lowly mushroom had never been studied carefully. She then decided to make a study of mushrooms, and, when she was graduated, she was offered an excellent position where she utilized her interest in mushrooms. Inventors often use this method. So does the man who sees a need for some particular kind of business in his community and then starts a business to answer that need. Thousands of problems in all the professions and businesses are awaiting solution. The man who determines to devote his efforts to answers to economic and social difficulties usually finds that he has found his vocation. A few of many such problems are listed as suggestions and not as a complete list:

1. Develop, through propagation, certain prolific weed plants into valuable food plants.
2. Work out and install better systems of training and promotion for employees of large concerns.
3. Much of the money now spent for advertising is wasted. Someone should develop laws of effective advertising, so that all money spent for advertising will be productive.

4. Find out how to make public school work more interesting, more cultural, and more related to life.
5. Develop better methods of settling difficulties between employers and workers.
6. Work out methods for improving the personal efficiency of certain classes or kinds of persons.
7. Teach and help people of this country to understand and appreciate art—the beautiful things of life as well as the practical.
8. Discover the bases of personality and help others to improve their personalities.
9. At present our educational system is adapted to the average child. Some cities pay special attention to the backward or poor student. Evolve a system that develops the exceptionally bright student to his utmost. Much of this latent ability is now being wasted.
10. Religion is in a different environment from what it has been heretofore. Some think that we must put religion on a basis that will appeal to the people of this age.
11. Prevent or decrease crimes and learn how to re-educate criminals.
12. Solve the parking problem in cities.
13. Invent sidewalks which are less trying to our feet.
14. Improve the lighting of rooms.
15. Invent better children's games, especially games to be played by small children while riding in an automobile.

We Americans have hundreds of unsolved problems, and the solutions of certain problems would give employment to thousands of workers. To the well-adjusted, intelligent worker, the pull of the future (toward the solution of a problem) should be more stimulating than the push from the past (his own adjustment tendencies). Unfortunately, however, most young people allow their own adjustment tendencies and the conventional occupational openings to determine the directions of their vocational efforts. Very few men devote themselves to the solution of some problem unless they first have had some profound emotional experience that pushes them in the direction of such devotion. For example, all of us recognize the need for greater safety in driving automobiles, but few among us will vigorously pursue safer driving as a life work unless we have had an intense emotional experience

with bad driving, such as the death of a
loved one in an unnecessary accident. Sometimes the vocational psychologist can recognize such adjustment tendencies, resulting
from severe emotional problems, which can
be utilized in solving a problem and giving
the individual a well-motivated and satisfying career.

Self-analysis

Many of the first attempts at vocational
guidance required the youth to answer a
long series of questions regarding his vocational interests. He was asked not only to
state whether he liked, disliked, or felt a
neutral interest in listed occupations, but
also to estimate himself in general traits as:

> Are you aggressive?
> Are you industrious?
> Do you have a pleasing personality?
> Are you neat in habits?
> Are you conceited?
> Do you coöperate with others?
> Do you look ahead?

Hollingworth and others have made studies of the reliability and accuracy of self-
estimates of general traits. He conducted
experiments wherein the individuals in a
group rated the other members of the group
and themselves in nine differnt traits. The
results indicated that people cannot rate
themselves with any great degree of accuracy. The natural expectation would be that
we tend to overestimate ourselves in desirable traits and underestimate ourselves in
undesirable traits. The following data from
his study of estimates of fifty people[2] show
the presence of a factor of constant bias in
self-estimation (See Table 11-2).

Hollingworth also found that the more admirable the trait the closer the relation between possession of the trait and the ability
to judge it in others. His subjects who had
reprehensible traits could not rate themselves very accurately in those traits. Of
course, we must bear in mind that people

TABLE 11-2

SHOWING CONSTANT TENDENCIES OR
BIAS IN SELF-ESTIMATION

Trait	Per Cent Over- estimating Themselves	Per Cent Under- estimating Themselves
Refinement	80	20
Humor	78	22
Intelligence	68	32
Sociability	68	32
Neatness	50	50
Beauty	50	50
Conceit	48	52
Snobbishness	36	64
Vulgarity	34	66

cannot rate others accurately in generalized
traits, and Hollingworth's experiment assumed that the group estimates of the raters
were correct. The consensus of the acquaintances who did the rating was accepted as the true impression that an individual made on others. It is quite probable
that, if objective measures had been available of Hollingworth's subjects in the nine
traits he studied, they would not have agreed
with the average ratings of the acquaintances.

The Allports' experiment confirmed the
principle that self-estimates in general traits
are not accurate.[3] Different people were
asked to estimate their own intelligence by
the rating scale method, and they were also
given intelligence tests. Then their self-estimates and their scores in the tests were compared. Those who were high in intelligence
tended to underestimate themselves and
those who were low in intelligence tended
to overestimate themselves. The correlation
between self-estimates of ability and scores
in the Otis Group Intelligence Test was —.67.
Self-estimates are not reliable, unless they
can be proved to be of sound predictive
value. To prove their value requires careful
statistical treatment, which has not yet been
given for most traits that are considered in
vocational self-analyses.

Even though self-estimates are not reliable, they may have some value in causing
the individual to grade and recognize his

own inclinations, tendencies, and characteristics in relation to an occupational choice. In some cases, it may be well for the individual to decide upon his personal likes and dislikes and to try to avoid those occupations that require traits that are definitely unpleasant or to seek occupations that require traits that are pleasant to him. For example, some persons dislike to handle other people physically, which is necessary in the work of the osteopath, the chiropodist, the barber, the nurse, and the hairdresser.

When the individual's self-analysis is made by means of a statistically treated list of occupational and other activities to which the individual reacts in terms of liking for (L), indifference toward (I), or dislike for (D), the method of self-analysis is called an *interest test.*

Vocational interest tests

The most widely used interest test is that of Edward K. Strong, Jr. There are two forms of this test, one for men and one for women. Each form of the test is an eight-page leaflet listing some 400 items covering occupations, school subjects, amusements, activities, peculiarities of people, and self-estimates of personal abilities and characteristics. The average time needed by most persons to fill in the test is forty minutes, though no time limit is set.

Norms have been developed for some forty-seven occupations and vocational groupings for men and twenty-five for women. Most of the occupations listed are on a professional level. This makes the administration of the test to a person of low intelligence or one with no prospect of professional training largely a waste of time. The test is best used with individuals of college age and above, though it may be used to advantage with selected high school groups.

The interest test is not a measure of aptitude or ability, and so is used, not to replace aptitude or ability tests, but to supplement them. Results of the test do, however, suggest that the person whose pattern of interest is similar to that of the men or women in the criterion group has greater chances for satisfaction and success in that occupation than in one where his interests differ widely from those of successful persons in that field.

Scores on the Strong test may be translated as standard scores, percentile ranks, or letter ratings. The ratings A, B, and C are more easily understood. An A rating means that the testee has the interests characteristic of persons successfully engaged in the occupation specified; B has a similar implication, but there is less certainty; and C means that the testee does not have such interests. Any occupation in which the rating is an A or B+ may be suggested to the testee for serious consideration. An occupation in which the interest rating is C should be chosen only after careful consideration of other factors, such as strong drives.

Numerous studies have been made of the permanence and predictive value of measured vocational interest and expressed vocational choice.

Strong made a follow-up study of seniors at Stanford University first tested in 1927 and freshmen first tested in 1930. He found that individuals who had "interests most similar to engineer, lawyer, or minister on the first occasion were the ones who had scores most similar to those same criterion groups on the retest—twenty-two years later. People expressed approximately the same order of work preference, according to occupational interest scores, for as long as twenty-two years."

At least two factors that affect permanence of the interest score are the time interval between the test and the retest and the age at the time the test was taken. Obviously, the older a man is when he is tested, the more permanent his preference is likely to be. Thus, the college seniors who ranged in age from 22 to 32 retained the same interests to a greater extent than did the freshmen who were between the ages of 19 and 28 when tested. Although permanence is less for younger men than old, it is still remarkably high among the former.[4]

Strong also made a follow-up study of men who had expressed some interest in engineering in 1930 and found that those with the highest scores were employed in engineering or closely allied fields nineteen years later. Men who had originally had little interest in engineering were usually working in offices, sales, or law. From these observations there would seem to be a high positive correlation between measured interest in engineering and the occupations in which these people were working almost two decades later.[5]

Trinkaus conducted an independent study to determine how permanent interests are as revealed by the Strong test. He compared the recorded interests of 212 Yale alumni who had originally been tested in 1935 and 1936 with their 1950 retest.

The scores were remarkably permanent over a fourteen or fifteen year period. The extreme scores, indicating great interest or lack of interest, were most stable. Of these, the low interest scores were more nearly the same. In the middle ranges where there was least stability the scores usually shifted downward.[6]

Another study has revealed a relationship between interest during adolescence, as measured by the Kuder Preference Record, and occupation seven to nine years later. Men in occupations covering 6 of the 9 test areas had significantly higher preferences for activities related to these fields than did men who were, at the time of the study, engaged in other occupations.[7]

The Psychological Service of Pittsburgh have also studied the stability of interests. They tested high school students with the Kuder Preference Record and made two follow-up studies of 130 pupils who went to college. The time lapse between the first follow-up and the original test was two years. The second retest was administered approximately four years after the initial one.

The Service reported that in these four years (the testees now seniors and juniors in college) preferences had stabilized, especially for females. The only significant change was on the persuasive scale among men. Other findings on stability of interest were:

Social service interests continue to be one of the least stable scales and artistic interest one of the most stable. The mechanical scale increased its value for males from the two to four year investigation and remained the most stable area for that sex. The group as a whole is characterized by a decline in clerical and scientific interest and a rise in social service preference when retested in college. The males gained in persuasive interests in both follow-up studies.

The study also indicated that job preferences of working women are more stable on a number of scales. This may be due to the fact that the women who fall into this group are those for whom the opportunity for wider experiences and stimulation is much less than for working men or college students. In this group are the women who, following high school graduation, enter clerical jobs and then marry. Because of this restriction of opportunity, their interest patterns and their job preferences would tend to stabilize.[8]

In a study of another interest test it was found that low scores in a particular area of vocational interest do not justify the assumption that the individual cannot derive satisfaction from work in that area. Nor does a high point in an interest test profile always indicate the most appropriate field for specialization.[9]

Interest tests are a helpful device in confirming stated interests as well as in calling attention to occupational interests which the individual may have overlooked. The vocational psychologist is also concerned about certain aspects of interests other than the score on a test, especially about "absorbing interests" or intensive drives which may have developed in the adjustment history of the individual.

Other tests for vocational guidance

Many people who seek vocational guidance think that the psychologist can test the capacities of anyone so that the person tested will know just exactly what vocation he can and should follow. The psychologists also at one time thought that they might be able to develop predictive testing to that stage, but the recent researches indicate that they were too optimistic. Professor Seashore and his colleagues have spent some fifty years in the analysis of musical talent. They have developed some tests with high predictive values, but the analysis of that one talent is not complete. If fifty years of research in one field have not produced wholly satisfactory results, we should not expect too much from the use of other tests which have had far less attention than the musical aptitude tests. Certain schools of music now use musical aptitude tests and find them very helpful, but psychologists have probably made more progress in musical testing than in any other aptitude. As stated in the previous discussion of tests, they do have some value, but they furnish a statistical prediction on the basis of what a group or number of individuals will do rather than what any single person can or will do. In vocational guidance we want to know what a group can do, but we wish particularly to know what a specific individual can do.

Another difficulty in vocational guidance, based upon tests only, is the fact that a person who tests high in a given trait that could be capitalized vocationally may not care for that vocation. Thousands of people are capable of becoming good undertakers, but most of them would object to it as a vocation because of emotional inhibitions. Similarly, psychologists might make more statistical studies of the kinds of men and women that can marry each other with the greatest chances of a happy marriage, but such tests would have little value in decreasing matrimonial failures. The persons whom scientific analyses would indicate as ideal mates might not care for each other at all and would refuse to go through with the ceremony. Scientific marriages would not be nearly so inviting to the masses of people as the old-fashioned method of romance and chance. Two individuals must be "drawn" to each other emotionally. The individual must also be attracted to his vocation emotionally.

This statement of some of the limitations of tests should not be construed as making them valueless. It is important to use tests as one factor to be considered when dealing with vocational problems. Tests are particularly useful in pointing out certain vocations in which the individual would have small chance of success. Certainly anyone who considers choosing music as a career should first have himself tested by someone who can administer the Seashore test or adaptations of it.

Other tests, helpful in certain problems of vocational analysis, can often be recommended by competent vocational psychologists and counselors.[10] However, when the vocational counselor attempts to find tests having unquestionable value in the vocational guidance of youth, he has difficulty in finding any that are conclusive. He must resort to the use of general intelligence tests. General intelligence has been defined in various ways, but chiefly as the ability to adjust oneself to the problems of one's environment, as the average of various abilities, as the ability to learn, and as the ability to do school work. Most studies indicate a definite relationship between general intelligence or mental ability and other desirable traits of vocational significance.

In cases of extremely high or low intelligence, we are safe in making certain predictions. A person with an intelligence quotient of less than 100 could not do good work in most colleges. Lack of intelligence can be compensated for, to some extent, by an exceptionally great amount of effort, but even superior effort would not enable a student of low intelligence to succeed in college.

The high school student who plans to enter college should try to select a college and a course that are in harmony with his intelligence level and high school marks.

The vocational psychologist often supplements intelligence, interest, and special ability tests with personality inventories such as the Bernreuter Personality Inventory, the Humm-Wadsworth Temperament Scale, social knowledge tests, and others. These are useful in making diagnoses regarding introversion, social adjustment, and similar personality characteristics of importance to the trained psychologist. He wants to know the pattern of temperament, intelligence, aptitude, interest, and other tests. Knowledge of such patterns may enable the counselor to suggest a suitable type of work within a vocation after the general vocational field has been chosen.

It was formerly thought that a person must have a certain set of personality traits and abilities to fit a particular occupation. Recent investigations have revealed that men with widely different characteristics may be equally successful in the same position. A man seems to be successful if he can supply the one thing that is particularly needed in a situation, with ordinary fitness for other requirements of the job. For example, a man may be a desirable member of an architectural firm if he is an expert draftsman, without any social ability or power of verbal expression. Another man may be equally desirable as a member of the same firm who has little ability as a draftsman but who knows how to meet people and explain building plans. A third member may specialize in drawing or esthetic appreciation. Legal firms have the same variety of talents. There is a great difference between a successful surgeon, a laboratory diagnostician, and a family doctor.[11]

We should recognize that vocational objectives and choices of college can be revised. Educational and vocational growth are intertwined. Civilizations and personalities are dynamic. Interests ripen. The satisfactions derived from exercise of intelligence and aptitudes vary with the individual's adjustments to new barriers in his development. This means that a study of adjustments, drives, and preferences should supplement any tests administered.

Adjustment analysis for choosing a vocation

The choice of a vocation, like the choice of a mate, often expresses the adjustment of the individual. For example, the son of many a very able and successful business executive does not care to become a businessman. He may want to become a scientist, even though he knows that his father hopes he will some day take over the business. When we also learn, as happens in some cases, that the boy has felt for years that he did not meet his father's expectations of him as a son, we can expect the boy to prefer a career in some line of work other than his father's. To such a son, the father's business may be associated with feelings of inadequacy. This appears to be most likely if the father has a dominating personality, is the kind of father who has often said to the child: "I don't understand why you can't do thus and so? Why when I was your age, I did that and more."

Such a boy in his adjustment development naturally turns to some activity which is not associated with the father's personality. Sometimes it is in the direction of political radicalism, because that kind of "conviction" on the part of the boy is one way in which the businessman-father can be "punished."

Of course adjustments such as these are made unconsciously. The boy, when asked to explain his own psychological development, cannot do so. The clinician can. Unfortunately, very few clinically trained persons are doing vocational counseling, and those who are realize that truly reliable insights into a person's motivations can be made only after considerable study of the individual.

Projective techniques such as the Rorschach ink-blot tests have been found especially helpful in making such studies,[12] but

"Young Raleigh," by John Everett Millais. This famous painting is reproduced to illustrate the fact that some individuals choose their vocation as the result of instructional influences. Of course the instructional influences are more likely to be acted upon when they fit into the individual's unconscious drives. (By permission of Gramstorff Bros., Inc., Malden, Mass.)

these require much clinical training for their interpretation and further validation of their results.

Stanley J. Segal reported findings from a study that was made to apply psychoanalytic theory to the vocational choices of accounting and creative writing students. A battery of projective tests was administered. The findings were:

1. Accounting students and writing students did not differ in general adjustment level.
2. It is doubtful that accounting students show greater acceptance of social norms than writing students.
3. Accounting students show greater attempts at emotional control, whereas writing students show greater awareness of feelings.
4. There were no differences in the use of compulsive defenses.
5. Writing students showed greater evidence of expressions of hostility.
6. Writing students showed greater tolerance for ambiguity and greater ability to deal with complex emotional situations.
7. There were greater signs of a more rigid fearful identification in accounting students and greater evidence of seeking for completion of multiple identifications in writing students.

The findings validate the idea that personality theory can lead to a more complete understanding of the role of personality factors as determinants of vocational choice.[13]

Most competent vocational counselors are aware of the influence upon vocational choices of the advisee's adjustments, such as his barriers, predisposing influences, substitute acts, frustrations, passive and aggressive hostilities, and so on. But they do not tell the advisee all that they know or think they know. The advisee must always retain the human right of living his own life in his own way.

Some clinical psychologists believe that vocational counselors are simply meddlers and that the individual should be allowed to follow the directions of the "Unconscious." They believe that all actions are determined by unconscious motives that follow definite patterns formed in the individual during childhood.[14]

The writer has attempted to assist several hundred persons in choosing a vocation. Some of these were students who were asked to have a vocational conference, but others, who heard of these conferences, requested

"Bonaparte, a Novice in the School at Brienne," by Realier-Dumas. This painting is reproduced to illustrate the influence of subconscious drives in choosing a career. Napoleon may have become a conqueror as a compensation for a number of unhappy childhood experiences. An inferiority complex is often compensated for by a career that satisfies the ego's needs. (By permission of Gramstorff Bros., Inc., Malden, Mass.)

guidance. Those who requested assistance in choosing a vocation certainly included an appreciable percentage of slightly psychoneurotic and inadequate-adjustment cases.

An estimate, based upon experience in this field, suggests that at least one third of the adults who voluntarily seek vocational guidance are really seeking an adjustment to life in general rather than a vocation only. This estimate is probably too low.

Adjustment analysis is of assistance to many persons who are vocationally unsatisfied because it may indicate the manner in which the person with a feeling of inferiority might attempt to compensate for his sense of inadequacy. It is probably partially true that Napoleon became the conqueror of a large part of the civilized world through his adjustment to the taunts of his playmates in his childhood. Some of our poets achieved their eminence because of physical defects. In fact, Adler cited many cases of compensation brought about by some organic inferiority and concluded that some psychic reaction makes up for the deficiency of the physical organism.[15] This theory hardly explains every successful person. Many of us develop our feelings of inferiority as the result of comparing ourselves with others. A person who has average artistic ability when

compared with other artists of the world may have a definite sense of inferiority because he knows that there are others considerably better than he. A person need not have any actual physical or mental inferiority in order to feel inferior.

Many a child, for example, who has a very studious brother or sister may believe that he is of low intelligence. Tests and adjustment analysis may show, however, that he has quite adequate intellectual capacity but he adjusted to his sibling rival by assuming that he was inferior.

Consider also the differences in personality needs on the part of the adults who, in childhood, were overdisciplined, were orphans and felt rejected, or were overprotected. Such feelings of inadequacy are almost certain to influence the individual's later choice of work and work environment. The inner needs of the individual interact with the potential satisfactions in the job. We can understand these people when we recall the typical adjustments discussed in Chapters 2-7.

The person who seeks a vocation that fits his personality should ask himself: What difficult or unpleasant experiences have I had for which I need satisfaction in my work? If he cannot answer the question

Personal problems

himself, he might consult a vocational psychologist. Each year it is found that several college students who are barely able to do college work and just manage to graduate wish to take additional postgraduate work in another college which has a reputation for requiring unusually hard work. This desired prestige of having done graduate work in a famous institution is merely an attempt to compensate for the feeling of inferiority engendered by their inability to do college work of ordinary grade. In most cases it has been difficult to convince these poor students that they wish to do graduate work not because it is essential to their careers but because the contrast between themselves and other college students causes them to think that they are inferior. Actually they are fine young men who have developed an abnormal attitude toward the importance of college degrees and the college aura.

Adjustment by projection explains many of the dissatisfactions with occupational life. A bank clerk, for example, who is not especially ambitious or intelligent and who knows it, may suddenly develop a dislike for banking. Further analysis may show that his home relationships have become strained and that he would like to get married and set up a home of his own. His dissatisfaction has not been caused by the uninteresting nature of bank work, but he has blamed his work for the fact that he does not have the courage to set up a new home on the available income.

Sometimes a person highly trained and successful in a given line of work suddenly tires of the vocation for which he has a high interest rating as measured by an interest test. His income and social prestige may also be excellent, but he refuses to continue in the work. In such cases, only an analysis of adjustment problems will reveal the true cause of his desire for a change.

Many a person has left a vocation and spent years in training himself for a new vocation because he thought that competition was far too keen, whereas he might have attained greater success by training himself more thoroughly in his original work. A typical example is a certain man who was a fairly successful printer. He blamed competition for his limited income, and decided to study dentistry. After six years of study and several years in developing his practice, he has become another average dentist. In the meantime, one or two printers in his city have become well-to-do. If he had devoted the same effort and capital to printing that he applied to learning dentistry, he might have become far more successful as a printer than he is as a dentist.

Whenever someone wishes to leave an occupation in which he is fairly well established, the counselor should look for the difficulty that the occupation symbolizes or represents to the person. The real reason for his eagerness to leave one job for another may be his irascible stepmother, a brighter sister, an unresponsive executive, or a fiancée who loves someone else.

In some cases a sudden interest in politics may be a protest against some injustice. A determination to travel may be an attempt to adjust to restraint or convention. A keen interest in the study of an obscure subject such as paleontology or Egyptology may be an attempt to prove to others that the individual is as bright as those whom he considers to be his rivals. By contrast with the knowledge of such unusual subjects on the part of most people, his meager fund of information gives him the intellectual recognition he unconsciously seeks.

The vocational psychologist frequently finds freakish interest on the part of persons who are dealing with a barrier, such as the crude man who wants to be an artist, the immoral person who wants to be a preacher, the homely girl who wants to be a beautician, and the failure who writes success books. Such attempts to gain adjustment through the vocation are not necessarily wrong. Many of the world's finest contributions have grown out of such troubled personality strivings. For example, Charlotte Brontë wrote some very successful novels, the result of an overflow of emotions engendered by her father's unfortunate influences. The father was a hypochondriac, a dyspeptic, and an ascetic. He did not believe in marriage and was particularly opposed to Charlotte's marrying. He was fond and jealous of her. He was unable to get along with his associates and so became a tyrant in his home. He tried to please her and showered her with attention, but he was moody and critical as well. She could not develop in a normal manner and was forced inward emotionally. She took refuge in books and fantasies. Her tragic childhood was stamped deeply upon her personality, and the books that she and her sisters wrote show the effects of a maladjusted father upon motherless children.

Vocational self-sabotage

Anyone who does vocational counseling of adults is certain to meet individuals who have high intelligence, pleasing personalities, seemingly good habits, and many good character qualities; but who always manage somehow to fail in their vocations. In contrast with them, other individuals of less intelligence, more irritating personalities, and poorer personal habits manage to succeed, regardless of their opportunities. Both types are difficult to explain as long as we use quantitative approaches only. When, however, we think in terms of unconscious motives, we get plausible explanations. We discover that many of the men who always manage to fail are really expressing an unconscious urge toward self-sabotage in their vocation.

Failure enables the maladjusted person to accomplish aims that are more important to him than success. Such aims have been revealed by Friend and Haggard in the systematic investigation of two classes of unemployed adults: those *high* and those *low* on eight basic criterion items of occupational adjustment.[16] One of the striking differences between the two groups was described, in part, in their findings.

Topping the many sharp contrasts in personality, the stronger tendency of the *Lows* to defeat themselves and spoil their job chances stands out as an indicator of adjustment at work. It is often evidenced by excessive drinking, quarreling, and illness. The *Lows* seem to marry the wrong person and to have families so large that they experience difficulty in supporting them. Correlational and other special analyses of the extent of the tendency toward self-sabotage link it with the extent of the following attitudes: parental rejection, antagonism toward the father, resentments both of dependence and domination of families, rigidity, buried fear of failure, and self-attack, unrealistic thinking about jobs, ambivalence, and reliance on pull. . . . Although the relationships suggested are not necessarily causal ones, these factors do seem to serve as devices through which the maladjusted individual accomplishes an aim. They seem to be ways of settling early parental scores; or of handling the guilt which demands constant failure; or of protecting himself against fears of being unable to cope with work. . . . This extreme type of "vicious-circle" behavior seems related to the well-known proclivity of those seriously disturbed emotionally (the *Lows*) to make things generally hard for themselves—a trait is slight in the *Highs.*

Friend and Haggard also call attention to similar findings on the part of psychiatrists:

Dr. Karl Menninger has discussed work as a valuable expression for the modified neutralized destructive tendencies of the individual and cites examples of job failure that illustrate the emergence of destructive and self-destructive elements in work motivation. After relating the numerous business failures of a patient, he says: "This man's aggressiveness, which was great, was carried out very largely in his work, but unlike the normal man who uses this drive as a means to success, this man made it his business to fail, losing not only his own money, but that of everyone who trusted him."[17]

In discussing another case, Dr. Menninger suggests that the work failure of the patient served to thwart the man's aggressive but indulgent father.

Whatever the explanations that may eventually be found most appropriate for the understanding of the adults who manage to fail, the fact is that they do manage to fail in spite of apparently excellent outward reasons for success. The only helpful psychological explanation, thus far, is that they themselves are unconsciously sabotaging their own efforts in order to attain aims more important to themselves.

The case method of vocational guidance

The evidence presented in the preceding discussions suggests that while some individuals do not need vocational guidance, many others do. We must not assume that all wholly normal persons need no assistance in choosing a vocation. The normal youth is not raw material psychologically; he was raw material at birth, but since birth he has developed many adjustments and conditionings. He has certain likes and dislikes, some feelings of inferiority, self-confidence in certain situations and not in others, a fairly definite level of intelligence, and accumulated experiences of all degrees of importance, so that his psychological composite in relation to his environment may not result in a happy vocational choice. In many cases he finds that he has difficulty in choosing a vocation. Even though he thinks that he knows what he wants to do, it may be well for him to attempt to obtain a bird's-eye view of himself and the world in which he lives. He really knows only a few occupations, and those he does not know comprehensively. Such a case study involves the following steps by a counselor:

I. Analyze the individual.
  A. History and general status.
    1. Health record.
    2. School record.
    3. Financial status.
    4. Leadership record.
    5. Hobbies and recreational activities.
    6. Psychological test scores.
  B. Vocational likes and dislikes—self-analysis.
  C. Estimates of associates and friends—ratings by others.
  D. Peculiarities of personality.
  E. Parental wishes.

II. Present the suggestions of the above to the advisee in a personal conference.
III. As a result of II, choose several occupations for the investigation of the advisee.
IV. After investigation of the several tentative occupations, choose one as a vocation.
V. Plan a program of training.
VI. Assist advisee to obtain a job or get started in the chosen field.
VII. Follow up advisee and revise his program as occasion demands.

College education as a part of a vocational program

When a high school graduate wishes to enter business and plans his vocational program, he must decide whether he will go to college or enter a field of work without college training. When successful men in one field are compared with the unsuccessful, investigations show that many of the successful individuals in business do not have a college education. We cannot say that a college education is a prerequisite for reaching the top. A recent survey of the men who run America's 500 largest corporations showed that 38.8 per cent of the presidents lack degrees. When, however, the percentages of degree-holding appointees are analyzed by decades since 1919, the data show that appointees of recent years have more formal education than their predecessors.[18] Statistics on the value of college training based upon men who graduated a generation ago are not entirely significant for modern conditions. Going to college then required more initiative and ability than it does today, when a college student is no longer a community marvel as he was then.

The main reason why college graduates make more money than high school or common school graduates is superior intelligence and personality. A youth with high intelligence and strong character traits is likely to go to college. He seeks the college degree as part of his program of personal development. College is the required or

The universities and colleges of America, both the large and the small institutions, have developed an increasing appreciation of the benefits rendered by a testing and guidance center.

Left, the reception desk for scheduling appointments at the Occupational Opportunities Service, The Ohio State University.

Right, the Rev. James E. Royce, S. J., Psychological Center, Seattle University, aids a young man in choosing an appropriate program of studies.

TABLE 11-3

RELATION BETWEEN SCHOLASTIC STANDING IN COLLEGE AND LATER SUCCESS

Deciles	"Who's Who in America"		"Who's Who in Engineering"		"American Men of Science"		*In all three volumes*	
	No.*	%	No.	%	No.	%	No.	%
1	68	15.3	128	16.1	123	23.8	20	22.0
2	60	13.5	108	13.6	85	16.5	13	14.3
3	45	10.2	87	10.9	67	13.0	16	17.6
4	49	11.1	93	11.7	62	12.0	11	12.1
5	26	5.9	63	7.9	39	7.6	6	6.6
6	19	4.3	45	5.7	26	5.1	3	3.3
7	23	5.2	46	5.8	23	4.5	3	3.3
8	30	6.8	54	6.8	23	4.5	6	6.6
9	26	5.9	53	6.7	23	4.5	5	5.5
10	96	21.8	118	14.8	44	8.5	8	8.8
Totals	442	100.0	795	100.0	515	100.0	91	100.0

From F. Alexander Magoun, "Scholarship and Distinction," *The Technology Review,* Massachusetts Institute of Technology, Cambridge, Mass., Vol. 37, No. 8 (May 1935).

* This column indicates the number of former M.I.T. students, from certain classes between 1868 and 1910, whose names appear in "Who's Who in America." Thus 68 persons (or 15.3 per cent of the total) stood in the 1st decile or top tenth of their class; 60 persons (13.5 per cent) stood in the 2nd decile or second highest tenth—and so on for all ten deciles. The table can also be read as follows: "Of 442 former M.I.T. men listed in 'Who's Who in America,' 96 or 21.8 per cent stood in the 10th or lowest decile, scholastically, of the members of their classes," and so forth.

accepted education for many superior individuals, and professional standards as well as many businessmen require college graduation for admission into many occupations.

The student who attains high grades in college and then succeeds in business probably does so not because the college trained him to think or gave him technical training but because he has superior intellectual and character traits. We should not advise every high school student to go to college. If a student barely manages to get through high school and if his general intelligence in abstract subjects is low, it may be inadvisable to recommend college training. It is interesting to know that high school graduates of both low and high mental ability plan to attend college. The desire to attend college is not a reliable criterion of the ability to do college work. Thousands of college freshmen are dropped each year because they are unable to do the work. However, if a youth has the intelligence and personality that will enable him to benefit from a college education, then he should by all means go to college, even though he may have to earn all his own funds for doing so.

The vocational program

The value of a definite vocational program is suggested by a study made several years before World War II; the writer made a statistical analysis of the records of 500 men who had registered for jobs with an employment agency. Their employment histories were accurately recorded because their records had been carefully investigated by the agency. A lot of facts were recorded about each man. Among the facts were answers to two questions:

1. What do you want to do five years hence?
2. What progress have you made in attaining your goal?

Approximately one half of the men stated a more or less definite ambition. When their salaries were analyzed in relation to age groups and ambitions, the following figures were found:

	Annual Average Salaries by Age Groups		
	20–29	30–39	40–49
The "definite ambition" men	$2,537	$4,021	$6,037
The "no definite ambition" men	2,443	3,792	4,853

The relations between average salaries and extent or progress made in attaining the definite ambitions were found to be the following:

Level of Progress Reported	Average Salary
"Preparing myself for it"	$1,832
"Have made no progress," or, "Little progress"	2,433
"Have made some progress"	3,390
"Good," "Very good," and "Fine progress"	5,664

Only thirteen men, all in the older age brackets, claimed they had attained their ambitions. Apparently most sensible men realize they are not likely to be very happy unless they are striving for goals that are ahead. As someone has said: "Success is a wonderful thing to strive for, but a terrible thing to gain."

Of course, a program in itself is of little value. However, persons of superior personality strengths are likely to utilize a program as an expression of their drive to achieve. The following conversation and appeal to a youth illustrates one kind of appeal that can be made when the counselor wishes the advisee to plan a definite program for training himself in his chosen vocation:

"Vocational success hinges partly upon not trusting your life to chance but knowing what you want and how to get it. The man of little ability who concentrates his efforts on one thing, in one direction, and on one goal is bound to succeed. He attains far greater height than the man of brilliant ability who lacks a goal.

"After you have chosen a vocation or selected your vocational goal, you should do what successful business concerns do—schedule your plans. Decide upon what you want to accomplish each year for the next few years. Determine upon what you will do each year in order to attain your goal. Set up standards for yourself. Set a date when you will accomplish each step and keep that schedule before you. Look at it occasionally, especially when you are failing.

"Whenever you find that your schedule needs revision, revise it. But follow a definite plan or you may drift, and drifting wood never reaches port." Table 11-4 shows a sample vocational program which will illustrate how one can plan a career.

Acknowledgments and References

1. Harry Dexter Kitson, *The Psychology of Vocational Adjustment*, J. B. Lippincott, Co., Philadelphia, 1925, p. 47.

2. Adapted from H. L. Hollingworth, *Judging Human Behavior*, D. Appleton-Century Company, New York, 1929, p. 52.

3. F. H. and G. W. Allport, *Journal of Abnormal and Social Psychology*, Vol. 16 (1921), pp. 6–40.

4. See Edward K. Strong, Jr., "Permanence of Interest Scores over 22 Years," *Journal of Applied Psychology*, April 1951, pp. 89–91.

5. For further information, see Edward K. Strong, Jr., "Nineteen-Year Follow-up of Engineer Interests," *Journal of Applied Psychology*, April 1952, pp. 65–74.
————, *Vocational Interests 18 Years after College*, Univ. of Minnesota Press, Minneapolis, 1955.

6. William K. Trinkaus, "The Permanence of Vocational Interests of College Freshmen," *Educational and Psychological Measurements*, Winter 1954, pp. 641–646.

7. Phyllis Rosenberg Levine and Richard Wallin, "Adolescent Vocational Interests and Later Occupation," *Journal of Applied Psychology*, December 1954, pp. 428–431.

8. See Frederick Herzberg and Arthur Bouton, "A Further Study of the Stability of the Kuder Preference Record," *Educational and Psychological Measurement*, Summer 1954, pp. 326–331.

9. Solomon Diamond, "Interpretation of Interest Profiles," *Journal of Applied Psychology*, Vol. 32, No. 5, October 1948, pp. 512–520.

10. For descriptions of the current developments in testing, refer to the periodical, *Test Service Bulletin* and the annual *Catalog of the Test Division*, both published by the Psychological Corporation, New York. See also the latest copy of *The Mental Measurements Yearbook*, Oscar Krisen Buros, editor, Highland Park, N.J.

11. Paul P. Brainard and Frances G. Stewart, *Manual of Instructions for Specific Interest Inventories*, The Psychological Corporation, New York, 1932.

12. Anne Roe, "Personality and Vocation," *Transactions of the New York Academy of Science*, Vol. 9 (1947), pp. 257–267. Goldie Ruth Kaback, *Vocational Personalities; An Application of the Rorschach Group Method*, Bureau of Publications, Teachers College, Columbia University, New York, 1946. Z. Piotrowski, B. Candee, B. Balinsky, S. Holtzberg, and B. Van Arnold, "Rorschach Signs in the Selection of Outstanding Young Male Mechanical Workers," *Journal of Psychology*, Vol. 18 (1944), pp. 131–150.

13. Stanley J. Segal, "The Role of Personality Factors in Vocational Choice," *The American Psychologist*, August 1955, pp. 365–366.

14. A. A. Brill, *Fundamental Conceptions of Psychoanalysis*, Harcourt, Brace and Company, New York, 1921, Chapter XIII.

15. Alfred Adler, "A Study of Organ Inferiority and Its Psychical Compensation," *Nervous and Mental Diseases Monograph*, 1917.

16. Jeannette G. Friend and Ernest A. Haggard, "Work Adjustment in Relation to Family Background," *Applied Psychology Monographs*, No. 16, Stanford University Press, Stanford University, Cal., 1948, pp. 58–59.

17. Karl A. Menninger, *Man Against Himself*, Harcourt Brace and Company, New York, 1938, p. 198. See also "Work as a Sublimation," *Bulletin of the Menninger Clinic*, November, 1942.

18. "How Top 500 Presidents Set off in their Long Climb," *Business Week*, June 9, 1956, p. 110. For a summary of recent studies of factors associated with attainment of executive positions, see *Personnel*, American Management Association, January 1956, p. 292 f.

TABLE 11–4

FACTORS TO BE CONSIDERED IN PLANNING MY VOCATION

Educational record:
High school graduate, college preparatory course.

Easy subjects:
English, history, languages.

Difficult subjects:
Math courses.

Grades:
Graduated in second quarter of class of 68 graduates. English grades highest.

Test results:
Otis S-A test of intelligence P.R. 90

Nelson-Denny Reading test, P.R. 92

Iowa Placement, English Aptitude, P.R. 86

Introversion, P.R. 62

Interest test results, rank order:
1. Copywriter
2. Advertising man
3. Journalist
4. Lawyer
5. Commercial teacher

Experience record:
Odd jobs in selling magazines, clerking in store.

Health record:
Children's diseases only. Good health.

Financial resources:
Father will supply money for most expenses. Must earn money for personal expenses.

Parental wishes:
Parents have no vocational preferences but they expect me to make high grades.

Special opportunity:
Uncle is in textile industry but I as nephew could not expect any special opportunity from anyone.

Past difficulties that developed drives of vocational value, habits, conditionings, feelings of inferiority, resentment, etc.:
Oldest child in family of four boys, like to show off. Believe that my parents are more or less indifferent to me. A younger brother is praised for his very high grades. Feel inferior regarding my lack of athletic ability. Fear that I will be a failure. Resent close supervision. Resent "poverty" of family.

Reasons for suggesting this vocational program: likes, dislikes, aptitudes, etc.:
High record in English.
Practical minded rather than a student of English only.
Like to study people more than I care to influence them in personal contacts.

EXAMPLE OF "MY VOCATIONAL PROGRAM"

Nature of the Career I Wish to Attain: *Advertising Copywriter*

My Job Program
Sequence of jobs to reach the main occupation:

For this year:
Obtain part-time job in retail concern.

For next year:
Obtain part-time job on newspaper or magazine.

Later:
Write ads for local concerns even though the pay is small.

Possible employers:
Previous contacts may suggest possible employers.

Employment bureaus to be consulted:
Study trade journals for employment bureaus that specialize in my field of work.

Places of work:
Do a good advertising job in my own community and hope to get an agency job in a big city.

Vacation jobs:
Work in a summer resort patronized by businessmen.

My Training Program
that prepares for the vocation:

Schools to attend:
Enter a four-year college of business that offers cultural as well as business training.

Courses to take:
Major in advertising. Courses in commerce, art, psychology, sciences, sociology, philosophy.

Books to read:
Burton, Kreer, and Gray, *Advertising Copywriting*, Prentice-Hall, Inc., Englewood Cliffs, N.J., 1949.
Hepner, H. W., *Modern Advertising; Practices and Principles*, McGraw-Hill Book Company, Inc., New York, 1956.

Trade journals:
Printers' Ink
Sales Management

Persons to interview or know:
Call on advertising men and women of home town. Associate with all types of people.

Writing to do:
Some themes in college dealing with the characteristics of consumers.

My Personality Development Program
List items, such as:
Friendships to make:
Establish friendship with business owners, advertising men, and salesmen.

Clubs to join:
Join local advertising or sales clubs. Later, join luncheon club.

Books to read:
Hattwick, Melvin S., *How to Use Psychology for Better Advertising*; Prentice-Hall, Inc., Englewood Cliffs, N.J., 1950.
Kleppner, Otto, *Advertising Procedure*, 4th ed., Prentice-Hall, Inc., Englewood Cliffs, N.J., 1950.

Tours to take:
Visit the advertising agencies of a large city.

Investment plans:
Save money when possible but spend in order to become acquainted with men and women in advertising and business. Attend trade convention.

Health plans:
Analyze my personality once a year in order to keep a healthy mind.

The Undesirable Aspects
of this program which should be anticipated:

Opposition to expect from family, friends, or employers:
Parents who help me through college will expect me to get a well-paid job upon graduation. This is not likely.

Effect on plans for marriage or home:
Will prevent my getting married for next eight or ten years.

Unpleasant conditions of work:
Will have to do many menial jobs in order to get my education.

Difficulties in making advancements:
Department heads such as buyers of stores often blame advertising man for their own failures.

Income difficulties:
Will be out of work at times. Must shift employers frequently.

PROJECTS

1. "Success in a vocation depends upon an adjustment to life in general rather than the fortunate selection of an occupation." Assume that this statement is true and prepare a list of mental habits that every person should acquire to be vocationally successful. Assume that the above statement is incomplete and add other forms of behavior that are essential.

2. "A rolling stone gathers no moss" and "A setting hen never gets fat." Which of these two epigrams is the more nearly correct? When should a man change his position?

3. Outline a program for obtaining valid occupational information that fits your needs.

4. Analyze yourself vocationally by means of the devices and suggestions presented in this chapter. Present the analysis in the form of a systematic report to a friend and ask him to criticize it. Then prepare a vocational program to fit your significant traits.

5. Study a number of friends who have achieved considerable success in their fields, and compare them with others who seem to be "marking time." What psychological differences can you discover between individuals in the two groups?

6. Compare the advantages and the disadvantages of going into business for yourself with those of working for an employer.

7. Study the student employment opportunities in your college or one near by. List all the ways the students earn money to help support themselves. Check the jobs that contribute valuable vocational experience as well as financial reward.

8. List some occupations which may diminish in importance within the next ten or fifteen years. Suggest how workers in those occupations might utilize the change to their advantage rather than suffer because of it.

COLLATERAL READINGS

Berrien, F. K., *Practical Psychology*, The Macmillan Company, New York, 1944, Chapter 18.

Burtt, Harold E., *Applied Psychology*, Prentice-Hall, Inc., Englewood Cliffs, N.J., 1948, Chapter 8.

Havemann, Ernest and Patricia S. West, *They Went to College*, Harcourt, Brace & Company, New York, 1952.

Lehner, George F. J. and Ella Kube, *The Dynamics of Personal Adjustment*, Prentice-Hall, Inc., Englewood Cliffs, N.J., 1955, Chapter 12.

Poffenberger, A. T., *Principles of Applied Psychology*, Appleton-Century-Crofts, Inc., New York, 1942, Chapters 12 and 13.

Shaffer, Laurance F. and Edward J. Shoben, Jr., *The Psychology of Adjustment*, Houghton Mifflin Company, Boston, 1956, pp. 567–573.

Smith, Henry Clay, *Psychology of Industrial Behavior*, McGraw-Hill Book Company, Inc., New York, 1955, Chapter 15.

Wrenn, C. Gilbert, "Trends and Predictions in Vocational Guidance," *Occupations*, Vol. 25 (1947), pp. 503–515.

CHAPTER TWELVE

Getting a job and gaining advancement

"How can I get a job when I haven't had any experience?" is the lament of many a young person when he leaves school or college. Actually, any normal individual who has a definite vocational goal, has seriously studied an industry, and developed a well-adjusted personality has excellent evidence of value to employers. But he must be able to present his worth in an effective manner.

Employers do not expect factory workers or uneducated applicants to use clever job-getting methods. Employers assume that such applicants use the old haphazard methods of seeking employment through employment agencies, help-wanted advertisements, labor-union headquarters, and applications at personnel offices. However, the college-educated and other superior job seekers are expected to demonstrate their superiority to some extent by means of their applications. The people who need superior techniques of making application are the more highly trained workers such as engineers, accountants, statisticians, technical salesmen, and professional workers. These should know how to present their qualifications intelligently.

The intelligent candidate in the course of making his application should regard the following admonitions:

1. Know the kind of work you want and why you want it.
2. Study the employer's problems and interests.
3. Present a letter of application which proves your interest in the employer's problems and your qualifications for his needs.
4. Participate in an interview which reveals mutual interests.

Stating the kind of work desired

Many an ordinary applicant is so ego-centered when he needs a job that he can think only of his own needs. As a result of his concern about his own needs, he thinks and talks about himself. His argument for a job is similar to that of a candidate for a political office whose placard read: "I am the father of nine children and I need your support!"

The intelligent applicant's major thought is to understand his abilities, limitations, and vocational goals so well that he knows the kind of work he wants and why he believes he can do it. One employment man explained the deficiencies of applicants in this respect as follows:

I interview hundreds of applicants, and when I ask them what they can do, a high percentage say "most anything." The answer is obviously false. I am not interested in the applicant who says that he can do anything, because that really means that he can do nothing well; nor does he know what he would like to do. But the applicant who says, "I have been studying motor transportation and I believe that I could be of help to your firm in cutting down your delivery costs," arouses a definite interest. Young people who leave school and college are especially weak in this respect. Many of them do not know whether they wish to work in a circus, a department store, a machine-shop, or a cheese factory. How can they expect to sell their services when they do not know what they have to sell?

The superior applicant, especially the one who has benefited from his college opportunities, knows the industry he wishes to enter and the kind of work he wants to do. His textbook readings, classroom lectures, and personal contacts with men in the field of his choice have stimulated him to learn more about certain aspects of the work and to associate with those who are already actively engaged in his chosen field. Such an applicant has read trade journals and attended trade association meetings, and there he has learned the names and addresses of the leaders in his chosen industry. Because of his genuine interest and informed background, he can approach the professional leaders or heads of the best firms and talk with them in terms that he and they understand. The reactions of executives approached by such an applicant are likely to be: "This man knows what he wants and is going after it.

He appears to be the kind of man we need in our organization. Let's try him out to discover whether he really means what he says."

Any college student who really wishes to use his college experiences in formulating definite vocational objectives can do so. Faculty members, friends in business, secretaries of trade associations, trade journals, psychological tests, and library books are usually available to him in his search to find himself in his work.[1]

Studying the employer's problems and interests

Whenever an applicant has decided what kind of work he would like to do, his knowledge will indicate which concerns would be logical employers for him. The advertisements and news articles in trade journals, listings in telephone directories, and suggestions from trade association secretaries will reveal names and addresses of many possible employers.

When the applicant has collected such lists, he should select several preferred prospective employers and learn all he can about them. He should investigate the history of each company, study each company's product, interview their customers, and find out why people use the product. Why did they buy the product? Would they buy the same brand again? If not, why not? Of course, the purpose of this kind of investigating is not to impress the employer but to write an effective letter of application and to ask intelligent questions during the interview.

For example, a certain young man registered at an employment office. He had had experience in the retail gasoline and oil business, but had sought work unsuccessfully for some time. As he wanted to obtain employment with a certain retail gasoline company, the employment director suggested that he take definite steps to make himself valuable to this company.

He was told that he should learn all he could about the business—if possible, find out if any of the company's local stations were not up to the usual company standards.

The young man found that a gas station belonging to the company where he had applied seemed to be getting less business than it should. To discover the reasons, he made a survey of all cars in the neighborhood to find whether their owners were buying gas from the station and, if not, whether there was any cause for dissatisfaction. When the survey was completed, the young man took it to the local manager of the gasoline company with a suggestion for increasing business at that station. The manager was impressed with the applicant's initiative and gave him a position to prove his worth. The young man made good at that job and at several other difficult ones. His work was so satisfactory that in a short time he had risen to a responsible position in the local office of the company.[2]

When looking for ideas of possible interest to the employer, the applicant can study the business by means of the trade journals of the industry. His local library probably has some copies on file.

If the applicant will also study the specific concern with which he would like to be associated, he will be able to offer some ideas which show that he is seriously interested in becoming a member of that organization. If possible, it is well to talk with the company's salesmen who, in many cases, will be glad to give the applicant helpful suggestions. Once the applicant has developed his ideas and checked them with some person who is acquainted with the problems of the company, he can approach the prospective employer as an inquirer who is anxious to learn more about the company. Of course, if he takes the attitude of an expert who tries to advise the management on how they should run the business, the employer is naturally likely to

assume that the applicant is too egotistical to fit into the company team.

The personnel manager of a large department store stated: "Not one person in a hundred who comes before my desk has any ideas. Yet it's the applicant with ideas who gets the job, the applicant who has intelligence and interest enough to spend some time in the store looking around before he comes to me, who can suggest ways we can improve our service, who at least will be able to say: 'I watched the clerks and customers in the jewelry department yesterday and I believe that I could sell in that line.' Most of them don't even do that."

When this question was brought up to the head of a publishing firm, he answered: "Ideas! Most job hunters don't know what the publishing business is. Less than one in a hundred will even go to the trouble of reading the most widely-used trade journal of the industry. Most applicants think they want to become editors because they do not know of the many other departments in the publishing business."[3]

Any applicant who takes the trouble to read the trade journals of the industry or to observe the ways in which the product is being used by the customers is bound to develop an application that is not only intelligent but outstanding. Most employers today are in need of applicants who show that they can think with the businessman rather than merely do what the boss wishes.

The letter of application

Many college students can write letters which are grammatically correct but fail to reveal an interest in the employer or in doing his work. The employer is seldom a student of English nor does he care about the niceties of phrasing. He has work to be done, products to sell, payrolls to meet, taxes to pay, customers to please, and bills to collect. He does not care particularly whom he hires—he does want to get his work done quickly and economically.

This letter, written by a college graduate and published in *Postage Magazine,* is typical of letters of application constantly written by ego-centered applicants who have had no training in writing to employers:

Dear Mr. Publisher:

I am seeking editorial (or writing) work on a magazine staff.

My age is twenty-four. I am a graduate of Grinnell College (Grinnell, Iowa), and since graduation have done irregular work at Chicago and Columbia Universities. My chief aim has been to improve myself in the ability to write and in comparative study of literature. I have also specialized in history, psychology, sociology, philosophy, and advertising. Recently I completed a long novel, which is at present at Doran's, having received one favorable reading.

My college record was good. I am a Phi Beta Kappa and a Sigma Delta Chi member, having edited the last-named organization's comic weekly during my senior year in college. Before that I worked on the staffs of certain local newspapers. I also sold automobiles for a time and can use the trade language with some facility.

I have no present business connections. Since I was fifteen, I have incessantly aimed at journalism. My writing style perhaps tends to the search of the color-bearing word and the ironic, but within controllable limits. I read very rapidly (120 pages an hour) and analytically.

I am willing to start in any position which promises an opportunity for development and offers a reasonable wage.

                                    Sincerely yours,

The comments of the recipient of this letter were:

This letter, written by a college graduate, contains eighteen "I's," "my's" and "myself's" but not a single "you." We can well imagine the publisher who wades through such a letter, searching for and finding the "ironic" word and using it without "controllable limit." Every year, millions of letters like this are written by young men looking for positions. We should like to recommend to every college in the land

that a business course on "How to Write a Letter" be delivered to its students, to cover the last six months of their term. Thousands of splendid positions are held by men who knew how to write a good letter and wrote it at the psychological time.

The following application letter, written by an alert college senior, was sent to the advertising managers of eighteen leading department stores and promptly resulted in offers of two jobs, one of which was accepted.

                        211 West 14th Street
                        Meldon, Massachusetts
                        July 5, 19—

Advertising Manager of (Name of Firm)
Street
City

Dear Sir:

Your advertising appeals to me. It suggests that you are following policies and procedures that would benefit the young advertising woman.

My ultimate goal is that of advertising manager of a retail store. To reach this point I realize that real experience is necessary.

I am anxious to have good supervision and direction in my training for this career and recognize the opportunities available in your store. Therefore, I am eager to attain any work in this line you can offer me.

As a beginner in your department, I offer the ability to take dictation and type. As your needs would demand, I could gradually make myself useful in writing copy or preparing advertisements. One of the sample advertisements for a local retail store is enclosed.

You will find further information and references in the attached personal data sheet. May I have your suggestions?

                        Very truly yours,
                        (Miss) Mary Doe

This applicant complimented the employer and indicated a genuine interest in learning *his* methods as an aid in her own development. Furthermore, the letter avoided the many "I's," "my's" and "myself's" through the use of a personal data sheet, an excellent device for most applicants.

Use of a personal data chart or résumé is important. A prospective employer likes to have facts about a candidate's past experience on paper in order to have it available for future personnel needs. The résumé lists personal data, and also employers and dates in reverse chronological order along with a short summary of the individual's responsibilities in each position. This, like any type of résumé, should be brief, and honest. Several briefs may be prepared for different types of jobs, with each stressing different aspects of background.

Many high school and college graduates claim that they cannot write a good letter of application because they cannot point to past experience as evidence of their ability. Some of these younger applicants visit employment offices where they are told that no jobs are open for inexperienced workers. These young applicants should recognize that the old answer: "Sorry, we have no opening now for persons without experience," often means that either the applicant did not appeal to the employment man or the applicant did not know how to present his qualifications effectively.

The intelligent inexperienced applicant who knows what kind of work he wants to learn and why, can, with reasonable persistence, find an interested employer. The youth has a most appealing argument whenever he applies to an employer with this type of approach:

"Mr. Employer, I have decided that I wish to learn the hardware business because I have worked in a hardware store during summer vacations and liked it. I know such simple details as the sizes of bolts and saws. I can drive a truck and check invoices. Besides my summer experience as evidence of interest, I read two trade journals in the hardware field. Three hardware dealers told me if they were young again and wanted to learn the hardware business they would come to you. So here I am for your advice and, if I meet your requirements, for your employment."

ADDRESS
DATE

NAME OF FIRM MANAGER
ADDRESS

Dear Mr. Blank:

I wish to apply for a position as Junior Accountant in your firm, and am submitting for your convenience a chart of my qualifications. [See page 232.]

This chart will, in a brief way, I believe, present the information desired.

Very truly yours,

Dear Sir:

I have just read your advertisement.

You evidently want someone who understands what are the real duties of a secretary. He must

—transcribe your dictation accurately, promptly.
—"proofread" his letters for possible errors.
—receive your callers politely, civilly.
—separate the important ones from those who should wait or come again.
—open and assort your mail.
—make a list of your engagements, reminding you of them at the proper time.
—keep your personal accounts.
—keep your business to *himself.*

My experience covers eight years of stenographic and secretarial service, with knowledge of bookkeeping. Age, 25 years. Unmarried.

Let me come and see you. I feel confident of fulfilling your requirements. My telephone is Main 6000.

Yours truly,

This letter leaves no doubt that the writer understands what a secretary is expected to do. The advertisement was simply for a secretary. Instead of making his letter the usual hackneyed statement of qualifications and experience, he tabulates the duties of the post and thus modestly conveys the idea that he can perform them.

Any youth can present his qualifications and evidence of interest in a given vocation in an original manner. He can prepare a loose-leaf booklet or pamphlet of his background and characteristics. It can be illustrated with pictures from advertisements and include character references, copies of school report cards, Boy Scout badges, maps, school term papers, and so on. Anyone's personal history offers many examples of good character and interest in performing honest work that leads to vocational growth and advancement. Thousands of employers are looking for young people who exhibit a spark of initiative and strategy in presenting their qualifications in original ways.

Below are a couple of attention-getting advertisements written by two clever young people seeking positions in the advertising or publishing fields.

THIS YOUNG MAN believing in the importance of a right start, is eager to go to work for an advertising agency at no salary until he has proved himself worthy of one. Twenty-two, college graduate, thorough training in advertising, background of retail sales experience, with character references of the best. Wrote for all college publications. Ambitious to do copy . . . start in anything leading up to it. Box 701, P. I.

ARE YOU PREJUDICED AGAINST A PHI BETA KAPPA KEY, University of Chicago? I confess I am—though I am a young woman who owns one.

I want to break into New York publishing or advertising or some similar employment—no matter how humble the starting place.

In extenuation, I offer:

1. One year's editorial experience on a Chicago publication.
2. Youth and enthusiasm—despite two years' public school teaching experience.
3. Some general business experience, including expert knowledge of typewriting.
4. A not unattractive personality—UN-ACADEMIC.

Will you grant me an interview? Box 432, Printers' Ink.

The interview

The main purpose of a letter of application is to obtain an interview. The interview is an occasion where employer and applicant consider each other's mutual problems and interests. The applicant is not asking a favor nor is the employer granting a privilege. Each has something to give and each has needs which may or may not be of mutual advantage.

Many applicants are nervous because they think of themselves during the interview. They can often overcome or avoid nervousness by anticipating the questions that are likely to be asked in the interview. Typical questions which are asked many applicants are the following:

1. Tell me all about yourself.
2. Why do you want to work for us?
3. What can you do?
4. Why did you leave your last employer? (Why do you want to leave your present employer?)
5. Do you have any good ideas on how to do this work for which you are applying?
6. May I see some samples or proof of your ability?

The first question should not be answered by starting with the date of birth, early life, and leading up to the time of the interview. Rather, the question should be answered by reference to the present: "I completed college this spring and I majored in finance. While I was studying finance I became interested in banking. Perhaps my interest in banking was stimulated by the speakers whom I heard at the state bankers' convention held in Blankville two years ago. The problems discussed with regard to financing farmers' crops interested me so much that I would like to learn more about the problems involved in loans to farmers. I myself was raised on a farm in Spring Valley and my father often felt financially handicapped in his plans for modernizing his farm," etc.

One hundred college students and graduates who had applied for positions were asked to list the problems they had encountered in their applications. The following list is made up of those problems most

PERSONAL DATA SHEET
John Richard Doe

ADDRESS:
TELEPHONE:

PHOTO

I. *Vocational Objectives:*

IMMEDIATE: To become a member of a management training program where I can learn a company's personnel, products and problems.

LONG RANGE: To become an executive in sales or some other department where I will have major responsibilities.

II. *Educational Background:*

Was graduated from Blank College with a B.A. degree. Major: psychology. Academic average: 90%. Psychology average: 93%.
Was graduated from John Adams High School in January 1941.
Was graduated from P. S. 121 in January 1937.
Both schools are on Long Island, New York.

III. *Military Background:*

Served in the Army for three years. Attained rank of Master Sergeant. Spent two years overseas.

IV. *Work Experience:*

Work experience has included working as undergraduate assistant in the psychology department at Blank College, vacation work as hardware salesman, and a six-month period as shipfitter's helper prior to being drafted.

V. *Extracurricular Activities:*

Psychology Club (assisted with programs).
Athletics (intramural—baseball, handball, football).
Outside Research (have read first sources in psychology beyond the scope of undergraduate academic requirements and have conducted small-scale experiments on my own initiative).

VI. *Hobbies and Avocations:*

Reading
Cooking
Athletics
Social Organizations
Bridge

VII. *Personal Data:*

25 years of age—married—no children—excellent health.
Height 5′ 9″; weight 155.
Willing to work at most any task.

VIII. *References:*

Three names and addresses.

PERSONAL DATA CHART

PHOTOGRAPH

AND

NAME

Past History

1. Scholastic Achievements:
   A. Grammar School—Valedictorian
   B. High School—Valedictorian
   C. Subjects Liked Especially Well:
      (1) Mathematics (All Forms)
      (2) Mechanical Drawing
      (3) Commercial Subjects
2. Interests:
   A. Athletics
      (1) Participation in all sports
   B. Social Interests
      (1) Church; Sunday School; Epworth League
      (2) Boy Scouts; Clubs; etc.
   C. Work: All kinds of odd jobs.

Future Ambitions

1. SUCCESS as a public-minded businessman and as a Certified Public Accountant

Present Status

Graduate of

Syracuse University; College of Business Administration; Accounting

Scholastic Achievements

1. Winner of two University Competitive Scholarships
2. Member of Beta Alpha Psi (National honorary Accounting Fraternity)
3. Member of Phi Kappa Phi (National scholastic)
4. Scholarship Rating—B

Wholly Self-Supporting

1. College education was wholly self-financed by means of summer work, working six hours daily during school year, and scholarships.

Activities

1. Athletics
   Wrestling '47, '48, '49
   Intercollegiate
      Champion . . . . '49
      Captain . . . . . . '49
      Soccer . . . . '47
2. Social Activities
3. Others: Scoutmaster

References

1. Name and address
2. Name and address
3. Name and address
4. Name and address

Personal Record

Birth—Jan. 30, 1927; Henderson, New York
Nationality—American
Religion—Methodist
Marital Status—Single
Height—5' 4"; Weight—135 lbs.
Health—Excellent; Defects—None.

frequently reported by the interviewees. Each general problem listed below is followed by its frequency and examples of the problem.

Before the Interview

1. The question of experience (27 times). Examples:
   a. Should I admit that I have had no experience and face the possibility of not being hired? Or should I try to lie and take my chances on getting by if I do get the job?
   b. Is there any way in which I can compensate for the lack of experience?
   c. How can I be sure that I am qualified to apply?

2. The question whether or not to tell the truth (19 times). Examples:
   a. Religious affiliations—should I mention membership in my church if I know that my prospective employer is an adherent of another faith? (The laws of some states prohibit the asking of this question; if it is asked in these states, it does not have to be answered.)
   b. Should I admit union membership if I am a member?
   c. Should I mention and discuss my political beliefs?

3. The interview itself (14 times). Examples:
   a. How can I best determine the type of approach to make?
   b. Should I emphasize my scholastic achievements?
   c. How should I sell myself?
   d. What type of references should I use?

During the Interview

1. The salary question (38 times). Examples:
   a. How can I answer, "What salary do you expect?"
   b. How am I to know that I will not ask too much? Or too little?
   c. Or should I ask for an approximate salary?

2. Reasons for choice of firm in making application (19 times). How can I answer, for example, the following:
   a. What can you do?
   b. Why did you choose this type of work?
   c. Why are you sure that you will like the work?
   d. Should I talk freely and frankly about what I consider my ability?

3. The job particulars (15 times). Examples:
   a. Should I ask questions about the job until I thoroughly understand all parts of it?
   b. Or should I wait until I get to the department to delve into the requisites of the job?
   c. Should I try to determine my chances for advancement, and its rapidity, while I am being interviewed?
   d. Should I ask questions about the firm during the interview? Or should I know many particulars concerning the firm before the interview?

4. Nervousness (15 times). Examples:
   a. How can I overcome nervousness?
   b. How can I best conceal my nervousness?
   c. How can I break down the formal attitude of the interview?

After the Interview

1. The interview itself (25 times). Examples:
   a. How can I judge the success of the interview?
   b. How can I tell whether the questions were answered correctly?
   c. What kind of impression did I make?

2. The results (23 times). Examples:
   a. Should I return and keep after the interviewer until he hires? If so, how soon?
   b. Should I have influential friends intercede in my behalf?

No one can offer blanket answers to these and other questions which are asked of applicants and which they ask themselves. Neither questions nor answers can be standardized. The applicant can seek the counsel of some experienced person with regard to appropriate answers to questions such as these. A discussion of the questions and possible answers will be a considerable help to many applicants. However, if the employer's question, "Tell me all about yourself," can be answered in the foregoing suggested manner, many other questions can also be answered sincerely and intelligently. All the employer's questions can be answered naturally when the applicant has developed a genuine long-term interest in the work for which he is applying. Getting a job is merely one stage in a series of efforts to become acquainted with specific kinds of vocational problems, employers, and occupational opportunities.

Some arts of personal salesmanship are helpful and many applicants can improve their abilities to sell themselves through a consideration of the following suggestions:

1. Think and talk *work*, not yourself. Try to think of yourself as a profitable investment to the employer, not of what the job means to you.

2. Consider getting a job as an investment —not an expense. Spend some time and money in getting a job. If necessary, borrow money to get the job you want.

3. Develop confidence in yourself by first studying your prospective employer's product or service.

4. Plan your campaign and follow the plan each day. Do not go about it in a hit-or-miss manner. Know where you want to apply each day for the next month until you get a job.

5. Consider it a sales proposition. If your first and second prospects do not want you, keep on trying. The fiftieth prospect may be just the one who needs you.

6. When asked to fill an application blank, fill it completely and cheerfully. Put a check mark in the blank spaces not applying to you. Then the interviewer will know you did not overlook any items.

7. Convince the employer you did not stop studying when you left school or college. Show him you are studying your work by means of books, magazines, and night-school or correspondence courses.

8. No one can write a good letter of application for you—you must write it yourself. You must "feel" what you write; then your letter will carry conviction. Study good letters of application, but write your own. If you really feel you are good for something, your letter will show it.

9. Have several friends criticize your letter. You'll probably revise it at least five times before sending it.

10. Always give your complete record and full information when asked to do so. Do not omit your activities of certain months or years.

11. When sending a photograph, send a good one. If the job is worth applying for, it is worth having a special picture taken for it.

12. When discussing salary, state what you have been getting and what you believe yourself worth to the employer. Do not haggle over salary too much, but if the employer is one of the kind who wants to pay less than people are worth, refuse his offer. The fellow who wants

something for nothing is not the kind of man you want to work for. Of course, he has a right to pay you a small salary until he knows what you are really worth to him. If you are a college graduate, your alumni secretary can probably give you some helpful figures on average or customary salaries of your fellow-alumni.

13. When you and the interviewer have discussed the vacant job to mutual satisfaction, the interviewer may hesitate to say, "Yes, you are the man we want." Many interviewers need subtle help in making decisions. If you feel that the interviewer really is willing to hire you but needs a "push" in your direction, you can help him by saying, "When would you want me to begin work if you decide to hire me?" The date of beginning work is a minor point but once the interviewer decides on the minor point he also usually hires you.

Gaining promotion

From time to time magazine publishers make surveys of the extent to which workers in America think they have chances for vocational advancement. Their findings are reported in current issues.[4] The economic status and advancement of 46,000 college graduates, eight years after graduation, has been studied by Federal government investigators.[5] This study indicated that most college graduates become employees rather than employers, hence, we shall discuss methods of gaining promotion with employers.

1. One factor that will greatly aid an employee in obtaining advancement is to work for an executive who likes him.

General Electric Company made a statistical study of 3,000 G.E. managers' records. Depth interviews also were conducted with a sample of 300 of them to find out what made them successful managers.

These managers were asked in effect: "How did you get where you are? What were the things that held you back? What do you consider were the strongest factors in your development to your present position?" and so forth. The answers were analyzed for significant factors.

Ninety per cent of these managers con-

The cash value of the degree.
It increases with age

EARNINGS

$7,000	
6,000	40 to 49 $6,152 50 and over $6,244
5,000	
4,000	30 to 39 $4,618
3,000	Under 30 $3,537
2,000	35 to 44 $2,845 45 to 54 $2,681
	25 to 34 $2,449 55 to 64 $2,344
1,000	20 to 24 $1,560

20 25 30 35 40 45 50 55 60
AGE

● MEDIAN EARNINGS OF MEN GRADUATES

■ MEDIAN INCOME OF ALL U. S. MEN

The study of college graduates reported by Ernest Havemann and Patricia Salter West included a comparison of the median earnings of 9,064 graduates of 1,037 colleges, and U.S. workers as a whole at various age levels. The data, analyzed by the Columbia University Bureau of Applied Social Research, indicate that college graduates earn more money almost from the first year on the job than the average man makes at the peak of his earning power. In the population at large, the peak period comes in a man's late thirties and early forties. But the youngest and least established graduates, those under 30 years of age, have a higher median income. In the second place, graduates get wealthier as they get older, while the average man's wealth begins declining after 45. According to the study, the graduates of the very oldest group, the 50-and-overs, have the best incomes. In the general population, the 50-and-overs are losing ground fast to younger men.

College graduate incomes excel the non-college worker not only job for job but also age for age. Even in their earliest productive years they earn far more than the average man at the peak of his earning power. After 45 the disparity becomes even more pronounced. At that age the average man's earning power is dropping fairly fast, but the college graduate's earning power is still going sharply upward.

Source: Ernest Havemann and Patricia Salter West, **They Went to College,** Harcourt, Brace and Company, Inc., New York, p. 29. Copyright, 1952, by Time, Inc. Reprinted by permission of the publishers.

sistently stated, "I got my best development when I was working for so-and-so and so-and-so."[6]

The employee who wishes to be promoted should seek the goodwill and admiration of his superior or find a new superior who does like him.

Some readers may say: "If there is anything I hate it's a bootlicker, a yes-man, or the employee who sticks around the boss." Yet we should not accuse the retailer of being a fawning flatterer because he dresses up his windows to attract those who are his logical buyers. The merchant merely utilizes some concrete advantages of his wares. Likewise the corporation employee should try to attract the prospective buyers of his services by appealing to his buyers in a way that can be understood.

The importance of working for someone who likes you does not, however, imply that advancement in a corporation depends upon favoritism—having relatives or friends in the firm who push you ahead regardless of your ability. The old adage: "It isn't what you know but whom you know" has been proven untrue. The study summarized by W. Lloyd Warner and James C. Abegglen, The Committee on Human Development, University of Chicago, of 8,000 top executives of large business and industry firms of the United States investigated the factors that are associated with advancement to the top.[7] The findings showed that the boards of directors and executives who direct our large corporations are not interested in "pull" or "drag"—they want men of ability who will produce profits for the company. The interest and support of a superior should be attained through the work situation—not by "connections."

2. The corporation clerical worker, salesman, or junior executive may be asking himself, "Why doesn't someone notice me?" If he is, he can answer his own question by asking himself, "What have I done that should bring about recognition or a raise?" "What new systems or methods have I devised that

will make more money or decrease costs for the employer?" The alert employee who seeks methods of making money or cutting costs often is surprised to find some good ideas which others have overlooked or "kicked around." It is well to pick them up, polish them, try them out, and present them to superiors with a description of their values and limitations.

In some cases the general manager and the unhappy sixty-dollar clerk have the same grade of brains. But the clerk tends to think in sixty-dollar channels—of his own needs, grouches, enmities, and desires for luxuries. How can he expect to merit a raise when his brain cells are working overtime on personal matters, while those of the big men in the company are active on company problems of volume production, sales resistance, net profits, and lower costs?

The employee obviously capable of advancement ought to learn to think like the higher executive and put himself mentally in the other's shoes. He ought to develop the ease in facing and solving problems that his superiors have.

3. If an employee is holding a mediocre job and the general manager does not know him, then he should not jump over the heads of his superiors in trying to get recognition from the key man of the company. He must always remember that chances for promotion are determined by his supervisory executive, because the "big guns" of the company consult their department heads before raising the pay or the job of an employee. This means that it may be necessary at times to neglect one's own "showcase" and help to trim that of one's superior. This is merely a part of the game of business.

4. A fourth possible way of advertising one's ability is that of making special reports on existing conditions of the business or conditions which may affect the business. Some executives have a fetishlike admiration for reports that present column after column of figures. Sometimes reports of this sort are not read, but they usually create a favorable impression at the time. A consultant related an experience in a concern where he was to study certain conditions. At the end of his job he gave the manager a complete report of the situation. Several days later, the manager told him that he had read the report with much pleasure, but that it failed to show him what to do in the future. The writer took the report from his desk and turned to the thirty-six pages where the details which were thought to have been omitted were given. As a matter of fact, the manager had not read the report. He just glanced through it and judged it very largely on the basis of its external appearance—its size, typing, charts, and quality of paper. The standards which he used in evaluating hours of mental toil gave a shock and a lesson which indicated that it is well to spend a large amount of time on the artistic aspects of reports. The colored charts may be unintelligible to a genius; but they should be beautiful enough to decorate the walls of an office carpeted with oriental rugs!

5. Another aspect of the report as a means of gaining recognition is that of the trade journal. Many office men think that it is necessary to be a professor of English or to use a Harvard accent to be able to write an article for a trade journal. Such is not the case. The trade journals are interested in shop talk, and any systems or ideas which have been of value to men in their field will be of interest to their readers. The good ideas should be described in as pleasing a manner as possible, but efforts should be concentrated on the ideas rather than the form. The editors will revise the article to fit the vernacular of the publication. Of course, one must be careful not to divulge information that should remain in the files of the employer. If in doubt on this matter, the manuscripts can be submitted to the proper authorities of the company before they are sent to the publisher. The average executive will probably be pleased to know that someone in his organization writes arti-

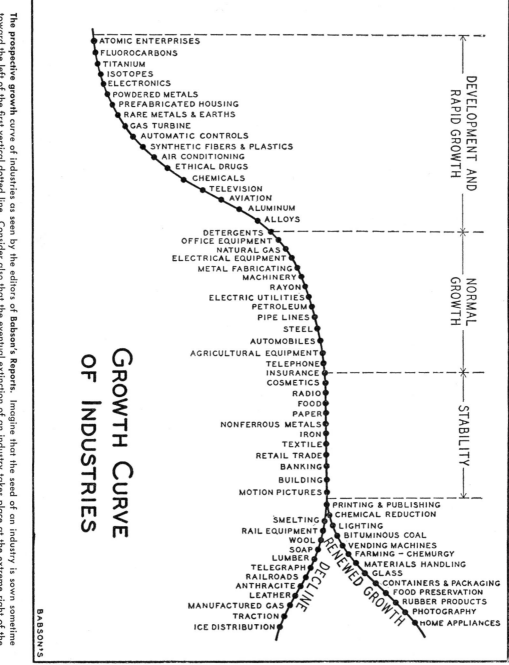

The prospective growth curve of industries as seen by the editors of **Babson's Reports.** Imagine that the seed of an industry is sown sometime toward the left of the first vertical dotted line. Consider also that the eventual extinction of an industry takes place at the extreme right of the chart beyond the end of the curve. Industries, like individuals, go through periods of development, rapid growth, normal growth, stability—and then into either a decline or new development. Here, in the opinion of the editors of **Babson's Reports,** is the present status of several dozen industries.

GROWTH CURVE OF INDUSTRIES

BABSON'S

DEVELOPMENT AND RAPID GROWTH

NORMAL GROWTH

STABILITY

ATOMIC ENTERPRISES
FLUOROCARBONS
TITANIUM
ISOTOPES
ELECTRONICS
POWDERED METALS
PREFABRICATED HOUSING
RARE METALS & EARTHS
GAS TURBINE
AUTOMATIC CONTROLS
SYNTHETIC FIBERS & PLASTICS
AIR CONDITIONING
ETHICAL DRUGS
CHEMICALS
TELEVISION
AVIATION
ALUMINUM
ALLOYS
DETERGENTS
OFFICE EQUIPMENT
NATURAL GAS
ELECTRICAL EQUIPMENT
METAL FABRICATING
MACHINERY
RAYON
ELECTRIC UTILITIES
PETROLEUM
PIPE LINES
STEEL
AUTOMOBILES
AGRICULTURAL EQUIPMENT
TELEPHONE
INSURANCE
COSMETICS
RADIO
FOOD
PAPER
NONFERROUS METALS
IRON
TEXTILE
RETAIL TRADE
BANKING
BUILDING
MOTION PICTURES

PRINTING & PUBLISHING
CHEMICAL REDUCTION
LIGHTING
BITUMINOUS COAL
VENDING MACHINES
FARMING – CHEMURGY
MATERIALS HANDLING
GLASS
CONTAINERS & PACKAGING
FOOD PRESERVATION
RUBBER PRODUCTS
PHOTOGRAPHY
HOME APPLIANCES

SMELTING
RAIL EQUIPMENT
WOOL
SOAP
LUMBER
TELEGRAPH
RAILROADS
ANTHRACITE
LEATHER
MANUFACTURED GAS
TRACTION
ICE DISTRIBUTION

DECLINE

RENEWED GROWTH

cles for his colleagues and competitors to read.

6. If possible to do so, it is well to attend some of the conventions of associations that influence the business. A good rule is never

to attend a convention without making a report of valuable facts to the management. One may neglect to do this because the speeches will be printed and sent to the company later on. This fact should not deter

Educational Testing Service, Princeton, N.J. conducts a wide variety of research and testing activities, primarily for educational and governmental organizations. Examples of tests are those used to determine aptitude and achievement, used extensively at the school and college levels.

ETS also prepared and administers selection and admission tests for college entrance as well as tests for admission to graduate schools including law, medicine, and business.

The photograph shows one of the activities of the Sponsored Scholarship Service division of ETS—the General Motors National Scholarship Plan. A part of the General Motors Scholarship Committee, composed of secondary school representatives and directors of admissions from leading colleges and universities, augmented by consultants from the ETS professional staff, is shown at work on the Scholarship Selection program.

one from making a report, because a delegate should study the undercurrents of the conferences and pick up valuable points that are not evident in the published reports. This is especially true of trends or tendencies of the times, which are seldom described in words but which the experienced technician uncovers when he meets experts in his field. The management should be given the benefit of the meetings attended even though the employee has to pay his own expenses to the convention.

7. To gain promotion, it is important to associate with the men and women who have demonstrated their abilities. The old-timers in the business world can give valuable pointers. Membership in pertinent trade associations will stimulate the employee to work and give him valuable contacts.

8. Work for an industry, or at least a firm, that is growing. Industries and companies are like individuals—they go through periods of development, rapid growth, normal growth, stability—and then either into a decline or into new development. All other factors being of equal influence, the man who works for a company whose growth has reached stability, or is declining, can hardly expect to advance to the same level or at the same rate he would in an industry that is in a stage of rapid growth or new development. See chart, "Growth Curve of Industries" as seen by the editors of *Babson's Reports*. Growth, these editors point out, is frequently as much a matter of management as it is of the industry, and companies that lead in engineering and market research have the best chances for survival and growth. An outstanding characteristic of growing companies is a continuing and aggressive search for new markets, new methods, and new products.

9. In the early years, seek work that gives good basic training in the fundamentals of the business, even though the pay may be lower than in other types of jobs. Many a young man graduating from college must

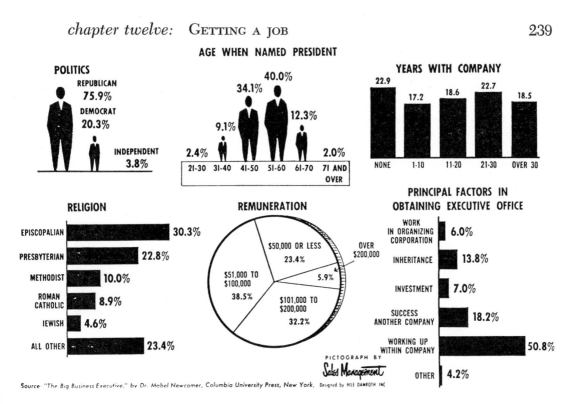

AGE WHEN NAMED PRESIDENT

POLITICS

REPUBLICAN **75.9%**
DEMOCRAT **20.3%**
INDEPENDENT **3.8%**

40.0%
34.1%
12.3%
9.1%
2.4% 31-40
2.0%

21-30 31-40 41-50 51-60 61-70 71 AND OVER

YEARS WITH COMPANY

22.9 17.2 18.6 22.7 18.5

NONE 1-10 11-20 21-30 OVER 30

RELIGION

EPISCOPALIAN **30.3%**
PRESBYTERIAN **22.8%**
METHODIST **10.0%**
ROMAN CATHOLIC **8.9%**
JEWISH **4.6%**
ALL OTHER **23.4%**

REMUNERATION

$50,000 OR LESS 23.4%
OVER $200,000 5.9%
$51,000 TO $100,000 38.5%
$101,000 TO $200,000 32.2%

PICTOGRAPH BY
Sales Management

PRINCIPAL FACTORS IN OBTAINING EXECUTIVE OFFICE

WORK IN ORGANIZING CORPORATION **6.0%**
INHERITANCE **13.8%**
INVESTMENT **7.0%**
SUCCESS ANOTHER COMPANY **18.2%**
WORKING UP WITHIN COMPANY **50.8%**
OTHER **4.2%**

Source: "*The Big Business Executive,*" by Dr. Mabel Newcomer, Columbia University Press, New York. Designed by HILE DAMROTH INC

Corporation Presidents—Where Do They Come from? Today's typical corporation president comes from a family of moderate means (only 36% of them have wealthy backgrounds; 12 per cent were poor). He's college educated (chances are three to one that he has had some college). He is Republican, Episcopalian, and an old-timer with his company. His occupational background is in administration (41 per cent), which includes sales (but 19 per cent were engineers, 12 per cent lawyers). He thrives on long hours, earns a good salary, and was elected to the top post when he was 52.

decide whether he shall take a high-paying job, such as factory labor, or a low-paying job, such as the executive training squad. Trainees are normally paid less than many other employees of the company, but the trainee should, all factors considered, advance more rapidly than the nontrainee. The chances for advancement to superior positions are so good in certain positions in companies that the ambitious, able beginner can well afford to work for a low beginning rate until he proves himself. A recent survey of plant managers and superintendents of the du Pont Company revealed that 46 per cent started as chemists, analysts, or technicians; 14 per cent as engineers; and the remaining 40 per cent as operators, laborers, clerks, office boys, and the like. Approximately 77 per cent are college graduates.[8] A study of 50 of the largest businesses in America (based upon an analysis of assets in the years immediately preceding World War II) showed that of the 143 executives who comprise top management of these companies, one started work for $1.50 a week, 11 others for less than $5 a week, 43 others for less than $10, and 81 others for between $10 and $25 a week. Only 7 received more than $25 a week—the highest getting paid $69.23 a week. "When you think of the head of a big business, think of a young man who once drew an envelope at the end of the week with $13.40 in it.[9] Training for management is, however, becoming increasingly important. Prof. Newcomer studied presidents and board chairmen of all large non-financial corporations in three business generations—1900, 1925, and 1950. She judged a corporation to be "big" if its assets totaled

$75 million in 1950, 50 million in 1925, or 25 million in 1900.

Her conclusion was that if managing is not already a profession, it is rapidly becoming one. The five solid pieces of evidence to back up this are:

The importance of wealth and family position has declined as a way to the top.
Formal educational requirements have increased.
More experience in the actual practice of managing is now required.
Managers today are a devoted, group of hard workers who like their jobs.
A professional code of ethics is emerging, although it's still somewhat amorphous.[10]

10. Another suggestion for the employee's advancement is illustrated in a recent occurrence. A certain department head operated his department with the same equipment bequeathed him some years before by his predecessor. The executive knew that his equipment and methods were slightly obsolete, but he thought that he was saving money for his employer by laboriously plugging along. He hated to ask his employer to spend money for needed machinery. The general manager finally decided that this department was too antiquated for the rest of the organization, fired the department head, and put a new man in charge.

The new man, realizing that he had to dress up the windows, at once spent all the money he could possibly get in making the department ultra modern. The new equipment could be seen and admired by his employer. It was tangible evidence of ability. Of course it cost a lot of money, but it was worth it. The new department head acquired the reputation of using progressive methods, and he was promoted again.

The advancement of any man in business depends upon his ability to please others. The owner of a business must please his customers. The employee of a corporation must please the man who is responsible for his efforts. His question should be, "What does this man want me to do?" not "What

should I do for my best interests?" If the boss wants his men to come to work at seven o'clock in the morning, then seven o'clock is the proper time to start work. If he dislikes men who wear mustaches and part their hair in the middle, then the employee should go without a mustache and comb his hair in a satisfactory manner. If an employer is whimsical, it is vastly easier to please his whimsicalities than to try to change him. Boss management is almost as important as scientific management. If adjustment to a superior's peculiarities is too difficult or degrading, then a new employer should be sought.

Every psychologically alert person becomes sensitive to the other fellow's moods and feelings. Only an obtuse introvert bursts in on the boss at his busiest time to ask for a raise in pay. The typical executive has certain free moments when he is likely to be relaxed and receptive. Annoying requests and suggestions for changed procedures should be timed accordingly.

Of course, every employer really wants results above all things else. If a special kind of bolt is needed for an emergency, it does little good to telephone all the local sources of bolt supplies and find that no one in the city can furnish the needed bolt. Excuses will not satisfy. The bolt must be obtained in another city or made to order. Most of the personal factors that produce results are not the work of genius but of habits of persistence and character in doing well the routine tasks of the job. However, an employee of a large corporation may be doing good work but the right executives may not realize it. Just as advertising is necessary in selling goods, so legitimate presentations of one's good works may be helpful to personal advancement in the large corporation.

Status symbols in business

Historically, the white-collar worker behind a desk has had more prestige and a higher income than the blue-collar worker.

The Paraphernalia That Goes With Rank

A shift has, however, taken place in recent years, particularly in earnings. Robert K. Burns has traced the income patterns for both groups since the 1890's, when average annual earnings of salaried employees were $860 a year, and wage earners were earning only $457. The income of the salaried employee rose rapidly during the 1920's but the wage earner's fluctuated and increased less rapidly. By 1928, the average salaried employee was making $2,398 a year, the wage earner, only $1,372.

During the depression differences were even more marked. While salaried employees' income fell to an average of $30 per week, wage earners were averaging as little as $18.

The recent data show, however, that the income of the wage earner has increased far more rapidly than that of the salaried employee. The biggest lift came during the war years. By 1943, the wage earners had already passed the salaried employees, receiving an average weekly wage of $45 as compared with the $43 of the salaried employees.[11]

The one major area in which the office worker still shows some advantage is in the fringe benefits—sick leave, holidays, vacations, and insurance—and such special details as better working hours, longer lunch period, less pressure, fewer penalties for tardiness, more pleasant surroundings, and a more generous attitude toward rest periods. For the production worker, weekend, overtime, and holiday pay is in general larger. Although various types of incentive bonus—higher pay for above-standard performance—are being applied increasingly to the production department they are still largely unknown in the office.

The office worker is more likely to have a formal merit plan for pay increases, with merit usually considered above length of service. It is also agreed that union seniority regulations may make rapid advancement difficult for the production worker.[12]

Employees who move upward into the supervisory and managerial levels are quite aware of the symbols of status. These symbols vary with the personality of the president. If he leans toward austerity, everyone adapts himself to the established customs. In most companies, however, there is a traditional pattern where privileges go with each rank. It is understood that the president has first call on the Cadillac in the company garage and that division managers usually get the Buicks. The roomiest, most comfortable offices belong to the brass, and are passed on to succeeding generations of brass.

Vice presidents, in certain companies, get an air conditioner, private stationery, an office on the brass-inlaid sixth floor, a davenport, a club membership, drapes, mahogany furniture, paneled walls, or a chance to turn in an un-itemized expense account. Their names appear on the lobby directory, their desks are larger and the desks have a water carafe.

In general, those of lesser status do not complain. Some expect to become members of the brass some day. They want the privileges to be there when they arrive. Furthermore, many employees realize that high level status also involves high level responsibilities and those in the lower ranks who do not seek heavy responsibilities tend to assume that special privileges should go to those who have extra heavy responsibility—they earn them.

Acknowledgments and References

1. H. W. Hepner, *Finding Yourself in Your Work*, D. Appleton-Century Company, New York, 1937, is one of many books available to college students who wish to refer to library books in setting up their vocational plans.

2. Charles H. Howard, "Help the Applicant to Help Himself," *Employment Service News*, December 1935.

3. These examples are taken from numerous sources; acknowledgment cannot be made to any one person.

4. For example, the surveys in *Fortune* beginning with the January 1947 issue.

5. Walter J. Greenleaf, *Economic Status of College Alumni*, Bulletin 1937, No. 10, Washington, D.C., U.S. Government Printing Office, 1939.

6. Reported by Moorhead Wright, Consultant in Decentralized Manager Education, General Electric Company, "Stop Looking for Loose Geniuses and Start Growing Your Own," *First Advertising Personnel Workshop*, Association of National Advertisers, January 26, 1956.

7. W. Lloyd Warner and James C. Abegglen, "Executive Careers Today: Who Gets to the Top," *The Management Review*, American Management Association, February 1956, p. 93.

8. *Du Pont Magazine*, October–November 1947.

9. "Has Management Gone Through the Mill?" *Trained Men*, No. 5 (1946), p. 13.

10. For further information, see Mabel Newcomer, "Professionalization of Leadership in the Big Business Corporation," *Business History Review*, March 1955. See also "The Mystery of Executive Talent," *Business Week*, May 21, 1955.

11. See *The Management Review*, American Management Association, January 1955, p. 22. Data from Robert K. Burns, *Journal of Business*, University of Chicago, 1954.

12. See "Strictly Personnel," *Personnel*, American Management Association, July 1952, p. 2.

PROJECTS

1. Select a business or industry which interests you vocationally, and gather the following data about it:

   a. Names and locations of the leading firms.
   b. Important individuals in the field.
   c. Names of trade associations related to the business or industry.
   d. Trade journals and associated periodicals.
   e. The closest local branches of the leading firms—the men in charge, and something about them personally.

2. From the list of questions about interviews which were asked by college students and graduates (see page 233), select those that you have encountered most frequently yourself. Prepare a well-thought-out procedure for use in your next interview.

3. Prepare a graphic presentation of your past history. Use an outline map to show the places where you have worked in the past.

4. Collect a number of unconvincing "situation wanted" ads from a newspaper or trade

journal. Diagnose the difficulty in each case and rewrite the ad for effective results.

5. Name some specific "showcase" items that you can utilize in your present work or in a position with which you are familiar. Analyze the probable effect of each.

6. Write a letter of application for a position you would like to have. Include a personal data sheet and a list of specific skills, or things you could do at once for an employer while working toward the type of position you are aiming at. Use the following check list and add to it any items you think would be helpful.

Men	*Women*
Operate an engine.	Sew.
Repair automobiles.	Cook.
Do concrete-mixing.	Take care of children.
Do physical labor.	Do housework.
Collect bills.	Be a telephone operator.
Run errands.	
Be a gas station attendant.	Do filing.
Repair radios.	Take care of the sick.
	Design clothes.

Both Men and Women

Do typing.	Invent new systems.
Do bookkeeping.	Versed in current events.
Do selling.	

Do clerical work.
Be an office machine operator.
Operate semi-automatic machines.
Do showcard writing.
Write a good letter.
Drawing, sketching.
Do window dressing.
Repair machinery.
Say a pleasant "Good morning."
Make a good first impression.
Use strategy in buying.
Know the rules of etiquette.
Talk interestingly.
Speak several languages.
Speak in public.
Invent new devices.

Do statistical work.
Write legibly.
Be an information clerk.
Drive a car.
Sort mail.
Be a cashier.
Be a sales clerk.
Be a helper to a skilled worker.
Drive a car safely.
Persuade others.
Act as a group leader.
Make many friends.
Supervise others.
Sell goods.
Use good English.
Invent unusual phrases.
Write.
Do research work.
Develop new services.
Manual dexterity.

7. Outline a program for obtaining a position. Include an unsolicited letter of application, trade journal advertisement, list of firms where you might apply, and a written description of the facts about yourself that you would try to present to the prospective employers.

COLLATERAL READINGS

Dickson, Carl, "What Employers Look for in the College Graduate," *Personnel and Guidance Journal*, April 1955, pp. 460–464.

Henry, William E., "The Business Executive: The Psychodynamics of a Social Role," *American Journal of Sociology*, January 1949, pp. 286–291.

Taft, R., and A. Mullins, "Who Quits, and Why," *Personnel Journal*, Vol. 24 (1946), pp. 300–307.

"Ten Rules for Getting Along with the Boss," *Changing Times*, the Kiplinger Magazine, May 1955, pp. 19–21.

"Time for You to Change Jobs?" *Changing Times*, January 1956, pp. 21–23.

Uhrbrock, Richard S., *Recruiting the College Graduate: A Guide for Company Interviewers*, American Management Association, New York, 1953.

Warner, W. Lloyd and James C. Abegglen, "Executive Careers Today: Who Gets to the Top?" *The Management Review*, American Management Association, February 1956, pp. 83–94.

CHAPTER THIRTEEN

Adjustments in dating, courtship, and marriage

The movies, novels, songs, and comics proclaim romance as a power that overcomes all obstacles. In these fictions, marriage is pictured as a continuous state of ecstasy. Actually, marriage is like work and other important arenas of life. It is an arena where we have special opportunities to learn to enjoy emotionally satisfying experiences such as companionship and to interpret life in new and exciting ways.

One interesting way to learn how adjustments affect the lives of men and women is to study couples during their courtship and marriage. In the case of a young couple courting each other, we can try to understand what each means to the other psychologically. Also, the college student usually knows his own parents well enough for him to appreciate, to some extent, what each probably meant to the other at the time of marriage and to observe some of the ways in which each parent's adjustment has affected his marital life. The college student who gains even a limited insight into the psychological factors involved in the courtship and marriage of other couples should have a somewhat improved perspective for the more intelligent direction of his own courtship and marriage. Certainly marriage itself cannot be the starting point for a discussion of the factors in a successful marriage.

Adjustment patterns that can be recognized in the behavior of couples

Almost all psychological adjustment patterns occur in the lives of persons, married or single. Some patterns, however, are especially influential in the choice of mate and the success or failure of the marriage. An objective awareness of these especially influential patterns can be acquired by any intelligent person who studies clinical findings, particularly those which are the mainsprings in the personality developments that lead to marital discord.

One of the first discoveries about marriage on the part of the psychological investigator is the fact that a boy and girl do not fall into love as a result of deep unfathomable forces. Rather, they fall into love with each other because each answers, or appears to answer, some of the dominant psychological needs of the other. A conventional example is the studious introverted boy, socially awkward, who is anxious to enjoy the company of a girl of his own age. He meets an extraverted girl, a poor student, who is vivacious. She helps him to enjoy himself socially. Perhaps she also builds up his feelings of self-worth because she tells him about her own shortcomings as a student and expresses admiration for his intellectual achievements. If he also has feelings of rejection by his parents and she mentions the ways in which her parents do not understand her, he may develop feelings of psychological kinship toward her and identify himself with her, thus forming ties that are likely to lead to further courtship and eventual marriage.

The individual's frustrations often find expression in the choice of the mate. The boy who was dominated by a stern parent or an older brother may prefer the company of a weak submissive girl because he can dominate her by telling her what clothes to wear, where she may go, and what she may or may not do. She, in turn, may enjoy his domination because her father was a tyrant over her. Her boy friend's tyranny allows her to live in terms of her earlier conditioning, but she likes the boy friend's domination better than her father's because she interprets the suitor's domination as proof of interest in her, not mere domination without sufficient interest.

Compensations are frequently demonstrated in the choice of a mate. The girl who feels that her family is socially inferior may prefer a mate of her own social class or she may seek one who appears to her to be of a higher class. If she feels inferior because her father was a plumber, she may prefer a bank clerk as a suitor even though he makes only half as much money as a plumber.

The girl who was reared too leniently or by parents who were inconsistent in their discipline may have pronounced feelings of emotional insecurity. She is not sure that she can depend upon anyone. Hence she may choose a man who has many fixed ideas, likes mathematics, lives his life in accordance with his formulas, is a firm disciplinarian and an army officer. His apparent self-assurance, even though it may actually be defensive on his part, is comforting to her. Actually, the two may be a well-mated couple.

Adjustments in courtship often demonstrate the previously stated principle (Chapter 2) that some persons react to an earlier environmental influence by antagonism toward it, others by adopting it. This is particularly evident in the case of a mother's domination of her son. One son may rebel against his mother's over-attentiveness and want to get away from home as soon as he can. He usually wants a mate who reminds him very little of his own mother. On the other hand, the son who enjoys his mother's attentiveness wants to remain with his mother as long as possible. If he does seek a mate, he is apt to seek a girl of the mother-image type. If he finds her, his courtship is likely to be of a vacillating kind because he finds his mother's company, after all, more comforting than the girl's.

Certainly every girl should know enough about the mother-fixation pattern to recognize it when she sees it. If she fails to appreciate its power for ill in married life and marries the man with an Oedipus complex, she is likely to find that his mother's apron strings become a noose around her life. Any bride who finds that her husband's comment about the pie she baked for him is: "Why don't you bake the kind of pie my mother baked?" should know enough to answer: "This is the kind of pie I bake for you. From now on you are going to eat 'em and like 'em!"

Every college man of courtship age ought to be able to recognize the behavior patterns of neurasthenia and functional invalidism when they are evident in the girls he dates. If he does not know enough psychology to recognize such adjustment patterns when he sees them, he will be lucky if he marries a well-adjusted girl. If he has enough insight to recognize patterns of serious maladjustment in a girl but decides to marry her regardless of such syndromes as neurasthenia or invalidism, he should appreciate the nature of the burden he assumes for life. Any hope he may have of curing her is just about as justifiable as that of the girl who marries a man in spite of the fact that she knows him to be a chronic alcoholic.

The adjustment mechanisms at work in the choice of the mate may be fairly obvious or very subtle. It is impossible to predict with one hundred per cent accuracy whether a given personality pattern on the part of a man will result in compatibility or incompatibility when matched with a specific pattern of a woman. We can predict only with greater or less likelihood of validity that two patterns may or may not result in a lasting marriage. Several psychologists and other researchers have investigated factors which indicate likelihood of success or failure in marriage.

Quantitative studies of marital success and failure

Different criteria for adjudging marital success or failure have been employed by different investigators. Clarence W. Schroeder used divorce as the criterion of failure in marriage in his study *Divorce in a City of 100,000 Population.*[1] Factors which he found to be positively correlated with marital success were: parents' marriage reported happier than average; parents not divorced or separated; sex instruction from mother or from books; education beyond high school; attendance at church three or more times a month; attendance at Sunday school beyond 18 years; and being reared in country or small town.

L. M. Terman[2] used the scores that 792 husbands and wives made on a marital happiness scale as the criterion of marital success. He found that the following factors were positively correlated with marital happiness: rated marital happiness of the parents; rated happiness of childhood; no conflict with mother; firm but not harsh discipline in the home; amount of attachment to father and mother; no conflict with father; frank attitude of parents toward early sex curiosity; relative mental ability where the husband is not inferior (with the wife's happiness) and where the husband is not much superior (with the husband's happiness); absence of severe and frequent childhood punishment; absence of disgust and aversion toward sex in premarital attitude of the subject; and, in the case of wife, absence of passionate longing.

Clifford Kirkpatrick[3] found that: (1) "in the case of women there is a marked tendency for greater intimacy with one or the other parent to be unfavorable to marital adjustment," and (2) "in the case of the males an excess or deficiency of friendship with the opposite sex is unfavorable to marital adjustment."

Hornell Hart, assisted by Wilmer Shields, used divorce as the criterion of marital failure.[4] He found that the optimum ages for entering marriage were twenty-nine for bridegrooms and twenty-four for brides. Men who were married when they were less than twenty-four years old, and women who were married when they were less than nineteen, were found to have a greater proportion of unhappy marriages than any other age groups.

In order to obtain objective information regarding the reasons for success or failure in marriage, Ernest W. Burgess and Leonard S. Cottrell, Jr. made a statistical and case history study of 526 married couples.[5] Their major findings were as follows:

1. Contrary to prevailing opinion, American wives make the major adjustment in marriage.
2. Affectional relationships in childhood typically of the son for the mother and the daughter for the father, condition the love-object choice of the adult.
3. The socialization of the person, as indi-

cated by his participation in social life and social institutions, is significant for adjustment in marriage.
4. The economic factor in itself is not significant for adjustment in marriage, since it is apparently fully accounted for by the other factors (impress of cultural background, psychogenetic characteristics, social type, and response patterns).
5. With the majority of couples, problems of

TABLE 13-1

STUDIES OF THE BEST AGE FOR MARRIAGE AS JUDGED BY MARITAL SUCCESS AND FAILURE

	Poor	*Good*	*Excellent*
Burgess-Cottrell (526 marriages)			
Men:	Under 22	22–27; 31 and over	28–30
Women:	Under 19	19–27	28 and over
Hart-Shields (500 marriages)			
Men:	Under 24	24–28	29
Women:	Under 21	21–23	24
Terman (792 marriages)			
Men:	Under 22	22 and over	22 and over
Women:	Under 20	20 and over	20 and over
Landis (409 marriages)			
Men:	Under 20	20–29	30 and over
Women:	Under 20	25 and over	20–24

From Judson T. Landis and Mary G. Landis, *Building a Successful Marriage*, second edition, Prentice-Hall, Inc., Englewood Cliffs, New Jersey, 1953, p. 107.

TABLE 13-2

DIFFERENCE IN AGE OF HUSBAND AND WIFE AND ADJUSTMENT

Difference in Age	Marital Adjustment			Number of
	Poor (per cent)	Fair (per cent)	Good (per cent)	Cases
Same age	13.1	39.1	47.8	46
Husband older:				
One to three years	21.4	31.0	47.6	168
Four to seven years	35.4	26.4	38.2	110
Eight years or more	31.1	17.8	51.1	45
Wife older	23.2	23.2	53.6	56
One or both, no reply	....	....	....	101
Total	28.5	28.3	43.2	526

From Ernest W. Burgess and Leonard S. Cottrell, Jr., *Predicting Success or Failure in Marriage.* Table 89 (Chart 36), p. 406. Copyright, 1939, by Prentice-Hall, Inc., Englewood Cliffs, N.J.

TABLE 13-3

DURATION OF KEEPING COMPANY AND ADJUSTMENT

Duration of Courtship	Marital Adjustment			Number of
	Poor (per cent)	Fair (per cent)	Good (per cent)	Cases
Under three months	39.3	28.6	32.1	28
Three to 11 months	42.9	23.8	33.3	105
One year to three years	28.9	31.8	39.3	201
Three to five years	12.6	30.6	56.8	111
Five years and over	17.2	27.6	55.2	58
No reply	....	....	....	23
Total	28.5	28.3	43.2	526

From *Predicting Success or Failure in Marriage*, Table 91 (Chart 38), p. 407.

sexual adjustment in marriage appear to be a resultant not so much of biological factors as of psychological characteristics and of cultural conditioning of attitudes toward sex.

6. Prediction before marriage of marital adjustment is feasible, and should and can be further developed through statistical and case-study methods.

Particularly important was their finding that similarity of cultural background was found to be of greater importance in a good marital adjustment than was similarity of economic background.

Landis has assembled data obtained from several studies of the best age for marriage as judged by marital success or failure. In general, the researchers seem to agree that the best marital adjustments are made by men who marry after they are about 28 or 29 and women who marry in their mid-twenties. Poor adjustments occur most frequently when the husband has married in his early twenties or teens and the wife, in her teens (see Table 13-1).

Burgess and Cottrell found that those who had the highest scores based on premarital background items, that is, those who seemed to have the most factors favorable to a successful marriage, actually did have more successful marriages.[6] They found that there was an increase in the number of divorces and separations as the prediction scores became lower. There was also an increase in the number of those who had *contemplated* divorce or separation as the scores became lower. It would therefore appear that it is possible to predict with some reliability the chances of success in marriage if certain factors are taken into consideration.

Factors in divorce

Divorce, although not actually encouraged in our culture, is condoned. During the period, 1944-1953, the number of divorces reported annually has ranged from 381,000 to 610,000. In addition, there were about 750,000 homes from which the husband was absent and more than 300,000 homes from which the wife was absent. This may not mean that more ill-advised marriages are being undertaken than heretofore, but that people are more anxious to be released from the marriage contract if they are disappointed in it. It appears that, in general, the longer the duration of a marriage, the greater is the possibility of its being permanent. The first six years of marriage are the crucial ones. There are more divorces during the third year of marriage than during any other, but the divorce rate remains high during the first six years of marriage.[7]

In connection with his study of psychological factors in marital happiness, Terman statistically evaluated domestic grievances of the 792 married couples who constituted his experimental group. Findings by Terman with regard to the grievances that are considered most important and least important are stated as follows:

Consider first the grievances that rank highest for seriousness. These are all personality faults of the complainant's mate, not the external circumstances or conditions of marriage. This holds for the entire first 20 in the husband's list, and for 19 of the first 20 in the wife's. A majority of the faults are of the kind commonly thought to be indicative of emotional instability, neurotic tendency, or marked introversion, as these terms are used in the current literature of personality psychology. Their position here lends support to the theory that one of the greatest dangers to marriage is the all-around unhappy temperament of one or both of the spouses. . . .

Most serious for husband's happiness are, in order: wife's nagging, lack of affection, selfishness or inconsiderateness, complaining, interfering with his hobbies, slovenliness of appearance, quick temper, interfering with his discipline of children, conceit, insincerity, too easily hurt feelings, criticizing, narrow-mindedness, neglect of the children, poor housekeeping, argumentativeness, annoying habits and mannerisms, untruthfulness, interference with his business, and spoiling the children.

Most serious for wife's happiness are, in order: husband's selfishness or inconsiderateness, lack of success in business, untruthfulness, complaining, failure to show his affection for her, unwillingness to talk things over, harshness with the children, touchiness, lack of interest in the children, lack of interest in the home, lack of (general) affectionateness, rudeness, lack of ambition, nervousness or impatience, criticizing, poor management of income, narrow-mindedness, unfaithfulness, laziness, boredom when she talks to him about her everyday life.

Only 6 items are found in the first 20 of both husband's and wife's lists: "not affectionate," "selfish and inconsiderate," "complains too much," "criticizes me," "is narrow-minded," "is not truthful."

Consider next the grievances that are least serious as causes of unhappiness. Here the spouses are in closer agreement. Of the 10 lowest in the respective lists, 7 are found in both.

The 10 things in order of least importance for the wife's happiness are that: husband is older, smokes, differs from her in tastes in food, is younger, differs from her in education, drinks, swears, is late to meals, is jealous, differs from her in religious beliefs.

The 12 least serious to husband's happiness are as follows in order of least seriousness: the wife is younger, drinks, smokes, is older, differs from him in tastes in food, is a social climber, works outside the home, swears, differs from him in education, is a poor cook, differs from him in religious beliefs, is unfaithful.

This list of things that are relatively so unimportant to the husband's happiness is one of the most interesting outcomes of our entire study. The striking fact about the list is that it is composed so largely of things which have long been regarded as among the most essential conditions of a happy and successful marriage.*

Divorce is indisputable evidence that one or both marriage partners have failed to adjust to the other, and to the institution of marriage. We have seen what some investigators believe to be factors militating for success in marriage, but the factors that contribute to a maladjustment, as in divorce, are perhaps even more difficult to ascertain.

One statistical finding about divorces is that a childless marriage has about 70 chances in 100 of ending in divorce; one with children has only 8 chances in 100.[8]

This means that a childless marriage has almost nine times as great a chance of culminating in divorce as does a marriage with children. The fact that no children are involved in most divorce cases may mean that these mates are selfish—so selfish as to be unwilling to make the adjustments necessary to a successful marriage. On the other hand, the fact that they have no children may mean that it is easier for them to consider divorce than it is for people with the responsibility of children. Regardless of the reasons, however, the fact remains that adjustments of the requisite number and scope are not made so that the marriage may be enabled to grow.

Terman, in his study of 792 married couples who had a mean length of marriage of 11.4 years, found that 8.8 per cent of the men and 11.5 per cent of the women had seriously contemplated divorce at some time during their marriage. When these 792 couples rated themselves as to the degree of happiness achieved, 95.5 per cent of the men rated their happiness from "about average" to "extraordinarily happy." Only 4.6 per cent of the men rated their marriage "somewhat less happy than average" to "extremely unhappy." Of the women, 94.4 per cent rated their marriage as "about average" to "extraordinarily happy," and 5.6 per cent rated their marriage "somewhat less happy than average" to "extremely unhappy."[9]

Husbands of good health make better adjustments than those less healthy. The health of the husband is shown to be more important than that of the wife, probably because of economic necessities.[10]

Statistical studies of divorces and other factors concomitant to marital conditions merely indicate likely relationships, not determining influences. This was shown in the Family Society of Greater Boston study of the Highs who adjusted well in their work in comparison wtih the Lows who failed

* By permission from *Psychological Factors in Marital Happiness,* by Lewis M. Terman, Copyright 1938, McGraw-Hill Book Co., Inc., pp. 101 f.

to adjust after counseling. See Table 7-1, page 131. The individual's own adjustments to his barriers were the determining influences, not such factors as family disruption, illnesses, or money troubles during childhood. These kinds of troubles plagued both the Highs and the Lows. The Highs developed a tendency to counteract and reverse negative early experiences, the Lows to re-enact unfavorable early family patterns. One important finding in regard to ability to adjust to barriers was that people seem to be able to adjust far more easily to outside pressures such as family disruption and money troubles than to inner emotional pressures like family antagonism or self-doubt.[11]

The person who adjusts best to marriage is the socialized person. Through his experiences with people in various groups he develops differently from the individual who participates but little in group organizations. He is more apt to be a stable personality and thus better suited to marriage.

Our choice of mates is restricted in our society by certain barriers that limit our acquaintances and friends. Although these barriers are not insurmountable, they are worthy of consideration.

Religion is one of these restrictive factors. While intermarriages do occur and many of them turn out happily, it is generally found that Catholics marry Catholics, Jews marry Jews, and Protestants marry Protestants. Many parents indoctrinate their offspring with the importance of marying "their own kind" for their own good. Serious friendships with young people of a different religious faith are usually disapproved. When two people of different religions do fall in love, however, and consider marriage, problems arise, particularly if the couple intends to have children. The question of which religion the children will be encouraged to adopt is a question that must be answered by the parents. Some couples feel that they cannot assume the responsibility of making such a decision and do not marry because

of the difference in religion. Other alternatives are: one may decide on conversion to the faith of the other; both may dismiss the problem of choice between two religions by subscribing to neither; each partner may retain his own faith. Another solution, more idealistic than practicable, is the adoption of the attitude that because of a mixed marriage the parents have something extra to add to the child's development—an appreciation and understanding of two religions instead of one only.

The chief obstacles to a successful religious intermarriage, or to any marriage, are psychological. Marriage is an adjustment. Even the most perfect marriage has its moments of difference and misunderstanding. If both partners share a common concern for the same values and are basically well-adjusted and love one another, there is a strong likelihood that they will be able to work out their problems. Yet it cannot be denied that a marriage concerns more than just the husband and the wife. The marriage involves the lives and relationships they have with their families and the religious communities in which the husband or wife had his origin and childhood association. Although churches, families and communities have only an indirect influence, they can do much to complicate and injure, or to support and further, the happiness of the couple. Young couples contemplating religious intermarriage should be fully aware of the pressures that may be brought on them. There are no national statistics to show just how the chances of an interfaith marriage compare with that of a marriage between two persons of the same religious fellowship. Experience has shown, however, that the more similar the background, interests and beliefs of the two individuals, the more likelihood there is that their marriage will be a success.[12]

It is a fact that couples having church connections have more stable marriages than those with none. The accompanying chart, based on a survey by the American Youth Commission,

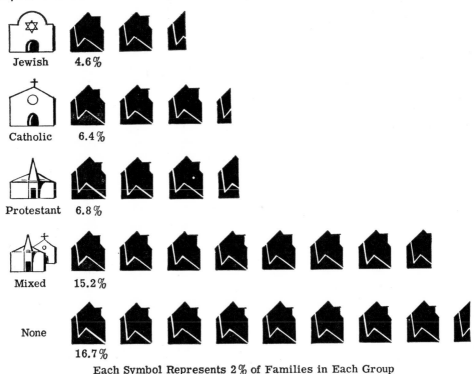

Jewish 4.6%

Catholic 6.4%

Protestant 6.8%

Mixed 15.2%

None 16.7%

Each Symbol Represents 2% of Families in Each Group

Religion and broken homes—from a chart by Graphic Associates for Public Affairs Committee, Inc.

shows the relation between religious affiliation and broken homes.

Finding a church home is an important part of building a marriage between people with religious needs and interests. Couples oftentimes would like to have a church home but after their marriage, especially if they come from different religious backgrounds, they find it difficult. He isn't at home in her church, nor is she in his, and so they settle it by having no church affiliation at all. This rarely solves the problem because most people need a larger interest outside themselves if they are to be happy. When trouble comes, that need becomes acute. You can feel terribly alone and helpless when a crisis comes. There is a desolation about death, sudden impoverishment, severe disappointments, and many family problems. At times like these, as well as in day-by-day living, religion is often a real source of comfort and support.

Finding a church home usually begins before marriage. When plans are being made for life together you talk about the church in which you will make your home. You visit each other's

church if you have not grown up in the same one. Together you plan for your joint membership. If the decision has been postponed until after your marriage, it is wise not to put it off longer.

Religious ceremonies at the time of the marriage, the dedication of the home, the christening of the children, the celebration of holidays, and in the everyday life of the home add richness and a sense of permanence to a marriage.[13]

Intelligent dating

Dating is a getting-acquainted period. High school and college students rate the ability to date successfully as a kind of status-gaining procedure. On some campuses, dating is largely an end in itself rather than an approach to courtship and marriage. College students, in most cases, must postpone serious thoughts of marriage until they complete their education and earn a livelihood. Dating enables the students to enjoy the company of the opposite sex and to engage in normal social functions until they reach the stage of educational and professional attainment which allows them to have more definite plans for marriage. Dating offers these young people excellent opportunities to note and evaluate the personality characteristics of the opposite sex and to surmise which ones would, as marital partners, be successful or unsuccessful.

The student who is psychologically alert should not go on a date and attempt to make amateur psychoanalytic interpretations of the dated partner and explain them to him (her). Such practice on the part of many college majors in psychology is evidence of immaturity. The mature student of psychology does not "psychologize" his friends and discuss his interpretations with them. Rather, he notes the cues to each friend's adjustment patterns, constantly adds to his understanding of the friend, increases his respect for him, and makes himself a better companion. Such a companionship is on a high level of mutual respect for the personality integrity of the other person. Dating experiences offer the student the opportunity to do some intelligent "field work" in the attainment of this high level of companionability and psychological insight.

Young people on dates often discuss their own childhood histories, their frustrations, resentments, disappointments, hopes, and other influences in adjustment. The alert listener can, in his own mind, note the patterns of behavior that control the other person's personality. The psychologically intelligent male student on a date will note significant factors in the adjustment development of his girl friends, such as the following:

1. *Her barriers:* Problems of health, physical appearance, limitations in mental capacities, birth of other children in the family, parental frictions, neurotic relatives, impa-

tient teachers, domineering associates, et al.

2. *Predisposing influences:* Cultural influences, standards of conduct insisted upon by parents, and especially her affect evaluation of herself when she was a small child. Did she, for example, behave as though she were the center of attention of the family; feel unwanted in the family, denied her rights, ridiculed, disciplined severely; or feel that she was helpless, sickly, and deficient as a child in comparison with other children?

3. *Precipitating influences:* recent factors such as failure, insult, loss, disappointment, fatigue, or success.

4. *Direct-attack adjustments* which she made or might have made.

5. *Positive substitute activities:* What means of adjustment were made of a positive, personality-strengthening nature, such as studiousness, in adjustment to real or imagined social failure or physical unattractiveness?

6. *Evasive or retreat adjustments:* What personality-weakening adjustments has she made, such as withdrawing from social contacts, habitual attendance at the movies, excessive alcoholism, constant fault-finding, exhibitionism, untruthfulness, wishing for death, or other negative-value activities?

If the dominating adjustments have been positive and personality-strengthening, she will need little aid from a future husband other than normal human companionship and consideration. If many dominating adjustments have been of an evasive nature and personality-weakening, she may require a great deal of helpful insight from a husband in order to make her happy or to enable him to be happy with her.

If she exemplifies the very common adjustment pattern of the child who felt inferior intellectually (barrier), was reared by doting parents who made her the center of attention (predisposing influence), now keenly enjoys being well dressed and pleasing others in social situations (positive value adjustment), she is very apt to continue the pattern after marriage. Her husband, in turn, will react to the pattern favorably or unfavorably, depending upon his own adjustment tendencies. If he has developed strong tendencies in the direction of stinginess in buying clothes and has little desire to have his wife impress others in social affairs, he is likely to find her behavior annoying. On the other hand, if he likes to spend money to buy nice things for his wife so that she becomes an ornament that impresses other people, he is likely to find her behavior quite gratifying to him.

Marriage does not change adjustment patterns. The individual takes into marriage the same patterns and techniques that he used before marriage. The girl who resorted to illness as an escape from difficult situations before marriage will also resort to illness as an escape after marriage. The youth who ran to mother for comfort or resorted to drink in emotional crises before marriage is likely to resort to the same techniques after marriage. But the patterns that one man needs in his mate may be quite different from the patterns that will complement the adjustment needs of another.

The one stage in boy-girl relations where our culture provides opportunity for the boy and the girl to evaluate each other objectively is the dating period, before courtship begins. Once their relation reaches the courtship stage, almost all objectivity in personality evaluation disappears. Evaluations of the other person in courtship become mere rationalizations.

Adjustments after marriage

Immediately after marriage the honeymoon takes place. This custom enables the young couple to get away from old environments, relatives, and friends. Marriage requires the changing of many habits, and the honeymoon provides the newlyweds some opportunity for learning how to live together in the first stages of their home life. As stated by Paul H. Landis:

"The first month isn't easy, you know," is a comment frequently heard from newlyweds. Being happy as man and wife does not come to most couples as a matter of course, but like success in any cooperative enterprise it comes only after considerable experience.

The readjustments of habits that marriage requires are sometimes disturbing, but, to establish any type of home routine, many habits accepted prior to marriage have to be readjusted to suit the new family situation. Habits of rising and retiring, the time of eating, likes and dislikes in foods, and numerous activities that make up daily living have to be adjusted. Failure of either member to make certain concessions is apt to become a source of friction.

Good husbands and wives are not born that way, nor is the transformation caused by courtship or the marriage ceremony. Some old folks on their golden wedding anniversary make flowery statements about never having disagreed on anything. The likelihood is that they have forgotten many things. Actually most couples disagree on certain points, and these differences may come to light early in married life.

Unfortunately, most courtship is carried on during leisure time so the young couple have opportunities to see each other only when they are in the best mood. During courtship they usually engage in pleasant activities. This is suddenly changed by marriage, when for the first time the marriage partners share every relationship of life: work, trouble, the daily grind of life, responsibility, duty, worry about finances, and all the other normal responsibilities that are a part of adulthood, as well as the leisure time and recreational periods.

During the early months of marriage much of the exaggerated romance wears off as the couple settles down to washing dishes, scrubbing floors, commuting, paying bills, and sharing the remnants of their days with one another. The young man and young woman come to see each other as human beings rather than as the idealized gods they appeared to be in the highly romantic phase of courtship. There was a tendency during courtship to oversell one's best traits to be sure of winning the other party. Now in day-to-day living both best and worse traits gradually appear.

Successful couples work out their disagreements or learn to accept and tolerate each other's differences in point of view. It would be unusual to find any relationship in which two people agreed on everything. Marriage is no exception. Few people like all of their own personal traits. It is unlikely that they will find

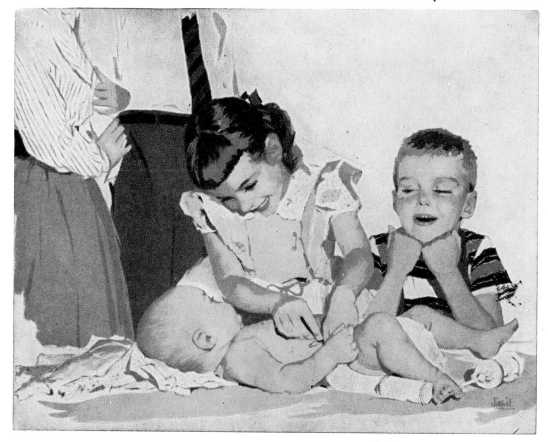

Nowadays, the bees are strictly for the birds

In former days, when parents were
   inclined to be tyrannical,
The facts of life, tradition held,
   were told in terms botanical.
(And, when disclosed, quite seldom brought
   about effects galvanical.)

Today, there's little subterfuge—
   no talk of bees or featherness.
The family climate's healthier, with
   a warm and sunny weatherness
That comes from interests shared—from what
   might best be termed "togetherness."

To face the economic facts
   of life with some profundity
And build a selling volume that
   develops real rotundity,
You now must reach the *family* as
   the source of sales fecundity.

Today, one magazine—McCall's—
   is edited exclusively
To comprehend all interests of
   the family unobtrusively
(Which may be why its advertisers
   praise it so effusively!)

everything exactly as they wish or had expected in the person they marry. Actually life would for many be a little dull if they always saw eye to eye.*

The fact that a man and woman marry and live together for many years may or may not indicate a happy marriage. Sooner or later, every marriage necessitates numerous adjustments on the part of each mate to the other. In our American culture, the husband usually expects his wife to be the dominant personality in regard to the home and the children. The wife expects the husband to be the dominant personality in regard to the earning of the income, the geographical area where they live, and the purchase of the home.

In the purchase of many commodities for the home, the home is a mutually operated enterprise.

When it comes to determining what shall be bought, surveys show that husbands and wives put their heads together more often than not. This is especially true when the item under discussion is of comparatively high cost, such as a refrigerator, a washing machine, or the family automobile. The purchase of toasters, electric irons, and, of course, cosmetics is usually decided by the wife. There is close agreement as to which spouse or whether both decide, as shown by the answers of the women and of the men concerning the purchase of four items. See Table 13-4.[14]

The extent to which the American home is a jointly operated enterprise is further indicated by the data from a mail survey of masculine readers of *The American Magazine.* Of the 2,003 men who answered the questionnaire, 94 per cent shop, or at times help to shop, for groceries. The majority, 63 per cent, prepare their own breakfasts. Eighty per cent claimed that they do some dishwashing, 62 per cent that they scrub out the bathtub, and about half that they scrub floors and wash windows.[15]

Men are somewhat more likely to help do household chores when the wife is employed. General Electric Company made a study of the household activities of working wives in comparison with those of full-time housewives and found that:

The husbands and families of working wives are slightly more helpful in getting the housework done than those of full-time housewives. But only slightly.

In the "garbage and trash emptying" department, the husbands of both wives show up best. The following percentages show which family member does the main part of this job.

	Working wives	Full-time wives
Wives themselves ...	40%	60%
Husbands	41	23
Other family members	19	17

When it comes to washing the dishes, 76% of working wives fall heir to the chore (as against 78% of full-time housewives). 9% of the working wives' husbands do the main job of dishwashing (7% of the full-time housewives' husbands). And other family members account for the job in 15% of both women's families.

88% of working wives do the main job of cooking meals (97% of full-time housewives).

Few couples are so perfectly mated that no frictions arise. Marriage calls for continuous adjustments as well as the performance of home responsibilities of good citizenship

TABLE 13-4

Item	Who Decides	As Answered by Women (per cent)	Men (per cent)
Automatic refrigerator	Both	88	88
	Men	3	6
	Women	9	6
Home deep freezer	Both	78	78
	Men	10	12
	Women	12	10
Automobile	Both	56	57
	Men	41	42
	Women	3	1
Electric iron	Both	24	29
	Men	1	4
	Women	75	67

* By permission from *Your Marriage and Family Living,* by Paul H. Landis, copyright 1946, McGraw-Hill Book Co., Inc., pp. 152–153.

and parenthood. The fact that it is easy for any interested observer to go into a restaurant and to differentiate the married couples from the unmarried does not mean that every young married couple need look forward to boredom or eventual separation. Nor should either party expect a completely problemless existence.

Sometimes a frank disagreement or emotionalized "spat" may clear the atmosphere and remove the unspoken grievances that have accumulated. Disagreement is a part of the process of marital adjustment. It helps to improve the unity of the family if it is a phase in the further adjustment of persons who are basically well adjusted in other respects. If the one partner always avoids open disagreement and merely suppresses his own feelings of frustration, the frustrations will in time affect his personal-

---

Working Wives: How Do They Manage Double Duty?

More than ten million American women lead double lives. They are working wives who run homes and hold jobs, too.

How do they manage double duty? General Electric wondered, too, so it cross-examined 700 to find out how they did it. Here are some things GE learned:

Less Housework? No, they do as much as full-time housewives do but at different times.

Less shopping? Only a little, about 30 minutes less a week.

Quicker meals? Very slightly. The stay-home wife spends only 12 minutes more a day getting meals than her working sister does.

Husband help? Not much. He may empty the garbage, but there are only 9 chances in 100 that he does the dishwashing.

More efficient? Nope. They're as lax as all-day homemakers about using labor savers. For instance, half never use the timers on their ovens and roasters. They bake pies and cakes almost as often as other wives. And they serve canned foods less.

Less fun? Hardly. They give nearly as much time to recreation and entertaining as one-job wives.

Well, then, how do they fit two lives into one day? And what, pray, are nonworking wives doing with their time?

Well, for one thing, nonworking wives spend nearly 8 hours more a week "just relaxing." And working wives spend 50 per cent less time with their children on weekdays, and 30 per cent less on week ends.

But double duty doesn't seem to wear down the working wives. Some 22 per cent say they are "exhausted" when bedtime comes. The percentage of full-time housewives in that condition is exactly the same. And more working wives than home-type wives report they end the day "pleasantly tired" or "wide awake."

From *Changing Times,* the Kiplinger magazine, May 1953, p. 18. Adapted from *Analysis of the Homemaking Habits of the Working Wife,* Copyright, 1952, by the General Electric Company.

ity. He must make some kind of adjustment, such as burying himself in his work. In that case he is likely to suspend his identifications with his mate, and their relationship becomes a conventional one. Success in his work, however, may give him feelings of adequacy that enable him to aid her by treating her objectively.

Most couples want to make their marriages successful. Marriages rarely become truly successful unless both, or at least one partner, is sufficiently well adjusted to facilitate the psychological well-being of the other. Both can grow best when they respect each other's personality and want the partner as well as the self to enjoy married life on its highest level—creative love.

The love life of the average individual passes through four stages: love of self, *babyhood;* love of parent, *childhood;* love of chum, *early youth;* and love of mate, *adulthood.* When the individual's love-object remains on the first level, self-love, he is an example of *narcissism;* when on the second level, attachment for a parent, the terms *Oedipus* or *Electra complex* are used to describe it; and when fixated on the third level, attraction for persons of the same sex, the general term *homosexuality* is used. The latter term is often used in a broad general sense and is contrasted with *heterosexuality,* attraction toward individuals of the opposite sex, but neither of these last two terms necessarily implies perversion or a specific sex relation.

The best-adjusted persons also attain a fifth stage of love-life, *creative love.* Each identifies his personality with that of his mate in absorbing tasks of rearing children, developing a happy home life, and pursuing successful vocational activities. Biologically, creative love is most commonly expressed in the rearing of children.

Sociological changes

From the sociological standpoint, American family life is changing in line with the influences of a changing society. Families in the United States in comparison with those of other countries have certain differential characteristics. These differential characteristics are largely in terms of process rather than of structure. One of the most distinctive trends is greater *urbanization.* The proportion of families living in cities and near-by urban areas has increased. Furthermore, rural families have adopted the urban way of life.

Instability is greater, as indicated by the increase in divorce. This instability within some families is set in sharper focus by the increased trend toward companionship, common interests, and emphasis on democratic relations. As one advertisement for a women's service magazine phrased the change: "The family climate's healthier, with a warm and sunny weatherness that comes from interests shared—from what might best be termed 'togetherness.'"

Several decades ago the father was undisputed head of the household. He dominated the family, and his preferences received first consideration. Today, this type of family is being supplanted by one that is more democratic. The father is slipping, or has slipped, from his throne as autocrat. He is now a companion rather than boss. His wishes are not the only ones which are considered when the family is involved. Each member can voice his opinion and have his desires acted upon, also. Or, if one member's interests are far different from those of the rest of the family, he can go off alone—within reasonable limits,—and do what he wishes. Ernest W. Burgess has described this aspect of the family in a changing society as follows:

The American family, both in its apparent variety and in its essential unity, needs to be viewed in the perspective of social change. It is in transition from older rural institutional forms to a democratic companionship type of family relations adapted to an urban environment. This great change in the mores is a vast social experiment, participated in by hundreds of thousands of families under the collective stimu-

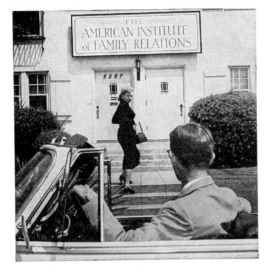

A client entering the American Institute of Family Relations, 5287 Sunset Blvd., Los Angeles 27, California.

Workroom at American Institute of Family Relations. Some of the Institute's more than 160 pamphlets may be seen in rack in background. The people in the picture are filling orders for pamphlets and other materials.

Mary Jane Hungerford, Ph.D. (with braids), directing exercises in connection with course on "Preparation for Parenthood." Photos by Gladys Tippett.

The American Institute of Family Relations, a national non-profit organization, will without charge put inquirers in touch with qualified counselors in their own communities. It maintains a comprehensive referral list in all of the states, and also in Canada and many foreign countries. It likewise publishes a monthly service bulletin, **Family Life,** edited by Paul Popenoe.

lation of the American ideology of democracy, freedom, and self-expression. This experimental situation places the emphasis upon the adaptability rather than upon the rigid stability of the family.[16]

Margaret Mead, anthropologist, has described further this aspect of the contemporary American family:

Great readjustment which is occurring in the family pattern is the terminability of American marriage. As the old religious sanctions which enjoined fidelity until death, regardless of such ephemeral considerations as congeniality or "happiness," have faded for large sections of the population and have been powerless to save many more marriages from dissolution, new ways of holding marriages together are developing. The life of a family is coming to be seen as a ship which may be wrecked by any turn of the tide unless every member of the family, but especially the two parents, are actively and cooperatively engaged in sailing the boat, vigilantly tacking, trimming their sails, resetting their course, bailing in storms—all to save something which is worth their continuous care. This new ideal, in which all the members of a family work together to keep alive an ever changing relationship, may in time provide us with the necessary new ethical sanction within which to give our changing family dignity and safety.[17]

Family life education and family counseling services

Married people should be educated to take advantage of the social service institutions provided to aid those with personal marital problems. There should be no stigma attached to visiting a marriage clinic or family service agency, as there should be no stigma to visiting a psychiatrist. An interview with a qualified counselor who can see the problem objectively may save many a failing marriage, or assure a successful one.

In this country there are relatively few marriage clinics as such, but there are two hundred and forty family service agencies affiliated with the Family Service Association of America.[18]

Luther E. Woodward, Field Consultant of the National Committee for Mental Hygiene, has stressed the need for more family counseling services that are educative and preventive:

It is seventy years since the first family society was organized in America, and in many of our cities family services have been operating continuously for forty to fifty years. That seems too long a time to go on correcting family difficulties without making concerted efforts on the preventive side. If leaders in the public health field had been as slow to undertake the education of the public in health measures many of us probably would have been victims of one or another epidemic. In the case of family and community pathology people do not die so quickly. But that is no justification for failing to educate for family living with a view to preventing serious family difficulties. The wisdom of a preventive program is apparent; yet after seventy years of family service extremely little education for family living is being undertaken by the staffs of family agencies.

This reminds me of a sanity test that the Cornwall coast natives are reputed to have used for a long time. Anyone suspected of mental imbalance was brought into a room where water was flowing from a faucet into a bucket. The patient was given a cup and asked to bail the water out of the bucket. If he first turned off the faucet before he began dipping, he was considered sane. If he proceeded to dip the water out while the water poured in from the open faucet, he was considered insane. Our neglect of education for family life hardly justifies a judgment of national insanity, but the point seems clear. To go on bailing out a third of the marriages through the divorce courts while a constant stream from the same potentials flows in hardly seems like good sense. . . .

As a result of his years of experience in the field of family counseling, he has also submitted a "Decalogue for Marriage":

I submit it not as the last word on psychological insight, but simply as evidence that the basic concepts of family life and of interpersonal relations in the family can be stated simply and succinctly enough so that hopefully they may be transmitted somewhat from mouth to ear. The whole story cannot be told in these simple epigrammatic statements, but they are, I think, suggestive of the kind of insight and understanding that can be fostered through education for family living. It can hardly be gainsaid that persons who acquire an appreciation of the truths embodied in these ten brief statements would, through such appreciation, greatly strengthen their own family life.

Decalogue for Marriage

1. Happy homes do not just happen. They are made by the understanding and cooperative zeal of the people who live in them.

2. Sex is as God-given and worthy as sight, hearing, or speech and like these is to be used intelligently and artfully for the enrichment of life.

3. In marriage all things add up: congenial conversation, sexual harmony, shared interests, practical helpfulness, and worship in spirit and truth are interrelated and strengthen each other.

4. Love fully and well, but make not a bond of love, for love is a quality of free spirits; and while love is the foundation of marriage and the home, demand not its constant expression for no one loves anyone 100 per cent all of the time.

5. As mates you need many interests in common which you share in the doing and others which you pursue separately and share only in the telling. Let each of you fully respect the individuality of the other for mates are not as two peas in a pod.

AM I WELL-BALANCED?

Your answers to these questions are a good indication of your emotional maturity, and so of one aspect of your fitness for marriage. Read each question carefully before you answer "Yes" or "No." Refer to page 627 for scoring.

1. Do you greatly dislike very bossy people?
2. Do you like to write personal letters?
3. Do you like people who are more clever than you?
4. Is it hard for you to like "yes" people?
5. Do you like to entertain friends at home?
6. Do you usually plan your work in detail?
7. Do you have great confidence in yourself?
8. Do you frequently attend church services?
9. Can you usually cheer up a depressed person?
10. Do you ever rewrite letters before mailing them?
11. Will you fight to get your own way?
12. Does praise or blame affect you very much?
13. Has anyone ever given you a very "raw deal"?
14. Do your friends think you are conceited?
15. Is it annoying to you to lose an argument?
16. Do your friends often talk about you behind your back?
17. Is it hard for you to keep your temper in check?
18. Do you dislike cautious and conservative people?
19. Do you believe present moral standards too strict?
20. Do you frequently feel miserable or grouchy?

6. Live fully today and mar it not by undue thought of tomorrow's difficulties, and "Let not the sun go down on thy wrath." Wrath there will be occasionally but let it not be stored up and carried into the morrow.

7. Strive for the grace of full acceptance of your mate notwithstanding his (her) shortcomings for these are likely then to disappear. And remember that while marriage and family living usually result in personality growth, obvious efforts to educate or "reform" one's mate are seldom successful.

8. Dwell upon the virtues and strengths of your mate and let them be praised to her (him) and to others, for we are all so made that we respond favorably to positive attention but are driven away or confirmed in our folly by criticism and nagging.

9. As the springs and tires on the family car take up the occasional bumps in the road and make them of little account, so members of a family must absorb and make of no account the occasional hostility and bad temper which one or another may show. To respond in kind is to make the road more bumpy.

10. Learn to share your feelings frankly be they feelings of affection, perplexity, or irritation, and be equally ready to accept those of your mate, for marriage can survive many troubles but cannot endure sham and pretense. Its greatest security is in being genuine and real.[19]

Acknowledgments and References

1. Doctoral dissertation, University of Chicago libraries, 1938.

2. Lewis M. Terman, *Psychological Factors in Marital Happiness*, McGraw-Hill Book Company, Inc., New York, 1938, pp. 167–266.

3. "Factors in Marital Adjustment," *American Journal of Sociology*, Vol. 43 (1937–38), pp. 270–283.

4. "Early Marriage and Happiness," *Journal of Social Hygiene*, Vol. 12 (1926), pp. 554–559. See pp. 115–117 for a discussion of this study.

5. Ernest W. Burgess and Leonard S. Cottrell, Jr., *Predicting Success or Failure in Marriage*, Prentice-Hall, Inc., New York, 1939, p. 349.

6. Judson T. Landis and Mary G. Landis, *Building a Successful Marriage*, Prentice-Hall, Inc., New York, 1953, pp. 284–288. Premarital and background items are based on factors in the individual's background such as education, employment history, participation in groups, and so forth.

7. By permission from, *Your Marriage and Family Living*, by Paul H. Landis, Copyright 1946, McGraw-Hill Book Company, Inc., New York.

8. Alfred Cahen, *Statistical Analysis of Divorces in America*, Columbia University Press, New York, 1923. See Paul H. Landis, *Your Marriage and Family Living*, p. 209.

9. Lewis M. Terman, *Psychological Factors in Marital Happiness*, McGraw-Hill Book Company, Inc., New York, 1938, p. 53.

10. Ernest W. Burgess and Leonard S. Cottrell, Jr., *Predicting Success or Failure in Marriage*, p. 118.

11. See Jeannette G. Friend, *Journal of Social Casework*, March 1948, p. 89, and *The Management Review*, American Management Association, September 1948, p. 459.

12. For further information, see Algernon D. Black, "If I Marry Outside My Religion," *Public Affairs Pamphlet No. 20*, 1954.

13. Evelyn Millis Duval, *Building Your Marriage*, pp. 25–26. Copyright 1946, by the Public Affairs Committee, Inc., New York.

14. *Family Management a Joint Affair*, Batten, Barton, Durstine & Osborn, Inc., New York, 1946.

15. *Tide*, October 1, 1945, p. 54.

16. Ernest W. Burgess, "The Family in a Changing Society," *The American Journal of Sociology*, Volume LIII, No. 6 (May 1948), pp. 417–418. This issue presents seventeen excellent articles on "The American Family" and should be read by the student who wishes to appreciate regional and ethnic family patterns.

17. Margaret Mead, "The Contemporary American Family as an Anthropologist Sees It," *The American Journal of Sociology*, Volume LIII, No. 6 (May 1948), p. 459.

18. Family Service Association of America has headquarters at 5287 Sunset Boulevard, Los Angeles 27, California.

19. Luther E. Woodward, "Strengthening Family Life by Educating for Family Living," *Journal of Social Casework*, December 1947.

PROJECTS

1. Make a list of the members of the opposite sex who have especially appealed to you as a possible marital partner. Then list some of their outstanding psychological characteristics. Can you note any significant factors in their appeal to you, factors that tie into your psychological background and needs?

2. In Dr. G. V. Hamilton's study of *What Is Wrong with Marriage* (A. & C. Boni, 1929), he asked 200 normal, intelligent married men and women the question: "If by some miracle you could press a button and find that you had never been married, would you press the button?" Thirty-five per cent said "Yes" or hesitated.

   Why do some married people fail to find reasonable happiness in marriage? List the psychological causes of incompatibility. Would companionate marriage be of real value? Prepare a set of rules for the young man or woman to use as a guide in choosing a life partner.

3. Observe women who are strangers to you. A good place for your observations is a bus or railroad station. Study the expression on each woman's face and decide whether she is married or single. After you have made your "guess," note whether or not she is wearing a wedding ring. Keep a record of your "hits" and "misses." Analyze your own criteria as to whether a woman "looks" as though she were married or single.

4. The chapter on counseling presents some suggestions for the person who must continue to live with an irritating personality, such as a boss or a neurotic mate. It is easier to live with a difficult boss than with a difficult mate because the identification with the mate is much stronger than with the boss. Irritating experiences with a mate break the ties of identification so frequently that the irritated partner must depersonalize the relationship. In such cases, the stronger partner may look upon the weaker person as a kind of "patient."

   This kind of adjustment enables many couples to remain married even though the relationship has lost its former mutuality. The stronger partner looks after the weaker one with a great deal of intellectual consideration but very little feeling of identification.

   What are some of the desirable and undesirable aspects of this kind of adjustment on the part of many American couples?

5. Clinical studies of marital relations indicate that many wives resent the husband's comment, "That's woman's work!" This resentment is especially pronounced in regard to the physical care of the baby. When a husband helps to take care of the baby, does dishes, and scrubs the kitchen floor, is he being unjustly domineered or is he really participating in the home responsibilities for the bringing about of a well-integrated home life?

COLLATERAL READINGS

Blood, Robert O., "Uniformities and Diversities in College Dating Preferences," *Marriage and Family Living*, February 1956, pp. 37–45.

Bowman, Henry A., *Marriage for Moderns*, McGraw-Hill Book Company, Inc., New York, 1954.

Burgess, E. W. and P. Wallin, *Engagement and Marriage*, Lippincott, Philadelphia, 1953.

Centers, Richard, "Marital Selection and Occupational Strata," *American Journal of Sociology*, May 1949, pp. 530–535.

Landis, Carney, and M. Marjorie Bolles, "Psychosexual Immaturity," *Journal of Abnormal Social Psychology*, Vol. 35 (1940), pp. 449–452.

Landis, Judson T. and Mary G. Landis, *Building a Successful Marriage*, Prentice-Hall, Inc., New York, 1953.

Landis, Paul H., *Making the Most of Marriage*, Appleton-Century-Crofts, New York, 1955.

Landis, Paul H., *Your Marriage and Family Living*, McGraw-Hill Book Company, Inc., New York, 1946.

Lehner, George F. J. and Ella Kube, *The Dynamics of Personal Adjustment*, Prentice-Hall, Inc., New York, 1955, Chapter 9.

Mace, David R., "What Is a Marriage Counselor," *Marriage and Family Living,* May 1954, pp. 135–138.

Monahan, Thomas P. and William M. Kephart, "Divorce and Desertion by Religious and Mixed Religious Groups," *American Journal of Sociology,* March 1954, pp. 454–465.

Peterson, James A., *Education for Marriage,* Charles Scribner's Sons, New York, 1956.

Popenoe, Paul (ed.) *Family Life;* monthly bulletins.

Rockwood, Lemo D., and Mary E. N. Ford, *Youth, Marriage, and Parenthood,* John Wiley and Sons, Inc., New York, 1945.

Shaffer, Laurance F. and Edward J. Shoben, Jr., *The Psychology of Adjustment,* Houghton Mifflin Company, Boston, 1956, pp. 578–581.

Tate, Mildred T. and Virginia A. Musick, "Adjustment Problems of College Students," *Social Forces,* December, 1954, pp. 182–185.

CHAPTER FOURTEEN

Facilitating the child's adjustments

The ability of the adult to deal effectively with behavior problems in children depends to a large extent on the adult's own adjustment to the problems in his personal experience. Is the adult strong enough to withstand the emotional shocks and attacks that he meets in children's disobedience, lying, stealing, sexual demonstrations, and defiance? The adult's social relationships with others, his sources of personal satisfaction, his strivings for recognition, his acceptance of authority, and his adjustment to love and sex life—all influence his ability to deal constructively with children and their problems.

The study of children's behavior is important to the student of psychology for many reasons. Their behavior often exemplifies in rudimentary manner the adjustments discussed in previous chapters. Any person who wishes to understand adult behavior can go some way toward it by observing children's problems and their adjustments to them. Indeed, one of the most helpful questions in the understanding of many an adult is, "What would this man's behavior mean if it were that of a small boy?"

Furthermore, most college students would be helped immeasurably in their own adjustments if they were to arrive at a better understanding of those of their own parents. A goodly percentage of students, for example, have been reared by the type of mother who was emotionally insecure and anxious. She found it necessary to protect her child from all sorts of real or fancied dangers, would not allow her child to play actively lest he become overheated and catch a cold, wanted to make sure that he ate enough of the right foods, and insisted that he wear rubbers and take his raincoat. At the same time that she fussed about her child's welfare, she also complained that she was a "slave" to her family and was unappreciated by her husband and children.

The person who has learned to view his parents' adjustment patterns in a clear-cut perspective is well on the way toward a clearer understanding of his own personality characteristics.

Later, when the student becomes a parent, he has the advantage of

264

greater insight and intelligent control of his methods in rearing his own children. If, for example, he has developed strong adjustment tendencies in the direction of dealing with his daily problems by means of formulas for behavior, strict rules of conduct, and mathematically exact answers, he should expect that he will seek a knowledge of *rules* for the rearing of his children. Once he has learned a rule, he will be apt to apply it with mechanical rigidity. Of course such a father is likely to develop either a pathetic duplicate of himself or a rebellious child.

Formulas and rules for child training are less helpful to the parent than an open-minded perspective toward typical childhood behavior and an intelligent ability to project oneself into the child's life.

Recently eighty parents were asked to respond to the California Personality Test as they thought their 12-year-old children would. A comparison of the parents' answers with those of the children indicates that parents do not understand their children very well. The mothers and fathers generally under-estimated their child's concept and feeling of self-adjustment, and over-estimated his social adjustment. On the whole, they were more accurate in describing the child's social adjustment than his personal adjustment. This is probably because they could observe their offspring's social interactions. The results of the study show that father-son understanding is closest, then comes mother-son, mother-daughter, and father-daughter in order from high to low.[1]

The clinically trained psychologist has these mental perspectives and abilities to feel as the child feels; many intelligent parents also acquire the same psychological acumen.

The parent who appreciates adjustment tendencies and feels himself into the growing child's mental life has a marked advantage over the parent who is psychologically obtuse. The latter may, sooner or later, discover that his child is a serious problem to him. If, for example, a ten-year-old boy fails to go home when he should because he finds the company of neighbors more satisfying than that of his parents, the father who lacks insight into childhood behavior may decide that punishment will induce more desirable conduct. It may not. The child may persist in his misconduct. In desperation the father may consult a person trained in child guidance. Perhaps he will be told that the boy feels rejected because of the recent birth of a baby sister. He may be advised to overlook some of the boy's bad behavior, become a better companion to the boy, and encourage him to participate in the family life. After pursuing the prescribed treatment for a day or two, the parents may decide that the boy is more mischievous than ever. The father reports that the recommended treatment is a terrible failure.

In such a case the contribution of psychology to the aid of the parents appears to have failed, but only because they lacked a proper appreciation for childhood adjustments. The father should gain an understanding of the adjustment concept as expressed by his son, so that he will have some basic principles of child training—a kind of working philosophy. If he does, he will persist in the application of these principles, because he will realize that no one can expect a child to change his deep-seated adjustment patterns suddenly. The patterns are too deeply ingrained. The father must appreciate that the boy continues to feel rejected and needs long-term assistance in developing the feeling that he is loved and wanted.

The mere application of rules for child training helps few problem children overcome their problems. The greatest aid to the parent is an intelligent insight into the dynamics of the problem child's behavior.

Predisposing influences in childhood adjustments

Parenthood increases each parent's responsibilities, involves some changes in standards of living, restricts freedom of certain movements, and compels each parent, particularly the mother, to perform many additional tasks at regular intervals. It also brings about important changes in the affectional relation between husband and wife. The new baby may become, in some ways, a rival for the affection of the mate. If the new father is lacking in his personality maturity, he may reject both the role of father and the child. Cases of such extreme rejections are not unusual in our clinics. Far more common, however, are the cases of children who realize that they were or are unwanted and develop feelings of rejection. Children who feel rejected tend to develop detached, seclusive personalities and to have few friends.[2] Many are unable to respond to the affection of others. Some are hyperactive, aggressive, rebellious, or resentful of authority. Rejected children are reported to show relatively a very high susceptibility to behavior disorders and delinquency.[3] Some of them develop characteristics with constructive value, at the high cost of being rejected, evidently as defense or compensation. Many seem able to survive rejection without serious personality damage.[4]

The behavior of a growing person is the result of many factors which operate throughout his life. One of the most important factors in helping him to attain the security he needs to develop well emotionally is to know that he is accepted by his parents. The importance of the home and the people with whom he lives is basic to his capacity for developing adequate adjustments to life's problems.

One of the most important predisposing influences in the life of the child is the attitudes of the parents toward each other. The broken home and the home filled with marital discord are statistically associated with the behavior of problem children.[5]

The child whose emotional loyalties have been torn between two quarreling parents is almost certain to have deepseated anxieties that motivate him in later adjustive situations.

Parents who are cold and impersonal toward the child, who dominate or belittle him or who make him feel incapable and rejected contribute much to the child's nonadjustive patterns. The child feels anxious and his anxieties spread to many activities and situations. The world and people appear to him to be very hostile. His negative value adjustments in later years are likely to be numerous and deepseated.

When the family atmosphere is congenial because the two parents are well adjusted and identify themselves with each other in the family relationship, few problem children occur—because in such an atmosphere a child feels secure, wanted, and is given consistent encouragement and discipline. He is likely to be given a share in making family decisions, a most important factor in happy character development.[6]

Several studies have shown that poor adjustments on the part of parents, with interparental frictions, tend to produce tensions in the next generation. The mental attitudes of husband and wife toward each other and their home are far more significant in the child's environment than their formal education, such as whether the wife has training in home economics.[7]

Some of the child's infantile experiences and tendencies have no noticeable bearing on the adult personality, but the majority of emotional disturbances found in adults arise from simple beginnings in early childhood. Appropriate changes in the home environment and skillful handling of the child, especially the child with a difficult problem, will enable him to attain satisfactory and even excellent personality maturity. If the parent is warned in advance about likely shifts in the child's behavior, he can improve his competence in meeting these developments.[8]

One of the major influences in the intellectual approach to the child on the part of the American parent of today is the emphasis on democracy in our government and culture. We believe in individual freedom, equality, and the right to pursue happiness, but such privileges for the child require a high level of emotional maturity and psychological skill on the part of the parent. Very few parents who believe in democracy in government and freedom for the individual have as yet learned how to conduct weekly house meetings which help to give each member of the family a feeling of belonging and of having an essential, respected part in making decisions about the home life. Once this practice becomes an integral part of our culture, many cases of problem children will be corrected.[9]

The direct influences of the parents' adjustments, expressed by their suggestions and examples, are less easily recognized than the direct influences learned from books and other formal instruction and expressed in the verbalized procedures. The former are acquired through each parent's adjustments throughout his life and are a basic part of his personality. The latter influences are intellectual and less basic, but can be discussed and acquired, as indicated by the large amount of published material now available for the treatment of childhood problems.

Hewitt's three patterns of maladjustment in delinquents

Three major patterns of maladjustment were revealed in the statistical analysis based upon 500 case records of children examined at the Michigan Child Guidance Institute by Lester Eugene Hewitt. This study presents one of the most thorough reports available in regard to the dynamics in the origin of fundamental patterns of maladjustment of the varieties found in child guidance clinics.

Hewitt's study revealed the three types of behavior syndromes or patterns of maladjustment: *I, overinhibited behavior syndrome; II, unsocialized aggressive behavior syndrome; and III, socialized delinquent behavior syndrome.* Psychiatric interpretations were made by Richard L. Jenkins as follows:

In Type I we see an individual who has an excessive development of the shell of inhibition. As a result of this the primitive impulses are denied adequate expression. Tension mounts within the personality and strong pressures develop in the struggle between the primitive impulses and the repressive forces. This individual is chronically in a state of internal conflict. Here we have the overinhibited individual likely to react to these internal conflicts by developing terror dreams or anxiety attacks, or to solve them by developing physical symptoms or illness, by conversion hysteria, or to defend himself from them by compulsive rituals. We do not as a rule see such well-developed neurotic symptoms in the child, but we see the milder overinhibited symptoms of shyness, seclusiveness, fears, clinging, tics, sleep disturbances, nail biting, and other common evidences of tension and anxiety with which the child guidance worker is familiar. The essential points are to recognize that the person with severe internal conflict is, as a rule, the overinhibited individual.

Type II represents the opposite of Type I. Type II represents the individual with an inadequate shell of internal inhibitions. As a result the primitive impulses come not only into consciousness but into expression very directly, providing there are no external pressures which constantly check them. Such an individual is unsocialized and aggressive in his actions and is continually coming in conflict with others—the authorities and the police—as a result of his freely giving vent to his primitive impulses. This represents a type of personality totally different from Type I, although many workers who use terms loosely will speak of this unsocialized, aggressive type of individual as neurotic.

Type III represents a more nearly normal type of personality structure than either of the foregoing. There is a normal shell of inhibition toward members of an in-group. Toward members of any out-group there is a deficit in the inhibitions, no sense of obligation and a free expression of the primitive impulses. In child guidance we see here the pseudo-social boy, the loyal gang member, the good comrade of the delinquent sub-culture who is socialized—often highly socialized—within a delinquent group and regards the rest of the world as fair prey.[10]

BEHAVIOR PROBLEMS CONCEIVED AS EVASIONS OF SOCIAL REQUIREMENTS

EVASIONS BY WITHDRAWAL	REQUIREMENTS IMPOSED ON INDIVIDUAL BEHAVIOR BY	EVASIONS BY ATTACK
Fearfulness	FAMILY	Temper tantrums
Sulkiness		Disobedience
Dreaminess		Overactivity
Shyness	NEIGHBORHOOD	Aggressiveness
Dependency on adults		Defiance to authority
Cowardliness	COMPANIONS	Fighting
Unsocialness		Delinquency
Dependency on routine		Rejection of routine
Pedantry	CHURCH	Pursuing own methods of work
Solitariness		Wanting to direct
Fear of criticism	SCHOOL	Breaking conventions
Suspiciousness		Antagonistic attitudes
Inability to carry responsibility	TRADITIONS	Exploitation of own authority
Inefficiency		Contentiousness
Social inadequacy		Egocentricity
	CUSTOMS	

REGRESSIVE ESCAPES	PRODUC-TIVE ACTIVITY	LAW	CONSTRUCTIVE ATTACKS	DESTRUCTIVE ATTACKS
Neurotic complaints	Invention	INDUSTRY	Competitive sports	"Psychopathic" tendencies
Economic dependency	Research		Exploration	"I won't work"
Alcoholism	Science		Industrial exploits	Crime
Drug addiction	Literature		Social and political reforms	
Functional insanity	Art			
Suicide				

From E. K. Wickman, *Teachers and Behavior Problems,* The Commonwealth Fund, New York, 1938.

According to the findings from this study, the *overinhibited personality* (Type I) typically develops in an atmosphere of parental repression in which the parents are cold and unsocial. Frequently the mother compensates for some rejection in her own life by overprotecting and over-restricting the child, and the father is perfectionistic and intolerant. Frequently there is jealousy of siblings. Illness is apt to be prominent in the environment and background of the child. The overinhibited child with parents who are cold, restrained, and unsocial, whose approval and acceptance can be gained only through strict conformance with their standards, learns to fear rejection consequent to any violation of the strict parental taboos. Security can be attained by

THE DIAGRAM on the opposite page roughly illustrates two characteristic methods by which the individual evades behavior requirements imposed by social forces.

The requirements set up for the individual, first as a child in the home, then in the school, and later as an adult in the greater social order, are represented in the central portion of the diagram. The two methods of evading requirements are shown in the columns to left and right.

There are listed only the more extreme examples of attacking and withdrawing behavior which may be observed to occur at various stages of individual development; lesser degrees of these evading tendencies may be detected in most individuals. There is no intention to attach moral or ethical values either to conformity to or evasion of requirements.

Behavior development leading to adult social maladjustment of the attacking or of the withdrawing type does not proceed along pure or regular stages as the diagram might suggest. Though there is a tendency for an individual to learn to respond characteristically by attack or by withdrawal, both kinds of behavior often occur together in the same individual. Early habits of evading requirements may work themselves out to constructive or productive ends and in that case they may modify the social requirements. Though art, literature, science, political and social reforms may represent evasions of social requirements in individual cases, the inference is not to be drawn from the diagram that such activities are always the product of conflict with social influences or social forces.

It is psychologically unsound to make fine distinctions between withdrawing and attacking forms of behavior, inasmuch as both represent individual modes of response to frustrations experienced on encountering social requirements. The distinctions between them are sharply made, however, by social attitudes toward the individual who responds in a manner that is interpreted as attack or withdrawal.

such a child only through very good, very much inhibited behavior. He therefore thwarts his primitive impulses, causing an acute internal conflict which may be relieved by neurotic disorders.

The *unsocialized aggressive* child (Type II) is the product of a background of overt, parental rejection, particularly maternal rejection from the time of his birth. He feels cheated, and expresses open hostility, bitterness, and aggressiveness. His hostility may be thought of as arising from three sources: from lack of love and acceptance, from the lack of a conscience, which has not been able to develop, and from the selfish and inconsiderate behavior which is this child's background of experience. It makes him feel insecure and anxious, and impels him to act in a hostile and uninhibited fashion.

The *socialized delinquent* (Type III) exemplified by the loyal gang member, is well adjusted to his own immediate associates or fellow gang members. It is only when his relationships with the larger social group in society are considered that he is maladjusted. In contrast to the unsocialized aggressive child, the socialized delinquent has had the benefit of an adequate relationship with his mother but not with his father, and it is the failure of the paternal relationship, coupled with neighborhood deviation pressures, that puts the child into a delinquent group for his adolescent socialization.

The method of psychotherapy used to alleviate these behavior problems depends on the dynamics of the particular behavior. Psychoanalysis is recommended for overinhibited children in order to engender feelings of security and reduce repressions. However, the unsocialized aggressive child needs outside pressure to help him build a stronger shell of inhibitions, which will stimulate socially acceptable behavior. The socialized delinquent or pseudo-social child needs help in enlarging his concept of the in-group.

Today, very often, the mother must work to supplement the family income. This means that she is away from home for a good part of the day. It has long been presumed that her absence will have a bad effect upon the children. Until recently, however, little actual research had been done on this question. Then, a thorough study of this problem was undertaken in California. In a school district which contained 16,000 pupils, there were 400 who were serious counseling problems. An analysis of the place of the mother in the home of these 400 was undertaken. The children were subdivided according to different family structures: Group 1—Employed mothers, Group 2—Step parents or guardians, Group

3—Lack of adult male, Group 4—A control group.

Having a working mother contributed to only ¼ of the total number of cases in need of psychiatric help. Apparently, there are an equal number of non-problem children whose mothers work. This seems to indicate that as long as the child is made to feel secure and happy, the mother's full time employment away from home does not create a serious problem for him.

According to the California Test of Personality which these children took, different personality components can be associated to a significant degree with the differing home situations. For example, the most serious problem of the group who lived with step parents was nervous symptoms (70%) and those children who belonged in families which lacked an adult male did not have as great a sense of personal worth as the others.[11]

For treatment to be effective, parents may need training in developing awarenes of the child's needs. A study of 21 delinquent and 21 well-adjusted children showed that problem children tend to have over-strict parents, or mothers who are not aware of their child's needs. (Awareness in this particular study was measured by the ability of the mother to predict her son's or daughter's preferences, ambitions, or fears. The number of items which both checked alike indicated how well she understood her offspring's needs.) When the mother is aware of her child's needs, the child is more satisfied, and he behaves better. Over-control frustrates the youngster. He rebels, for he is being too restricted. The result of insufficient maternal awareness with over-strict control—poor parent-child relationships.[12]

Children who have happy relations with their parents seldom resort to delinquent forms of behavior as a means of satisfying their repressed aggressions. Their anxieties tend to find normal outlets. In contrast with those who have happy relations with their parents, the children who have developed deepseated hostility toward the parents may turn to delinquency as a means of "punishing" the parents. Girls who feel unwanted and unloved often find it easy to indulge in flagrant sexual delinquency as a means of punishing the parents as well as gaining a kind of temporary affection. The problem behaviors of delinquents are adjustive and can be understood only in terms of the individual's problems, emotional needs, and attitudes.

Children who are referred to child guidance clinics fortunately are in the minority. Most parents need seek only the kinds of understanding which are essential in the common problems of sibling rivalry, thumbsucking, and discipline.

Sibling rivalry

The only child can be made to feel that he is a functional part of the family set-up, but his integration is upset at the birth of an interloper called "your baby brother" or "your baby sister." Both mother and father of necessity must direct greater attention toward the new baby. Under these circumstances the older child resorts to aggressive or regressive tactics in order to regain a lost sense of significance or even to avenge his displacement.[13]

His attempts to regain his lost importance may be expressed in vocal form as "Throw the baby away," in bodily attacks on the baby, or in ignoring its presence. Sewall's analysis of jealousy took as subjects a group of seventy small children consisting of one third nursery school children and two thirds clinical or "problem" children.[14] Of the seventy children who had younger siblings, thirty-nine were reported to be jealous and showed their jealousy in the following ways:

1. Bodily attacks on the younger sibling 26
2. Ignoring the presence of the sibling 2
3. Denying having a younger sibling 2
4. No outward manifestation toward the sibling, but definite personality changes at the time of its birth 9

The last-mentioned group of cases showed a wide variety of personality changes, such as more temper tantrums, more destructiveness, changes to withdrawal types of behavior—daydreaming, shyness, or timidity. Sewall found that when the ages of the children at the birth of the youngest child were studied: "Jealousy seems to be associated with an age difference of from eighteen to forty-two months, for two-thirds of the children of that age difference were jealous, as compared with one-third of all the children whose age differences were greater or less than that amount."

This finding may indicate that when children are closer together in age than eighteen months they share the same interests, and that children more than four years apart in age have interests that do not clash. If the younger child is sufficiently younger, the older child may not arouse enough competitiveness to cause resentment.

Additional findings from Sewall's study indicated that four fifths of the children whose mothers were oversolicitous were jealous. Similarly, four fifths of those subjected to inconsistent discipline were jealous. When the families were divided into two categories, well adjusted and poorly adjusted, it was found that ten per cent of the children in the well-adjusted homes and sixty-three per cent of the children in the poorly-adjusted homes were jealous. "The inference seems justified that there is a tendency for jealousy to develop in an atmosphere of maladjustment, such maladjustment often meaning an overprotective mother, a negative father, some marital or other discord, and inconsistent discipline."

As Murphy and Newcomb concluded, after summarizing several investigations of jealousy in children:

. . . a background of maladjustment is apparent against which jealousy stands out, not as the inexplicable fruit of a field devoid of other personality difficulties, but as a growth well nourished by the soil in which it and *its* ilk are found.

TYPICAL ADJUSTMENTS OF A FIRST-BORN CHILD
TO THE BIRTH OF A SECOND CHILD

1. The first child is in a pleasant state of ongoing activity. He is the center of attention.

2. After the baby appears, he loses the center of attention. He has a problem barrier, and will make an adjustment as 3, 4, 5 or 6.

3. Direct attack in the form of helping to take care of the baby will give him new recognition.

4. Positive substitute activities, such as reading or games with playmates is a more likely adjustment than direct attack.

5. Substitute activities of negative value, such as "naughtiness," are very likely to appear.

6. If adjustments exemplified in 3, 4 and 5 do not produce satisfaction, he can still resort to a powerful method of regaining attention—invalidism.

From such studies as these it is clear that competitiveness, standing up for one's right in the family groups as elsewhere, is normal and within limits acceptable to adults; that when it begins to make trouble either because of its intensity or because of inept or troublesome expression it is given the name of jealousy and becomes "problem behavior."[15]

Intelligent parents prepare the older child for the birth of the younger before it takes place. They prepare him for the inevitable change in his status:

It is better for the child to know ahead of time that a baby is expected so that he can get used to the idea gradually. This helps less than an adult would expect because the small child's imagination may not create anything like the reality. He may visualize an animated doll to tote around or a full fledged companion. Even if he knows and loves a neighbor's baby, he is apt to find that his mother's baby evokes entirely different feelings. Most professionals in the children's field feel that the child should know that the baby is growing within the mother's abdomen. This is not primarily for the sake of abstract honesty but because it is known that many children beyond the age of 3 and some under 3, suspect the truth anyway, through a combination of shrewd observation, slips in the conversation of adults, and perhaps a touch of intuition. One supposedly innocent 3-year-old will call attention to his mother's changing girth with hints, partly questioning, partly accusatory. Another will suddenly hit at her abdomen as if already jealous of what he suspects is there. The child who is hesitantly coming to his own conclusion that the new baby is growing in the mother is likely to become troubled. It is not that he cannot take the truth. What worries him is his mother's evasion in continuing to talk about the stork theory or the hospital theory in an unconvincing tone when he is pretty sure the baby is coming from elsewhere. Many parents refrain from telling the child the truth for fear that it will open the door to other embarrassing questions. This is an unjustified fear. The child before the age of 6 years will not put his parents on the spot to explain conception. The likely question will be, "How did the baby get in there?" to which at this age the most understandable answer is that the baby grew from a seed which was there all the time. To the question, "How will it get out?" the answer might be, "Through a special place." Incidentally, parents should be warned against predicting the sex of the baby ahead of time since a wrong guess may lead to long-lasting disappointment.

Some mechanical readjustments in the household are usually necessitated by the arrival of a baby. Wherever possible these should be made several months before the baby's birth and presented to the older child as evidence of growing up. If he is to move into another room or into a big bed, he should graduate to them because he is a big boy and not be dispossessed by the rival in person. If he is to enter a nursery school he should become well established there before his mother's confinement. Then when the baby arrives, even though the older child feels somewhat slighted at home, his satisfying life at nursery school will help to ease the pain. If he is sent off to nursery school after the baby's arrival, he may resent it as banishment, resist going, resist fitting in.

It is vital, particularly when the older child is in the neighborhood of 2 years, that he feel comfortable and secure with the adult who will care for him while his mother is in the hospital. If a relative or maid is coming into his home, she should either be someone whom he knows well and loves, or she should come two or more weeks ahead of time and take over his care gradually. When a very young child is abruptly left in the care of a stranger, he may behave well while his mother is away, but when she returns all his latent anxiety suddenly comes to the surface. Such a state may last for many months and make even more difficult his other problem of adjusting to the baby.

First impressions are most important. When a mother and father bring the new baby home from the hospital there is usually a great deal of hectic confusion for at least an hour. The older child is lost in the shuffle. No one has time to fuss over him and he stands by, looking wretched. If possible he should be off on an excursion during this time and come home when his mother is able to take him in her arms and give him her undivided attention.

Now that the baby is at home what are the parents' cues? The first principle is to play down the importance of the baby. This means talking about him as little as possible, enthusing over him as little as possible, taking care of him casually when the older child is around. The hardest thing for many children to take is seeing the baby nursed, especially when this is at the breast. Often the older child will want a bottle, too, and it is a wise mother who cheerfully provides it. If this is well handled the child will not repeat the request often since he finds that the bottle is not really a delight.

Even though one advises the mother to feed and care for the baby as much as is practical when the older child is preoccupied with other activities, she should, of course, be equally warned against shutting him out of the nursery whenever he has the desire to see what is going on there. If there is a relative or nurse helping out in the early weeks, it is usually best to have this person taking care of the baby, allowing the mother to give as much attention to the older child as she used to.

Then there are the other relatives. When the father comes home from work he should resist the natural impulse to greet the older child in the front hall with the question, "How's the baby been today?" but should stop to play with him for a while before he drifts in to see the newborn. When Aunt Nellie telephones to arrange a visit to the baby, the mother can remind her that the older child is still counting on being her favorite and will appreciate a present much more than the baby will.

So often Aunt Nellie in her thoughtless enthusiasm greets the older child with the breathless question, "Where's that darling baby sister of yours? I have brought her a present." For these situations the mother might have a box of ten-cent store toys from which to produce a gift each time one arrives for the baby.

Many parents have already heard of the value of letting the child share in the ownership and care of the infant. It is fine for the older child to bring the bottle from the icebox or the towel to the bath provided he enjoys his work and does it spontaneously. Another child will overcome the feeling of being an outsider by an elaborate care of her doll which follows her mother's care of the baby to the last detail.[16]

When the older child feels that he is really secure again in his family constellation, wanted and loved by his parents, he usually loses his more severe sibling jealousies. Sibling rivalry probably never entirely disappears, but the relations between siblings may develop into rich companionships. Most siblings soon learn to protect each other in the impacts with neighborhood gangs and school factions. They learn to share each other's persecutions and conspiracies. Their mutual problems and interests should help them to develop a better sense of belonging to both the family and the community, especially when the parents appreciate the drastic adjustment required on the part of the older child on the arrival of a rival.

Disciplining the child

Children neglected because of a broken home, disinterested parents, or other abnormal conditions are likely to misbehave, but most children are reared by parents who try desperately to make their children "good." These latter parents often seek counsel in their child training, and many of their questions center around discipline. To them, "discipline" means punishment. Actually, it means to learn.

Some parents who believe in rigorous discipline do have children who are "good" in the sense that they have withdrawn into themselves to so great an extent that they cause the parent little trouble. Almost any parent of low intelligence and strong muscle can have a well-behaved child of the fearful, subdued type. Severe bodily punishments are employed by parents who are either too lazy or too dull to learn how to use more intelligent methods in guiding the child. Case studies of children who have a decided withdrawal pattern of behavior show that very many have suffered from abusive treatment: physical punishment, loud scoldings, and threats. Persistent states of fear have been developed that cause the child to react fearfully in many later situations.

As pointed out above in the discussion of sibling rivalry, if the psychological atmosphere of the home is positive, guiding the child becomes relatively easy. The parental example is one of the strongest influences on the child's developing patterns of behavior. However, parents may be unusually well-balanced emotionally, highly intelligent, and constructive in their techniques, and still have many problems in child training. One kind of problem is exemplified by the parent who says: "Why is my toddler good as gold for a while and then suddenly becomes perverse and puzzling?"

An explanation of basic significance is

available from the years of systematic research by Dr. Arnold Gesell and his associates of the Yale Clinic of Child Development.

Gesell has found that children do not grow in a mechanically steady manner. Children grow by shedding old habits and taking on new ones. The child's mind grows by making forward "thrusts." During a "thrusting" period the child is in disequilibrium, discarding old ways and reaching for new ones. In such periods, he is in a state of confusion and instability. As he gradually masters new patterns, his equilibrium improves, and a period of stable behavior continues until another forward thrust brings about disequilibrium with its problems for the parent.

Stages in stable and unstable equilibrium are likely to occur in a typical infant at more or less alternative ages: sixteen weeks, relative equilibrium followed by a transitional period in which he shows a dawning sensitiveness to strangers. By twenty-eight weeks he is again more composed and in a state of balance. Periods of lessened equilibrium and reorganization recur at the age of two and one half, three and one half, and six years. Children who are confused by their inner drives need added love and security, not spankings.

Periods of reorganization are usually characterized by negativism in the preschool child. He will not do what he can do, and he cannot do what he wants to do. When the two-and-a-half-year-old child seems particularly perverse, it should be remembered that his mental life organization is poorly developed. This also accounts for the regression in toilet habits which frequently occurs at about this age. Even though he knows what is expected of him, the child's inner confusions inhibit his behavior and make him appear to be obstinate. Sometimes there are extraordinary factors, such as illness or emotional crises, which may be influencing the child's behavior. If present, these factors should be investigated; however, if no factors which would be expected to militate against the child's good behavior are present, general health-preserving care is indicated.

In addition to the typical negativism of young children, all children suffer frequent frustrations and may adjust to them by aggression. This may happen when adults impose their wishes, often unreasonable to the child, at times when he is already in a state of mental uncertainty. The average parent regards the misbehaving frustrated child merely as disagreeable or naughty, and punishes him. If the parent could only appreciate the fact that the frustrated child has a problem, he could help the child make adequate adjustments through expressions of understanding, examples of what to do, and encouragement in doing the right thing.[17]

Thumb-sucking

Some of the "bad" behavior of children grows from the effects of previous mishandling by the parent. Thumb-sucking is an excellent example.

Levy's investigations convinced him that the main reason for thumb-sucking was the infant's dissatisfaction with the amount of sucking he was getting from breast or bottle. His studies showed that babies who finished their bottles in the shortest periods of time were more apt to suck their thumbs than babies who took longer to complete their feedings. These latter, satisfied with the amount of sucking they got in the course of their feeding, did not resort to thumb-sucking. He also found that those babies who had infrequent feedings were more apt to suck their thumbs than those who were fed more frequently. Puppies, too, require a certain minimum of sucking satisfaction; when they are fed through a medicine dropper, they compensate for their deprivation by sucking on parts of their own and seek other's bodies.[18]

Of those children studied by Yarrow, the ones who had the shortest feeding period were the most severe and persistent thumb-suckers. He did not find any relationship, however, between the age at which the child was weaned and thumb-sucking, or between thumb-sucking in those children who were breast fed the median of three months and those who were not breast fed at all. His study did reveal, though, that thumbsucking was less severe and was discontinued sooner among infants who were breast fed six months or more.[19]

If the infant's dissatisfaction with his quota of sucking is the reason for his thumb-sucking, he should be provided with longer and more frequent nursing periods. The breast-fed baby should be allowed to nurse as long as he desires, rather than being forced to stop after an arbitrary number of minutes. The bottle-fed baby should be provided with new nipples for his bottles, as the chances are that the holes in his old nipples have become enlarged with age.

If the baby is just beginning to suck his thumb, but is ready in other respects to be taken off the 10 P.M. and 6 A.M. feedings, the incipient habit may be discouraged by retaining the old feeding schedule to guarantee the continuance of at least as much sucking satisfaction as he has been getting. If thumb-sucking continues despite these measures, his instinct should not be thwarted by physical means, such as "thumb guards."

When thumb-sucking still persists at one year, it can be assumed that it is no longer a satisfaction for the sucking instinct, but a comfort in fatigue, frustration, or boredom. Therapy is therefore different. Parents should make sure that the child feels secure and happy, and that he has enough play space, playthings, and playmates to keep him absorbed in his daily activities. Ordinarily the child gives up the habit as he acquires inner security and interest in the world as he learns to know it. If parents are dismayed to find the habit persisting despite all these measures, they will be well-advised to follow a laissez-faire policy, since the child will eventually outgrow it, and nag-ging, physical restraints, and moral intimidations are futile.

Children's developmental phases

Stages in development are obvious in the life of the toddler and the adolescent. These stages tend to produce confusion for the child and the parent. Furthermore, the parent's confusion is often accentuated by the child's ambivalent behavior.

Ambivalence, or manifestations of double feelings toward the same person, refers to reactions in which opposing trends of emotion appear simultaneously. Almost all children show ambivalence by statements such as, "I am going to kill my daddy." Such feelings are most pronounced in the affectional relations of children, but also appear in adult behavior, as exemplified by the sweetheart who says to her suitor whom she really loves, "I hate you." Reactions such as these are normal and do not merit a reprimand on the part of the suitor or discipline of the child by the parent.

Children of older ages as well as toddlers are constantly undergoing mental reorganization. Many college students can recall "thrusting" stages in their development. The adolescent's typical drives are toward complete independence. He wants to make his own decisions without interference from his parents. He wants to decide when and where he will go and when he will return. He likes to belittle his parents and their ideas. Even the furniture at home and the clothes of the parents are ridiculed. In certain stages of adolescence the child can just barely tolerate his parents.

When the adolescent boy reaches the quiet, secretive phase of development, he does not want his father to be a pal. He wants pals of his own age. "At this stage of his son's adolescence, the wise father will begin to fish and to golf alone again—or with pals of his own age."[20]

In a later stage of adolescence, the young person tries to improve his adjustments by intellectual analysis of himself and the world. He believes that he could construct a much better social and economic order than the one in which he lives. He has ready solutions for many of the problems that have bothered the great thinkers of his age!

Behavior problems of the aggressive and withdrawal varieties

Man is born with a capacity to react with a variety of emotions. He has within him the lion (the will to fight) and the rabbit (the will to flight). He exhibits three major emotions in response to a threatening situation: Anger directed outward toward others —rage; anger directed inward toward himself—depression; and anxiety—fear. The bodily changes produced in anger are different from those produced by depression or fear. Man's early childhood experiences largely determine in which of these ways he will react under stress. His emotional development is not finished at birth, but is developed as he grows older. Young children are usually more outwardly aggressive than older ones. The older ones are usually more anxious and direct their hostilities inward. The latter emotions are a result of the acculturation of the child; he is becoming an adult and conforming to the society in which he lives.[21]

Young children express a great deal of aggression. As they become older, they become more inhibited. When the child is three, he is probably more openly aggressive than he will be at any other age. As the child grows up, the forms of his aggression change and become more varied. Crying and direct counterattack give way to leaving the scene, verbal expressions, appeals to an adult for help, and general inhibition of his feelings.

Evidently the kind and amount of frustration and punishment a child experiences are very important in determining what his ag-

gressive and dependent drives will be like. In a study of forty children in preschool laboratories, Sears and his colleagues found that the mothers treated boys and girls very differently after the first year of life. They believe that this difference is a major determinant of radical sex differences in aggressive and dependent behavior in boys and girls.[22]

If, for example, a boy sees his father acting in a rough and tumble manner and imitates him, he may receive praise for this. If, however, a girl tries to act the same way, she may be reprimanded. After this happens enough times, the girl will adopt other behavior patterns that earn her approval.

Almost every child resorts to temper tantrums when thwarted. If the outburst gives him some satisfaction, even though the satisfaction entails severe punishment by the parents, he may continue the practice of defiance. The punishment suffered may be endured willingly in order to enjoy annoying the parents. Increasing the severity of the punishment may cause the child to increase his endurance and resistance, or to withdraw into himself, an adjustment practice more dangerous than aggression.

Adjustments of the hostile aggressive variety are exemplified in disobedience, fighting, rejection of routine, delinquency, contentiousness, and refusal to coöperate. Clever parents and teachers avoid open conflict and try to direct the established tendencies into competitive sports, exploring the world of pets, or other interests. The parent who remains calm when faced by defiance and rage can often relieve the situation through humor, or through actively participating with his child in some diverting activity. A funny story or an appeal to take part in some interesting sport will help the rebellious child far more than the use of brute force.

Withdrawal adjustments are closely related psychologically to aggression, in the sense that both represent hostile modes of response to the social situations. Hostility may be expressed by overt aggression or by passive resentment. Parents, teachers, and other adults evaluate the two modes of response quite differently, imagining that the passively hostile child is a "good" child. The child who deals with his problems by means of withdrawal—fearfulness, sulkiness, daydreaming, shyness, solitariness, fear of criticism, and overdependence on adults—is usually liked because he does not annoy others. He is, however, very unhappy within himself. After attaining adulthood, he is apt to be beset with nameless fears and acute anxieties. He is likely to nourish his suspicions and to develop neurotic complaints. Of course, many people who adjust by withdrawal reduce their tensions in the course of development by seeking relief in the quiet nonsocial activities of reading in libraries, enjoying laboratories, art, or inventing. Unfortunately, some also develop escapes from reality in the forms that lead to alcoholism, drug addiction, and insanity.[23]

Obviously, the child who adjusts to his social situations by withdrawing into himself needs systematic and continued encouragement and invitations to participate in normal social activities. He may still need discipline from time to time, even though his withdrawal stemmed from former discipline. However, he especially needs discipline in the spirit of, "This act is wrong, but I love you." The wise disciplinarian can discipline the child for his wrong acts; others merely discipline the child.

To most parents and teachers, discipline is a personal issue rather than an objective procedure. This results in causing the child to feel that the disciplinarian does not like him. Effects of this harmful procedure are revealed when the child says, "My dad doesn't think very much of me," or, "Nothing *I* do would ever please my mother." Discipline should not humiliate the child. He ought to feel that he is still loved and that the discipline was fair.

When discipline is needed we should not think of children as "good" or "bad," but as "learning." They need constructive discipline. The child gets a sense of security when he has consistent discipline that teaches him the limits in his behavior. The pressures exerted by intelligent loving parents give him patterns for his conduct. If he knows and obeys the rules of society, he will feel more at home in his society.[24]

Recent investigations by mental hygienists of the values of discipline refute the erroneous inference that the "new psychology" advises parents to let children do as they please. Rather, parents who use no discipline and no restraint tend to rear playboys, delinquents, and psychopaths.[25]

Parents who abdicate their authority and allow the child to run wild lose the child's respect and fail to give the child the development necessary for orderly happy living. Nor should the parent utilize pleasant rewards only to bring about desired behavior. Good conduct purchased by means of frequent rewards is only a veneer because it does not arise from an inner conviction on the part of the child.

Dealing with the child's fears

To the child, the unknown is fear-provoking. The parent can remove many fears of the unknown by encouraging the youngster to ask questions. The adult, by his answers, can alleviate much of the ignorance which makes the child feel insecure.

Children need confidants to whom they can unleash their fears. Talking over an accident or a disturbing event helps the child. Even more than talking, acting out the feared situation—like a visit to the dentist's office—helps to lessen the anxiety.

After a scare, a child needs relief and reassurance. Shaming him does not help. Although it may sometimes seem to work, it actually adds insult to injury. It causes suppression of the fear, but does not remove it. The underlying fear may come out in nightmares, temper tantrums, timidity, tension, or stuttering.

It is important for parents and teachers to make an effort to discover the basic causes of a child's anxiety and remove them. If the real causes are not uncovered, the child may easily transplant his fears from one person or object to another—especially from a loved one to someone whom it is safer to fear.[26]

How to interpret the child's behavior to the child

College students and parents who have taken a few courses in psychology are apt to attempt psychological analysis of the child to the extent that they become amateur practitioners of psychotherapy. Such practice is dangerous. Dr. Rudolf Dreikurs, Professor of Psychiatry, Chicago Medical School, offers an excellent explanation of what the parent should and should not do in regard to interpretation:

Psychological interpretation should not be confused with attempts to analyze, to pry into the unconscious, to dig into deep sources of motivation. We do not advocate psychological analysis on the part of anyone who is not thoroughly trained and qualified to conduct psychotherapy. But we must distinguish between *psychotherapy*, which is a tool of psychiatrists and trained psychotherapists, and *interpretation*, which everyone who is dealing with children should be able to make. The main distinction between the two is the kind of psychological mechanisms and problems which are examined and analyzed; only psychotherapy can reveal the *past* development, the formation of deep-seated concepts, of the life style of the person, child, or adult. Interpretation, on the other hand, is concerned solely with *present attitudes and immediate purposes*.

Every parent and educator should have some psychological knowledge and some understanding of the probable nature of a child's personality. In difficult cases, this knowledge may be obtained through the services of a psychiatrist or trained child psychologist. But analytical knowledge should never be used for conversations between you and your child; it can

serve only as a guide for your general management of the child. You must take cognizance of the child's actions and attempt to influence them. Discussing the questionable action with a child is one of the most successful ways of changing it. An effective discussion, however, should never investigate *why* a child acted in a certain way, but only explain *for what immediate purpose* he did that. The distinction between "why" and "for what purpose" may seem, superficially, to be insignificant. However, it indicates the complete difference between emphasis on the past and on present goals. There may be a thousand reasons which led to a present attitude of a child; but there is only *one* purpose possible for his actions. The search for the "why" is, for the untrained person, mere guesswork; the recognition of the purpose indicates understanding.

The child responds in a different manner to an explanation of *causes* than to an explanation of *the goals* of his actions. Explanations such as jealousy, lack of self-confidence, feeling of being neglected, dominated, or rejected, feelings of guilt or self-pity, regardless of how accurate they may be in explaining the child's behavior, are accepted by the child at best with friendly indifference. It tells the child only what he is. His reaction is quite different when told what he *wants*: to get attention, to show his superiority, to be the big boss, to demonstrate his power, to get even or to punish others. Such interpretations of his true intentions, when correct, evoke immediately a very definite and characteristic reaction on the part of the child. This reaction is immediate and automatic, a "recognition reflex," and indicates the correctness of the interpretation. It consists of a roguish smile and a peculiar twinkle of the eyes, characteristic of the cat who swallowed the canary. The child need not say one word, or he might even say, "No"; but his facial expression gives him away. This discernment of his psychological attitude generally leads to an immediate change in the particular behavior, especially in a young child. Even very young children, as soon as they comprehend the meaning of words, that is, at two years of age, are capable of conscious understanding of their intentions and are inclined to change their attitudes when they are made aware of them. That does not imply a complete change of the life style, but it may lead eventually to a change of basic concepts in relationship to other people.

Even psychological interpretations must be

used with care. If repeated or overdone, they no longer are revelations. They should never have a humiliating or belittling effect and should never be translated by the child as fault-finding and criticism. It is generally advisable not to make a definite statement, "You do that because you want to . . ." Much better are remarks of vague conjecture, "I wonder whether you don't want to . . . ?" Could it be?" Such discussions never can do any harm. If you are on the wrong track, you just do not get any reaction. Then you can make another conjecture and the child's reaction will indicate which one was correct.

Two boys, nine and ten years old, annoyed their mother by using bedtime for fighting in their beds. Mother could not stop it and did not know what to do. I had a talk with the boys. I asked them why they went on fighting after going to bed. I did not expect the correct answer to this question, but wanted to hear what they had to say. They both explained that it is so much fun to fight in bed when it does not hurt to be thrown down on the pillows. That was their rationalization.

I asked them whether they would mind if I told them the real reason. Of course, they wouldn't mind. Then I ventured, "Maybe you do it just so that mother will come several times to remind you to be quiet." The younger one said indifferently, "It could be." The older one said nothing, but beamed. One should know that the older one was the favorite of the mother and depended upon her, while the younger one felt somewhat excluded and relied upon himself for his position in the world. Generally, the younger was the one who started the fights, but in this particular situation the older brother obviously had instigated the fights for the sake of getting his mother's attention, bringing her back to the bedroom every so often. Nothing more was said or done about it; but after our short discussion the evening fights stopped and never were resumed. That does not mean that the older boy suddenly became independent of his mother. But this particular method was no longer useful once he recognized his purpose.[27]

No parent should expect a child to answer correctly the question, "Why did you do that?" The child cannot be expected to know why he behaves in a certain way. He needs help in order to understand himself and the purposes of his conduct. The wise parent does not try to give the child such understanding immediately after some act of misconduct. Nor should the parent be angry or excited at the time.

Child training is one of the great arts of mankind. Few peoples and few persons have mastered it. Our modern scientific investigators have developed many principles of value for the present-day parent. A very brief summarization of some of these findings for the benefit of the modern parent indicate that the child needs:

1. Full satisfaction of his sucking instinct. Not only must sucking periods be of sufficient length and frequency to satisfy the infant, but they must be administered while the mother gives her close attention so that both mother and child may exchange warmth and affection.

2. Unhurried training of the functions of excretion. Toilet training should not be pursued militantly. Socialized habits cannot be taught until the child is physically and emotionally ready.

3. A long period of consistent mothering by one individual, which satisfies the child's psychological and biological needs. This stimulates mutual growth and gratification of mother and child.

4. Parents who are so well-adjusted to each other that they may be capable of setting a consistent pattern for his love development.

5. Absence of harsh disciplinary measures at his infantile manifestations of sexuality. He can learn effectively what is expected of him by parental example and societal attitudes.

6. Treatment commensurate with his position as a person of some importance of his own. He should be credited with needs, rights, and feelings, and should be given adequate explanations of parental authoritative measures.

7. Truthfulness, honesty, and sincerity, which are essential in dealings between parents and the child.

Acknowledgments and References

1. Louise M. Langford and O. W. Alm, "A Comparison of Parents' Judgments and Child Feelings Concerning the Self-Adjustment and Social Adjustment of 12-year-old Children," *Journal of Genetic Psychology*, 1954, pp. 39–46.

2. See summaries and bibliographies in L. Wolberg, "The Character Structure of the Rejected Child," *Nervous Child*, Vol. 3 (1944), pp. 74–88; F. Clothier, "The Treatment of the Rejected Child," *Nervous Child*, Vol. 3 (1944), pp. 89–110.

3. A. Simon, "Rejection in the Etiology and Treatment of the Institutionalized Delinquent," *Nervous Child*, Vol. 3 (1944), pp. 119–126; M. Field, "Maternal Attitudes Found in Twenty-five Cases of Children with Behavior Primary Disorders," *American Journal of Orthopsychiatry*, Vol. 10 (1940), pp. 293–311.

4. Norman Cameron, *The Psychology of Behavior Disorders,* Houghton Mifflin Company, Boston, 1947, pp. 34–35.

5. J. Macfarlane, "The Relationship of Environmental Pressure to the Development of a Child's Personality and Habit Patterns," *Journal of Pediatrics*, Vol. 15 (1939), pp. 142–154; L. Kanner, *Child Psychiatry*, Thomas, Springfield, Ill., 1935, pp. 87–105; D. Baruch and J. Wilcox, "A Study of Sex Differences in Preschool Children's Adjustment Coexistent with Interparental Tensions," *Journal of Genetic Psychology*, Vol. 64 (1944), pp. 781–803; D. Baruch, "A Study of Reported Tension in Interparental Relationships as Coexistent with Behavior Adjustment in Young Children," *Journal of Experimental Education*, Vol. 6 (1937), pp. 187–204.

6. Andrew W. Brown, Joan Morrison and Gertrude Crouch, "Influence of Affectional Family Relationships on Character Development," *Journal of Abnormal and Social Psychology*, Vol. 42 (October 1947), pp. 422–428.

7. A. S. Jensen, "How Is Psychology Used in Home Life?" in *Psychology in Use*, J. Stanley Gray, ed., American Book Company, New York, 1941.

8. Benjamin Spock, "Preventing Early Problems," *American Journal of Orthopsychiatry*, Vol. 17 (1947), pp. 575–579.

9. E. S. Rademacher, "Democracy and Mental Hygiene in the Home," *American Journal of Orthopsychiatry*, Vol. 10 (1940), pp. 466–471.

10. Lester Eugene Hewitt, *Fundamental Patterns of Maladjustment—The Dynamics of Their Origin,* published by the State of Illinois, 1946. The chapter on psychiatric interpretations and considerations of treatment was written by Richard L. Jenkins.

11. For further information see Jack Rouman, "School Children's Problems as Related to Parental Factors," *Understanding the Child*, April 1955, pp. 50–55.

12. For further information, see Loretta K. Cass, "Parent-Child Relationships and Delinquency," *Journal of Abnormal and Social Psychology*, January 1952, pp. 101–104.

13. D. Levy, "Studies in Sibling Rivalry," *Research Monograph No. 2, American Orthopsychiatric Association* (1937), pp. 1–96; D. Levy, "Hostility Patterns in Sibling Rivalry Experiments," *American Journal of Orthopsychiatry*, Vol. 6, No. 2 (April 1936), pp. 183–257.

14. M. Sewall, "Some Causes of Jealousy in Young Children," Part I of "Two Studies in Sibling Rivalry," *Smith College Studies in Social Work*, Vol. 1 (1930), pp. 6–22.

15. Gardner Murphy, Lois B. Murphy, and Theodore M. Newcomb, *Experimental Social Psychology,* Harper & Brothers, New York, 1937, p. 389.

16. Benjamin Spock, "Avoiding Behavior Problems," *The Journal of Pediatrics*, October 1945. This excellent article is available in reprint form at a nominal charge from New York Committee on Mental Hygiene of the State Charities Aid Association, 105 East 22nd Street, New York 10, N.Y. It offers the parent valuable suggestions concerning the following problems: early feeding problems, weaning conflicts and thumbsucking, bowel-training, kidney-training, anxieties in the early years, and jealousy of the new baby.

17. Arnold Gesell and Frances L. Ilg, *Infant and Child in the Culture of Today,* Harper & Brothers, New York, 1943. See also Gladys Denny Schultz, "Why Pre-Schoolers Are Bad," *This Week*, January 6, 1946, pp. 28 f.

18. Benjamin Spock, M.D., "Avoiding Behavior Problems," *The Journal of Pediatrics*, October 1945. See also David M. Levy, "Experiments on the Sucking Reflex and Social Behavior of Dogs," *American Journal of Orthopsychiatry*, Vol. 4 (April 1934), pp. 203–224.

19. Leon J. Yarrow, "The Relationship Between Nutritive Sucking Experiences in Infancy and Non-Nutritive Sucking in Childhood," *Journal of Genetic Psychology*, 1954, pp. 149–162.

20. George E. Gardner, "The Mental Health of Adolescents," *Mental Hygiene*, October 1947, p. 535.

21. Daniel H. Funkenstein, "The Physiology of Fear and Anger," *Scientific American*, May 1955, pp. 74–80.

22. R. R. Sears, J. W. Whiting, V. Nowles, and P. S. Sears, "Some Child Rearing Antecedents of Aggression and Dependency in Young Children," *Genetic Psychology Monographs*, 1953, Vol. 47, pp. 135–234.

23. E. K. Wickman, *Teachers and Behavior Problems*, The Commonwealth Fund, New York, 1938, p. 25.

24. John B. Geisel, "Discipline Viewed As a Developmental Need of the Child," *The National Elementary Principal*, December 1946.

25. Robert P. Knight, M.D., "Behavior Problems and Habit Disturbances in Pre-Adolescent Children: Their Meaning and Management," *Bulletin of the Menninger Clinic*, November 1944, p. 189.

26. For further information see Helen Ross, *Fears of Children*, Science Research Association, Chicago, 1951.

27. Rudolf Dreikurs, M.D., "The Challenge of Parenthood," pp. 88–91. Reprinted by permission of the publishers, Duell, Sloan and Pearce, Inc., New York. Copyright 1948, by Rudolf Dreikurs.

PROJECTS

1. Discuss reasons why many children will not go to their parents to discuss problems. What are the characteristics of parents that encourage, and what of those that discourage, the child in the bringing of problems to them?

2. Why do children react disdainfully to the parent's assertion, "When I was a child. . . ."? What can the child do about it when the parent harangues him about what *he* did as a child?

3. Certain effects are likely to show up in the personalities of children who were reared too leniently, as well as in the personalities of those who were reared too strictly. List some of the likely later problems or characteristics of children reared under each of the two extremes.

4. Discuss techniques of reprimanding the child in the spirit of, "The act is wrong, but I love *you*," versus, "I am punishing you for what you did."

5. What are the effects on the child's psychological development when he is punished by the "silent treatment"—when the parent will not speak to him for several days?

6. How can the child be integrated into the life of the home through the performance of chores? What chores or tasks can the city child be required to do?

7. What is the effect on the child when the parent almost never gives a definite "no" or "yes" to the child's request for permission to do something which he is uncertain about? Also, what is the effect when the parent habitually withholds permission for several hours or days before granting it?

COLLATERAL READINGS

Aquilera, Augusta and Katherine G. Keaneally, "School Failure—Psychiatric Implications," *Journal of Child Psychiatry*, Vol. 3, 1954, pp. 88–93.

Baldwin, Alfred L., "Socialization and the Parent-Child Relationship," *Child Development*, Vol. 19, pp. 127–136.

Bergman, P., "Neurotic Anxieties in Children and Their Prevention," *Nervous Child*, Vol. 5, 1946, pp. 37–55.

Bro, Margueritte H., *When Children Ask*, Harper & Brothers, New York, 1956.

Cameron, Norman, *The Psychology of Behavior Disorders, A Bisocial Interpretation*, Houghton Mifflin Company, Boston, 1947, Chapter 2 and pp. 113–120.

Child Study, A Quarterly Journal of Parent Education, Child Study Association of America, New York.

Dreikurs, Rudolf, *The Challenge of Parenthood*, Duell, Sloan and Pearce, New York, 1948.

Gesell, Arnold, and Frances L. Ilg, *Infant and Child in the Culture of Today: The Guidance of Development*, Harper & Brothers, New York, 1943. Also any other books by Gesell.

Individual Psychology Bulletin, Individual Psychology Association of Chicago.

Jersild, Arthur T., *Child Psychology*, 3rd ed., Prentice-Hall, Inc., New York, 1947.

Landis, Paul H. and Joanne Haer, *Helping Children Adjust Socially*, Science Research Associates, Chicago, 1954, pp. 3–6.

Lehner, George F. and Ella Kube, *The Dynamics of Personal Adjustment*, Prentice-Hall, Inc., New York, 1955, Chapter 9.

New York Committee on Mental Hygiene of the State Charities Aid Association, New York. Booklets on behavior problems available at moderate cost.

Rockwood, Lemo D. and Mary E. N. Ford, *Youth, Marriage, and Parenthood*, John Wiley and Sons, Inc., New York, 1945.

Ross, Helen, *Fears of Children*, Science Research Associates, 1951.

Sears, Robert R., et al., "Effect of Father Separation on Preschool Children's Doll Play Aggression," *Child Development*, Vol. 17 (1946), pp. 219–243.

Shaffer, Laurance F. and Edward J. Shoben, *The Psychology of Adjustment*, Houghton Mifflin Company, Boston, 1956.

CHAPTER FIFTEEN

Hiring the employee—the interview

Alfred P. Sloan, Jr., General Motors chairman, in an annual report (1946) to stockholders stated: "In our existing industrial economy the only difference of fundamental nature between one business and another operating in the same general field is people. The same sources of raw materials are available to all. The same equipment will be furnished to anyone who may buy. The existing standards of technology are largely a matter of common knowledge. The same markets are available with the same instrumentalities to capitalize them. The same reservoirs of capital are available to those who can qualify. All these means are open to everyone, and generally speaking, on equal terms. The one major difference is people. . . . Management is a most consequential problem as affecting the long-term interests of any business."

Of all the methods used to appraise an individual's qualifications for a job, interviewing is the oldest and most widely used. It is an art which many persons, particularly employment interviewers, believe that they can practice with a high degree of reliability. Actually, studies by psychologists some decades ago indicated that when two or more interviewers conduct the experiment of appraising the same applicant, their appraisals often do not agree.

One of the earliest experiments of this kind was made by H. L. Hollingworth; in his experiment fifty-seven applicants for sales positions were interviewed individually by twelve sales managers.[1] Each interviewer conducted his interview in the manner that he wished. At the end of the interview, the sales manager assigned each applicant a rating with respect to his suitability for the position in question. These ratings were recast so that it was possible to assign each interviewee a rank ranging from one to fifty-seven. The results revealed very little agreement on the part of the interviewers. One applicant, for example, was rated as first by one interviewer and fifty-third by another.

When Walter Dill Scott had six sales managers interview thirty-six applicants, the results showed that in the case of twenty-eight of the thirty-six, the interviewers disagreed as to whether the applicant should be rated in the upper or lower half of the group.[2]

In addition to the proved unreliability of the traditional interview as usually conducted, the validity of interviewers' judgment is also dubious. And yet many employment interviewers believe that their interviewing experiences give them an ability to judge people more accurately than inexperienced interviewers can. Some even imagine that their abilities are uncanny, as expressed in this statement:

Not every man has a head for mathematics, and not every man has a sense of logic necessary for the practice of law. Just so, not every man has what I might call the "sixth sense" necessary to judge what I truly believe is a series of psychic waves which flows from one man to another when in conversation.

Psychologists have been unable to find anything that would correspond to "psychic waves." It is possible, but has never been demonstrated in the laboratory, that the facial expressions, general bodily movements, bodily posture, and changes of pitch, intensity, rapidity, and inflection in the voice are noted by those who have daily contacts with people and analyze their motives. Some executives have said that they tend to suspect the man who makes a statement and then leans back. Others have claimed that, when a lie is told, the speaker catches his breath. Salesmen say that they know when the prospect is sold by the fact that he leans toward the salesman. The writer decided to test the theory that experienced interviewers can detect false statements more accurately than inexperienced interviewers. Arrangements were made to have eleven experienced credit men and fourteen experienced employment interviewers, eighteen inexperienced men students and seven inexperienced women students, interview several hundred college students. These students who were to be interviewed were instructed to answer all the questions that any interviewer might ask, but to answer some truthfully and some falsely. The interviewers had the privilege of cross-examining the students.

The questions varied in nature, but were of the kind that could be answered in a definite manner, such as, "How old are you? How long have you been in college? How much money did you earn during your summer vacation? What were your grades in your college courses last semester?" Both the interviewer and the interviewee kept a written record of the questions and the answers, so that it was possible to record the interviewer's accuracy in judging the answers to each question. Records were tabulated of the interviewers' estimates of 3,205 answers to questions. Of the four classes of interviewers, the experienced credit men were wrong in 34 per cent of their judgments; the employment men in 42 per cent; the inexperienced men in 34 per cent; and the inexperienced women in 47.5 per cent.

A careful analysis of each interviewer's judgments showed that some of the interviewers were better detectors of false statements than others. The experiment indicated the following points of note:

1. The experienced interviewers were unable to detect false statements when the "applicant" wanted to lie. His detection was largely a matter of chance.

2. An interviewer should depend upon records and objective information in evaluating statements of applicants rather than upon his "hunches" or "feel" or "atmosphere" or the movements of lips and hands. One interviewer claimed that he could detect false statements from the movement of the lips. The results showed that he was one of the poorest interviewers in the group.

3. The individual interviewers who made the best records in judging the statements of the students were those persons who had had previous experience in interviewing students and knew the general facts of student life. This indicates what one would expect: an interviewer should be acquainted with the facts concerning the type or class of people whom he interviews.

4. The individual interviewers who made the poorest records seemed to be the "fatherly" trusting type of person who did not cross-examine the applicants. Conversely, the interviewers who made the best records were those who cross-examined the applicants, looked them in the eye, and pursued a policy of compelling the applicant to prove his statements.

READ THEIR RECORDS . . .

These are facts matched with models who closely resemble the actual salesmen for a leading manufacturer of aids for handicapped people.

FORMER DOCTOR Salesman A started with company 8 years ago after struggling for years to make a living as a doctor in a low-income town. Age, 45. Married: 4 children. Lives in a rented house. Has thorough knowledge of the physiological causes of the malady to be helped. Keeps up-to-date on medical advances. Extremely interested in the clients, maintains close contact with them.

SOCIAL REGISTER Salesman B has been with the company for 3 years. College-educated, social background. Member of country club, alumni association, and political party. Married; 1 child; lives in own house; has independent income. Came to the job through a personal friendship with the president. Formerly worked in bank. Seldom mingles with other salesmen in the company. Said to be snobbish.

SMOOTH OPERATOR Salesman E has sold everything from can-openers to vacuum cleaners. Knows all the tricks. Worked for competitor for 3 years. Widower for many years; no children; lives at hotel. Is active in local sales organization. Good dresser; big spender. Not receptive to directions, likes to do things his own way, resents criticism of any kind.

ROSE FROM RANKS Salesman F has been with the company ever since he first started to work. Began as clerk, rose steadily if not rapidly. Asked for opportunity to enter selling 6 years ago. Married; 1 child. Interested in advancing. Studies and takes courses regularly. Carries heavy life and accident insurance. Intense hobby, stamp collecting.

...THEN RATE THEM AS SALESMEN

HAD OWN BUSINESS Salesman C formerly owned his own drug business. Wiped out when large chain moved into the neighborhood. Came to the company 6 years ago. Has wide acquaintance in the community. Is well liked. Is known as a mixer; active in church. Married; no children. Middle-aged. Lives in rented house. Supports parents. High-school education. Is a poor manager with regard to money. Harassed by debts.

VETERAN Salesman D came to the company after discharge from the army. Wounded in action. No visible sign of disability. Held rank of corporal. Age 25; college graduate; single. Had no previous experience in business. Father who worked for the company had recently died. Now helps to support his mother; lives at home; is youngest member of big family. Ambitious and anxious to learn.

(Reproduced by permission from **Modern Industry**, October 15, 1945. Photographs by Ewing Galloway.)

FORMER FAILURE Salesman G had a bad record when he came to work 5 years ago. He never seemed to last on a job, couldn't seem to figure out why. Hired as a favor to a friend. Financially burdened. Supports wife, 2 children, and his wife's parents. Usually in debt and beset by home and family worries. Well-liked by other salesmen, but not by clients.

OLD-TIMER Salesman H knew the current company president when he was a "pup," the sales manager when he was just another salesman. Married; father and grandfather. A little wary of new methods, but excellent with people. Still in fine health, has good record on absenteeism. Good humor and spirit. Never forgets a client's face, name, or history.

5. The best of the interviewers made bad mistakes in their judgments of statements made by students who were adept in talking with strangers and who wished to baffle the interviewer. The experiment clearly demonstrated that, if a person wished to falsify his statements, the interviewer could not differentiate the false from the true unless he could check the statements objectively.

When interviewers depend upon their impressions, without reference to records of the applicants' past behavior, they succeed more often than they fail, because the majority of applicants want to tell the truth rather than not.

Several investigations of interviewing have shown that interviewers disagree among themselves regarding the same applicants, that some interviewers vary in the consistency of their judgments and in their ability to judge the applicants accurately. Many experienced employment men realize that they cannot judge applicants with any great degree of accuracy on the basis of the interview alone. They try to obtain dependable information from former employers or to hire the applicant for a probationary period. In spite of the unreliability of the interview, it will continue to play an important part in modern hiring. Somehow human beings want to see each other even though the meeting may not elicit valid information. They want to find out whether or not they would like to work with each other. Furthermore, studies of the interview—the conversation with a purpose—prove that interviewing ability can be improved. Improvability varies with the kind of interview used.

The various kinds of interviews for employment are the following:

1. The free interview

This is the customary informal interview as practiced by the average employment interviewer, a man who has had approximately two years' high school education. He worked as a clerk for some years and was transferred from record-keeping to interviewing.[3] This type of interviewer has had no systematic training for his work and no constructive coaching. He has read no books on interviewing techniques. He has no understanding of basic psychological concepts, such as the adjustment pattern. He follows no organized plan and asks whatever questions come to his mind. He himself may have emotional maladjustments that cause him to be biased and lacking in objectivity in his judgments. He is a likely victim of common pitfalls in interviewing such as the following:

a. PERSONAL BIAS. Each of us, in the course of our psychological development, collects certain likes, dislikes, preferences, and beliefs that in our more objective moments we recognize as unfair or unjustified. Prejudices are an important factor in personal bias. If the employer recently has hired a man who once sold cash registers but failed on the job under consideration, he is apt to be prejudiced against all men who have sold cash registers. One executive claimed that all men who had mustaches had failed him. Dozens without mustaches, whom he had hired, had failed him too, but he still believed that a mustache was an indication of poor material for his organization. Some executives dislike applicants who have red hair or bad teeth, or wear bow ties, green socks, pink shirts, and so on. It is fortunate for applicants that executives differ in their prejudices, because if one employer rejects them they can always go to some other employer who may like the very trait for which they were previously rejected.

Some sales personnel men never hire a man who has worked for a competitor. They believe that the man who has been trained under one set of conditions will cling to those former beliefs and habits and refuse to become a teamworker in a new organization. Some managers will not hire salesmen who have had a systematic training course where they had to learn a standardized sales talk. On the other hand, one life insurance company found that 20 per cent of the men who had had previous life insurance selling experience turned out to be successful.

Other executives do not hire recent college graduates because they believe that college men require three years in which to orient themselves. In this view college men are believed to want immediate promotions and to loathe doing routine work. In college they studied international problems, the progress of civilization, the boundaries of the universe, great social forces, and historical movements; hence small wonder that they are bored when they must spend hours checking detailed bills in a butter-and-egg firm. Once a college graduate finishes about three years of floundering, these executives will hire him without very much quizzing about his past failures. It is believed that he is then ready to fit himself into the business picture without demanding a front seat.

One executive claims that young single men succeed better than young married men. He assumes that the young married man is either too greatly interested in his wife to study his job or he is ambitious to buy his wife expensive articles for her adornment.

One executive may take applicants for important positions to dinner and gauge their ability by their table manners. Another may argue with the applicant to discover how he conducts himself toward an unruly stranger. The empirical rules for hiring vary with the executive. Most of these rules are merely the result of a few dramatic instances. Many are without sound statistical basis.

Prejudices often affect findings from interviews that are supposed to be so systematic as to overcome subjective influences. Rice[4] made an analysis of the findings of twelve trained interviewers as to the cause of the downfall of 2,000 vagrants who had applied for free lodging. The interviews were standardized, but different investigators obtained different results. One interviewer, a socialist, reported that 39 per cent of the men were down and out because of industrial conditions, and 22 per cent because of excessive use of alcohol. Another interviewer, an ardent prohibitionist, attributed but 7 per cent of the failures to industrial and economic conditions and 62 per cent to drink. Prejudices were even more significantly revealed when we note that, according to the socialist, the *vagrants themselves* gave as the cause of their downfall: industrial conditions, 60 per cent; drink, 11 per cent. But according to the prohibitionist, the *vagrants themselves* blamed industrial conditions in 42.5 per cent and drink in 34 per cent of the cases. Obviously, each interviewer influenced the interviewees to give answers in line with his own biases.

The interviewer should note and compensate for his own prejudices, such as likes or dislikes for applicants who have mustaches, wear a vest, reveal tobacco-stained fingers, or belong to certain racial classes. He should hire people who do good work rather than those who satisfy his own idiosyncrasies. Of course, if the interviewer is hiring applicants who are to be supervised by department heads, the interviewer must hire in accordance with the idiosyncrasies of each department head.

b. pseudo-sciences. These are phrenology, palmistry, numerology, astrology, and physiognomy. The ideas that a low forehead, receding chin, large ears, or any other physical features indicate certain mental traits or behavioral tendencies are merely blithe assumptions, like the myth that shifty eyes betoken dishonesty. Investigations indicate that college students have some tendency to be influenced in their estimates by the physical factors of appearance, such as the wearing of glasses. Wearing glasses tends to cause persons to be rated as more intelligent and more industrious, but not more honest.[5]

c. the illusion of previous experience. Most interviewers tend to assume that the applicant who has had previous experience on a similar job is bound to be a better em-

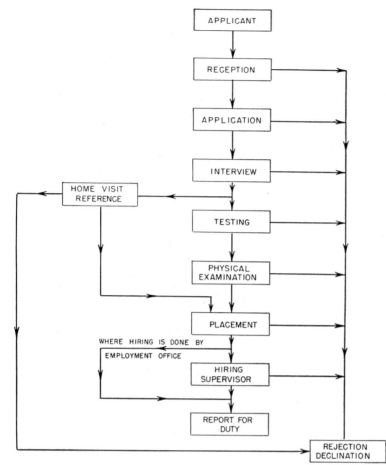

Flow chart of an applicant through the employment office.

ployee than any other applicant who may have superior potentialities but lacks experience. When a secretary is desired, the interviewer chooses the applicant who claims secretarial experience in preference to the stenographer, who may actually be brighter and more competent.

Actually, previous experience when taken in conjunction with other pertinent factors is an extremely valuable indicator of future performance, *but it is not, of itself, a guarantee of ability to do a job well.* Mediocrity is tolerated in much of the world's work, and *experience* too often cloaks such mediocrity. There is danger, therefore, in making a criterion of the fact that an applicant has done similar work in the past. The applicant who is willing to accept a job on the same level as his previous one is as likely to be below average in performance as above average. The tendency to *over-value* previous experience in weighing qualifications should be discouraged, for it may be costly to a company in terms of valuable talent lost and of commonplace or inferior performance perpetuated.[6]

The list of pitfalls in the free interview can be increased by observing any interviewer who is untrained in his art. He may use the interview as a means for expanding his ego by talking to impress rather than analyze the applicant. He even may be so inept as to suggest the answers desired to his own questions or to hire the people who need jobs rather than the ones who can do the work.

2. The area interview

Some free interviewers discover that certain areas of the applicant's background and personal characteristics are more significant in predicting job success or failure than other areas. They gradually learn to ask more and better questions about the important areas.

The questions are asked not haphazardly but according to an organized procedure. The interviewer is guided by an interview blank and jots down answers as given, thus making a record of the results of the conver-

---

THE INTERVIEWER'S GUIDE

Name . . . . Address . . . .
Position wanted . . . . Date . . . . Interviewer . . . .

1. Give me the names of your past employers. Begin with the last employer and go backward for the last five years.
2. Describe the work you did for each.
3. What did you do in your spare time: evenings, Saturdays, and Sundays? (Look for side lines and hobbies, reading of trade journals, clubs.)
4. What general education have you had?
5. What technical education have you had?
6. What is state of your health? How much time have you missed from your work because of sickness during the past two years?
7. For what other jobs have you applied with other concerns recently?
8. What is your financial condition: savings accounts, life insurance, investments, speculations, own home?
9. With what merchandise firms do you have credit accounts?
10. What are your plans for the future, vocationally?
11. What suggestions have you made regarding improvements in operations for your former employers?
12. Why do you want to work for us? Interviewer's deductions:

Be near friends	Just needs a job . . . .
For home reasons	Seems restless . . . .
Likes the community	Floater . . . .
Regularity of work	Family reasons . . . .
Self-expression	More pay . . . .
More prestige	For opportunity . . . .
Union reasons	Other reason . . . .

13. What pay do you expect?

                  Overestimates his worth . . . .
                  Underestimates his worth . . . .
                  Fair estimate . . . .

DECISIONS FOR THE INTERVIEWER TO MAKE DURING THE INTERVIEW

14. Would his personality fit our organization? . . . .
15. Is applicant eager for the job? . . . .
16. Does the applicant fit the job that is open? . . . .

Too good for the vacancy	Undoubtedly satisfactory . . . .
Not suited to vacancy	Probably a safe man to hire . . . . . .
Unable to do the work	Hire, if no better applies . . . .

17. Remarks: . . . .
     . . . .

FORM 69
(9-1-44)

INTERVIEWER'S EVALUATION OF APPLICANT

DATE 6-27 19 44

NAME OF APPLICANT Helen Francis Davis

LOCATION 1631 Arch St., Phila.

JOB CONSIDERED FOR Telephone Operator

INTERVIEWER Stella Burns

AREAS TO CONSIDER	FINDINGS	INTERPRETATION OF FINDINGS
I VOICE MANNER & APPEARANCE	Voice clear, tone pleasing, enunciation good.	Meets voice requirement for operating
1 VOICE AND SPEECH PLEASANT CLEAR, DISTINCT NO ACCENT		
2 MANNER COURTESY SPEECH, GESTURES, FACIAL EXPRESSIONS	Manner courteous, responsive, and composed.	Conversational ability and attitude should result in satisfactory customer contacts.
3 APPEARANCE POISE, DRESS, CLEANLINESS FEATURES	Well groomed and dressed in good taste.	
4 PHYSIQUE WEIGHT HEIGHT REACH, STRENGTH HANDEDNESS		
5 VISION AND HEARING	Slender, average height, no noticeable defects of sight or hearing	Size satisfactory.
6 PERSONAL CHARACTERISTICS (COOPERATIVENESS FRIENDLINESS ADAPTABILITY TEMPERAMENT AGGRESSIVENESS, NERVOUSNESS)		
II WORK HISTORY	One month in insurance office, filing forms and correspondence.	Filing experience not significant for operating, but might help in C&P B
1 KIND OF JOB OR HOME DUTIES (APTITUDES SKILLS AND COOPERATION REQ D)		
2 WORKING CONDITIONS HOURS, HAZARDS SURROUNDINGS SUPERVISION)	Hours 8:30 to 5:00. Saturday 8:30 to 12:30. Supervision close, helpful and considerate, co-workers congenial.	Work less confining, better hours, used to close supervision. Apparently, got along well with supervisors and co-workers
3 REASON FOR LEAVING JOB (INCOMPETENCE INSTABILITY, TEMPERAMENT FRICTION WITH SUPERVISION LAY OFF)		
4. ATTENDANCE RECORD		
5 MILITARY EXPERIENCE (DATES OF SERVICE BRANCH STARTING AND FINAL RANK, DUTIES AND RESPONSIBILITIES KIND OF DISCHARGE)	Temporary job, during school vacation only.	may be co-operative Employee left job to return to school.
6 EMPLOYER REFERENCES (DATES OF EMPLOYMENT TYPE OF WORK, PAY, WOULD HE RE EMPLOY)		
III SCHOOLING	Two years high school. Liked English, Math., History, Latin, reading assignment and book reviews. Favorite subject English.	Meets educational requirements. Liking for English and reading should insure good usage of English in customer contacts.
1 FORMAL SCHOOLING (AMOUNT AND KIND DATES)		
2 SPECIALIZED TRAINING OR ON JOB TRAINING	Left school to aid family financially.	Financial need may assure motivation and permanence.
3 MILITARY TRAINING		
4 BEST AND LEAST LIKED SUBJECTS IN SCHOOL)	Honor student, elected to student council.	Intelligence probably adequate.
5 REASON FOR LEAVING SCHOOL		
6. ATHLETIC AND SOCIAL ACTIVITIES, SPECIAL INTERESTS (IN SCHOOL)	Engaged in gym, soft ball, tennis.	Physically active, healthy, co-operative
7 SCHOOL REFERENCE REPORT (STANDARD TESTS, CLASS STANDING, ATTENDANCE, PERSONAL RATING)	Never late - attendance good.	Probably dependable.
IV SPARE TIME ACTIVITIES	Knits for Red Cross; sells War Stamps and Bonds two nights a week at neighborhood movie.	Interest in helping others. Likes contact work. Co-operative.
1 HOBBIES		
2. CHURCH ACTIVITIES		
3. COMMUNITY ACTIVITIES	Sings in church choir.	Conduct wholesome.
4 TYPES OF READING		
5. SOCIAL ADJUSTMENT FACTOR (GREGARIOUSNESS SECLUSIVENESS, PARTIES, SOCIAL HABITS)	Reads biography and fiction.	May indicate desire for self-improvement.

Courtesy of N. A. Moyer, The Bell Telephone Company of Pennsylvania, from his article "Non-Directive Employment Interviewing," **Personnel,** American

sation with the applicant. He tries to ask questions that require factual answers as given, thus making a record of the results of the conversation with the applicant. He tries to ask questions that require factual answers rather than opinions. In some cases he adds some problems which are of a semi-trade nature. The questions in *The Interviewer's Guide*, page 291, were prepared by a group of employment men and executives who wished to have a list of definite questions to guide them. The thirteen suggested

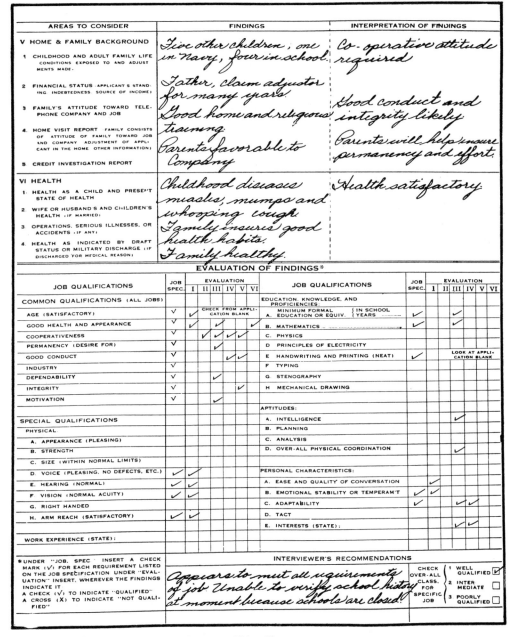

Management Association, March, 1948, p. 379. The two exhibits, "Interviewer's Evaluation of Applicant," and reverse side, are from the same article. See "3. The nondirective interview," pages 294–295.

questions may be used in conjunction with the usual employment blank. The questions may be phrased to suit the interviewer and the applicant, but it is essential that the interviewer ask each question and record the answer while he is conducting the interview. If he does not adhere to a definite procedure, he is apt to let the interview become a hit-or-miss procedure—a conversation that will not give him complete information. Of course, the interview may be ended long before the last question if the applicant is obviously unfit.

Some area interviewers develop special sets of questions that apply to the personality and aptitudes of the applicant as revealed during the interview. Examples of two sets of area questions, developed by R. S. Uhrbrock, for use in interviewing recent college graduates are the following:

Is he keenly analytical?

- a. What college courses demanding analytical ability has he taken?
- b. What special problems has he worked on that required careful analysis?
- c. Has he taken many "cinch" courses?
- d. What special reports, term papers, etc., has he prepared? To what extent do these deal with numbers and statistics?

Initiative and originality:

- a. Did he try to interview the interviewer?
- b. Did he ask any questions, or make any observations that distinguish him from the ordinary run of applicants?
- c. Did he ever make tentative plans for a new mechanical device that he thought might be patentable?
- d. Did he ever undertake to sell any article? If so, with what degree of success?

If the interviewer is unusually able and scientifically trained, he may even make statistical studies of his questions of specific areas, as exemplified by the "Diagnostic Interviewer's Guide" developed by Hovland and Wonderlic.[7] If he does make such a study, he raises his interview to a higher scientific level and probably uses the patterned or standardized interview.

The area interview may be conducted in the manner of a free association, with the questions arranged under certain headings. Or it may be a phase of the most advanced variety of the patterned or standardized interview.

3. The nondirective interview

This kind of employment interview stems from the nondirective counseling interview developed by Carl R. Rogers and his disciples.[8] The few employment interviewers who use it claim that an applicant's story can best be obtained through a conversational type of listening when the interviewee is relatively free from direction by the interviewer. The applicant is encouraged to talk without constraint on whatever subjects interest him. It is believed that the applicant will spontaneously cover most of the topics of interest to the interviewer.

In the early stages of the interview, the interviewer may stimulate the applicant by means of conventional questions about his work history, or by: "We are interested, as we assume you are, in finding the job for which you are best suited. Instead of my asking you a lot of questions, why don't you tell me the story of your background and experience in your own words?" N. A. Moyer of the Bell Telephone Company of Pennsylvania has described the technique in detail.[9] To keep the applicant talking he recommends suggestions such as the following:

> Give entire attention to the applicant.
> Listen.
> Never argue.
> Do not interrupt or change the subject abruptly.
> Use questions sparingly.
> Allow pauses in the conversation.
> Phrase responses briefly.

The last-mentioned admonition is explained in a manner that exemplifies the nondirective interviewer's typical responses:

> Responses should be brief and should refer to the applicant's interests or feelings. It is often helpful to repeat the last few words of the applicant's statement, make a short comment, or ask a brief question, such as:

> "Tell me more. "
> "That's interesting."
> "What were the circumstances?"
> "What happened then?"

"Exciting wasn't it?"

". . . until 11:00 p.m.?"

"You say, 'It's not worth the effort'?"

"H-hm."

Even though the nondirective interviewer appears to function in a free manner, he actually structures the interview to some extent. Furthermore, his final evaluation of the applicant also is influenced by findings from home visits and investigations of school and employer references. The evaluation form itself is quite detailed and involves an extensive and systematic investigation of the applicant's characteristics. See pages 292 and 293.

Some specific values reported, in part, from a nondirective interviewing program are the following:

1. The percentage of turnover cases which could be ascribed in whole or in part to faulty selection, while the labor market was growing tighter, has declined steadily.

2. The department supervisors say that they are getting people better fitted for the work. Follow-up studies bear this out.

3. Interviewers who have used both the questionnaire and nondirective method say the latter enables them to make more effective appraisals.

4. Applicants frequently tell interviewers they liked the interview because it did not seem like an interview. They had expected to be asked a lot of questions; instead, they just had a pleasant chat.[10]

4. The patterned or standardized interview

This type of interview usually requires the following: careful preparation of questions, the use of printed forms that contain specific items to be covered, a uniform method of recording information and making judgments, prepared manuals that describe the procedures to be followed and the use of directions for interpreting the applicant's responses. One of these instruments, called the "Diagnostic Interviewer's Guide," was developed by Hovland and

TABLE 15-1

PATTERNED INTERVIEW RESULTS

Percentage of Individuals (1) Still on Job, (2) Resigned, and (3) Dismissed in Various Categories of Scores on D.I.G.

Classification	*Scores on D.I.G.*				
	0–10	12–16	18–22	24–28	30–34
	%	%	%	%	%
On Job	38.9	42.9	47.2	48.6	59.2
Resigned ..	22.2	25.7	29.2	29.4	34.7
Dismissed ..	38.9	31.4	23.6	22.0	6.1
Number ...	18	35	89	109	49

From C. I. Hovland and E. F. Wonderlic: "Prediction of Industrial Success from a Standardized Interview," *Journal of Applied Psychology,* American Psychological Association, Inc., Vol. XXIII (October 1939), pp. 537–546.

Wonderlic as part of a selection program of the Household Finance Corporation, a large personal loan organization.[11]

The general construction and layout of the D.I.G. blank can be seen from the accompanying illustration (page 296) showing the first of four general areas of the applicant's background and personal characteristics: (1) work history, (2) family history, (3) social history, and (4) personal history. It will be observed that at the top of each section there are a series of standardized questions which the interviewer asks the applicant.

After the interviewer has collected the significant information, he asks himself certain specified questions about the applicant and assigns prescribed values to his judgments. A quantitative score is obtained for each area, and the sum of all the scores for all areas yields a total score for the applicant. The validity of the D.I.G. is indicated by Table 15-1.

This table for 300 individuals shows that "there is a progressive increase in the percentage of applicants who are still on the job the higher the score on the D.I.G. at the time of employment. More striking is the progressive decrease in the percentage of individuals who are dismissed as the scores increase."

Robert N. McMurry has published some

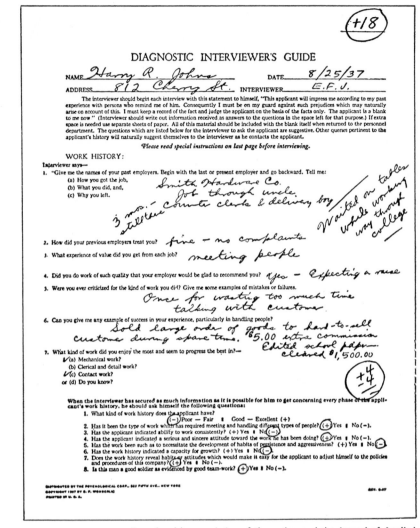

of the results of his experience with the patterned interview and has shown that interviewers trained in the use of this kind of interview tend to obtain reliable and valid results. Table 15-2 depicts the relationship between interviewers' initial ratings and those made by foremen one and one-half years later with 407 cases still on the job.

On the basis of three separate studies in the hiring of metal workers, truck drivers, and workers in the needle trades, McMurry concluded that "a properly conducted

and evaluated *planned* interview is a statistically reliable selection instrument." He has described the advantages of the patterned interview:

The *patterned* interview endeavors to overcome the weaknesses of the ordinary employment interview in several ways: First, the interviewer works from definite job specifications; he knows what qualities each job requires. Second, he has a plan; he knows what questions to ask. Third, he has been trained in the techniques of conducting an interview—i.e., he knows how to put the candidate at ease, how to make him talk, and how to extract pertinent information. Fourth, prior to the interview, he has checked with outside sources (previous employers, schools, etc.) and already knows a great deal about the applicant. Fifth, he has a series of clinical concepts—e.g., that of emotional immaturity—which provide him with a yardstick for interpreting and evaluating the information obtained from the candidate. Sixth, the interviewer himself has been carefully selected to assure that he has adequate intelligence and is emotionally well-adjusted.

Moreover, it is not necessary that the interviewer be a psychologist or psychiatrist to obtain good results. Actually, if he makes full use of all available techniques for assembling relevant facts about the applicant, in nearly every case the final decision concerning his qualifications can be made on strictly common-sense grounds.[12]

After reviewing research which has been done on the value of the interview for assessing personality and occupational fitness, K. A. Yonge concluded that the most valuable interview is the one which uses a standardized form. The form should be designed to assess complex, dynamic constellations of traits rather than relatively isolated, static traits. If properly used, he states, the interview can play a reliable part in the over-all assessment of an individual's qualities.[13]

In spite of the statistically demonstrated values of the patterned interview, certain critics object to it on the grounds that some interviewers will follow the pattern slavishly and without insight into the dynamics at work in the applicant's personality. This objection is overcome of course when interviewers are properly trained for their work as recommended by McMurry. Properly handled, the patterned interview draws out the applicant's prejudices, motives, drives, and adjustment history more clearly than an unpatterned interview.

5. The probing interview

Questions of a probing nature are used by psychologists for two different purposes: as tools in a clinician's attempts to discover the underlying drives in the psychodynamics of the interviewee's personality, and as a kind of performance test in the selection of men in industry. Examples of the first type of probing are the questions: "If a former high school principal were to ask you to address the school's assembly of students, what do you think your subject or topic would be?" and, "When you have

TABLE 15-2

COMPARISON OF INITIAL INTERVIEW SCORE WITH SUCCESS RATING

(Men and Women Combined)

	Interviewer's Rating			
	1	2	3	4
Foremen's Success-on-the-Job Rating				
Outstanding	6 (35.3%)	8 (47.1%)	3 (17.6%)	
Above Average	2 (1.2%)	88 (53.0%)	75 (45.2%)	1 (.6%)
Below Average		13 (6.6%)	175 (88.8%)	8 (4.6%)
Very Poor			4 (14.8%)	23 (85.2%)

In the table above, as may be seen, the relationship is unusually close. The Pearson coefficient of correlation is .68 ± .02. (From Robert N. McMurry, "Validating the Patterned Interview," *Personnel,* American Management Association, January 1947, pp. 263–272.)

children of your own, how do you plan to raise them, in comparison with the way you were reared?" Answers to questions such as these tend to reveal some of the individual's fundamental reactions to his school and home situations.

The second type of probing interview, as practiced in industry, usually involves the asking of related questions that are slanted so as to force the applicant to reveal his attitudes, judgments, and knowledge of procedures as applied to typical job situations.

When the interviewer asks how the applicant's previous supervisors and associates treated him, his main interest is in what the answers reveal about the applicant's adjustment tendencies. The answers enable the interviewer to judge how effectively the person can deal with others in face-to-face situations, as indicated by his speech, mannerisms, persuasiveness, enthusiasm, and so forth. An example of a probing question used in selecting first-line supervisors is:

If you had a worker who wouldn't do something you asked him to do, what would you do?
Probing: What if he still wouldn't do it? What if he said union rules forbid it?

Another probing question, used with applicants for selling, is:

Suppose a salesman has a customer who seems interested in buying, who needs the product, but who seems to find it impossible to make up his mind. How should the salesman handle the customer to make a sale?
Probing Question 1. What if he still wouldn't sign the order?
Probing Question 2. What if he said, "Come back next week?"
Probing Question 3. What if he said, "I want to think about it some more?"

When selecting applicants, the interviewer should use the probing interview before he has learned anything about the applicant's background or experience. To avoid bias, the interviewer should not ask questions about the applicant's personal history nor see his application blank previous to the interview. A committee of several interviewers should conduct the interview, and each interviewer should make an independent rating of the applicant. The interview should last at least twenty minutes.[14] Care must be taken to obtain rapport with the applicant, and he should be told that the interview is only part of the selection procedure. The interviewer should note the applicant's emotional reactions as well as the content of his statements.

Inasmuch as the probing interview is still a relatively new technique in industry, reports concerning its validity are not as yet in published form. The interviewers who have used it in selection practice like it because it seems to indicate what the applicant is likely to do in actual work situations. To some extent, it is a kind of performance test that appears to be particularly useful in selecting salesmen and supervisors.

Practices that improve the interview

A good interviewer has a plan. He knows, before he talks to the applicant, the kind of information he wants and the methods he intends to use to obtain it. Furthermore, he has in his own mind some basic framework, such as the adjustment concept (Chapters 2 to 6), for interpreting the information that he obtains. He has developed skill in stimulating the applicant to talk freely. He tends to follow practices such as the following:

1. He puts the applicant at ease in a natural manner. If the applicant has filled in an application blank, the interviewer may use some fact recorded on the blank as the basis for his first comments. Examples are former places of employment or recreational activities. If the applicant is obviously tense, the interviewer may give him time to pull himself together by picking up the application blank and saying: "Do you mind if I look at this so that I need not ask you questions that you have answered on the application form?"

The universal need for improved interviewing procedures has caused psychology departments of several universities to establish institutes for the teaching of effective techniques. Here are pictures, for example, taken at the Personnel Psychology Services Center, University of Houston.

At the left is a staged setting of one of the sessions. Dr. Ronald Wilson is lecturing. The doors in the background lead to three of six especially designed interviewing rooms. This room was planned with the Interviewing Institute in mind and all PPSC institutes are held here. All the interviewing rooms are equipped with one-way glass windows, intercom systems, and facilities for tape recording from and monitoring to all six rooms at one time.

At the right are some of the Institute members watching a practice interview through a large one-way glass window located in the front of the conference room. The young lady and man are sitting in a classroom situated next to the conference room. A microphone set-up in each room enables the institute group to hear the practice interview.

Some interviewers facilitate the applicant's adjustment to the interview by purposely asking a question that makes the applicant feel a bit better informed than the interviewer. An example might be: "I see that you come from Blank City. Several years ago, I spent two days at the main hotel—it had an Irish name. Was it the Hotel Murphy?" When the applicant answers, "You must mean the Casey House, because that's the main hotel there," he is more apt to feel that he has established his adequacy in the interview situation.

2. He asks many open-end questions, especially in the early stages of the interview. Direct questions are avoided. Instead of saying, "What was your job with your last employer?" he may phrase the inquiry in a less directive manner as, "Tell me about your last job and the kind of work you did there." After the applicant has answered the question, the interviewer can elicit further revealing responses by saying, "Tell me, how did you feel about that job?"

3. When open-end questions have not revealed a clear picture of the applicant's work record, the interviewer asks questions of a specific nature, such as, "In your job with the XYZ Company, just exactly what did you do? Please tell me in detail."

4. When the applicant stops talking, the interviewer asks exploratory questions that keep the conversation moving in the direction desired by the interviewer. Examples are: "Of all the jobs you have held, in what ways did any of them give you chances to develop your abilities?"; "Compare the last two jobs that you had. Tell me some of the things you liked better about the one than about the other"; and, "In what ways do you think that you bettered yourself when you changed some of your jobs in the past?"

5. The good interviewer avoids or has few questions of the following kinds:

a. Questions that can be answered with an unqualified "Yes" or "No."

b. Questions that invariably elicit the same answer from all applicants. Example: "Do you drink liquor to excess?"

c. Trick questions that compel the applicant to defend a former statement or admit an error in an earlier statement.

d. Leading questions, such as: "You finished high school, I assume?"; "Did you make good grades in college?"; "Would you be willing to work in an office where most employees are much older than you are?"; "Were you an accountant or a bookkeeper on your last job?"; and, "Don't you agree that the job I described would be very interesting?"

6. The good interviewer carries on a conversation which results in true exchanges of ideas on the part of both the interviewer and the applicant. He does not dominate the applicant but encourages him to describe his actual feelings, preferences, hopes, abilities, and inabilities. This kind of exchanging of ideas means that the interviewer's statements consume less than 50 per cent of the interviewing time, preferably less than 25 per cent.

7. The good interviewer evaluates his own techniques by means of moving picture and sound recordings of some of his interviews. These objective records enable him to observe his characteristic mannerisms. He can note whether or not his facial expression is friendly, his tone of voice encouraging, and his manner one that gives the applicant a favorable impression of the company. Furthermore, the recordings will give him evidence as to whether he spends too much time talking to the applicant or in inducing the applicant to do most of the talking. Is he stimulating applicants to express themselves so that their abilities can be judged accurately, or is he merely delivering unimpressive monologues to strangers?

8. The good interviewer recognizes that the employment interview has two major divisions or phases: the appraisal of the applicant before accepting him for employment; and, if the applicant is hired, the accepting phase.

In the appraisal or sizing-up phase, the interviewer controls the situation in a manner which causes the applicant to realize fully that he is being appraised rather than hired. The careless interviewer is apt to allow the applicant to assume that he is being hired by an overly friendly manner or by the way he asks the applicant to take various tests or questions him about the amount of pay he would expect if hired. As a result, the applicant gets an emotional jolt when he discovers that he has not been hired.

The good interviewer, on the other hand, keeps the applicant subtly aware of the fact that he is still being appraised and that no decision about his employment has as yet been reached.

Once the decision has been made to accept the applicant for employment, the interviewer begins the induction of the new employee into the company. The applicant is made clearly aware that his status has changed from that of applicant to new employee. At the same time, the interviewer gives the applicant ample information about the company and the job, thus enabling him to make his decision to work there more definite, or, as happens in some cases, to come to the conclusion that he does not want the job after all.

9. The good interviewer is a member of the management team. He not only selects employees who fit well into the organization but also prepares the new employee for the kinds of personalities whom he will meet. When, for example, the interviewer knows that the new employee's supervisor has a brusque hard-boiled manner, he explains the supervisor's personality characteristics so that the new employee can adapt himself to his new boss with understanding and develop respect for whatever admirable qualities the supervisor may have.

In reviewing the interview, we can conclude that few interviewers have developed the art of interviewing to the extent that it deserves. Anyone who studies interviewing practices is likely to conclude that modern industry has been productive in spite of rather than because of its employment procedures. Many applicants who have been hired by the present inadequate methods and become productive workers do so because most human beings are adaptable; not because they have been well chosen for their tasks. Furthermore, even though some statistical studies of interviewing have indicated that improved techniques, such as the standardized and probing interview, are better than unguided procedures, a selective interview of some kind is better than none at all, as proved by a study at the Aircraft Warning Unit Training Center at Drew Field, Florida.[15] About one fourth of the men assigned to this school were chosen at random to fill quotas. Thereafter, a four-week study was made to compare the success of these men with those selected by the classification interviewers. It was found that only 29 per cent of those selected at random completed the course, while 84 per cent of those selected by interview completed the courses successfully.

Letters of application

Our discussion of interviewing would be incomplete without some mention of the letter of application. Carefully conducted investigations show that the letter of application cannot be judged with any great degree of accuracy. If, for example, thirteen experienced employment men are asked to rank several letters of application, the letter that stands at the head of the list of one interviewer is at the bottom of the list of another. No executive has the right to assume that he can pick the wheat from the tares in letters of application. He can eliminate some of the decidedly unfit, but when he rates the remainder he is apt to commit serious errors.

Eight letters of application were received in answer to the following advertisement:

"Required, Secretary to Employment Manager of Large Factory. Apply, stating particulars, to Box ——."

These letters were ranked in order by thirteen experienced employment managers, none of whom knew any of the applicants personally. Half the applicants (four out of the eight) were ranked at both the top and the bottom, that is, first and eighth.

When a company advertises for applicants, no single executive should eliminate and rate the letters of application. A group of executives or other raters should select the letters whose writers are to be investigated further.

The *weighted application blank* has been developed for the selection of salesmen, but for few other applicants. The procedure for adapting the application blank to improved salesman selection is as follows: A group of at least one hundred salesmen are divided into sub-groups such as good, average, and poor, on the basis of such factors as their sales records and supervisor's opinion. Each man's background then is analyzed by examining personnel records or by interview. The purpose is to ascertain certain facts, such as age, height, occupation, dependents, and so forth, and whether or not any particular fact or facts are significant characteristics of any particular sub-group of men. It may be found, for example, that height is positively correlated with volume of sales.

The significant items, those that distinguish potentially successful men from potentially unsuccessful men, are put on a weighted personal history blank. Usually such blanks have only from ten to fifteen items.

As in most weighted personal history forms, a man's score is obtained by adding the weights of the various items. If the total does not amount to the minimum score decided upon as the criterion, the man is eliminated from further consideration unless there are special extenuating factors.

Before adopting a weighted personal history blank for use in selecting salesmen, a company should realize that a formula that has given good results to one company will not necessarily give good results to another. Each company has its own problems, and items that distinguish potentially good salesmen for one company may be valueless criteria for another. It is for this reason that every company must develop its own weighted blank.

Letters of recommendation

An instance of the questionable worth of letters of recommendation came to the attention of the writer when employed by a rubber company. An executive had hired a secretary who was exceptionally competent but was very temperamental. On several occasions he transferred her temporarily to other executives of the company who were friends of his, told them that she was difficult to handle, and asked them to discharge her. The other men refused to discharge the girl because they did not wish to withstand her fiery temper. Finally the executive who was responsible for her employment decided to have vengeance upon a friend, employed as an executive in another concern, who had beaten him in a poker game, by giving the girl an excellent letter of recommendation to him. When she applied for a position, her personality impressed the friend favorably and she was hired, largely because of the excellent letter of recommendation from her employer! This case is exceptional, but it illustrates the fact that many letters of recommendation and many references are given which do not tell the true story of the employee's past record.

Many companies check references by telephoning to employers. Companies who use this plan believe that telephoning is better than writing a letter for the reasons:

(1) It is faster. The average time required to check two references by telephone is 12 minutes. The correspondence method requires from three days to months.

(2) Response is more certain. Almost one-quarter of the mail inquiries are not answered. Almost everyone will answer questions asked by telephone.

(3) The man who is on the hiring side can modify his questions and ask them more freely in order to get the facts he needs.

(4) The former employer feels that he can act naturally and spontaneously. He will speak more frankly about former employees on the telephone than he would in a written letter.

(5) Telephoning saves money. The direct cost of securing references by mail, when combined with the money lost in hiring people who later are found to have poor references, is greater than the cost of telephoning for reference checks. This is true in spite of the additional telephone expenses.

One industrial concern found that even though an extra employee has to be hired for the job, checking applicants' references by telephone is cheaper in the long run than using a mailed check form.

A mailed reference check, the company found, cost only 9 cents per applicant, but only 76.6 per cent of the forms were returned. Because of the time lag involved in getting back the answers, applicants had to be hired on a probationary basis. Of 1,239 new factory employees hired during the period under study, 90 were dropped by the company. Twenty-eight of these were rated as poor risks by former employers. Reference checks had not been returned for 36 of the 90. On the reference forms returned, only 26 of the 90 had been rated "Fair" to "Good."

If the company had not hired the 28 who eventually were reported as poor risks, an estimated $3,640 would have been saved.[16]

One sales manager who hires salesmen

in all parts of the country telegraphs his requests for information from former employers who are given as references by applicants. He has found that he must demand about eight references and follow up each reference very carefully if he wishes to avoid hiring men with bad records. On one occasion he sent telegrams to eight references regarding an applicant whom he wished to hire. Two of the references did not reply at all, but telegrams from four were as follows:

"Glad to hear Walter K. has applied to you for a position. I can recommend him highly as regards honesty and workmanship. He is 100%. Has worked for me 3 years."

"Walter K. was with us for two months. Character and dependability very good. Would recommend."

"While Walter K. was with us he was very satisfactory."

"I recommend Mr. K. very highly in every respect."

These telegrams from the references were quite satisfying to the employment man and he was about to hire the applicant when he received a long-distance telephone call from one of the former employers. The former employer described Walter's conduct with his firm and told how he had failed even to attempt to do the work for which he was hired, had led an immoral life, owed the company money, borrowed money from customers, and had been discharged for incompetency. A few hours later, another former employer telephoned the employment man and gave a similar report of gross misconduct. These executives refused to put their reports in writing, but used the telephone in an honest effort to save time and money for a prospective employer. This employment man frequently requests former employers to telephone him at his expense if they prefer to do so rather than write or telegraph him. He claims that he has saved his company thousands of dollars by asking for

telephone answers, because former employers will give more honest reports in oral than in written form.

Most executives write a general letter to a person given as reference, and the person answering usually gives a general reply, selecting those good points in the applicant's history that may be stressed without harming his chances for another job. A slightly better method is to use a special report form that asks for information on specific points, as:

1. Was the applicant discharged by you, let go because of decrease in work, or did he leave of his own accord?

2. Does he owe you any money now? *No. Yes.*

3. Would you rehire him if you needed a person for a vacancy that he had the ability to fill? *No.   Yes.   Possibly.*

4. How long did he work for you?

5. What date (month and year) did he leave your employ?

6. He states that his salary or income from you was . . . per month. Is this correct? *Yes. No.*

7. Did he use alcohol to any extent? *Yes. No.*

8. How do you rate his moral conduct? *Very good.   Satisfactory.   Questionable.*

9. Do you think that he possesses the ability to fill a job with us which is . . . .*Yes.   No.   Don't know.*

10. How would you rate his record with your firm?
   a. Very satisfactory.
   b. Satisfactory.
   c. Fair.
   d. Questionable.
   e. Unsatisfactory.

These questions should be made part of a two-page letter to the previous employer, the first page giving the name of the former employee and assuring the answerer that his report will be kept confidential. The questions and answers suggested may be varied, but they should deal with objective factors rather than ask for opinions. The possible answers should be suggested on the form so that the correct answer can be checked by the writer or written with a minimum of effort. This type of letter to a reference does not allow the previous employer to select the pleasant parts in the former employee's record and ignore the bad parts. Such forms have been used by a few progressive firms, but many employment men still accept a general letter of reply from persons given as references. They assume that, when an applicant has a bad record, the person answering will phrase his letter so that it is possible "to read between the lines" and grasp the real story. Such an expectation on the part of executives may be unfair to the applicant and it requires too much time on the part of the previous employers.

When letters are addressed to former employers of an applicant, they should be addressed to the "Employment Manager" rather than to individuals within the company. Some applicants who do not wish their real record to be revealed to prospective employers often give the name of a friend in the company as a reference. This friend is usually a person of no responsibility and his statement has no weight as a reference for a discharged employee.

Summary

The hiring of employees is still mostly in the hands of the empiricists of business. The old rules-of-thumb and prejudice prevail. A few progressive concerns have made statistical studies of the factors which correlate highly with successful employment records. Some have improved their hiring procedures through more systematic interviewing and the use of psychological tests to eliminate the unfit and to reduce labor turnover, but such modern aids are likely to be found in the larger and better-managed employment offices where trained experts are in charge of hiring. However, any executive or employment manager who wishes to improve his hiring techniques can do so by standardizing his procedure, keeping records of his findings, and then making statistical studies of his records. He can at least use several interviewers rather than depend upon the evaluations made by any one man. Such attempts will yield results more valuable than those of the present haphazard treatment of the interview, letter of application, and letter of recommendation.

Certain companies who are especially desirous of developing cohesive work groups also insist that each applicant must be endorsed by three employees. This policy results in the development of a friendly shop, where even the newest worker feels that he is accepted.

Acknowledgments and References

1. H. L. Hollingworth, *Judging Human Character*, D. Appleton and Company, New York, 1923, p. 268.
2. Walter Dill Scott, "The Scientific Selection of Salesmen," *Advertising and Selling*, Vol. 25 (1915), pp. 5–6, 94 f.
3. Richard Stephen Uhrbrock, "The Personnel Interview," *Personnel Psychology*, Vol. 1, No. 3 (1948), p. 274. The two sets of questions for interviewing recent college graduates, quoted under "the area interview," are from this article, p. 286.
4. S. A. Rice, "Contagious Bias in the Interview," *American Journal of Sociology*, Vol. 35 (1929), pp. 420–423.
5. G. R. Thornton, "Effects of Wearing Glasses Upon Judgments of Traits," *Journal of Applied Psychology*, American Psychological Association, Inc., Vol. 28, No. 3 (June 1944), p. 207.
6. *Manual of Employment Interviewing*, Research Report Number Nine, American Management Association, New York, 1946.
7. Carl Iver Hovland and E. F. Wonderlic, "Prediction of Industrial Success from a Standardized Interview," *Journal of Applied Psychology*, American Psychological Association, Inc., Vol. XXIII, No. 5 (October 1939), pp. 537–546.
8. Carl R. Rogers, *Counseling and Psychotherapy*, Houghton Mifflin Company, Boston, 1942.

9. N. A. Moyer, "Non-Directive Employment Interviewing," *Personnel*, American Management Association, March 1948.

10. *Loc. cit.*

11. Carl Iver Hovland and E. F. Wonderlic, "Prediction of Industrial Success from a Standardized Interview," *Journal of Applied Psychology*, American Psychological Association, Inc., Vol. XXIII, No. 5 (October 1939).

12. Robert N. McMurry, "Validating the Patterned Interview," *Personnel*, American Management Association, January 1947.

13. K. A. Yonge, "The Value of the Interview: An Orientation and Pilot Study," *Journal of Applied Psychology*, February 1956, pp. 25–31.

14. The examples and instructions for the probing interview were obtained from Richardson, Bellows, Henry & Co., Inc., and Jay L. Otis.

15. Richard W. Putney, "Validity of the Placement Interview," *Personnel Journal*, Vol. 26 (1947), pp. 144–145.

16. See *The Management Review*, American Management Association, May 1955, p. 335. Data provided by Howard P. Mold.

PROJECTS

1. Collect some letters of application. Ask friends or executives to rank them in the order of estimated desirability of the applicants. Discuss the differences in the rankings.

2. Make a list of some of your own tendencies toward bias in interviewing. What means might you use to overcome such tendencies?

3. Assume that you are about to establish a small manufacturing enterprise employing between 50 and 100 persons. Outline your plans for:
   a. Selecting the women you wish to hire.
   b. Making special provision in the plant and working schedule for the women.

4. Read material concerning lie detectors and evaluate their usefulness and limitations. List other methods you have heard of for telling when a person is lying.

5. Write a *Help Wanted* advertisement to obtain women factory employees and a similar

advertisement for male employees. How do they differ?

6. To prevent politics in business, some managers hire employees of all kinds of religious and racial affiliations. What "mixtures" of religions, races, sexes, etc., would you consider to be most desirable to prevent company politics?

7. Find pictures of several famous persons of whom you have heard but whose physical features you have not seen. In which cases were you disappointed by the pictures and in which were you pleased? Give possible reasons for your reaction in each case.

8. Collect handwriting specimens of persons whom you know. Analyze the writing according to the system of analysis presented in a book on graphology. Estimate the value of the system.

COLLATERAL READINGS

Bellows, Roger M., and M. Frances Estep, *Employment Psychology: The Interview*, Rinehart & Company, 1954, Chapters 10 and 11.

Covner, Bernard J., "Nondirective Interviewing Techniques in Vocational Counseling," *Journal of Consulting Psychology*, Vol. 11 (1947), pp. 70–73.

Crissy, William J. E., and M. J. Wantman, "Measurement Aspects of the National Clerical Ability Testing Program," *Educational and Psychological Measurement*, January 1942, pp. 37–46.

Dictionary of Occupational Titles, 3 vols., United States Employment Service, Washington, D. C., June, 1939. (Note: Two companion manuals and several volumes of job descriptions supplement the *Dictionary*. According to a recent announcement, the *Dictionary* now defines some 17,542 jobs. The supplementary job descriptions cover occupations in job machine shops, job foundries, the retail trade, the construction industry, the laundry industry, the automobile industry, and the cotton textile industry. A sample occupational interview illustrating the application of the *Dictionary of Occupational Titles* and the use of oral trade questions has been transcribed on phonograph records by the National Broadcasting Company.)

Fear, Richard A., and Byron Jordan, *Employee Evaluation Manual for Interviewers*, The Psychological Corporation, New York, 1943.

Ghiselli, Edwin E., and Clarence W. Brown, *Personnel and Industrial Psychology*, McGraw-Hill Book Company, Inc., New York, 1955, Chapter 6.

Lawshe, Jr., C. H., *Principles of Personnel Testing*, McGraw-Hill Book Company, Inc., New York, 1948.

Manual of Employment Interviewing, Research Report Number Nine, American Management Association, New York, 1946.

Smith, Henry Clay, *Psychology of Industrial Behavior*, McGraw-Hill Book Company, Inc., New York, 1955, Chapter 15.

Tiffin, Joseph, *Industrial Psychology*, 2nd ed., Prentice-Hall, Inc., New York, 1948.

Thorndike, R. L., *Research Problems and Techniques in Personnel Selection*, New York, John Wiley and Sons, 1949.

CHAPTER SIXTEEN

Hiring the employee–the use of tests

When psychological methods are used in an employment office, they should always be looked upon as supplementing—not replacing—other methods that are in use. No psychologist who has thought at all about the problems of modern industry would seriously suggest that present employment procedures should be eliminated. . . . But the fact that these methods, though excellent in many respects, are still not perfect is proved by the marked individual differences among employees which any study of differential production will reveal. A considerable amount of research, both in industry and in the laboratory, has shown that still further improvements in employment methods can be attained when psychological tests and methods are used as supplements to other employment procedures.[1]

Companies that wish to improve their hiring procedures often turn to psychological tests as instruments of prediction. A psychological test does not evaluate all of the person's ability, but merely tests parts, samples, or symptoms of ability. The psychological test is very similar in nature to the tests made by the assayer of minerals. If a man wished to purchase a vein of silver ore, he would first obtain samples of it and have these analyzed by some competent chemist. On the basis of the samples, he would decide upon the value of the ore and the price he would be willing to pay for it. Obviously he could not test all the mineral in the vein of ore. Similarly, the psychologist tests samples of a person's abilities rather than all of them.

Psychological tests and aptitude tests are terms often used loosely by modern businessmen and even by scientists. In many cases, a businessman thinks he is using psychological or intelligence tests when actually he is merely asking a number of random questions. For example: a businessman may find that he needs a new secretary. Accordingly, he advertises in the usual manner; when he arrives at his office the next morning he may find an applicant there. He then opens his morning mail, chatting with her while he takes a casual glance at the letters which await his attention. Then, deciding that it would be well for him to "test" the applicant, he picks up one of the letters which he must answer and dictates a reply. The applicant types the letter and gives it back to him; he examines it for errors and appearance. He then dismisses the first applicant and awaits the coming of the second one, at which time he answers another letter—an entirely different one. In this manner, he "tests" five applicants, after which he makes his decision. He thinks he has given each one of the applicants a psychological test. As a matter of fact, he has not done so at all. If he were to develop a psychological test for the hiring of stenographers, certain factors would have to be standardized for all applicants, namely:

1. *Materials.* The same letter and appliances must be used for each person.

2. *Instructions.* Each applicant must receive the same instructions regarding speed and accuracy. Instructions should be read.

3. *Technique.* The speed of dictation, enunciation, and so forth must be kept the same.

4. *Conditions.* Distractions should vary as little as possible.

5. *Interpretation of score.* The score of each applicant must be compared with scores of other stenographers of high, medium, and low ability.

Any test, to be of value, must fulfill three requirements: it must be *objective,* so that personal opinion is held to a minimum in the scoring; it must be *valid,* that is, it must test the trait that it is supposed to test; and it must be *reliable,* that is, it must give the same results on repetition, regardless of the particular individual who administers the test. Many of the tests that are published in magazines do not fulfill these three requirements. Such tests are still in the experimental state. They may have promise of future results, but they should not be used as a basis for hiring until their predictive value has been statistically determined.

A psychological test is any problem or series of questions that has been tried out on persons who possess a known degree of the trait being tested. It has been shown that the test scores made by these persons are stable and correlate with their records in that trait. Therefore, one of the chief requirements for preparing psychological tests is that of statistical training.

Many businessmen and scientists have been using tests for many years, but the terminology is not very well standardized. The various terms used to describe tests are: intelligence, aptitude, efficiency, mental alertness, information, specific ability, performance, mental, job, trade, and army tests. These terms usually refer to diverse kinds of tests.

Kinds of tests used in employment

One helpful way to classify tests is to think of them in regard to what they are supposed to measure: (1) *Intelligence, mental alertness,* or *scholastic aptitude* tests are designed to measure a person's ability to deal with abstract relationships, sometimes referred to as the ability to do "mental gymnastics." As mentioned before, a good definition of intelligence is "The degree of availability of one's experiences for the solution of immediate problems and the anticipation of future ones." (2) *Aptitude* tests are tests concerned with the capacity to acquire certain specified knowledge or skills, such as stenography, salesmanship, chemical engineering, or some limited aspect of these or other occupations. Some users of the term assume that it embraces intelligence, personality, and interests, because these must also be included in the prediction of potentiality for learning skills and acquiring knowledge.[2] (3) *Proficiency* or achievement tests intend to measure actual ability to do certain kinds of work or to perform specified skills such as typing, comptometry, grammar, or carpentry. When these tests are applied to the work of the artisan they are also called "trade tests." (4) *Vocational interests* are exemplified by the E. K. Strong test. (See Chapter 11.) (5) *Personality* or temperament tests usual-

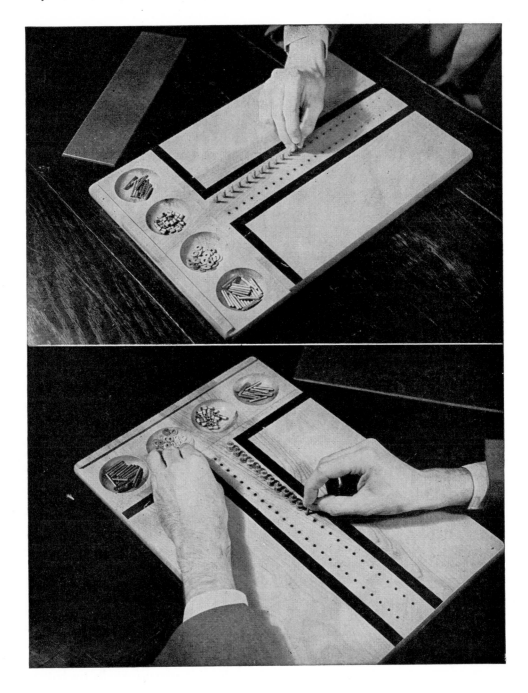

The "Purdue Pegboard" Test measures certain basic aspects of manipulative dexterity. Separate measurements may be obtained for right hand, left hand, and both hands. The test can be given to ten or more persons simultaneously. When test boards were available in one office, a single examiner administered the test at the rate of fifty applicants per hour. See Joseph Tiffin, **Industrial Psychology.** Englewood Cliffs, N.J.: Prentice-Hall, Inc., 1947, pp. 126 f.

Salesmen differ from engineers. The scores on the base line represent a combination consisting of measures of interest in advertising, attitude toward sales work, knowledge of selling methods, accuracy, aggressiveness, confidence, emotional stability and liveliness of disposition.

Edwin G. Flemming, of the Burton Bigelow Organization, Management Consultants of New York City, uses a battery of eight tests in his service designed to aid executives in the selection of salesmen, sales managers, and other executives. When he compared the test data obtained from batteries or sets of tests answered by applicants for jobs as salesmen with that from engineer applicants, he found significant differences between the test scores of the two groups.

After appropriate statistical treatments were given the test data, the average score for engineers was found to be 1125; for salesmen, 1376.—The data showed that salesmen and engineers are distinctly different, not only in the pattern of their major interests, but also in their accuracy, their knowledge, their attitude toward their work, and their personalities.

Dr. Flemming's experience with the practical problem of selecting salesmen for many employers of all sizes in many different kinds of selling operations indicates that sales engineers—those salesmen who must have a technical training in engineering, but whose primary job is to sell—are likely to be found in the area of overlapping of the two curves in the chart, between the scores of 1150 and 1300.—**Chart and data by Edwin G. Flemming, Director, Division for Sales Personnel Selection, Burton Bigelow Organization, New York.**

ly refer to adjustment tendencies that more or less characterize the individual's behavior, as exemplified by terms such as introversion, sociability, and emotional stability. Temperament refers to one's tendency to act in certain characteristic ways, not at any one instant but over a long period of time.

Stages in the development of testing in industry

The history of testing for the appraisal of job applicants and employees has had three overlapping stages:

1. *Single tests,* such as those for the measuring of intelligence, proficiency, and personality. Thousands of tests, of varying validity, have been published and used. Examples of single tests may be found in the appendix of this book.

2. *The battery of tests* with a profile of test scores. This procedure, developed by psychologists in recent years, means that a number of single tests are administered as a battery. A single test usually measures but a limited facet of the individual's psychological make-up. Under the battery method, the scores of several standard tests, given one individual, are plotted on graph paper in the form of a profile. This test profile is then compared with the master test profiles that are typical of successful and unsuccessful employees. See figures on page opposite,

SUCCESSFUL VS. UNSUCCESSFUL SALES MANAGERS

Direct to the Consumer

These curves show the differences between successful and unsuccessful district and branch managers in direct-to-the-consumer selling operations. The heavy perpendicular line represents the median score made by 1040 salesmen.

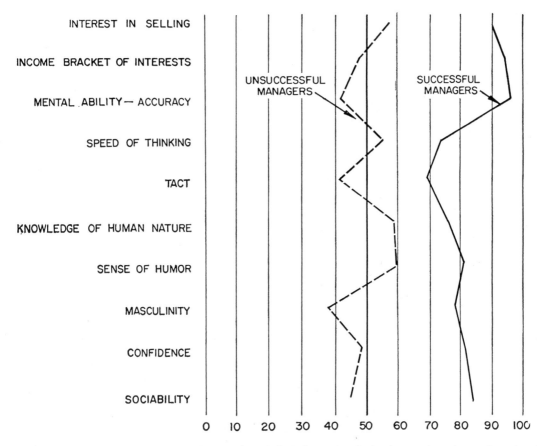

"**Criticism has sometimes been leveled** at the use of psychological tests in selection because investigators have found no very high correlations between scores on single tests and criteria of success in selling. It is true that very significant correlations seldom are found for single tests, but it needs to be pointed out and emphasized that a score on any one test is not necessarily critically significant in determining a man's potentialities for success in selling. The important thing is the pattern of scores revealed by a battery of tests. No one score may be critically important, but the pattern is. By a pattern we mean the interrelationships of scores and the relative strengths and weaknesses of the traits, interests, and tendencies revealed by the complete battery of tests."—From Edwin G. Flemming and Cecile White Flemming, "Test-Selected Salesmen," **Journal of Marketing**, April 1946. Chart is not included in this article, but was prepared by Edwin G. Flemming for use in this book.

and 312. When this procedure is used by an experienced psychologist, the psychologist may interpret also the profile for management, writing a one-to-five page report on the significance of the test findings.

3. *Projective tests.* These tests are called projective because through them the person being analyzed tends to project his own unacknowledged motives and traits into a response to a vague and undefined situation. The Thematic Apperception Test, for example, consists of a series of standard pic-

PATTERN SALES PROFILE BASED ON 400 SPECIALTY FOOD SALESMEN.

> **Shaded area**—above-average hiring area.
> **Line** separating shaded from unshaded areas—median scores.
> **Unshaded area**—acceptable hiring area within average range.

The entire profile represents the inter-quartile range or the middle 50 per cent of those employees who were considered above average. This technique was used to eliminate the atypical cases who are unusually high on one hand or unusually low, thus making the profile more indicative of a homogeneous above-average group.—When applicants are plentiful, the shaded area is used. It is also used for upgrading. When applicants are few, the entire pattern, including the unshaded area, may be used.

The criteria used to determine the above-average individuals were above-average production on the job and managers' ratings. Four or five managers' ratings were available for every individual. These ratings pertain to more intangible personal characteristics, which very often are not revealed in production figures themselves or sales volumes, as the case may be, and include such factors as loyalty to the company, willingness to follow managerial policies, stability, willingness to work, planning, personal appearance, etc.

The success of this method in application has been substantiated in one company by the fact that throughout six years of conscientious and controlled application it was possible to reduce the turnover in the sales field from 13 to 1 to 5 to 1. It costs the company around $2,500 to hire and train a salesman over a six-months period. On a yearly basis, the reduction in turnover has saved the company approximately $150,000. Of course there are other intangible benefits, such as increased versatility in the new men who are now hired as compared to the old type.—Chart and data by Richard S. Solomon, Consulting Psychologist, Dayton, Ohio.

For the second picture (photograph, Museum of Modern Art, New York) the subject is asked to tell a dramatic story. It is thought that even though he may not be aware of it, he endows the story with needs and stresses that he experiences at the time. From expressions of needs and stresses, generalizations are made about his behavior patterns.—Projective techniques are used in clinical practice and offer one way of getting at the individual's hidden or non-conscious behavior dynamics. The subject has little or no control over his responses. However, much basic research in this area is needed before these techniques can be fully trusted. (Painting shown is "Landscape," a watercolor by Kasimir Malevich.)

Two examples of response cards for projective techniques. The ink blot has no meaning in its own right, but it is thought to induce responses that enable the clinical expert to make deductions concerning the subject's imaginative processes and gain clues to the individual's personality. Scoring of responses includes not only response-content, but also such factors as size of area responded to, movement, detection of shading, and others.

tures, most of which contain human figures. The person being studied is told to make up a story about each picture. When the person makes up the stories, he also reveals important attitudes, feelings, tendencies, strivings, conflicts, and frustrations. The expert clinical psychologist can learn much of value about a person from this type of test.

One of the earliest projective tests is the well-known Rorschach or ink blot visual stimulus technique. Other examples of the projective technique are those of finger-painting, word association, and the psychodrama.[3]

The projective techniques have been given considerable publicity in business recently as a result of the work done by several personnel researchers, particularly Dr. Burleigh Gardner and his associates in Social Research, Inc., a consulting service of Chicago.

A technique employed by these scientists consisted of a short, nondirective interview, a special analysis by means of several traditional personality tests, and the Thematic Apperception Test, developed by H. A. Murray and associates of Harvard University. Use of the TAT test requires interpretation by experts. As a result of a program of testing executives with this type of test, Gardner and his associates found that the following list of characteristics is typically possessed by a good executive:[4]

1. He must accomplish and achieve in order to be happy.
2. He accepts authority.
3. He has a strong drive toward achievement, material rewards, and prestige.
4. He is able to bring order out of chaos.
5. He is decisive—but he doesn't necessarily have to make snap decisions.
6. He is sure of his convictions and decisions.

7. He has a constant drive to be moving and doing.

8. He may have a pervasive fear of failure —a lingering doubt of his ability to do as good a job as he wants to do.

9. He has a strong sense of reality.

10. He identifies himself more with his superiors than with subordinates. His superiors represent a symbol of his own achievement.

11. He feels and acts on his own. "In a sense, a successful executive is a man who has left home."

On the other hand, an unsuccessful executive is likely to have these traits:

1. He cannot grasp the over-all picture, cannot see the forest for the trees.

2. He fails to carry his load of responsibilities.

3. He has an unconscious desire to be something else.

4. He has an unconscious desire to be someone else.

5. He is unable to coöperate with his associates.

6. He is so ambitious that he is impatient with and intolerant of routine tasks.

7. He cannot accept supervision from his bosses.

8. He is arrogant with his subordinates.

9. He may have a deep-rooted, fixed idea that hobbles him in dealing with his duties. He may, for example, suspect that some colleague is out to "knife" him, or that his background is not adequate.

10. He may keep his nose too close to the grindstone. Overemphasis on work often results in breakdowns. A successful executive must have outside interests and relaxations to sustain his energy, balance his activities.

11. He may, through some quirk of a youthful background, be subconsciously bent on self-destruction.

12. He may have some mental disorders that only a psychologist can pry out.

Obviously, the work of the projective technique users is very technical. Few companies can afford to hire the services of experts of this order. Furthermore, the use of projective techniques in industry is new, and they are still to be regarded as experimental. In some studies, their use failed to discriminate accurately between good and poor performers.

Extent to which tests are used in industry

Most employers who do testing limit their testing programs to the use of several single tests or, at most, to batteries that have been found helpful in hiring applicants for certain occupations. Several investigators have made surveys at irregular intervals by means of mailed questionnaires to learn the extent to which companies use tests for selection.

These surveys are usually limited to companies that have well developed personnel policies,[5] are large concerns, or are members of specific industry classifications. The surveys do, however, indicate trends. Generally, the use of tests for hiring is on the increase for clerical and sales positions. Mental (intelligence) tests are being used increasingly but trade, dexterity, and performance tests are used decreasingly. Even though less than one-half of the country's employers are using tests in hiring, their use has increased as indicated by surveys and the sales of test publishers. A list of test publishers and their addresses is given in the references for this chapter.[6]

The United States Employment Service developed norms for occupational aptitude tests and trade tests. The aptitude test batteries are of two kinds: the General Aptitude Test Battery and specific aptitude test batteries. The General Aptitude Test Battery has norms in terms of 22 occupational aptitude patterns covering over 500 occupations. Since not every different occupation requires a completely different set of aptitudes and abilities, those occupations requiring similar abilities are grouped together into a family of occupations requiring the same pattern of abilities. Each occupational aptitude pattern is expressed in terms of the three key aptitudes required for the performance of the jobs within the family and the minimum qualifying scores required for each aptitude. In counseling an applicant, it is possible to determine his aptitudes for many different occupations on the basis of relatively few tests.

Specific aptitude test batteries consisting of tests from the USES General Aptitude Test battery are used in the selection of applicants for specific jobs. In some instances, training time of new employees has been reduced by a third or even a half by using these tests to select the right man for the right job. The use of these tests has also facilitated the work of those who select workers for upgrading, promotion, and so on. In over 1200 local offices of the State Employment Services throughout the United States at which testing is done, employers can arrange with the local office to administer specific tests that have been developed for a particular occupation and to refer test-selected applicants for specific job openings. This service is free to both the employer and the applicant. Inquiry at the local office will reveal the testing services available.[7]

Personality tests in industry

Much work has been done in the development of personality tests for use in industry. The Humm-Wadsworth Temperament Scale, as an example, is an attempt to measure potential work attitudes, social adjustment, and coöperative capacity.[8] The use of the test is restricted to those who have had some training in psychiatric principles.

Much research must still be done in this kind of testing, but the employment interviewer should become acquainted with this field of human analysis. The chapters on adjustment (2 to 6) present a general background for this type of testing and interview.

One study of the Guilford-Martin Personnel Inventory indicated that the test classified as having "undesirable temperaments" 82 per cent of the workers who had, in management's opinion, demonstrated that they were troublemakers and soreheads. However, also in the group whose scores indicated that they had "undesirable temperaments" were 38 per cent of the workers whom management had labeled satisfactory.[9]

Dr. Joseph E. King and his associates, Industrial Psychology, Inc., have developed batteries of tests for hiring clerical, mechanical, sales, technical, and supervisory personnel. One test, called Neurotic Personality Factor, was designed to spot the neurotic and maladjusted employee, and to select individuals of high stability and responsibility. The work of Cattell and Stice, measuring the performances of small groups, shows that even when neurotic employees do not actually make trouble, their presence considerably lowers the morale and productivity of the group. Various job areas have different demands in terms of the amount of stability required, and companies can use the N.P.F. for job areas where maladjustment is a serious problem and cost factor.[10]

Personality tests are not as yet as well perfected as some other types of tests. The experimental or statistical shortcomings of many of the studies of personality tests justify a cautious attitude toward the results obtained, but the fact cannot be ignored that the inventories usually do make some definite contribution to psychiatric screening. The evidence that some of the inventories were found useful in the military situation encourages the hope that similar inventories may prove to be useful in civilian practice.[11]

Values of testing in industry

In American industry, tests alone are not sufficient for hiring or rejecting an applicant in most firms. They are merely one of the factors that must be evaluated, just as age or education must be weighed in the composite score. The tests may have greater predictive value than any other one variable, but in most firms the other variables are considered in the total picture of the applicant. However, tests have been found helpful for the following purposes:

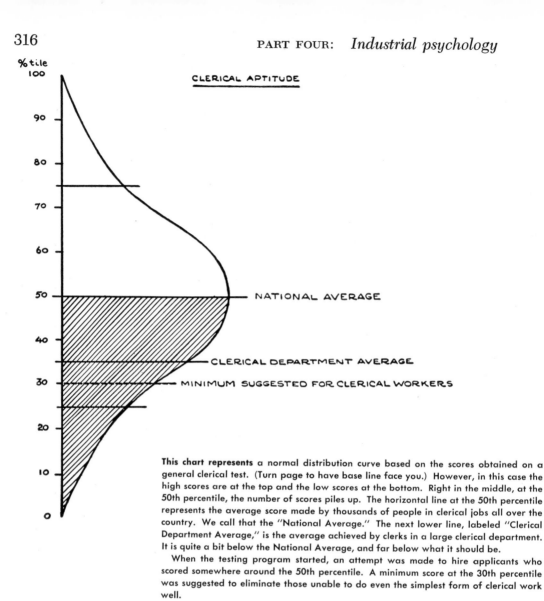

%tile
100

90

80

70

60

50

40

30

20

10

0

CLERICAL APTITUDE

NATIONAL AVERAGE

CLERICAL DEPARTMENT AVERAGE

MINIMUM SUGGESTED FOR CLERICAL WORKERS

This chart represents a normal distribution curve based on the scores obtained on a general clerical test. (Turn page to have base line face you.) However, in this case the high scores are at the top and the low scores at the bottom. Right in the middle, at the 50th percentile, the number of scores piles up. The horizontal line at the 50th percentile represents the average score made by thousands of people in clerical jobs all over the country. We call that the "National Average." The next lower line, labeled "Clerical Department Average," is the average achieved by clerks in a large clerical department. It is quite a bit below the National Average, and far below what it should be.

When the testing program started, an attempt was made to hire applicants who scored somewhere around the 50th percentile. A minimum score at the 30th percentile was suggested to eliminate those unable to do even the simplest form of clerical work well.

1. Weeding out of the unfit applicants. For example, persons who have an intelligence quotient of less than 105 seldom succeed in clerical jobs of average difficulty.

One personnel manager for a public utility firm reported that when tests were used in selecting applicants, less than 10 per cent of those hired failed on the job. Without tests, the long-term record of failures in hiring approached 30 per cent.[12] At one time, the Woodward Governor Co. of Rockford, Illinois, found that they were hiring too many tramp mechanics and other undesirables. Later The Psychological Corporation made a study of the company's personnel needs and recommended the use of tests which, according to the general manager of the company, succeeded in weeding out 85 per cent of the untrainable men who applied for work.[13] Similarly, the Lockheed Aircraft Corporation averaged twelve successful hirings out of twenty before testing. With testing, the average rose to nineteen out of twenty.[14]

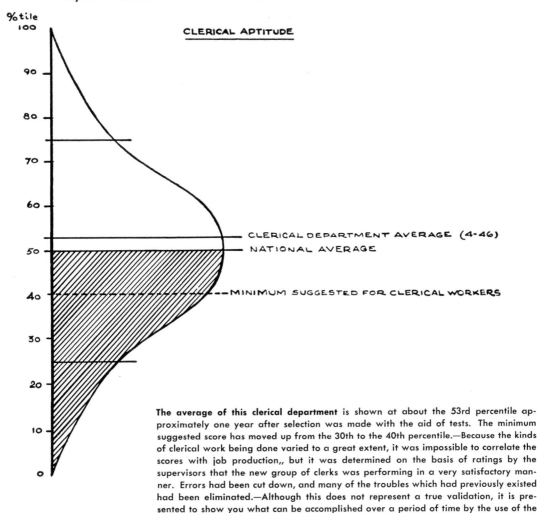

The average of this clerical department is shown at about the 53rd percentile approximately one year after selection was made with the aid of tests. The minimum suggested score has moved up from the 30th to the 40th percentile.—Because the kinds of clerical work being done varied to a great extent, it was impossible to correlate the scores with job production,, but it was determined on the basis of ratings by the supervisors that the new group of clerks was performing in a very satisfactory manner. Errors had been cut down, and many of the troubles which had previously existed had been eliminated.—Although this does not represent a true validation, it is presented to show you what can be accomplished over a period of time by the use of the norms published with some of the good clerical tests.

2. Tests reduce the costs of training new employees through the selection of applicants who can learn the work. When, for example, a camera manufacturer hired twenty-six persons to learn film spooling, all were subjected to taking a finger dexterity test. Seventeen failed the test. Because of a shortage of labor at the time, all were hired. Ten weeks later each had left the job. The cost of the make-up pay alone, the difference between the minimum hourly rate of pay and what they actually earned, was more than one thousand dollars. Indirect costs to the company amounted to several thousand dollars more. Moreover, a cost greater than dollars was the fact that some of the failing employees were unnecessarily subjected to the experience of failure in their work.

3. Tests enable the personnel manager to spot unsuspected talent within the organization. For example, one third of the line supervisors of the Pacific Lighting Companies first attracted attention through results of their tests.[15] Several large concerns use tests in selecting employees for apprentice, sales, or executive training.

4. Several investigators have developed tests which reduce accidents in bus and

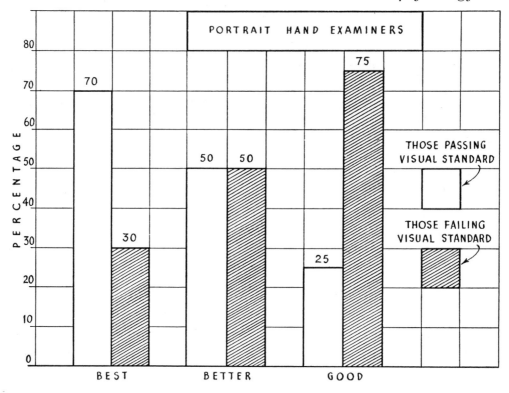

This chart illustrates the relationship between scores made on the Ortho-Rater vision test and production on an inspection job. In each one of the columns, the white area represents the percentage of that group of employees who met all the visual standards established for the job. The shaded area of each column represents the percentage of that group who failed to meet the visual standards. The three columns, reading from left to right, represent three different groups of employees designated as "best" group, "better" group, and "good" group, on the basis of quality of work. As can be seen, the percentage of each group passing the visual standards increases as the quality of the work increases. There is a definite relationship between excellence of vision and quality of work on this particular job. This illustrates the importance of vision. It does not make any difference whether a clerical job, a machine job, or an inspection job is being studied. A positive relationship between vision and excellence of work is often found. If such a relationship has been proved, the majority of the better workers meet the vision standards of the job, and the majority of the poorer workers fail to meet these standards.*

truck driving through the selection of fewer accident-prone drivers. In one study it was found that the highest tenth of the drivers (according to composite profile scores) had had 21.2 per cent fewer chargeable accidents than the lowest tenth.[16] A comparison of the average yearly accident rate for the year following the tests and the three preceding years showed an improvement with respect to chargeable accidents of 28.8 per cent. Another psychologist, C. A. Drake, developed a series of tests which

reduced the average accident index rate 70 per cent for new employees during the first three months of their work.[17]

5. Psychological tests decrease favoritism in hiring and place the securing of a job on an objective basis rather than on sentiment. Tests are a convenient device for avoiding pressure from friends and politicians who may have some protégé who needs a job. Definite standards which every applicant must meet will enable the executive to say to the man who has an

* David W. Cook, *Psychology Challenges Industry*, Personnel Series No. 107, American Management Association, 1947. Charts on pages 316 to 318 and explanatory captions reproduced by courtesy of David W. Cook and the American Management Association.

incapable nephew who needs a position: "We shall be glad to have the young man apply to us for a job, and if he meets the standards we have set up, we will find a place for him." However, the main value of tests is in locating good applicants and employees. Furthermore, there is considerable evidence to indicate that when a testing program is installed it tends to draw better applicants to the company.[18] A self-imposed selection takes place among applicants who know that the company uses tests.

6. Tests can be used to determine needed areas of training on the part of new and old employees. Usually, tests of information and proficiency are used for this purpose. However, personality tests are helpful too, particularly in those occupations that require certain personality characteristics, as in selling and research.

7. If a personnel department does counseling of inadequately adjusted employees, tests are essential to diagnosis. When used for this purpose, testing contributes to the development of happier and more effective workers.

8. Test findings and interpretations are especially helpful to effective supervision. The use of tests often reveals vital information for management. Guy W. Wadsworth, Jr., president of the Southern California Gas Company, pointed out their value when he stated:

Generally speaking, low-grade supervisors tend to attract and to favor low-grade men. Their most favorable reports may be expected to concern subordinates much like themselves, who offer little potential rivalry. A keenly intelligent applicant placed under such a supervisor is often quickly classified as a "smart aleck." Thus there may be an unlooked-for wastage of manpower, in which technical fitness is not an issue. In any case, within our experience, the use of standardized tests has provided a most effective personnel audit, disclosing not only abilities which may not be called into play in the immediate assignment, but which would have remained obscured for other thoroughly human reasons.[19]

Limitations of tests

Psychological tests have demonstrated their values in many phases of business, but are especially helpful in reducing labor turnover. However, when a critical score is once determined and an executive decides that no applicant shall be hired unless he scores above that point, the executive is also apt to go to the opposite extreme and try to hire only those who score considerably above the critical point. This practice may result in a high turnover, for it is desirable to have a maximum score as well

TABLE 16-1

Test Score	Average Length of Service in Days
10 to 19	3
20 to 29	91
30 to 39	156
40 to 49	142
50 to 59	107
60 to 69	100
70 to 79	96
80 to 89	87
90 and above	35

From Harold E. Burtt, *Employment Psychology*, Houghton Mifflin Company, Boston, 1926, p. 289.

as a minimum score or an *optimum range* (see Table 16-1). One employment manager started to use tests for hiring and then hired only persons with high intelligence for all his jobs. His method resulted in a high turnover, because few of the jobs were worthy of a person of high intelligence. The well-manned corporation is like a well-manned army; it consists of one general, a few high officers, many junior-grade officers, and the great mass of the organization made up of people with average or below-average intelligence. An elevator operator should have the intelligence needed for operating elevators and not very much more. If this country should suddenly embark upon a eugenics program and breed only people of very high intelligence, we might be worse off than we are now, because many jobs in a technological civilization require only average and below-average intelligence. Examples of such jobs are truck-driving, elevator-operating, factory machine-tending, and so on.

When intelligence tests are used for selective purposes, it is well to know whether environmental conditions have been eliminating the unfit of the group to be tested. The use of intelligence tests for the selection of students for admission to college does not result in very high correlations between scores in the tests and scholastic records. One reason for a low correlation is the selective process that has been operating through the school system. The students of lowest intelligence find grammar school and high school work too difficult for them and tend to drop out according to the degrees of intelligence possessed. Hence, when a student is able to apply for admission to college, he has already survived a process of selection. Only those above the average of intelligence are able to finish high school and apply for admission to college.

If an individual has a certain minimum of intelligence for a given occupation or job, his success depends upon other characteristics, such as temperament and personality. The intelligence of the executive is merely one of several factors in his composite behavior pattern, as suggested in the chapters (2 to 6) on adjustment patterns.

Executives who decide to use psychological tests for hiring often want to take the tests themselves. The experience of the writer has been that, if the executive interested in the tests happens to make the highest score of all the employees, he then believes that the tests are good. The executives who happen to score lower than one or two employees lost interest in the use of tests. Such an attitude is wholly unscientific and unsound. If the executive could only realize that the purpose of the tests is to hire employees of a behavior pattern type requiring qualities of a different nature from his own, he might not be so easily

elated or offended over the results of the test procedure.

One of the most frequent criticisms of psychological tests is that they are unfair to the nervous applicants. It is claimed that a person may be in an unusual mood. His digestion may be bad or he may be in a state of worry and therefore not do justice to himself. Experience indicates that very few persons are emotionally disturbed while taking the tests administered by an experienced examiner. Tests may frighten employees and applicants when they are given without the necessary preliminary explanation of their limitations and values. However, when tests are properly handled, very few applicants object to taking them. A person of an especially timid or psychoneurotic nature may object, but such applicants are in a decided minority. In many situations it is not essential to tell the applicant that he is about to take a psychological test. It is better to ask him whether he objects to taking a short examination of his general fund of information or speed in figuring.

In order to ascertain workers' attitudes toward employment tests, 575 employees in eight organizations were polled by means of an anonymous questionnaire. The evidence suggests that workers feel that personnel selection tests are helpful rather than harmful. Only one out of five workers stated that he did not like to take employment tests. Over half of those quizzed felt that they were more satisfied with their jobs when they had been placed there by tests. Only four per cent were less satisfied. Most workers reported that they felt more secure in their jobs after they had been selected by tests. Having to take a test in order to gain employment does not deter seven out of ten workers from going after a job. Two out of three declared that tests are beneficial to both the employer and the employee.[20]

Employees who have been tested should

not be given their scores. Such results should be kept in the personal file of a major executive of the firm. As previously stated, if a person has a certain accomplishment level of intelligence, his success and advancement may depend upon factors which are not measured by the tests. When an employee or lower-rank executive is given his own test score and he knows how he compares with other members of the organization, he assumes that those employees who happen to be a few points above or below him are also above or below him in ability or chances for promotion. No tests are available that measure so fine a degree of differentiation. Their chief value is that of classifying individuals into broad or general groups.

Good scholastic records and high scores on intelligence tests are an indication of ability to do the kind of learning that requires some grasp of abstractions. However, ability to learn certain important business operations does not correlate with intelligence tests. The best example of this is stenographic ability. Many students of superior mental capacity make low marks in shorthand, and many who make high marks in shorthand have relatively low intelligence test scores.[21] This simply means that individual companies who use intelligence tests for hiring should supplement them with specific ability and skill tests.

Thus far, personnel men have not been able to obtain tests that measure character traits such as honesty in handling the employer's funds. Obviously, character as well as intelligence and personality must be considered in hiring cashiers, bank tellers, and salesmen. Experiments have been conducted with tests of character. Some people are high in intelligence but of unreliable character. In general, however, we do find that most socially desirable traits go together. People of high intelligence tend to be of good character and are better-looking, easier to get along with, and healthier. However, a high rating in intelligence does

not prove that a given individual will be honest in his business relations, for these correlations are not high. It merely indicates that the chances, statistically speaking, are somewhat greater that he is of good character than that he is not. Some of the first character tests dealt with school situations.

Children in school have been tested in deceit by giving them an examination, collecting the papers, making copies of each child's answers, returning each child's papers to the child, giving each a key to the correct answers, and asking each child to score his own paper. The child's own scoring was then compared with the office copies of the scores and definite discrepancies between the two scorings were noted. It was found that some children would correct their own papers while scoring them: some would put dots over the letter "i" when it was a part of the test, others would cross the letter "t," others would write in extra words, and the worst offenders would erase writings in ink and write in the correct answer in pencil. In most of these tests, the amount of dishonesty varied with the degree of motivation. When children were impressed with the tremendous importance of making a high score, they cheated far more than when they were allowed to think that a high score in the examination was of no importance. This is in harmony with the businessman's experience. The executive who wishes to hire an employee for a position where, if he chooses, he can manipulate the company's finances for his own benefit does well when he selects a man who lives within his income and saves some money rather than a man who plays the stock market or happens to have a "social climber" for a wife. Our dishonesty tends to increase as the pressure for it increases.[22]

At present, tests are not available that tell the businessman whether an applicant is honest or dishonest. Honesty, like all character traits, is of a complex nature. It varies with the situation. A man may be

1st Trial _____
2nd Trial _____
3rd Trial _____
4th Trial _____
5th Trial _____

An example of a character test. Close your eyes. Move a pencil around the square three times without touching the paper. With eyes still closed, try to put a dot in each circle. Do this for each of five trials. You must put a dot in each of the five circles on each trial in order to have a plus score for any one trial. Refer to the Appendix for the answer. *(Adapted from V. M. Cady, "The Estimation of Juvenile Incorrigibility," **Journal of Delinquency**, Monograph No. 2, April 1923).*

scrupulously honest about paying his gambling debts and exceedingly lax about paying his room rent. One test will not measure any one character trait, because character traits are specific in their applications to situations. Knowing whether a person will cheat in an examination does not tell us whether he will steal money. A "battery" or number of tests is needed to measure any one character trait, such as aggressiveness, although Moore and Gilliland got excellent results with an eye-control test. To use this test, select ten persons who are very aggressive and ten who are not aggressive. Let each applicant, while he adds simple numbers and gives the answers aloud, face the examiner and look him in the eye. For example: ask the applicant to begin with 38, add 11 to it, and continue to add 11 to each sum, looking you in the eye meanwhile, until you tell him to stop. Have him do this for three trials of one minute each. Count the number of times he shifts his eyes from yours. In the Moore and Gilliland experiment, twenty-six persons were tested. Thirteen were known to be

very aggressive, and thirteen to be lacking in aggressiveness. The average number of eye-movements for the aggressive persons was .5, the average number for the nonaggressive persons was 5.5.[23]

All tests are limited by the fact that they give a group prediction rather than a prediction for a specific individual. A test that has high positive predictive value indicates that anyone who scores high in the test tends to be high in the trait with which the test correlates. The high score means that, of one hundred persons who score high in the test, a certain percentage will also be high in the correlating trait.* If an employer hires a large number of employees for a specific job, as one does in life insurance selling or factory operations of large standard process shops, a set of psychological tests should be developed for the hiring of applicants; but most American business concerns do not have a large number of employees who do the same work. They have a few stenographers, several bookkeepers, a janitor, an office boy or two, and a larger number of miscellaneous

* We shall not discuss the meaning of negative coefficients of correlation here, but leave that for the statistician who wishes to have a thorough knowledge of tests. However, the last chapter of this book presents some of the factors involved in evaluating tests.

machine operators. Unless the firm employs about fifty persons on the same kind of operation, it is difficult and expensive to develop reliable psychological tests and standards. Even in the larger corporations, it is often arduous to invent profitable tests for more than one or two classes of employees.

Psychologists recognize this limitation of tests and govern their decisions accordingly; but the novice who uses tests is apt to apply the prediction to specific individuals rather than to group relations. In general, no especially difficult technique is required to administer group psychological tests after they have been statistically treated; but to give them statistical interpretation requires more technical application than most businessmen care to give. Executives should obtain the services of a trained tester if they wish to have any worthwhile results from psychological tests for hiring purposes. This is one reason why tests have been much discussed in business publications but have been used relatively little. Another reason is that tests do not measure the will to work, a trait which is often more important to the executive than the capacity to work.

In conclusion, we can say that testing does not supplant, but supplements, other steps in hiring. Common sense in the use of tests in industry has been summarized in regard to the more common errors, which are: (1) taking over completely test batteries that have been used successfully in other organizations, (2) thinking that anyone can administer tests, (3) not interpreting test results in the light of the whole situation, and (4) expecting too much from tests. Tests may make definite contributions, however, as: (1) a check on educational background, (2) a check on reported occupational experience, (3) a means of comparing the applicant with workers already employed, (4) an indication of particular abilities, and (5) a device offering some clues to temperament and personality characteristics.[24]

David W. Cook has listed the kinds of questions that management must answer before undertaking a testing program:

First:—Does top management really want such a program? Have you a *sincere desire* to put testing in the personnel program or are you merely trying to "keep up with the Joneses?"

Second:—Does your anticipated program fit in with your present personnel policies? For example, if it is your present policy to hire only friends and relatives of your employees, you may find that a testing program will conflict with it. Sometimes your brother-in-law shouldn't be given a job—are you able and willing to go along with such decisions?

Third:—Are you willing to provide the space, the equipment, and the salary of a director? Such space and equipment should be adequate to carry on the testing under controlled conditions.

If you can answer all of these questions satisfactorily—if you are really in earnest—then you are ready to plan a testing program; and in planning the program, here are some rules which you will find it helpful to follow:

1. Get a qualified director; give him cooperation and a free rein.

2. Enlist the support of your union if there is one. Employees worry about new things and very often ask for information from union stewards rather than from their supervisors. It is only right that the union officials should be informed of the program.

3. Validate the tests; that is, make some scientific study to prove that there is a positive relationship between test scores and job success. Your test director will take care of this matter.

4. Accept tests with their limitations. Don't expect perfection in the results. Remember that all testing can hope to accomplish is to raise your batting average in selecting good employees.[25]

The competent personnel man who uses tests also systematically improves his interviewing practices, evaluates the items on the application blank, and checks his appraisals by means of work histories and all available objective data. Truly to succeed, a personnel testing program must include the development of improved supervisory and labor union relations as well as be sound scientifically.

Acknowledgments and References

1. Joseph Tiffin, *Industrial Psychology*, 2nd ed., Prentice-Hall, Inc., New York, 1947, pp. 46 ff.

2. A. G. Wesman, "What Is an Aptitude?" *Test Service Bulletin*, The Psychological Corporation, August 1948.

3. J. E. Bell, *Projective Techniques*, Longmans, Green and Company, Inc., New York, 1948.

4. See William E. Henry's article, "The Business Executive—A Study in the Psychodynamics of a Social Role," *The American Journal of Sociology*, January 1949. Also, "What Makes a Good Executive?" *Business Week*, July 17, 1948, p. 24.

5. See William R. Spriegel and Alfred G. Dale, "Trends in Personnel Selection and Induction," *Personnel*, American Management Association, November 1953, pp. 169–175.

6. A catalog or descriptive literature about personnel tests can be obtained from the publishers by making such a request on company letterhead, signed by one of the executives. Typically, the test catalog will also state any purchase restrictions, and the price of the various test forms. Some of the major test publishers in the United States are listed below:
    California Test Bureau, 5916 Hollywood Boulevard, Los Angeles 28, Calif.
    Cooperative Test Division, Educational Testing Service, Princeton, N.J.
    Houghton Mifflin Company, 2 Park Street, Boston 7, Mass.
    Industrial Psychology, Inc., Box 6056, Tucson 6, Ariz.
    Institute for Personality and Ability Testing, 1608 Coronado Drive, Champaign, Ill.
    Psychological Corporation, 522 Fifth Avenue, New York 18, N.Y.
    Science Research Associates, Inc., 57 West Grand Avenue, Chicago 10, Ill.
    United States Employment Service, Washington, D.C.
    World Book Company, 313 Park Hill Avenue, Yonkers 5, N.Y.

7. "New Aptitude Tests at USES," *Industrial Relations*, April 1948, p. 34.

8. Guy W. Wadsworth, Jr., "Hidden Abilities of Clerical Workers," *Office Management Series No. 88*, American Management Association, 1939; and Herbert Moore, "Experience with Employment Tests," *Studies in Personnel Policy*, No. 32 (March 11, 1941), National Industrial Conference Board.

9. H. G. Martin, "Locating the Troublemaker with the Guilford-Martin Personnel Inventory," *Journal of Applied Psychology*, American Psychological Association, Inc., December 1944, p. 465.

10. From Industrial Psychology, Inc., Box 6056, Tucson 6, Arizona, 1954.

11. Albert Ellis and Herbert S. Conrad, "The Validity of Personality Inventories in Military Practice," *Psychological Bulletin*, September 1948, p. 421.

12. Guy W. Wadsworth, Jr., *op. cit.*

13. "Testing for Talent," *Fortune*, January 1941, p. 96.

14. *Loc. cit.*

15. Guy W. Wadsworth, Jr., *op. cit.*

16. H. R. DeSilva, R. G. Claffin, and W. J. Simon, "Making Safer Bus Drivers," *Transit Journal*, November 1938, pp. 1–3.

17. Charles A. Drake, "Testing for Accident-Proneness," a paper presented before the American Association of Applied and Professional Psychology, University of Minnesota, August 31, 1937.

18. Eleroy L. Stromberg, "Testing Programs Draw Better Applicants," *Personnel Psychology*, Spring 1948.

19. "Hidden Abilities of Clerical Workers," *Office Management Series No. 88*, American Management Association, New York, 1939, p. 8. See also "Supervisory Selection Programs," *Personnel*, September 1955, p. 113.

20. For further information, see Raymond H. Van Zelst, Otto J. Kroh, and Willard A. Kerr, "Workers Attitudes Toward Employment Tests," *Personnel Psychology*, Autumn 1951, pp. 261–271.

21. Raymond J. Worley, "Prognosis in Shorthand," *The Journal of Business Education*, September 1931.

22. T. H. Howells, "Factors Influencing Honesty," *Journal of Social Psychology*, Vol. 9 (1938), pp. 97–102.

23. H. T. Moore and A. R. Gilliland, "The Measurement of Aggressiveness," *Journal of Applied Psychology*, American Psychological Association, Inc., Vol. 5 (1921), pp. 97 ff.

24. F. H. Kirkpatrick, "Common Sense About Tests," *Personnel Journal*, Vol. 21 (1943), pp. 277–281.

25. David W. Cook, "Psychology Challenges Industry," *Personnel Series No. 107*, American Management Association, 1947.

PROJECTS

1. Assume that all the employees of a large bank are to be given several psychological tests. Outline the complete plan of procedure for the administration and use of these tests.

2. A sales manager asks you to select some psychological tests for hiring salesmen. Outline the main steps in the procedure you would follow in attempting to give him what he wants.

3. Intelligence test results are sometimes expressed in terms of IQ and sometimes in terms of percentiles. Which would you select in each of the following cases? Offer reasons for your choice. In the case of percentiles, define each group used as the base.
   a. For applicants for a night watchman's job.
   b. For admission to the graduate school of a university.
   c. For selecting soldiers for officers' training schools.
   d. For discovering mentally handicapped children.
   e. For rating stenographers in an office.

4. Try the Moore and Gilliland eye-control test on some friends and record the result. Evaluate the worth of the test for hiring purposes.

COLLATERAL READINGS

Bellows, Roger M., *Psychology of Personnel in Business and Industry,* Prentice-Hall, Inc., New York, 1954, Chapter 13.

Blum, Milton L., *Industrial Psychology and Its Social Foundations,* Harper & Brothers, New York, 1949, Chapters 16 and 17.

Ghiselli, Edwin E. and Clarence W. Brown, *Personnel and Industrial Psychology,* McGraw-Hill Book Company, Inc., New York, 1955, Chapter 7.

Harrell, Thomas Willard, *Industrial Psychology,* Rinehart & Company, Inc., New York, 1949.

Maier, Norman R. F., *Psychology in Industry,* Houghton Mifflin Company, Boston, 1955, Chapters 9 and 10.

CHAPTER SEVENTEEN

Merit ratings

The ambitious employee does not want managerial sermons or copybook maxims about how to become a big businessman. He needs definite and organized explanations regarding the actions he should take in order to deserve and achieve a feasible promotion. An inventory of personnel should be as important as a physical inventory.

The writer once had the temerity to suggest to the general manager of a firm having three thousand employees that he ought to have a promotion and training system. His answer was: "Training and promotion? Bosh! Nothing doing. Why, do you know what I did several years ago? I arranged for several training courses to be given, hired the teachers, rented a special room in the center of town, and put a slip in the pay envelopes telling the employees that anyone taking the course would be directly in line for promotion and higher pay. The whole proposition was free. I almost begged some of them to take the training. About 50 per cent of our men are foreigners or too old to take any courses, but I estimated that about 1,200 could benefit by courses I had planned. Of the 1,200 possibilities, how many do you suppose took the courses? Well, you couldn't guess. I'll tell you. Eight started and two finished."

The experience of this manager is not exceptional. Many employees will not exercise the self-discipline necessary to merit important positions. Most employees do not seek responsibility. Some must be persuaded to accept it. However, certain intelligent employees do desire promotion. When higher-grade applicants are hired they often ask: "Where does this job lead to?" The most frequent answer is one of evasion, such as, "You do your work well and keep your eyes open and you'll be promoted when you really deserve it."

A more truthful statement to the applicant would be: "We have no well-planned system of promotion or advancement. We have never taken the trouble to study our employees and to explain how they can make themselves worth more to us. If you work for us and make good, it may be that in time we shall have an opening somewhere in the organization where we can use you. Of course, someone may have to die or leave before you can be promoted, but if you live long enough and work hard enough, you may get there. On the other hand, someone else may appeal more to us than you do, and then the other fellow will get the promotion. We think we know who the good men in our company are, but we don't always know, so you must make a good impression on someone farther up. You must be able to sell us your ability as well as do good work."

Most employees recognize this situation and, even though they are not decidedly ambitious, they would like to know how well they do their work and what management thinks of them. That is one reason why a salary increase is so keenly desired by many employees—it is a token of management's esteem for the employee. Granted that most employees do want more money for their economic needs, they also want more money as a means of satisfying certain psychological needs. That is why surveys of employee morale often reveal that a very high percentage would like to find out answers to the question, "How am I doing?" Of course they want more than a report of the quantitative variety—they want to have the benefits of an interview with a responsible executive who will discuss the employee's potentials and work habits in a friendly, constructive spirit. Many managements, too, would like to do this for each employee. As a means of satisfying these and other needs, merit ratings have been developed.

Merit ratings, to a large extent, must depend upon personal estimates because many important traits of employees cannot be measured by objective tests. Rating scales must be used. *A rating scale is a systematic method of estimating character or personality traits.* It is not a measuring device but only a standardized means of communicating and reporting opinions about individuals.

The benefits of a rating scale

1. Executives are prone to classify all employees into two large groups: the "good" and the "no-good." The executive may call the "no-good" group "passable," "tolerable," or "just satisfactory," depending upon the mood he is in at the time. Obviously, employees are neither wholly good nor wholly bad, but each has some traits to a high degree and others to a low degree. The use of a rating scale compels the executive to analyze his employees and to obtain a more accurate picture of each person under his supervision.

2. A rating scale also compels an executive to analyze his employees at regular intervals. Many an executive walks by some of his employees every working day for years and never thinks of their specific characteristics. If an employee commits a serious error or refuses to join a labor union, the executive may then hear of the matter and gauge the employee by a single dramatic incident. In most cases, the dramatic incident is an isolated defect of the employee's conduct, because his good qualities are taken for granted. Too many executives are negative-minded toward their employees. They can recite their weaknesses or failures, but are unable to list their positive points.

3. The periodical use of a rating scale discovers the good men sooner and makes them available for the company. These men can be given special training, extra compensation, executive recognition, or opportunities for additional responsibilities or duties.

4. The executive can check or verify his own analyses of employees. If he should rate a man high one month and then rate him low six months later, the cause should be known. Perhaps a trivial incident has changed the estimate of the executive, or he may not really know the employee well enough to rate him. Having a record of his estimates of employees will enable the rater to ascertain his ability to analyze others. His ratings can be compared with those of other executives and his tendencies toward high or low ratings can be discovered. If an executive is a poor judge of human behavior, the rating scale will cause him to realize his peculiarity.

5. Just as the rating scale enables the executive to improve his ability to analyze the employee, so the employee also learns the particular qualities he should develop or eliminate. Few employees know their own strong and weak characteristics. They do not improve themselves, because the management does not tell them what to improve or how to do it. The "Success" books and pep lectures are too general or too inspirational to enable the employees to make direct and tangible applications to their own jobs.

Kinds of rating scales

Many different rating scales have been invented, but most of those in current use can be classified into five basic types:

1. RANKING: The rater is asked to list employees in rank order from "best" at the head of the list to "poorest" at the bottom of the list, in regard to some defined characteristics. This method is seldom practiced today.

2. MAN-TO-MAN COMPARISONS (paired comparisons): This method is similar to the first but applied to a group. By this, the individual members of groups are compared to each other, one at a time. This technique was developed during World War I and was used by the army at that time to assess officer ability. It is extremely laborious and time consuming. Hence, it is rarely used today.

3. FORCED CHOICE RATING: This device usually sets up five statements in a section and the rater is requested to check two in each section that best describe the individual. Raters do not like this method, for it is often difficult for them to know when they are rating a person favorably.

4. GRAPHIC RATING SCALES: This is the most widely used and abused technique. Series of traits or characteristics important in assessing employee performance are listed. Each listing is divided into degrees.

For example, "co-operative" might be divided into degrees such as: "always co-operative," "usually co-operative," "often co-operative," "seldom co-operative," "never co-operative." Thus, in effect, a quantitative measuring scale is provided for each trait.

5. BEHAVIOR CHECK LIST: Experimentation with this form has been going on during recent years. The check list utilizes definitive statements felt to be typical of poor, average and good performance. The rater is instructed to check whether the person being rated does them or how well he does them.[1] One important advantage of this form is that it gives the rater and ratee helpful ideas to talk about in an interview. This particular variety of rating type was developed for the Army in World War II. One of its purposes was to overcome bias by means of a system that would compel the rater to give descriptions of a person's performance without being able to know how the final rating would turn out. Reign Bittner, who participated in the development of this type of rating form, has explained it further:

It was believed that errors resulting from interpretations of trait names and points on the trait scales could be pared to the bone by not using trait scales. Instead, descriptions of behavior commonly used in describing performance on the job should be used.

Let us see what kind of merit rating procedure resulted from these ideas. A number of groups of four statements descriptive of supervisors were set up, like the following:
1. Avoids responsibility.
2. Inspires pride in the organization.
3. Lacks sense of humor.
4. Offers suggestions.
The rater was then asked to choose from each group of four statements the one that was most descriptive of the person to be rated and the one that was least descriptive.

Now two of the statements are favorable to the person and two of them unfavorable. The two favorable statements look equally attractive to the rater and the two unfavorable look equally unattractive. At least they would if they had been paired on the basis of research. The important point is that only one of the fav-

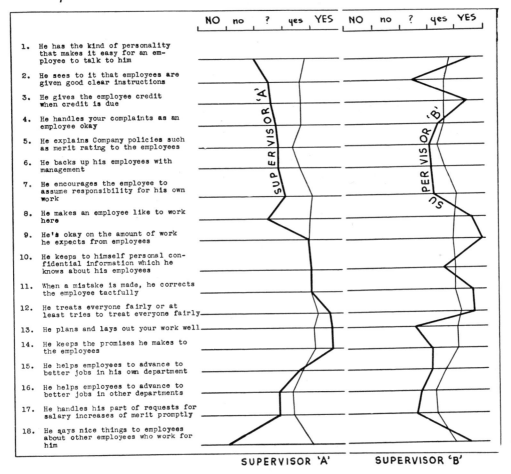

	NO	no	?	yes	YES	NO	no	?	yes	YES

1. He has the kind of personality that makes it easy for an employee to talk to him

2. He sees to it that employees are given good clear instructions

3. He gives the employee credit when credit is due

4. He handles your complaints as an employee okay

5. He explains Company policies such as merit rating to the employees

6. He backs up his employees with management

7. He encourages the employee to assume responsibility for his own work

8. He makes an employee like to work here

9. He's okay on the amount of work he expects from employees

10. He keeps to himself personal confidential information which he knows about his employees

11. When a mistake is made, he corrects the employee tactfully

12. He treats everyone fairly or at least tries to treat everyone fairly

13. He plans and lays out your work well

14. He keeps the promises he makes to the employees

15. He helps employees to advance to better jobs in his own department

16. He helps employees to advance to better jobs in other departments

17. He handles his part of requests for salary increases of merit promptly

18. He says nice things to employees about other employees who work for him

SUPERVISOR 'A'   SUPERVISOR 'B'

Personality patterns of two supervisors are shown in the two profiles for supervisors A and B.—When a training program for supervisors was organized, the supervisors were asked to choose the traits on which they would like to be rated by their own employees. The supervisors, in the course of discussion, selected the list of eighteen traits shown above.— Each supervisor's employees rated him without revealing their identities. The ratings were given to the psychologist in charge of the ratings and training sessions. He calculated the average numerical rating for all supervisors. See the thin vertical line. The average rating on each trait for each supervisor was also computed and plotted on the above scale. See the heavy line.

When the profile for the average rating of individual supervisor A, heavy line on left of chart, was compared with the average for all the supervisors, thin line, it was found that A's profile was typical of the technically well trained but impersonal supervisor, such as a cold unresponsive engineer or accountant. Supervisor B, on the other hand, had a profile characteristic of the warm, friendly, but overly lenient supervisor. His employees criticized him for not requiring them to do as much work as they could do with ease.—The training sessions dealt with techniques of supervision but also included suggestions concerning the personality development, or adjustment pattern, of the individual supervisor.

orable statements counts for the person and only one of the unfavorable ones counts against him. But the rater does not know which these are because the scoring key is not revealed to him. So he is forced to decide solely on the basis of how *he* describes the man. If he is biased, he cannot mark the one that will reflect his bias because he does not know which one

that is. He does not have to wrestle with trait names or the problem of how many points to give because he is merely asked to choose which of four rather dissimilar statements best or least describes the person.

The trick, of course, is to set up these groups of four statements, and much research must go over the dam before this is achieved. . . .

The efficiency of this type of rating scale was compared with the results obtained with two different trait rating scales, a ranking system, and a system involving a combination of trait scales and a performance check list. The results showed that this new type yielded more accurate ratings than any of the others.

What are the prospects for using this type of rating scale in industry? My feeling is that it is a coming thing, but it has not yet arrived. There are several reasons for my attitude. In the first place, this rating scale will work only when the method of scoring the rater's evaluations is kept secret, and I am not at all sure that industry is ready to do this. It would certainly take a real job of selling to convince the rater and labor unions that this was either wise or necessary. In the second place, the research necessary to develop the rating scale will prove a barrier for many companies, especially if they are small. Perhaps a general scale that will apply to supervisors wherever you find them will eventually be developed, but at the present time it is believed that each organization must have one tailor-made to its own measure. Finally, the techniques are so new that there are few people qualified to conduct this research.[2]

Of the 130 employee rating plans reviewed in a recent study, 85 per cent of the companies reported that they employed graphic-rating techniques, 9 per cent the check-list, 2 per cent forced-choice, and 1 per cent used either man-to-man comparisons or ranking.

The need for further research in the development of this kind of scale is illustrated by the finding that when 900 behavior items like "Can't take suggestions" and "Resents criticism" were used in rating by a group of Army officers, 600 of them had to be discarded because they were not observable, not universally applicable, or both.

A survey of 75 companies ranging in size from 130 to 196,000 workers was made to determine how rating scales were actually being used. Among these companies, 130 plans were in operation. Some plants had more than one type in use. The companies reported[3] they used the scales for the following purposes:

	Companies reporting
In connection with merit increases	28
To tell employees where they stand	27
To determine training needs	23
To determine promotability	21
To evaluate employees	18
To determine advisability of transfer	13
To determine layoff or recall	7
To improve departmental efficiency	7
To determine who should be demoted	7
To determine disciplinary action	6
At the end of probationary period	6
To determine specific talents	4
To validate psychological tests	3
To assure proper placement	2
Miscellaneous	4

The choice of form to be used should be determined by the main purpose of the rating system. Most purposes tend to fall into one of four main classes:

1. To obtain a measure or estimate of job performance for administrative use, as in the case of the Lincoln Electric Company's "Bonus Merit Rating Scoring System" (see pages 332 and 333). A general trait scale is usually used for such purposes. When the main purpose of the rating is for administrative use rather than training or interviewing, discussion of four or five general traits is sufficient. As stated by Bittner:

1. In a study of a 12-trait rating scale applied to over 1,100 men in industry, a factor analysis showed that only two traits were really being measured. These were called "ability to do present job" and "quality of performance on the job." This result was due to the great overlapping or inability of the raters to distinguish between the traits.

2. In a study of a 10-trait rating scale applied to 2,000 Army officers, factor analysis revealed that only three traits were being measured—namely, "sense of duty," "physical and mental endurance and ability," and "leadership." It was also found that "ability to obtain results" correlated .90 with the total score on the 10 traits, and four of the 10 traits predicted the total score almost perfectly with a correlation of .97.

3. In another study of a 12-trait rating scale applied to Army Air Force officers, factor analysis showed that only four traits were being measured—namely, "sense of duty," "physical and mental stability and endurance," "leadership," and "judgment and common sense."

4. In developing a new Army rating scale, 900 behavior items—statements like "can't take suggestions," "resents criticism"—were rated by a group of officers on observability and universality, and it was necessary to throw out 600 of them as being not observable, not universally applicable, or both.

The import of these and similar studies is that only a few traits will be included in the rating scale if the three criteria—observability, universality, and distinguishability—are observed in selecting them. Add more if you like, but you end up with essentially the same result (and often misleading results) at the cost of considerably more effort. A few companies have recognized this and applied it in their rating procedure. At least one company I know rates on only two traits—"ability to do present job" and "promotability."[4]

2. To select employees for promotion, transfer, or layoff. The ranking method is most commonly used.

3. To provide a basis for a training program, as exemplified by the "Employees' Ratings of Their Supervisor" (see page 329). In this case, each employee rated his supervisory superiors. The employees' ratings of each supervisor were charted to show whether he was above or below the average for all supervisors of the company. The results of the ratings on all traits were not given in any one training session. To stimulate the supervisors, the results for trait number one were given in the first session, and so on to the end of the training course of eighteen sessions.

In another company, study of the 2,000 ratings prepared in one year for 308 employees revealed the following list of weaknesses:

126 were weakest on dependability.
 81 were weakest on coöperativeness.
 76 were weakest on industry.
 10 were weakest in accuracy.
  8 were weakest on attention to pertinent detail.
  7 were weakest on accuracy of judgments and decisions.[5]

The management decided that these employees were in need of development in regard to their attitudes, and a training course was set up for that purpose.

4. To provide a basis for a constructive interview with the employee. Some kind of behavior check list or other type that provides a wide variety of specific descriptive phrases is most helpful.

The chief value of ratings which are made on specific characteristics rather than general behavior is that they enable the executive to give the employee definite suggestions as to what he should or should not do. To tell an employee that he should improve his appearance is not so effective as to tell him that he should shave more frequently or press his clothes regularly. To tell him that he should be more industrious is not so effective as to ask him to do less "visiting" in the office or to come to work on time. When abstractions are rated and the supervisory executive wishes to have an intimate advisory talk with a subordinate, he usually preaches a sermon. However, if he discusses definite items with the employee, he lets him know just exactly what he should do to improve his chances for promotion.

General principles for using and making ratings

Some of the principles stated may appear to be dogmatic and academic; but experience in the use of ratings and a desire to avoid technical dissertations warrant the brevity of the statements.

1. THE PURPOSE OF RATINGS IS CONSTRUCTIVE RATHER THAN CRITICAL SO FAR AS THE EMPLOYEE IS CONCERNED. Many executives who use ratings for the first time give the employees the impression that they are being spied upon. Employees do not like to be analyzed merely for the benefit of the employer. They resent being catalogued. They do not want to be analyzed and then labeled and forgotten until the company needs a person of their classification. Employees suspect that ratings are merely a device for getting rid of those who are not up to the required standard of efficiency. Therefore, rating scales should not be ap-

BONUS MERIT RATING SCORING SYSTEM

Incentive pay—One's share in the incentive pay depends upon his wages in the twelve months prior to November 1st and a merit rating given each employee. Wages depend upon the base rate of one's job, the individual's effort on the job, and the hours worked. Merit rating applies equally on all individuals so that it is possible for a trucker to have as high a rating as a highly skilled diemaker.

There are four factors that go to make up this rating:

    A. Job Knowledge and Performance
    B. The Quality of Work Done
    C. The Quantity of Work Done
    D. Cooperation

The rating is carefully and separately done by the men in four different departments: Foreman, Inspection, Cost Reduction, and Production. Four separate lists are made for each department and are given out for grading. Points are given to each individual from 8 to 42, the average grade being 25. This is done by using the attached rating sheet. After these lists are graded, each is returned to the head of the Personnel Department. It is imperative to have a fair comparison between departments so point scores must be reduced to a comparable basis and still not change the relative position of individuals within the group. To do this, the points for each factor are totalled and divided by the number of employees. If this average comes out less than 25, an equal number of points will be added to each person's score. If the average is over 25, an equal number of points will be subtracted from each individual to bring the average number of points to 25. An example will show how this does not change the relative position of an individual within the group.

| | DEPARTMENT Y | |
Individual	*Grade as Received*	*Grade as Corrected*
A	22	23
B	23	24
C	24	25
D	24	25
E	25	26
F	26	27
	6)144	6)150
	24	25

Then the four grades for each individual are totalled, and thus we have possible scores from 32 to 168 points with 100 points being average. For the factory, these grades are checked separately by Messrs. Giles, Steingass, and Kneen for accuracy and fairness.

H. F. Kneen

Job Knowledge and Performance	Quality of Work	Quantity of Work	Coöperation
Supervision rates:	Inspection rates:	Production rates:	Time Study rates:
Experience, training, ability, judgment, versatility, initiative, personal requirements.	Workmanship, accuracy, dependability, spoilage, scrap.	Output, effort, helpfulness in maintaining production, attendance, tardiness.	Willingness to accept changes, attitude, suggestions, cost consciousness.
Little experience, requires detailed instruction and much supervision. 8 9 10 11 12	Only gets by, bears watching, careless, often makes mistakes. 8 9 10 11 12	Low production, slow worker, too often absent. 8 9 10 11 12	Fails to cooperate, unwilling to accept changes. 8 9 10 11 12
Requires additional experience and training, regularly requires supervision. 13 14 15 16 17	Acceptable, work usually meets specification, small amount of spoilage. 13 14 15 16 17	Fair production, below par, wastes time, away from job more than necessary, fair attendance. 13 14 15 16 17	Cooperates passively, reluctant to change, needs urging. 13 14 15 16 17
Informed on job, needs some assistance and supervision. 18 19 20 21 22	Work meets specifications, occasional mistakes. 18 19 20 21 22	Fair speed, regular production, steady worker, occasionally absent. 18 19 20 21 22	Cooperates, accepts changes, follows instructions. 18 19 20 21 22
AVR.— Good working knowledge on job, well rounded experience, requires little supervision. 23 24 25 26 27	Good quality, does good job most of the time, seldom makes mistakes. 23 24 25 26 27	Speed and production consistently good, helpful, seldom absent. 23 24 25 26 27	Willing to accept changes and try out new ideas. 23 24 25 26 27
Considerable knowledge, well experienced and trained, only needs direction. 28 29 30 31 32	High quality, usually does excellent job, rejects rare. 28 29 30 31 32	Fast, high production, efficient worker, high effort, very helpful, rarely absent. 28 29 30 31 32	Cooperates actively on changes, good teamworker. 28 29 30 31 32
Expert on job, self starter, needs practically no supervision. 33 34 35 36 37	Consistently does good work, excellent quality, never makes scrap. 33 34 35 36 37	Top output, applies exceptional effort, extremely helpful, always on job. 33 34 35 36 37	Enthusiastic about changes, ready to try new ideas. 33 34 35 36 37
Same as above, but requires no supervision, helps others. 38 39 40 41 42	Always does job perfectly. 38 39 40 41 42	As above, but helps eliminate work above call of duty. 38 39 40 41 42	As above, but submits many good ideas on own initiative. 38 39 40 41 42

TOTAL ....

333

plied in any organization unless the employees have had an adequate explanation of the purposes of the ratings. Employees should be told that the company wishes to help each one to help himself; that sermons are not to be preached, but rather that the management wants to give the employees who desire it definite help and counsel in obtaining a promotion through merit.

If the executives can rate the employees without their knowledge, well and good. However, very few companies can conduct systematic ratings without the knowledge of the employees, and, if it is not done openly, the employees will soon spread rumors of spies and detectives having been hired to catch them in any negligences or petty infractions of rules. The better plan for the management is to put all the cards on the employees' table, explain the ratings, their constructive purpose, and then rate only those employees who wish to be rated.

2. HAVE A JOINT COMMITTEE DEVELOP THE RATING PLAN. Many companies that operate successful rating systems have developed the plan through a committee which uses the advice of executives, supervisors, and employees. As reported in *Business Week*:

A cardinal feature of all plans, quoted again and again, is that "the employee must understand and approve of what is being done." And, in a growing number of such efforts, the labor unions are offering their help.

Summing up the results of such plans, administrators seem agreed that certain results are found in the following ways:

a. Guesswork and doubt are removed in raising or reducing compensation. If a man is refused a raise, there is a definite reason which can be proved to him. And, if he is entitled to more money, he knows how to prove it.

b. Careful judgment of each man's ability, habits, and adaptability often indicates a weak point which can be corrected. Thus his right to advancement in position and pay can be more easily determined and gratified.

c. The rate of "turnover" of misplaced workers is greatly lowered.

d. Grievances resulting from unfair differentials are reduced, and the settlement of such complaints is greatly aided.

e. The jobs of the foremen and supervisors are made easier, as they learn to interpret the evaluation and rating method to the employee.

f. If an accurate and fair means of judging the higher-salaried employees can be worked out, the charges of some classes that "executives are paid too much" can be answered without guesswork. Further, complaints from some salaried people about too loose a system of evaluation and payment can be ended.[6]

A more favorable attitude on the part of employees toward a rating system can be fostered by using a positive and pleasing title for it, such as "Employee Progress Review" or "Employee Development Plan."

Rightly used, the development of a rating system can be made the basis of an extensive company educational program.[7] When employees do not participate in management's rating and educational plans, the employees do not respond wholeheartedly to management's well-meant efforts. The violation of this basic principle explains why the manager mentioned in the beginning of this chapter failed to get a worth-while response to his new training courses.

3. THE TRAITS TO BE RATED SHOULD BE OBJECTIVE RATHER THAN SUBJECTIVE. Most experienced users of rating would prefer, for example, "Moral Conduct" to "Moral Attitude" as a rating item. Generally, traits for which we would normally have some external or objective evidence are the ones most likely to be judged with good chances for reliability. Rating an individual on his ideas or attitudes generally is likely to produce appraisals of dubious value.

4. RATINGS SHOULD BE BASED UPON PAST ACCOMPLISHMENTS RATHER THAN UPON WHAT THE INDIVIDUAL MAY BE ABLE TO DO IN THE FUTURE. It is important to know what a person may be able to do, but we must judge the future by the past. When necessary to make predictions concerning the future possibilities of an employee, it is well to do

it on the basis of all the known information concerning the employee—ratings, years of service, production, age, attitude toward the proposed new job, and so on. In large organizations it is also well to have rating scales adapted to the various kinds of workers. In most firms it is necessary to have four different rating forms—one for the factory workers, one for the executives, one for the salesmen, and one for the office workers.

5. ONLY THOSE WHO KNOW THE EMPLOYEE SHOULD RATE HIM. It may sound absurd to specify that strangers to the individual should not rate him, and yet, in many firms, it is difficult to find persons in executive positions who know all the employees of large departments. If necessary, ratings may be made by supervisors or even by fellow employees. In a department store, the rating made by a floorman is apt to be more accurate than that made by a buyer. A buyer has so little direct contact with the sales clerk that he does not know him from every angle. Teachers are often asked to rate students or former students, but their ratings should be limited to the classroom contacts and should not include the many outside activities. When a teacher has a large class, he seldom becomes acquainted with the students. Occasionally he does have direct associations with a student in his home or on the athletic field, and then the classroom estimate may be modified very decidedly. The ratings made by ministers and doctors have little value, because they know people under limited conditions only. Few of us conduct ourselves normally when in the presence of preachers and physicians.

Ronald Taft reviewed the literature concerning the ability of people to judge others and described five different types of methods of measuring this ability. He found that the following characteristics appear to be related to the ability of a person to judge the personality characteristics of others:

High intelligence and academic ability. This is positively related to ability to determine another's characteristics analytically, but not to non-analytic ways of judging. Probably perception and attitude are more important in determining the latter than abstract intelligence.

Emotional adjustment. The better adjusted person is the better judge.

Insight into one's own status. Evidently those who can rate themselves accurately on individual traits can also rate others fairly well.

Social orientation. Good judges of others have a greater social orientation than the poorer judges.

Social skill. The ability to predict how subjects will respond to opinion items is consistent with measures of social skill such as leadership, salesmanship, and popularity. This might also be due to projection on the part of the skilled people.

Apparently the ability to judge another's personality characteristics accurately depends on more than the possession of certain traits in the person judging. It is more than the right proportions of general intelligence to social intelligence to intuition that is needed. The judger needs, in addition, appropriate norms, such as a similar background, and he should be motivated to judge accurately and be free to do so.[8]

6. EMPLOYEES SHOULD BE DEALT WITH ON THE BASIS OF MORE THAN ONE PERSON'S RATINGS. No matter how impartial or intelligent the rater may be, he is apt to commit serious errors, because of the special conditions under which he deals with the ratee. The rater is also conditioned by his own childhood experiences and has certain unconscious prejudices that will influence his ratings in spite of his effort to be fair. To prevent unfair and erroneous estimates, it is necessary to have at least three persons rate each employee. If the specific behavior

form of rating scale is used by three or more raters, then only those items checked or underlined by two or more raters should be recorded for the employee. If only one rater attributes a trait to an employee, that trait should be disregarded, as it is not indicative of the group estimate.

7. RATINGS DO NOT TELL THE MANAGEMENT WHAT AN EMPLOYEE ACTUALLY IS OR DOES. They show what acquaintances think of the employee. However, in many situations, the attitude or estimate of the group is more important than what the person is or can do. If an applicant for a job gives people the impression that he is dishonest or incompetent, they will treat him according to their estimate of him rather than according to his actual qualities. When tests can be given the applicant or employee, it is better to do so than to use ratings, because ratings are a substitute for the measurement of qualities for which no tests now exist. In the course of time, scientific research may produce tests that will be more accurate and objective than our present recourse to group estimates.

8. THE "HALO ERROR" IS COMMON TO ALL RATINGS. The general impression of an individual markedly colors our evaluation of his specific traits. If a person impresses us favorably in a general way, or because of some specific quality that we know he possesses, or because of an outstanding experience with him, we then tend to invest his entire personality with a luster that causes us to overestimate his desirable traits and underestimate his undesirable characteristics. One executive was asked why he rated a certain employee so low in all traits. His answer was to the effect that he did not like people who have small mouths and the particular employee had a small mouth. Some previous experience caused small mouths to become associated with the undesirable kind of personality and this experience colored his estimates of people who

had that incidental trait. As we all know, if we like a person, we are apt to attribute all good traits to him. Conversely, if we dislike him, we tend to assign to him all negative traits.

The halo influence on graphic rating scales can be overcome to some extent if the rater will fill in the rating blanks for all employees by judging the employees on one trait at a time. For example, if twenty employees are to be rated on ten traits, the first trait on the scale being initiative, the judge should rate all twenty on initiative, and so on for each trait. It is natural for the executive to consider one man at a time rather than one trait at a time, but that procedure increases the halo effect. This danger also suggests that raters need systematic instruction before they make the ratings of their employees.[9]

9. THE ONE BEST RATING PLAN IS STILL TO BE INVENTED. When executives decide to use a merit rating plan, they naturally want the "one perfect plan." Unfortunately, no one system or form has as yet been proved to be valid or appropriate for all or even for many organizations.

The rating plan that is best for most companies is the one that most members of the organization will use constructively.

Thomas A. Ryan, after reviewing the various merit rating plans and finding them all deficient in some important respects, recommended the simple common-sense procedure shown on pages 338 and 339. This form is nothing essentially new, but it has certain sensible values:

It is an attempt to secure some of the advantages of a standardized rating technique without depending so heavily upon the assumptions required for the graphic scale-point method of evaluation.

The writer [Ryan] believes that this "Inventory of Personnel," though still having flaws which cannot be entirely eliminated, is more defensible than the graphic rating scale. It obtains an over-all estimate of the value of men in a job from the supervisor, which, in view of the halo effect, is all we can confidently expect of the graphic rating technique. It requires the supervisor to make only broad groupings, which, in the light of the known reliabilities of the graphic scale, are the only groupings justified. (If three groups are felt to be too broad, the same technique could be used with four or five categories instead of the three major groups illustrated on page [338].) The method obtains these broad groupings without resort to dubious point-rating scales.

The method also allows us to obtain useful information upon special traits without forcing the supervisor to rate all workers on each trait. He can thus designate those who show noticeable excellence or deficiency, without being asked to make ratings on these traits where no information is available.

Last, but by no means least, this procedure should reduce the amount of "paper work." Though the supervisor has to write names instead of making check marks, he is not overwhelmed with a rating-form for each man. One form can serve for all the men on a job or a related group of jobs, so long as sufficient space is provided for listing the names. At the same time, the supervisor is required to consider each man because the form requires that each man must be listed somewhere.[10]

The post-appraisal interview

Ratings should be used once they are gathered. If the company records the ratings on the personnel records of the employees, some benefits can be derived. When a promotion is to be made, the executives do not have to make snap judgments. Ratings should be filed in advance of any emergencies. But their greatest worth may be obtained through a friendly discussion of the ratings with each employee. This kind of post-appraisal interview is far more difficult than most people appreciate.

When the Industrial Relations Section, California Institute of Technology, had completed a total of 25 surveys in 18 different companies, covering over 50,000 employees, the Section formulated a number of conclusions based on all of its studies of employee opinion. One of these was that "Employees want to know from their supervisors how they are doing on the job and how they can improve." Supervisors will not do this task, which appears disagreeable to them at first, unless they have been properly trained and unless there is a planned procedure for rating employees and for discussing these ratings with them.[11]

Most post-appraisal interviews are conducted on the assumption that it is sufficient for the employee to be told, or asked, or otherwise persuaded to do better. Actually, a man will not change his behavior—except superficially, perhaps—until he has acquired objective insights into his own shortcomings. The post-appraisal interview is one of the most difficult of all interviews, but only a very few firms provide a guide or instruction for conducting it.

Most companies merely take it for granted that supervisors are equipped to handle this function and leave it up to them. This laissez faire attitude regarding coaching is in sharp contrast to the highly formal techniques and paperwork the same companies use in *appraising* the subordinate.

Spencer J. Hayden has described some of the current faulty practices and the more effective procedures, in part, as follows:

What do most of us do when we "coach" a subordinate after rating him? Well, usually we begin by calling him in for a special interview. (How did *you* feel the last time your boss scheduled such a meeting—anxious and on the defensive?)

Next, we "put him at ease" by rambling on about the weather, his kid's progress in school, and such. Then we pointedly compliment him on some minor matter. All of this is a prelude to getting down to the dirty work. (How did *you* feel when you were on the receiving end of this—were you fooled? Were you mentally preparing your defense?)

Then we lower the boom: tell him what's wrong, his "strengths and weaknesses," and what he ought to do to improve. (How did *you* feel when you got the works—cooperative on the surface but hurt underneath; confused, upset, resentful?) . . .

When someone tells you that you are doing wrong, he is really disapproving of you. There-

INVENTORY OF PERSONNEL

Department .... (This should be a single job or group of
Jobs .... similar, related jobs. Jobs requiring unrelated skills or training should be con-
sidered independently.)

I. All-round Value

1. *Outstanding Men:* List names of the men who are doing an exceptionally good job,
   and whose all-round value to the department is very high. Consider their present
   ability and skill, not what you think they might develop later. Men placed in this
   group should be in about the top 10 per cent of men in this line of work *anywhere,*
   and not only in this shop. If you are doubtful about any man's belonging in this
   group, *do not include him.* List these men in order from top down if that is possible.
2. *Poor Workers:* List the names of all men who are doing an exceptionally poor job,
   and whose all-round value to the department is very low. Consider present ability
   and skill, but do not include those who are poor because they do not have sufficient
   training or experience. These will be listed separately. As in the top group, if you
   are doubtful about a man's belonging in this group, do not include him. The men
   in this group should be those who would be considered as about the bottom 10 per
   cent of men in this occupation *anywhere,* but they may include more or less than 10
   per cent of your own men.
3. *Average Workers:* List all men who have not been included in the first two groups,
   except those who are not fully trained or who lack experience. As you list them, consider each one so as to make sure that he does not belong either in Group 1 (exceptional men) or Group 2 (poor workers).
4. *Trainees and Inexperienced Workers:* Include here all those who have not finished
   the normal training period, or who have not worked long enough to show what they
   can do. Mark those who show promise with a *G,* and those who do not appear to
   make normal progress with a *P.*

From Thomas Arthur Ryan, *Work and Effort,* page 247. Copyright, 1947, by The Ronald Press
Company, New York.

---

fore, he becomes a threat to your self-esteem. When this happens, the perfectly normal tendency is to react defensively. And the more a person is on the defensive, the less advice he is able to accept from the threatener. In other words, the person who tells you your weaknesses is doing you no favor. He has created a barrier, unless the weaknesses are so minor, and mean so little to both parties, that the criticism cannot be taken seriously. At any rate, the boss's telling does not help the subordinate learn how to criticize himself, to solve his own problems, or to think more objectively about his performance, now or in the future. . . .

At any rate, in the ordinary post-appraisal interview, the boss carries the ball, does all the work, does all the thinking, does all the planning—even though it is the *subordinate* who

should be doing the learning. Somehow, this type of interview must be converted into a situation in which the subordinate does the work: the appraising, the evaluating, the thinking, the learning, the planning. And this will not happen unless he does almost all the talking.

To put it differently, when someone "advises" you, or pleads with you, or "suggests" that you do something, all these approaches involve *his* ideas rather than yours. Ever try advising a problem drinker? Or pleading with him? Or suggesting that he stay away from alcohol?

The point is this: everyone has a behavior pattern that reflects his personal adjustment to the problems of work and life. Until he *feels* differently about these patterns he'll continue them or substitute similar ones. If forced to abandon or change his ways, by being told to,

II. Special Qualifications and Abilities

Listed at the left are a number of special characteristics which may be important considerations in making promotions or transfers. List, for each of these qualifications, the names of those men in the job you are considering who are outstanding in this quality, and those who are especially poor in this respect. The names listed are not necessarily the same names you have given in your over-all estimates of the value of the employee on page 1. (Reverse side.)

Quality*	Outstanding Men	Poor workers
1. Dependability. (Does he follow instructions without close follow-up?)		
2. Ability to get along with others. (Is he respected and trusted by fellow workers?)		
3. Specialized technical knowledge of the job.		
4. Ability to instruct others in his job.		
5. Interest in his work and in the department.		

* Other traits to be added to meet the needs of a particular organization. Instructions to be revised after conferences with supervisors and experience in application of the forms.

or ordered to, or advised to, the change is usually insincere, uncomfortable, and only temporary.

What, then, can be done to help or motivate people to change . . . assuming that straightforward telling or suggesting doesn't really come to grips with the basic problem? The answer lies in the fostering of the man's own *insight*, that is, in the maturing of his own self-perception, so that he sees himself, his behavior and the consequences of his actions in a clearer and more objective light, and eventually frees himself from the tangle of needs and emotions that determines the things he does. No one learns about himself from another. No one can be "analyzed" by another, because no two people have the same feelings about things, the same history, or the same problems. A man has to analyze himself. A counselor's role (the post-appraisal interviewer's role) is to stimulate this self-appraisal. . . .

Attitudes are not changed by telling, advising, or showing. They are not changed by the process called "training." They are changed only by *education*, a long-range process that takes into account the whole man, his home life, goals, fears, hopes, history, and concept of himself. We call this type of education "counseling." It is man-centered rather than work-centered. It aims at the source rather than the result of performance. It doesn't ask "What should this man do to improve?" It seeks the answers to the questions: Why does he act this way? How far does he recognize the nature of his trouble? . . .

The most important thing is *a man's own appraisal of himself*. This, rather than anyone else's rating, should form the basis of a counseling relationship. Let *him* rate himself. Let *him* initiate the discussion of his own rating. As an example, some rating forms carry printed directions requesting the man to turn in his rating to his superior. This provides a somewhat less objectionable situation than the scheduled visit or summons to the boss's office. If a man initiates his own post-appraisal interview, he may feel a little surer of himself. He can wait until he's ready and feels that things are "right" for the meeting.

The objectives of post-appraisal interviewing should be a personal recognition of limitations and a self-propelled motivation toward improvement. The senior man should listen sympathetically and encourage the subordinate to "think out loud." With freedom of speech and a relaxed atmosphere, certain things will be said and brought to the surface that ordinarily would be hidden. The senior man's task is to help the other man to *see* the hidden significance of things that are said. "What did you mean when you said . . . ?" "How did you feel when that happened?" "Tell me more about that."

No matter how wrong the subordinate seems, he should *not* be told that he's wrong. Instead, the questions should go on. "Why do you feel that way?" "Why did you say that?" The questions should seldom be of the kind that can be answered by a "Yes" or "No." The emphasis throughout should be on feelings, not on facts. Facts here are relatively unimportant. How the man *sees* and feels and interprets the facts are what count . . .

Two Basic Approaches

There are two other types of counseling that come to mind: Both can be classified as requiring the subordinate to explain himself to the

superior. Therefore, they represent a healthier approach.

1. *The boss can be a passive listener.* Some people pride themselves on this skill. And, indeed, it may be pleasant and even a little helpful to a man to pour out his thoughts and feelings to another. However, unless some special assistance is given, the speaker may fail to grasp the significance of all he is saying. He mentions and then *fails to capitalize on* some problems and feelings he brings up in the interview. He should be asked to "explain further" about the things that seem upsetting to him. The completely passive listener isn't the ideal counselor.

2. *The boss can be an active listener.* That is, by skillful and tactful questions and comments, he can focus attention on key feelings. He does not quibble over facts. He does not rebut the arguments and contentions of the speaker, even though the latter's position could easily be crushed. Instead, he strives for better understanding and insight on the part of the man being counseled.[12]

Acknowledgments and References

1. For further information, see Roland Benjamin, Jr., "A Survey of 130 Merit Rating Plans," *Personnel*, American Management Association, November 1952, pp. 289–294.

2. Reign Bittner, "Developing an Employee Merit Rating Procedure," *Personnel*, American Management Association, January 1949, pp. 290–291.

3. For further information see Roland Benjamin, Jr., "A Survey of 130 Merit Rating Plans," *Personnel*, American Management Association, November 1952, pp. 289–294.

4. Bittner, *op. cit.*, p. 281.

5. Gustav C. Hertz, "Planning for a Successful Merit Program," *Personnel*, American Management Association, March 1949, p. 368.

6. "How to Rate Worker's Value," *Business Week*, February 25, 1939, by special permission.

7. An example of the development of a rating system by cooperation between foremen and labor union workers is presented by C. S. Slocombe in "Psychology of Cooperation," *Personnel Journal*, Vol. 16 (1938), pp. 325–332.

8. Ronald Taft, "The Ability to Judge People," *Psychological Bulletin*, January 1955, pp. 1–21.

9. W. V. Bingham, "Halo, Invalid and Valid," *Journal of Applied Psychology*, American Psychological Association, Inc., Vol. XXIII, No. 2 (April 1939), points out that not all halo is invalid because the person rated may be evaluated with regard to a specific position. This study indicated that ". . . it is not the rater alone whose reactions to the candidate are in question. He is but typical of others—clients, subordinates, fellow employees—who will react to the subject not as a bundle of isolated traits but as a person with certain duties. The judgments and responses of all these people will unconsciously and inevitably manifest a halo effect which is, in part at least, valid."

10. Thomas Arthur Ryan, *Work and Effort*, pp. 247–249. Copyright 1947 by The Ronald Press Company, New York.

11. Excerpt from Project 5, "Surveys of Employee Opinion," *Annual Report 1953–1954*, Industrial Relations Section, California Institute of Technology.

12. Spencer J. Hayden, Training Director Metal & Thermit Corporation, New York, "Getting Better Results from Post-Appraisal Interviews," paper delivered before the AMA Special Conference on Training held Dec. 9–10, 1954, at Atlanta, Georgia, and published in *Personnel*, American Management Association, May 1955, pp. 541–550.

PROJECTS

1. Examine several graphic rating scales for general traits such as initiative, personality, and so on. Select the traits that are objective in nature and those that are reactions to persons. Select several general traits and break them down into the specific forms of behavior to which they may apply.

2. Perhaps you think that a person can be judged more fairly by means of an anecdotal behavior journal, a cumulative record of characteristic behavior patterns, than by means of rating scales. If so, write several paragraphs that describe one or two persons whom you know well. Show them to someone who knows the ratees. Does that person think that your anecdotes are truly descriptive of each person you described?

3. You may, without experience with the post-appraisal interview, think that it is easily conducted. To appreciate its difficulties have some friends rate a person on a standardized rating form. Then conduct an effective post-appraisal interview with the ratee. Let several observers evaluate your skills and discuss possible improvements that you should make.

4. Discuss reasons why some students may disagree with an instructor regarding marks given in a course. Most students consider their marks satisfactory but a small percentage do not, as indicated by one study[*] of opinions of a group of college students concerning their marks. Students in education in the Eastern Illinois State Teachers College were asked to list courses taken in the winter quarter and to state (anonymously) whether they considered the marks too high or too low and why. Of 396 students, 80 per cent considered the marks satisfactory, 5 per cent too high, and 15 per cent too low. The percentage of satisfaction varied with the height of the mark. Slightly more men than women were dissatisfied. The reasons given for thinking the marks too high were: "Did too little work," "Received lower marks during the quarter," and "Knew too little about the course." The reasons given for thinking the marks too low were: "Received higher marks during the quarter," "Worked hard," and "Did as well as others."

5. Make a study of several people you know. Ask them to rate themselves on several traits such as those listed on a merit rating form. Then ask some of their close friends to rate them on these same traits. How similar or dissimilar are the ratings? Which people tend to overrate themselves? Which tend to underrate themselves?

[*] E. Reinhardt, *School and Society*, Vol. 46 (1937), pp. 447–448.

COLLATERAL READINGS

Bellows, Roger M., *Psychology of Personnel in Business and Industry*, Prentice-Hall, Inc., New York, 1954, Chapter 17.

Ghiselli, Edwin E., and Clarence W. Brown, *Personnel and Industrial Psychology*, McGraw-Hill Book Company, Inc., New York, 1955, Chapters 3 and 4.

Maier, Norman R. F., *Psychology in Industry*, Houghton Mifflin Company, Boston, 1955, Chapter 8.

Mandell, Milton M., "Supervisory Characteristics and Ratings," *Personnel*, American Management Association, New York, March 1956.

National Industrial Conference Board, *Employee Rating; Methods of Appraising Ability, Efficiency, and Potentialities*, Studies in Personnel Policy No. 39, 1942.

Poffenberger, A. T., *Principles of Applied Psychology*, Appleton-Century-Crofts, Inc., New York, 1942, Chapter 14.

Ryan, Thomas A., *Work and Effort, the Psychology of Production*, The Ronald Press Company, New York, 1947, Chapter 11.

Spriegel, William R., and E. Lanham, *Job Evaluation in Utility Companies*, Bureau of Business Research, College of Business Administration, The University of Texas, Austin 12, Texas, 1954.

CHAPTER EIGHTEEN

Job evaluation, motion study, and wage incentives

A man's job and his pay are important links between him and his company. They are integral parts of his life. They mean so much to him psychologically that when anyone evaluates or changes either his job or his pay, his emotions are aroused. Usually, the emotions have defensive significance but it is also possible to arouse favorable reactions to the changed job situations.

JOB EVALUATION

Job analyses for employment and promotion purposes

In recent years, job evaluation has been given much attention by management. Certain conditions have compelled this attention. One reason is that both management and employees want wage rates to be consistent throughout the organization. Some jobs are easy, others are difficult; some can be learned in a few minutes, others in decades; some require much physical strength, others little; some are enjoyable, others are dull and unpleasant; and so on. The rate of pay therefore should be in line with the requirements for doing the work.

Even though a management may, at some past time, have established equitable rates of pay, the rates soon get out of alignment. Some employees are more aggressive than others and get increases in pay for themselves. Some supervisors are very anxious to reward their employees and obtain pay raises for them. Furthermore,

> . . . some union representatives try to raise wages for a handful of jobs. If they are successful—through management yielding out of weariness, or through an arbitrator's award—the relationship between jobs will become distorted, the wage curve will have out-of-line bumps in it. Next step by the union is to seek removal of these "inequities" by pushing the whole wage structure up to meet the above-the-line wages.

Many a union request for a raise for one individual or group is made because some squeaking wheel in the union demands greasing, and hopes enough noise will get him results. If wages in the plant are set arbitrarily, it may be worth the union's while to gamble. But if jobs are evaluated systematically, with employee participation and approval, the union leaders may be less willing to upset the balanced wage structure they have helped establish.[1]

There are several kinds of job analyses, depending upon the purposes for which the analyses are made. The most common variety is that of the industrial engineer who analyzes jobs for the improvement of working processes and methods. He prepares, through time and motion studies, performance standards which show him how much work an employee should produce and the best way in which to produce it. The job analyses of the psychologist or personnel man are for the human relation values in selecting new employees; in promoting, transferring, discharging, and training present employees; and in the establishment of health and equitable wage standards. In this discussion we shall give emphasis to job analyses for the purpose of promotion.

Merit rating obtains appraisals of employees, whereas job evaluation measures the jobs. Each may be used without the other but to promote employees systematically requires several general steps:

1. Know the employee: ratings, tests, past record, and so on.

2. Know the jobs in the organization: the one the employee is now holding and the ones to which he might be promoted if he were qualified.

3. Interview employees periodically, so that the manpower may be utilized for the benefit of employer and employee.

Strictly speaking, a *job analysis* is simply an abstraction for a variety of operations made by the analyst. It is the process of collecting information about the jobs in a company. A *job* or *occupational specification* is a written statement of the facts obtained in the job analysis. The job specification has

two main parts—description of the job and description of the qualifications of the ideal person to fill the job. The written report or estimate of the qualifications of the ideal person to fill the job should not be confused with the qualifications of the person who is actually on the job. The person who now holds the job may or may not have the desired qualifications.

The job analysis procedure usually begins with the preparation of a work sheet wherewith the analyst can go into the shop or office and obtain the pertinent facts of the jobs in the organization. The analyst takes a supply of the work sheets to the department head or foreman and explains the purpose of the job analysis. By discussing the work and the kinds of jobs of the executive's department, the analyst obtains a general idea of the activities of the jobs and the relationships of the jobs which he is about to analyze. The employees on the several kinds of jobs are then interviewed and the work sheets are filled in in preparation for the typing of the complete job specification. In sixteen of twenty-three aircraft companies surveyed, the most common method used to obtain information for job descriptions was to interview the supervisors. Next most popular method, used by thirteen firms, was to interview the employees for their analysis of their own jobs. Some companies used both methods.

Six major functions of the jobs which are most often rated are: (1) responsibility, (2) knowledge, (3) effort and skill, (4) physical conditions, (5) personal and social conditions, and (6) supervision. Some companies have a further breakdown of these factors; others do not.[2]

When the data have been collected, written on the work sheets, and arranged in logical order, the revised work sheets or job specifications are then taken to the responsible department head for correction and approval. In most cases some corrections must be made. The data on the corrected work sheets are then typed on the final work sheet, which is now considered to be the job specification, as it includes the qualifications of the ideal person to fill the job. One specification is made for each kind of job in the organization.

The guide for classifying the jobs, or master job-classification chart

When the specifications have been completed for the various jobs in the organi-zation, each job must be graded or zoned. The purpose of zoning or grading is to determine the relative value and importance of the jobs. The guide for classifying the jobs is a description of typical grades of jobs in the company. The classification chart is a kind of scale which enables the management to grade the jobs, determine the salary ranges for each zone, and prepare promotion charts for the development of each employee. Wage or salary studies can also be made of

---

TYPICAL WORK SHEET FILLED IN FOR A JOB SPECIFICATION

(R for required. D for desired. X for items that apply to job.)

GENERAL:

Name of Position—**In Charge of Suggestion Division.** Symbol . . . .
Dept.—**Better Letters Bureau.** Div.—**Suggestion.**
No. in Position—**1.** Number of Subordinates—**2.**
Immediate Superior—**Manager Better Letters Bureau.**
Time Required for Inexperienced Person to Learn Work—**3 years.**
Time Required for Experienced Person to Learn Details of Work Here—**18 months.**

QUALIFICATIONS

R Male   D Married   Age Limits—**27 to 40**   Beginner
  Female   Single   R Experienced
                                                                      Expert

EDUCATION: Common   High School   College
Required—None 6 7 8   I II III IV   A B C D   Desired   D
Courses Required—**Psychology, English.**
Courses Desired—**Salesmanship, Better Letters, Office Manager's Course, Factory Course.**

EXPERIENCE:

Required—**On Policy and Product. 1 Year in Division as Assistant.**
Desired—**Office Manager, Salesman, Newspaper Work.**

Manual	Meets Public	x Desk	x Indoors
Clerical	xx Meets Employees	Standing	Outdoors
Correspondence		Stooping	
x Promotional	x Plans Broadly	x Walking	Travels Much
x Supervisory	x Attends Details		xx Travels Little
Technical		xx Varied	
Research	Major Responsi-	Routine	Artificial Light
	bility		
Managerial	x Medium Respon-	Automatic	x Natural Light
	sibility		
Executive	Minor Responsi-		
	bility.		

DESCRIPTION OF JOB:

    1. State duties of supervision and responsibility. 2. Operations in work. 3. Occasional duties. 4. Machines and appliances used. 5. Relationship to other jobs.

Works under supervision of Manager of Better Letters Bureau. Is responsible to the Board of Control for making a preliminary survey of all suggestions submitted by employees of the General Offices, branches, and service stations; for tactfully informing employees of action taken in regard to their suggestions; and for the proper publicity of the suggestion system.

Eliminates only those suggestions which are obviously of no value; the others are investigated as to their worth and reviewed by the Suggestion Committee (a committee of three men, the man in charge of the Suggestion Division having an equal vote with the other two members). All decisions are subject to review by Board of Control at any time.

Submits a detailed report every week to Board of Control showing in regard to suggestions: the number submitted, their value, the departments affected, reason for action taken, and a résumé of each.

When a suggestion is received, it is copied on a standard form and sent to qualified members of the organization, who report its worth. Follows up these investigations to see that contents are made so that Suggestion Committee can make an intelligent and tactful reply to every person who submits a suggestion.

TABLE 18–1

COMPARISON OF THE FOUR BASIC SYSTEMS OF JOB EVALUATION

Ranking System	*Classification System*	*Point System*	*Factor Comparison System*
The Job Analysis: A narrative description of the job with the duties, responsibilities, degree of difficulty, and required qualifications clearly brought out.		*The Job Analysis:* A narrative statement of duties and qualifications. In addition, the job is broken down into the important compensable factors, such as required experience and training, mental effort, and physical effort. The amount to which each factor is present in the job is indicated by a short narrative statement.	
Method of Relating Jobs	*Method of Relating Jobs*	*Method of Relating Jobs*	*Method of Relating Jobs*
Jobs are ranked in their order of relative difficulty or value to the company, and grade levels are sometimes defined after the jobs have been ranked.	Jobs are allocated to grade levels which are defined arbitrarily prior to evaluating jobs.	Jobs are related by factorial analysis. A restricted number of fairly specific factors are selected for application to a limited number of types of work. The point values are predetermined before analysis of jobs and are decided arbitrarily, and the degree of each factor is expressed by a definition.	Jobs are related by factorial comparison. The factors used are assumed to be fundamental to all jobs and of universal application, the point values are set after analysis of jobs from existing rates of "key" jobs, and the degrees of each factor are expressed by sample jobs.

From *Informational Manual on Industrial Job Evaluation Systems,* War Manpower Commission, Bureau of Manpower Utilization, Division of Occupational Analysis and Manning Tables, U.S. Government Printing Office, August, 1943.

all the jobs in the company, as some employees who receive a Grade 4 salary may be doing Grade 5 work, or vice versa.

If the management wishes to succeed in increasing the efficiency of the individual employee, some responsible executive must know the nature and grade of the job of each employee. He should be able to evaluate correctly any job in relation to the other jobs in the organization and in relation to the jobs in other industrial concerns. It is very easy to overestimate the importance of low-grade jobs and to underestimate the higher-grade jobs. Example: when an employee says that he is "Clerk on the Outgoing Requisitions of the Purchasing Department," it may mean that he is a little higher than the office boy or it may mean that he is an assistant purchasing agent. By means of the guide for classifying jobs and the job specification, any job may be properly classified as to grade or zone of importance.

When jobs have been fully described, they must be evaluated and graded. Five main kinds of job evaluation systems are available:

Kinds of Systems	Examples of Common Denominators

1. Nonquantitative evaluation measures
   a. Ranking
   b. Job classification
	Duties, responsibilities, working conditions, etc.

2. Quantitative evaluation measures
   a. Factor comparison
   b. Point-evaluation
	Education, experience, mental effort, physical effort, skill, etc.

3. Basic Abilities	Specific abilities and knowledge[3]

Both quantitative systems are widely used. The point system is the most popular. A survey of 23 aircraft manufacturing companies showed why certain plans were chosen. The major reason, 32.5 per cent, for selecting a plan was that it was used by other companies in the field. Almost as important, 29.7 per cent, was the fact that one plan was better suited to company needs than another. Management consultants' recommendations were dominant factors in 13.5 per cent of the selections. Ease of understanding by the employees was significant in only 10.8 per cent.[4]

By means of one of these systems of job evaluation, levels of job grades are established appropriate for the specific employees. The technical aspects of job evaluation are very numerous and are treated in other books,[5] but the kind of job grade classification used in the U.S. Civil Service is shown in Table 18-2.

A system of evaluated jobs has great value in industry. It provides definite systematic and factual data for determining the relative worth of jobs. Thus it creates equity in salary administration and improves and standardizes the latter. Such a system establishes bases for placement and promotion. It is especially valuable at times of layoffs in a unionized plant.

Many unions prefer to insist that all layoffs be made on the basis of lowest seniority. Managements prefer a more flexible procedure because of the evils of "bumping." "Bumping" is a common expression for the procedure of an employee of greater seniority employed in one department forcing during layoff periods an employee of lesser seniority in another department to be laid off so that the former may have his job. In many cases, the "bumped" employee is more efficient and cooperative than the one who takes his place. If a company has both merit rating and a complete system of graded jobs, management and the union can negotiate a contract which is more just both to the employer and to the employees. In one company, for example:

An agreement with its union provides a lay-off register, set up in four parts. Straight seniority governs in the first four labor grades. Other workers are grouped together as follows: Those with less than 50% of possible numerical score are laid off first, with union retaining right to appeal; those with good ratings (75% or better) are touched last; and people with fair ratings (50 to 75%) are considered on basis of seniority.

Under this system 900 were laid off last year. Only 53 cases were appealed. Management's decision was upheld in 27.[6]

The installation of job evaluation also may involve serious psychological problems, chiefly because accepted social relations of employees are upset. Employees evaluate jobs in their own ways long before the jobs are graded for them. Their evaluations are exceedingly important to them as stated in this example by a union leader:

One of the great difficulties of labor relations has been the disregard with which executives have treated the problem of human organization. They have attempted to inflict all sorts of radical and material changes upon employees, without the active participation or consideration of the individuals affected.

A case in point involved a metal-working establishment in a midwestern city organized by the machinists and other crafts. The management had been sold on a job evaluation and classification plan which would "properly and scientifically" align the jobs in the factory—from least skilled to most skilled. The objectivity of the plan, however, flew straight in the face of the customary and traditional working relationships in the establishment.

In one department all jobs had been paid the same rate prior to the job evaluation. The engineers moved in and set up 12 jobs and 12 rates where one existed before. Immediately, production declined, and employee discontent and hostility increased. Upon further investigation, it was found that the employees had always functioned as a team; they were capable of operating each other's machines, and they there-

TABLE 18–2

THE PAY SCALES OF THE CLASSIFICATION ACT OF 1949, AS AMENDED MARCH 1955

GENERAL SCHEDULE

Grade	Basic Pay Rates							Longevity Rates		
	a	b	c	d	e	f	g	x	y	z
1	2,690	2,775	2,860	2,945	3,030	3,115	3,200	3,285	3,370	3,455
2	2,960	3,045	3,130	3,215	3,300	3,385	3,470	3,555	3,640	3,725
3	3,175	3,260	3,345	3,430	3,515	3,600	3,685	3,770	3,855	3,940
4	3,415	3,500	3,585	3,670	3,755	3,840	3,925	4,010	4,095	4,180
5	3,670	3,805	3,940	4,075	4,210	4,345	4,480	4,615	4,750	4,885
6	4,080	4,215	4,350	4,485	4,620	4,755	4,890	5,025	5,160	5,295
7	4,525	4,660	4,795	4,930	5,065	5,200	5,335	5,470	5,605	5,740
8	4,970	5,105	5,240	5,375	5,510	5,645	5,780	5,915	6,050	6,185
9	5,440	5,575	5,710	5,845	5,980	6,115	6,250	6,385	6,520	6,655
10	5,915	6,050	6,185	6,320	6,455	6,590	6,725	6,860	6,995	7,130
11	6,390	6,605	6,820	7,035	7,250	7,465		7,680	7,895	8,110
12	7,570	7,785	8,000	8,215	8,430	8,645		8,860	9,075	9,290
13	8,990	9,205	9,420	9,635	9,850	10,065		10,280	10,495	10,710
14	10,320	10,535	10,750	10,956	11,180	11,395		11,610	11,825	12,040
15	11,610	11,880	12,150	12,420	12,690			12,905	13,120	13,335
16	12,900	13,115	13,330	13,545	13,760					
17	13,975	14,190	14,405	14,620						
18	14,800									

The table above shows the pay rates (1955) for the various services and grades. There is a maximum and a minimum for each grade with intermediate levels. A federal government employee begins in a position at the minimum of a grade and promotions within the grades are made according to the steps shown.

fore expected the same rate of pay. The employees had established a social organization among themselves which lent assistance whenever a fellow member of the team was in distress. This was the hub of their daily activities; their sentiments and attitudes flowed from their associations in the work unit.

When advised of the reasons for the drop in production, top management remained adamantly behind the job evaluation system. The employees through their union opposed its continuance just as vehemently. With discussions deadlocked, the foreman of the department was called into the controversy. He stated that if the new job structure was continued, it would be impossible to maintain production standards. In view of the practical and experienced approach of the foreman, the management decided to reinstall the original method of operation.

The job evaluation method of rating such factors as responsibility, skill, mental requirements, physical demand, working conditions, and supervision fails to treat as relevant the very things that give meaning and substance to the individual's work. In their haste to pigeonhole each individual in the productive process, the industrial engineers lose sight of that which makes effective collaboration possible: the complete integration of the individual in the technical and social organization of the establishment. A rigid job evaluation procedure which overlooks such basic factors as the seasonality of employment, the prospects for advancement, the established routines of work, and the traditions of workmanship and fellowship in the shop, fails to recognize that a man's job is often the main pivot about which his life revolves.[7]

When new job evaluations are made, workers in one department compare their increases with gains made by other departments. They do not compare job content. They do not see the evaluation system as an automatic functioning of a fixed formula. Rather, in unionized plants, they think of increases as a measure of one group's influence over the union compared with some other group's influence. They believe that the union can and should exert its influence, especially in borderline cases. Thus, the new rates can often upset relationships between workers and their union.

Wage is a symbol of status in the plant, and workers use it as a reference point.

They equate drastic changes with injustice. As the new evaluation program is put into effect, job classes become the new standard of value, for they give the wage structure clear definition.

The job evaluation program, seniority agreements, and company promotional policy are all tied into the employee's ideas of promotional ladders in the plant. A change in any one of these has an immediate effect on how he evaluates his present job and future chances in the company.

Furthermore, not only do workers compare job rates within the plant, but they also compare them from plant to plant. Thus, the new rates have to take into account community evaluations of particular jobs.[8]

Most managements that install a job evaluation system try to convince employees of the values of such a system to them.

Among the methods of convincing workers that a new job evaluation system is valuable to them, the following are popular:

To win the support and confidence of non-supervisory employees, the president of the company may send letters and memos to the workers, or have stories featured in employee publications. Descriptive literature about the plan is often distributed. Usually the management holds meetings and gets the employees to participate in the installation of the new program. The company may schedule individual interviews with employees to explain the system. Sometimes the evaluation plan is incorporated into the union contract. The usual method of trying to convince them is to have representative employees participate in the development and inauguration of the plan.

To help employees identify themselves with the company there is no substitute for a clear-cut promotion system which any employee can understand. Even though an employee may not be interested in becoming anything other than what he is, a concern which has a promotion system rates higher in his estimation than the firm where promotions are mysterious things that seem to be acquired by the "lucky fellows with a pull." Children go through school by doing the work of the specified grades. Promotion is systematic. Each child has a definite scholastic goal before him. The method of getting into the next grade is known to all pupils. In industry, the method of getting into a higher job is largely a mysterious thing about which nothing definite is understood. A promotion chart, based on job evaluation, takes the mystery out of promotions.

There are some operating difficulties. The management must insure, as far as possible, uniform interpretation of the program, and get changes in jobs and the creation of new jobs reported promptly to the evaluation division. It has to resist pressure to increase individual rates above the maximum rates for the job. Experienced personnel are needed to administer the plan. Executive and supervisory personnel have to be kept sold on the job evaluation program, and everyone should be informed about changes that occur in it.[9]

A promotion system connected with a training system

Some company managers try to follow a rigid policy that all promotions should be made from within the organization. Such a policy is likely to result in an unhealthy in-breeding and an excess of deadwood in the supervisory force.

It has been our experience that promotion-from-within [without a training program] re-sults in a very mediocre grade of supervision. Occasionally we were fortunate to get an out-standing man, but to most of them supervision is only a higher degree of performance on their previous occupation. They lack the breadth of viewpoint, and other inherent characteristics of management usually apparent in men who are capable of assimilating good educational background and experience.[10]

In view of the dangers mentioned above, some personnel managers have a definite policy to the effect that approximately 20 per cent of all promotions are made from the outside. Employees have the policy ex-plained to them and the reasons for it. Al-most every organization needs the stimulat-ing effects of "new blood" occasionally. On the other hand, some companies believe that a long history within the company is essen-tial to the company's welfare.

[On the whole,] the policy of our company throughout the years has been one of promotion from within its own ranks as higher positions of responsibility have become vacant. A ma-jority of our officers and principal employees have a long history with the company—many of them having come in as students or apprentices at young years. This is true not only of execu-tives, but, in not a few cases, of men who are in high technical positions. . . .

There is, however, no question in our minds whatever but that our Works Supervisors who come up from within the organization are those in whom we can put the greatest dependence.[11]

It is apparent from the above and similar statements by industrial executives that de-veloping effective supervisors and at the same time using promotions to increase incentive among the wage-earners is a continual process of careful selection for promotion from within, with sufficient in-filtration of new employees qualified for pro-motion into the supervisory level. More and more companies are making a special effort to employ and train college graduates for management jobs. When these better-edu-cated employees are the only ones who are encouraged to prepare for advancement, there is usually some feeling of bitterness among other employees. When a plan of promotion from within applies to all em-ployees and upgrading in all classes is ac-cording to acceptable technical require-ments, then there seems to be little criticism against the special training program for col-lege graduates.

The development program of every interested employee

In most modern concerns, many em-ployees have already reached the limit of their capacity. Some employees recognize this and are contented. Others do not realize their limitations and picture themselves as sales managers or factory managers. The latter group must be handled very tactfully, and, inasmuch as they really are seeking some means of self-expression rather than responsible managerial jobs, the counselor of the personnel should explain these facts to the employee and help him to express his individuality in some manner which fits his capacity and circumstances.

A certain percentage of the employees, as shown by the ratings and job specifications, will be found capable of greater achievement. These are the employees most worthy of attention and are the ones the company will need most in the future. The executive in charge of personnel should try to understand and appreciate these employees and outline a plan of development for each one of this group.

MOTION STUDY

The subtle factors in efficiency—attitudes, feelings, adjustments, team spirit, and others —are potent influences and of special interest to the industrial psychologist.[12] However, the psychotechnologist also realizes that a worker may be happy, admire his supervisor, like his work, and yet may perform his tasks inefficiently. We all know that workers left to their own devices seldom hit upon easy and economical methods of performing their work. The unguided worker is apt to make many unnecessary motions, waste time, and develop needless fatigue from his efforts. True time and motion study is not a mere speeding up of the worker but a systematic approach to *the one best method of work*. Motion study has been defined as "a common-sense method for analyzing operations performed by the left and right hands and for determining 'the one best way' of doing work, through elimination of all unnecessary motions and by rearranging

all necessary motions into the most economical sequence."[13]

Motion study is not a newly discovered system of magic that will automatically reduce hand-operating costs 50 per cent. It is a modern method of practical analysis which has assisted the good judgment of thousands of executives in their search for better ways to produce standard-quality products with the least possible expenditure of time and energy for the worker. It has repeatedly produced savings from 10 to 70 per cent of production costs. Motion study has been extensively used in machine shops, foundries, and mechanical assembly work, and in a wide range of other industries.

The literature on modern scientific management began at the turn of the past century. The classic reference is Frederick Winslow Taylor's investigation of handling pig iron for the Bethlehem Steel Company. As an outgrowth of the Spanish American War, the company was confronted with the necessity of speeding up the loading of pig iron onto freight cars. Taylor was hired to make a study of the process of handling pig iron.

His analysis of the process, based upon his principles of scientific management, suggested that a first-class worker should be able to carry 48 long tons a day.[14] The men on the job were carrying only 12½ tons. Taylor experimented with several workers and, at the start, offered one man an appreciable increase in pay if he would agree to follow directions in carrying the pig iron and resting. As a result of experiments with this man, Taylor was able to raise his average daily output to 47½ tons. Ultimately, Taylor was able to train an entire group of workers to function according to a planned work-and-rest program which enabled them to maintain their output at Taylor's original estimate.

Taylor's major contributions to scientific management related to "time study" and the investigation of better tools to perform work. Later, Frank B. and Lillian M. Gilbreth originated what they called "Motion Study." Its purpose was to eliminate waste and to balance the development of the use of power, machines, and better methods with the development of the human element. This work is a combination of industrial psychology and industrial engineering. This is illustrated by its three divisions: *Fatigue study* is an endeavor to eliminate unnecessary fatigue and to provide for recovery from necessary fatigue. It includes investigations of the usefulness of rest periods, work and rest chairs, and a survey designed to determine sources of fatigue. *Motion study* has to do with utilizing the time and energy of the human being to produce most efficient, profitable, and satisfying work. It employs process charts for visualizing work problems; the micromotion method for making films recording work and analyzing them into the seventeen component elements of a work cycle which are then recorded on the simultaneous motion cycle chart from which standards are derived. *Skill study* considers the derivation, transfer, and increase of skill, which is defined as knowledge plus dexterity plus adaptability to meet changing situations. It utilizes the stereochronocyclegraph method to record skill and the motion model as a teaching device to facilitate its development and transfer. Through the work in these three areas the Gilbreths and those who are carrying on this work are endeavoring to teach people to be motion-minded and to improve their own techniques of work and of leisure.

One of the outstanding Gilbreth studies dealt with bricklaying, one of the oldest of all skilled trades. By changing the placing and handling of the materials, Frank Gilbreth brought the average number of bricks laid per hour from the traditional standard of 120 to 350 per man and reduced the number of movements in laying one brick from 18 to 4.

Gilbreth early recognized the importance of breaking down a total act into its components and the value of a short-hand

method of designating the motions. As a result of his analysis of work movements, he analyzed all acts into 17 different component movements and devised an arbitrary shorthand symbol for each. These elements of movement were termed *therbligs* (Gilbreth transposed).[15] These symbols are still used by some investigators in recording their observations of a worker as he makes his movements in performing a task. Slow-motion picture cameras, split-second timers, and stereoscopic devices also are used to chart movements and discover "the one best way of work."

An understandable example of motion-study technique as applied to hand packaging of drug products is given on page 352. A and B, showing the "old method," are chiefly significant in showing that the right hand was idle during a large part of the packaging process. C, D and E, the "new method," indicate how a re-planning of the worker's movements resulted in a busy right hand. The actual savings brought about from this application of motion study to the hand packaging example was a production increase from 120 boxes an hour to 215 boxes an hour, or a unit package cost decrease of 44 per cent.[16]

The use of time and motion study has resulted in some spectacular increases in output as well as marked decreases in fatigue of the workers. Improvements made in these studies have been along the lines of giving both hands useful work to do, prepositioning tools and materials, arranging foot-pedals to relieve the hands, designing containers for materials whereby materials drop into the worker's hands, training the worker in making rhythmic movements of hands, and arranging for a suitable body position of the worker. All of these aids to the worker tend to reduce his fatigue as well as increase his production.

Production often can be increased by eliminating obviously unnecessary operations of workers. At one plant, for example, a worker asked why green tags attached to

A. Table set-up of product and supplies under the old method of working. Letters identify the following: S—box sleeves, P—partition, A—ampules, F—files, C—circulars.

B. How the operator performed the packaging operations under the old method. Note the random distribution of materials and the absence of fixtures which would hold these materials in the most convenient position for use.

D. Contrast the new location of materials with that of A. Since the new method calls for assembly of two packages at once, some supplies are stacked in duplicate fixtures, gravity feeds being used for box sleeves.

E. Position of the operator's hands and arms in relation to the new material locations is clearly shown. Note how operator selects two box sleeves at the same time.

C. The chart shows normal and maximum working areas for operators working at assembly tables when properly seated. Supplies should all be available within the maximum area and performance of handling operations should, if possible, occur within the normal work area.

COMPARATIVE SUMMARY	OLD		NEW	
	L.H.	R.H.	L.H.	R.H.
Total number of transportations	13	2	15	13
Total number of operations	17	9	17	17
Total cycle time	.50 mins.		.56 mins.	
Number of pieces per cycle	1		2	
Cycle time per box	.50 mins.		.28 mins.	

SAVED—.22 mins. per box, or 44% of old method time.

F. The comparative summary shows a saving of 44 per cent of old method time since the adoption of the new method. Note that while cycle time has increased fractionally, each new method cycle produces two finished packages.

Principles of motion study applied to hand packaging are illustrated in Diagrams **A—E.** Note the savings in time and motions as shown by the comparative summary table for old and new methods.—From Clifton H. Cox, "Motion Study Applied to Hand Packaging," **Modern Packaging,** July 1939.

gas cylinders had to be filled out with figures giving gross weight, tare weight, and net weight. On investigation, it was found that neither the manufacturer nor the customer had any need for the information. All that was necessary was for the worker to mark the tag *Full.*

Sometimes both executives and employees resist the elimination of wasted effort—management because of established habits and

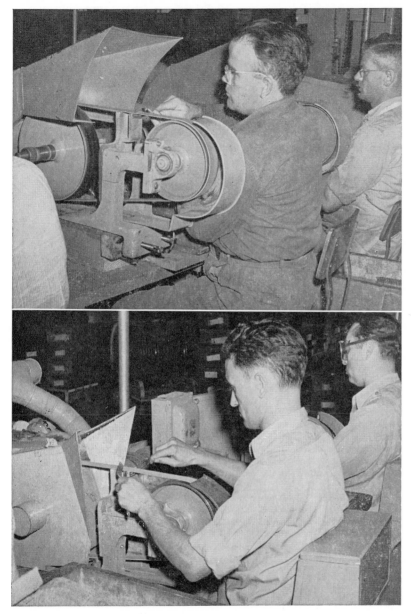

Better workplace for finishing tines of forks replaces set-up shown in top photograph. Benefits of change include 20 per cent output boost, easier training, better quality.

Old method forced worker into tiring positions.

New method provides low, adjustable chairs; allows use of both hands on productive work.

—From "False Moves that Cost You Money," **Modern Industry**, November 15, 1945. Photographs courtesy of Oneida, Ltd.

employees because of fear of losing jobs. Methods engineers, therefore, are putting more emphasis on the selling of methods improvement. Both managers and workers must be sold on the idea that higher productivity tends to bring about more profits and more jobs.

Time and motion techniques have become a permanent part of our modern industrial economy. Obviously, the psychological factors must be considered in the use of such techniques with workers. Failure to obtain the coöperation of the workers when time and motion studies are made may bring about breakdowns of morale with resultant decreases in production. A classic example is that of the efficiency expert who proved to a group of laborers that they could shovel

Before change, operator was in cab hidden behind boom structure, often experienced difficulties as a result.

After change, operator has clear field of view of bucket at all times, can spot dragline safely and accurately.

A dragline operator is responsible for the efficient, safe, continuous operation of a machine that costs over one million dollars. To improve his work, the president of a company that does mining engaged Dunlap and Associates, Inc., a research-consulting firm of Stamford, Conn., to work on the problem.

Dunlap and Associates studied control of the dragline, applying to it the principles of "human engineering" that the firm's president, Dr. Jack W. Dunlap, had helped to develop.

Human engineering may be regarded as the design and layout of equipment with the abilities and limitations of the human operator in mind so that the man-machine system that results will develop the greatest possible efficiency.

Human engineers apply, in a systematic way, the knowledge and techniques of fields such as psychology, physiology, industrial engineering, and probability statistics. Their aim is to design equipment that can be operated easily, quickly, accurately, and safely.

Almost at once, it was apparent that the operator's visibility was too limited to permit most effective shovel operation. His vision of the cut in which he was digging was obstructed by the position of the cab and by the position of his seat in the cab. The boom was in his way, as well as the catwalk on the boom and the catwalk in front of the cab. He couldn't see below or behind the shovel at all.

For further information, see R. H. Ramsey, "Revolution in Control," **Engineering and Mining Journal,** April 1954. Courtesy of Bernard J. Covner, Dunlap and Associates, Inc.

more sand when they shoveled *his* way. They admitted that he was right, but when the expert left the workers, each worker cut an inch off his shovel blade just because he disliked the expert personally! The expert had failed to make his methods an accepted part of the group's culture.

Alex Bavelas has stressed the importance of the unique culture of each industrial plant when changes are made in the worker's established habits. A plant's culture consists of ways of working, coöperating, loafing, and so on, and even though not formalized it regulates and stabilizes the organization. New employees have to learn it and adjust to it even though at first it may seem amusing or trivial. After they have been integrated into it, they may become unaware of the over-all cultural pattern, even though the pattern regulates thought and action during the working hours.

Changes in work must be fitted into this cultural framework. Small changes can be made without disturbing the framework, but larger ones (fundamental or widespread) may cause some ado, even to the point that the framework is threatened or destroyed.

To avoid the latter eventuality, two courses are possible: "A long period of gradual accommodation to the idea of the change before the change itself is introduced," or "Group decision."[17] Both of these methods have one thing in common. They aim to "establish the new frame of reference before the change occurs."

Typical of the "accommodation" approach is the way a new type of machine might be introduced. First, the idea of a new machine and the need for it might be broached and explained so that employees appreciate its values for them. Next, the machine might be placed in the work area, but not installed. This would give employees an opportunity to "get used to the idea" of having the machine around without feeling that their present social framework was threatened. While on view prior to installation, the machine and problems relating to its use could be discussed. The machine then might be installed for trial operation.

The "group decision" approach is based on the psychological concept of participated decision. To be effective it must be actively shared by the group concerned. Through their decision, group members can feel that they are participating in a positive action which should eliminate their feelings of being threatened and enhance their security during the period of adjustment. Thus a drop in production can be prevented and morale can be strengthened.

WAGE INCENTIVES

Wage incentives differ from bonuses and profit sharing plans in that they are plans providing payments for exceeding "normal" work requirements, established by time study. This "normal" work requirement on any job is called the "standard." For example, an increased earning of 25 per cent means that the worker has made 25 per cent more units in a given time than would be expected of him if he worked at a "normal" pace. Or, stated differently, he has made a given number of units in 80 per cent of the allotted time.

A major difference between wage incentives and a piece rate system is that the worker's base rate is guaranteed. Even though he earns no increase until he exceeds the standard, he receives the base pay, regardless of his output.

Wage incentives cost more to install and maintain than do bonuses or profit sharing plans, but they also can bring greater benefits in higher production, better use of machines, and fewer grievances.

Some labor unions prefer an incentive system of payment rather than piece work payment because of the bargaining advantage it gives the employee. When the employee increases his productivity, he does not have to bargain with the employer in order to get a wage increase. The increase comes to him automatically. Another reason why some unions like an incentive system is that it enables the employee to obtain higher earnings without appreciably raising labor costs. Most organized unions recognize that the jobs of their members depend on the ability of organized plants to meet competition. Wage incentives enhance this ability and at the same time give workers an opportunity to make more money. A further psychological incentive for the worker is that he acquires a feeling that in a way he is his own boss. As a result, labor relations are likely to be better, and foremen under such a system do not have to supervise the employee so closely.

Wage incentives have some psychological hazards. Some managements use incentive plans as a means of bringing about a speed-up; that is, productivity may be increased 100 per cent while the wages of the worker are increased only 25 per cent. Also, if concern over unemployment becomes an important factor in the workman's thinking, he is likely to withhold extra effort because he feels that his greater productivity may be depriving someone else of a job.

Poorly conceived and carelessly administered incentive plans may disrupt labor relations and restrict production. However, when wisely organized and systematically operated, the plans tend to raise production, to lower costs, and to create more harmonious employee-employer relations. In general, increased earnings of 120 to 130 (20 per cent to 30 per cent above the base rate) are usually considered the objective of an incentive plan.

This amount should represent what a worker of average skill can earn if he performs his job well and without too much effort. There are, of course, always a few cases where workers make two or three times the base increases. If such superiority arises from abilities which the average worker cannot duplicate, most managements do not attempt to bring the earnings back into line. The superior worker makes a special contribution and is entitled to whatever he can earn. Of course, when rate cutting has been done because of unusually high earnings of individual employees, the incentive system is naturally opposed.

Workers often find short-cuts on the job. These short-cuts are really changes in the methods of work rather than merely the effects of increased effort or skill. If management simply appropriates these short-cuts and changes the methods accordingly, the workers will stop having productive ideas.

Some managements try to iron out the difficulty by paying the worker for each short-cut, as an idea or suggestion, apart from the incentive system. Management then changes the standard. When this is done, the worker is given a liberal reward, usually at least 50 per cent of the labor saving over an extended period. Some contracts with unions arrange for such sums of compensation. Most managements, however, believe that once a standard has been set, it should not be changed. If a mistake has been made, management intends to abide by the original arrangement with the employee. Changes in standards are made only when substantial revisions have been made in work needs, material, or equipment.

Some guiding principles for the successful operation of an incentive system are the following:

1. Workers and management must be in complete agreement on the desirability of developing a wage incentive plan, and the operating terms of the system must be developed by the employees as well as by management. Where a union exists, the union must want the plan and be a partner in working out the method of operation. If no union exists, management somehow must ascertain the wishes of the workers and make sure that they want and like the plan before it is installed.

2. The plan must be simple enough to be understood by the employees. Each employee should be able to determine his own wages at the end of each day of work. If conditions within the plant require that the incentive plan involve abstruse mathematical and engineering formulas, the union representatives should be trained to understand the system so that they in turn can explain it satisfactorily to the employees, or at least convince the employees that the plan is adequate and fair.

3. The plan should include a guaranteed base hourly minimum wage, which should be high enough to give workers the assurance that they always will earn approximately as much as paid in similar jobs of the area.

4. The incentive rates that are set should provide earnings in the same proportion above basic rates as the worker's production is above standard. That is, each one per cent increase in production should increase the worker's earnings one per cent. The increased production is presumed to be due to the worker's extra effort, and he naturally believes that he should get a proportionate increase in wages.

5. The wage incentive plan, whatever its

nature, must be geared to a sympathetic understanding of how the men in the plant react toward the management and the plan. The most important factor in the success of any incentive system is the coöperation of every member of the organization.

Wage incentive plans have been used in both large and small companies, such as Lincoln Electric, Cleveland, Ohio; The Dunmore Company, Racine, Wisconsin; and the Pittsburgh Plate Glass Company, Pittsburgh, Pennsylvania.

Wage incentive plans also bring headaches for management and employees. For example, in one steel mill, it was found that one shift was breaking all production records and the pay envelopes of workers on this shift were bulging. The workers on the second shift, however, were disgruntled because their production was below standard. The reason was that the employees on the crack shift skipped the housekeeping and speeded up every production step, leaving for the following shift clean-up work that cut its tonnage. Management had to correct the situation by placing all shifts on an equal footing and applying the incentive to the total tonnage of all shifts.

Managements cannot hope to use a wage incentive system as a substitute for efficient management practices—cannot, for example, use it to compensate for obsolete equipment or poorly developed methods of work.

Since the use of incentive plans is becoming more widespread, it is important to know how effective they are. Recently the staff of the Methods Engineering Council of Pittsburgh interviewed representatives of 100 companies about their companies' incentive plans. The majority—60 per cent—believed that it was accomplishing its purposes. Of these, however, 17 per cent qualified their comments and added that the benefits of the plan fell short of justifying the bonus paid.

The companies who were pleased with their systems thought that the greatest benefits of the incentive plan were reduced costs and increased production. Even half of those firms which were dissatisfied with their plan indicated that production had increased. Two benefits of the plan listed by one-fourth of the companies who had ineffective plans but omitted by *all* of the companies with successful plans were: the plan brought about more effective supervision and it gave the management a better conception of what a fair day's work is.

The design of the plan itself was judged by both groups to be the most important factor in its failure or success. Along with the design goes intelligent administration. Insufficient coverage was thought to be a major cause of failure by 75 per cent of the dissatisfied managements. It was also listed as one of the chief day-to-day problems which they encountered. Another big problem for the dissatisfied managements related to wage inequalities for employees.[18]

Bruce Payne, management consultant, has reviewed some of the causes of failure and success for incentive plans, and comments in part:

Reviewing industry's experience with wage incentives, it is certainly very clear that there have been countless instances of failure. For example, not long ago an extensive survey of wage incentives in over 300 businesses and industrial companies was completed. It was found that nearly four out of five plans had failed or developed major weaknesses within fifteen years—a large percentage, within five years. The immediate causes ranged from inept human relations (for example, employee misunderstanding) and poor administration (for example, method changes were not co-ordinated with standards) to technical deficiencies in the plan itself (for example, inaccurate measures of work).

Also, there is no doubt that many efforts to increase productivity and reduce costs *without* incentives have succeeded. Many managements have brought costs down 10 per cent or more in the face of the greatest obstacles without the benefit of any sort of incentive pay plan. Also, as everybody knows, there are hundreds of well-run companies in the Midwest whose workers are paid on a straight hourly basis.

On the other hand, many parts of the record of industry's experience seem to make an excellent case *for* incentives. In a large number

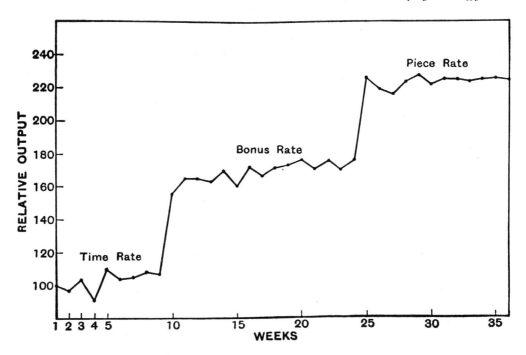

Effect of different systems of payment on production.—From S. Wyatt, assisted by L. Frost and F. G. L. Stock, **Incentives in Repetitive Work, A Practical Experiment in a Factory,** Industrial Health Research Board (Great Britain), 1934, Report No. 69. Reprinted by special permission of the Controller of His Britannic Majesty's Stationery Office.

of companies, incentives are working without a question. Managements all across the country have achieved great results with them. At business conferences one frequently hears about how effective incentives are; productivity increases of 20 to 30 per cent per worker are often cited. Costs can be cut. The workers are better paid, but the work force is smaller, fewer machines have to be used, fringe benefits are not so great. . . .

There is growing evidence, despite all the talk we hear about quality being adversely affected by incentives, that where quality control does break down, the trouble lies not with the incentive plan but, usually, with supervisory training. It is significant, too, that only a little over 2 per cent of 246 companies reporting trouble with incentive plans considered quality of work to be a major problem.

In addition, the reactions of employees to the incentive idea are significant. I have never found a worker who did not want to earn an incentive premium. Moreover, there are signs that unions are coming around to a different view of incentives. We often hear the union castigated for wrecking an otherwise good in-

centive plan, but a study of causes of failure today will, I believe, show that it is rarely possible to pin primary responsibility on the union. In addition, unions are tending more and more to accept (reluctantly, perhaps) well-engineered standards, upon which incentives should be based; there is also a growing number of instances where union time-study stewards are making time studies or Methods Time Measurement analyses that are as acceptable as those of the company industrial engineer. . . .

But if we go beneath the record and study the underlying causes for failure of incentives as well as the common characteristics of the plans that succeeded, we can reach some clear and definite conclusions. For example, take those 246 companies in the survey where wage incentive plans had failed or developed major weaknesses. Go behind the immediate reasons for failure—inaccurate work measures, misunderstanding about the plan, and the others—and it will become apparent that in every case the company had failed to complete one or more of the following steps before establishing incentives:

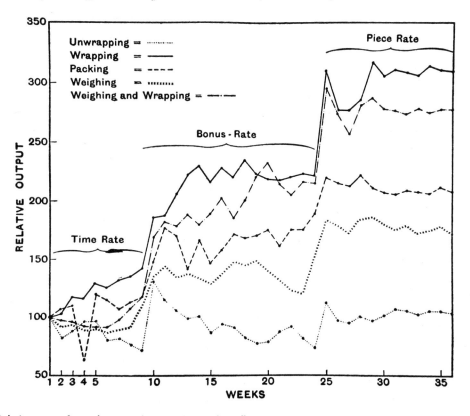

Relative output for each process in successive weeks. Effects of incentives on work that is considered useful, wrapping, and on work considered destructive, unwrapping. The incentive of extra pay was ineffective in the case of the work disliked by the employees.—From S. Wyatt, assisted by L. Frost and F. G. L. Stock, **Incentives in Repetitive Work, A Practical Experiment in a Factory,** Industrial Health Research Board (Great Britain), 1934, Report No. 69. Reprinted by special permission of the Controller of his Britannic Majesty's Stationery Office.

1. Trained an effective industrial engineering group;

2. Measured all work carefully;

3. Analyzed methods for possible improvements and made supervisors methods-conscious;

4. Trained operators in the new methods.

Conversely, in the cases of the companies where incentive plans had succeeded, this four-step preparation for incentives was conspicuously present.[19]

The investigations by the Industrial Health Research Board, Great Britain

Of all the numerous experiments conducted on the relations between conditions of work, including forms of pay incentives,

and production, the best and most basic have been those of the Industrial Health Research Board, Great Britain. Some of these experiments are reported here because of their fundamental significance.

1. In one experiment by the Industrial Health Research Board, Great Britain, conducted for the purpose of studying the nature and causes of workers' reactions to various types and conditions of work, the workers were studied with regard to effects of different methods of payment.

The piece-rate method of wage payment was found to be by far the most effective incentive to high productivity in a candy-making plant. During the investigation of

Effect of different methods of payment on output during the work day.—From S. Wyatt, assisted by L. Frost and F. G. L. Stock, **Incentives in Repetitive Work, A Practical Experiment in a Factory,** Industrial Health Research Board (Great Britain), 1934, Report No. 69. Reprinted by special permission of the Controller of His Britannic Majesty's Stationery Office.

incentives in monotonous work, three methods of payment were studied over a 36-week period: time rate, bonus rate, and piece rate. Time rate established a uniform but low level of performance; the bonus brought about a new level approximately 50 per cent higher; and the piece rate brought a new level of achievement some 40 per cent above the bonus level. The investigators of this study concluded that only under the piece-rate system were the workers stimulated to produce at top speed.[20] See figure on page 358.

2. Although the system of payment has a direct effect on productivity in simple manual work, the type of task being done was found to have great bearing on increased productivity because it is closely related to the employees' attitudes toward the task assigned. For example, the greatest contrast in productivity in a certain factory was

found to exist between those who wrapped and those who unwrapped pieces of toffee. Employees thought of unwrapping as destructive and aimless. Their mental set created a disinclination to work which was not altered noticeably even by different wage-payment systems. See lowermost line of figure on page 359.[21] In general, employees caused the most trouble and wasted the most time on processes that they disliked. Conversely, they showed the greatest increase in productivity when working on those jobs they liked most.

3. In the same study, it was found that a typical daily work curve under the three wage-payment systems showed a relatively low early-morning output under the time-rate system. As can be seen from the figure on this page,[22] production dropped just before mid-morning in this investigation. Employees' reactions gave an explanation.

Performance in packing razor blades by eight girls under time rate, competitive bonus, and piece-rate methods of payment. Chart reproduced by courtesy of the National Institute of Industrial Psychology, London.—From J. H. Mitchell, "An Investigation of a Packing Process," **The Human Factor**, Vol. X, No. 3 (March 1936), pp. 106–113.

They were bored. Prospects of lunchtime motivated them to increase production until the lunch hour. Examination of bonus-rate and piece-rate morning work curves also shows a general decline except for brief pre-lunch spurts, but progressive fatigue seemed to investigators to be the explanation.

Comparable results can be observed in the afternoon curves. Thus it would appear that even though the time-rate method of payment is more conducive to boredom than the other two methods of wage payment, the work curve of those who are more bored than fatigued is similar to the curve for those who are more fatigued than bored.

In another series of experiments in a British factory, girls wrapping razor blades were studied with regard to the effect of time-rate, competitive bonuses, and piece-rate methods of wage payment.

The time-rate method, a fixed wage for a stipulated work week, was used from the time the factory started until there had been no improvement in speed of working for several weeks. This created a plateau on the work curve. (See *A*, figure on this page.) To improve speed of working, a competitive bonus was introduced. Under this system, the girl with the highest production for the week was paid the biggest bonus, the next highest received the next biggest, and so on

down to the eighth girl, the lowest producer, who received only the basic wage. With the adoption of this system, production jumped each week for five weeks, after which the curve flattened again. (See *B*.) Seven weeks after improvement stimulated by the competitive bonus system had ceased, straight piece-rate wages were introduced. Still greater improvement was obvious. It continued for 10 weeks before Plateau *C* was reached.[23]

The fact that output for the group increased under the competitive bonus system and again under piece rates does not mean that each employee's production increased under each system. Individual differences must be kept in mind. Some workers do not like piece work at all, and some are temperamentally so unsuited to it that their production suffers. This suggests that the personnel man should try to allocate workers to jobs paid by time or to jobs paid by piece according to how they react to these systems of payment.

Wages and jobs have so many connotations for employees that personnel men often turn to psychologists and other consultants for assistance. They are gradually building up basic knowledge, such as this chapter has outlined, that will enable managements to utilize incentive plans more and more effectively.

Acknowledgments and References

1. "What's New in Job Evaluation," *Modern Industry,* June 15, 1947, p. 46.

2. See Elizabeth Lanham, "Policies and Practices in Job Evaluation," *Personnel,* American Management Association, May 1953, pp. 492–499.

3. For further information, see Ralph W. Ellis, "Simplified Job Evaluation," *Personnel Series, No. 140,* American Management Association, New York, 1951, pp. 9–21.

4. *Loc. cit.*

5. Jay L. Otis and Richard H. Leukart, *Job Evaluation,* Prentice-Hall, Inc., New York, 1948.

6. "Sifting Good Workers from 'Duds'," *Modern Industry,* August 15, 1945, p. 52.

7. Harvey W. Brown (President of the International Association of Machinists) in *Labor and Nation,* November–December 1947, p. 25:3. See also "A Labor Leader Looks at Industry's Human Relations," *The Management Review,* American Management Association, March 1948, p. 122.

8. For further information, see Leonard R. Sayles, "Worker Values in Job Evaluation: Impact of Job Evaluation on Worker Attitudes," *Personnel,* American Management Association, January 1954, pp. 266–274.

9. *Loc. cit.*

10. Helen Baker, *Company Plans for Employee Promotions,* Industrial Relations Section, Princeton University, 1939, Report No. 58.

11. *Loc. cit.*

12. Chart and comment on Mayo's data taken from Sidney L. Pressey, J. Elliott Janney, and Raymond G. Kuhlen, *Life: A Psychological Survey,* Harper & Brothers, New York, 1939, pp. 542–3.

13. Frederick Winslow Taylor, *Principles of Scientific Management,* Harper & Brothers, New York, 1911. Presents a summary of many of Taylor's principles used in his pig-iron study.

14. *Loc. cit.*

15. The 17 therbligs are *search, find, select, grasp, position, assemble, use, disassemble, inspect, transport empty, transport loaded, release load, prepare for next operation, plan, unavoidable delay, avoidable delay,* and *rest* for overcoming fatigue. See F. B. Gilbreth, *Motion Study,* D. Van Nostrand, New York, 1911.

16. Examples and illustrations reproduced by courtesy of Clifton H. Cox and *Modern Packaging* magazine under the title "Motion Study Applied to Packaging," in the issue of July 1939.

17. Alex Bavelas, "Some Problems of Organizational Change," *Journal of Social Issues,* Vol. 4, No. 3 (Summer 1948), pp. 48–52.

18. See "Is Your Incentive Plan Headed for Success or Failure?" *Factory Management & Maintenance,* May 1955, pp. 128–130.

19. Bruce Payne, "The Why and How of Wage Incentives," *Dun's Review and Modern Industry,* January 1954, pp. 60–74.

20. S. Wyatt, assisted by L. Frost and F. G. L. Stock, *Incentives in Repetitive Work, A Practical Experiment in a Factory,* Industrial Health Research Board, Great Britain, Report No. 69 (1934).

21. *Loc. cit.*

22. *Loc. cit.*

23. J. H. Mitchell, "An Investigation of a Packing Process," *The Human Factor,* Vol. X, No. 3 (March 1936), National Institute of Industrial Psychology, Aldwych House, London W. C. 2, England, pp. 106–113.

PROJECTS

1. If you were working in a company where employees on jobs of the same grade were paid inequitably, what would you do about the inequalities that applied to your job?

2. Construct a work sheet for the analysis of jobs within a company whose personnel problems you know. On it analyze and describe a particular job.

3. Describe the differences between a job analysis work sheet and a blank for an employment application.

4. Describe a number of comparatively recent changes in automobile design which have saved effort and eliminated waste motion for the driver and made for greater safety and better control.

5. If you were making a study of the subjective factors in efficiency of sales clerks in a large department store, what sort of information would you gather? List the items and explain what value each might have for your research.

6. Study carefully some work you do regularly, such as washing dishes or folding letters and placing them in envelopes. Work out an improved procedure by applying some of the general principles of time and motion study. Evaluate the results in terms of both subjective benefits.

7. Have you ever worked in a place where employees had a wage incentive plan? If you have, discuss ways in which it appeared to increase the employer's profits or detract from the welfare of employees. Consider also the positive values of the plan to employees. What method of wage payment do you prefer?

COLLATERAL READINGS

Bellows, Roger M., *Psychology of Personnel in Business and Industry,* Prentice-Hall, Inc., New York, 1954, Chapter 9.

Blum, Milton L., *Industrial Psychology and Its Social Foundations,* Harper & Brothers, New York, 1949, Chapter 6.

Ghiselli, Edwin E., and Clarence W. Brown, *Personnel and Industrial Psychology,* McGraw-Hill Book Company, Inc., 1955, Chapters 2, 10 and 11.

Haire, Mason, *Psychology in Management,* McGraw-Hill Book Company, Inc., New York, 1956, Chapter 7.

Harrell, Thomas Willard, *Industrial Psychology,* Rinehart & Company, Inc., New York, 1949, Chapter 7.

Lawshe, Jr., C. H., and A. A. Maleski, "Studies in Job Evaluation. 3: An Analysis of Point Ratings for Salary Paid Jobs in Industrial Plant," *Journal of Applied Psychology,* Vol. 30 (1946), pp. 117–128.

Maier, Norman R. F., *Psychology in Industry,* Houghton Mifflin Company, Boston, 1955, Chapters 11–14.

Otis, Jay L., and Richard H. Leukart, *Job Evaluation,* Prentice-Hall, Inc., New York, 1948.

Poffenberger, A. T., *Principles of Applied Psychology,* Appleton-Century-Crofts, Inc., New York, 1942, Chapters 22 and 24.

Smith, Henry Clay, *Psychology of Industrial Behavior,* McGraw-Hill Book Company, Inc., New York, 1955, Chapters 1 and 6.

CHAPTER NINETEEN

Making working conditions favorable for employee efficiency

Employee morale is lowered by unfavorable working conditions. This situation is the more serious because often the employees who are affected are unaware of the true cause of their grouchiness and dissatisfaction . . . the physical surroundings of a job may result in a general lowering of employee morale in a way which is not revealed by ordinary questioning of the men. The conclusion we may draw is that when an unfavorable morale condition is found to exist, it is wise to examine carefully the physical surroundings to determine whether some unnatural condition may be at fault.[1]

Many investigations, similar to those of the Hawthorne studies, have indicated that the factor of motivation is more important in productivity than simple physical changes in the environment. When workers feel that they are participating in a significant project and that they are important as persons, they are likely to be so highly motivated as to ignore mere physical conditions. Of course we cannot assume that environmental factors are of no consequence. As specified by Whitehead, "in order to maintain a satisfactory material situation . . . the total physical situation at any time must be within the indifferent range of the individual experiencing it."[2]

LIGHTING—ILLUMINATION OF WORK

Good lighting often helps the worker do more work with less effort. Furthermore, inadequate lighting is depressing to many people. Obviously, lighting should be adequate, constant, evenly distributed, and without glare. Contrary to popular opinion, direct sunlight does not always meet these four requirements, so that it often must be supplemented with artificial lighting.

Many managements fail to realize the effects of lighting on output, quality, costs, morale, and safety. Dirty lamps and bad lighting are claimed to account for more serious production losses than strikes. When

364

neglected lighting fails to furnish the illumination that is necessary for high production, man hours and materials are wasted every day. Every kind of working situation is likely to have its unique lighting problems, and we cannot assume that what is good lighting for one worker and his work is also good lighting for the next worker and his work. However, many studies of lighting have indicated that better factory lighting tends to increase production.

Vision checks of more than two million workers by the American Optical Company indicated that about one third of all American industrial employees have poor eyesight. Some workers admit that they obtain their glasses without an eye examination, and some wear spectacles borrowed from friends or relatives.[3] Among 200,000 employees in diversified industries, about 55 per cent had normal or 20/20 vision without glasses; 20 per cent had normal vision with glasses; and 25 per cent had defective vision which was not corrected with glasses. Another typical survey of nearly 15,000 adult employees showed that 25 per cent had 20/30 to 20/40 vision.[4]

Motorola, Inc., became aware of the need for a vision test when its employees began complaining about various eye discomforts. At the same time, the company decided to do something about field complaints concerning their product. They had traced these to the production line inspection department.

Results of Motorola's vision examinations revealed that 30 per cent of the workers in that department could not see well enough to do their job effectively. Of those with inadequate vision, 63 per cent had been rated below average workers by their supervisors. The company records also pointed up a relationship between below-average sight and above-average absenteeism. When the men's vision was corrected, their absences dropped. The number of complaints from the field about defects in Motorola sets

dropped eight per cent below that of the previous year. Employee turnover decreased 10 per cent in spite of the hiring of many additional workers. Machine accidents declined by one-third.

The company feels that the $5,000 it originally appropriated to give financial aid to employees in correcting their vision with glasses has paid off, both in material savings and the good will of employees. The plant has gained a reputation for having high vision requirements, yet this evidently does not deter applicants for employment. Of those job applicants who were rejected because of faulty vision, 42 per cent purchased corrective lens in order to be able to pass the vision examination and work for the company.[5]

The Department of Psychology of the University of Texas occupied its new building, Mezes Hall, in 1953. The offices, classrooms, laboratories, clinics, shops, and library of the department are housed in this building. Specialized research rooms—soundproof, constant temperature, surgery, and submammalian laboratories—are located in the basement; the machine shops and graduate research rooms on the fifth floor. This building offers facilities for the study of psychological factors that influence work effort.

In many cases of reported improvements in efficiency as a result of better lighting, only the lighting is mentioned, even though the most important factors such as changed improvements in lighting, like any other additional changes are made. Sometimes methods of work are ignored. Furthermore,

Session of The Industrial Vision Institute, Division of Education and Applied Psychology, Purdue University. This short course enrolled people from companies that were installing or operating a vision program that made use of the Bausch & Lomb Ortho-Rater. This instrument is shown on the desk in front of the group. It accurately measures twelve visual skills of an employee in an average of less than six minutes.

marked improvement in conditions of work, tend to result in increased efficiency. Marked increases in efficiency as a result of improved working conditions are not always permanent, because the "lift" in morale is likely to wear off after several months.

One significant study was that in which the National Society for the Prevention of Blindness coöperated with several government agencies in an experiment on the effects of improved lighting in a government office. The employees were girl workers in the card punch subsection of the Bureau of Internal Revenue. Originally, their room had little to recommend it: lighting was old-fashioned, ceilings and walls were badly soiled; and equipment was crowded. The illumination varied from four to 26 foot-candles.

When the conditions of work were improved, the walls were painted and new lighting fixtures were installed. The illumination was raised to 33 to 58 foot-candles. The eyesight of all workers was tested and corrective eyeglasses furnished to all those who needed them. The floor and the desks were made light in tone and the tabulating machines were changed from black to a light greyish green.

Careful measurements were made before and after the corrective steps were taken. Production records of the workers in the

room were kept daily and turned over to the public health service officers for analysis and interpretation.

The experiment indicated that the effects of the change on the workers was marked: morale was better and production was higher. Unfortunately, an exact mathematical measure of the increase in output was not possible, the reason being that the forms on which the girls worked were changed during the second year of the test. The new forms were considerably more complex. Despite the fact that the job had become more difficult the second year, there was an increase of five and one half per cent in the total number of cards produced per hour. Estimates indicated that had the work remained the same during the two years, the output would have been increased between 20 and 25 per cent.[6]

Surveys of lighting of homes, offices, factories, and schoolrooms have revealed many examples of inadequate and harmful illumination. The three aspects of lighting which most often are unhygienic are brightness or intensity, quality or color, and distribution or diffusion of illumination.

Intensity of light

Intensity of light is measured in foot-candles. Foot-candle is a technical term which refers to "the amount of light illuminating a surface by a standard candle at a distance of one foot." A green grass lawn under the full sunlight of midday in midsummer may have a level of illumination of 8,000 foot-candles.[7] Instruments for measuring brightness level, *light meters,* are available. Another instrument, the *visibility meter,* now makes it possible to specify the foot-candles necessary for various tasks so they may be performed with approximately the same degree of ease of seeing. Visibility can be roughly illustrated by holding a newspaper at arm's length. Most persons can read all the print regardless of the size of type, but the largest type obviously is of higher visibility than the smaller type.

The visibility meter makes it possible to reduce the visibility of any object or task by gradually reducing the contrast (and brightness) until you can barely see it. This threshold is a measurement which can readily be made. We can determine when the object or task is barely visible when it is viewed through this visiblity meter. . . .

Thus there is now available a means for scientifically specifying the foot-candles necessary for various tasks to be performed with approximately the same degree of ease of seeing. . . .

It has been found that reading large print for prolonged periods is easiest when the level of illumination is more than 100 foot-candles. However, let us use as our very conservative standard the visibility of 8-point type (a type size slightly larger than that used in the average newspaper) when illuminated by only 10 foot-candles. The foot-candles necessary for various tasks to be of the same visibility are presented herewith.

FOOT-CANDLES NECESSARY FOR THESE TASKS TO BE OF EQUAL VISIBILITY

	Foot-candles
Reading 8-point type, well printed on white paper [e.g., this line of print]	10
Reading 6–point type, well printed on white paper . .	20
Reading average newspaper printed on newsprint	30
Reading handwriting with average pencil . . .	50
Reading newspaper stock quotations	80
Distinguishing black thread on dark cloth . . .	500

It is seen from the foregoing that the foot-candles required for doing various tasks of the same visibility vary enormously. As the standard is raised, all the values are raised. For example, a black thread on dark cloth would have to be illuminated to a level of 4,000 foot-candles (approximately the average level of daylight outdoors) to make its visibility the same as that of 8-point type on white paper, and illuminated to a level of 100 foot-candles.

Recommended Foot-candles

100 Foot-candles or more—For severe and prolonged tasks, such as fine needlework, fine engraving, fine penwork, fine assembly, sewing on dark goods and discrimination of fine details of low contrast, as in inspection.

50 to 100 Foot-candles—For severe and prolonged tasks, such as proofreading, drafting, difficult reading, watch repairing, fine machine-work, average sewing and other needlework.

20 to 50 Foot-candles—For moderately critical and prolonged tasks, such as clerical work, ordinary reading, common benchwork, and average sewing and other needlework on light goods.

10 to 20 Foot-candles—For moderate and prolonged tasks of office and factory and, when not prolonged, ordinary reading and sewing on light goods.

5 to 10 Foot-candles—For visually controlled work in which seeing is important, but more or less interrupted or casual and does not involve discrimination of fine details or low contrasts.

0 to 5 Foot-candles—The danger zone for severe visual tasks, and for quick and certain seeing. Satisfactory for perceiving larger objects and for casual seeing.[8]

Generally, lighting engineers advise 50 to 75 foot-candles of glareless light for reading, writing, or any other close work. In laymen's terms, this means from five to 10 times more light than is available in the typical home. The best way to overcome such a lack is to set aside a corner of the living room or den for reading purposes.

A lamp is good for reading if it meets these three specifications:

Reflects the maximum amount of light from a standard 100-watt bulb. Diffuses the light into an abundance of glareless illumination. Shields your eyes from the glare of the bulb.[9]

Direct Glare . . . It is no new problem to have too much light in a worker's eyes, too little on his work. The first step to effect a cure . . . is to shade lamps properly, put the light where it belongs . . . save as much as 60% of light that may otherwise be wasted.

Reflected Glare . . . is a problem in two phases . . . often more objectionable than direct glare, and frequently more harmful. A change from concentrated light sources to a large-area light source is the first and best cure. Adequate covering, to assure diffusion, plus proper placing of offending supplementary units, can help.

Daylight Glare . . . Improper placement of drafting boards, desks, etc., can cause time loss due to glare from direct daylight. The cure . . . to shade the window or, wherever possible, shift working surfaces to put natural light on working plane instead of in the worker's eyes.

Dirt . . . Commonest of all lighting bottlenecks and easiest to cure. Dirty lamps and fixtures or windows frosted with grime can cut lighting levels as much as 50% . . . a regular soap and water schedule is essential, and for many installations equipment must be taken down for thorough washing.

CHECK THESE FIRST-AID RECOMMENDATIONS

Reflected Daylight Glare . . . is natural light that bounces from work plane to eyes. Its only cure is shading the source or providing a high enough indoor intensity to offset as much reflected daylight as possible. (Sketches to be interpreted as plans, not as elevations.)

Point-light Source Reflections . . . Light reflected from curved work surfaces is concentrated by a point-light source . . . can be minimized by shifting the lamp, shading, diffusing or changing to a long light source.

Shadows . . . Every worker knows the problem of "standing in his own light." Belts, beams, cranes, and tool racks all aggravate this trouble. The complete cure is adequate general lighting. The next best remedy is to increase the number of light sources.

Procedure Chart Lighting . . . Here eyes must change focus constantly, look through the pool of light over machine at a less highly illuminated procedure, blueprint, or scale table. The cure . . . to equalize the illumination on machine and chart.

From **The Magazine of Light**, No. 3 (1942). Lamp Department, General Electric Company, Nela Park, Cleveland. Recommendations verified June 17, **1949.**

Light distribution

Distribution of light is exceedingly important and can often be achieved with little effort. Unevenness of distribution is the most common error in lighting. Failure to maintain a proper diffusion of light produces eyestrain and decreases visual efficiency. Simple re-arrangements of work and changes in lighting fixtures often eliminate glare and the bright areas and shadows within the visual field. Tinker has summarized suggestions for certain improvements in distribution as follows:

The uncomfortable effects of bright spots of light above or off to the side of the line of vision while reading, doing other visual work, or even when no visual discrimination is involved, is common experience. Elimination of this disturbing peripheral illumination is necessary if hygienic vision is to be maintained. When these side lights become brighter or are moved closer to the line of direct vision, the immediate working surface, the fatiguing effects become greater. Furthermore, the greater the number of such peripheral light sources, the more detrimental is the effect upon vision.

Uncomfortable glare and loss of visual efficiency also result from highly polished or glazed objects within the field of vision. Examples are nickle-plated metal parts of a typewriter and glazed printing paper. Such glare is reduced by maintaining well-diffused illumination in the work room.

Visual fatigue and lessened efficiency are produced by brightness contrast within that portion of the visual field where critical vision is required and also within the immediate surroundings. When the eyes must shift back and forth from bright to dark areas or when there is a sharp division between dark and bright portions of the working area, the eyes must constantly re-adapt to the different degrees of brightness. Eyestrain soon results. Examples are (1) white paper on a dark desk, and (2) a dark undersurface of an opaque eye shade used in a brightly lighted room.

The following will aid in eliminating glare effects: (1) Avoid peripheral light sources, such as wall brackets and low-hanging fixtures which reach down into the field of vision. (2) Avoid as far as possible the use of glazed paper, polished metallic objects, and marked contrasts of brightness within the visual field. (3) Avoid strictly local lighting like that produced by most desk lamps with opaque shades. The latter produce a circle of bright light surrounded by dimly illuminated areas and shadows. (4) Maintain, in general, as equal a distribution of light as possible over the working surface.[10]

Researchers have used various criteria for the determination of the most desirable lighting conditions. One criterion frequently used has been the production or output of the worker under different conditions of lighting. However, studies of lighting based upon factors such as output, rate of performing useful work, and speed of reading must be supplemented with additional criteria. Psychological factors often are more difficult to measure than the relatively simple objective environmental factors.

COLOR

Like lighting, color has been used in industry to help reduce employee fatigue, increase efficiency, decrease accidents, and improve housekeeping. Many industrial plants are too dull and dark for efficient seeing. Even the most modern lighting system is ineffective if light falls only on dull, dark walls, workbenches, and floors. Such surfaces may absorb rather than reflect and spread light. Color in industry often is used to improve "see-ability" rather than merely to provide more aesthetic surroundings. Color use should be planned to be functional and to fit the needs of the industry.

. . . Data show that with the use of color it is possible to recover light otherwise wasted and increase the actual illumination 100 per cent without changing the lighting equipment or increasing the wattage.

. . . Frequently eyestrain, which can create dangerous fatigue and nervous tension, is the result of constant, involuntary adjustment of the eye muscles caused by wrong color contrast, or distracting, glaring horizon colors, even where there is sufficient light.

In the inspection room of a North Carolina textile mill, girl operators scan blue denim hour after hour, as it moves rapidly under their eyes. Thinking to provide the maximum light, the

Pittsburgh Plate Glass Co.

COLOR HATH CHARMS . . . After the paint job at right, which "defined limits" of the stair well, the behavior of junior-high-school students on the stairs definitely improved, their teachers say.

Several years ago, one of the country's largest paint makers, the Pittsburgh Plate Glass Company, joined forces with a group of psychologists at Johns Hopkins to find out, one way or another, whether the color scheme of a room really does affect the people who work in it. The Pittsburgh people developed a system of color decoration to which they gave the trade name "Color Dynamics." It involved tailoring paint colors individually to each situation in which paints were to be used, taking into account such factors as light, space, furnishings and equipment, and the purposes to which a room was to be put, on the theory that the performance of persons working amidst such planned colors should appreciably improve.

To test their theory, Pittsburgh asked the Hopkins psychologists to make a lengthy statistical study of a large group of people at work. The first idea was to conduct the study in a factory, since industry had already done a great deal of experimenting with colors, especially in an effort to increase the safety of workers on dangerous machines. But the psychologists felt that the tests would require several years, and it would be almost impossible to find an industry whose work force, equipment, output, and other factors were likely to remain stable for that long.

So the experimenters decided to conduct their tests in schools.

The elementary schools showed a very strong reaction to the experimental decoration. Kindergarten pupils improved most of all, suggesting that the younger the person the greater may be his response to color.

Surprisingly, these young pupils improved more in scholarship than in behavior. Average ratings for history, spelling, music, and even arithmetic were up from eight and a half to twelve per cent, while "social habits" brought up the rear with an improvement of less than six per cent.

In five out of six areas of comparison, the same situation prevailed: the unpainted school stayed about as it had been, the conventionally painted one improved somewhat, and the experimental school improved appreciably more.

An unexpected discovery was that boys often responded more to the new colors than did girls.

The teachers overwhelmingly expressed pleasure with the new paints, and the great majority of them felt strongly that the appearance of a building plays a big part in the morale and loyalty of both teachers and pupils.
—For further information, see "New Colors in the Classroom—Psychologists and Paint Makers Study Hues' Effects on School Work," **Johns Hopkins Magazine,** May 1954, pp. 10–12.

operators of the mill had painted the walls of the room white. But when the girls looked up momentarily from the blue cloth to the white wall for a rest, a peach color swam before their eyes.

This is the visual phenomenon called "after-image." The human eye, ever-stimulated by one color, registers the opposite or complementary color as a means of readjustment. When the girls looked back at the work, it took them several seconds to regain normal vision. A color engineer greatly increased the time the girls could work effectively and without strain at this job by providing what their eyes demanded: peach-colored walls.[11]

To avoid eye fatigue, colors directly in line with the workers' eyes should be about the same brightness as the bench-top or working area.

When a desk worker, for example, works with white paper on a desk with a dark green surface, he will constantly be seeing strong contrasts. In terms of the eye, this means a constant opening and closing of the pupil or lens-opening. The excess of mechanical movement within the eye contributes to fatigue. Soft shades, such as light gray, pale green, and light blue, are restful, line-of-vision colors.

Eyes may become overworked by staring too long at two objects of the same color and trying to differentiate between them. A too brilliant reflection, such as sun rays on snow or light on a painted surface, may produce marked strain. An important factor in improving the working environment is to provide a color harmony that does not tire the eyes. Color engineers have developed certain effective principles:

The idea that colors on the red side of the spectrum are warm and stimulating, while those at the opposite blue-green end are cool and relaxing, is accepted as a rule-of-thumb by all color practitioners. In a chain of restaurants, waiting lines formed outside telephone booths. When each booth interior was painted bright red, conversations speeded up so that the signs asking users to be brief were removed.

Another group of restaurants in New York adopted their striking red-and-yellow scheme on the advice of a color consultant. Originally a chaste gray-green, the restaurants were popular, but patrons were inclined to linger and the turn-over wasn't fast enough to suit the management. When the decorating was changed to stimulating colors, traffic speeded up and business increased. . . .

Though most animals, including bulls, are color-blind, color has its effects on certain insects. Blue appears to be repugnant to flies. Recently a Chicago cheese manufacturer painted a large factory window blue, to screen out the ultra-violet rays. It was discovered that flies no longer congregated outside this window, though they were as thick as ever around other windows. Mosquitoes, however, seem to like blue. During the war the Navy withdrew blue shirts from men working at shore installations in malarial districts and substituted white, after tests showed that the incidence of mosquito bites was considerably higher among men wearing blue.[12]

Generally speaking, the warm colors (yellow, orange, etc.) are those that stimulate and promote efficiency. When properly used, they create a most pleasant environment. Of all colors, green apparently has the most relaxing effect on mind and body. Nature's extensive use of green in field and forest is ample evidence of this. Various shades of green such as Eye-Rest, Vista and Seafoam form the basis of properly engineered office color patterns. Blue is a calming color and can be used extensively in the form of Cascade Blue and Stratosphere Gray in offices to promote peace of mind and a calm, quiet atmosphere conducive to efficient work. The cool tints of Mist Gray could be used on the ceilings to counteract the too-warm effect of southern light. Cool expanses of Seafoam Green on the walls would rest the eyes of the personnel when they glance up from their desks or typewriters. To emphasize further the eye-rest factor, the walls which the workers face could be treated as a focal center and finished in an Eye-Rest Green. The floor could be a dark shade of green to harmonize with walls and ceilings. This combination would effectively offset the feeling of too much warmth created by the exposure and the broad expanse of desks. . . .

. . . In one instance, an office manager changed a drab office color scheme to a cool, relaxing pattern featuring blue. The office was painted in August; when winter came, the girls complained of feeling too cool. The normal temperature was 70 degrees Fahrenheit; this was raised to 75. The girls still felt cool. After much discussion and study the color scheme was changed to warm yellows and restful greens. The temperature was left at 75 degrees. Soon the girls protested it was too warm; it was dropped to normal and complaints ceased. This is just one of many instances showing the psychological effect of color.[13]

. . . In another plant, workers lifting black metal boxes filled with rough-cut brier pipes complained that they strained their backs. One weekend the foreman had all the boxes painted a pale green. On Monday several men said to the boss: "Say, these new lightweight boxes make a real difference." . . .[14]

Sometimes a more intense lighting is not the key to bettering a work situation. When one progressive manager brought daylight lighting into his shop, he got the wrong effect. Instead of production going up as he had intended, it went down. His error came in considering only the lighting of his shop and not the lighting in harmony with color. When a color engineer, Faber Birren, was called in, he had the colors changed: the yellow walls were subdued to a two-tone green, (light green top and medium green dado). Instead of the relatively non-reflective black, floors were changed to a durable gray. Machines were painted a deep gray-green. The ceilings were made an off-white to distribute the light evenly. Thus, through judicious use of color, the quality of the workmanship in the shop improved, accidents were reduced, maintainance simplified and production increased.—See T. Metaxas, "Color: Paint Plants Scientifically," **The Iron Age,** May 7, 1953, pp. 142–4.

If the factory interior is cold looking, warm colors, such as ivory or buff, should be substituted if the illusion of warmth is desired. If working conditions involve high temperatures, cool colors, such as blues and greens, should be used.

"Working with dark objects, the surroundings should not be too brilliant, or the [iris] opening will become too small, with the result that vision will be taxed, production will suffer, and general tension and fatigue increase. The ideal situation is that in which illumination is ample and the surroundings a trifle lower in brightness than the object of concentration. Where dark materials are used, supplementary lighting may be necessary."[15]

Faber Birren, who has done outstanding work in color conditioning in industry, recommends that walls should not be too bright for the particular type of work. For example, bright, glaring white walls are not good for types of work that require the handling of dark objects. If the lighting is ample, walls can be toned down; if walls are on the dim side, supplementary lighting may be necessary.

Colors rarely should be pure, because these are likely to distract the worker. Soft grayish blue-green is recommended because it is neutral and stimulating.

If the work is of a type that demands much close work with the eyes, walls should provide a resting place for the eyes—for "space-gazing." Eyes need at least 20 feet to gaze through and a cool color to see.

Faber Birren emphasizes that painting with different colors will pay larger dividends in accident prevention than in any other one phase of industrial application. He cautions against overuse of color in industry however. When this happens, the worker does not see the things he is supposed to. His eye is distracted by many colors clamoring for his attention.[16]

The color program at Master Lock Company in Milwaukee is credited with contributing to this company's excellent safety record. Master Lock has a lower accident rate than any comparable plant in the nation. It was one of the first companies to experiment with yellow in place of red as a danger signal. Some of its findings have modified safety standards set by city and state codes and insurance companies.

Unlike other factories where machines are painted in dark shades, this company uses bright tones. The giant padlock-making machines are painted in flamboyant brights to show dust and soot rather than hide them. "If they see the dirt, they'll clean it"—and the workers do. Although there is no company rule requiring employees to play housekeeper, the plant is immaculately clean.

Two standards were used to determine the efficiency of a particular color or combination: workers' preferences and production records. What finally developed was an eye-rest green for machinery with buff and yellow to point up guards and other units. Pipes and conduits gleam in iridescent greens and yellows.[17]

Oil refineries are leaders in the effective use of color in industry. The Baton Rouge refinery of Esso Standard Oil has developed a paint schedule to designate specific units and tank markings using nineteen different colors that harmonize together. Redecorating programs have resulted in greater worker pride in the colorful surroundings, keeping the plant cleaner, providing a pleasant change for workers, and helping to prevent accidents. Night workers, particularly, are benefiting from proper color schemes. Distinctive colors are being used to designate equipment, show what liquids are flowing through particular pipes, warn of the presence of stairwells, and aid visibility in dark areas.[18] Color standards, once adopted, should be rigidly adhered to, especially in accident prevention. Once workers learn the meanings of color signals and rely on them, the accident frequency rate should decline.

NOISE

Work in almost every factory and office involves a certain amount of noise. Executives have recognized that noise is a distraction to many employees. Accordingly, some executives have attempted to overcome the problem by sound-proofing offices and other places of work.

Everyone knows, too, that the worker may become adapted to noise and that certain noises do not distract some workers. Experiments by psychologists indicate that the nature of the noise and the attitude of the individual toward the noise are of paramount importance regarding the distracting effects. A continuous noise may not have any harmful effects whereas an intermittent or unusual noise may. The steady noise, such as that of a battery of typewriters, is not likely to be as disturbing as irregular noises from automobile horns, strangers entering a room and banging a door, or persons talking more loudly than usual. Noise may even facilitate the individual worker's output if he has adopted a favorable attitude toward it.

Many workers accept a certain amount of noise, thinking of it as a necessary background for the work of the day. Several investigators have found that the significance of the noise for a particular individual rather than its intensity or nature determines its effects on the individual listener. Most of us have at some time been annoyed by a power shovel or hoisting machine. However, it is probable that if the listener who is annoyed by the power shovel were the inventor or manufacturer of the shovel, he would enjoy the noise rather than consider it a distraction.

The Industrial Health Research Board, Great Britain, found during its experiments on the effect of noise on the efficiency of industrial workers that, although noisy working conditions usually do not markedly impair worker-efficiency at simple motor tasks, noise consistently does have the effect of decreasing efficiency to some extent. Loud noise, particularly mechanical irregular noise, was found to be prejudicial to efficiency roughly in direct proportion to the difficulty of the work involved; and even though differences in performance of work with and without noise were not statistically

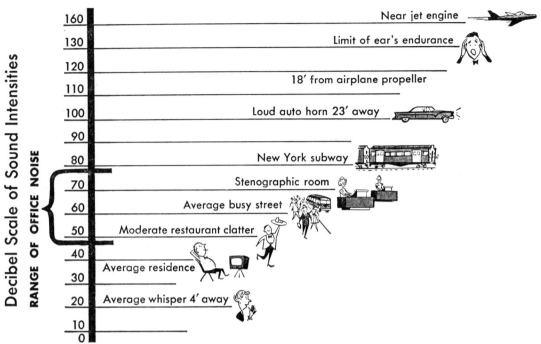

Decibel Scale of Sound Intensities

RANGE OF OFFICE NOISE

160	Near jet engine
130	Limit of ear's endurance
120	
110	18' from airplane propeller
100	Loud auto horn 23' away
90	
80	New York subway
70	Stenographic room
60	Average busy street
50	Moderate restaurant clatter
40	
30	Average residence
20	Average whisper 4' away
10	
0	

Courtesy of U.S. Department of Commerce and the Carpet Institute, Inc., New York.

significant, a trend was evident. The trend, however, does not indicate as deleterious effects as often are charged.

Loud noise appears to be most distracting when first heard. This is equally true of unpleasant noise, such as irregular mechanical noise, and pleasant noise such as music. However, because of man's powers of adaptation, he soon accustoms himself to distracting influences such as noise, and its detrimental effects shortly disappear. This disappearance seems to be caused more by a decrease in interest in the noise than in a change in sensory reaction.

Certain forms of mental work consistently are more affected by noise than are simple mechanical tasks, apparently because motor tasks, with a moderate amount of practice, become almost automatic, whereas even simple mental tasks are relatively complex in their demands upon the worker. However, as in simple motor tasks, in simple mental tasks the worker adapts himself quite readily to noisy conditions. Sometimes noise-caused irritation or annoyance results

in better than usual performance of work because the worker expends greater than usual effort in order to counterbalance environmental conditions. On the other hand, if the worker does not increase his expenditure of effort his performance may be worse than usual. If the work being done is highly automatized and there is no increase or decrease in effort expenditure, performance will remain within normal range. Thus it can be seen that performance in a noisy environment depends not upon the noise itself, but upon the worker's attitude toward the performance of the work.[19]

Various investigations of noise have pointed out that it should not be assumed, when a worker accepts noise as a background for his work, that his passive acceptance signifies an increase in efficiency. Furthermore, they have found that an increase in output often is accompanied by a considerable increase in the expenditure of energy involved. Several clever experiments of this kind have been conducted with keyboards. For example, the operator pressed appropriate keys similar to typewriter keys when he was given a designated stimulus. Careful measurements indicated that the operator exerted more pressure under distraction of noise than he did without the distraction.

Laird studied the air exhaled by typists and inferred from the greater consumption of oxygen during the noise periods that the typists expended more energy at a given task when conditions were noisy than when conditions were quiet. When typewriter keys were used to transcribe a code, J. J. B. Morgan found no difference in learning capacity when the room was noisy, but recorders attached to the keys indicated that more muscular pressure was then exerted by the operator. However, loudness and annoyance do not wholly go hand in hand. Loudness in relation to the background is often simply the dominating measurable feature of noise.

We can conclude, therefore, that when a noise really distracts the worker, a decrease in output or an increase in the expenditure of energy is likely to result. Also, when the noise is considered a background for the worker's activities, the sound which is noise for one observer may be a kind of pleasant environment for the person who has become adapted.

When noise of work cannot be reduced sufficiently to satisfy workers, the sufferers may gain some advantage by using ear defenders or plugs. Certain solid types of defenders are useful for relieving discomfort from intense noises and explosions. The wearer may still hear conversation. Complaints of traffic noise usually come from office workers in rooms facing the street, the sound usually being transmitted through windows or other openings. Closing the windows often keeps out the noise. Panes of heavy glass are helpful in further decreasing the noise. The best remedy is to use double windows and keep them closed, providing ventilation by quiet fans or vent ducts. When employees complain of noise

from office appliances used by other members of the staff, annoyance can be reduced by the use of absorbent materials on the ceilings and walls. The absorbent materials may be tiles of a soft, porous nature or canvas, or perforated metals. Also, the machines can be insulated by means of bands of felt placed under them. An experienced sound engineer may discover many additional ways of reducing noise and making working conditions more comfortable.

Employees' reactions to noise were studied systematically in six industrial plants. In three of the plants, studies were made before and after sound conditioning. Results indicated that acoustical treatment improved ease and accuracy of understanding of conversations in noisy areas. Discomfort and annoyance from noise were decreased. No evidence, however, was obtained from the study to show that production was increased.[20]

The effect of noise reduction on the personal output of a group of ten weavers was studied by Weston and Adams.[21] The output of the group was charted for twenty-six weeks; on thirteen alternate weeks the weavers wore ear plugs to reduce the noise.

The average hourly output per weaver for the group studied in this investigation shows an increase of approximately one per cent when the loom noise is reduced by the use of ear defenders. Weaving is largely a mechanical process, and it is probable that in other occupations, comparable in regard to the intensity of noise but depending less upon the mechanical and more upon the human factor than weaving, the effect of noise upon output may be considerably greater than that demonstrated by this investigation.

A study of the hourly variation of output during the day under conditions of reduced noise, as compared with normal conditions, is very interesting. Over half of the gain in output occurred during the first three hours of the work day, while some increase occurred every hour of the day but one. This

Average Performance of Ten Weavers

Average Performance of Ten Weavers

Ear defenders (a special type of ear plug) were given to ten weavers whose job was highly mechanized and involved the use of noisy machines. The output rate was slightly greater when noise was reduced every hour during the day except for one; 9:30 to 10:30. See figure on left. This figure also shows the difference between the morning and afternoon production. Figure on right shows that the subdued noise conditions resulted in a more nearly straight-line production curve, a finding that is considered ideally desirable.—From H. C. Weston and S. Adams, **Two Studies in the Psychological Effects of Noise, II. The Effects of Noise on the Performance of Weavers,** Industrial Health Research Board (Great Britain), 1932, Report No. 65. Reprinted by permission of the Controller of His Britannic Majesty's Stationery Office.

distribution suggests the important conclusion that, even after years of work in a noisy environment, the worker does not become completely adapted or acclimatized to noise but goes through the process of adaptation daily.

Owing to the increased output with re-

TABLE 19-1

NOISE CREATED BY TWELVE INDUSTRIAL SOURCES

Source of Noise	Decibel Level 3 ft. from Source
Airplane riveting guns	94–103
Drop hammers	99–101
Bumping hammer	100
Hydraulic press	130
Automatic riveters	95– 99
Lathes, average	80
Automatic screw machines	93–100
Airplane riveting guns	94–103
Airplane propeller grinding	100–105
Looms	94–101
Wood planers	98–110
Wood saw	100

From "Your Plant Doesn't Have to Be So Noisy," *Industrial Relations,* January 1948, p. 23.

duced noise, the type of work curve characteristic of the relatively quiet experimental period is better than that of the noisy period, since it is smoother and tends to approximate more nearly the theoretical ideal straight line.

Further data and study of the general significance of noise would permit more specific conclusions; however, noise must be recognized as one of the factors which can exercise an appreciable influence on an individual's job performance, particularly at times when other factors combine to lower personal efficiency.

The American Standards Association defines noise as "undesired sound." To the engineer or physicist noise is a sound whose characteristics can be defined and whose properties can be measured with standard instruments:

(1) Decibel levels are usually determined by electronic measurement, i.e., by a microphone, an amplifier, and a calibrated meter. The complete instrument is known as a sound-level meter.

A subject participating in a sound-localization experiment in a specially constructed chamber at the Psycho-Acoustic Laboratory, Harvard University.

Reflected sounds are carefully controlled. Soundproof chambers of this type are also used to measure noise such as the sound coming from a motor. Photo by courtesy of S. S. Stevens, Director of the Laboratory.

(2) The average office has a background noise level of about 50 decibels.

(3) At a level of 120 decibels most people get a feeling of discomfort.

(4) Around 140 decibels, the feeling becomes painful.

(5) The ear drum may be ruptured at a level of 160 decibels.[22]

The Workmen's Compensation Board of New York State has adopted standards on the relation between deafness and industrial noise. Based on recommendations by a committee of 5 specialists who studied the problem for more than a year, injurious noise starts above 90 decibels. These standards set forth that permanent hearing damage results as follows:

Most persons exposed to over 120 decibels of noise for several hours daily will suffer permanent damage in a matter of months. An "overall" din of 100 to 120 decibels for several hours daily over a long period can permanently damage hearing of a considerable portion of workers. A few very susceptible persons may be permanently damaged by exposure for many years to noises between 90 and 100 decibels.[23]

Several states have legislation that allows compensation for partial loss of hearing by a worker who can prove that his hearing loss was caused by the noise of the factory equipment he operated. In most other states, complete loss of hearing in either or both ears must be proved.

Some sources had concluded as early as 1952 that a prolonged 85-decibel sound will injure a worker's hearing. There is some evidence, however, that a noise level as high as 100 decibels is not injurious even after considerable periods of exposure. The important factor is noise frequency (cycles per second or pitch) rather than decibel rating (volume).[24]

Sleight and Tiffin made a comprehensive survey of the literature on industrial noise and hearing.[25] They found that some experiments have indicated that the harmful effects of noise have been overemphasized, but that the weight of experimental evidence indicates that there are many circumstances wherein noise is deleterious. They suggested that the following actions be taken by employers confronted with the noise problem: (1) noise measurement; (2) institution of noise elimination or reduction measures; (3) establishment of hearing testing programs.

There are several sources from which the employer may draw assistance in approaching his noise exposure problem. Among these:

1. The industrial hygiene division of the state's board of health or its equivalent can help him establish a conservation of hearing program.

2. Trained specialists supplied by insurance companies can be of particular assistance in occupational hearing-loss problems.

3. Trained acoustical consulting engineers, in general, can render assistance on all types of problems.[26]

MUSIC IN INDUSTRY

Hundreds of plant managers have used music to relax tensions and to stimulate production. Stevedores, cotton workers, and others know that music often helps to reduce

fatigue. Managements of some department stores, banks, and other firms regularly devote a period of the working day to mass singing. Night clerks in some post offices handle mail to the music of the radio. We all know that many school children also study their lessons with an ear "glued" to the radio.

One of the beneficial effects of music in industry is that it tends to reduce the strain of factory noises. The irritating din of a factory contributes to fatigue. Factory noise consists of irregular pulsations that lack rhythmic form and regularity. Music, on the other hand, consists of regular pulsations. It has rhythmic sequence. Even in the midst of industrial clatter, the human ear tends to follow a pleasing melody and ignore disagreeable noises. Almost all types of industrial work are adapted to music, with the exception of riveting and other operations that have loud, intermittent noises, sounds of definite pitch, loud squeaks or scratches, or high continuous sound. The explanation for this lies in the acoustical difference between sound and noise.

A helpful fact is that people working constantly in a noisy environment grow accustomed to the noise—in reality, develop a psychological deafness to it—and therefore are able to hear other sounds above the noise far more readily than someone unused to it. For this reason, adjustments in loudspeakers should be made in accordance with the ability of the plant workers to hear the music clearly, rather than with that of the sound engineers who have come in from the outside. Expert sound engineers are aware of this.[27]

Because of the acoustical difference between musical sound and noise, *Rustle of Spring* can be heard through the sound of pneumatic hammers, and *The Skater's Waltz* through the 102 decibels of a worsted mill weaving shed.

Authorities in the field of music and industry do not agree as to the optimum lengths of periods of music. Some prefer twelve to twenty minute periods; others use forty-five minute music periods.

In many companies, the periods from 9:30 to 10 A.M. and 2:00 to 2:30 P.M. are considered major fatigue periods—the periods when music is needed most and is likely to be most effective. This is especially true when the fatigue is mental and is induced by the boredom of repetitive work. Obviously, these fatigue periods do not occur at the same relative time in all plants, but they are usually in the middle of the morning and the middle of the afternoon. Sometimes, production graphs indicate the time when music is likely to be most helpful to the employees.

Some companies follow the practice of scheduling pre-fatigue music—an hour or so after the beginning of each half-day of work. Music for the minor fatigue periods is generally of shorter duration. The most important music periods appear to be those at the opening or closing of the shift, because next to overcoming the tedium of monotonous work, the most important objective is to have workers start and end the day in a pleasant frame of mind.

Those who plan music programs for industry differ somewhat in their planning.

R. L. Cardinell recommends music of progressive stimulation for fatigue periods, asserting that by starting with a selection of moderate stimulation and increasing the pace gradually to the end of the period the program will have a carry-over effect of an hour or more. Other authorities in program planning work on the principle of a gradual decrease in stimulation from the beginning to the end of the day.[28]

Work music should have a clear-cut, singing melody. The tunes should be of a nature that overrides plant noises. Highly stimulating music, such as that of the jitterbug type, is too distracting. *Deep in the Heart of Texas* is usually considered taboo as work music because some workers cannot refrain from stopping to clap hands in the chorus. Religious music, except when used on Sunday morning shifts, tends to slow down production.

The musical selections preferred by employees vary considerably with the individual company. Each management must determine by means of questionnaires the selections and types of music that are preferred.

Scientific tests of the effects of music on work and workers are difficult to make. Those investigators who report greater productivity and less absenteeism after music has been introduced often tend to overlook the presence of other factors which may be influencing the productivity or attendance.

One carefully conducted study of music was made in relation to employee attitudes, piece-work production, and industrial accidents. The influence of an industrial music program, which systematically varied the amount, type, and distribution of music played, was studied in a plant of approximately one thousand employees over a twelve-week period. An effort was made to determine effects of music on employee attitudes, piece-work production, and industrial accidents. Some of the important findings, presented in the summary of the report by Henry Clay Smith, were the following:

Employee Attitudes

A questionnaire concerned with attitudes toward music was sent to every employee before the music program began. Somewhat over 70 per cent of these questionnaires were completed and returned. An analysis of the replies showed that:

1. Almost all of the employees (98 per cent) thought that music during working hours would be at least "mildly pleasant," and 74 per cent thought that it would be "extremely pleasant."

2. The intensity of interest in music while working decreased somewhat with age. The oldest group preferred semiclassical, nonvocal, and quiet music more than the younger groups.

3. No sex differences in the intensity or type of musical interest were found.

4. Personal interviews with a sample of employees at the end of the twelve weeks showed no decrease in the desire for music while working.

Piecework Production

Music in relation to production was studied on a highly repetitive assembly line operation which was on incentive pay. Two separate shifts with an average of 21 employees on each

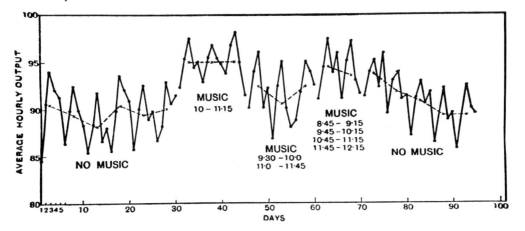

Effects of music on output of workers performing repetitive work on a straight piece-rate basis of pay.—From S. Wyatt and J. N. Langdon, assisted by F. G. L. Stock, **Fatigue and Boredom in Repetitive Work,** Industrial Health Research Board, Great Britain, Report No. 77, 1937. Reprinted by permission of the Controller of his Britannic Majesty's Stationery Office.

shift were studied simultaneously for twelve weeks. The results showed that:

1. Production under varying conditions of music increased from 4 to 25 per cent. The average increase on the day shift was 7, on the night shift, 17 per cent. The increases were statistically significant and large enough to be of economic importance.

2. Maximum production increases were found when music was played 12 per cent of the time on the day shift, 50 per cent of the time on the night shift.

3. Production tended to decrease with a large increase in the number of semi-classical selections but did not vary with a large increase in the number of vocals. Waltzes were more effective at the opening of the shift than marches.

4. Production increases varied with the hour at which music was played and were greatest during the hours of low production.

5. The more an employee wanted music, the more music tended to increase her production; the lower the employee's production, the more music tended to increase her production; the more the employee's job permitted conversations while working, the more music tended to increase her production.

6. The greater effectiveness of large amounts of music on the night shift corresponded with a greater demand for music on the night shift; the greater effectiveness of varied music corresponded with an expressed preference for varied rather than for special types of music; the greater effectiveness of certain distributions of music corresponded with an expressed preference for such distributions.

Conclusions

Music during working hours will generally improve production where repetitive work is common. Properly administered in such situations, it not only will increase production but also will provide widespread employee satisfaction. Music probably produces its major direct effect when the individual's capacity for attention is not absorbed by his work; in this circumstance, music appears to divert unused attention from brooding, talking, or off-the-job activities. Although music, on the average, had no influence on the accident rate, the relation of music to accidents was not entirely clear in the present study.[29]

An investigator who studied the attitudes of employees toward music in several industrial plants offered the following recommendations: Music should be provided for work areas in which the work is manual and monotonous if a majority of employees want it; the music preferences of employees should be measured rather than approximated; the music needs of night-shift workers should receive special attention; selection of bass and soprano announcers should be avoided; and industrial music should be regarded as a factor favorable to quantity of production in the typical repetitive operations of industry.[30]

Perhaps the best indication of the positive value of music for morale is the fact that

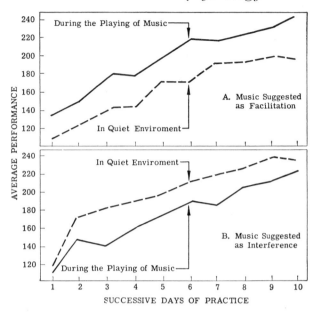

The effect of attitude on performance in mental arithmetic as shown by the production of ten subjects in a quiet environment and during the playing of music (**a**) when music is thought by the subjects to facilitate performance, and (**b**) when subjects believe music interferes with performance. Note that the music facilitates when subjects believe it to, and interferes when they believe it an interference.—Adapted from K. H. Baker, "Pre-experimental Set in Distraction Experiments," **Journal of General Psychology,** Vol. 16 (1937), pp. 471–486. Sidney L. Pressey, J. Elliott Janney, and Raymond G. Kuhlen, **Life: A Psychological Survey.** Harper & Brothers, New York, 1939, p. 533.

once the employer has provided music for the employees, in only rare instances has he discontinued it.

The beneficial effects of music on industrial output seem to have a direct relation to the degree of monotony caused by the work. Relatively simple, mechanized work is most aided by music, but as the task becomes more complex and requires more thought, the beneficial effects of music become less perceptible. This relation seems to hold true because music relieves monotony; it distracts the mind from what seems to be an interminable working day.

When music first was introduced for seventy-five minutes in mid-morning, twelve factory employees on repetitive work, paid on a straight piece-rate basis, increased their average hourly output by 6 per cent over their former average. As shown on page 381, production later dropped when music was played twice a day, but it was still 2.6 per cent higher than when no music was played. Production increased again to 4.4 per cent over that of the non-music period when music was introduced during alternate half hours.[31]

Dance music may be a distraction or an aid to concentration, depending upon the worker's attitude.[32] This fact was brought out in an experiment in which one group of subjects was told that music facilitated arithmetical calculations, and another group was told that it interfered with them. Charts allegedly based on a previous experiment in which the appropriate finding was made were shown to each group to help create the mental set.

The subjects reacted in accordance with the suggestion in both cases. All those who were told that music was an aid to more work produced more work. All those who were told that music would interfere did more under normal conditions of quiet. The subjects who were told at the beginning of the experiment that their performance without music would probably exceed their production with it appeared to work harder under conditions of quiet. Their remarks, changes of posture, and appearances of concentration gave this impression. The subjects who were led to believe that music would increase their output stated afterwards that it had helped to keep their minds on their work. See chart on this page.

It appears that "the changes in attitude

and accompanying changes in motivation may be all that is necessary to account for differences in performance under various experimental conditions."[33]

ACCIDENTS

Many managements have considered industrial accidents as a phase of faulty or inadequate machine design, the lack of proper machine guards, failure to safeguard hazardous areas or the conditions of work such as night work. Recent studies by insurance companies, the National Research Council, and the Industrial Health Research Board of Great Britain have agreed that from 80 to 90 per cent of all accidents are due, not to defective machinery or to a physical or mental defect or lack of skill in the worker, but to an *X factor* in the person injured.[34]

Accident proneness on the part of certain individuals has been indicated by findings such as the following:

1. Analysis of accidents among 946 employees of one mill revealed that employees who had disabling injuries averaged 6.5 minor injuries in the year, while those who had no disabling injuries averaged 3.1 minor injuries. Employees who had one or more doctor's care injuries averaged 5.5 minor injuries and those with no doctor's care injuries averaged 3.0 minor injuries. Evidence indicated the fallacy of the chance distribution theory of accidents and favored the theory of unequal liability: 49 per cent of the employees accounted for 94 per cent of the accidents, 29 per cent of the employees for 80 per cent of the accidents, 11 per cent of the employees for 50 per cent of the accidents, and 3 per cent of the employees for 24 per cent of the accidents.[35]

2. The reason why insurance companies are reluctant to accept automobile policies for drivers who have a record of previous accidents is adequately demonstrated by the results of a group study completed by the Personnel Research Federation. Four and one-half per cent of the drivers had 30 per cent of the accidents —seven times their quota. In another group, 800 drivers had 4,000 accidents—an average of 5 per driver; 400 had 3,200 accidents—8 per driver, and 800 had 10,800 accidents—13½ per

driver! One hundred drivers who had accidently killed one person each had previously killed three, and had had 38 other accidents. One Connecticut study showed that 4 per cent of the drivers were responsible for 36 per cent of all accidents.[36]

3. One large company which employs a great number of truck drivers became concerned about the high cost of its automobile accidents and tried to analyze the causes of accidents in order to reduce their frequency. The company examined the accident records for each driver and finally transferred those who had the most accidents to other occupations. While this reduced the company's auto accident rate, interestingly enough, the drivers who had had a high accident rate retained their accident habit in their new occupations. This would seem to be another clear indication that there exists an accident-prone person[37] and that these individuals are accident-prone in any occupation—and in their everyday life.[38]

Children who are accident prone seem to exhibit a different pattern of behavior from those who have few accidents. When he studied two groups of children who were matched according to age, sex, and accident history over a four-year period, one researcher found that children who had had repeated accidents were generally freer and less inhibited in a doll play situation than the others. Their play was less stereotyped. The accident-prone children expressed their aggression more readily than did the accident-free. The former were more verbally aggressive.

The child's background was found to be related to his behavior, too. Accident repeaters seem to come generally from larger families, were born in somewhat later birth order, came more often from broken homes, and transferred schools frequently. They had been, in many instances, referred to home and school counselors in public schools.

The author suggests that if these characteristics identified in children with accidents were also found in adults, accident liability might be considered continuous from childhood to maturity.[39]

Several significant clinical studies have

Gas Training School which is in the Blast Furnace, Coke Oven and By Products area of the Steel Division, Ford Motor Company. This training goes on continuously all the year round and the objective is to make the employees thoroughly familiar with the use of breathing equipment so that they will put it on and use it just as they would put on a jacket or overcoat without excitement or confusion. Major gas leaks are not common but when they do take place the company wants employees to go about their jobs calmly and methodically and without fear or panic.

been made of accident-prone persons. Alexandra Adler, for example, studied 100 such industrial workers of Europe and 100 Massachusetts applicants for workmen's compensation.[40] Some of her findings were:

Among American accident-prone workers, over one fourth were over-fearful. She found that fear of accidents can produce them. More than 23 per cent of American accident-prone workers had a fatalistic attitude that they were unlucky. Almost 20 per cent wanted to be pampered. More than 13 per cent had a revengeful attitude toward parents or teachers.

Among the European workers, a revengeful attitude was responsible in 56 per cent of the individuals. These men were bitter, antagonistic, revengeful, particularly toward parents and educators.[41]

Flanders Dunbar, a researcher in the field of psychosomatic medicine, has made extensive investigations of the personality profiles of accident-prone and other hospital patients. In one study of 1,600 patients that led to the development of distinguishing profiles, she found that 80 per cent fell into recognizable profiles of significance in regard to accident record:

It is clear from a brief review of these personality profiles that two important diagnostic points are: the sphere of life in which the patient had his major conflicts, and his characteristic means of reaction and of attempting to solve these conflicts. The area of focal conflict of patients with the accident habit is in the realm of authority. The authority may be, first, parents, then school, and later, church, job, wife or husband. The characteristic response to these difficulties is to strive for independence and autonomy outside such relationships and to minimize and avoid conflicts with authority whenever possible, although without submitting. . . .

Any dynamic formulation relative to the profile of these accident-prone personalities should begin with an investigation of the nature of their defenses. By focusing their values on immediate concrete experience, striving to find satisfactions and security outside the authoritarian hierarchy, and avoiding any marked submission or domination in vocational or social roles, accident-prone persons get along without serious conflicts with authority. The defenses work most of the time. When thwarted, deprived, or subjected to unusual strain such as unemployment, or the pressure of a mother-in-law in the family, these persons "do something" to modify the situation or get away from it instead of keeping their anger bottled up inside. It is significant that these patients have a health record far above the average.

When the characteristic defenses fail and conflict with authority becomes unavoidable, the accident happens. Aggressiveness may break out in an act which appears to punish the victim or those responsible for his frustration, or both. Or it may come near enough to the surface to cause the kind of confusion which leaves the person defenseless in the danger situations normally encountered from day to day. Unlike depressed persons who consciously attempt suicide, the accident-prone individual usually reports no conscious premeditation. It is interesting, however, that he occasionally reports a dream or a "hunch" that "something was going to happen today" or that he "was going to have bad luck." This trend is illustrated by the statement made so frequently by these patients after the accident has happened: "You can't get around fate; I got mine today, you'll get yours tomorrow. . . ."

. . . These profiles may be useful to the physician not trained in psychiatry, as an aid in knowing what kind of questions to ask, which emotional problems should be approached first and what *not* to do in general therapeutic management of the patient. Too often if a mother-in-law or a sexual problem turns up, the psychosomatic-minded internist or surgeon concentrates on this and fails to realize that although he may make the patient happy by listening, he will do nothing that is effective in curing the accident habit unless he attempts to deal with the fundamental problems of his patient in terms of both the area of the patient's greatest sensitivity and the inadequacies in his habitual manner of attempting to solve his conflicts.[42]

Night blindness, a factor contributing to some accidents, has been difficult to diagnose, since those affected by it do not always realize it. Electroretinography, which is especially useful in identifying night blindness, was made possible by the introduction of the contact lens electrode for use on human beings in 1941. For the first few years, the laboratory of the Department of Psychology, Brown University, was the only one carrying on this work, but since the war the technique has spread to other laboratories in universities, medical schools, and military installations. The photograph shows electrodes in position for recording the electroretinogram.—See Lorrin A. Riggs, "Electroretinography in Cases of Night Blindness," **American Journal of Ophthalmology,** July 1954.

In a recent study, Dr. W. A. Eggert and Dr. A. H. Malo of the Lumbermens Mutual Casualty Company studied more than 1,400 route salesmen, getting their reactions to situations and to questions involving personality characteristics and then correlating the replies with their accident frequency over a three-year period. Some of their findings were:

High-accident-frequency drivers have more frequently experienced parental divorce. They think that women expect too much of their husbands. They make spur-of-the-moment decisions. They tend to avoid meeting some people face-to-face. They may blush easily. They are easily disturbed by minor irritants, and they tend not to be comfortable in the presence of the opposite sex.

They blow their horns or yell at other drivers. They are more interested in driving than in other aspects of their job. They tend to be irresponsible and to worry only about accidents in which they might be at fault. They are not as considerate of their customers as they should be.[43]

HOW MANY UNSAFE PRACTICES CAN YOU SEE? unsafe working practices are illustrated in the manner of the old picture puzzle. One employee found 34 violations of safety in the above bottling house scene. See Appendix, page 627, for his list. Courtesy of Joseph S. Finch and Company, Schenley, Pa., Stanley S. De Vault, Safety Director. Cartoon by William Wilson.

Several investigators have tried to find psychological tests that identify the accident-prone person. Farmer, summarizing the results of studies on industrial workers, air pilots, and drivers, indicates that "people who are slow and inaccurate on certain sensorimotor tests tend to have a higher accident rate than others," although "the predictive value of these tests is not high." They discriminate well only on the extreme ends of the distribution. "Nervous instability" is also assumed to be related to accident rate, and Farmer[44] expects that progress in the diagnosis of accident proneness will be derived mainly from a direct study of the affective make-up.

Results of the use of tests of this kind have been reported recently. One study was made of bus operators of the Third Avenue Transit Corporation of New York City. Of 178 operators employed in 1954 one group acted as a control. They were selected by the older method of selection, while another group acted as an experimental group. The latter was selected by the old method plus the addition of three written psychological tests. In evaluating these groups the frequency of accidents per man per month was a major criterion. An analysis of the various accidents involving these two groups showed that the accident rates of bus operators who passed the three tests were better than the control group who did not take the tests.[45]

Of two groups of 100 automobile drivers studied in Canada, one group had been involved in four or more accidents, the other in none. When their names were submitted to various legal and social service agencies it was found that 60 per cent of the accident repeaters had been in various other difficulties, as against only 9 per cent of the accident-free group.

The credit bureau knew 34.3 per cent of the repeaters, 6 per cent of the accident-free; social service agencies knew 17.7 of the repeaters, 1 per cent of the non-repeaters; the adult courts (exclusive of traffic violations)

knew 34.3 per cent of the repeaters, only 1 per cent of the others; and even the public health clinic knew 14.4 per cent of the repeaters, but none of the accident-free group.

Follow-up studies over two or three years have shown that these people tend to continue their poor performance. The authors of the study concluded that a poor accident record was only one manifestation of an inadequate "method of living."[46]

Current thinking concerning accidents seems to be that some persons do have more accidents than others, that tests to spot the repeaters do not as yet identify most of those who will have accidents, and that the factors associated with their occurence are not well established. There is also considerable disagreement over just what an "accident-prone" person is. One investigator may use the term in an empirical sense merely to identify persons with a history of accidents. Another may use it in a diagnostic sense, referring to a supposed clinical entity. Empirical descriptions would seem more advisable until sufficient data have been accumulated to make etiological distinctions. Hence we should regard a person with a history of accidents as an "accident-repeater" rather than "accident-prone."[47]

NIGHT WORK

Scientific study of the effect of night work on production is difficult to make because many uncontrolled variables prevent it. However, *Modern Industry* editors surveyed a number of plants to find out what problems are posed by night shifts and how the problems are handled. In some plants night shift workers appear to be more relaxed than day shift workers. Occasionally, they act as if they are doing the company a favor by being on the shift at all.

In general, night workers equal the quantity production of the day shift, but the quality of the work record is usually not as good. For that reason, simple routine jobs may be the best choice for the night shift. Surprisingly, night workers seem to have fewer accidents than the day shift. Perhaps this is because there is less movement of materials at night.

Personnel experts estimate that less than 25 per cent of all workers actually want to work at night. Most of the rest won't do it at any price. Today the usual night-shift premiums (4¢ to 10¢ an hour, or 5% to 10% of earnings) provide little incentive to the worker who doesn't like the night shift to begin with. That's particularly true of the third shift.

Neither does it seem to make much difference whether shifts are rotated so men work each shift for a certain number of weeks, or permanently set, with men definitely assigned to one shift or another. Each has a few things to recommend it, and a good many drawbacks. . . .

When shifts are permanently set, workers with most seniority and highest skill will get the preferred day jobs. That leaves the less-experienced, less-skilled workers for the night shifts. On the credit side, there is that small, reliable corps of men who actually prefer night work. And permanent assignment to it lets them arrange their lives accordingly.[48]

Rotating shifts assure good workers on all shifts. However, because foremen and lead men do not usually rotate, it's harder to build teamwork between workers and supervisors. Also, when shifts rotate, workers must constantly change their eating and sleeping habits.

Because top management, engineers, and production specialists are not regularly in the plant at night, it is difficult to keep night-shift workers informed of company plans and policies. A special effort should be made to get such information to the night-staff— both by word-of-mouth and by means of bulletins and memos.

FATIGUE AND BOREDOM

Certain biology teachers have likened man to a machine and tried to compute his efficiency in a manner similar to that used in measuring the efficiency of motors. In terms of chemical energy consumed, the Diesel engine and the high-compression automobile engine surpass man's efficiency as a machine. In terms of chemical energy consumed as food and converted into external mechanical energy, man's efficiency usually ranges from 15 to 20 per cent.[49]

The term fatigue has various meanings. To the layman it simply means "feeling tired." Researchers usually call this type *subjective fatigue,* and it may be thought of with reference to certain muscles only, or it may be rather general and involve drowsiness. Laboratory experiments often show that subjective fatigue may be quite pronounced but that the person having such feelings actually may be doing as much work as ever.

Subjective fatigue often is distinguished from mental fatigue, the tiredness that develops from work of a mental rather than a muscular nature. The fatigue that results from doing accounting or writing a book may be considered to be somewhat different from the subjective fatigue caused by the use of muscles. Perhaps the difference between the two is only one of degree or source. At any rate, mental workers often wish to change to some other activity, but the other activity at the time may have a greater appeal simply because of vague psychological influences and not because of physiological changes in the body.

Of course, physiological conditions have pronounced bearings on the feelings of fatigue. For example, in hot industries workmen are given salt in tablet form or in drinking water in order to remedy the deficiency of body salt lost through perspiration. Glassmaking, baking, steel, and similar industries furnish salt to workers, especially during heat waves. Some football trainers feed salt, or bouillon, which is more palatable, to football players.

In some fatigue experiments, the subject of the experiment may not feel tired but may do considerably less work. This decreased capacity for work because of exhaustion of energy-producing materials such as sugar products, especially glycogen, and the ac-

An Alertness Indicator has been developed by Tufts University. The Indicator, the device pictured in the middle of the photograph at right, works in such a way that when the subject becomes drowsy or less alert, a relay is tripped. This relay could conceivably be connected to signal the individual or another person that the subject's state of alertness had deteriorated. The meter might have application in any situation where human safety and economic loss would occur if continuous alertness were not maintained, e.g., as in automobile driving or radar watching.

The Alertness Indicator is set up so that the muscle potentials from the subject's forehead and the total integrated electrical output may be read from a meter in the upper right-hand corner of the instrument. For research purposes, Tufts University can also record the bio-electric activity from the Cathode-ray Oscilloscope (shown at the left of the picture) and on an ink recorder shown in the background. Information and photo by courtesy of Prof. Leonard C. Mead.

cumulation of waste products, mostly carbon dioxide and lactic acid, is called *objective fatigue.* Objective and subjective fatigue do not always correlate, especially when the individual is offered a greatly desired reward for continued output.

In most cases, psychological and physiological factors in fatigue are closely interrelated. Differentiation is difficult. However, the "feelings of fatigue" and "boredom" have been differentiated by Brozek:

Boredom is characterized by discontent, restlessness and yawning, whereas the "feeling of fatigue" appears as weariness and can be relieved only by rest. Fatigue which accompanies heavy or very intensive work is regarded as a subjective sign of physiological changes produced by the work. In some cases, such as sprinting, it is possible to identify and measure some of the physiological changes such as the rise in blood lactate, oxygen debt, and so on. . . .

What are the personal characteristics of the boredom-prone individual? Wyatt and Langdon[50] investigated four personality traits: general intelligence, divided attention ("ability to think of other things while working"), perseveration (interference of the preceding activity) and introversion-extraversion. The differences between the average scores of "least bored" and

"most bored" workers were found to be statistically significant for the first and last traits studied. Higher intelligence and extroversion tend to be associated with greater susceptibility to boredom.

Individuals who were classified as "most bored" registered also a higher number of complaints against working conditions. In three plants where studies were made on sub-groups comprising 54, 34 and 26 workers, bored workers registered on the average, 19 per cent, 23.7 per cent, and 21.3 per cent more complaints.

Workers spontaneously develop antidotes to boredom such as talking, singing and daydreaming. Features introduced and tested experimentally in previous investigations included such factors as rest pauses and changes in the form of work.[51]

More work is done per hour when authorized rest periods are given to clerks than when there are no authorized rest periods.

Even when the length of time consumed by pauses is added to the length of the working day, this increase holds true. These findings were made for a group of sixteen women, comptometer operators, who were computing applications for crop loans in a government agency.

When the experiment was started, the only authorized rest pause was the 45-minute

An air conditioned room, insulated with cork all around, and capable of maintaining temperatures from 35 to 160°F with dew points of from 35 to 120°F.

Temperature and humidity affect the amount of work a man can do. When both temperature and humidity are high, a worker accomplishes less than he does when the temperature is at the same high level but the humidity is low. A man capable of performing 100 units of work under comfortable temperature and humidity conditions, can produce 90 units of work at 100°F with 30% relative humidity, but only 70 units at 100°F with 60% relative humidity.

When the environmental temperature approaches body temperature humidity is much more important than temperature in affecting the amount of work a man can do.

For further information, see C. P. Yaglou, "Beat Summer Heat Now," **Factory Management & Maintenance**, June 1955, pp. 102–103. Photograph and information courtesy of C. P. Yaglou, Department of Industrial Hygiene, Harvard University.

noon recess. Observers noted that the women took rest pauses when it was convenient. During the second part of the experiment, rest periods were installed from 10:22 to 10:30 A.M. and from 2:23 to 2:30 P.M., and the fifteen minutes thereby consumed were added to the length of the workday. During this part of the experiment a decrease in the amount of unauthorized rest and an increase in the amount of production per hour was proved. Although in this particular case only six of the sixteen operators preferred authorized rest periods, the complaints of the majority were directed not at the system itself but at the crowded restroom. Such negative aspects of the work situation

should, of course, be corrected if authorized rest pauses are inaugurated.[52]

Rest periods in industry

Practices in regard to the granting of rest periods vary for office and factory workers.

The Office Management Association of Chicago made a recent survey of 170 companies, employing a total of 82, 636 employees. Of these 170 companies, 128 said they had policies providing for regular rest periods, while 23 more, although allowing employees to take time off, had no formal policy governing such matters. Only 19 companies did not grant rest periods.

Two-thirds of the companies stated they allow rest periods of 15 minutes twice a day. Ten per cent give 20-minute rest periods. Breaks, where scheduled, normally are not allowed to begin less than an hour after the beginning of the working day, and they must be completed at least an hour before lunch or quitting time.[53]

Robert M. Smith, a time study engineer, sent a questionnaire to 96 companies, selected at random from Moody's list of industrial firms, concerning rest periods in factories. Of the 96 questionnaires sent out, 50 were completed:

On the question of allowances for piece-work time standards, the survey showed that the granting of a certain amount of compensatory time for fatigue and personal needs is generally accepted practice. An additional allowance is sometimes given for unavoidable operating delays. These allowances may vary according to the individual operation or may be the same for all operations and established plant practice. The over-all average allowance for both personal and operating delay factors was reported to be 11.7 per cent of the total working time.

The average allowance specifically allocated to personal and fatigue delays was 8.5 per cent; four plants varied this allowance according to the nature of the operation. Two other plants allowed a flat 3 per cent for personal needs. One company had established 24 minutes as sufficient time for personal needs in an eight-hour shift. Most other respondents gave similar personal and fatigue allowances except, as might be expected, where hot and dirty work was involved. One airplane manufacturing plant, for example, granted a 25 per cent personal allowance on certain welding operations.[54]

REST PERIOD ACTIVITIES. Forty plants made coffee and soft drinks available during rest periods; seven did not. Of the former, two specified that soft drinks only were available; one specified milk and one dispensed free coffee. In addition, 35 plants allowed snacks at the bench, and again seven did not. In no case were there lounge rooms for the use of male workers during working hours, and in only one plant was there a lounge for female workers.

Plant rules on smoking are shown in the following breakdown:

	Plants
Smoking permitted, except in hazardous areas	17
No smoking, except in men's room	13
Smoking not permitted, except in designated areas	6
Smoking permitted during rest period only	4

The reasons given for installing scheduled rest periods were:

	Plants
Belief that such rest periods are necessary because of health, fatigue, and morale factors	7
To control the time workers spend away from their work place	4
Area practice	3
Union request	3
Belief that production would be increased	2
In effect a number of years and initial reason unknown	4

Although rewards such as rest pauses and bonuses facilitate production markedly, they have little effect on reported feelings of tiredness and boredness. This was found in an experiment in which subjects were told to "work as hard and as fast as you can" at monotonous laboratory work that simulated the type of work done by many industrial workers daily. The study was made to determine the effects of various suggested attitudes or mental sets on work productivity and boredom. Authors tested eighty-eight college students—divided into groups to test various attitudes and conditions. The manual work (motor tasks) performed were simple, but equipment prevented it from becoming automatic even toward the end of the four-hour test period.

Under ordinary working conditions, reported feelings of tiredness and boredness were found to be in inverse proportion to the amount of work done. There also was found to be an inverse relation between observable boredom and tiredness as rated by experimenters and amount of work done. Additional findings were:

Knowledge that a rest pause is imminent retards production for the period immediately preceding the pause.

Indulgence in activities such as talking or

laughing tends to objectify the working situation and also tends to inhibit to some extent reports of tiredness and boredness.

The introduction of positive motivation, in the waking state, facilitates production considerably, and produces fewer reports of tiredness and boredness.

The introduction of negative motivation, in the waking state, inhibits production significantly but has little effect on reports of tiredness and boredness.[55]

Workers often reduce their boredom at repetitive work through conversation. They provide their own rest pauses if management does not systematize rest for them.

Coffee breaks

Approximately one half of 170 companies surveyed in Chicago distribute coffee from a central location such as a cafeteria or snack bar. Others arrange to have coffee brought in from the outside. Less than ten per cent serve it at the employee's desk. For many offices and plants, the automatic coffee-vending machine is the answer to the mid-morning coffee problem. Machines require no more employee time than the moment required to put a coin in the slot and carry the drink back to the machine or desk.

Desk-side coffee service at Mutual of New York.

One company, Mutual Life Insurance of New York, estimated that the coffee break saves $130,000 a year in over-all labor costs when the coffee is delivered to the workers' desks.[56] Of course this number of dollars saved does not show up on the company's accounting books—it is an estimate of the value of the time lost when 800 employees spent 20 minutes a day getting a "second breakfast."

The extent to which the coffee break increases productivity is not clear even though some surveys indicate that it does reduce fatigue and increase productivity. Most companies do think that it has some effect in improving company morale.

Caffeine is often used to overcome fatigue or to increase alertness. In general, caffeine, when administered as the raw alkaloid or as caffeine citrate, tends to reduce simple motor-sensory reaction time from 6 to 8 per cent, depending upon the individual.[57] Hollingworth has reported studies of differential effects of dosages and found that the speed of performance at typing was quickened by doses of one to three grains of caffeine but retarded by larger doses of four to six grains. Small doses seemed to decrease errors and increase speed in typing, but doses greater than six grains had opposite effects.[58]

In general, the effects of caffeine appear to be slight on the average, but they vary greatly with the type of work performed and the person involved.

SMOKING

Tobacco is used by many persons as an aid to efficiency in work. Numerous experimenters have tried to investigate its effects by setting up controlled conditions, using control subjects for comparisons, and attempting to eliminate influences of suggestion. Most of these studies have failed to exclude the influences of variables such as habit, attitude toward smoking, body weight, suggestion, and others. Accordingly, a few researchers have used rats as subjects for experiment. Nathan W. Shock has summarized the studies regarding many of our psychophysiological relations, including certain experimental results on effects of tobacco:

Pechstein and Reynolds[59] exposed rats to tobacco smoke over a period of 30 minutes to 3 hours daily for 30 to 60 days. The animals were exposed to smoke from 5 gr. of tobacco, so there is no indication whether the effects were produced by nicotine, carbon monoxide, pyridine, or some other combustion products of tobacco. After fuming, the animals were transferred to the maze, and learning curves were obtained. It was found that rats fumed with a limited amount of tobacco smoke excelled all normal and experimental groups in maze learning. Animals who were fumed over longer periods of time were less effective in learning, with greater variability in the female group. The authors concluded that tobacco smoke to a small degree acts as a stimulant and enhances learning, while excessive smoking depletes learning capacity to the point of inability by the fourth generation.[60]

Professor Raymond Pearl, biologist at Johns Hopkins University, published several studies showing that tobacco smokers do not live as long as non-smokers:

This conclusion was based on life tables for the number, out of groups of 100,000 non-smoking men, 100,000 moderate smokers (men), and 100,000 heavy smokers (men), who were still alive at each age level after 30 years. At age 60, for example, 66,564 of the 100,000 non-smokers were still living; 61,911 of 100,000 moderate smokers were living; and 46,226 of 100,000 heavy smokers were still living. The studies show that smoking is associated with a definite impairment of longevity. This impairment is proportional to the habitual amount of tobacco usage by smoking, being great for heavy smokers and less for moderate smokers, but even in the latter sufficient to be measurable and significant. The effect of tobacco smoking on length of life is different from that of alcohol in that moderate as well as heavy smokers live less long than non-smokers, whereas moderate drinkers do not have appreciably shorter lives than total abstainers, although heavy drinkers do.

The effect of hard physical labor on length of life was also studied by statistical methods. Up to the age of about 40 years, hard labor either indoors or outdoors has no effect on life expectation, but after about age 40 such labor "definitely and considerably" shortens the length of life of the individuals.[61]

Although no conclusive findings have been made regarding the effects of smoking on the human body, the general consensus in the medical profession is that smoking has no outstandingly beneficial effects. Two physicians, Kahn and Gildea, believe that smokers fall into two categories, the lusty and the tense.[62]

The lusty smoker enjoys the so-called good things of life, such as excellent meals and pleasant company, whereas the tense smoker is characterized by inner tensions. The lusty smoker, who prefers cigars and pipes to cigarettes, smokes for sensual pleasure, whereas the tense smoker smokes to alleviate tension. The latter can be distinguished from the lusty smoker by the quick, nervous way he takes the cigarette from the package, lights it, and inhales the first puff. He smokes half absentmindedly, half ritualistically.

If the tense smoker wishes to discard the smoking habit, the factors such as work or home difficulties that have created his tension usually must be removed, or he must adjust himself so as to be comparatively free from tension. Getting to the cause of tensions is ordinarily difficult, but must be done if the tense smoker is to give up smoking. Because people do not realize the true causes of their tensions their efforts to give up smoking are unsuccessful. This is the reason why the substitution method—chewing gum or sucking candies—by itself practically never effects a cure. It does not get to the root of the habit. If a fundamental cause of tension is suddenly removed, as by an inheritance or dissolution of an unfortunate marriage, breaking the habit may be easy. However, in most cases fundamental causes of tension cannot be eliminated entirely, so that relaxation must be achieved through cultivation of a hobby or a new interest.

Breaking the habit should be done on the basis of *one* decision, and at once. If it is done for reasons of physical health, a physician can aid the patient to make the decision and emphasize the strength to quit smoking. He can do this by helping the patient to gain insight into the reasons for his smoking. After the cause of tension has been determined, past conditioning must be overcome. Long-established smoking habit patterns must be rechanneled. Substitution of something other than tobacco now will help. Instead of pulling out a cigarette and putting it in the mouth, one may substitute a mint, peanut, or toothpick. Occasionally an old habit may be given up by substituting a new one, but this requires stronger motivation than ordinarily is available.

Summary

In general, we can say that fatigue and efficiency of the individual are influenced by many chemical and psychological influences. Furthermore, the individual can accommodate himself to almost any conditions. Man has permanent settlements in towns that frequently have winter temperatures 50 degrees F. below zero and in deserts with sun temperatures of 150 degrees. Attitude is exceedingly important toward the adaptation. An experienced stevedore, for example, can toss freight all day without appreciable fatigue but will be worn out by several hours of simple effort while on a shopping trip with his wife who is looking for a hat!

In the case of industrial workers, Britain's Industrial Health Board has summarized the findings of researchers on the effects of working hours and similar factors on output of workers as follows:

It used to be thought that worker's and employer's interests were opposed—the worker wanting plenty of leisure and pay, the employer wanting the most work for the least expenditure. But now psychological researches into industry have shown that the best conditions of work for the greatest output are exactly the same as those that give health and a low accident rate to the worker.[63]

Industrial psychologists have concluded that bad working conditions do not in themselves produce bad morale nor do good working conditions produce good morale. Rather, the *psychological climate* determines the kind or degree of good or poor morale. A company may, for example, recognize that certain employees have to work over a chemical bath that gives off unpleasant fumes. When an exhaust system is installed to draw off the fumes, morale goes up or down depending upon whether the workers think that the exhaust system was installed for their benefit or to boost output only. When workers are suspicious of the reasons behind management's moves, the improvement of working conditions will not change morale.[64]

Many executives, in their labor relations thinking, still pay too much attention to physical frills and not enough to human feelings. The frills can make a factory or office a more comfortable place in which to work, but the best morale and highest production come out of a homey atmosphere of friendliness and personal understanding between management and workers. It is, of course, much easier for an executive to install a system or device of some kind than for him to change his cold personality to a friendly understanding one.

General Motors, using its own 79 plants as a laboratory, conducted an interesting study on the effect of physical environment on productivity. The company has some plants that are the last word in employee comfort as well as other, older plants where there is less emphasis on the mechanics of comfort. The survey showed that there was no difference in output between the slick and the staid plants. Workers who are impressed by swank factories and bowling leagues will normally gravitate to such plants, it seemed, while others, who do not care for externals or sports, take jobs with companies that do not go in for showmanship. The study showed that while frills and fringes made no dent one way or the other in individual productivity, the degree of camaraderie in the department or plant made a tremendous difference in ultimate output.[65]

Acknowledgments and References

1. Joseph Tiffin, *Industrial Psychology,* 2nd ed., Prentice-Hall, Inc., 1947, pp. 475 ff.

2. T. N. Whitehead, *The Industrial Worker,* Harvard University Press, Cambridge, Mass., 1938, Vol. I, p. 94.

3. *Modern Industry,* December 15, 1947.

4. Matthew Luckiesh, "Footcandle Levels Threshold, Ideal, Optimum, and Recommended," paper presented at the National Technical Conference of the Illuminating Engineering Society, New Orleans, September 15–19, 1947. General Electric Company, Cleveland, Ohio.

5. See Kenneth Piper, "Motorola's Vision Program Pays Off," *Advanced Management,* September 1951, pp. 24–25.

6. *The Influence of Lighting, Eyesight and Environment Upon Work Production,* Public Buildings Administration and the Public Health Service, Washington, D.C., 1947. See also *The Magazine of Light,* Vol. 17, No. 1 (1948).

7. Matthew Luckiesh, *op. cit.*

8. Matthew Luckiesh, *Seeing,* Lighting Research Laboratory, General Electric Company, Nela Park, Cleveland, 1931. See also Matthew Luckiesh and Frank K. Moss, *Light, Vision and Seeing,* Lighting Research Laboratory, General Electric Company, Nela Park, Cleveland, The Year Book Publishers, Inc., Chicago, Illinois, 1942.

9. See *Business Week,* Aug. 6, 1955, p. 144.

10. Miles A. Tinker, "Illumination Standards for Effective and Comfortable Vision," *Journal of Consulting Psychology,* Vol. 3, No. 1 (January–February 1939), pp. 17 ff. Quoted by permission of the author and the *Journal.*

11. "Color Punches the Time Clock," *The Management Review,* American Management Association, September 1947, p. 452. After Lloyd Stouffer, *Popular Science,* June 1947, p. 124–6.

12. *Loc. cit.*

13. "Color in the Office," *The Management Review,* American Management Association, September 1948. After C. E. Seghers, *Office Management Association of Chicago Monthly Bulletin,* April 1948.

14. *Loc. cit.*

15. Faber Birren, "Color Conditioning in Modern Industry," *Dun's Review,* July 1942. See also *The Management Review,* American Management Association, Vol. 31, No. 8 (August 1942).

16. See Faber Birren, "Color in Your Plant," *Factory Management and Maintenance,* February 1954, pp. 110–112.

17. See "Making Color Pay Off in the Plant," *Safety Maintenance and Production,* April 1955.

18. See "Industry Dresses Up with Color," *The Management Review,* American Management Association, February 1955, p. 77.

19. K. G. Pollock and F. C. Bartlett, H. C. Weston and S. Adams, *Two Studies in the Psychological Effects of Noise,* Industrial Health Research Board, Great Britain, Report No. 65 (1932).

20. Robert B. Sleight and Joseph Tiffin, "Industrial Noise and Hearing," *Journal of Applied Psychology,* American Psychological Association, Inc., Vol. 32 (1948), pp. 476–489.

21. H. C. Weston and S. Adams, *Two Studies in the Psychological Effects of Noise, II. The Effects of Noise on the Performance of Weavers,* Industrial Health Research Board, Great Britain, Report No. 65 (1932).

22. Albert E. Bachmann, "Quiet, Please!" *Harvard Business Review,* May–June 1955, p. 69.

23. See John F. Goldsmith, "New and Noteworthy," *Factory Management and Maintenance,* February 1954, p. 132.

24. See K. W. Bennett, *Iron Age,* July 7, 1955, p. 51.

25. Robert B. Sleight and Joseph Tiffin, *op. cit.*

26. For further information, see Albert E. Bachman, *op. cit.,* pp. 68–74.

27. "Your Plant Doesn't Have to Be So Noisy," *Industrial Relations,* January 1948, p. 23.

28. R. McDaniel, "How Music Increases Office Production," *American Business,* Vol. 15 (April 1945), pp. 22 ff.

29. Henry Clay Smith, "Music in Relation to Employee Attitudes, Piece-Work Production, and Industrial Accidents. With a foreword by Joseph Tiffin," *Applied Psychology Monograph,* No. 14, Stanford University, published for the American Psychological Association by Stanford University Press, 1947.

30. Ernest M. Werner, *Work Music by Muzak, 1945–47, a Research Study of Its Effectiveness and Acceptance,* Muzak Corporation, New York, 1948, p. 23.

31. W. A. Kerr, "Psychological Research in Industrial Music and Plant Broadcasts," *Journal of Psychology,* Vol. 17 (April 1944), pp. 243–261.

32. S. Wyatt and J. N. Langdon, assisted by F. G. L. Stock, *Fatigue and Boredom in Repetitive Work,* Industrial Health Research Board, Great Britain, Report No. 77 (1937).

33. K. H. Baker, "Pre-experimental Set in Distraction Experiments," *Journal of General Psychology,* Vol. 16 (1937), pp. 471–486.

34. Flanders Dunbar, "Susceptibility to Accidents," *The Medical Clinics of North America,* 28; 659–661 (May 1944). Published by W. B. Saunders Company, Philadelphia.

35. C. E. Jurgensen, "How Much Do We Know About Accident Causes?" *National Safety News,* Vol. 52, No. 5 (1945), pp. 26–27, 80, 82, 84.

36. *The Management Review,* American Management Association, July 1948, p. 375.

37. Alexander Mintz and Milton L. Blum have made a critical examination of data establishing the principle of accident-proneness. They have shown the need for better quantitative criteria to establish estimates of differences in accident liability. See their article "A Re-examination of the Accident Proneness Concept," *Journal of Applied Psychology,* American Psychological Association, Inc., June 1949.

38. "What Psychiatry Has to Say about the Accident Habit," *Personnel,* American Management Association, May 1949, p. 407.

39. See Vita Krall, "Personality Characteristics of Accident-Repeating Children," *Journal of Abnormal and Social Psychology,* January 1953, pp. 99–107.

40. Alexandra Adler, "Accidents in Industry," *Science,* Vol. 94 (September 5, 1941).

41. *Ibid.,* p. 12.

42. Flanders Dunbar, *op. cit.*

43. "New Light on the Accident-Prone," as reported by A. H. Malo. See *Personnel,* American Management Association, July 1954, p. 65.

44. E. Farmer, "Accident Proneness and Accident Liability," *Occupational Psychology,* Vol. 14, No. 121 (1940), p. 125. See also Joseph M. Brozek, "Psychological Factors in Relation to Performance and Fatigue," reprinted from *Federation Proceedings,* Vol. 2, No. 3 (September 1943).

45. Harold Brandaleone and Edward Flamm, "Psychological Testing—Effect on the Accident Frequency of Bus Operators," *Industrial Medicine and Surgery,* July 1955, p. 296.

46. From *The Insurance Index,* January 1954. See also *The Management Review,* American Management Association, March 1954, p. 175.

47. See John C. Larson, "Industrial Accident Research: How Can It Be Improved?" *Personnel,* American Management Association, September 1955, pp. 135–138.

48. "Making Night Work Pay," *Modern Industry,* January 15, 1948, pp. 41–44.

49. J. D. Ratcliff, "What Makes You Tired," *Collier's,* December 21, 1940, p. 43.

50. S. Wyatt and J. N. Langdon, "Fatigue and Boredom in Repetitive Work," Industrial Health Research Board, Great Britain, Report No. 77 (1937), p. 86.

51. Joseph M. Brozek, "Psychological Factors in Relation to Performance and Fatigue," *Federation Proceedings,* Vol. 2, No. 3 (September 1943).

52. William McGehee and Edwin B. Owne, "Authorized and Unauthorized Rest Pauses in Clerical Work," *Journal of Applied Psychology,* American Psychological Association, Inc., Vol. 24 (October 1940), pp. 605–614.

53. See *The Management Review,* American Management Association; reported in *Office Management* July 1955, p. 471.

54. Robert M. Smith, "Rest Periods in Industry: A Survey," *Personnel,* American Management Association, July 1955, p. 49.

55. James H. Taylor, Claude E. Thompson, Dimiter Spassoff, "The Effect of Conditions of Work and Various Suggested Attitudes on Production and Reported Feelings of Tiredness and Boredness," *Journal of Applied Psychology,* American Psychological Association, Inc., Vol. 2 (1937), pp. 431–447.

56. *The Management Review,* July 1955, p. 471.

57. W. Shilling, "The Effect of Caffeine and Acetanilid on Simple Reaction Time," *Psychological Review,* Vol. 28 (1921), pp. 72–79.

58. H. L. Hollingworth, "The Influence of Caffeine on the Speed and Quality of Performance in Type-writing," *Psychological Review,* American Psychological Association, Inc., Vol. 19 (1912), pp. 66–73.

59. L. A. Pechstein and W. R. Reynolds, "The Effect of Tobacco Smoke on the Growth and Learning Behavior of the Albino Rat and Its Progeny," *Journal of Comparative Psychology,* Vol. 24 (1937), pp. 459–469.

60. Nathan W. Shock, "Some Psychophysiological Relations," *Psychological Bulletin,* Vol. 36, No. 6 (June 1939), pp. 447–476.

61. "Smokers Less Long-Lived; Heavy Drinkers Die Earlier," *Science News Letter,* March 12, 1938.

62. Eugen Kahn, M.D., and Edwin F. Gildea, M.D., "How to Overcome the Smoking Habit," *The Connecticut State Medical Journal,* Vol. V., No. 12 (December 1941), pp. 886 ff.

63. Marjorie Van De Water, *Science—Supplement,* Vol. 92, No. 2396, p. 12.

64. See *The Foreman's Letter,* National Foreman's Institute, New York, December 6, 1954, p. 3.

65. See Lawrence Stessin, "Good Feeling Is Key to Productivity, Survey Suggests," *Forbes Magazine,* Oct. 1, 1952.

PROJECTS

1. Conduct a study among fellow students or associates regarding effects on efficiency of listening to the radio while reading or studying. Note the kind of music listened to, the loudness, and other pertinent factors.

2. List the factors in lighting that tend to improve productivity in industry. Which recommended factors or principles are you violating in the lighting of your own study or work environment?

3. Consider the colors of walls, ceilings, and furniture in your study or work situation. Are the colors conducive to study or work? What improvements would you like to make in the colors of your work or study environment?

4. What kinds of noises do you usually have in your study or work environment? If certain ones distract you from study or work, how do you try to adapt yourself to them? Do you simply ignore them? Does ignoring them appear to affect your productivity or your comfort? Have you ever been in a work situation in which the noise factor was a major problem? How was it solved?

5. What is the effect of music on your mental efficiency? Do your tastes in music annoy anyone else who studies or works in your environment? If others are annoyed by your preferences in music, what reasons can you suggest for the different preferences?

6. What period of the day can you do your best mental work: early morning, mid-morning, noon, mid-afternoon, late afternoon, early evening, or late at night? When is your mental efficiency lowest? Do you try to schedule difficult mental tasks accordingly?

7. Do you know an automobile driver who has had several automobile accidents? If you do, describe any psychological factors that may be influential in his high accident rate. If you were a traffic court judge, what sentences would you impose on traffic law violators who are "repeaters"?

8. If you use tobacco, how does it seem to affect your mental efficiency? If you were the executive in charge of a large office, what rules would you have about smoking?

COLLATERAL READINGS

Ghiselli, Edwin E., and Clarence W. Brown, *Personnel and Industrial Psychology,* McGraw-Hill Book Company, Inc., New York, 1955, Chapters 9–12.

Poffenberger, A. T., *Principles of Applied Psychology,* Appleton-Century-Crofts, Inc., New York, 1942, Chapter 20.

Ryan, Thomas A., *Work and Effort, The Psychology of Production,* The Ronald Press Company, New York, 1947, Chapters 3 and 4.

Tiffin, Joseph, and S. Edgar Wirt, "The Importance of Visual Skills for Adequate Job Performance in Industry," *Journal of Consulting Psychology*, Vol. 8, No. 2 (March–April 1944), pp. 80–89.

MUSIC IN INDUSTRY

Benson, Barbara Elna, *Music and Sound Effects in Industry*, McGraw-Hill Book Company, Inc., New York, 1945.

Kerr, W. A. "Three Studies in Plant Music," *Factory Management Maintenance*, Vol. 101, No. 11 (1943), p. 280; *passim*.

———, "Psychological Research in Industrial Music and Plant Broadcasting," *Journal of Psychology*, Vol. 17 (1944), pp. 243–261.

———, "Experiments on the Effects of Music on Factory Production," *Applied Psychology Monograph*, No. 5 (1945), p. 40.

Kirkpatrick, F. H., "Music in Industry," *Journal of Applied Psychology*, Vol. 27 (1943), pp. 268–274.

Music in Industry, Industrial Recreation Association for American Industry, Chicago, 1944.

Smith, Henry Clay, *Psychology of Industrial Behavior*, McGraw-Hill Book Company, Inc., New York, 1955, Chapter 13.

Werner, Ernest M., *Work Music by Muzak, 1945–1947, a Research Study of its Effectiveness and Acceptance*, Muzak Corporation, New York, 1948.

FATIGUE

Bartley, S. Howard, and Eloise Chute, *Fatigue and Impairment in Man*, McGraw-Hill Book Company, Inc., New York, 1947.

Blum, Milton L., *Industrial Psychology and Its Social Foundations*, Harper & Brothers, New York, 1949, Chapter 10.

Harrell, Thomas Willard, *Industrial Psychology*, Rinehart and Company, Inc., New York, 1949, Chapter 9.

Maier, Norman R. F., *Psychology in Industry*, Houghton Mifflin Company, Boston, 1955.

CHAPTER TWENTY

Group dynamics in industry

The behavior of each worker takes place in a social context. Researches have demonstrated the importance of recognizing the group dynamics and the individual group member's expectations. The potentials for action within the individuals of the group can be utilized in order to build an effective work team.

Industrial psychologists and members of management have, in the main, concentrated their efforts on the individual. Many psychologists in industry have confined themselves to such activities as interviewing, testing, rating, and counseling the worker. Management men, too, have thought in similar terms. Of necessity, the individual always will be a focus of interest to both the psychologist and the executive.

Until recently groups of employees have been considered mainly as work units, and employee relations programs have been concerned with wage payment plans, unionization, company sponsored social affairs, and recreational programs. All of these relations of management to employees as a group or groups are pertinent to good morale and productivity. Investigations have shown that they are not in themselves, however, sufficient to assure either good morale or high productivity. It has been found necessary to consider the function of the group in other aspects of the work situation.

Considerable research is now being done in industry and in the military concerning factors that influence work carried out by teams rather than by individuals only. Team members must be able and willing to anticipate the expectations of other members as well as make their own needs known to them.

Within the group are certain powerful dynamics such as the degree of cohesiveness or the extent to which members of the group stick together as a team in order to attain their objectives. The psychological climate, the extent to which employees participate in making decisions about their work, the role of the leader, and the attitudes of workers toward the group are examples of the kinds of influences that currently are being studied in the area of group dynamics.

Historically, the growing interest in group dynamics can be dated from the research studies made by the Harvard investigators in the Hawthorne plant of the Western Electric Co. These studies began in 1927 and lasted five years. The stated aim at the time was to find "the relation between conditions of work and the incidence of fatigue and monotony among employees."[1]

Temperature, humidity, and hours of sleep were to be studied to learn the effects of these factors on output. As the experiment progressed, it was discovered that productivity is influenced by a wide variety of factors including attitudes, motives, interpersonal relations, and strong forces from within and without the group itself.

Some of their first experiments dealt with the introduction of unaccustomed rest pauses. Later, variations were made in length of working days and weeks. The wage incentive was also considered as an influence on output, but the investigators concluded that the wage itself was not adequate to account for output changes.

Social relationships in a factory: a study of an industrial group[2]

The most provocative aspects of these experiments have been described by Whitehead and are here summarized as follows:

In a special test room designed for the experiment, five girls assembled telephone relays at a work bench. Trays containing parts for assembly were opposite them. A sixth girl procured necessary parts for the assemblers and performed other routine duties. A male supervisor and one or two assistants sat facing the assemblers. The supervisor in charge obtained and kept numerous records relating to quality of output, reasons for temporary stops, length of time spent in bed by each girl every night, periodical medical reports of their physical condition, and other factors. Room temperatures and relative humidities were taken hourly. The supervisor and his assistants made extensive daily notes of conversation and of the relations developing among the workers. The workers were also occasionally interviewed in a separate room by an experienced interviewer. Furthermore, an automatic device recorded, to a fraction of a second, the instant at which each girl completed each assembled relay. Hence, a minute-to-minute record of output with supplementary information was available for each girl over a five-year period.

When the production of each worker was charted in graphic form, it was found that wave-like irregularities were exhibited by each graph. Some of the waves lasted for months; others only a week or two. The output figures also showed that similar irregularities occurred with durations of as little as a minute or two.

At first it was supposed that these variations in working speed might be related to the experimental changes deliberately introduced, or possibly to other changes in physical circumstance such as temperature or the worker's physical state. However, careful analysis of the data showed that irregularity in output failed to correlate with any known changes of physical circumstance.

When this negative conclusion was reached, the researchers next considered changes in the girls' social relationships. Study along these lines produced positive results. It was found that speed of work varied markedly with changes in the sentiments entertained by the workers toward each other, toward their supervisors, and toward the group. A social history of the test room from 1927 to 1932 offered an explanation of the major fluctuations found in the graphs.

Certain graphs showed an average increase in speed of about 30 per cent. The curves were not learning curves, because all the workers had had several years experience in the work before they came into the test room. The plateaus and spurts in output were decidedly suggestive, and analysis showed that:

Average weekly output of five workers assembling telephone relays, who received much individual consideration under a variety of work conditions. The following summary describes the various "periods" of work:

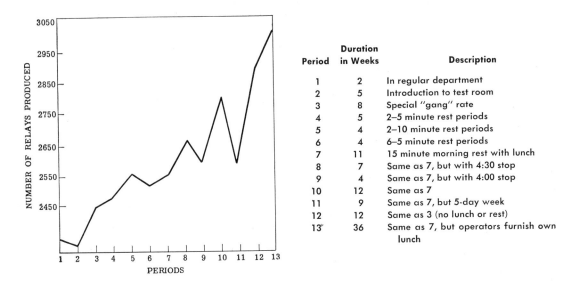

Period	Duration in Weeks	Description
1	2	In regular department
2	5	Introduction to test room
3	8	Special "gang" rate
4	5	2–5 minute rest periods
5	4	2–10 minute rest periods
6	4	6–5 minute rest periods
7	11	15 minute morning rest with lunch
8	7	Same as 7, but with 4:30 stop
9	4	Same as 7, but with 4:00 stop
10	12	Same as 7
11	9	Same as 7, but 5-day week
12	12	Same as 3 (no lunch or rest)
13	36	Same as 7, but operators furnish own lunch

In this study extending for more than two years, a group of workers were placed with usual equipment in a separate room, shown friendly individual consideration, and repeatedly interviewed regarding their opinions of various incentive conditions that were being investigated. The noteworthy thing is that **regardless** of the incentive or the work conditions introduced, **output continued to increase!** As an outgrowth of this study, the company has since instituted a plan of widespread interviewing of individual workers.—Data from Elton Mayo, "Supervision and Morale," **Human Factor,** Vol. 5 (1931), pp. 248–260. Chart and comment on Mayo's data taken from Sidney L. Pressey, J. Elliott Janney, and Raymond G. Kuhlen, **Life: A Psychological Survey,** Harper & Brothers, New York, 1939, pp. 542–3.

. . . It was the organization of human relations, rather than the organization of techniques, which accompanied spurts in these cases. This illustrates the futility of attending exclusively to the economic motivation of workers, or to their physical conditions of work. These things are of high importance; but no group of workers can be expected to remain satisfied, or co-operative, unless their social organization and sentiments are also protected at the working level.[3]

As the experiment progressed, the girls developed common interests and loyalties. The girls took their discipline out of the hands of the supervisor and supervised themselves. For example, when a girl wished to have a half day's leave she had to obtain permission from the supervisor. However, the girls themselves developed a custom whereby no girl could ask for such leave unless the group approved the request.

In general, the output of individual workers was directly related to their sentiments toward each other. The feelings of *approval, antagonism,* and *indifference* toward each other influenced their individual variations in output. One of Whitehead's final generalizations was the following:

Perhaps the main conclusion to be chosen from this type of analysis is the vital importance of human relationship as a factor in the motivation of an industrial group, and in its ultimate stability. The logical motive in economic activity is financial; and endless ingenuity has been expended in devising schemes of payment, designed to secure a maximum of employee satisfaction and efficiency. But, in the last analysis, buying power is largely a means for satis-

The observed and the observers are shown in the Group Dynamics Laboratory, as several students and staff members from the Group Dynamics Research Center, Institute for Social Research, University of Michigan, demonstrate the use of this research facility. The camera shows a teacher conducting a small group meeting as it is seen through one of the vision screens. In the photograph opposite, Mrs. Jane Corfield and Dr. Sidney Rosen look on from one of the observers' booths.

 The Laboratory is used both for teaching and research by the Research Center for Group Dynamics.

 The observation rooms are equipped with the one-way vision screens, sound proofing, an intercommunication system, and necessary ventilating equipment.

 Primary purpose of the laboratory is to make possible additional research on the psychology of group life. The Research Center for Group Dynamics, which was established at Michigan in 1948, is interested in discovering the basic principles of group behavior—those which affect the formation, change or dissolution of groups, or which influence the relations of one group with others and of members within a group with each other.

 Some of the research programs of the Center for Group Dynamics have to do with group productivity, communications and spread of influence within and between groups, inter-group relations, and adjustment of the individual to the group.

 A good deal of this research is accomplished by means of field studies, as for example in the armed forces, in a telephone company, in a clothing factory, and in a housing development. Other projects, however, are carried on in the laboratory under carefully controlled conditions.

For further information, see **University Record,** University of Michigan, December 1952.

fying social sentiments; and money incentives will never secure a full measure of activity and contentment until firms are organized with greater regard for the social stability of their own working groups, *at the working level.*[4]

The same company conducted an experiment with fifteen young men who did wiring, soldering, and inspecting of electrical apparatus, and obtained quite different results from those found in the experiment with the women workers.

Nine wiremen were organized in three groups of three men. Each group of three wiremen had one solderman. Two inspectors judged the work of these twelve men, and one supervisor was in charge of the fourteen employees. All fifteen men worked together in a small shop. Payment was on the basis of group piecework. Within the group, the supervisor had the highest official status, the inspectors ranked second, the nine wiremen third, and the three soldermen lowest. However, a more elaborate social organization soon developed. The group split into two cliques. These cliques were not divided according to the social status levels but cut across one of the wiring groups and across the various occupations. Each clique had its own leader.

The customs that developed within the group related mainly to the organization and performance of the work. Output and performance of the work were soon controlled through the customs which developed among the men. Certain levels of output from each individual were decided upon and controlled by the men themselves. They maintained their output at the levels they determined through breakdowns, interruptions, and other behavior that wasted time. If any worker indicated that he was exceeding his allowance of work, he was "disciplined" by the others. The supervisor, too, was more or less forced to accede to the workers' control. The control of output which was exercised by the workers was largely for the purpose of protecting the group from managerial interference. They jealously guarded what they believed to be their rights and privileges as workers. In short, the workers were not protecting themselves against economic injustice but against social ignorance on the part of management.

The contrasting results of the experiment with the two groups of workers of the same company, the five girls versus the fifteen men, cannot be attributed to a sex difference but rather to the fact that the girls' group ways and sentiments were integrated to a much greater extent with the economic purposes of the management.

One lesson revealed and emphasized by the experiment with the fifteen men is that the administrator should appear to the members as one who is guarding and developing *their* life and the emotional character of *their* group, rather than representing only the economic policies and wishes of the management. The men resisted outside threats to the character of *their* group. This suggests that an executive should not only promote the efficiency of his employees but should also guard and develop their social sentiments toward each other.[5]

Effects of Western Electric Company's experiments on thinking about human relations in industry

The result of these experiments was to force later investigators to pay more attention to the attitudes of workers, to the role of the work group, and to study the social organization within the factory situation. The experiment showed that the strength of the work group was more powerful than the wishes of management. The group often operated quickly and effectively to protect itself from violations within the group as well as from the outside.

When it wished, the group restricted the output of its individual members by means of ridicule and ostracism.

When reports of these researches were published, thinking about industrial problems was improved. Productivity was no longer assumed to be solely an effect of changes in illumination, physical fatigue, hours of work or pay. Supervision became recognized as a more important factor in output.[6]

New methods of measuring the network of relations among individuals within a group were developed by researchers.

The most important change that occurred after this series of experiments in the Western Electric Company was that a large number of men, trained in the fundamentals of psychology, turned their researches toward groups at work. These psychologists enlarged their thinking about industrial problems above the traditional tests and individual differences approach to the more meaningful studies of adjustment,

motivation, and psychological ties among individuals as members of functioning groups. Many men contributed to this development; one who deserves particular attention was J. L. Moreno. He found ways of identifying the kinds of bonds that exist between group members. His sociometric technique maps these relationships, for example, by having each member list the persons in the group whom he likes most and those whom he likes least. The reactions that hold accepted members in the group and those that tend to expel rejected members can be diagrammed.

The sociometric technique

This technique which J. L. Moreno devised is a method of studying relationships that exist between persons within groups. This procedure, and modifications that have been tested by other psychologists for measuring the amount of group organization and the interplay of personalities within groups, is known as the sociometric test.

Its purpose is to analyze a person's relationship to other members of a group. At the same time certain facts about the group are clarified, such as to what extent it is cohesive, whether there are cliques and cleavages, and who the dominant personalities are. Bronfenbrenner defines the sociometric test as a method for discovering, describing, and evaluating social status, structure, and development through measuring the extent of acceptance or rejection among individuals in groups.[7]

It must be emphasized that only a test that tries to ascertain feelings of group members toward one another and to ascertain them in respect to the same criterion (that is, for a concrete situation in their group life) can be called sociometric. The feelings and attitudes of the testees are of prime importance, as it is on them that validity of the whole test rests.

In order to make a sociometric test, all members of a group are requested to select a certain number of persons whom they want to associate with in the context of a particular situation. Ideally, subjects participating in the test should have some reason for expressing their interpersonal likes and dislikes truthfully. Their choices should, in some way, affect their lives. For example, if all testees are living in assigned quarters, they might be informed that their choices will be the basis for reassignment in accordance with their own preferences instead of the convenience of the assigning authority. It is reasoned that, if the subjects are given the opportunity to improve their own life situations through the test, their choices will be truthful and the test will not incur the odium commonly felt for a test.

After choices have been made by each group member, they are calculated and charted, and a definite pattern of group and subgroup formation can be observed. The fact that some members are highly regarded and desired by many members emerges. These much-chosen individuals are the "key" individuals. They are in many situations also the actual leaders; in some cases they are not. But they usually are the ones whom the leader must attract and direct in order to exercise influence and attain power. Other members may be chosen by no one. These are the "isolates." Between these two extremes are many intermediate statuses. For example, one individual is chosen by one person and himself chooses that same person. In other cases a person chooses only one person and that person does not choose him. Obviously, in the latter case, such persons are not wanted by others as colleagues in the situation for which the choices were given.

Thus the cohesiveness of a group in its interpersonal structure can be tested. If many group members are linked in mutual chains of preference forming a network to which the large majority of members are connected, a fairly cohesive group exists.

By classifying an individual in relation to others on the basis of his associates' opinions, his importance as a unit in the group is measured, and his part in the sociodynamic situation in which he lives for at least part of the time can be evaluated. Inevitably the individual acts upon the group of which he is a member, and the group acts upon him. Thus the extent to which he accepts the group and the group accepts him determines whether individual growth and constructive group activity will be encouraged, or whether membership in the group will militate against good adjustment of both individual and group. As Bronfenbrenner has stated: "The sociometric test, while it may show where people stand in the group, does not indicate why they are placed there. In other words, a person may be the 'star' or 'isolate' for a wide variety of reasons—some of them good, others bad. The natural tendency to interpret rejection as an indication of unsatisfactory adjustment and wide acceptance as signifying superior social relationships is therefore not always justifiable."

Different experimenters have employed varied techniques in the testing situation.[8] Some have set no limit on the number of choices allowed group members, and some have allowed expressions of rejection in addition to expressions of choices. Some have retested the same group after an interval of several months in order to ascertain the extent to which choices remain the same over a period of time.

While doing sociometric work for the Navy during World War II, Jenkins formulated the nominating technique. Although it is similar to all sociometric methods, it is particularly adaptable to solving the problem of selecting suitable industrial leaders.

Under Jenkins' direction, members of a group made four selections apiece. Each named two persons, inside or outside the immediate group, with whom he most preferred to work. He also named two with whom he most disliked the thought of working.

Modifications often are made in the method by framing the question in accordance with what is desired to be learned, e.g., "Who, in the group, would be the best foreman?" Number of choices allowed each person also varies in accordance with the purpose of the experiment.

Results are graphically illustrated by representing each group member as a circle and a number. An arrow is drawn from the circle representing the chooser to the circle representing the one chosen. When all choices have been charted it will usually be apparent that one person is chosen more often than others. "Isolates" and "mutual admiration societies" appear also by this modification of the original Moreno technique. Cliques and cleavages within the group are also exposed. The figure on this page is a sociogram.

Little imagination is required to envision how useful this method might be in choosing a leader. He would be the most highly regarded, thus the one likely to get greatest co-operation.[9]

Although leaders of social groups in our culture are usually chosen by the group of which they are a part, this is not true of leaders in industry. Leadmen, foremen, superintendents are usually selected by some person or group in authority. The desires of the group which is to be led or supervised are not of prime importance, although the chosen leader must not be so unacceptable to the group that he will be ineffective in the leadership role. The fact that leaders and supervisors in the work situation are not chosen by the group as they are in social situations contributes to much of the jealousy and divided loyalty found in industry. This is accentuated when leaders are seemingly arbitrarily appointed or removed. As already stated, leadership is a function of the group. The leader must fulfill the needs of the group. If the group has mental reservations about its leadership, it will

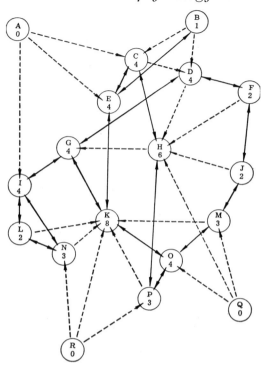

Sociogram above shows a work group of eighteen carpenters, from data collected by Raymond H. Van Zelst. Each circle represents one man. Each member of the group was requested to nominate the three men with whom he would most like to work. Arrows indicate the direction of choice, broken lines indicate one-way preferences, solid lines indicate mutual choices. Total number of votes for each individual is shown in the circle. "R" chose "N," "K," and "P." "R" is an isolate because no one chose him. Raymond H. Van Zelst, "An Interpersonal Relations Technique for Industry," **Personnel,** American Management Association, July 1952, pp. 68–77.

probably not operate with optimum efficiency. If, in addition, there is petty feuding and overtly expressed discontent, all possibilities of a smooth-functioning unit may be disrupted.

Snags of this type of tension arise when, for reasons of economy, the number of supervisors is reduced. For example, the foremen in a certain industry were told to reduce the number of leadmen (foremen's assistants). Accordingly, one foreman assigned two of his leadmen back to their old jobs as mechanics. He explained to them that they had been selected for demotion because they had less seniority than the other leadmen in the department. One of the demotees continued to help the men who formerly had been under him. They wanted him to do so and he was pleased. The leadman to whom these men had been newly assigned was delighted at the help. However, when the demotee asked the foreman for a raise and was refused, he became antagonistic toward the foreman, and his ex-subordinates imitated his attitude. The foreman met this antagonism by staying away from the clique.

The other ex-leadman has apparently been much disliked. So great was the display of enmity toward him by two of his former operators that he asked their present leadman to intervene in his behalf. When this proved unfruitful, he spoke to the foreman. The afternoon that the foreman reprimanded the men, a bolt was thrown at him. Next the disliked ex-leadman sprained an ankle as a result of a peculiar "accident." After all this, the foreman decided that things were out of his control. He took his troubles to the superintendent.

Although the superintendent advised the foreman to clarify to his department reasons for the demotions and to talk with the disliked ex-leadman about his personality, he informed the foreman that the real reason for all the departmental trouble was that he had lost touch with the men under him. Even though pressure of other types of work may make it difficult, contact with the group, individually and collectively, must be cultivated if the group is to be a harmonious, cohesive unit. It will be torn with major and minor strife unless there is sufficient personal contact to breed understanding and mutual respect.

The discerning foreman or executive utilizes the functional leaders in his group and thereby prevents the development of cliques. He eliminates cliques by integrating the functional leaders into the life of the larger group.

Van Zelst's use of sociometric procedures in a study of construction workers

The building trades are particularly well adapted to a study by sociometric procedures because they are not subject to the same limitations that are typical of mass industry where a regrouping means that a worker must learn an entirely new job. The subjects of this study by Raymond H. Van Zelst were four total work groups: a carpenter group of twenty members, another carpenter group of eighteen members and two separate groups of bricklayers, each having sixteen members. These men were working on the same housing project, but were split into two separate groups by a highway running through the middle of the site. In housing construction the foreman normally assigns men arbitrarily to work crews, but in Van Zelst's study the men were asked to indicate their first, second and third choices as to preference for teammates. The foreman assigned workers into these new groups, respecting each man's choices as far as possible.

The graphs on the next page show the results in terms of costs. The savings in both materials and labor are quite evident. Furthermore, the men liked the new system much better than the old.

Van Zelst found that using sociometric procedures resulted in increased satisfaction for the worker and greater financial returns for management. The company's chief constuction engineer in his report to management stated:

. . . savings due to this psychological procedure have exceeded those of any previous work saving device or any combination of five previous work saving methods. Financial benefits are such that we are now constructing every 29th building entirely free from labor and materials costs. Even greater financial gains would occur were it possible to evaluate monetarily savings due to the great reduction in turnover. . . .[10]

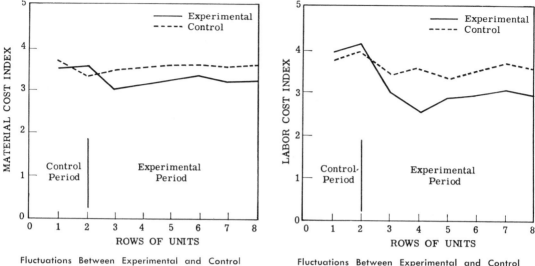

Fluctuations Between Experimental and Control Groups on Materials Costs Compared for Entire Three-Month Period

Fluctuations Between Experimental and Control Groups on Labor Costs Compared for Entire Three-Month Period

The figures above show cost differences in the work done by an experimental group on which sociometric procedures were used and a control group where these procedures were not used. Both groups worked on the same housing project during the same time. They were separated from each other by a highway. Note that the cost indexes for both materials and labor were lower in the experimental group—the one which received the benefit of sociometric techniques.—Raymond H. Van Zelst, "An Interpersonal Relations Technique for Industry," **Personnel**, American Management Association, July 1952. See also "Validation of a Sociometric Regrouping Procedure." **Supplement to the Journal of Abnormal and Social Psychology**, April, 1952.

The level of group output was definitely superior after the regrouping. At no time during the experiment did actual costs even approximate previous costs or the engineers' estimates. The decline in production costs was probably due to the success of improved techniques for the incorporation of isolated and newly hired workers into the work force.

Careful employment of human relations procedures increased the worker's sense of belongingness and molded worker and management together into a mutually satisfied group solidarity. There was less turnover. The men seemed more satisfied with their job and work situation. The end result of this study was a happier and more productive worker and a reduction in total production costs by 5 per cent.

The way the workers felt was summed up by one of the men:

"Seems as though everything flows a lot smoother. It makes you feel comfortable work-ing—and I don't waste any time bickering about who's going to do what and how. We just seem to go ahead and do it. The work's a lot more in-teresting too when you've got your buddy work-ing with you. You certainly like it a lot better anyway."[11]

The methods of sociometry permit the worker to express his needs and interests. He can determine to his advantage his part in the social structure of the group in which he operates.

Sociometric techniques can be used also for supervisory selection, assigning of buddy-workteams, and for selecting malad-justed employees for counseling. They are used in certain researches on the informal organization of a company to determine the traits of successful and unsuccessful leaders.

George F. F. Lombard and his group of researchers made a study of interpersonal relations in the children's wear department of a modern department store.[12] The in-vestigation revealed numerous misunderstandings and misevaluations on the part of supervisors and buyers. From the standpoint of group dynamics one interesting finding was that the older salesgirls often tried to mother and to help the junior executive who resented the older salesgirls for their better knowledge of the business.

Cohesiveness of a group does not assure high productivity

Recently, the Institute for Social Research, University of Michigan, has made outstanding research investigations which have thrown new light on group dynamics in industry. One approach has been to study the characteristics and performances of high-producing and low-producing work groups. In one series of researches the degrees of cohesiveness of different work groups were studied by asking each employee questions like: "Would you rather remain in this work group than move to another one even if you can get the same pay and do the same kind of work?"

Strangely, one of the findings from the study of cohesiveness has been that the cohesive work groups produced on the average the same as the groups that were not cohesive. Some of the closely-knit groups showed both very high and very low extremes of productivity. Robert Kahn, director of this program of research for the Institute, found that one characteristic of the cohesive work group is that the individual workers in it will tend to produce at the same level. Group ways of regulating production take over. The level of production that is chosen by the group is influenced by several factors; one that is especially important is the supervisor.

Think of it this way: a group can get together tightly and stick together for a lot of reasons. One is in response to some external threat or against some external enemy. We're certainly familiar with this at the national level. Sometimes the group gets together and forms this kind of alliance in defiance of the foreman, and for the express purpose of frustrating the company's goals. But we also know that some of the tightest groups are put together when the effort is not to frustrate the organization's goals but to achieve them. The athletic team, for example. So there are two important kinds of cohesive work groups. One is the kind where it is the group against the foreman. The other is the kind that has developed, not apart from the foreman, but including the foreman, and he may even be the leader who has had the skill to bring the thing off.[13]

We do not as yet know all the factors that cause a group to be either nonproductive or highly productive but we do know that under certain conditions, some groups restrict their production while others increase it. Let us now consider some findings regarding restriction.

Group restriction of production

Obviously, the attitude of the individual worker toward the amount of work he should produce is often influenced by the group with which he works. The Western Electric Company experiment with the fifteen men who did wiring, soldering, and inspection indicated what every production executive knows, namely, output and performance of the individual worker are often controlled by what the group members believe to be fair. The effect of such social influence on the worker is illustrated by the figure on next page. In this case, the output of a girl increased greatly when group pressure was removed. As stated by Lippitt from the study by Coch and French at the Harwood Manufacturing Company:

We see the day-by-day production curve of a girl belonging to a work group with a group production level of 50 units per hour represented by the dotted line. On the 11th and 12th days her production began to rise noticeably above the group standard and when she on the 13th day, hit standard production of 60 (a psychologically very important deviation for the other members) she became a scapegoat of the group with a great deal of social aggression directed toward her. Under this pressure her production decreased toward the level of the other group members. After 20 days the work group had to be broken up and the members transferred to various other units. The scapegoated

Effect of group expectations on member productivity (Sewing Factory)

operator remained on the same job, alone. As can be seen, her production shot up from about 45 to 96 units per hour in a period of 4 days. Her production stabilized at a level of about 92 and stayed there for the remainder of the 20 days. Clearly the induced forces on behavior from a strong subgroup may be more powerful than those induced by a progressive friendly management, and by personal needs for economic reward.[14]

Evidence that the group influence often restricts the production of the individual members is available in almost every factory, but we should not assume that the group influence is restrictive only. Sometimes it aids productivity very decidedly. This has been proved by several laboratory experiments where group members participated wholeheartedly in the solution of complex problems such as code problems. Group effort was found to be more productive than solitary effort.[15] The benefits of group participation are pronounced when problems require originality, insight, and the rejection of incorrect ideas.

We now know that a modern factory is a social enterprise. The worker comes there not only to earn money but also to be recognized as "one of the fellows." To be so recognized he must conform to the group's standards of conduct and as to what constitutes a fair day's work. If his output exceeds the group norm, he becomes known as a "rate-

buster." In some plants this kind of nonconformist is likely to have narrow escapes from accidents, his wife may be given the silent treatment when she goes shopping, and his children may lack playmates. While he is at work, his machine may be broken so often that he cannot earn a normal rate of pay.

On the other hand, if he is accepted as a regular member of the group, he will be given aid by his fellow workers when he needs it. This aid may even extend to allowing him to earn extra take-home pay during an emergency such as illness in the family. Such a concession is, of course, only temporary.[16]

Participation as a factor in productivity

The importance of participation by the individual in those matters which are important to him and of the participation of the individual in the group life has been revealed in numerous researches in group dynamics.

One of these is the Western Electric Company study. Other studies have revealed the influence of interpersonal relationships in employee productivity. An industrial organization is a social unit, governed by laws of social interaction. Good personnel management includes recognition of the individ-

The effect of participation on production. By permission from **Human Relations**, Vol. 1, No. 4 (1948).

ual as well as the social structure among the employees. This kind of recognition has been investigated at the Harwood Manufacturing Company, Marion, Virginia, under the direction of Dr. Alfred J. Marrow, president. When he was a graduate student in psychology, Marrow came under the influence of Dr. Kurt Lewin, one of the pioneers in the study of social psychology in industry.[17]

A significant study, made by Coch and French in the Harwood factory, indicated the importance of member participation in the setting and accepting of new work standards upon transfer to a new type of job. For the simplest type of job in the plant, the average learning time for beginners was 5 weeks. Yet when experienced operators were transferred to this same type of job, 38 per cent required an average of 8 weeks to reach standard production. The remaining 62 per cent either became substandard operators (regardless of their record before transfer) or quit during the relearning period. Furthermore, there was marked resistance to transfer, expressed in grievances about the standards, restriction of output, and aggressive reactions toward management. Analysis indicated that skill was a minor factor and that motivation was a major factor in determining the rate of recovery. A real-life action experiment was designed to study the problem.

The experiment consisted of selecting four groups of operators, one control and three experimental groups. The four groups became experimental transfers:

1. For the *control group,* the usual factory routine was followed. A group meeting was held in which the employees were told that a change was necessary because of competitive conditions and that a new piece rate had been set. The new piece rate was explained by the time study man. Worker's questions were answered.

2. *Experimental Group 1* was represented in the planning of the change by selected group members. The planning included a dramatic explanation of the need for change, and group agreement was reached concerning savings that could be made by removing "frills" and "fancy" work from the garment. The plan for the new job and piece rate included participation of the employees in the development of the new methods, having the time study made on them, and having the trained workers help train their co-workers in the new methods.

3. *In experimental Groups 2 and 3*, the above plan was followed except that the groups were smaller and all workers in each group were the "special" operators who participated in the actual designing of the new job. They also were the workers whose performance of the new job was studied by the time study man.

The results of the experiment were fairly clear. The control group dropped in production immediately upon change, and by the end of the experiment showed no appreciable amount of recovery. Resistance developed almost immediately. There were marked instances of aggression against management, deliberate restriction of production, lack of cooperation with the supervisor. Nine per cent quit during the first 15 days after the change. Grievances were filed about the piece rate which, upon checking, was found to be even a little "loose."

The recoveries for Groups 2 and 3 were dramatic. Both groups recovered to their pre-change level of production the second day after change, and by the end of the experiment they had actually surpassed their pre-change level by about 14 per cent. They worked cooperatively with their supervisors, there was no indication of aggression, and there were no quits during the 15-day period.

Group I required more time to recover (possibly because of an unavoidable operational problem), but reached the pre-change level by the 14th day after change, and by the end of the experiment had exceeded its pre-change level. Here, too, no quits were recorded. One act of aggression was observed which was neither prolonged nor serious. . . .

The success of the experiment seemed to be attributable largely to the fact that experimental transfers were given the opportunity to participate in planning the change, in planning their own work future. Thus, where such external motivating forces as monetary rewards, management pressure, and other means had failed, group involvement and decision developed internalized motivation for the accomplishment of a goal mutually desirable to management and worker.[18]

Robert E. Schwab has summarized some of the ways in which the principle of participation was applied in a typical industrial situation:

We've always known that some supervisors got better results with their people than others.

When we begin to look objectively at the supervisor who is building highly motivated work groups, or a division, or a department, we find he is likely to be a sort of fellow who

> Goes to bat for his employees;
> Shows an interest in how they get along;
> Lets his employees know what he thinks of their work, and
> Gets his employees' ideas and does something about them.

These are only typical of the personal characteristics of the supervisor who gets best results with his work group. The significant finding is that sincere concern for the employee as an individual and consideration for his point of view are essential elements in motivation. We can hardly expect the other fellow to be concerned with our point of view unless we show a little interest in his.

In examining further the human relations principles which are present in the high-morale, high-productivity situations, we find one kind of activity that is almost always present. There is a good deal of sharing of problems and plans with those who will be most affected by decisions. This is a practice which most top managements recognize as valuable for building a strong top-management team, but we have not been fully aware of its importance for high motivation at every level in the organization . . .

Belief in the principles of good human relations and awareness of the special significance of participation has led us during the past five years to extend our understanding and activity in these four ways:

1. The training of all supervisors, from top management down, in human relations in supervision. The purpose of the training was to develop understanding of and skill in sharing certain job problems with employees.

2. The involvement of all supervisors and, on occasion, employees in the development of a number of company personnel policies and benefit plans.

3. The feedback of results of a company-wide attitude survey to supervisors and employees for consideration, comments, and recommendations.

4. Continuing investigation of the relationship between participation and desirable attitudes or action on the part of supervisors and employee . . .

Once the effectiveness of participation was demonstrated, ways of sharing problems with the group were discussed, and supervisors were encouraged to try the method on their own problems. A great many examples of the successful application of participation to the solution of problems in work groups resulted. As supervisors experienced success in using this method, they began using it more in their relations with their subordinates. Some problems successfully solved in this way included:

1. Distribution of disagreeable jobs.
2. Selection of vacation periods.
3. Office arrangement.
4. Reduction of paperwork.
5. Lunch schedules.
6. Equal distribution of work.
7. Care of equipment.
8. Correction of errors on bills of material.
9. Responsibility for company-owned tools.
10. Wash-up time.
11. Selection of men to be transferred.[19]

Schwab has pointed out that participation also causes problems. Once employees have the satisfaction of being "in" on things, they tend to resent it when, for some reason, they are not consulted. He found, however, that these limitations have not offset the advantages that have been gained. They are perhaps the result more of limited understanding and skill on the part of the individuals involved rather than of any basic fault in the principle itself.

Lombard's study of developing teamwork among employees

Every leader of men who has supervised many groups of employees has recognized that some groups have excellent team spirit; others very little. When he has had good teamwork, he has had high productivity and good morale. Supervision was a pleasure.

Several scientific studies have been made of the psychological factors that underlie and influence teamwork. One outstanding investigation in this field was made by Mayo and Lombard in the aircraft industry of Southern California in relation to labor turnover. They found that teams are of three classes:

1. The "natural" group, arising spontaneously in a small group of workers, limited apparently to 6 or 7, the work of each individual clearly related to the work of the others.
2. The "family" group, larger in size, based on the presence of a core of relatively long service workers whose behavior is respected by, and sets the example for, the behavior of newer workers. Formation of this group is limited to situations where the whole group can stay together long enough, for a minimum of possibly 6 months to a year, for the example of the older group to be effectively communicated to the newer workers.
3. The "organized" group, where a supervisor with skill and understanding consciously conducts his administration to secure the group integrity and spontaneous coöperation of his workers.[20]

In Lombard's study, one department, Department IV, had an exceptionally good record regarding attendance and productivity. The output per man-hour was 100–105 per cent efficiency in a plant where the average was about 80 per cent. The high level of teamwork in Department IV was due mainly to a "leadman," Z, a college man who did not rank as a supervisor. This man thought of himself as having three chief activities: first, helping the individual worker in such ways as listening to him, introducing him to his companions, getting him congenial work associates, and dealing with his personal problems; second, adjusting technical difficulties; and third, handling for members of the group their contacts with inspectors, time-study men, the department foreman, and others outside the work center. The leadman also arranged trips for the worker to other parts of the plant so that he could see in place on finished assemblies the parts he produced.

Supervisory practices that have been found effective in developing teamwork in other plants are: insisting that foremen shall listen patiently to individual workers; having employees participate in deciding which day each individual may have as his day "off"; making sure that each employee is content with his work; not transferring or

(Above and right) The National Training Laboratory in Group Development is sponsored by the National Training Laboratories of the Division of Adult Education Service of the National Education Association of the United States.

The NTLGD's two three-week intensified summer laboratory training sessions on the campus of Gould Academy at Bethel, Maine, are devoted to the more effective development of human relations knowledge, insights, and research on the part of various professional and volunteer leaders—whether in industry, labor, government, education, or civic groups. The whole training design is based on the National Training Laboratories' beliefs, borne out by research, that (1) our nation's need for practical, effective, and democratic leaders in all occupations is constantly on the increase, and (2) effective leadership depends on face-to-face working relations in small groups. For its faculty it draws persons from both educational and applied fields.

lending employees to other departments; letting employees control their own rest-pause system; consulting and discussing the work with the employees; and giving them a sense of mutual responsibility and teamwork, as shown in the Hawthorne Plant, Western Electric Company "test room" experiment.[21]

This experiment began with a high number of attendance irregularities on the part of the employees. When, however, the new worker at No. 2 bench of the test room assumed informal leadership of the group and identified the team wholeheartedly with the company experiment, attendance irregulari-ties stopped and casual absences sank to a fraction of their former number and to a fraction of the rate in the department outside the test room. "A change in morale had also been observed. No longer were the girls isolated individuals, working together only in the sense of an actual physical proximity. They had become participating members of a working group with all the psychological and social implications peculiar to such a group." The effect of the mutual responsibility thus created was remarkable: the layout girl, for instance, had been absent, before the teamwork began, 85 times in

Play acting their roles as pressure groups, these NTLGD delegates push hard for their interests in a training session.

Instructor states problem precisely and obtains a quick response. Moral: if you direct a group, make the objective crystal clear.

For further details, write to: NTL, 1201 16th Street NW, Washington 6, D.C. For further published information, see "What Makes a Small Group Tick," **Business Week**, Aug. 13, 1955, pp. 40–46.

Foremen of the American Brake Shoe Company discussing the principles of bottom-up management with William B. Given, Jr., President.

32 months; after it began, she was not ever absent during 16 months.

Lombard's findings, as well as those of many industrial leaders, have shown that teamwork can be developed by management. Teams can be directed so that employees take over responsibilities, not only for discipline but also for production and attendance. Once the team takes over such functions successfully, their performance immediately becomes an important source of satisfaction to the workers.

Numerous examples of the effectiveness of participation in industry are available. One company, for example, received for years only a hostile response to programs to reduce scrap. When, however, a workers' economic education program explained in understandable terms why keeping scrap low was necessary to maintain the firm's competitive position, the workers realized that it was in their own self-interest, as a measure to protect their jobs, that scrap should be kept as low as possible. From then on such scrap programs made sense to the workers and were not looked on as "speed-up" programs but as necessary in their own interest.[22]

Bottom-up management

The importance of the individual employee in contributing to the success and progress of the organization is receiving greater recognition in American managements. The American Brake Shoe Company, as an example, has been successful in developing and applying a management philosophy which encourages employee participation in the management activities of the company. William B. Given, Jr. has explained and shown the effectiveness of this kind of management.[23]

In bottom-up management, top management tries to release the thinking and initiative of the employees so that ideas flow from the bottom up through the organization. It is the job of executives, plant managers, division chiefs, and supervisors to make the objectives of the organization clear, chart the course, and hold the group to it. It is also their job to stimulate a feeling of personal freedom, freedom to think, freedom to defend ideas and plans, freedom to take calculated risks, and freedom to fail. Numerous examples indicate that the company is sincere in trying to carry out this philosophy and that it is successful both socially and profit-wise.

The fact that the American Brake Shoe Company is a highly decentralized organization with plants in many villages and cities makes bottom-up management all the more applicable. As decentralization increases, control from the top solely by one man or by a small group of executives increases in difficulty and complexity. The answer to this problem, as Mr. Given indicates, is to encourage management responsibility as far down the line as possible.

One difficulty with this kind of management, not mentioned by Mr. Given, is the desire by some plant managers and department heads to adopt this run-it-like-your-own-business philosophy too literally, and to the point where little if any regard is shown for other parts of the parent organization.

In the case of the American Brake Shoe Company, the possibility of a break of this kind in the company structure is not likely because of the techniques used to hold the company together. A service unit from company headquarters acts as a consulting group for outlying plants on problems of budgeting, staffing, and items for new development. Foremen and supervisors are brought in on any revision of company policy, by means of manuals and specified procedures. Plant managers and division chiefs are given the responsibility for making their own budgets and these are not arbitrarily reduced by the home office.

It has often been said that the American worker of today will not tolerate the close supervision which he experienced several decades ago. His better pay and shorter hours are enabling him to have more freedom in his relationships with managements as well as more humility, and less of the know-it-all attitude of the old-time boss. Bottom-up-management is one answer to this trend.

William Given has presented the case for encouraging initiative down the line, for allowing scope for mistakes if unavoidable,

and for building a sense of participation at every level. He has presented evidence of the workability of this philosophy on a practical basis, as manifested in his own plants and foundries. He has explained the flexibility of the plan and shown how it can be adapted to the needs of other forms of business.

Generally, a group which has a leader who mixes with his men, who has informal relations with them, who encourages their ideas, and is interested in their welfare is regarded as the more effective one.[24]

Also, how members of a group feel towards one another affects the extent to which various methods and characteristics will change the efficiency of the work group. In pleasant working situations, high efficiency is more likely to occur when the group believes that it is regulating the behavior of individuals in its own midst. That is, the members as a group could place restrictions on each member's freedom of behavior. To a lesser extent, this is true in groups where membership is characterized by griping, complaining or unpleasant feelings.

Regardless of the atmosphere in the group, however, if the equipment facilities are not adequate and the skills of the individual not applicable to the job, the efficiency of the group is reduced.

Of course, individuals in top management positions who do not basically believe in this kind of philosophy toward employees or other individuals in general should avoid any attempt to promote bottom-up management in their organization because the long odds of failure will be against them.

Some individuals are more responsive to group pressures than others

The evident influences of group dynamics in industry should not cause us to imagine that every member of the group is equally susceptible to group pressures. In any industrial group, certain employees will

SUBJECTS WERE SHOWN TWO CARDS

One bore a standard line. The other bore three lines, one of which was the same length as the standard. The subjects were asked to find this line.

EXPERIMENT PROCEEDS AS FOLLOWS.

The subject (center) hears the rules of the experiment for the first time.

He makes his first judgment of a pair of cards, disagreeing with the unanimous judgment of the others.

He leans forward to look at another pair of cards.

He shows the strain of repeatedly disagreeing with the majority.

After 12 pairs of cards have been shown, he explains that he has to "call them as I see them." This subject disagreed with the majority on all 12 trials. Seventy-five per cent of experimental subjects agree with the majority in varying degrees.

invariably go along with majority opinion; others tend to identify and side with management in so far as they can without antagonizing their colleagues. Some few will even choose management's points of view at the risk of losing the friendship of their colleagues.

Social scientists have investigated the effects of group pressures on the responses of specific individuals and have found some interesting differences. Solomon E. Asch, for example, has reported some of his experiments with college students. He used groups of seven to nine men, assembled in a classroom for what was supposed to be a "psychological experiment," in visual judgment. The experimenter told the students that they would compare the lengths of lines on a series of large white cards.

One card of each pair had a single vertical line—the standard whose length was to be matched. The other card of the pair had three vertical lines of various lengths. The subjects were to choose the one line of the same length as that of the standard line. See figure opposite (size is reduced).

When the experiment began, the subjects announced their answers in the order in which they were seated in the room. On the first trial, everyone chose the same matching line. On the exposure of the second pair of cards, the opinions were again unanimous. After that, all the members of the group except the one who was the real subject of the experiment gave incorrect answers.

Some of Asch's findings reported by him at the time of the study are the following:

What the dissenter does not know is that all the other members of the group were instructed by the experimenter beforehand to give incorrect answers in unanimity at certain points. The single individual who is not a party to this prearrangement is the focal subject of our experiment. He is placed in a position in which, while he is actually giving the correct answers, he finds himself unexpectedly in a minority of one, opposed by a unanimous and arbitrary majority with respect to a clear and simple fact. Upon

him we have brought to bear two opposed forces: the evidence of his senses and the unanimous opinion of a group of his peers. Also, he must declare his judgments in public, before a majority which has also stated its position publicly. . . .

How do people respond to group pressure in this situation? I shall report first the statistical results of a series in which a total of 123 subjects from three institutions of higher learning were placed in the minority situation described above.

Two alternatives were open to the subject: he could act independently, repudiating the majority, or he could go along with the majority, repudiating the evidence of his senses. Of the 123 put to the test, a considerable percentage yielded to the majority. Whereas in ordinary circumstances individuals matching the lines will make mistakes less than 1 per cent of the time, under group pressure the minority subjects swung to acceptance of the misleading majority's wrong judgments in 36.8 per cent of the selections.

Of course individuals differed in response. At one extreme, about one quarter of the subjects were completely independent and never agreed with the erroneous judgments of the majority. At the other extreme, some individuals went with the majority nearly all the time. The performances of individuals in this experiment tend to be highly consistent. Those who strike out on the path of independence do not, as a rule, succumb to the majority even over an extended series of trials, while those who choose the path of compliance are unable to free themselves as the ordeal is prolonged . . .

Which aspect of the influence of a majority is more important—the size of the majority or its unanimity? The experiment was modified to examine this question. In one series the size of the opposition was varied from one to 15 persons. The results showed a clear trend. When a subject was confronted with only a single individual who contradicted his answers, he was swayed little: he continued to answer independently and correctly in nearly all trials. When the opposition was increased to two, the pressure became substantial: minority subjects now accepted the wrong answer 13.6 per cent of the time. Under the pressure of a majority of three, the subjects' errors jumped to 31.8 per cent. But further increases in the size of the majority apparently did not increase the weight of the pressure substantially. Clearly the size of the opposition is important only up to a point. . . .

In a variant of this procedure the trials began with the majority unanimously giving correct answers. Then they gradually broke away until on the sixth trial the naïve subject was alone and the group unanimously against him. As long as the subject had anyone on his side, he was almost invariably independent, but as soon as he found himself alone, the tendency to conform to the majority rose abruptly.

As might be expected, an individual's resistance to group pressure in these experiments depends to a considerable degree on how wrong the majority is. We varied the discrepancy between the standard line and the other lines systematically, with the hope of reaching a point where the error of the majority would be so glaring that every subject would repudiate it and choose independently. In this we regretfully did not succeed. Even when the difference between the lines was seven inches, there were still some who yielded to the error of the majority.[25]

This and other experiments show that there is a strong tendency on the part of most individuals to conform to group pressures. Some persons have, as a result of their observations of group behavior, hypothecated the functioning of a "group mind."

The "group mind" fallacy

The fact that we often see examples of unusual group behavior such as "mob hysteria" does not mean that such group action must be interpreted in terms of a "group mind" concept. The individual member of each group retains his emotions, motives, and perceptions. He acts as an individual.

Ross Stagner has ably explained the need for thinking in terms of individual psychology by means of a typical conflict situation in industry:

A picket-line example. A brief consideration of a specific incident will clarify our emphasis on the distinction between group and individual understanding, and our concern to reject the group-mind hypothesis. Suppose that a strike is in progress at a small manufacturing plant. The company has taken the position that it will try to operate; the union places a picket line across the gate. Some employees, not members of the union, try to drive in to go to work. The car is stopped, tipped over, and badly damaged; the non-strikers are mauled around, as are the police trying to protect them.

This kind of incident is often referred to as an example of a "group mind" or "mob hysteria." The point is made (correctly) that the union members did things under the influence of the group situation that they as isolated individuals would never do. Joe Jones and Sam Smith are honest, quiet, law-abiding citizens. They would not damage a neighbor's car or beat up strangers whom they had never seen before. Yet as members of a picket line they may do just such things. How can we reconcile these two sets of observations without saying that the men were under the influence of a "mob spirit?"

Psychologists, while agreeing that Joe Jones acts differently in the group situation, reject the notion that any new principles are needed to understand his action. Here are the main points of an analysis adequate to understand his behavior as a picket:

1. *Intensity of motivation.* Although it is true that Joe would not *ordinarily* attack another man individually, it can happen under strong motivation—to protect his money, his family, or his life. To some extent the striker protecting his job sees all three of these involved. The strikebreakers are seen as snatching the bread from the mouths of his children.

2. *Mutual reinforcement.* The tension level is reinforced by the group situation. Other men are shouting angrily. Joe hears their voices, sees their facial expressions. Each encourages the other to act in a violent manner. People are pushing and shoving. The physical contact intensifies the emotional response.

3. *Distortion of perception.* Under the stress of excitement and strong motivation, the strikebreakers are perceived as alien, inhuman. They are criminals. It is not only permissible, it is actually righteous to attack them.

4. *Lifting of inhibitions.* The group situation acts in two different ways to relieve the normal inhibitions against violence. One is the neutralizing of "conscience" or superego restraints against antisocial actions. Conscience is a social product. Group pressure instills in us a reluctance to damage property or use force against other human beings. But in the mob situation there is an illusion of group approval of violence, just as in wartime people get medals for killing. Hence the normal internal inhibition against violence is diminished or neutralized in the group setting.

The fear of punishment for violence is also lessened. Guilt in our culture is an individual matter; but when many participate simultaneously in an act, it will be difficult to identify and punish individuals. The individual feels anonymous in the mob. He thinks (correctly) that his chances of being punished are rather small.

This skeletonized analysis of a typical group incident serves only to show that the concepts and methods of individual psychology are adequate to give us a basis for the understanding of behavior in groups.[26]

Acknowledgments and References

1. F. J. Roethlisberger and W. J. Dickson, *Management and the Worker*, Harvard University Press, Cambridge, Mass., 1939, p. 5.

2. This title was used by Whitehead for a paper read before Section J (Psychology) of a British Association meeting in Norwich, England, September 1935, and later published in *The Human Factor*, National Institute of Industrial Psychology, London, Vol. IX, No. 11.

3. *Ibid.*

4. *Ibid.* The author's summary of this outstanding experiment in worker efficiency has of necessity omitted many important aspects. The reader should read the more complete and accurate reports listed in Roethlisberger and Dickson, *op. cit.*

5. *Ibid.*

6. For further information, see B. B. Gardner and W. F. Whyte, "Methods for the Study of Human Relations in Industry," *American Sociological Review*, 11 (1946), 506–512.

7. Urie Bronfenbrenner, *The Measurement of Sociometric Status, Structure and Development*, Beacon House, New York, 1945.

8. Charles P. Loomis and Harold B. Pepinsky, "Sociometry, 1937–1947," *Sociometry*, Vol. XI (August 1948), pp. 147–191.

9. J. G. Jenkins, "The Nominating Technique: Its Uses and Limitations," paper presented at Eastern Psychological Association in 1947.

10. Raymond H. Van Zelst, "Validation of a Sociometric Regrouping Procedure," *Supplement to the Journal of Abnormal and Social Psychology*, April 1952.

11. Raymond H. Van Zelst, "Sociometrically Selected Work Teams Increase Production," *Personnel Psychology*, 1952, pp. 175–185.

12. George F. F. Lombard, *Behavior in a Selling Group*, Graduate School of Business Administration, Harvard University, Boston, 1955.

13. *Modern Management*, The Bureau of National Affairs, Inc., Washington, D.C., Aug. 15, 1955, p. 2.

14. Lester Coch and J. R. P. French, Jr., "Overcoming Resistance to Change," Human Relations, Vol. I, No. 4 (1948), after Ronald Lippitt, *Current Trends in Social Psychology*, University of Pittsburgh Press, Pittsburgh, Pa., 1948.

15. For examples, see Marjorie E. Shaw, "A Comparison of Individuals and Small Groups in the Rational Solution of Complex Problems," *American Journal of Psychology*, Vol. XLIV (1932), pp. 491–504; and R. W. Husband, "Cooperation versus Solitary Problem Solution," *Journal of Social Psychology*, Vol. 11 (1940), pp. 405–409.

16. For further information, see William Whyte, *Money and Motivation*, Harper & Brothers, New York, 1955.

17. Alfred J. Marrow, "Human Factors in Production," *Personnel*, American Management Association, March 1949, pp. 343–344.

18. *Ibid.* See also Ronald Lippitt, "A Program of Experimentation on Group Functioning and Group Productivity," *Current Trends in Social Psychology*, University of Pittsburgh Press, Pittsburgh, Pa., 1948, pp. 14–22.

19. Robert E. Schwab, "Motivation and Human Relations Principles," *Personnel Series*, No. 155, American Management Association, 1953, pp. 31–34.

20. Elton Mayo and George F. F. Lombard, *Teamwork and Labor Turnover in the Aircraft Industry of Southern California*, Bureau of Business Research, Harvard University Graduate School of Business Administration, Boston, Mass. Copyright 1944 by the President and Fellows of Harvard College.

21. Roethlisberger and Dickson, *op. cit.*, p. 83 f. See also Thomas North Whitehead, *The Industrial Worker*, Harvard University Press, Cambridge, Mass., 1938.

22. See Father Edward S. Keller, CSC, "What Makes People Do the Things They Do?" Bureau of Economic Research, University of Notre Dame, South Bend, Ind., *Personnel Series, No. 155*, American Management Association.

23. William B. Given, Jr., *Bottom-Up Management*, Harper & Brothers, New York, 1949.

24. For further information, see Bernard M. Bass, "Feelings of Pleasantness and Work Group Efficiency," *Personnel Psychology*, Spring 1954, pp. 81–91.

25. Solomon E. Asch, "Opinions and Social Pressure," *Scientific American*, November 1955, pp. 31–35. Photographs and quotations by courtesy of the author and the publisher.

26. Reprinted with permission from Ross Stagner, *The Psychology of Industrial Conflict*, Copyright 1956 by John Wiley & Sons, Inc., New York, pp. 8–10.

PROJECTS

1. Make a study of some small group with which you are acquainted, such as a fraternity or class. Use the sociometric technique. Can you plot the choices of members of the group? If you were to put the group to work in a factory or office, would your sociometric findings be of value to you?

2. Think of a place where you have worked or are now working. Describe the group culture; the employees' unwritten rules about the amount of work to be done, when loafing is permissible, when employees may be absent, the conditions under which employees may appear to cooperate with management but actually modify management's programs, and so on.

3. List some of the difficulties and dangers to management of attempts to use group dynamic influences in supervising employees.

4. List incidents which you have observed or read about that would appear to substantiate the "group mind" concept.

COLLATERAL READINGS

Cartwright, Dorwin and Alvin Zander, *Group Dynamics: Research and Theory*, Row, Peterson and Company, Evanston, Ill., 1955.

Gordon, Thomas, *Group-Centered Leadership*, Houghton Mifflin Co., New York, 1955.

Haire, Mason, *Psychology in Management*, McGraw-Hill Book Company, Inc., New York, 1956, Chapter 6.

Kornhauser, Authur, Robert Dubin and Arthur M. Ross, *Industrial Conflict*, McGraw-Hill Book Company, Inc., New York, 1954, Chapter 28.

Lombard, George F. F., *Behavior in a Selling Group*, Harvard University, Division of Research, Graduate School of Business Administration, Boston, 1955.

Maier, Norman R. F., *Principles of Human Relations*, John Wiley Sons, Inc., New York, 1952, Chapter 10.

Stagner, Ross, *The Psychology of Industrial Conflict*, John Wiley & Sons, Inc., New York, 1956, Chapter 7.

Thelen, Herbert A., *Dynamics of Groups at Work*, The University of Chicago Press, Chicago, 1954.

CHAPTER TWENTY-ONE

Supervising employees

Good management organization, by reliance on authority instead of skilled and understanding leadership as the basis for handling men, easily destroys the desire for cooperation. A higher type of leadership adapted to democratic conditions is necessary. Management, if it is to be successful in the years which lie ahead, must rely less on authority and more on leadership which transcends authority.[1]

Anyone who has worked under the supervision of several foremen or executives knows that each supervisor tends to develop a work-situation that has a unique psychological atmosphere.[2] Just as every home that one visits has a psychological atmosphere of its own, so each work environment has its distinctive atmosphere. It may be one that is tense because it is dominated by an authoritative boss or a neurotic fellow employee. Or a relaxed, cheerful atmosphere may result where democracy prevails, every member enjoys the confidence of his colleagues, and group decisions govern conduct. When the supervisor of such a place arrives at work, a current of enthusiasm fills the place. Faces become brighter. Movements become faster. Work seems to flow along more smoothly. Other supervisors have the opposite effect: fears arise in employees; they become tense; their work becomes harder and gloom settles over them.

The importance of proper "atmosphere" is exemplified by an experience reported for one company:

A simple questionnaire was handed out to employees. The idea was to find out how the men got along from the standpoint of coöperation. Employees were asked to describe the attitude of their fellow-workers, whether friendly or unfriendly, and to comment on working conditions.

Replies revealed these surprising facts:

Departments with friendly and coöperative operators had a far better all-around production record than those departments in which employees showed a disgruntled attitude toward one another. The "friendly" departments produced an average of 10 per cent more, with spoilages about 40 per cent less than the "non-coöperative" departments.

423

In these latter departments, the foreman's lack of friendliness was often commented upon. One worker had this to say (since the questionnaires did not need to be signed, he felt free to get his gripe off his chest): "Who does our foreman think he is? The big cheese himself? Why don't he get wise to himself? He's no better than any of us here. He acts like it costs him money to say good morning to us."[3]

When the Industrial Relations Section, California Institute of Technology, had completed a total of 25 surveys in 18 different companies, covering over 50,000 employees, the Section formulated a number of conclusions based on all of its studies of employee opinion. One of these was that "The morale of supervisors is usually higher than that of employees, but the morale of employees is related to that of supervisors: the higher the morale of supervisors, the higher the morale of their employees."[4]

The typical foreman in American industry is recognized as a key factor in employee morale. He, rather than the heads of the company, represents the company to the individual employee.

Foremen have important responsibilities but many of them have serious problems in management's relations with them as shown by a recent survey made by the National Council of Industrial Management Clubs, composed of some 140 foremen's and supervisors' clubs that draw their membership from a widely diversified group of industries in 32 different states. Questionnaires were administered to 1,602 industrial supervisors in 11 major labor market areas in New England, the Middle Atlantic, Southern, Midwestern, and Far Western regions. The results of the survey were broken down on the basis of supervisory rank, earnings, seniority, education, and a number of other variables. An opportunity was thus afforded to contrast the attitudes of foremen with those of higher-ranking supervisory personnel as well as with those of others in various pay categories.

The results of this survey, when viewed as a composite, leave a predominantly positive impression, but the findings also indicate a considerable amount of dissatisfaction on the part of industrial supervisors with important aspects of their jobs—their pay, their treatment by management, and their role in industrial relations. The results showed that supervisors as a group may be loyal to their companies and management and at the same time be acutely aware of the deficiencies existing within the organization.

The data from this survey are too extensive to present in complete form, but several significant findings have been reported by James H. Mullen.

1. *Communication of Company Policies*
The problem of proper communication of company policies was stated in the following question.

Whenever I am faced with a problem which requires the application of company policy:

	All Supv.	Foremen
a. I am always certain what the company policy is	18%	13%
b. I usually know what the company policy is	62	62
c. I'm as likely to be wrong as right on what company policy is	12	15
d. I can seldom be sure what the company policy is	6	8
e. I can never be sure what the company policy is	2	2

The answers to this question reflect a real failure in the communication process. This becomes particularly true if the neutral response (c) is included. Even though the statement is technically "neutral," most executives would agree that a situation where one is "as likely to be wrong as right on what company policy is," is essentially an unsatisfactory one. Twenty per cent of the entire survey group and 25 per cent of the foremen indicate that they are frequently at a loss to know which company policy is applicable to a given situation.

2. *Knowledge of Job Status*
[One of the questions reported here] dealt with a facet of the communications process— the responsibility of the upper-level supervisor to communicate adequately to his subordinate supervisors about their job performance.

When it comes to knowing how I am doing on my job:

	Answers	
	All Supv.	Foremen
a. No one ever mentions it to me	15%	17%
b. I am told only when something goes wrong	21	23
c. I am told occasionally how I am doing	40	40
d. I am told often how I am doing	12	9
e. I am kept fully informed on how I stand	12	11

The fact that as many as 80 per cent of the supervisors surveyed are not being kept adequately informed about their job performance is symptomatic of a very serious failure in the relationships within the management organization. Though the extent of dissatisfaction seems somewhat higher among foremen than among higher-level supervisors, over-all results indicate that the difficulty is by no means confined to lower levels of supervision.

3. *Role in Policy Formulation*

The role of the industrial foreman in the discussion and formulation of new policies emerges from the following question.

When new policies are formulated, supervisors are given an opportunity to present their thinking and experience before they are put into effect:

	Answers	
	All Supv.	Foremen
a. Almost never	8%	9%
b. Usually not	20	22
c. About half the time	16	16
d. Usually	35	36
e. Practically always	21	17

4. *Supervisory training programs*

In my opinion, the program in my company for training supervisors in such matters as labor and human relations, grievance procedure, how to apply the union contract, etc., has been:

	Answers	
	All Supv.	Foremen
a. We have no such program	27%	31%
b. Excellent	12	12
c. Good	29	26
d. Only fair	18	17
e. Rather inadequate	9	7
f. Definitely poor	5	7

This question yields a response which emphasizes a serious deficiency in industrial training and indirectly points to a lack of appreciation on the part of management of the importance of the supervisor's role in industrial relations. . . .

Summary

The foreman's answers to a number of questions which deal with the broader aspects of his job and his company show him to be loyal to his company and, in fact, rather proud of his relationship with it. He appears to be satisfied that his company's policies toward its employees are generally fair and that his company takes a genuine interest in its employees' welfare. His over-all attitude toward his own superior is also positive, and on the whole he seems to like his job. On economic questions, his thinking is, by and large, consistent with the philosophy of the capitalistic enterprise system.

Underlying this over-all pattern of satisfaction, however, are some very important qualifications and reservations. His answers point to a feeling of frustration with regard to his position in the management organization. He seems very frequently to be at a loss to know which policies to apply in different situations. He also appears to be consulted only infrequently about policies and changes in policies which affect him directly. There are evidences of considerable dissatisfaction because management has not encouraged his participation and has restricted his initiative and discretion in important management functions. He also appears to feel somewhat frustrated by his own superior's failure to keep him informed of his status and progress on the job as well as the fact that his contributions frequently go unrecognized by his supervisor.[5]

Most foremen are aware of the importance of human relations in industry. They want to better their own performance in this respect and they have a desire for closer integration into the management team. When surveys of attitudes of foremen are analyzed, the typical foreman recognizes his own limitations and indicates his desire to do a better job.

A fundamental concept of the modern foreman or supervisor is that he is a teacher and a leader—not a boss. He realizes that if he is a poor leader, his record will show his weaknesses in the form of lowered production, higher costs, increased absenteeism, and numerous grievances. If he is a good leader, he also knows that he can prove the effectiveness of his supervisory methods by means of favorable production figures. Furthermore, he enjoys handling people. He

The four steps below were made famous during World War II in the Training Within Industry Program. They are one means of instructing a learner in a job. Not only do they seem applicable to teaching a job, but to all cases where an idea is being transmitted.

FOUR-STEP METHOD

The four steps	How each is accomplished
1. PREPARATION: Prepare listener to receive new experience.	1. Put learner at ease. 2. Tell him the title of job. 3. Explain the purpose of the job. 4. Explain why he has been selected to learn. 5. Help him relate his past experience to the job.
2. PRESENTATION: Set the pattern in his mind.	1. Introduce him to tools, materials, equipment and trade terms. 2. Demonstrate the job, explaining each step slowly and clearly. 3. Review with him what he should know up to this point: Title of job, Purpose of job, Steps to be taken.
3. APPLICATION: Help him form habit.	1. Supervise his doing the job. 2. Question him on weak and key points. 3. Have him repeat until he has developed the manual skills and/or habits of thought.
4. TEST: Check the success of your instruction.	1. Have him do the job alone. 2. Inspect job against standards of performance. 3. Discuss with him where he goes from here, whether to production work or new learning experience.

Robert P. Cort, "How to Get an Idea Across," *Personnel*, American Management Association, July 1951, pp. 46–51.

gets as much thrill from a skillful handling of an "ornery" employee as a fisherman gets from landing a game fish.

Schuyler Dean Hoslett has described examples of good and poor supervisory procedures. The first uses role-playing.

1. Here are two examples of the foreman's problems in human relations:

EVELYN: (Getting up reluctantly and going over to Anne at the desk.) Well, Dottie, you only made 30 units yesterday. Did you have any special trouble? After I brought you all your work, too.

ANNE: I didn't feel good.

EVELYN: Did you have any machine trouble or anything?

ANNE: Yes, I did.

EVELYN: Well, why didn't you put your little red light on?

ANNE: I don't know. I guess I forgot. And the thread breaks all the time.

EVELYN: Well, you should tell me about those things so I can help you. You'll do that after this, won't you? And you'll try to do better too, won't you?

ANNE: Yes, but I don't know if I can. It's hard to do.

TRAINER: That's fine. Now let's talk about this case.

The role-taking continues with suggestions of using check studies and additional training. In the discussion of "making excuses," the Personnel Manager thinks the supervisor should find out whether the girl has any personal problems. Because the trainer knows that Evelyn has caused resentment by prying into personal affairs of her girls and because he wants to criticize the argumentative technique without criticizing her personally, he sets up a special situation.

TRAINER: Let's see how Mr. Jones (the Personnel Manager) would tackle this problem. I'll be the girl, the same girl Anne was last time. (Sits at the "machine.")

MR. JONES: Well, it just seems to me this way. There's lots of things that might be holding the girl back. Possibly she got a letter from her boy friend that had bad news in it, or something like that.

TRAINER: Well, let's try it out and see how it works.

MR. JONES: (Getting up from his chair.) What did you say your name was?

TRAINER: Dottie Sholley.

MR. JONES: (Now acting the role of supervisor.) I have some bad news for you here, Dottie. It seems you have fallen down a little in your units. What seems to be the trouble?

TRAINER: Well, I didn't feel so good.

MR. JONES: But when you asked me to be your supply girl you seemed to be feeling well enough.

TRAINER: Well, I got some machine trouble and that slows you up. And these old threads break all the time. You can't do much when that happens.

MR. JONES: (Pauses for a moment.) Did you go to the show last night?

TRAINER: No.

MR. JONES: Anyone in your family sick?

TRAINER: No.

MR. JONES: Did you have a date last night?

TRAINER: No! I'm married.

MR. JONES: And you say you haven't been feeling well?

TRAINER: No, I wasn't feeling well, but that was just yesterday.

MR. JONES: You don't feel sick most of the time?

TRAINER: No, that was just a little stomach trouble. There's nothing wrong with me.

MR. JONES (*laughing*): You're sure bucking me. I give up!

BILL: If you let them get into an argument with you, you'll never get out. They answer and answer and answer.

TRAINER: Thanks. I certainly was being a tough one. Now let me give you my reactions. When you came up saying you had bad news I felt nervous. I didn't like that, so I was sort of on the defensive. I was thinking, now what am I going to say? I thought of something, and then while I thought of that I thought of something else to have ready for the next question. Then he asked me about my family and that scared me. I thought maybe something was wrong. Then he asked me if I had had a date, and I was married. That made me so mad I nearly slapped him. And when he asked me again about my health I tried to assure him that I was in good health because I was afraid maybe he would fire me if he thought I was sick all the time. Now, this is the toughest kind of case you will get. A girl who doesn't do what she can do, and you just can't find out why. Now would you like me to try the skunk oil method?

BILL: Yeah, I think so.

TRAINER: O.K. You be the girl, Bill.

BILL: Sure, I'll answer your questions.

TRAINER: You try to be the same girl that Anne was and that I was. Be as tough as you want to.

BILL: O.K. (*Sits down at the table.*)

TRAINER: (*Approaching Bill with the sheet in his hands.*) Hello, Dottie. Here's the unit sheet for today. Let's see, where is your name? (*Turning the sheets with Bill's help.*) I guess it's over on another page. What have you been doing?

BILL: Well, I made 30.

TRAINER: How does that compare with what you've been doing? Is that good for you or not so good?

BILL: Well, I have done better.

TRAINER: How long have you been on the job?

BILL: Oh, about eight or ten weeks, but they change me around so much.

TRAINER: How long have you been on this job?

BILL: About six weeks.

TRAINER: Well, it usually takes a girl three or four months to make 60. You say you have done better?

BILL: Yes.

TRAINER: Have any trouble yesterday?

BILL: Yes, the thread breaks all the time. And I had such little bundles. I had to get more all the time.

TRAINER: Oh, I'm sorry. I told you yesterday I was going to bring you a lot.

BILL: But they're too little. You run through them in no time.

TRAINER: What you want to do is not worry about your progress one day or another day. How much do you suppose you will make a week from today? Maybe you'll get some small bundles and maybe your machine will give you trouble, but counting that in, what do you suppose you will make in a week?

BILL: I don't know. I might make 40 or 45.

TRAINER: You think you could make 40 or 45! Why I've known girls who have taken three or four weeks to get up there from 30! What's the best you have made?

BILL: I think it's 48.

TRAINER: Well, maybe you could then. How'd you like to try and make 40 by next Friday?

BILL: You mean just do 40 by next Friday?

TRAINER: Yes, that gives you a good chance in spite of machine trouble and those things that you can't help that come up. Do you think you could do it?

BILL: I believe so.

TRAINER: Now I don't think you can do it if you have troubles that aren't your fault. Now on the matter of thread breaks, sometimes that's the way you hold your cloth and sometimes the trouble is with the machine. When you get trouble like that, we can call the mechanic in or we can get the trainer over to see what's wrong. You want to have perfect working conditions. I'll come over Friday to see if you've made it, and I'll come around every other day, too, to see if I can help in some way. (*End of role-playing.*)

MR. JONES: Fine!

TRAINER: I don't think I did that very well, but I was trying to use a different technique. Now what's the difference?

MR. JONES: Well, you weren't on the defensive all the time.

TRAINER: You mean Bill didn't put me on the defensive?

BILL: What he means is when you were the operator you answered him back. And I could answer all your questions to me this time, but there never was any blame on me.[6]

The discussion continued for fifteen minutes on the details of how to avoid arguments, putting a person on the defensive, the use of production goals, why the trainer tried to make a goal out of the *lower* of the two estimates given by the girl, and so on.

Conclusion:

There is no standard spiel which can fit every situation, no standard spiel that will work with every kind of personality. More important than the specific words are the attitudes the supervisor brings to this kind of discussion. If he tries to build up a fellow instead of tearing him down, if he sets up a goal the worker can accomplish, the chances are pretty good he will get cooperation.[7]

2. A boss is usually the center of the men's attention. For one thing, his word carries more weight than theirs; he has authority. And for another, he, either actually or from the men's point of view, knows more and is a more able person in one way or another; he is their leader. This being the case, it is difficult for him not to prompt in others—in at least some others—a variety of emotional stirrings that seem to have nothing to do with the boss-worker relationship.

Wherever you look, you will find that authority and leadership always generate in the followers feelings of jealousy, need for personal attention, desire for help and assistance, wish for praise, and so forth. And when you honestly appraise your reactions to the man whom you consider endowed with authority and leadership, you probably will admit to yourself that he is the man to whom you would like to take your troubles, whose personal attention and interest please you, whose praise you want and whose criticism you fear. In a way, your feelings toward him are not unlike the feelings you used to have toward your father. . . .

To give an illustration:

A foreman had noticed that one of his men displayed an indifference and hardly-concealed resentment for which there seemed to be no reason. He couldn't get any clue to the fellow's strange behavior and he finally decided to pay the man a visit at his home. Being within his own domain, the foreman thought, the fellow would probably feel free to say what was on his mind.

Much to his surprise he found that the worker's wife greeted him with a great deal of reserve. And it was she who almost immediately launched into long and intemperate remarks about "snobbishness and favoritism." It seemed that she was sore at him because he, the foreman, had failed to play with her kids at the company's last picnic. But he did spend a lot of time romping around with the kids of another fellow, "not half as good a worker as my husband."

The foreman didn't laugh; he didn't even feel like laughing. To be sure, the complaint wasn't any too reasonable. But then, from the man's and his wife's point of view, it was important that he, the foreman, should act as just the person for whom they had previously felt a great deal of respect and admiration. Because the foreman had failed to pay any attention to their children, he had shown himself unworthy of the good sentiments the man and his wife had had for him. They felt cheated, neglected and hurt.

Just how persuasive the foreman's explanation of his own conduct at the picnic was, he did not know. He only noticed that, having spoken her piece and having listened to his comments, the woman seemed to be somewhat mollified—and her husband looked as if he would find great pleasure in having a tooth pulled. At any rate, the talk proved to be a great success. The man again turned into the cooperative and attentive worker he had been before.[8]

Some findings from the Institute for Social Research, University of Michigan

This organization is conducting systematic research on what a good management does that makes the difference between high and low productivity, between high and low morale, and the principles and practices of leadership that are responsible for high productivity and high job satisfaction.

Studies have been conducted or are under way in a wide variety of organizations: public utilities, an insurance company, an automotive company, a heavy machinery factory, a railroad, an electric appliance factory, and some government agencies. The work of the organizations studied has varied from routine clerical and assembly operations to complex scientific research.

In this program of research, two major criteria have been used to evaluate administrative effectiveness:

1. Productivity per man-hour or some similar measure of the organization's success in achieving its productivity goals.
2. The job satisfaction and other satisfactions derived by employees or members of the group.

The findings show that a consistent pattern of motivational principles and their application is associated with high productivity and high job satisfaction, irrespective of the particular company or industry in which the study is conducted. Some of the generalizations that are emerging from this research are summarized in these condensations and excerpts from one of the Institute reports:

1. Very little relationship, *within a company*, has been found between employees' attitudes toward the company and their productivity. The more productive employees or sections do *not* have appreciably more favorable attitudes than do the less productive employees. A favorable over-all attitude toward one's company and job does, however, result in less absence from the job.

2. In some situations at least, there is a negative relationship between the extent to which employees participate in a recreational program and their productivity. The less-productive sections participate in recreational activities more often than do those sections that are more productive.

3. In contrast to the two above-mentioned patterns involving factors of a nonpersonal nature, there is a marked relationship between the kind of supervision an employee receives and both his productivity and the satisfactions which he derives from his work. When the worker (or a person at any level in a hierarchy) feels that his boss sees him only as an instrument of production, as merely a cog in a machine, he is likely to be a poor producer. However, when he feels that his boss is genuinely interested in him, his problems, his future, and his well-being, he is more likely to be a high producer.

My supervisor...

... recommends promotions, transfers, pay increases ...
61%
22%

... informs men on what is happening in the company ...
47%
11%

... keeps men posted on how well they are doing ...
47%
12%

... hears complaints and grievances.
65%
32%

■ HIGH MORALE GROUP   □ LOW MORALE GROUP

Supervisory relations as seen by high and low morale groups. University of Michigan findings show significantly higher percentages of highly productive workers, both in office groups and section gangs, had pride in their groups, than did those with low production records. Chart above shows difference in attitudes towards supervisors, company communications, and grievance procedures among machine shop employees with generally high and generally low morale. Chart reprinted with permission from **Dun's Review and Modern Industry**, July 1956, p. 43.

4. The employee-centered supervisor not only trains people to do their present job well but tends to train them for the next higher job. He is interested in helping them with their problems on the job and off the job. He is friendly and supportive rather than being punitive and threatening.

5. Close supervision tends to be associated with lower productivity and more general supervision with higher productivity.

Low productivity may at times lead to closer supervision, but it is clear that it may also cause low productivity. In one of the companies involved in this research program it has been found that switching managers of high- and low-production divisions results in the high-production managers raising the productivity of the low-production divisions faster than the former-high-production divisions slip under the low-production managers. Supervisors, as they are shifted from job to job, tend to carry with them and to maintain their habitual attitudes toward the supervisory process and toward their subordinates. This suggests that supervisory attitudes and habits tend to be the causal influence.

6. The superior's skill in supervising his subordinates *as a group* is an important variable affecting his success: the greater his skill in using group methods of supervision, the greater are the productivity and job satisfaction of the work group.

7. For both blue-collar and white-collar workers, there is a marked relationship between worker morale and how much employees feel that their boss is interested in discussing work problems with the work group.

8. Work groups with high group pride and loyalty are the more productive. One reason is that the workers cooperate more and help one another in getting the work done. Work groups with high group loyalty show more teamwork and more willingness to help each other than do those with low group loyalty. In the high-loyalty groups there tends to be a flow of work back and forth between the workers depending upon the load. In groups with low group loyalty there tends to be more of a feeling that each worker is on his own and that how he gets along with his work is his own responsibility.

9. In high productivity groups, workers help one another. When foremen were asked, "How does your section compare with other sections in the way the men help each other on the job?" the answers showed a marked relationship to group productivity. The foremen of high-production groups reported much more often than the foremen of low-production groups that their men helped one another in getting the work done.

The workers in the high-production work groups not only have greater group loyalty and help one another more but give this help on their own initiative.

As might be expected, work groups with high group loyalty have more favorable attitudes toward production than do groups with low group loyalty. Thus we find that high-loyalty groups differ from groups of low group loyalty in having higher production goals. Their opinion as to what is reasonable production is higher and is more nearly the same as that of their foreman. Moreover, the high-loyalty groups have a more favorable attitude toward the high producer.

We are finding that the high-loyalty groups differ from the low in ways that form a consistent pattern. In addition to the differences already mentioned, the following characteristics have been found. The groups with greater group loyalty are more likely to

—Have greater identification with their group and a greater feeling of belonging to it.
—Have more friends in the group and in the company—rather than outside the company.
—Have better interpersonal relations among the members of the work group.
—Have a more favorable attitude toward their job and their company.
—Not only have higher production goals but produce more with less sense of strain or pressure.

10. When a superior treats subordinates as human beings, it results in greater group loyalty and pride. When supervisors stay sufficiently close psychologically to their workers to be able to see the problems of the workers through the eyes of the workers, they are better able to develop good group loyalty.

11. The good supervisor is able to identify with his employees and keep psychologically close to them. This seems to foster a good team spirit with open communication. It permits the supervisor to understand problems as employees see them and to interpret for top and middle management the employees' points of view. The supervisor who fails to identify with employees becomes psychologically far from them. This makes him incapable of seeing and dealing with problems as employees see them and hence unable to help middle and top management to see problems as employees see them and thereby to help management to arrive at policy decisions which will be mutually satisfactory.

12. There are, of course, many other factors which are important in developing group loyalty and team spirit. Scattered research in industry and elsewhere indicates that commonly recognized methods of group leadership will yield good group loyalty when used. These methods and skills include those developed and taught by the National Training Laboratory in Group Development. Among the most important of these methods are those involving group participation in decisions affecting the group. There is evidence that group participation and involvement are beneficial at all levels in an organization. One of the best ways, for example, to have supervisors become aware of the job that needs to be done by their work group and to have them accept responsibility for it is to involve them in decisions where the functions and responsibilities of their work group are examined and reviewed. . . .

An examination of the results presented here and of results from other research shows that every human being earnestly seeks a secure, friendly, and supportive relationship and one that gives him a sense of personal worth in the face-to-face groups most important to him. The most important face-to-face groups are almost always his immediate family group and his work group. If his formal face-to-face work group is hostile, he develops new friendly informal groups. Human nature seems to motivate each of us to establish and maintain these friendly supportive relationships in those face-to-face groups in which we spend most of our lives. Either we successfully establish these friendly and supportive relationships or we crack up.

It is not surprising, therefore, that we see people generally striving for a sense of dignity and personal worth. We all seem to seek recognition and a sense of importance in terms of the values and goals which we cherish and which our most important face-to-face groups also cherish.

To say that people seek friendly and supportive relationships does not mean that they seek to be coddled. Quite the contrary. People seek to achieve a sense of importance from doing difficult but important tasks which help to implement goals which they and their friends seek.[9]

Research findings are an important means for discovering sound principles in dealing with problems in human relations. The Institute for Social Research, University of Michigan, is now in the process of experimenting with ways in which members of management can use these and further research findings to influence the thinking of the various management levels in business organizations.

GROUP METHODS OF TRAINING SUPERVISORS

Numerous procedures for training supervisors, particularly factory foremen, have been developed in industry. The first and most commonly used methods naturally repeat the schoolroom procedures. Executives or teachers hired for the purpose give lectures or conduct classroom instruction of an informative nature. These traditional methods have not been so successful in industry as in the academic fields, chiefly because the teaching of supervisors is not mainly a problem in giving information. Supervisors need a kind of stimulation that causes them to drop old habit patterns and to adopt new attitudes toward human relations. Mere verbal understanding and acceptance of new ways of dealing with employees is not sufficient. What the supervisor does in everyday contacts with employees is the important measure of the effectiveness of the training program.

Lectures have little effect on the kind of foreman who, for example, is 60 years of age, attained his foremanship the hard way while working on a night shift, is now arbitrary and set in his habits. Such a foreman's supervisory tactics were described by a college student who worked for him one summer.

Incident 1.

FOREMAN (*To a man on the loading crew, paid on an hourly rate basis*): "Want to go on piece rate?"

EMPLOYEE: "Yeah, sure."

FOREMAN: "You paint tomorrow." (*The next night the worker came in T-shirt and dungarees, not suitable for spray painting. The foreman made a vague reference to mask and goggles and the man started to work without them. After several hours of hard work during which the worker got smeared with black paint, the foreman came over.*)

EMPLOYEE: "Hey, boss, what's the rate on this stuff?"

FOREMAN: "It ain't been timed yet. Yur're on your regular hourly rate." (*The material was in regular production and the employee knew it had been timed.*)

EMPLOYEE: "The hell it isn't timed."

FOREMAN (*Indignant*): "I said it ain't timed."

EMPLOYEE (*Throwing the spray gun in a bucket of thinner*): "I quit."

FOREMAN: "Wash up and report to the loadin' dock."

The following night as the worker reported for the job:

FOREMAN: "Yur paintin' tonight."

EMPLOYEE: "I am like hell—it took me the whole damn day to get clean."

FOREMAN: "I said you paint."

EMPLOYEE (*Walking away*): "I quit."

FOREMAN: "Go on help Mike unload steel."

Incident 2.

A crew of men who had been working hard unloading a boxcar decided to sit down for a smoke. While they were smoking, a worker from another crew came over and bummed a cigarette. He was generally disliked for his subservient attitude toward the foreman. Shortly, he disappeared in the direction of the foreman's office, and a little later the foreman appeared followed by this man. The foreman then reprimanded the crew in unprintable terms.

FOREMAN (*Turning to the informer*): "Ya go on piece rate tomorrow!"

Incident 3.

The men were paid on Friday night by a short well-dressed man, with an overbearing attitude, who casually tossed the pay envelopes to the men as they came in. It was his habit to leave as soon as possible, often before 5 P.M. when the work started.

EMPLOYEE: "Hey, where the hell is the paymaster?"

FOREMAN: "He's went."

EMPLOYEE: "I didn't get no pay, and I need it for groceries."

FOREMAN: "Come tuh work on time."

EMPLOYEE: "But I need it."

FOREMAN (*Turning away*): "Come tuh work on time."

The authoritarian type of supervisor believes in the old philosophy that men will work only when they are controlled by a firm disciplinarian who uses fear as a motivator. Fortunately, modern managements gradually are developing supervision directed toward democratic leadership. Democratic leadership means that the foreman strives to satisfy the egos of the members of the working group and de-emphasizes his own ego. He does little shouting at people, sits quietly, listens to people, gives them a sense of participation in solving the fascinating problems that are the daily part of the job.

The authoritarian person tends to regard others as either superior or inferior to him, and he adopts conduct adapted to the situation. The authoritarian person does not love or respect others. "In the last analysis, the alternatives are to fear or be feared."[10]

The democratic supervisor endeavors wherever possible to share with his group the decision-making about work planning, assignment and scheduling. Where a decision must be made by him, he helps the group to understand clearly the basis for his decision. He is careful to develop as much participation, opinion-giving and decision-making as possible, and a feeling of responsibility for the success of the work on the part of everyone. He is concerned that each employee clearly understands his work and has opportunities for success in it. His praise and criticisms are always delivered objectively in terms of work results and never personally in terms of what he may or may not like. He encourages worthwhile suggestions and the development of new procedure.[11]

The traditional training techniques of the past failed to develop the desired changes in attitudes and behavior of foremen and other supervisors. Foremen could be convinced intellectually that they ought to greet employees with a smile when they reported for work, discuss common problems with them, and behave in ways which show an interest in people, but still fail to supervise their workers in that manner. The latter obviously recognized their insincerity, because their words and actions did not express their underlying attitudes. After all, employees often react to a supervisor's attitudes rather than his words and actions.

The attitude of the supervisor is highly important in another respect. Not only do his actions tend to reflect his attitude, but his attitude also influences the way he will view or interpret the behavior of employees. For example, loafing, insubordination, failure to cooperate, disregard of company property, and being unwilling to do a full day's work are largely supervisory interpretations of actions which might also be interpreted, respectively, as resting, face-saving, lack of skill, an accident, and a re-luctance to begin a job that cannot be completed. The differing interpretations are highly important, since the problem which confronts the supervisor depends on his interpretation rather than on the actual behavior. The procedure that the supervisor will follow depends in turn upon the problem he sees, so that inaccurate interpretations invariably result in inadequate procedures.

Interpretations of behavior are greatly influenced by an attitude of suspicion. When employees do not trust supervisors and supervisors do not trust employees, misunderstandings in great numbers are created. Grievances that seem small and childish to management are seen as fundamental issues by workers. When mutual trust is present, grievances are rare, and when they do appear, remedies are easily found. Trust is an attitude that must be developed, and when the supervisor has this trust, his attitude is recognized and it develops mutual trust.[12]

Recent advancements in training supervisors are designed to influence attitudes as well as teach techniques for dealing with people. These training programs are of three general kinds:

1. Conference
2. Permissive (nondirective)
3. Role-taking

1. The conference

The conference may be defined as a group training method in which problem situations of common interest to the supervisors are discussed in an effort to formulate a solution through the contributions of all members of the group.

Advantages claimed for the conference method are:

1. The subject matter is of immediate interest to supervisors.

2. Opportunity for participation by members is provided.

3. The supervisors themselves do most of the talking.

4. The level of discussion usually matches their learning speed.

5. The method tends to develop qualities

of self-reliance and the ability to recognize and solve problems.

A typical conference usually consists of four steps:

1. The conference leader shows why a given problem or subject applies to the members of the group.

2. The nature of the problem is discussed and defined.

3. The discussion centers around wrong and right methods of handling the problem.

4. Analysis is made of right and wrong ways for the prevention of the problem in the future.

The conference method enables the leader to present informative material as well as conduct a discussion. Principles may be developed and emphasized. Problems involving the principles may be used for emphasis. When doubts arise concerning the applicability of a principle, the leader can clarify the principle more fully and illustrate its applicability to everyday situations in the plant. The leader also may give special assignments which are to be carried out on the job. Later, the supervisors may present the reactions to their attempts to carry out the assignment. During the discussions the leader encourages the whole group to participate. His role is to keep the discussion on the problem or topic under consideration, to bring about opportunities for face-saving, and to make contributions which clarify the issues or emphasize neglected aspects of the discussion. In some cases, he functions as a democratic leader and in other instances as an expert.

When attitudes or habits are to be changed, discussion is especially important as shown by the kind of experiment conducted by Kurt Lewin during the war. He worked with the National Research Council program on food conservation. Consumers' food habits were to be changed. One problem was to persuade housewives to use beef hearts, sweetbreads, kidneys, and other animal organs in family diets. Three groups of women were given lectures that stressed the health value of these meats, demonstrated various menu applications, and linked the nutrition problem to the war effort. In another experiment three comparable groups of women took up the question in group discussion, rather than lecture, and talked freely about their aversions. A follow-up showed that of the women who had heard the lectures, only 3 per cent served one of the meats never served before. Of those women who had had group discussion, 32 per cent of the women did so.[13]

One of the important advantages of the group conference, as practiced in the better concerns, is that the leader or secretary of the group can summarize the principles learned in the meeting. These principles can be mimeographed and reviewed by the supervisors and members of management. The supervisors can be provided with a textual guide which can be reviewed and re-emphasized. Most supervisors like to have some kind of written statement which summarizes what they think they have learned.

An effective conference includes a summary of the conclusions developed by the group. Conferees will feel that the conference was worthwhile and that something definite was accomplished if they are given a formal statement of the thoughts and conclusions brought out in the discussion. Such a formal statement usually includes the recommendations of the conference leader as exemplified in the following statement, which was developed during several discussions on disciplinary problems of supervisors:

As a supervisor, you are the leader of your men. Most of your contacts with them deal with the work and the ordinary everyday instructions to them. Most of your thinking and conversation with employees is of a positive friendly nature.

Occasionally, however, you find it necessary to handle problems that involve discipline, problems on the part of employees who have violated some company regulation or failed to do what is expected of a good employee. These problems in violation or failure must be handled with good judgment and offer you a chance to give employees the kind of leadership that builds strength and loyalty to you and the company.

Here are some suggestions and principles that may help you handle the fellow who gets out of line:

1. *Believe in the rules or practices which you expect employees to obey.* Every good rule or regulation has sound reasons back of it.

If you understand the reasons for the company's rules and expectations, you can wholeheartedly represent the company in regard to the expected practices by employees.

Employees are very smart. They soon recognize whether the supervisor really believes in a rule or is willing to shut his eyes and ears at certain times. Most employees naturally fall into line with what they think is expected of them.

Of course, if a rule has become a dead letter and everybody ignores it, somebody ought to find out whether the original reasons for the rule have changed and, if they have, the obsolete rule should be declared null and void. Review the old doubtful rules with your superior and get his decision about the rules that appear to need review.

If you yourself understand the soundness and fairness of the rules that your superior wishes you to enforce, your part in enforcing them will be easier.

2. *Getting employees to obey rules is an educational matter; not a policing job.* Years ago, a lot of plant foremen and other supervisors thought that the main part of a boss' job was policing employees. As a result, those old bygone foremen had a lot of policing to do. The employees were like the small boys in the old schoolmaster's schoolroom—they often raised hell because their teachers were poor teachers. The good teachers kept the boys so interested in their work that they forgot most of the hellraising.

The same principle applies to the good supervisor of today—he keeps his employees so busy and interested in their work that they usually do the right and neglect the wrong. The good supervisor is a good teacher who explains the right so enthusiastically that employees do the right. And he explains the right before, not after, trouble arises.

3. *The good supervisor has good discipline and still has most employees like him.* A lot of poor supervisors think that the employees do not like the supervisor who expects employees to obey the established rules. Actually, most employees have more respect for the supervisor who takes good discipline for granted and en-

forces it on the part of the few employees who need disciplinary attention.

Bear in mind that the children who usually have the least respect for the parent are the children who are allowed to do as they please. Employees who know that they can get away with anything usually have little respect for the supervisor who lets them get away with it.

4. *Disciplining an employee who needs it is not only a matter of being fair to him, but a matter of being so fair about it that the other employees approve of it.* Now and then, it becomes necessary to fire an employee. Every supervisor and personnel man who fires a man hopes that he can do it in a way that makes the fired employee feel that he was treated fairly. In addition to making the employee feel that the drastic treatment given him was fair, it is also necessary to make the other employees feel that the treatment was fair.

No one wants to punish an employee for his bad conduct just for the sake of punishing him. We do not punish our grown-up friends who work with us, but we do find it necessary to tell them that we will have to get along without them until they learn that we insist on working with each other in ways that are fair to all of us· fellow employees, the company, and customers.

5. *Good housekeeping and good discipline tend to go together.* The supervisor who keeps his equipment and materials in clean orderly fashion usually finds it easier to have his employees work in an orderly manner.

The supervisor who allows employees to get into sloppy habits of work in surroundings unnecessarily dirty, where raw materials are wasted and unused tools litter the place, must expect his employees to ignore a lot of good rules essential to efficient production.

6. *When the good supervisor finds that one of his best employees has lied to him or violated an important work rule, the good supervisor thinks of himself as also partially guilty.* He thinks of himself as also partially guilty because every employee under his supervision cooperates because his supervision is good. And the bad employee is also partially bad because of bad or poor supervision.

When a normal employee lies to his supervisor, it means that the supervisor has not established the kind of relationship that produces frankness and confidence on the part of the employee. (Of course the chronic liar is another kind of problem.)

When a good employee knowingly breaks a work rule, the good supervisor realizes that he failed to train the employee to appreciate the sound reasons for the rule.

In the long run, the good supervisor tends to attract and hold good employees. And the poor supervisor tends to attract and hold poor employees.

To the supervisor who finds that he has too many problems in discipline, the following "Don'ts" may be of help:

1. *Don't threaten* an employee. Explain. State the facts. Let the plain facts tell their own story. If repeated explanatory statements of the facts do not produce satisfactory results, act. Weak men make threats and use sarcasm.

The parent who constantly threatens his children seldom gains obedience. The parent who teaches the right and holds his children to good conduct gets the desired action without threats.

2. *Don't criticize or find fault only—point out the right.* Stress the right. When an employee has knowingly failed to do the right, let him explain his side of the story before the reprimand or criticism is made. Perhaps special circumstances were involved.

3. *Don't blame "higher-ups" for the rules.* The poor supervisor hides behind the old dodge: "Don't blame me for the rules—I didn't make 'em!" And every time the supervisor says that or its equivalent, he admits that he is not really a full-fledged member of management. Any rule that ought to be obeyed has a good reason back of it and the average employee knows it. The average employee has greater respect for the man who stands on his own two feet than for the supervisor who passes the buck to someone else in management.

4. *Don't try to make the wrongdoer feel guilty—try to get him to see the right.*

Perhaps you've seen a mother grab her small son by the shoulders, stare in his face, and yell at him: "Tell me you're sorry or I'll do so and so." In most cases, the mother is more interested in building up her own ego by wringing an admission of remorse than in getting the child to do right. The child must learn to understand why right is better than wrong.

The supervisor who likes to make the wrongdoer confess his guilt is likely to be the kind of sinner himself who feels bitter about his own sins when others confess their sins to him!

5. *Don't carry the whole discipline load on your shoulders.* Let the employees feel responsible for their own conduct and the conduct of their fellow employees.

A good supervisor respects his own employees. He shows by his manner and conversation that he likes them, trusts them, and expects

them to conduct themselves sensibly. His manner of brotherhood toward them helps to develop a feeling of brotherhood on the part of the employees toward each other. Sometimes their suggestions and influence will help to keep one of their fellow employees in line.

Discuss your problems of discipline with your superior. Keep him informed and ask his advice. The two of you usually can handle any disciplinary problem within reason.

2. The permissive method

In recent years many psychologists have given a good deal of attention to the use of nondirective techniques in psychotherapy. The usefulness of these methods has been demonstrated in dealing with some inadequately adjusted individuals. In the nondirective technique, the individual subject or client is encouraged to think through his own problem and develop a solution or procedure that appeals to him rather than to the counselor.

A few psychologists have applied the method of nondirective or permissive principles to the training of supervisors. One of these, Nathaniel Cantor, University of Buffalo, has prepared a series of audio-visual aids for discussion leaders on the development of morale in industry. Permissive conferences differ from most other conferences in the fact that the leader does not attempt to teach principles verbally; he stimulates the members of the group to develop their own principles.

After the audio-visual material has been presented to the group, the leader allows the members of the group to develop their own discussion and to discover answers for themselves. The leader is cautioned to remain silent and wait for the members of the party to take hold, even though they may flounder. Even if the leader is asked to give help, he refuses to start the discussion. A basic principle is that what the leader tells is not important; rather what the group members want to know must indicate where discussion should start.

The leader does not take the position of a

teacher or tell the group members what is right or wrong. They must find out for themselves what is right. They must participate, explain to themselves, and develop their own insight. When the leader remains neutral and refuses to agree or disagree with the member of the group who makes a statement, the latter is left free to decide his answers, to decide how he feels, and what position he wishes to take on any issue. The leader does not take sides because taking sides is likely to start an argument. When an argument is started, some persons will disagree but remain silent. Instead, the leader compels members of the group, by his silence, to sweat through their own problem and take the position which they themselves finally choose. Cantor gives several examples of the typical leader who takes a position versus the leader who does not take a definite stand on a question.

The problem used by him in this example of the directive *versus* the permissive method relates to the importance of seniority:

When the Directive Leader Takes Over

FIRST SUPERVISOR: Shouldn't the fellow with seniority be the one to get the promotion?

LEADER: Of course. He's been on the job longest and should be the first one to be upgraded.

SECOND SUPERVISOR (*A foreman who is having trouble because he wants to by-pass an older employee and recommend a younger one in point of service*): I don't agree. A worker with seniority isn't necessarily the most competent for the job.

LEADER (*Who feels embarrassed since his authority and judgment have been questioned in front of the group*): Well, you're wrong. A man who's worked longer will be more skilled.

SECOND SUPERVISOR: That's not so. I know a lot of guys who've been here a long time and they just haven't learned their job.

THIRD SUPERVISOR: Well, that's not my experience. The older men do know more.

LEADER: Sure, it is reasonable to suppose that the longer you work at the same thing the more competent you'll become.

SECOND SUPERVISOR: That might be your experience. It's not mine. The newer men in my department are way ahead of the older men. They're faster, they've caught on quicker, and they're producing more. And you can't convince me otherwise.

LEADER: Well, if you're going to feel that way, I don't suppose there's any point in arguing about it.

SECOND SUPERVISOR: I don't want to argue either. I know my crew and I know I'm right.

This leader did a very poor job in the above discussion. He took a definite stand on the question of seniority. This led to a heated argument. His judgment was immediately questioned and he was put on the defensive. It is easy to imagine that others wouldn't participate in the discussion because they felt they'd be on the spot, too. The easiest thing to do was to keep quiet and take no chances of getting into hot water either with the leader or their fellow-supervisor.

Now let's see how a more skilled leader, who realized he should not take sides, would have handled this question.

When the Leader Uses a Permissive Technique

FIRST SUPERVISOR: Shouldn't the fellow with seniority be the one to get the promotion?

LEADER: (*Waits a few seconds to see if anyone would reply—but no one does*).

SECOND SUPERVISOR: I don't agree. A worker with seniority isn't necessarily the most competent for the job.

LEADER: I see what you mean. This is becoming very interesting. Some of you feel seniority should count and others feel that merit should count. What do the rest of you think? I guess this isn't an easy question to answer.

THIRD SUPERVISOR: Well, maybe there's something to both sides of the question. Maybe seniority and merit both play a part?

SECOND SUPERVISOR: Sure, seniority should count provided the guy knows his job, too.

LEADER: You mean that as between two men equally competent the one in service longer should get the promotion?

SECOND SUPERVISOR: Naturally, seniority should count in that case.

LEADER: Are all of you agreeing, then, that seniority is an important factor but not the only one, that merit must be considered, too?

In this instance you will notice that nowhere does the leader take sides on this question. He merely makes clear what the different speakers are saying and expresses the issue very clearly. He leaves it to the group to decide on the importance of seniority versus merit in the matter of promotion. The leader by keeping his own views out doesn't pre-judge the matter. The group members don't have to fight *against* his position. They are free to express their differences. And if the leader doesn't put them on the spot by his views they are more likely to modify their original position.[14]

Cantor illustrates the effectiveness of the permissive technique in his discussion of why the leader should not argue with any member of the group even though the group criticizes the technique being used:

Do not argue. As a rule, when people argue what they say is much less important than how they feel. To contradict a speaker is to invite a restatement of what he said. People want to feel important. When they speak, they want to be respected. To argue with what they said, especially in a group, is to "show them up." It is to be expected that the speaker will resent this. Do not try to "sell" a point to anyone. People must convince themselves. All the leader can do is *to offer* another way of looking at the issue and leave the speaker free to disagree at the time. Let's turn to an example or two.

(*A film on Morale in Industry has just been concluded.*)

SUPERVISOR: I don't think supervisors need this kind of high-fallutin' stuff. We know how to handle our men!

LEADER: Yes, but the guy who wrote this is a specialist and he ought to know.

SUPERVISOR: I'll bet he's never been on an operating line in all his life. He's read something in books.

LEADER: Well, even so, we can learn something out of books, too.

SUPERVISOR: No, not on this job.

Now let's look at what took place. The supervisor made a statement. The leader argued for his position. The discussion ended just where it began. Here is the way a skilled leader might have handled the same question.

SUPERVISOR: I don't think supervisors need this kind of high-fallutin' stuff. We know how to handle our men!

LEADER: I see what you mean, Joe. You feel it sounds completely foolish and it's a complete waste of time?

SUPERVISOR: Oh, I wouldn't go that far and say it's completely foolish.

LEADER: You mean there may be something to it, after all?

SUPERVISOR: Oh, I guess we could still learn something new.

Here the leader doesn't argue. He simply shows Joe that he respects and understands how he feels, and therefore, helps *the supervisor* to modify his former rigid position.

SUPERVISOR: This business of morale is a lot of baloney. Give the worker a living wage and he's got all the morale you want.

LEADER: Well, I notice that supervisors get a living wage and still they're not doing such a grand job. Production has fallen in several departments. How about that?

SUPERVISOR: You said it. Production has fallen because the men aren't satisfied with their take.

LEADER: No, I meant the supervisors aren't doing *their* job.

SUPERVISOR: Oh, yes we are. But you can't get the work out of people who aren't paid a decent wage.

It's obvious in the above example, that the leader is unskilled in handling the issue of morale. He is fighting the supervisor and the supervisor fights back. The leader really starts the argument. A more skillful leader would have handled this question differently.

SUPERVISOR: This business of morale is a lot of baloney. Give the worker a living wage and he's got all the morale you want.

LEADER: I see what you mean. The only thing that interests a worker on the job is the money he gets. He's not interested in the kind of supervisor he works for.

SUPERVISOR: Oh, sure, that makes a difference, too.

LEADER: You mean, he'll be more satisfied and happier on the job if he has a square shooter for a supervisor than a crab?

SUPERVISOR: Naturally. That's just common sense.

LEADER: Then, if I understand you, you are saying that besides his wage he wants to have good relations with his foreman?

SUPERVISOR: Sure, that's right.

LEADER: And that's good morale?

SUPERVISOR: I see what you mean.

In this instance, you will note, the leader doesn't argue but helps the supervisor to see for himself that the relationship between supervisor and worker is important.[15]

One of the chief values of the permissive or nondirective technique is in the contribution which the technique makes to the personality development of the leader himself. Very few discussion leaders can use a nondirective technique effectively unless they have a personality development that characterizes individuals who are emotionally secure. A leader who attempts to use the nondirective technique with a discussion group cannot have a temperament that is characteristically on the defensive. He first of all must feel secure within himself as a person and be able to hear criticism of himself without emotional disturbance on his own part. Discussion leaders who have learned to use the nondirective technique are likely to be individuals who have an unusually high type of emotional control and poise in social situations or they acquire such a level of social development. True personal leadership and long-term patience in getting benefits from it are necessary for the effective use of the nondirective technique. As yet, its application to the training of supervisors has not been widely used, but it gives promise of considerable future effectiveness.

3. Role-taking

Role-taking (also called role-playing) is a grown-up form of "Let's Pretend." In the training of supervisors, the supervisor acts out a situation that involves a human relations problem. The basic principles used are very old. Companies have used them for years to teach salesmen. Psychotherapists have employed them in the psychodrama technique. In recent years, studies made by Alex Bavelas, of the Massachusetts Institute of Technology, and his associates used the "Do and Learn" technique in the training of supervisors in handling human relations problems. In the role-taking, the

supervisors not only discuss the techniques which supervisors should use in dealing with employees but they also demonstrate them in the presence of their colleagues.

Several large industrial concerns have used the Bavelas studies as a basis for their supervisory training. In the American Type Founders Company and in other companies, the principle works as follows:

1. The staff-training department calls a meeting of the foremen to set up principles for handling a certain type of case.
2. A foreman is briefed to be the "worker" in the role-taking—usually from actual case histories of labor disputes.
3. Two other foremen, one at a time, are called on to hear the "worker's" grievance, and deal with it.
4. Recordings of the discussions are played back, and criticized by the two foremen-players first, then in open discussion.
5. The group then decides how the grievance should have been handled. If there's time, a foreman and "worker" play the roles that way.[16]

When supervisors are inducted into this form of training, they at first tend to dislike the idea. They feel that they are not actors and that the whole idea is a lot of foolishness. However, after several sessions have been conducted, the members of the group learn to enjoy the role-taking and begin to volunteer for roles. Sometimes a competitive spirit makes the sessions quite lively. Of course, some supervisors refuse to change their beliefs merely because they have seen others play a role with which they did not agree.

Allan H. Tyler, training supervisor at American Type Founders, after the plan had been in operation about a year, noted considerable improvement in the ways in which supervisors handled their grievances. Qualty and quantity of production rose. Supervisors spoke up at meetings with other management men. One of the last foremen to accept the principles developed under role-taking instruction was a tough old-timer who ran his battery of machines and crew of men in the traditional manner. The first

1

"Damn it!" the irate employee at ATF, Inc., yells at his foreman in the familiar way a grievance is initiated almost everywhere, "I'm getting a bum deal."

2

"It happens out there all the time," the foreman reports to his superior—and how well management knows it. In getting supervisors to handle grievances effectively, ATF had the same problem that most employers have experienced. That's why the company sought a better way to make each foreman a human-relations expert.

3

ATF thinks it has found the answer in role-playing: a development in psychotherapy which the company aims at its specific training objectives.

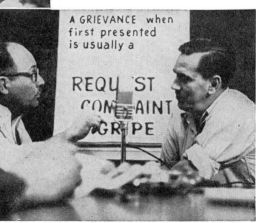

4

Role-playing is a modern version of childhood's play-acting—with a serious purpose. Here the foreman acts out the role of the irate employee, pouring it on a younger foreman, who handles his part as he would do it in the shop.

5

Still acting as the aggrieved employee, the foreman tries the routine on a supervisor who is an old hand. Unabashed, the old-timer mobilizes his experience, lays his argument on the line like the capable veteran he is.

6

The old-timer and the younger foreman hear a recorded playback of their exchange with the aggriever. They are critics of each other and of themselves. This gives them a chance to stand off and check their own performance, to see what they did wrong.

7

How they have handled their parts is measured against company standards for best ways to settle grievances.

8

A discussion, led by training experts, clarifies what good practice is, and how it's best achieved.—**Business Week**, April 9, 1949.

time this foreman played a role, he had to handle a charge of carelessness: a worker accidentally had dropped a wrench into a machine, damaging it. The foreman, in demonstrating the role that he would play in such a situation, promptly fired the man in five acrid sentences.

Then the old-timer watched while another supervisor took over the same role. The new man reprimanded the "worker" and showed him the right way to handle a wrench. After the playback, the old-timer still insisted he was right: A dope who damaged a machine ought to be fired. But the group voted him down; it decided a reprimand and short layoff would be enough penalty for a first offense. At this point, the old-timer relented a little—maybe he had been too rough. Since then, Tyler reports, the foreman has mended his ways somewhat. Tyler credits the role playing with the change.

Tyler believes the great value of role playing is this: Supervisors learn, by practice, to think on their feet. They never know what the "worker" will say next, hence they learn to make quick decisions under realistic pressure and anxiety. Then, too, they learn by seeing how others cope with situations. And—when they act an employee's part—they put themselves in the place of a worker and see his point of view.

Other companies have had much the same experience. Role playing is firmly set in training programs at Owens-Corning, Armstrong Cork Co., General Foods Corp., Sharp & Dohme, Inc., Esso Standard Oil, and elsewhere. The Michigan Industrial Training Council recommends it to its member-training directors. The American Society of Training Directors recently gave considerable time at a convention in Cleveland to a demonstration of the technique.

At least one union has adopted role playing. The Pulp, Sulphite & Paper Mill Workers (A.F.L.) uses it to teach shop stewards how to handle workers who fancy they have a grievance, and how to put grievances effectively to foremen.[17]

Role-taking is a process in which supervisors spontaneously act out problems that face them. It differs from demonstrations in the fact that demonstrations are previously prepared. In role-taking, one of the group takes the part of the supervisor and the other member the role of the employee. The

scenes are discussed by the members of the group and the skills and principles pertinent to the particular type of problem are clarified and stated. One of the chief values in role-taking is that it enables the supervisory trainee to participate in his own training.

The results of a survey of 107 companies who use or had used role-playing show that the chief benefit of this technique is in developing human relations skills. There are other benefits, too: The members of the group participate more, they become interested in their co-workers and subordinates, and they gain confidence in handling problems in interpersonal relations. Over half the companies polled thought that role-playing was useful in handling morale, teamwork, attitude improvement, and grievance problems.

There are disadvantages to role-playing, also. Among these are the fact that it takes too long and it fails to present the material in true perspective. Hence, it is unnatural. Some management men feel it is unwise to use this device because it produces occasional embarrassment. A few are reluctant to use it because it takes too long to get the group to feel at ease. The authors, however, thought that most of the disadvantages were of the sort that could be overcome if the role-playing procedures were improved.[18]

The effectiveness of personal relationships in industry depends upon specific social skills. Like other skills, they may be learned by practice. Thus far, the most effective method for teaching these skills appears to be the common-sense one—"Watch others, let others watch you, discuss and evaluate differences, and try it again." Alex Bavelas has described the principles and procedures of role-playing in several published articles. Excerpts from one are:

. . . Group discussion may effect considerable changes in motivation, and may raise the group's level of understanding regarding the problems of face-to-face relationships, but it is not very effective in transmitting behavioral skills. It is this defect in the discussion method that has led individuals interested in the problem of training social skills to experiment with role-playing. The central idea of role-playing is the assigning of roles to various members of the training group and the acting out of problem situations. . . .

. . . Whatever the form of role-playing, [strictly-defined roles, or highly-spontaneous roles] if it is well planned and directed, the following advantages for teaching are usually gained:

1. Playing a role before an "audience" makes an individual self-conscious. Since the purpose of role-playing is not to present a finished performance, this self-consciousness is desirable because it makes the individual aware of his actions in a new way. . . . He becomes as it were, "sensitized" to himself.

2. . . . The foreman who is playing the role of a *worker* can report how it made him feel when the *foreman* treated him the way he did. This helps the trainees to get a better insight into the effects of their actions on others.

3. Rotation of roles causes certain factors to operate:

a. the individuals waiting for their turn take full advantage of the chance to see what the fellow "at bat" will do, and thus eliminate errors from their own performance.

b. the individuals who have already been at bat, elated with their success or chagrined at their errors, are also only too ready to find and point out the good and bad points in the current play.

c. very often an individual who has just played the role of *foreman* takes the role of *worker* in the very next play. For him this offers the stimulating experience of "feeling the difference" between the foreman's and the worker's position in a difficult situation.

4. Role-playing shows you how to *do* something rather than *telling* you how to do it.

5. People learn by *doing*.

. . . Several years of trial and error in the use of role-playing in management training seems to indicate that an effective procedure for teaching specific skills requires (1) the use of carefully planned "stereotype" situations as basic training material, and (2) rather close controls of all roles being played, with the exception of the role primarily under consideration—that one being left entirely free to be played as the individual sees fit.

. . . And there is always the task of constructing the situations which will be acted out. Almost always they must be planned anew for each group and organization, and it is not easy to find the problem situations which will yield the most fruitful material. It may appear on the surface that certain types of problems are common to all foremen—attendance, discipline, work delegation, employee training, etc. But in reality these are areas of responsibility, not problems. . . . The planning of situations for role-playing rests finally not upon generalizations from the picture of industrial management as a whole, but upon individual diagnosis of the organization in which the training is to be done.

. . . The question often arises "Granted that role-playing is an efficient training method, can individuals be trained to use it?" The answer is a qualified "yes," based upon both failures and successes. Attempts to train individuals to direct-role-playing yield very questionable results when reliance is placed upon lectures, demonstrations, and trainers' manuals. Experience indicates what should have been self-evident: that the directing of role-playing can best be taught by the use of role-playing itself.[19]

Sensitivity training for supervisors

One of the most promising methods of training supervisors by the group method has been developed by psychologists in a workshop for executives at the University of California, Los Angeles.

"Sensitivity training" is an approach to supervisory development programs which emphasizes that supervisors should see themselves and others realistically, understand their own feelings and prejudices, and be sensitive to the ways people relate to each other. As the trainees examine themselves and the impact they have on one another, they also develop specific skills for the handling of various human relations problems. This novel training approach, clinical in its orientation, has resulted in far-reaching changes in the ways in which people work together on management teams.

Aims of Sensitivity Training

1. Each trainee should get a better picture of the kind of person he is.
2. The trainees should check the accuracy of their perceptions as to what other people are like.

"Sensitivity Training for Top Executives," a program limited to 15 persons, makes possible a high level of individual involvement.

Unstructured discussion among participants helps them to gain a new feeling about their human relations problems. Here a small group of Los Angeles industrial executives, working with Dr. Robert Tannenbaum (in light coat at extreme right, facing camera), of the University of California at Los Angeles faculty, utilize an octagonal table arrangement to promote conversational atmosphere.

3. Trainees should obtain more factual data.
4. Each trainee should develop new "human relations" skills, including ways of dealing with conflicts and tensions.
5. The trainees should be helped to become more aware of "group process," those forces unique to a group which ultimately may result in its success or failure.

The Nature of the Training Process
1. The training is "feeling-oriented" as well as "content-oriented." The participants learn to deal not only with specific cases and examples from their "on-the-job" situations, but also to analyze their own reactions and feelings toward one another and toward the situations in which they become involved at the training session.
2. Each person attempts to keep his concept of himself intact, and little training impact can be expected unless the trainee is able to examine his "self-concept," to reevaluate it, and to instigate those changes which he feels would benefit him.

3. The training design is partly unstructured. Opportunities are provided for the trainees to decide what they want to talk about, what kinds of problems they desire to deal with, and what means to use in reaching their goals.
4. Auxiliary training devices and techniques are utilized to facilitate the interaction process among the participants.
5. A permissive atmosphere is maintained.

Experience shows that if participation in the training process has been effective, the first impact will probably occur in the trainee's own perceptions about himself and others. His new self-assessment may lead to more confidence and security, and to less anxiety in his day-to-day relations on the job. Next, the repercussions of such insights will probably be felt by those with whom he deals. He may "blow up" less often, turn an attentive rather than a deaf ear to suggestions, or play a more constructive role in staff meetings. As he begins to feel his way and explores new behavior patterns, he must be supported by his co-workers to utilize the understanding and skills which he has learned. He needs an environment where human relations practices are part of the total organizational philosophy, where "gimmicks" and manipulative devices are recognized and deprecated for what they are.

As yet, the results of sensitivity training have not been subjected to a rigorous scientific analysis to ascertain the specific type and direction of changes which have undoubtedly taken place. However, reports from both trainees and co-workers indicate that this method of training does lead to greater "human relations" know-how, which in turn often seems to be followed by higher productivity, better morale, and lower turnover. Sensitivity training, of course, is not a "cure-all" for every organizational problem; there are too many other technical and administrative aspects to effective management. We do see it, however, as an exciting development in executive training—with a future rich in promise and in potential rewards.[20]

To be effective, the training of supervisors must be done in a favorable leadership climate

Members of the Personnel Research Board, Ohio State University, made an unusually careful study, with the cooperation of the International Harvester Company, of the effectiveness of a training program for supervisors. This research program dealt with the leadership of first-line industrial supervisors and measured relationships of the different kinds of leadership to the morale and efficiency of the workers.

On the basis of earlier statistical studies of leadership, two leadership factors were extracted. One identified as "consideration" included such characteristics between supervisors and subordinates as friendliness, mutual trust, and respect. The other, termed "initiating structure," involved establishing patterns of organization, channels of communication, and ways of getting things done.

A major interest of the company in promoting the research program was investigation of the effectiveness of the central school for supervisors.

The results showed that foremen who operated under leadership climates high in consideration scored significantly higher themselves in both consideration attitudes and behavior. In other words, a boss who was considerate tended to have foremen who were that way. With reference to initiating structure, the trend was the same. In a climate high in initiating structure the foremen had initiating structure attitudes. Their behavior showed the same tendency although that trend was not statistically significant. . . .

The foreman is more responsive to the day-to-day climate in which he operates than to any special course of training he may have been given. To a considerable extent, the specific training in human relations is wasted unless the environment in the plant is also strong in human relations. . . .

With reference to training in human relations, our study yields one clear implication. Such training conducted in isolation from the practical situation falls short of its objective. It does not take much to upset whatever the training seemed to have accomplished. It is necessary to involve the social situation in which a person is going to operate. Our foremen developed a point of view in school but lost it on their return to the plant if their supervisor had a different point of view. All this suggests that to improve social relations almost anywhere, it is important to work on the whole social setting. It is not possible to pull people out of this setting, tell or teach them some ideas, and then return them to the setting and consider everything fixed. In fact, if we are concerned with a supervisory hierarchy, it looks as if we should really begin working on the leadership attitudes at the top, so that the favorable leadership climate will spread down to the first-line supervisors, because certainly it will not spread up the line in the usual industrial organization. Leadership behavior is not a thing apart but is imbedded in a social setting.[21]

Paradoxically, several studies of the effectiveness of certain training programs for supervisors have indicated that the supervisors were less effective after than before training! The reason for this finding can be attributed to the kind of leadership climate to which the supervisor returns after training.

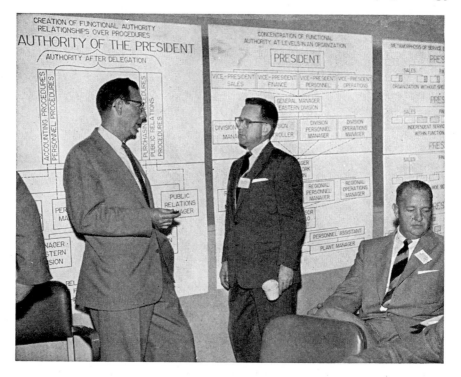

Training in industry is not limited to skilled workers and foremen. Executives holding responsible positions in industry are attending workshops, classes and discussion group meetings in order to improve their own abilities.

Here is a picture of a discussion that continued into the break period for three of the Southern California executives who were members of one of the groups attending the "Executive Program in Business Management," University of California, Los Angeles.

The program is designed primarily for men in the executive and middle ranks of management, including both line managers and staff specialists.

Members of the past groups had an average age of 43 and 40 per cent were either presidents, executive vice-presidents or general managers of their firms.

Similar workshops, seminars and conferences are conducted in the East by the American Management Association, New York, and by other industry associations and universities.

If his superior is authoritative, arbitrary, and production-minded rather than employee-centered, the supervisor will fit his practices into the established pattern, not into the pattern taught him in the training program.

The conflict between his situation as he feels he must function in it and his new desires to adopt better methods may cause him to become confused. He may adjust to the problem by some form of aggressive behavior.

Many a supervisor has said of his train-ing program: "A wonderful program but when does my boss get it!"

The kind of superior under whom the foreman or other supervisor operates is more closely related to his behavior than the kind of training course he has taken. This indicates that the answer to the improvement of supervision in industry must include top management men as well as the supervisors.[22] Many companies are doing this through the numerous workshops for executives such as those conducted by the American Management Association.

Acknowledgments and References

1. Wallace B. Donham, Elton Mayo, and George F. F. Lombard, *Teamwork and Labor Turnover in the Aircraft Industry of Southern California,* Harvard University Bureau of Business Research, Boston, Mass., 1944, foreword.

2. Douglas McGregor, "Conditions of Effective Leadership in the Industrial Organization," *Journal of Consulting Psychology,* Vol. 8, No. 2 (1944), pp. 55–63.

3. *The Foreman's Letter,* National Foremen's Institute, Inc., Deep River, Conn., November 1945.

4. Excerpt from *Annual Report 1953–1954,* Industrial Relations Section, California Institute of Technology, Project 5, Surveys of Employee Opinion.

5. James H. Mullen, "The Supervisor Assesses His Job in Management, Highlights of a Nation-Wide Survey," *Personnel,* American Management Association, September 1954, pp. 94–108.

6. Schuyler Dean Hoslett, *Human Factors in Management,* Harper & Brothers, New York, 1946, pp. 107–111.

7. *The Foreman's Letter,* National Foremen's Institute, Deep River, Conn., November 6, 1947.

8. *Ibid.,* May 4, 1949, pp. 3–4.

9. Rensis Likert, "Motivation: The Core of Management," *Personnel Series,* No. 155, American Management Association, Inc., 1953, pp. 3–7.

10. A. H. Maslow, "The Authoritarian Character Structure," *Journal of Social Psychology,* Vol. 18 (1943), pp. 401–411.

11. John M. Pfiffner, "A Pattern for Improved Supervisory Leadership," *Personnel,* American Management Association, January 1948, p. 271.

12. Norman R. F. Maier, "A Human Relations Program for Supervision," reprinted from *Industrial and Labor Relations Review,* Vol. I, No. 3 (April 1948).

13. For further information, see *Fortune,* August 1950, p. 46.

14. Nathaniel Cantor, "Manual for Discussion Leaders on Human Relations in Industry," *Human Relations Films,* Buffalo, N.Y., 1948.

15. *Loc. cit.*

16. *Business Week,* April 9, 1949, pp. 102–103. By special permission.

17. *Op. cit.*

18. See Gustav R. Stahl, "Role Playing in Training Supervisors, *Factory Management and Maintenance,* January 1954, pp. 102–105.

19. Alex Bavelas, "Role Playing and Management Training," *Publications in Social Science,* Series 2, No. 21, Department of Economics and Social Science, Massachusetts Institute of Technology, Cambridge, Mass. See also *Sociatry,* Vol. I, No. 2 (June 1947), pp. 183–191.

20. Irving R. Weschler, Marvin A. Klemes, and Clovis Shepard, "A New Focus in Executive Training," *Advanced Management,* May 1955.

21. Edwin A. Fleishman, Edwin F. Harris, and Harold E. Burtt, *Leadership and Supervision in Industry,* Ohio State University Studies, No. 33, 1955.

22. See *Personnel,* American Management Association, September 1955, pp. 95 f.

23. Glenn Gardiner, "Reaching the Individual Worker," A paper delivered before the Second Annual Greater Philadelphia Safety Conference, May 27, 1935.

PROJECTS

1. Discuss the good and bad aspects of the foreman's procedure described in the following example.

   I recall a situation where a foreman in charge of an unloading crew went to the superintendent and recommended that inasmuch as certain roller conveyors had been put into use in the unloading of cars, a reduction in the tonnage rate paid to workers for unloading cars should be put into effect. His recommendation was accepted and a reduction in rates was installed.

   In announcing this reduction to his workers, the foreman explained to them that the superintendent had called him in and told him that rates would have to be cut.

   "In spite of everything I could do and in spite of every argument I could put up against this cut in rates, the superintendent insisted it had to be done anyhow," the foreman explained.[23]

2. Construct a rating scale for the use of a supervisor who wishes to have his employees

rate him on his supervisory characteristics and ability. Keep the tone and purpose of the rating scale constructive rather than critical in nature.

3. Tell how you would deal with the following kinds of employees who are in need of executive attention:
    a. The employee who asks for a raise but does not deserve it.
    b. The employee who thoughtlessly gives a company secret to a competitor.
    c. The rank-and-file employee who masquerades as an important executive of the company.
    d. The salaried employee who was absent because of intoxication.
    e. The employee who pads his overtime card.

4. What rules should the supervisory executive follow, in order to be certain that his instructions to an employee are thoroughly understood by the employee?

5. What should be done by the executive who happens to appear unexpectedly among a group of workers on a day-wage basis of pay and finds that most of them are loafing on the job?

6. Tell how the autocratic type of executive might handle the cases listed in this chapter. What would be some of the possible reactions of the employee in each case? How could an intelligent, well-adjusted employee handle himself in such circumstances?

7. The foreman is a key figure in labor relations. Work out a system for selecting foremen in a large factory. Describe specifically each quality you would want to consider and how you would use it in the selection plan.

8. Experiments indicate that employees tend to do more work when they have a supervisor who gives them little close supervision, allowing them to feel responsible for their own work. What are some of the dangers or difficulties in such supervision?

9. Review the characteristics of one of your former supervisors or a present supervisor. To what extent does he apply the supervisory practices that develop teamwork?

COLLATERAL READINGS

Bellows, Roger M., *Psychology of Personnel in Business and Industry*, Prentice-Hall, Inc., New York, 1954, Chapter 4.

Ghiselli, Edwin E., and Clarence W. Brown, *Personnel and Industrial Psychology*, McGraw-Hill Book Company, Inc., New York, 1955, Chapter 13.

Haire, Mason, *Psychology in Management*, McGraw-Hill Book Company, Inc., New York, 1956, Chapters 3 and 5.

Harrell, Thomas Willard, *Industrial Psychology*, Rinehart & Company, Inc., New York, 1949, Chapter 16.

Maier, Norman R. F., *Principles of Human Relations*, John Wiley & Sons, Inc., New York, 1952, Chapters 1–8.

Smith, Henry Clay, *Psychology of Industrial Behavior*, McGraw-Hill Book Company, Inc., New York, 1955, Chapters 10 and 11.

CHAPTER TWENTY-TWO

Communication in industry—morale surveys

Five thousand years ago an ancient Egyptian by the name of Ptah-Hotep wrote:
"If you are in the position of one to whom petitions are made, be courteous and listen
to the petitioner's story. Do not stop his words until he has poured out all that is in his
heart and has said all that he came to say. A man with a grievance loves the official
who will accept what he states and let him talk out his trouble fully. A kind word will
illuminate his heart, but if an official stops the flow of his words people will say, 'Why
should that fellow have the power to behave this way?' "[1]

Systematic surveys of employee attitudes began in the early 1920's. Now
similar investigations are made each year in hundreds of companies with
thousands of employees. One reason for the rapid growth of attitude surveys in industry is exemplified in this incident:

Recently I inquired of one of a certain company's drill press operators, "Joe,
how's the food in the plant cafeteria?"
"Food's okay," he replied. "But the prices they soak us is terrible."
"Aren't they less than you'd have to pay outside?" I pressed him.
"Maybe so," he agreed reluctantly. "But with the company able to buy in
quantity, they must get everything cheap. Us guys figure they're makin' plenty
of dough right out of the food they serve us!"
Later this same day the company's President said to me, "Our workers know
we're sincerely interested in their welfare. Take our plant cafeteria. We operate that entirely for their convenience. It's losing us just under fifty thousand
dollars a year."

Clearly here was a case where management had failed to explain itself
to its labor. Here, too, was a case where, because of this failure, labor was
resentful toward management. And finally, here was a case where management was entirely unaware of its workers' antagonism.[2]

If you have been at all alert to social situations, you have had the experience of talking to a person who did not respond to what you were
saying. You talked and he talked but you realized that he did not get
meaning from what you said. Perhaps you, too, failed to get meaning
from what he said.

449

Communications can be defined as the conveying and exchanging of meanings. Recently, it has become a highly appreciated problem in modern industry. Actually, the problem is as old as civilized life. Civilized life has always depended on communication. The reason why the problem is now gaining more attention is not because of a change in the nature of the problem but in our constantly developing complexity of modern industrial life. We now realize that as work teams have grown in size our techniques have not kept pace with the needs for intra-team and individual communication.

The need for improved communications in industry

Many communication relationships between managements and men are based on the assumption that the employees are interested in the same things as management: profits, lower prices, efficiency, and free enterprise.

Actually, the individual employee does not see things the way management does. The things important to management are not necessarily important to the employee. Management does *not* have an obligation to reform the employee who sees his situation in a manner quite different from the way management sees it; management *does* have the obligation to arrange its relations with employees so that both management and men can work together harmoniously and effectively.

The ability to communicate effectively with others—to understand and convey meaning—is essential to everyone, but it is especially important for the executive because he can get things done only *through other people*. He must learn not only how to get acceptance of his ideas but also how to gain willing, enthusiastic cooperation that results in benefits to all concerned with the work team and its production.

Effective communication is a fundamental skill of modern management. Productivity in industry is largely a result of work team performance, the work team consisting of all members of an organization: officials, executives, supervisors, department heads, rank-and-file employees, and all their colleagues. Communication as a term used in industrial situations usually implies the two-way conveying of ideas: upward to management as well as from management downward to subordinates.

To function effectively, a work team must be coordinated in thinking and action. In many companies, work teams are widely separated, even distributed over widely scattered geographical areas. Communication is maintained among members of the work team by means of conversations, interviews, committee meetings, conferences, written instructions and reports, handbooks, booklets, bulletin boards, employee magazines, public address systems, suggestion plans, telephones, and other devices. In many cases the situation is of a nature that makes the choice of the technique a simple matter, as in a foreman's need for instructing an employee. The oral communication may be so simple and appropriate that the conveying of ideas takes place without further consideration of other available techniques. In other situations that necessitate communication, the selection of the most effective technique may require investigation, even research.

The effectiveness of communication often depends upon psychological factors such as attitude, motivation, skill, and the psychological climate where the words are used. Anyone, for example, who has participated in labor negotiations between an employer and a union knows that weeks of discussion may have taken place but there may have been very little real communication. There may have been much talk and little listening on the part of both parties to the controversy. Round the clock negotiations may have produced no agreement because deep-seated resentments prevented a meeting of minds.

Personality characteristics influence and

are related to a person's attitudes and beliefs. Several research studies have demonstrated such relationships. Social scientists have, for example, studied the connections between attitudes toward big business and personality. Personal factors condition attitudes and beliefs as reported in this example:

Suppose a man tells the interviewer that prices are too high, that big business is running everything these days, that the small fellow gets no break, and that all labor unions are run by gangsters. If this is all we know about the man, we are not very near to understanding him. We can perceive his bitterness and know that he probably does grind an axe when these attitudes are tapped. But we cannot see any sources of his feelings; and, most of all, we are still in the dark completely on how one might seek to change his attitudes.

Suppose further, however, that we discover that this man feels isolated, is a poorly paid low-ranking clerk, feels left out of the main stream of life, and that he has risen from a manual laborer's background, though he does not feel he has lived up to his own expectations. We can now better understand the connection between his expressed attitudes and his private world.[3]

Studies such as this one have emphasized to business leaders the need for training in psychological insight into the factors that color and control attitudes. Communications research has given impetus to the need for training in sensitivity to the other person's wants, to the need for facing frankly one's own wants, and to the establishing of a system of "feedback" in industry whereby the employee can give the communicator—the executive—a better understanding of the employee's ideas and needs.

Management men who think that they have developed good lines of communication downward, upward and horizontally within their own organizations, often find that bottlenecks block the channels. The bottleneck may be in the form of individual supervisors who garble the message transmitted or they may be in the form of human motives, attitudes, and aspirations that management has failed to appreciate. The higher a man goes into management, the more he becomes dependent on the accurate exchange of information on all levels of his organization.

Every experienced person in industry knows that status relationships of superior-subordinate—formal organization structure—slow down the free interchange of information, ideas, suggestions and questions. The subordinate tends to tell his boss only what the latter is interested in hearing, and to cover up mistakes, failures, and bad news. He distorts information going up. This distortion also takes place in information going down. The superior does not always explain his problems to his subordinates.

In progressively managed companies, these status differences are not especially prominent in boss-employee relations. Each looks upon the other as a colleague in performing work. Well-managed companies realize that the spirit of colleagueship and openness of communication channels are not always operating as well as possible. Surveys of the situation are necessary to reveal bottlenecks, irritation points, and the effectiveness of management's messages.

The need for such investigations was revealed in an experiment by the Borden Company when the public relations department prepared a series of messages for use on bulletin boards. The series was shown to a group of top management men and to a group of employees. Each group guessed which of the messages would receive most effective acceptance by the employees. The messages were then displayed to the employees. A few weeks later a test was made among the workers to find out which of the notices had had the most effective impact. The management favorites were at the bottom of the list in order of effectiveness.[4]

Top managements believe in the values of communication

That managements recognize the importance of effective communication was indicated by answers to a questionnaire mailed to presidents of 100 of America's leading corporations by the Industrial Communication Research Staff of Purdue University. The total number of replies received was 73. Of these, 20 came from company officials other than the president himself. Some of the questions and answers were the following:

Is there a relationship between communication and employee productivity? Ninety-six per cent of respondents saw a "definite relationship"; and 4 per cent, a "slight relationship."

Is there a relationship between breakdowns in communication and labor disputes? Ninety-four per cent replied in the affirmative; 79 per cent saw a "definite" relationship, while 14 per cent believed the relationship to be "slight."

What is the nature of communicative ability? An analysis of the responses to this question, which was accompanied by a list of seven alternatives to be checked, showed that these presidents believe that:

(1) Not all managers can communicate effectively (only 12 out of 51 thought that nearly all top managers possess this ability).
(2) While natural talent is a factor in communicative ability, it is not the only factor.
(3) Greater communicative ability can be developed through training and experience.

Should training in methods of communication be provided for management personnel? Every respondent replied in the affirmative to this question. . . .

How much does the personal regard listeners have for a communicator affect the reception of his ideas? Nearly 98 per cent of the executives believed that the personal regard the listeners have for the communicator is of some importance. Seventy-three per cent of the group thought that this factor was very important.

To what extent is the effectiveness of management personnel dependent upon ability in oral communication? The vast majority of the respondents indicated that effectiveness of management personnel is greatly dependent upon ability in oral communication. Many executives affirmed their belief that oral communication is more important than written communication in the performance of certain managerial tasks.[5]

The attempt by management men of large companies to improve employee communications highlights an increasing desire to return to the face-to-face relationships that existed when plants were small. As one investigator stated: "We have to find a way to help the employee think of the business as though he were the boss, and to help the boss look at things as though he were an employee."

A few industrial giants have developed integrated communication programs. Some firms employ staff communication experts. General Electric Company, for example, has installed "managers of communication" at more than half of its plants, besides employing five "communication consultants" whose job is both to teach "communication theory" to employees and to trouble-shoot when bottlenecks in communication occur at any particular plant.

Methods of keeping track of morale

One investigator defined morale as the feeling of well-being that an individual experiences when his needs are being filled to his satisfaction.[6] Other investigators regard morale as a synthesis of employee attitudes toward the employment situation. In general, it is regarded as a combination or complex of employees' attitudes which arise from the ways in which they perceive the factors in their work situation.

Several methods have been developed for getting factual reports of what employees think about their jobs, their supervisors, and their working conditions and of what they like or do not like about them.

The standard methods used to keep track of morale conditions are three:

ANALYSIS OF COMPANY RECORDS. Ups and downs in employee attitudes can be deduced to some extent from production and spoilage records. Marked changes in the production output of employees and increases of rejects from inspection of work produced are signals that something is happening to morale.

Attendance records may be significant.

A morale sag may show up in increased failures to report for work regularly, excessive sick leaves, habitual tardiness, long lunch periods, and early quitting. Safety records, too, bear examination.

EMPLOYEE COMMITTEES. These are used in some of the larger corporations. Committees, consisting of members from employee ranks, can indicate morale, spot causes of dissatisfaction, and help correct them. Any number of committees, each with a special field to cover, can be set up.

A large department store, for example, was dissatisfied with employee morale as reported by members of the personnel department and by supervisors. The management set up 22 committees, each with 20 members, to work on every conceivable phase of the morale problem. In the first two months, 500 specific complaints were received and processed. The store eliminated over half of the trouble spots at a cost of a few hundred dollars.

MORALE SURVEYS. The most widely used systematic method is the employee attitude survey, or opinion poll, administered in questionnaire form.

This type of survey consists of a list of carefully prepared, written questions about the work situation which employees are usually asked to answer on an anonymous basis. If properly administered, tabulated, and interpreted, these responses give a representative picture of what employees think about the areas covered by the survey questions. The survey responses thus become a report of employee opinion or morale. The survey is usually conducted for a company by an outside consultant such as a psychologist or by an industrial relations consulting firm. In most cases, technical know-how is required. Furthermore, outsiders are better able to keep the operation on a strictly confidential basis.[7]

Generally, the survey is conducted so that no information can be traced back to the person who gave it. Employees must be assured that they can express criticisms without any retaliation being possible. Also, they should understand why their answers are sought, that management is sincere in asking the questions, and that complete frankness will be helpful to both management and employees.

Typical findings from surveys

Eugene J. Benge, consulting psychologist, has conducted employee attitude surveys over a period of several decades in many companies. The findings show roughly that 20 to 30 per cent of employees seem to be somewhat on the unhappy side—that is, they check more negative than positive responses. Additional findings are:

We find that women have better morale than men as a group; that the lowest morale appears between the ages of twenty and twenty-four and that it is higher before and after this age period; that employees start in jobs with high morale and that morale falls for a period of about five or six years before it starts to rise again; that low paid and high paid employees have higher morale than the medium paid; that the closer an employee approaches in earning power to his immediate supervisor, the lower his morale is likely to be. We also found that small companies tend to have better morale levels than big companies and that night shifts tend to have better morale than day shifts, contrary to usual thinking. Usually the latter is associated with the fact that night shifts approach working teams much more than do day shifts. By indirect reasoning we are sure that those who have left or are about to leave a concern have much lower morale than the average of that concern.[8]

The above findings represent a composite for the employees of a large number of factories, commercial and financial institutions, offices, and sales forces. When the Industrial Relations Section, California Institute of Technology, had completed a total of 25 surveys in 18 different companies, covering over 50,000 employees, the Section formulated a number of conclusions based on all of its studies of employee opinion. One of these was that "Morale is affected by length of service. Employees with less than a year

Science Research Associates, Chicago, publishes the SRA Employee Inventory, the most widely used employee attitude survey instrument. It has been used to survey over 600,000 employees. Through the aid of interpreters it has been used to survey the attitudes of foreign speaking employees—Japanese, Chinese, Spanish, Italian, and Philipino.

The Inventory is distinctive in that the percentage of favorable attitudes among any employee group toward various aspects of their employment can be compared with national norms. This enables management to identify more accurately the specific areas of strengths and weaknesses within the company and within departments of the company.

SCIENCE RESEARCH ASSOCIATES

SRA Employee Inventory

FORM A

Make no marks on these pages!

1. The hours of work here are O.K.

2. Management does everything possible to prevent accidents in our work....

3. Management is doing its best to give us good working conditions

4. In my opinion, the pay here is lower than in other companies...

5. They should do a better job of handling pay matters here

6. I understand what the company benefit program provides for employees

7. The people I work with help each other out when someone falls behind or gets in a tight spot

8. My boss is too interested in his own success to care about the needs of employees

9. My boss is always breathing down our necks; he watches us too closely

10. My boss gives us credit and praise for work well done

11. Management here does everything it can to see that employees get a fair break on the job

12. If I have a complaint to make, I feel free to talk to someone up-the-line

13. My boss sees that employees are properly trained for their jobs

14. My boss sees that we have the things we need to do our jobs...

15. Management here is really trying to build the organization and make it successful

16. Management here sees to it that there is cooperation between departments

17. Management tells employees about company plans and developments

18. They encourage us to make suggestions for improvements here

19. I am often bothered by sudden speed-ups or unexpected slack periods in my work

20. Changes are made here with little regard for the welfare of employees

21. Compared with other employees, we get very little attention from management

22. Sometimes I feel that my job counts for very little in this organization

23. The longer you work for this company the more you feel you belong

24. I have a great deal of interest in this company and its future

25. I have little opportunity to use my abilities in this organization

26. There are plenty of good jobs here for those who want to get ahead

Go on to the next page

Companies who use the SRA Employee Inventory can graph the morale of individual departments on profile charts like this one. Here the solid line indicates how one department feels about jobs, pay, and the company management. The dotted line shows how the employees as a whole reacted to the same questions. As you can see, workers in this department, a warehouse and shipping unit, have strong loyalty towards their immediate supervisors and fellow employees. On the other hand, they are not enthusiastic about management or working conditions. SRA scores the survey and delivers a report of results along with follow-up recommendations for management's consideration.

The set of 78 questions provides a comprehensive survey, and space for an additional twelve special questions insures the instrument's flexibility.

The **Employee Inventory** uses easy-to-understand language. Since it requires only a few minutes to administer, it can be given during working hours with little disruption or loss of production time. The brief time required for answering the questions is equally important where the **Inventory** is given to employees on their own time. Because employees are asked not to sign their names, they are willing to answer frankly. Management can use the **Employee Inventory** to: (1) Measure morale for a company as a whole; (2) Compare morale between departments or plants in an organization; (3) Compare morale in a company with the average of others, particularly in the same industry.

By using the **Employee Inventory** to find out what employees really think, companies can pin-point weak departments, increase the effectiveness of supervision, learn if communication is adequate, discover training needs, improve employee relations, build community good will, and cut employee turnover.

The **SRA Employee Inventory** was prepared by the Employee Attitude Research Group in the Industrial Relations Center, University of Chicago. This group has members from both the University and industry.

The **SRA Employee Inventory** is published by **Science Research Associates, Inc.**, 57 W. Grand Avenue, Chicago 10, Illinois. Copyright, 1951, by the Industrial Relations Center of the University of Chicago.

of service have almost as high morale as employees with 25 years of service or more. The morale of employees declines with length of service, reaching its low point after 10 to 15 years of service. After this point, morale tends to increase."[9]

Individual companies that make a morale survey usually tabulate answers so that comparisons can be made by departments, men versus women employees, by wage brackets, and other factors.

Interestingly, one of the most common causes of low morale is the employee's inability to do good work because of poor equipment. Poor maintenance of equipment has marked effects on employee morale. Employees resent having to put up with an unnecessarily high percentage of down time due to machine failure, off-standard quality of materials used in work, and similar delays beyond their control. When they are unable to do good work, their morale is likely to be low as indicated by their adverse comments, absenteeism, tardiness, and high quit rates.[10]

Surveys of employee attitudes, opinions, and morale are made in many companies. These surveys are a means of analyzing not the employees but the effectiveness of management in its communications.

Most employees recognize that their welfare is largely dependent upon the prosperity of their employer. When it is explained that these inquiries are directed toward improving plant operations and the ability of the firm to compete successfully—which, in turn, means greater security for every employee—their willingness to cooperate is practically assured. When management shows interest in their employees' opinions on such key issues as working conditions, the quality of supervision and the effectiveness of plant operations, the employee tends to have a warmer feeling of closeness toward his management. . . .

For proof that employee attitude studies are beneficial to management I would like to cite some figures reported by the National Industrial Conference Board which have a bearing on this point. One hundred and eleven companies were asked about their experiences with employee attitude studies. Ninety-five per cent feel that employee attitude studies are a good thing; 91 per cent say that these studies do *not* upset the employees—start negative thinking, increase griping, nor do they awaken "sleeping dogs." Instead, reporting executives say that the employee attitude studies definitely *boost* morale. Four out of every five companies report that employees show interest in attitude surveys and 40 out of 43 union leaders who were questioned also say these studies are a good idea. . . .

All evidence points quite clearly to the fact that employee attitude studies *improve the feelings of employees toward the company* by making it possible to establish good lines of communication. Ideas from the employees have an opportunity to be shared by management. The employees, in turn, have an opportunity to better understand the policies and aims of their management. So long as there is rightness in the company's operations, this improved two-way communication makes it possible to achieve understanding and harmony.

The companies conducting regular employee attitude studies find that they can establish good lines of communication with the workers and by so doing are able to improve both the workers' understanding of company problems and management's understanding of employee problems.[11]

Managements' opinions of morale surveys

The Dartnell Corporation reported a survey of 55 companies which had conducted one or more employee opinion surveys. In most instances, the companies had used printed questionnaires which employees filled out. Very few of these surveys involved personal questioning of employees by interviewers, a much more expensive method. Of the 55 firms, 45 had some help from outside consultants—especially in regard to planning the survey and constructing the questionnaire as well as in analyzing and interpreting results.

Practically all companies participating in this survey said they obtained new information about employee attitudes, and that results were helpful in giving a more exact measurement of attitudes that were known or expected prior to the survey. Employees' answers in most cases were analyzed by departments, divisions, or other work groups, to pinpoint the information from the survey.

About half of the companies were surprised by the level of their employees' morale. Only two found morale consistently worse than expected, 10 found it better than anticipated, and 17 found it better in some areas, worse in others.

A large majority of respondents, 45 of the 55, said they made changes in personnel policies or practices as a direct result of the survey. Also, as a result of the survey, 40 companies gave special information to employees regarding various personnel policies or practices.[12]

The National Industrial Conference Board made a study of the reactions of production workers of two plants. The workers and plants were matched except for the one factor of communication. In Plant B the foremen had conducted monthly work-unit meetings in which reports were made on company matters such as vacation schedules, receipt of new orders, scrap reports, and so on. Also, workers were encouraged to make suggestions and offer their ideas. Plant A had no communication program of this nature. The Board prepared a questionnaire which was filled in but not signed before mailing it directly to the Board. The questions dealt with reactions to various aspects of communication and morale.

Typical questions and percentages of answers for the two plants were the following:

1. *Question. Have you been able to get your ideas up to the top men?*

Answers	Plant A	Plant B
I can almost always get my ideas up	21%	49%
I can sometimes get my ideas up	31	28
I can hardly ever get my ideas up	32	13
I am not interested in trying to get my ideas up	16	10

2. *Question. Does your company do a good job of telling you what's going on and what's being planned?*

Answers	Plant A	Plant B
It does a very good job	18%	55%
It does a fairly good job	60	31
It doesn't do much of this at all	22	14

3. *Question. Do you feel a part of your company?*

Answers	Plant A	Plant B
I feel I really belong	29%	62%
I feel I just work here	42	14
Sometimes I feel one way and sometimes the other	29	24

4. *Question. Generally speaking, how does your company compare as a company to work for compared with other companies that you know about or have worked for?*

Answers	Plant A	Plant B
One of the very worst	1%	0%
Worse than average	4	3
Just average	35	19
Better than average	40	33
One of the very best	20	45

One of the goals of communication is to develop a team spirit—to increase positive feelings toward the organization. The investigators concluded that the findings evidenced that communication is a powerful factor that affected the ideas and attitudes of employees of the two plants.[13]

Putting morale survey results to work

Obviously, making an attitude or morale survey is only a first step in the improvement of communications within a company. Business concerns have been making surveys among their employees for several decades but the literature concerning their follow-through is sketchy. Generally, managements agree that at least two uses can be made: one, the findings can be reported to the employees and two, remedial actions can be taken to improve the situations that need it.

Some managements conduct meetings with supervisors and employees in order to clarify the reasons for negative findings. Shortcomings on the part of management are

. . . for the Garrett Corporation, AiResearch Manufacturing Plant, Los Angeles. Consulting firm, Psychological Services, Inc.

1. Survey begins when industrial relations staff formulates questions. From left are John Muchmore, staff assistant; Chuck Wetmore, industrial relations manager, Phoenix; Duke Reynolds, vice-president, industrial relations; Jerry Bradley, industrial relations manager, Los Angeles. Division managers often help.

2. Mail room (right) addresses and sends surveys. No one in The Garrett Corporation will ever again see them.

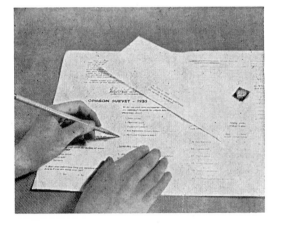

3. Employee fills out survey in privacy of his home. Best results are obtained when questions are answered as soon as received.

4. When mailed, the completed survey goes to Psychological Services Inc. Maximum return means maximum value of survey.

5. Mail clerk at office of Dr. Floyd Ruch, head of Psychological Services, removes completed questionnaire from envelope, which is destroyed along with postmark and return address.

MAKING AN EMPLOYEE OPINION SURVEY . . .

6. Answers to specific questions are punched onto tabulation cards for statistics necessary to evaluate survey results. Verbatim comments are ignored at this point.

7. Verbatim comments are transcribed by a typist at Psychological Services so there will be no way of recognizing handwriting. Comments are grouped by departments, but no other information supplied by employee is used here. There is no way to connect verbatim answers afterward with such information as employee's length of service.

8. Dr. Floyd Ruch personally supervises burning of the questionnaires. The last step in the program of scientific secrecy has been taken, assuring accuracy of the survey.

9. Comments and statistics are combined into summaries for all divisions. First copy goes to head of the company. Condensations go to all employees.

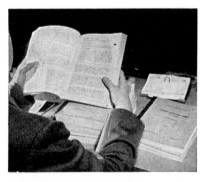

10. Conferences are held with department and division heads. Herb Stout, AiResearch Los Angeles machine shop general foreman, maps action on needed improvement with Don Bromley, personnel. All comments must be investigated.

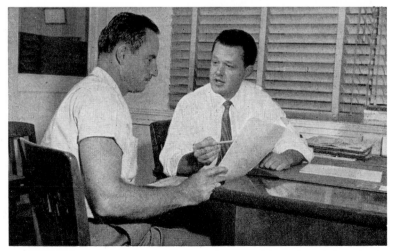

brought into open discussion and improvements in managerial practices and communications are developed. If such "feedback" sessions are conducted in a sincere and constructive spirit, later surveys of employee morale are likely to produce higher percentages of favorable reactions to conditions that were previously found to be "least liked" by the employees.

Crucible Steel Company of America, for example, conducted and followed up on a supervisory opinion survey. The first step in the follow-up of the survey was the publication of the results. Each respondent was given a printed copy of the survey results, entitled, "Let's Look at Your Supervisory Jobs." A feedback program of about 50 separate meetings was conducted for more than two months. Experts of the company answered the questions asked by the supervisors. The men were encouraged to pull no punches and every effort was made to disseminate the information and knowledge that was apparently lacking. Reactions to the feedback were immediate and favorable. Comments received were such as "I never understood the program before" and "It looks like top management really does care what we think."[14]

Anyone who participates in feedback sessions of this kind is likely to become convinced that the results of morale surveys can be made far more beneficial to employees and employers than speeches by executives or educational conferences.

Experimental study of the value of feedback of attitude survey results

Relatively few experiments have been set up to measure the benefits of attitude survey feedbacks. Robert E. Schwab has reported one of several studies of this type.

The Institute for Social Research, Survey Research Center, University of Michigan, made an intensive survey of the attitudes of employees and supervisors of a company:

Written questionnaires were administered to all non-supervisory employees, and all supervisors and members of management were interviewed concerning their work attitudes. In addition, 10 per cent of the non-supervisory employees from groups identified through the questionnaire as having high or low morale were given personal interviews. The resulting information about attitudes of employees toward their jobs, their supervisors, company benefits, pay, their chances for promotion, and various other factors in the work situation was sent back down the line for discussion. Comparisons between departments and work groups were made available, and both supervisors and employees were asked to interpret the results and make recommendations for the solution of problems which were present. Here again many changes were made which resulted in better understanding and improved working effectiveness.

In one department, a controlled experiment was set up in which supervisors of certain work groups held a series of discussions with employees about their own group attitudes as revealed by a survey. In other work groups the results were reported back to employees but without the opportunity for group discussions led by the supervisor. In those groups where discussions were held over a period of several months, there was a measurable improvement in the attitude of the employees toward their jobs, their supervision, their opportunities in the company, and various other factors in the work situation. In those groups in which discussion was not held, relatively little change in attitude took place.

This experiment would seem to indicate that sharing of a group's own problems with them and freedom to discuss such problems with the supervisor result in more favorable attitudes in the work group. Another very interesting fact was that greater change in employees' attitudes occurred in this situation than in other departments where employees' attitudes were studied after their supervisors were given training in human relations.[15]

Limitations of a morale survey

Even though a morale survey usually produces some benefits it also has or may have some drawbacks. These are:

1. Its impersonality. The employee who fills in a questionnaire which he does not sign may fail to get the satisfaction that is obtained from face-to-face communication

On the other hand, many employees will state criticisms anonymously on paper that they would not state in face-to-face situations.

2. In too many cases, surveys are made and the results are filed but the employee never again hears or sees any evidence that his criticisms and recommendations were acted upon. As a result, the individual employee feels that he has been whistling into the wind. Managements that ask for criticisms are obligated to act upon them or to explain why they cannot be acted upon.

3. Results are usually presented to management and employees statistically. Majority responses are studied more carefully than minority findings. And yet a minority feeling that is intense, such as a strong resentment against a wage differential, may give rise to action that overwhelms the majority of employees.

4. Questionnaire attitude surveys indicate the nature of some broad problems such as whether morale is high or low, but they do not, as a rule, break the problems down in terms of the individual employee and his needs. The individual employee is a member of a group and has certain group relations but his problems are personal and individual. Even though he has strong group loyalties, he still wants to be treated as an individual.

5. Certain pitfalls must be recognized when evaluating results of questionnaire attitude surveys. One of the most difficult to avoid is the wording of questions in such form that the desired response can be indicated. Another pitfall is the oversimplified question that forces employees to make absurd or unrealistic choices. For example: "Would you rather have the company spend its available money for new machines in the plant, for more parking space, or for a better technical library?"

6. The time lag in collecting the data and writing the report causes interest in the survey to cool off. The results of a survey are not available for a month or two. During this time, the interest of management and employees is likely to cool. Executives, for example, may say, "Things have changed during the past sixty days. Hence, the findings no longer apply."

7. Certain aggravating situations cannot be corrected because of financial or other limitations. Bad working conditions such as the need for air conditioning cannot be corrected unless the company can afford it. The company may not have the money to buy the equipment. Executives may agree to the desirability of the recommended changes but the money needed to make them is not available. Similar difficulties occur in regard to poor supervision. A specific supervisor may be very competent in so far as his technical abilities are concerned but a poor leader of men. And yet, his job may require his technical abilities even more than good supervisory skills.

8. Surveys do not emphasize the mutuality of working interests between management and men. Instead, they put the management on the defensive. The very nature of a survey implies that it is up to management to correct every disliked condition. Actually, both management and men have to work together to do a better job. Some managements assume that morale can be achieved by having the company do kindnesses *for the employees* or by solving all their problems. Many executives fail to realize that morale is highest when employees also do things *for the company*. Morale and loyalty are best when employees as well as executives devote their efforts to the success of the company, when employees realize that they as well as management are essential to the company's success, and when management and employees work together in a spirit of operating a mutual enterprise.

Management can gain little by a display of fatherly generosity toward employees who are treated as children. On the other hand, both management and employees gain growth and competence when management treats employees as colleagues in their joint economic enterprise.

At its best, however, a morale survey is a device that helps management to listen. And to communicate effectively, management must "listen." The ability to "listen" is also essential to the understanding of the other person's motivations.

Current programs for improving management's "listening"

Numerous programs are being conducted by psychologists for improving techniques for the study and improvement of morale. Several universities are conducting studies in this field. The Institute for Social Research, University of Michigan, is one example. The one business organization that has an active program for improving communication in industry, particularly "listening," is the American Management Association.

The AMA conducts courses and conferences in executive communications. The businessmen students have learned that to be effective in communication it is necessary to know far more than rules for writing memos or for making an effective presentation in a speech. These men repeatedly say they feel a lack of the insight into human motives, attitudes, and aspirations that is needed for good communication.

It is information in these areas, rather than methods of making surveys or analyzing data from questionnaires, that psychologists try to supply.

What businessmen say they must now perfect are: sensitivity to the other party's wants; frankness in facing one's own wants; thorough planning and outlining; the establishment of a suitable climate; a system of "feed-back" that enables a communicator to check for understanding.

First, Listen—In the welter of new information being presented to communication-minded management, one philosophy occurs so frequently and in so many applications, that it seems to sum up the new thought. This is its keynote:

To communicate effectively, you must first of all "listen."

This means far more than a sympathetic ear. It contains one group's demand that you rigorously inspect your own motives—that you "listen" to yourself. In this, the stress is on introspection.

To another group, it means that you should tune up all your "listening" apparatus—eyes, ears, memory, and emotions. Here the emphasis is on observation, awareness.

You can almost wrap up AMA's Executive Communication course under the title "Listening," if you take the broadest sense of the word.

Ways to Do It—AMA—tells its conferees to look inside their own minds, to "listen" to themselves—not haphazardly but with method—to get the main threads of a thought sorted out. Next, AMA insists you get participation from others in sharpening the solution or communication. This adds new facts to those a communicator already has in his head. Also, it sets the stage for the communication that will follow.

Management, by the AMA definition, is the art and science of getting things done through people—thus the emphasis on participation follows naturally.

"Remember," one AMA conference leader points out, "the higher you get in management, the more dependent you are on accurate exchange of information."

Getting Results—To wrap up good executive communication, you have to be pretty good at motivating people and measuring the results of your communication on them, AMA feels . . .

Motivation is probably the most recent part of business communication to get emphasis. This is where your ability to "listen" counts. When you can understand what motivates people, you're better able to get across your points. You can present your ideas more in the lights of their understanding, biases, ability, ambitions, etc.[16]

Morale and productivity

The work of early researchers into human relations, and the studies which grew out of the classic Western Electric Company Hawthorne experiment, have tended to confirm the common-sense point of view that a satisfied worker is more productive than a dissatisfied one. However, recent investigations have indicated that the relationship between morale and performance is not so self-evident or so simple as was once assumed. Cases have been found where high morale has been found to accompany either high or low productivity; and, conversely, low morale has been found where productivity is either high or low.

Arthur Brayfield and Walter Crockett, of Kansas State College, made a comprehensive survey of attitude studies.[17] They concluded that there is little evidence that employee attitudes of the *type usually measured in morale studies* bear any simple—or, for that matter, appreciable—relationship to performance on the job. This finding should be expected in some companies because statistically-measurable changes in productivity depend upon many factors other than morale: the alertness of management, the competence of employees, and the motivational drives of the individual executives and employees. After all, lazy and incompetent workers may be just as satisfied with their work situations as the industrious and competent members of a work group.

A key finding of the studies by the University of Michigan, Institute of Social Research, has been that there is a marked relationship between an employee's productivity and job satisfaction on the one hand and, on the other, the kind of supervision he receives. The highest productivity and the highest morale have consistently been found to result from employee-centered supervision as opposed to supervision of the production-centered type.

Research in the area of employee attitude and output suggests that there is an unrealized potential for improving productive effectiveness while at the same time making work less burdensome. This potential can be utilized when we have achieved and applied a better understanding of the basic factors which motivate an individual to accept the goals of the organization of which he is a part, and the conditions which allow these motivating factors to operate fully. High levels of production seem to be obtained through improvement in the immediate job situation of an employee, rather than through the impact of broader, impersonal policies and programs.[18]

The present stage of research indicates that companies cannot look to specific types of morale-building programs for a complete solution to the problem of building a productive and satisfied work force. Instead, it must be recognized that morale has its origins not in any particular "program" but right on the job—in the relationship between the supervisor and the worker. Furthermore, this relationship must be carried on by competent, well-motivated individuals who function in a favorable psychological climate. This suggests that if morale and productivity are to be linked together, management must find ways to select and develop more supervisors and workers who are capable of putting the principles of sound communications and good human relations into practice. The media of communications, such as employee publications and bulletin boards, do not in themselves bring about high morale and productivity—they are useful aids in the hands of intelligent managements and employee-centered supervisors.

Acknowledgments and References

1. Quoted from Glenn Gardiner, *How to Handle Grievances*, Elliott Service Company, 1937.

2. A. Corning White, "Auditing Employee Relations," *Dun's Review*, March 1949.

3. Burleigh B. Gardner and Lee Rainwater, "The Mass Image of Big Business," *Harvard Business Review*, Nov.–Dec. 1955, p. 62.

4. See *Employee Relations Bulletin*, National Foremen's Institute, Inc., April 15, 1953.

5. Paul E. Lull, Frank E. Funk, and Darrel T. Pierson, *Business and Industrial Communication*, Purdue University, June 1954; *Advanced Management*, March 1955; and *The Management Review*, American Management Association, May 1955, pp. 289–291.

6. See O. J. Gordon, "Factor Analysis of Human Needs and Industrial Morale," *Personnel Psychology,* Spring 1955, Personnel Psychology, Inc., Baltimore, Maryland.

7. Louis A. Allen, "Action-Oriented Attitude Surveys," *Personnel,* American Management Association, September 1952, presents a good set of directions for making attitude surveys. For a description of various methods of attitude measurement, see Irving R. Weschler and Raymond E. Bernberg, "Indirect Methods of Attitude Measurement," Institute of Industrial Relations, University of California, Los Angeles, 1949.

8. Eugene J. Benge, Asheville, N.C. From letter dated April 3, 1956.

9. Excerpt from *Annual Report 1953–1954,* Industrial Relations Section, California Institute of Technology, Project 5, "Surveys of Employee Opinion."

10. See G. S. Odiorne, "Some Effects of Poor Equipment Maintenance on Morale," *Personnel Psychology,* Summer 1955, for a study on this aspect of morale.

11. Patrick Coyle, "Employee Attitude Studies," *Forbes,* Sept. 15, 1954.

12. W. M. Longman and L. F. Van Houten, "Analysis and Staff Report: Experience of 55 Companies With Employee Opinion Surveys," The Dartnell Corporation, Chicago.

13. Stephen Habbe, "Does Communication Make a Difference?" *Management Record,* National Industrial Conference Board, November 1952. See also "Communicating with Employees," Studies in Personnel Policy No. 129, National Industrial Conference Board, Inc., New York, pp. 36–40 and Frank E. Fischer, "A New Look at Management Communication," *Personnel,* American Management Association, May 1955.

14. See Robert H. Milligan and John E. Osmanski, *Personnel Journal,* July–August 1954. See also, "Experience with Employee Attitude Surveys," *Studies in Personnel Policy,* No. 115, The National Industrial Conference Board, New York, 1951.

15. Robert E. Schwab, "Motivation and Human Relations Principles," *Personnel Series, No. 155,* American Management Association, 1953, pp. 36–37.

16. "Executive Communications: Fit the Method to the Need," *Business Week,* April 23, 1955.

17. Arthur H. Brayfield and Walter H. Crockett, "Employee Attitudes and Employee Performance," *Psychological Bulletin,* September 1955.

18. See "Morale, Productivity—and the Missing Link," *Personnel,* American Management Association, January 1956, p. 291.

PROJECTS

1. Visit an industrial plant in your community and note evidences of the management's program for maintaining high morale among employees. Write a report suggesting additions to or improvements in the existing program.

2. A Canadian Mountie is credited with the statement: "Human beings are only twelve meals away from the dumb animal stage." To what extent do you accept this point of view? How does it affect industrial relations?

3. Ask a number of women who are employed what they like the most and what they like the least about their jobs. Were the replies concerned chiefly with personal relationships or with methods and things? Assume, in each case, that you are the woman's supervisor, and tell what specific action you would take in the light of the information received.

4. Should the employer attempt to obtain the good will of the wives of employees? How can he do so? What are the dangers of such an attempt?

5. Andrew Carnegie wrote his epitaph for himself:

> *Here lies a man*
> *Who knew how to enlist*
> *In his service*
> *Better men than himself.*

What attitudes are necessary for an executive to pursue such a policy?

6. How can the management convince the employees that "pull" is not essential for promotion?

COLLATERAL READINGS

Bellows, Roger M., *Psychology of Personnel in Business and Industry,* Prentice-Hall, Inc., New York, 1954, Chapter 7.

Blum, Milton L., *Industrial Psychology and Its Social Foundations,* Harper & Brothers, New York, 1949, Chapter 3.

Green, Harold E., "21 Steps for Obtaining Opinions and Facts about Employees," *Printers' Ink*, November 28, 1947, pp. 35 ff.

Harris, F. J., "The Qualification of an Industrial Employee Survey," *Journal of Applied Psychology*, April 1949, pp. 103–113.

Kornhouser, Arthur, "Psychological Studies of Employee Attitudes," *Journal of Consulting Psychology*, May–June 1944, pp. 127–143.

Maier, Norman R. F., *Psychology in Industry*, Houghton Mifflin Company, Boston, 1955, Chapter 3.

McMurry, Robert N., "Management's Reactions to Employee Opinion Polls," *Journal of Applied Psychology*, Vol. 30 (1946), pp. 212–219.

Roethlisberger, F. J., and William J. Dickson, *Management and the Worker*, Harvard University Press, Cambridge, Mass., 1941, Chapter 15.

Whyte, William F., editor *Industry and Society*, McGraw-Hill Book Company, Inc., New York, 1946, Chapter 2.

CHAPTER TWENTY-THREE

Communications: media and methods

In former days, managements assumed that if an item of information was posted on a bulletin board, the employees would read, understand, and believe it. Later, executives discovered that bulletin boards must be supplemented by other media and methods of communication. This search for effective media and techniques has, in too many cases, obscured the importance of the basic influential factors in communication: the psychological climate and the face-to-face relationships.

The term "communication" connotes many media and methods. It is applied to any kind of behavior that leads to exchange of ideas and includes media such as personal telephone calls, feature stories in a company publication, office memoranda, speeches to employees, and group conferences. Communication in itself is not an end or a goal. Rather, it is a universal tool for conveying meaning and—particularly for management—a factor in inducing action. Problems in communication may arise from poor acoustics, semantic confusion, emotional resistances, and bottlenecks in channels of transmitting messages.

In industry, the channels of communication are of three types,—up-line, down-line, or cross-line, depending on the direction from the source to the ultimate receipt of the information. Unless each avenue of communication is kept clear and is used effectively, serious problems may result. A block in the up-line channel, for example, may leave top executives feeling walled off from their employees, while a break in down-line or cross-line communications may damage morale and increase the traditional friction between line and staff members.

Obviously, treatment of all aspects, problems, methods, and media in communications would require several volumes. In this chapter, the major emphasis will be placed on those that involve management's means of communicating information, action plans, and attitudes to employees—that is, down-line communications. Two methods of achieving up-line communications will also be discussed.

What do employees want to know?

When the Industrial Relations Section, California Institute of Technology, had completed a total of 25 surveys in 18 different companies, covering over 50,000 employees, the Section formulated a number of conclusions based on all of its studies of employee opinion. One of these was that "Employees are eager to know more about the plans of their company, its products, and processes, and other items which affect security of jobs, the stability of employment, and that may provide an opportunity for advancement. This interest also extends to a desire for increased information about the American business system. Very few employees feel that they are receiving too much information."[1]

Numerous other surveys indicate that an especially important interest of employees is the security of their jobs and the factors about the company which enable them to think that their jobs are even more secure than they had thought.

Generally, employees not only feel that they should know more about the company for which they work, but they also want information *regularly* about manufacturing operations, about future company plans, about new products and the story behind the progress being made in the development of new products.

Most employees have a sincere interest in the company's competitive position and long-range outlook. They want to know the company's products and plans well enough to discuss them intelligently when they talk with people on the outside. An employee has an opportunity to feel important when he can answer the questions of his family and friends about the company's plans and prospects.[2]

An intelligent executive of today realizes that as a leader he should transmit not only the information that employees seek but also certain information that they may not be consciously seeking. He should anticipate their wishes by providing information that improves their working relations even though they are not always aware of what they need. A good leader has the larger perspectives that enable him to use his initiative in setting forth those facts and interpretations that strengthen the team spirit.

So the role of communication in your management job becomes that of "bridging the gap" between your interests and those of your workers—of finding where the different interests meet.

It's very interesting that the word "communication" comes from the Latin word *communis*, meaning "common." In communicating, we're trying to establish a common meeting ground for understanding—for sharing facts, ideas, attitudes—for exchanging meaning.

For instance, a recent survey by the Opinion Research Corporation showed that a majority of the industrial employees felt that management generally couldn't be counted on to look out for employees' best interests—with one notable exception. That exception was *safety*, on which management has done the most consistent and dramatic job of purposeful communication—of tying employees and management interests together—of "bridging the gap."

TABLE 23-1

COMMUNICATIONS MEDIA FOR HOURLY WORKERS—NATIONAL SURVEY OF 519 REPRESENTATIVE COMPANIES

Media Used	No.	%
Total Replies	519	100.0
Bulletin board	511	98.5
Letters or bulletins to employees	335	64.5
Payroll insert	311	59.9
Meetings	240	46.2
Employee handbook	210	40.5
Special booklets (other than safety)	152	29.3
Employee magazine	148	28.5
Safety manual	145	27.9
Reading racks	127	24.5
Films	115	22.2
Employee newspaper	102	19.7
Public address system	75	14.5
Special financial reports to employees*	47	9.1

*These are separate reports in booklet form, addressed to employees, and reports addressed jointly to employees and stockholders.

From "Personnel Practices in Factory and Office," fifth edition, *Studies in Personnel Policy*, No. 145, National Industrial Conference Board, Inc., 247 Park Avenue, New York 17, N.Y., Table 161, p. 54.

On the other hand, industry is spending literally billions of dollars on all types of benefit programs. Yet, because of a lack of down-to-earth communication (try to become interested and understand the actuarial language in many pension booklets, for instance) industry gets little credit. In fact, surveys show that the vast majority of employees don't even know what benefits they're entitled to. The "gap" in understanding certainly has not been bridged in this area.[3]

The wished-for development of true understanding between management and labor is a big and continuous task. A complete solution has not been found, but better communication—the sharing of meaningful information by both parties—moves in a helpful direction. Some of the ways in which this is being attempted are discussed in the following sections.

DOWN-LINE COMMUNICATIONS

Employee publications

To supplement other methods of communication, many firms have utilized the company house organs of the employee publication variety. Though some date back to the turn of the century, widespread use of company magazines is relatively recent. The precise number of such publications is not known, but one investigator estimated the total as 10,000. This includes those of small companies as well as medium and large firms.

Claude Robinson estimated that approximately three out of four companies having assets of $5,000,000 and over have company publications. In companies of this size, there are 6,000 magazines for employees, representing an investment by employers of $100,000,000 and reaching some 40,000,000 people. Moreover, surveys show that 85 per cent of employees read their company paper or magazine.

In the interest of bettering morale, 99 per cent of company publications run personal recognition stories; 90 per cent use recrea-tion stories for this purpose; 90 per cent use department and division news; and 85 per cent use "personals."

Robinson reported that in 1947, only 57 per cent of the publications gave information about the company to employees; today all of them do. Informative material includes articles on safety, profits, expansion programs, product improvements, employee benefits, business outlook, the company's role in national defense, company policies, and union-management news. Fifty per cent of all publications carry stories on the role of taxes and financial reports on the economics of business, 20 per cent give information on competition and profits. In giving information on national problems, 57 per cent of the publications discuss the need for higher productivity, 40 per cent deal with government controls, 32 per cent publish material on the duties of citizenship, and 31 per cent discuss inflation.[4]

An employees' magazine can be entertainingly educational as well as merely entertaining. For instance, many employees believe that advertising is a waste of money and that their wages could be raised if those funds were added to the wages. Many others think that orders are easy to get, that any business can borrow plenty of money, that the government could operate all businesses more cheaply than private concerns, that there is a fixed amount of money in the world, and that factory workers have all the "grief" and office workers all the "snap" jobs. Such erroneous impressions can be corrected by including humorous comic strips or chatty articles in the magazine which drive home the point. To an extent, some of the editors have seemed to realize this need and have attempted to experiment with cartooning and other features. But most editors, while close to management in the sense that they identify themselves with management, paradoxically have done a poor job of selling management to the employees.

Such editors have limited their pages to friendly personals, bowling scores, or editorials on plant safety. This type of news is good to a degree. But more and more of these editors are beginning to realize the great potentialities of their media. They are beginning to report such news as information on new orders, installations of modern equipment, certain data on the cost of producing and selling the products, and the allocation of the company's income dollar. In short, these more enterprising editors have taken it upon themselves to explain to the employee the factors operating in a free enterprise system. Some editors have ventured to discuss even labor problems—legislation and strikes—in their pages.

The humor page is a standby of the less venturesome and nonprogressive editors. The joke used as "filler" appears to be disappearing. Communications people are disposed to agree that a joke page or jokes used as fillers are essentially space users and nothing else. The joke page does have high readership but it does not serve any useful purpose beyond that of entertaining.

The sports page, when done properly, is a genuine readership builder, and surveys have indicated that such pages help to pull male readers into the rest of the publication.[5]

The *company's magazine advertisements* to the consumers and the trade are reproduced in many employee publications. These reproductions show the end products to the people who helped create them. When this is done, experience indicates that it is well not to publish the advertisement without a special explanation for the employees. The explanation should be presented in an adjacent block of copy where the advertisement appears. This block of copy tells where the advertisement has appeared, how many people it may reach, and the purposes that lay behind its creation. The employee and his family have a real curiosity about the company's product and take pride in making a product that is used by thousands or even millions of customers.

The "question box" idea has been used by some managements as a means for conducting a continuous morale survey. They invite employees to ask questions. Answers to the questions are given on the "question box" page of the employee publication.

Extensive use of the individual question-and-answer technique is made by one airline management. Every payday, 15,000 employees receive a blank form in their pay-envelope. On it they are urged to submit any questions they want to have answered. In each issue of the company's publication for employees, the president answers 10 to 30 questions in an 1,800 to 4,500 word department that begins on page 2 and takes up as many as three and one-half pages of the magazine.

Within a few months, he had more than 800 responses to the pay-envelope invitation, and each questioner either received a personally dictated answer or, if his question was of general interest, was answered in the employee magazine. Today the total of questions runs into the thousands, and so far, he says, there has not been a crank letter among them. Suggestions, requests for clarification, plugs for unions the company deals with, and blasts at the unions, inquiries about business prospects, personal and group gripes—all are answered, with due consideration for the authority of supervisors below as well as for the appeals-court nature of a query to the president.[6]

For the open "question-box" policy to be effective, management must be ready to accept and answer any question and to be irritated at none. The executive who accepts the assignment of answering questions must answer all questions; those which are stupid or unfair as well as the ones that are sensible.

To help employers evaluate the job their employee magazines are doing, the Association of National Advertisers, Inc., surveyed six major companies, interviewing a total of 1,800 employees. The researchers found that most employees feel that the plant magazine or newspaper is their best source of information about the company; 53 per cent of those surveyed mentioned it as their major source. The believability of employee publications is high; some 97 per cent of workers stated they felt they could believe what they read. Readership is faithful; 78 per cent of employees reported that they read their publications regularly. Home readership is sizable. Employees reported that an average of 1.4 family members read the publications.

Signed editorials on socialism, profits, and so on, do well, while economic news does even better. When one company published a feature telling about contracts the company bid for and won or lost, it got a phenomenal 84 per cent "read some" and 83 per cent "read most" scores for the feature.[7]

Experience indicates that the company organ or magazine should avoid being so management-conscious that the employees feel that they are receiving only company platitudes. The idea is not to propagandize the employees, but to create harmony between the employees and management. Whenever the executive of a company has an impulse to explain some policy in the pages of the magazine, he should first discuss the matter with his editor. This editor should be free to express his honest opinions to superior officers.

The theme for house organs to emphasize is simple: management cannot get along without the employees, and the employees cannot get along without management. Each complements the other. It is to their mutual benefit to make the relationship a happy, profitable one.

Financial reports about the company to employees

Many business leaders believe in the doctrine of sharing operating facts with their employees. They publish financial reports for the benefit of employees as well as stockholders. They make surveys of the rate of profit that the employee considers fair and show that the rate actually made by the employer is less than that. Yet, when this fact is pointed out to the employee, he still believes that the company makes too much!

This attitude has been extremely disconcerting to executives who sought to gain the good will of employees by means of published reports about the company, its profits, plans, and so forth.

The procedures, mostly ineffective, used by managements in attempts to gain acceptance by their employees of facts favorable to the company have been the following:

1. Managements have presented the facts in a "protestation of virtue" manner, particularly about profits made and salaries paid officers of the company.

2. The basically sound reasons for the effectiveness of free enterprise as an economic system have been used as an argument for friendliness toward the employer.

3. Managements have thought of security in terms of sickness benefits, old-age pensions, and guaranteed annual wages. Employees have thought of security as a sense of job satisfaction. As Keith Powlison stated:

Isn't it possible all of this means that job security—from the standpoint of wage protection, sickness benefits, and so forth—is not so important as the feeling of amounting to something as an individual, the feeling of pride that comes with recognition of and reward for a job well done? A retirement plan is not a substitute for a sense of satisfaction in today's work. Furthermore, the reference management usually makes to security is a negative appeal to the emotion of fear, and that is no foundation upon which to build long range, constructive employee relations.[8]

4. Managements have assumed that the technical terms of accounting and finance are beyond the comprehension of most employees.

Business leaders, particularly those in the accounting fields, have recognized the psychological ineffectiveness of current methods of giving information to employees. Accordingly, the Controllership Foundation, Inc., made a special survey of the problem. They discovered that 71 per cent of the factory laborers and 41 per cent of the white collar employees never see the annual report. These employees indicated that their company's report never reaches them.

Those employees who did see their company's financial reports (40 per cent white-collar employees; 16 per cent factory employees) like the brief version of the annual report, but table and complicated statistical treatment of the reports were disliked.[9]

TABLE 23-2

FINANCIAL REPORTS TO EMPLOYEES—
PRACTICE IN AMERICAN INDUSTRIES

	For Hourly Workers		For Salaried Employees	
	COMPANIES		COMPANIES	
	Number	Per Cent	Number	Per Cent
Provide financial reports to employees	178	34.3	144	34.2
No financial reports to employees	341	65.7	277	65.8
Total	519	100.0	421	100.0

From a survey reported in "Personnel Practices in Factory and Office (Revised)," *Studies in Personnel Policy,* No. 145, copyright, 1954, National Industrial Conference Board, Inc.

Ross G. Walker made a study of the Controllership Foundation, Inc., report. A few of his more significant conclusions are:

That there appears to be general agreement with the premise that lack of understanding and acceptance of the facts and figures of business are not altogether due to the way reports are prepared; but that this is part of a larger problem with which management is confronted; viz., that of creating acceptance for, and instilling confidence in, our American capitalistic system.

. . . That in the case of employees, personal contact is regarded as being more effective than written messages.

. . . to me the survey findings make one conclusion unavoidable: that management is typically bent on looking for appropriate remedial action in handling the misinformed employee exclusively within the agreeable master-servant framework. If there is a failure of "confidence" at the lower levels of organization, management feels it must be from some error in the direction of affairs within that framework, and whatever action is taken must be consistent with the basic acceptability of that framework as an industrial way of life.[10]

Of course employees will not believe facts presented to them as long as the employer presents them in the master-servant framework. The employer can hope to gain acceptance of facts when he keeps in mind the old psychological principle: "People believe as they participate." Facts in themselves are not sufficiently forceful in changing the attitudes of employees toward the employer. The devices of communication such as financial reports, conferences, and house organs cannot be effectively used as ends in themselves nor even as means toward educating employees and supervisors to understand management. Rather, the devices of surveys and communication should be incidental parts of a social philosophy of management. The philosophy should be one of a desire to exchange ideas, to participate mutually in the work of the enterprise, to understand and respect each other in the daily face-to-face relationships.

Information racks

Some companies operate information racks in order to supply reading material of interest to the employees. These are similar to the "reading racks" commonly seen in churches, union halls, and social service organization meeting places. Usually, the booklets are free. General Motors has been a leader in the use of information racks or "idea cafeterias." One and one-half million copies of booklets ranging in topics from "Fishin' for Fun" to "Profits for Customers" are distributed each month.

Materials in six categories are offered: (1) information about the company itself, including the stockholders' report; (2) home and family material; (3) inspirational literature; (4) health and safety; (5) technical and mechanical information; and (6) economic and social material. The social and economic material outpulls all other divisions, about 35 per cent of the total distribution being in this classification.

Most companies set up special screening

committees of three or more members to select material for the employee information racks.

Information racks should be easily accessible to employees and, like the bulletin board, be located where the majority of the employees pass at least once a day. Generally, however, racks should not be placed at entrances or exits because employees are in too great a hurry, coming or going, to stop and select pamphlets.

Records should be kept on how many copies of each pamphlet are picked up by employees. These serve as a basis for ordering future supplies and show the relation between the total number of employees whom the racks serve and the number of pamphlets picked up on a particular subject.

Bulletin boards

Bulletin boards are an essential means of communication to most plants. To be effective, however, their use must be supervised. If notices are allowed to accumulate on them for months, employees will decorate them with witty remarks and cartoons. Hence, when an important notice is posted, it is likely to be neglected by the workers.

The bulletin board should be painted, enclosed in glass, and lighted. The inside of the board should have a number of brass nails upon which small colored boards can be hung. Every bulletin should be tacked to one of these colored boards. As the colors are changed, they gain attention for the new notices. Several headline boards should be prepared for special types of notices—"Read the bulletin today," "The cause of an accident," "See our national advertising," or "What our competitors are doing."

The bulletin board should have photographs to illustrate the principles of safety. Broken goggles and old shoes may be displayed if they have played an important part in an accident. Human interest pictures of employees who have caught a big fish while on a camping trip, the bride and groom of a recent plant marriage, and valuable suggestions made by employees are examples of items that can be posted. The bulletin board never should be used for sermonizing by the general manager. It should be kept inviolate for the interest and information of the employees. As a rule, all notices should be changed or reserved for change every three days.

The boards should be located where the employee traffic is heavy but slow. The area of the time clock is a poor choice because traffic is fast. Restrooms are likely to be good locations.

The bulletin board and similar forms of written communication have definite limitations. When management wants its employees to grasp changes in a company policy, it rarely succeeds by simply passing on the information in written form. The most effective way of transmitting information is by combining oral and written methods, according to a study which included 1,030 Purdue University students; 84 employees of a corporation in Lafayette, Indiana; and 528 employees in a mail order-chain store firm—Spiegels, Inc., of Chicago. These last-mentioned employees were in the warehouse facilities, not in the retail departments. If use of this combination of methods is not possible, then oral communication is next-best. Just writing a message is the least effective of these three methods.[11]

CROSS-LINE AND UP-LINE COMMUNICATION

The grapevine

The "grapevine" is a familiar variety of communication that peddles news and gossip wherever a working force consists of more than one person. The term "grapevine" probably arose because it was thought to be a long, winding means of communication from one point to another—like a real grapevine. But it is now recognized that the grapevine is often faster and more direct than so-called direct, formal channels of information.

The grapevine is typically considered to apply to workers, but investigations indicate that it is also active among management. Wherever there are people, there are grapevines.

Grapevines are likely to be especially troublesome in plants where union officials and management representatives distrust each other. Where management and employees get along amicably in union as well as in other relations, grapevines are not so likely to function irresponsibly. In the absence of suspicion and distrust, the natural tendency is for both parties to talk over their problems regularly, calmly, and objectively. Hence, the evils of rumor-mongering are diminished.

The grapevine works fast. Keith Davis cited an example of a plant manager's wife who had a baby at 11 o'clock one night. By 2 P.M. the next day, 46 per cent of the management group at the plant knew of the event![12]

Most employers realize that the information the grapevine passes along is frequently disturbing to employee morale and to the company. Quite often it is misleading if not downright wrong.

One evil inherent in grapevines is that they become vehicles by which office "politicians" conduct whispering campaigns. Sometimes they reveal management secrets before the time appropriate for official announcement. They may even ruin reputations of individual employees or executives.

Grapevines do have one value. They are an effective safety valve at times when a management plans to make changes in policies or programs but is uncertain as to how employees will react to them. If the plans "leak out" and are discussed, the results may become a trial balloon. Just as some management attitudes are passed down through the grapevine, so also employee reactions are passed up.

When the Industrial Relations Section,

California Institute of Technology, had completed a total of 25 surveys, previously mentioned, the findings indicated that

From 10 per cent to almost 40 per cent of employees indicate that they now get most of their information about their company from fellow employees. In spite of the efforts of many companies to improve communication, the grapevine has never been less than third in rank order and in some cases has been second and even highest in response as to how information is actually being transmitted. In contrast, hardly any employees indicate that they prefer to get information from other employees. Only a few items such as newspapers have ever received a lower vote in terms of preference.

Employees want to receive information through their supervisors either in conversations or in group meetings. They are willing to accept such information through bulletin boards, plant papers, or special bulletins and letters. They do not want to depend upon the grapevine.[13]

Obviously, the grapevine is likely to stay in spite of its many evils and few virtues. As a result, managements today are trying to learn how to live with it. In some cases, it can be made to work for employer and employee benefits. From management's point of view, the main problem is to supply the grapevine with facts in order that misinformation may not be relayed. Plans that have been tried by managements are the following:

1. *The rumor clinic.* In small group meetings, employees are asked what rumors they have heard recently. Such discussions may report that the plant is going to be moved or that a 10 per cent raise is coming through. If a rumor is true, management fills in any details which may be lacking so that the full story may become known. If there is no basis for the rumor, management presents the true situation.

2. A *"Sounding Board"* for rumors is part of the employee communications program at Argus Cameras, Inc. Feeling the need of a speedier method for dealing with rumors than was provided by existing employee communications devices, management posted "Rumor Boards" at key plant loca-

tions, with the legend: "Rumors flying? Get the *right* answers here." Attached was a pencil and a pad of paper with the instructions: "Write down the question or rumor you want answered in the space below."

A few days after the rumor boards were put up, rumors began flying—onto the rumor boards. One employee asked, "Is it true that a labor union has filed notice with the company of its intentions of attempting to organize here?" Another said, "I heard there is going to be an extended vacation period this year due to layoffs." Neither of the rumors was true; both were the type of question which the company had hoped to get from employees.

As might be expected, however, many questions which employees post on the boards are not strictly rumors. Some are complaints, some are criticism. But seldom are the boards empty.

Strangely, perhaps, trivial or nonsensical questions and gripes which occasionally appear on the board seem to irritate or embarrass the employees much more than they do management. Often after such a question is asked, employees themselves reprimand the questioner with a comment on the board—or mention to members of the personnel department that such a question deserves no answer.

The board is checked daily by members of the personnel department, who contact the proper person to answer the question, type the answer, and post it on the board. The question is usually answered the same day it is posted on the board.[14]

3. *Putting the grapevine to constructive use* may be accomplished by having meetings with the "natural leaders" in employee ranks. Management tries to keep these key employees informed on the theory that this will ensure that the facts reach other rank-and-filers in undistorted form.[15]

The grapevine is especially fast and active when news is significant, which means that it will undermine a formal system for significant news unless the formal system is kept flexible

and fast. The grapevine quickens its pace when people are insecure, as when a reorganization is "in the wind" or a reduction in force is probable. Since the grapevine has no reliable source to which participants can refer to confirm facts, the grapevine carries rumor or distorted information rather easily. Since participants in a grapevine cannot easily be held responsible for distortion, as they could be in formal communication, each participant is freer to treat facts lightly.

In the management group the grapevine is more spontaneous and flexible than formal communication. For example, it can easily by-pass managers in the chain of command because it is not confined by formal procedure. Under certain conditions, this can be beneficial, but often it short-circuits other managers and undermines executive relationships.

Studies show that the management grapevine can be influenced because its patterns are partly predictable. For example:

1. People talk most when the news is recent.
2. People talk about things that affect their work.
3. People talk about people they know.
4. People working near each other are likely to be on the same grapevine.
5. People who contact each other in the chain of procedure, tend to be on the same grapevine.

No matter what the causes of grapevines, they will continue. Grapevines represent a normal management activity.[16]

Robert Hershey has suggested the following methods as means of controlling and reducing the harmful effects of rumoring:

Keep the normal channels of communication open—rumors are found in the absence of reliable information.

Don't use public address systems to debunk a rumor; this method seems to make the rumor better remembered than the refutation.

The best way to debunk a rumor is to present fact upon fact about the topic, rather than to try to disprove the logic of the rumor.

Prevent idleness and monotony in the work force wherever possible.

Campaign against rumors and ridicule rumor-mongering.

Educate your supervisors in the dynamics of rumor.

Distract people's attention from the rumor area.

An official denial alone will never debunk a rumor.

And the most effective: Interpret the rumor as a psychiatrist would interpret a symptom. Ask yourself, "What anxiety or attitude does this rumor reflect?" Then, try to relieve the tension by correcting the situation which caused it.[17]

Information from unions

Employees' organizations, the labor unions, also present their views of industrial relations questions to employees and the public.

The labor union organizer deals with the workman's most vital interests. He is often a better student of labor psychology than the employer, for the organizer directs his appeals to the worker's problems and interests. And labor has developed a fairly extensive scheme of propaganda.

No positive figure is available as to how many labor papers there are, how many people they reach, or what effect they have on their readers. Herbert Little, director of the Office of Information of the Department of Labor, says the department has a mailing list of more than 800 periodicals. He estimates their total circulation as anywhere from 20 to 30 million.

Generally, union journals today not only print news of interest to their readers, such as goings on within the union itself, news of labor elections and contracts won, but also decry the high cost of living, plump for wage increases, and attempt to win membership support for labor-approved candidates for political office and for labor-approved legislative programs. They are used by the leadership both to stir up trouble and to pour oil on waters already troubled.

The news of a labor publication, in short, is tailored to fit the occasion. If a business man resists the union's attempts to organize his plant, the union's publication may well call him every name under the sun in order to steam up his workers. The same thing may apply during contract negotiation time. For the rest of the year, however, the publications can afford to be charitable.[18]

Some labor editors do an effective job of selling their story to their followers. Their language is uninhibited. They come to the point quickly and pull no punches. For example: commenting on a NLRB ruling regarding freedom of speech for employers, one labor paper said, "You've got to sit and listen to the boss raise unshirted hell about your union if he calls you and your fellow workers together on company time for such a purpose."

Company editors and the businessman could learn much from the labor press. As Martin Dodge says, "When the businessman takes the trouble to find out what is being said about him, he also will come upon the whole gamut of gripes, aspirations and delusions that labor harbors, for they are all spelled out in the union press."[19]

It is fair to say that, on the average, each one of the country's unionized workers gets at least one labor paper. This may be either the official organ of the international union to which he belongs, a local labor body publication, or the paper of the state federation. In most cases, union dues entitle the member to a subscription. Distribution usually is through the mail or by hand-out at union meetings. In most cases the paper is taken home and carefully and sometimes laboriously read and reread, for labor editors fill their sheets with information close to the interests of their readers. About half of these publications accept local and national advertising.

The labor press is frankly propagandistic, in fact supplementing the never ending organizing work which many unions conduct. The function of the labor press is to bring workers information about their trade and industry and to interpret for them their economic interests in such affairs. On the whole, they see their job as counteracting what they consider to be the "anti-labor bias" of the daily press, the radio, and the movies, and as anchoring the member's loyalty to his union.

In view of the two differing emphases in the communication of employers and of union organizations with workers, it is not surprising to find that leaders of both groups see the same situation in differing lights. When a survey was made of about 100 labor and 100 management executives, a few of the highlights were:

Leaders of both groups have plenty of complaints about "irritations" with the *personal* characteristics of the other side's leadership. Almost all of the specific gripes hit at the morality of the other group, or at its *behavior during negotiations.* Name-calling and the use of stereotyped epithets like 'labor racketeers' and 'business autocrats' are almost universal. Union leadership is especially resentful of the *lack of respect* shown it by management. Company leadership clearly expressed this disrespect, and cited the 'irresponsibility' of labor's executives as a justification. These *personal feelings* are reflected in the *policy demands* of both groups. Neither group is particularly realistic about what the other feels, thinks, sees, or hears.

Both sides live in private information *worlds.* Overwhelmingly, management and labor trust sources of information which are identified in advance with their *own point of view.* . . . Thus labor has more confidence in government information; management in the daily newspaper and periodical press.

What comes out of this study as 'cause for alarm' is not the body of issues in dispute between union and company officials. The most disturbing result is the existence of highly charged emotional attitudes on both sides which will interfere with the reasonable solution of whatever issues there are. . . .

The ways out of this impasse lie along the road to clarification and greater familiarity between both sides. . . .

But above all else both sides must have a day-to-day common meeting ground at the plant, industry and national levels. There must be a medium which introduces them to one another, and in which they can both have confidence. Information breeds understanding; understanding produces respect; respect is the sole foundation on which a workable machinery for meeting the nation's industrial problems can be built.[20]

Face-to-face communications

In our preoccupation with media of communication we are likely to slight the basic problem: improving face-to-face communications between the employee and the supervisor. Nine-tenths of industrial communications take place face-to-face.

Face-to-face communications are not simple because they are as complex and as varied as the human beings who take part in them. The basic attack on communication problems must begin in these daily face-to-face relationships. In order to do this, more attention has to be paid to motivations of individuals as outlined according to the adjustment concept in Chapters 2–8.

Productivity depends on effective teamwork that arises first and foremost in the on-the-job dealings between an individual and his supervisors. All need practical guidance on every aspect of interpersonal communication, including giving orders that are accepted wholeheartedly, handling grievances, making rumors work constructively, counseling on job performance, and reporting results to upper management.

Company publications, speeches by executives, bulletins, and letters are important media of communication, but they are only aids to the day-to-day relations. Both the executives and the employees communicate most of their meanings by the words they say and how they say them. Attitudes are communicated by the tone of voice, facial expression, and the manner of presentation.

The true leader knows this principle and practices it naturally. One example is that of a superintendent of a leather plant who has the reputation of being tough on quality. He has developed the reputation through such acts as taking a foreman and his crew off their down-the-line jobs and taking them into the sorting room, the final step of the operation. "Isn't that a beautiful piece of leather?" he'll ask, with pride expressed by his voice and manner. He has communicated his own high regard for good workmanship by his manner rather than by his words and has enabled the workers who produced the leather to experience pride in themselves for their contribution to its high quality.

Workers judge an executive by what they *think* his motives are. If they sense that he is for them, they will put a good construction on what he says. If they sense that he is basically disinterested in them, they will read negative meanings into his words and efforts even though what he says and does would appear to be favorable to them otherwise. Employees sense the psychological climate from daily personal contacts rather than from formal media of communication.

The written word is not a substitute for sound face-to-face relationships. Written communications to employees are not accepted unless there is first a foundation of trust and confidence, an understanding psychological climate where management and workers can function effectively and happily.

The psychological climate

Each company has a unique psychological climate. As someone has said, "A business organization is like a home—it has a characteristic atmosphere. In some homes, the head of the household and all its members are vitally concerned about politics, religion, or some other interest—the occupations of the individual members being only of minor interest. In others, where the personality of the head of the household dominates the activities and spirit of the members, the opposite occurs. Like any group, a business organization has its own culture, traditions and, to some extent, its own language and climate."

In some companies everyone from top management to the shipping room is concerned with production. In others, the dominant interest is marketing—even the machine operator in the factory knows who will buy and use the product made by his machine.

Some companies have a lively team spirit in regard to sales. Employees use the editorial "we" in a manner that connotes a firm identification with the company and its struggle against competition. In others, each employee is an individualist who seeks his own satisfactions without very much thought about the other members of the team or management's sales goals.

Similarly, each organization has its own tempo in seeking its goals. The pace set in one may be active, energetic, fast. The employees who advance most rapidly are the dynamic-mannered individuals. In others, the tempo of work and manner is slower. Most of the employees are seeking security rather than rapid development. The pace is a "congenial" one.

Some organizations are conservative in their consideration of new products and new ideas. They react only as they have in the past. They continue to function as they did years ago, making only minor changes in their products and methods. Other companies place much stress on research in all areas of the business, particularly in the development of new products. New products are always in the laboratory or pilot-plant stage, and these companies often plunge into new production and distribution programs without much apparent thought.

Of course, pay scales vary from company to company of the same industry. In one, the pay scales for employees may be above the average, year after year. In another company that makes the same kind of product, the pay scales are always below the average for the industry. The salary scale of a company may be low, but its prestige level may be high. These two aspects, salary and prestige levels, do not, however, always appear in reverse. Many companies can be found that are relatively high or low in both respects.

Companies differ markedly in their attention to public relations and publicity for their products and policies. Some managements put forth extra effort to send out press releases and have their executives make speeches at conventions. Others avoid both, and every employee soon learns to keep quiet about company matters.

Company managements also differ in regard to factors such as the top education of the executives. Some companies are headed by men who never went to college and they are proud of it. Other organizations have so many college graduates that the employee with a bachelor's degree feels inferior because he does not have a doctor's degree!

Some companies set the pace for their competitors. They are the first to develop the new design and to break from tradition. Others wait until the new products and methods are well established and then follow suit. Sometimes the slow-to-change companies make more profits than the pioneers, but American business has moved forward because pioneers and innovators refused to abide by tradition.

Some companies are so volume-minded that each executive gets ulcers unless the output curves on his charts are ever upward and his cost curves ever downward. "Bigger and better" is the motto that seems to hang on the wall of every office.

Numerous additional criteria for evaluating and characterizing the climates engendered by different managements might be listed. Each person who becomes a member of an organization soon learns to sense and to adapt himself to the existing atmosphere. If he does not, he is likely to be unhappy and soon leave it.

Some managements adhere strictly to lines of authority and thereby can stifle self-development. Such rigidity creates confusion since a man does not know how far he can exercise his talents and assume responsibility. Other managements operate through a flexible organizational structure where each man may take on extra responsibilities which might be viewed as encroachments on someone else's responsibilities.

Some managements are so busy doing something about testing and training techniques and other tangible tools like appraisal forms and job specifications that they pay only a lip service to the really basic nourishment employees need. In some companies no one expresses his criticisms or gripes. These are suppressed. In others, the orientation of new employees includes frank analyses of grievances which have been filed by regular employees. The grievances are discussed to impress newcomers that it is not shameful to gripe so long as the expressed gripe leads to constructive action.

Psychological climate is the best way to classify these feeling tones in a company. Climate and team spirit are created by the top management in its relations with supervision. Supervisors must have adequate daily knowledge of each worker's personality and performance—knowledge that comes from daily *direct observation*, not from formal company communication programs.

When the Industrial Relations Section, California Institute of Technology, had completed a total of 25 surveys, previously mentioned, one conclusion based on all of its studies of employee opinion was that

Wages, hours of work, working conditions, benefit plans, grievance procedure, supervision, and equipment affect morale. All of these items are essential for good morale, but they are insufficient to produce the highest morale. With these conditions present, the catalyst that is needed to produce effective high morale is a sincere, day-to-day interest of top management in its employees as individuals. Under these circumstances the minor irritations can be quickly recognized and eliminated before they become serious, the employees receive both economic and non-economic recognition as individuals; and owners, managers, and employees work together to produce goods and services at reasonable costs.[21]

Acknowledgments and References

1. Excerpt from *Annual Report 1953–1954,* Industrial Relations Section, California Institute of Technology, Project 5, "Surveys of Employee Opinion."
2. See W. A. Earl, "A Blueprint for Action." *Personnel,* American Management Association, March 1951.

3. Tom Wolff, "Are You Getting Across to Your Workers?" *Personnel,* American Management Association, September 1955.

4. From a talk by Dr. Claude Robinson before the American Association of Industrial Editors and reported in *Personnel,* American Management Association, March 1953, p. 452.

5. See Robert Newcomb and Mary Sammons, "Dos and Don'ts of Publishing a Good Employee Publication," *Industrial Marketing,* March 1955, p. 97.

6. See Alfred G. Larke, "How to Learn by Listening," *Dun's Review and Modern Industry,* April 1955.

7. See *The Management Review,* American Management Association, February 1954, p. 84.

8. Keith Powlison, "How Can We Help Workers Grasp the Truth about Profits?" *Sales Management,* September 1, 1947, p. 143.

9. *A Report on What Information People Want about Policies and Financial Conditions of Corporations,* Vols. I and II, The Controllership Foundation, Inc., New York, 1948. This condensation from *The Management Review,* American Management Association, August 1948, p. 427.

10. Ross G. Walker, "The Misinformed Employee," *Harvard Business Review,* May 1948.

11. See the study by Thomas L. Dahle, "Transmitting Information to Employees," *Personnel,* American Management Association, November 1954.

12. Frank M. Kleiler, in *The New York Times Magazine,* October 31, 1954, pp. 19–22. Reprinted in *The Management Review,* American Management Association, April 1955, pp. 265–266.

13. Excerpt from *Annual Report 1953–1954,* Industrial Relations Section, California Institute of Technology; Project 5, "Surveys of Employee Opinion."

14. Personnel Administration Service, The Dartnell Corp., Chicago, Ill., in *The Management Review,* American Management Association, March 1955.

15. See Frank M. Kleiler, *loc. cit.*

16. For further information, see Keith Davis, "Communication within Management," *Personnel,* American Management Association, November 1954.

17. See Robert Hershey, "Heed Rumors for Their Meaning," *Personnel Journal,* January 1956.

18. Booton Herndon, *Nation's Business,* June 1954, p. 66.

19. Martin Dodge, "Labor's Fourth Estate," *Personnel,* American Management Association, January 1949.

20. Nejelski and Company, *Must Labor and Management Fight?* New York. See also *Tide,* May 31, 1946, p. 70.

21. Excerpt from *Annual Report 1953–1954,* Industrial Relations Section, California Institute of Technology, Project 5, "Surveys of Employee Opinion."

22. Quoted from *Management Record,* National Industrial Conference Board, August 1939.

PROJECTS

1. Collect copies of employees' magazines or plant organs and analyze them as to style, selection of material, illustrations, size, and so on.

2. Employees can be made conscious of costs involved in the use of their equipment. Do you think that college students could be made cost-conscious through the use of the method of Monarch Machine Tool Company?

   "Employees operating costly machines rarely have any conception of the amount of the company investment entrusted to their care. Believing that a realization of the value of equipment would result in more care being exercised in its use, the Monarch Machine Tool Company tried the experiment of attaching to each machine in its own plant a plate showing what the machine cost the company when it was purchased. Results have been so gratifying that customers are beginning to request that machines purchased from the company be similarly equipped."[22]

3. Would the morale of the employee be improved by employee meetings at which some of the older men of the company describe their experiences and advancements with the company?

4. In one company the coal bill had increased 30 per cent when the board of directors ordered an investigation. The chief fireman reported that he had been shoveling more slate than coal. He knew that the coal was inferior, but he did not think it was his place to report it. Analyze this situation as to possible causes of such an attitude on the part of the employee. How can such attitudes be prevented?

COLLATERAL READINGS

Bellows, Roger M., *Psychology of Personnel in Business and Industry*, Prentice-Hall, Inc., New York, 1954.

Blum, Milton L., *Industrial Psychology and Its Social Foundations*, Harper & Brothers, New York, 1949, Chapter 5.

Carlucci, Cosimo, and William J. E. Crissy, "How Readable Are Employee Handbooks?" *Personnel Psychology*, Winter 1951.

Ghiselli, Edwin E., and Clarence W. Brown, *Personnel and Industrial Psychology*, McGraw-Hill Book Company, Inc., New York, 1955, Chapter 15.

Haire, Mason, *Psychology in Management*, McGraw-Hill Book Company, Inc., New York, 1956, Chapters 2 and 4.

Harrell, Thomas Willard, *Industrial Psychology*, Rinehart & Company, Inc., New York, 1949.

Industrial Relations Research: Ten Years of Progress. Industrial Relations Center, University of Minnesota, Minneapolis, Minn. 1955. Included in this overview of the activities of the Industrial Relations Center during the decade 1945–1955 are an account of the research program, a summary of annual conference highlights, and a comprehensive bibliography of the publications of the IRC and its staff members.

Stagner, Ross, *The Psychology of Industrial Conflicts*, John Wiley & Sons, Inc., New York, 1956, Chapters 2–5, and 10.

CHAPTER TWENTY-FOUR

Employee relations–formal programs

Two real comrades know all about each other and are tolerant. Each knows what the other is up against and, understanding each other, wanting to work out the common task which is theirs, they make allowances as one man to another. Then there is fun in the day's work, there is that sense of going places with other men, there is a click in the job. That is great; that is a priceless possession. When it exists among men in industry, so-called "personnel management" is simple. But you cannot define this relationship; you cannot blueprint the course of comradeship. It is a mistake to try. But we can create the physical environment that is conducive to comradeship. We can have good "personnel management" and then give comradeship a chance.[1]

Systems of personnel management in industry are relatively unimportant. A given company may have the finest industrial relations mechanisms or formal systems and still have poor industrial relations. Another company may have almost no personnel management mechanisms and yet have fine industrial relations. If the executives have the kind of managerial leadership that inspires comradeship and confidence between management and men, the formal methods of supervision are incidental. Many examples of this fine relationship exist in American industry.

At the same time that some of our largest corporations have been beset by costly labor controversies, other companies of the same industry have had few or no disturbances. And yet the company that has a pleasant industrial relations history may have no special plan or system to account for the results. It may have no formal suggestion system, no employee relations counselors, no music or public address system in the shops, and no athletic association. There may be no printed statement of labor policy or procedure, no codified rules of conduct, and no commitment on the part of the company or its workers except the intent to comply honestly and fairly with a simple arrangement or practice regarding wages and working conditions. It may, however, have many spontaneous get-togethers that provide opportunity for fellowship. In such a company, the relationship between management and men is likely to be surprisingly informal. The psychological climate is right—management and men work together in a spirit of mutual confidence.

481

Managements of other companies who would like to bring about a more favorable psychological climate in their organizations often turn to some formal plan as a means toward achieving the desired relationship between employees and the company. The plans to which they turn are typically profit sharing, stock ownership, and suggestion systems.

Profit-sharing

Profit-sharing is not a new idea; the plan was in operation in agriculture in England during the thirteenth century. Records show that it was used in shops in England in 1870 and in France as early as 1842. The first plan instituted in the United States was that of Albert Gallatin, who introduced it in his glassworks at New Geneva, Pennsylvania, in 1794. In 1889, the United States had thirty-two recorded schemes for profit-sharing. Most of these schemes were short-lived, although one St. Louis firm has been operating on a profit-sharing basis since 1886. The Procter & Gamble plan was begun in 1887, but it has been modified several times since then. Few schemes now operating were started before 1900.

In most cases, profit-sharing should be distinguished from bonuses, which are given as a reward for high production by an individual worker. It is not part of a wage system. True profit-sharing is an agreement between the employer and the employees under which the profits allocated to the

TABLE 24-1

PERSONNEL PRACTICES BY COMPANY SIZE

Personnel Practice	Per Cent Having Practice By Number of Factory Employees				
	1–49	50–99	100–499	500–999	1,000 and over
Formal Pension Plan	16	14	34	57	83
Compulsory Retirement (Male Workers)	5	10	17	48	48
Group Life Insurance	55	80	77	99	100
Sickness & Accident Insurance	43	73	82	91	96
Incentive Wage Plan	36	53	54	75	68
Safety Program	32	54	74	95	96
Formal Suggestion System	15	14	26	48	70

Personnel practices differ from industry to industry and among companies of different sizes. The extent of the differences appears in a study by the Associated Industries of Cleveland, covering the personnel practices of 338 firms in the Cleveland area, an area considered generally representative of U.S. industry.

The table shows, for seven selected personnel practices, the proportion of firms in five size categories reporting each. Only those practices were chosen which showed a clear-cut and significant variation in frequency according to company size.

Large companies, to a far greater extent than medium-size and small ones, carry on formal safety programs, conduct physical examinations for new employees, maintain formal suggestion systems, provide recognition for long-service employees, and make use of interviews, and so on. Pension plans were more than five times as frequent among the largest companies as in the smallest ones. In all size groups, non-contributory plans predominated, but the frequency of contributory plans was materially greater in firms having fewer than 100 employees.

Frequency of insurance plans in the largest companies was pretty consistently about twice what it was in the smallest firms. An exception was hospitalization insurance, reported by almost every firm.

There was no significant variation in the proportion of firms having non-contributory as opposed to contributory insurance.

Compulsory retirement for male employees varied directly with size of company. Nearly one-half of the largest firms had this requirement, as against only one in 20 of the smallest ones. On the other hand, the mandatory retirement age tended to be 65 in the smallest firms, 68 or 70 in larger ones.

Source: *Labor Policy and Practice,* The Bureau of National Affairs, Inc., September 8, 1955.

workers rise or fall in proportion to the increase or the decrease in the profits realized by the employer.

Most profit-sharing plans can be divided into two classifications: current distribution and deferred distribution. Under the first, the older type, the profits are paid in cash at regular intervals. In the second type, the employee's share of the profits is deposited in an irrevocable trust and the employee, or his beneficiaries, does not receive his shares until some future time: termination of employment, disability, retirement, or death. Combination plans that pay a portion of the profits in cash but also have a deferred element appear in some cases. Plans to which the employees contribute toward deferred benefits are more common in large than in small companies. Small companies are more likely to have current distribution plans.

Many of the plans have been started in the hope that efficiency would be increased, costs decreased, and the working force stabilized. Some were begun by wealthy employers who wished to share their success with the employees whose hard work contributed toward the profits of the enterprises. The employers' motives were an attempt to give social justice and to increase their own sense of well-being. Where such an attitude prevailed, and was coupled with reasonable managerial efficiency, some benefits actually accrued from profit-sharing and similar plans of employee relations. The plans started by such humanitarians were usually abandoned at their deaths, when inevitable changes in management took place. In a few instances, the owner of the business provided for the perpetuation of the plan after his death.

In general, profit-sharing has not been so successful as many of its advocates anticipated. One important reason is that employees prefer to have a definite salary or wage that is known in advance. They declare "a bird in the hand is worth two in the in the bush." In the years when the company makes unusually large profits, the money distributed is accepted as a gift from a kind, industrial Santa Claus; but when profits are negligible or a deficit must be written on the books, the employees may be sorely disappointed. To say the least, an employee will be shocked if, after he has spent his anticipated profits, he finds that the practice of distributing profits has been suddenly discontinued. When profits are shared for a long time, they are often confused with or considered as a part of the wages.

When the profits of the company do not allow any distribution to the employees, the employees tend to doubt the honesty of the management, particularly if they note that the president or the general manager of the company has purchased a new house or a new limousine. They do not, as a rule, have access to the accounts of the employer; but even if they did, they would not be able to understand the accounts. A negligible number of the employers who have a profit-sharing plan have a disinterested accountant audit their books and prepare a report, which he presents to the employees. However, the great masses of workers cannot understand how profits in modern business are made or computed. It is only natural, therefore, that they should be suspicious of the management when the plan of distribution remains a mystery to them.

The individual employee can seldom see any relationship between his own daily efforts and the profits at the end of the year. In most plans, the profits divided are a small fraction of the annual wages. In one-third of the plans studied, it was found that the dividends amounted to less than 6 per cent of the annual wages of the participants. Hence the interested employee who decides to work hard in order to increase the company's profits at the end of the year, a proportionate share of which he will receive, finds that the lazy worker by his side receives a check just as large as his own. As a result of his discovery, during the following year he may decide to work as slowly and as carelessly as the poorest workman in the shop. Thus profit-sharing, under some conditions, tends to bring the efficiency of the best workers down to the level of the poorest rather than to raise the efficiency of the poorest workers. The profit-sharing sun shines just as brightly on the undeserving as on the deserving. It is for these and other reasons that profit-sharing for workmen has been found deficient as an incentive to work. The only type that appears to have incentive values for modern business is that of managerial profit-sharing.

The General Foods Corporation, whose headquarters at White Plains, New York, is shown above, manages its personnel, who work in some 85 locations throughout the world, through a Corporate Department of Personnel Administration. The Department, with offices in the White Plains building, includes a very active division for Personnel Research and Communications, headed by Roger M. Bellows. Functions of the Division include personnel research and planning, communication through corporate publications, supervisory and safety training, executive development, and salary administration.

The making of profits in modern business is largely beyond the control of the factory workers. Profits depend upon the managerial ability to purchase economically, to organize the whole scheme of production efficiently, to sell the goods at a satisfactory profit, to finance the operations during the depressions that are bound to occur in business, and to find new markets to take the place of contracting markets. The key executives of a business—the sales manager, the production manager, the comptroller, the purchasing agent, and a few others—can see the direct relations between their own efforts and the profits made. They are the men who are responsible for profits and losses, rather than the workers in the factory. For wage earners, profit-sharing is largely incidental to a humanitarian motive or managerial attitude of fairness toward the employees. As a rule, it does not by itself give the workers a strong sense of participation in the enterprise.

Many employers who adopted profit-sharing did so, not with the hope of obtaining more material gains from employees, but to improve the *esprit de corps* and to express management's sense of colleagueship with employees.

When the National Industrial Conference Board made a study of 167 companies having profit-sharing plans, approximately one-third of the managements reported some dissatisfactions with their plan. The largest single group of complaints consisted of employee attitudes such as taking the plan for granted, inability to see the connection between company profits and individual effort, amount of profits, and greater interest in current wages.[2]

The Profit Sharing Research Foundation recently analyzed over 300 profit-sharing plans in industries employing a total of three-quarters of a million workers.

They found that large companies rated their plans successful more often than small companies. Success ratings were larger in proportion among financial and professional enterprises than among manufacturing or mercantile enterprises. Some companies with unions have successful profit-sharing plans, but the success rating of nonunion companies is higher than for the unionized companies.

To make a profit-sharing plan work satisfactorily, the following recommendations by investigators have been offered:

PROVIDE A HEALTHY PSYCHOLOGICAL CLIMATE BEFORE SETTING UP THE PLAN. Both management and workers should have confidence in each other, before the directors and officers can expect profit-sharing to be beneficial. To succeed, profit-sharing must be consistent with the way the business is done and the way management and employees feel about each other. Companies that succeed with profit-sharing would, in most cases, also succeed without it.

BE WILLING TO GIVE EMPLOYEES ALL FACTS ABOUT THE BUSINESS. A willingness to share all the facts in the financial situation is necessary. A willingness to give limited facts only is likely to result in doubt and disbelief, thus defeating the aim of profit-sharing.

PROVIDE A SOUND COMPENSATION PLAN. An equitable wage and salary plan should be developed before profit-sharing is introduced. A poor compensation plan that is bolstered by the contingent compensation from profit-sharings is likely to cause trouble. If the pay structure is sound, a profit-sharing plan will supplement it. If the pay structure is unsound or inequitable, profit-sharing will only accentuate its inequities.

HAVE EVERYBODY SHARE ALIKE. The same number of dollars per employee is not necessary, but the same percentage is. If the pay structure is sound, a profit-sharing plan may improve it, especially if the percentage of wages rather than a scale of wages or salary brackets is used to determine the profits per employee.[3]

In spite of the fact that some profit-sharing plans have not worked out to the complete satisfaction of all employers or employees who have adopted them, certain companies have demonstrated the effectiveness of the idea when it is part of some more comprehensive plan of employer-employee relations. The Lincoln Electric Company is an example. There, as in other successful uses of profit-sharing, the idea is only part of a greater philosophy. As the Lincoln Electric Company states, ". . . if all employees of any organization, from top to bottom, will work together and do as much as they can, instead of as little as they can, everyone in that organization will be better off. As a result, such an organization will be outstanding among all others of its type."

Employees' stock purchase plans

It has been argued that stock ownership, rather than profit-sharing, is more advantageous to the employee for the following reasons: Under the latter plan, although the employee may gain a little by sharing in the profits, he is not required to expend any extra effort or to take any risks. Thus the profit-sharing plan does not give him any feeling of responsibility in the management of the company. On the other hand, under the stock purchase plan, the employee, by being allowed to purchase some stock, is made to regard himself as a partner in the business; consequently he naturally takes an active interest in the affairs of the business and acquires a sense of importance as a budding financier!

Advocates of the plan claim that stock ownership would be an incentive to the employee to eliminate waste, to be more industrious, to attend work regularly, not to quit for a better job, to criticize the employer less, and to refuse to harm the company's property in case of a strike. Some advocates even think that by purchasing enough stock, the employees could have direct representation on the board of directors and in the management of the company.

Dramatic instances of the benefits to employees of stock ownership are published from time to time.

General Robert E. Wood, when chairman of the board of trustees of the Sears, Roebuck and Co. savings and profit-sharing pension fund, described how the company's fund was created in 1916 and built up from 5 per cent pay deductions supplemented by a 5 to 10 per cent share of the company's profits before taxes.

With the fund invested largely in Sears stock, the 123,800 participating employees with more than a year's seniority owned 26 per cent of the company. At the time, total resources of the fund exceeded $600,000,000, despite employee withdrawals of $351,000,000 since 1916, against employee contributions of $191,000,-000. After citing an instance of a little Polish girl who started to work "in the old days" for $6 a week, and who had accumulated $121,000 in the fund, General Wood summarized: "In fact, every employee who has been with us over 30 years gets out, no matter how humble his position, with a minimum capital of $50,000, which may go up to $150,000. In other words, we are making capitalists every year."[4]

Most companies who do have a stock ownership plan cannot, of course, point to such dramatic benefits.

The main reasons for instituting employee stock ownership plans are a desire (1) to make employees partners in the business, so that they will have greater interest in and loyalty to the company; (2) to promote employee thrift; (3) to educate the workers on the advantages of the free enterprise system; (4) to provide a hedge against inflation; and (5) to obtain working capital for the company.

The Brookings Institution studied the extent of stock ownership in the United States and found that some 6.5 million Americans own stock in publicly-held corporations. Of these individuals, about 4.9 million have incomes of less than $10,000 a year. More than one million families with incomes of less than $4,000 own shares.

In industry, out of the 9.3 million who are classified as foremen and skilled workers, only 410,000 were found to be shareholders. Housewives showed a better percentage of ownership among members of their group than the leading group of industrial workers.

The extent of employees' ownership of stock in the companies for which they work varied in the early 1950's as follows:

Industry	Number employed— millions	Per cent owning stock in their own companies
Manufacturing	16.9	1.4%
Public utilities	1.1	15.9
Banking and finance ...	1.7	8.6
Professional business service companies ...	1.2	6.4
Petroleum companies ...	.9	5.8
Transportation companies	2.6	3.1
Total	24.4	3.2

According to this study, only one worker in 70 in manufacturing owned stock but one utility worker in six was a shareholder. In the telephone companies about 21 per cent of women employees owned stock as against 12 per cent of the men.[5]

These figures, of course, do not tell the whole story of business ownership. Approximately 3 million people have shares in private, closely-held companies. Many of these also own stock in publicly-held corporations. In addition, other millions own small businesses. These are the proprietors and partners who own an overwhelming share of the almost 4 million businesses operating in the United States. Economically, too, other tens of millions of Americans have an indirect share in the ownership of American industry in the form of life insurance policies and bank accounts.

One of the principal complaints made against the stock purchase idea is that not enough wage earners participate. When, for example, the National Industrial Conference Board made a survey of 33 companies which provided company stock plans, only a quarter million, or 26.6 per cent of employees, were buying stock under the company's latest stock offerings. Only one of four eligible employees took advantage of the offer. The percentage of employees buying stock, however, ranged for different companies all the way from 1.1 per cent to 92.5 per cent.[6]

Actually, some employee stock ownership plans have not worked out as anticipated. It has been found that employees purchase stock mainly for three reasons: as a speculative investment; in the hope of attracting the

Advisory Council, Industrial Relations Center, University of Minnesota, in one of its regular quarterly meetings. The advisory Council is composed of some 18 representative citizens of the state. The Council advises the Center on major questions of policy. The Center's research program is carried on through its six major laboratories.

The Center serves to integrate and coordinate the services of the faculty and facilities of the University in providing training and carrying on research in the field of industrial relations.

The Industrial Relations Center was established because it has become clear that neither training nor research in this field can be provided within the limits of any single department. The members of the Faculty Committee, which is charged with full responsibility for the Center's policies and program, have been drawn from eight departments of the University whose resources are thus combined in training and research in the industrial relations field. The departments include Economics, Business Administration, Law, Psychology, Public Administration and Political Science, Engineering, Sociology, and Agricultural Economics.

Dale Yoder, Professor of Economics and Industrial Relations, is Director. Published reports of studies may be obtained from University of Minnesota Press, Minneapolis.

good will of management and of gaining promotion; and as a nest egg for old age. The extent to which these hopes have been dashed in some unfortunate instances is illustrated in the case of the employees of a company that suffered severely in a business depression. When the company was only a few jumps ahead of the sheriff, the executives had to retrench and, consequently, many of the employees were dismissed.

Certain employers who have sold negotiable stock to employees have found that the employees have become interested more in the market value of the stock than in in-

creasing its real value through extra diligence. At the very time when the employer has needed employee loyalty—a keen desire on the part of the workers to pitch in and lift a little harder—he has found them busy watching the stock market! In a few cases, employees have made paper profits that would have given them substantial annual incomes had they sold at the right time; but they held on, hoping to make still more or fearing that the employer would look upon their transactions as disloyalty to the company. When the paper profits were wiped out, the former "well-to-do" employees lost heart in their work and blamed the company for their misfortune.

Or consider, from an editorial in a financial journal, this danger of stock ownership programs for employees:

It is self-deceptive to think that, because an employee has a few shares of his company's stock, he considers himself a capitalist, or that his interest becomes the same as the investor's. . . . The time when an employee will most need to rely on his savings or capital is the time when he is out of a job. If he has become unemployed because the company has cut its payroll, the same condition will militate against the value of the stock. Thus he will suffer a double loss, and have double disillusionment in the company and in capital generally.[7]

Most stock ownership plans for employees, inaugurated before the market crash of 1929, had to be dropped because of the later decline in security values. Many of the employee purchases had been made at peak market prices, with the result that many employees suffered severe losses. However, by the late 1940's a small number of companies had revived interest in employee stock ownership because stock market price levels appeared to be stable and favorable to the employees.

Some stock purchase plans are open to selected employees, such as managers, department heads, salesmen, or others whose services are highly respected or who can afford to stand a loss in case of a decline in value. Stock purchase plans can give the employee a sense of participation in the industry only when he has rights in shares in which the public does not participate, a partnership psychologically as well as economically in the business. Otherwise, the employees who are encouraged to purchase stock should be of the higher income class, who are mentally capable of understanding the fluctuations in stock prices and able to absorb their losses.

Despite the misfortunes suffered by stock purchase plans in the depression of the 1930's, many companies continue to be interested in the idea of employee stock ownership. They still think it can be a good way to promote employee thrift and help the worker to identify his own welfare with that of his company. Managements, of course, are aware of the hazards in stock ownership plans and hope to set up plans that avoid disasters.

The recently-developed plans are based on the regular savings of the worker, augmented by a contribution from the company, and invested in varied types of securities. Many of the plans are called "thrift plans" or "savings plans."[8]

Most employers realize that they cannot hope to develop an effective profit-sharing or stock ownership plan. They appreciate that none of these or other formal plans have proved to be of measurable direct productive value. They know that any plan in itself is effective in the extent that it helps to develop a favorable psychological climate in which management and men can work together productively. For most companies stock ownership and profit-sharing are big and serious ventures—too big for their capacities. Many of these managements do, however, want to work toward a better psychological climate. They want their employees as well as the company executives to have the benefit of a sense of participation in the business. They therefore turn to the suggestion system idea.

Suggestion systems

Ideally a suggestion system should be unnecessary. Management and men should work so closely with each other that each makes suggestions regarding the work as the work is carried on. Practically, such ideal relations seldom exist. A suggestion system may, to some extent, enable alert employees to participate more actively in the operation of the business. The extent to which employees participate depends upon the attention given to the suggestion system by management. Some companies get ideas from about 50 per cent of their employees in the course of a year, but so high a percentage of participation is unusual.

The average rate of adoption reported by the National Association of Suggestions Systems has been 20 per cent.

Corning Glass Works, for example, asked its 13,000 employees, "What's your big idea?" The result was 27,687 suggestions for new glass products in the course of a five-month contest at Corning's 18 plants. New glass products suggested by Corning employees ranged from vases and lipstick holders to septic tanks, dog dishes, and structural beams. About 10 per cent of the total number of suggestions submitted were worthy of further consideration. Of these, 5 per cent were in the outstanding or excellent category. Duplication ran very high.[9]

Employees will not offer ideas unless they have learned through years of experience that suggestions are welcome. The executive who calls employees into his office and makes a direct request for suggestions is likely to be disappointed for several reasons. One is the fact that most employees are like students; they try to give an answer that they think will agree with the questioner's ideas.

Again, employees who are paid on a piece-rate basis may be able to make suggestions that would speed up their work, but they have learned that the new method would bring about a retiming of the job and a lower rate of pay. They can make more money by keeping the discovery to themselves and retaining the old rate of pay than if they were to be paid a small reward for the suggestion.

To operate a successful suggestion system, the management must do more than merely hang up a few tin boxes with a sign, "Suggestions Wanted." Considerable managerial thought and effort are essential to the operation of a satisfactory suggestion scheme.

1. Small concerns have found it best to conduct a contest for suggestions. The contest should start and end on definite dates. Announcements should state that rewards are given for each accepted suggestion and also prizes for the best of these suggestions. The disadvantage of this method is that awards cannot be made until all the suggestions have been considered; and many suggestions require considerable time for study and investigation.

2. Large concerns find it better to conduct extended campaigns and to award prizes at definite periods, or simply to pay for suggestions when they are accepted or put into effect.

3. It is well to obtain the cooperation and good will of the foremen and other executives. Many a department head considers an employee's suggestion for improvement as a reflection upon his ability. This really is not true, but foreman lethargy and company politics can be quite effective in throttling employees' suggestions. To overcome employees' fears, some companies request that all suggestions be submitted on a standard three-part form, each bearing the same number. The largest part of the form is reserved for the description of the suggestion; each of the two smaller parts is for the name of the employee and the number of the suggestion blank. When the suggestion form is submitted, it is first sent to one of the higher officials of the company, who tears off the parts which include the name of the employee, files one of these in a private safe, and sends the other to the employee, ac-

knowledging its receipt and expressing appreciation for the suggestion. The employee is also told when the suggestion will be given its first hearing by the committee in charge. By using this plan, the committee does not know the name of any of the suggestors, and therefore it will more easily avoid unfair personal influences.

4. The announcements and requests for suggestions should explain to the employees the specific kinds of suggestions that are desired. A mere invitation to employees to *think* does not stimulate them to think. The management that really wants employees to think should list and describe problems that are within the employees' areas of experience. Descriptions of specific plant problems can be posted on bulletin boards with an urgent request for suggested solutions. This kind of notice gets thoughtful attention, especially when diagrams, cost figures, and amounts of awards are stated.

One company increased its suggestions for reducing costs of paperwork by presenting questions like these to clerical employees:

Is any record or file you keep identical with another kept in your office?
Are there some files or records on which you never get calls?
Do you find some records unreliable, so that you have to use other sources?
Are you making too many copies of some records?
Do you know why you do each paperwork job? Does it help you in your duties? If you're not sure, have you asked your supervisor?

Employees usually find it easiest to think up ideas for improving operations involved in their own job because they are the only ones who can observe everything that happens in their operation during the working day.[10]

They can often make valuable suggestions for their improvement, however, especially when they are invited for their ideas about preventing machine breakdowns or damaged goods. Some companies even offer awards for the employee's statement of problems which he himself cannot solve.

5. When suggestions are considered by the appointed committee, complete records of proceedings should be kept in order that copies of the minutes and other records may be submitted to the management. Each item of business should have an identifying number; thus all activities of the committee can be traced. Monthly and annual reports can be made from the proceedings of the recorded meetings. These reports will be available for guidance in the elimination of duplicate suggestions. The foreman in charge of each department should be informed of all suggestions that are made by employees of his department, and he should be congratulated when his employees make good suggestions.

6. When a suggestion is rejected, the reason for the rejection should be explained in writing to the employee. A member of the suggestion committee should discuss the rejection personally with the employee in order that he may understand why the suggestion was not acceptable. Few things will cause a suggestion scheme to die more quickly than to ignore or to forget the employees who make the suggestions. An important factor in the rejection interview is the personality and the manner of the rejector. His manner may stimulate the employee to submit additional ideas or discourage him permanently.

7. The employee should have the right of appeal when his idea has been rejected. If he cannot be convinced that his idea is valueless, he should have the privilege of preparing new charts, drawings, or evidence of its worth.

8. The members of the awarding committees should include several employees. The employees then will know that they are represented in the determination of awards. If they are not thus represented, some of the employees may suspect the company of stealing their brilliant ideas.

9. The employees who make the best suggestions should receive publicity in the plant paper, on the bulletin board, or at a general meeting. A few firms give no financial reward for accepted ideas, but consider promotion, prestige, and personal pride a sufficient reward. Such a policy is often harmful, because it stimulates the sycophants rather than the more balanced personalities.

10. The awards or rewards should be commensurate with the value of the idea. If the company demands from each employee a waiver of rights for a patentable idea, the flow of suggestions is certain to decrease. If a suggestion has little cash value to the company, the reward may be modest, but not less than five dollars. The employee who is given too small a reward is likely to be teased by his fellow workers; for example, "Well, Bill, are you gonna buy a new house and car with that two dollars and a half you got for your bright idea?"

Mill and Factory recently surveyed 364 industrial firms representing a cross-section of American industry, and found that 46 per cent had employee suggestion programs and that 62 per cent of these paid workers for acceptable ideas. Thirty-five per cent solicit suggestions from rank-and-file workers, 4 per cent from supervisors only, and 61 per cent tap both groups. In 90 per cent of the cases the amount of the award is scaled according to the savings effected.[11]

A point which easily escapes employee attention is the company's lack of ability to pay off on imagination and ingenuity alone. Most improvements become valuable only by their cumulative impact on a large number of operations. This fact makes it necessary for managements to explain to employees the reasons for its system of awards.

The formulas used to calculate awards vary considerably. However, a study of fifty-three companies revealed definite relationships between award practices and the number of suggestions submitted:

1. The granting of low minimum awards, sometimes called token awards, such as some

companies offer for safety suggestions, tends to increase the total number of suggestions received.

2. The granting of even an occasional high award also tends to increase the number of suggestions received.

3. As the number of suggestions received increases, the acceptance rate tends to increase. (Part of the increase in the acceptance rate may be attributed to the granting of token minimum awards.)

4. As the number of suggestions received increases, the average award tends to decline. (Part of the decline may be attributed to the granting of token awards by companies receiving a larger number of suggestions.)

Sixty-five per cent of the concerns responding in this survey calculate the amount of the award on a percentage basis of savings to the company. Of interest is the fact that the firms using a net saving formula receive, on an average, 530 suggestions annually per 1,000 employees, whereas those employing a gross saving formula receive only an average of 250 suggestions per 1,000 employees.[12]

Suggestion systems, like all other group methods of influencing employees, depend for their success upon the alertness and ability of the management. One of the country's leading manufacturers of a highly technical product receives about forty suggestion letters a day. An expert examines each suggestion to determine whether it is of any possible value to the company. This company has found that it pays to examine one thousand ideas in order to find six that are definitely valuable and can be adopted with satisfactory results to the company. The management of this company, however, is "on its toes" in many respects, and its careful consideration of submitted ideas is simply one phase of an aggressive outlook.

Summary

Many formal methods of dealing with employee relations are available to management and employees. The extent to which various methods or plans are used and factors to consider in their use may be studied from reports published by scores of research organizations. Among the organizations that report valuable studies of industrial relations are the National Industrial Conference Board, Inc., The Brookings Institution, The American Management Association, and The Policyholders Service Bureau of the Metropolitan Life Insurance Company. Those who deal with employee relations should become acquainted with the publications of these and other sources of information, such as the current professional and business journals.

Studies of such publications indicate that industrial relations activities are a mark of alert management rather than of a desire to exploit workers. Intelligent managers wish to supply pleasant working conditions, vacations with pay, rest rooms, physical examinations, insurance, and pensions for employees. The money spent for such provisions is not necessarily taken out of the employees' pay envelopes. At least one study showed that the companies which engage in industrial relations activities pay higher wages, on the average, than companies which provide few activities such as bonuses, profit-sharing, vacations with pay, and group life insurance.[13] This study also indicated that a weak management cannot bolster itself by the use of welfare devices. On the other hand, the strong management tends to be intelligent in its employee relations as well as in its customer and financial relations.

Whenever industrial psychologists have studied methods of management, the usual result has been that the spirit back of the methods has been more important than the method itself. After all, we should expect this to be true. Employees are human beings. When owners and managers prefer to continue to operate their businesses in the old boss-subordinate manner, difficulties

The clubhouse that was never used. It was built by an employer for his employees, but they were not grateful for the gift, and objected to the club fee of one dollar a year. In time the employer demolished the entire clubhouse.

tend to develop, and owners may wonder whether they should quit entirely.

Generosity alone does not produce good employee relations

In 1910, a certain successful factory owner in a Wisconsin town decided that he would like to do something big and fine for his employees. He had become so wealthy that the making of money appeared to be rather easy. He had more or less "made his pile." After some consideration, he realized that the town offered his employees very little suitable recreation. Accordingly, he decided that he would build a beautiful clubhouse for the use of his employees—to show his gratitude to those who had helped him make his fortune.

He owned a valuable plot of land that was near the center of the town's business section and an ideal location for a clubhouse. He engaged architects, approved their plans, selected the materials, made contracts, and paid the costs of construction. In the course of construction, he told the employees about the recreation center that he was having built for them. When the building was completed but still unequipped, he announced the rules for the use of the clubhouse and stipulated that each employee should pay a

membership fee of one dollar each year as a partial payment of the cost of operating the clubhouse.

Some of the employees immediately criticized the "rich old man" for his gift. "Why doesn't he pay the cost of operation?" they said. When the employer learned of the attitude of his employees, he became discouraged by their lack of gratitude and announced that he would not give the clubhouse to them. He then offered the building, which could be used for a gymnasium, to the local high school on the condition that the community would raise ten thousand dollars to cover the cost of the equipment, which had not yet been installed. The high-school students were delighted at the prospect of receiving a much-needed gymnasium. The students were allowed thirty days in which to raise the money for the equipment. They solicited energetically during this time but were able to raise only about seven thousand dollars in subscriptions, and requested an extension of thirty days for additional soliciting. The students had encountered considerable difficulty in getting subscriptions because the "donor" of the clubhouse was not well liked by many of the well-to-do people of the town, and at the end of the sixty days of hard soliciting, they were still more than a thousand dollars short of the specified amount. They reported their failure to the philanthropist and tried to make a suitable "arrangement." But he was obdurate; he was through.

Some time later, workmen were hired to demolish the building. The building materials were sold or dumped into the river. In a short time, the excavation for the foundation was filled in, and sod was placed on the site. The beautiful new clubhouse was gone and the experience had cost the employer approximately one hundred and seventy thousand dollars!

This incident from American industry illustrates an old principle that many employers have had to learn through costly experience; namely, that *employees must be mentally prepared for the employer's well-meant human relations plans.* The employer cannot assume that his employees are thinking as he is thinking. All proposed plans for the improvement of employee relations must fit into the wishes, attitudes, and behavior patterns of the employees. The employer must develop a feeling of genuine colleagueship through employee participation in dealing with the problems of the business.

Acknowledgments and References

1. Roderic Olzendam, *The Importance of Personnel Administration to Public Relations,* Weyerhaeuser Timber Company.

2. For further information, see *Profit Sharing for Workers, Studies in Personnel Policy,* No. 97, National Industrial Conference Board, 1948.

3. For further information, see P. A. Knowlton, *Profit Sharing Patterns,* Profit Sharing Research Foundation, 1718 Sherman Avenue, Evanston, Illinois, 1954.

4. See *Monthly Letter,* First National City Bank, New York, July 1955, p. 76.

5. For further information, see *Business Week,* July 19, 1952, p. 176.

6. See "Stock Ownership Plans for Workers," *Studies in Personnel Policy, No. 132,* National Industrial Conference Board, 1953.

7. *Trusts and Estates,* January 1947. See also *The Management Review,* American Management Association, April 1949, p. 213.

8. See "Employee Savings and Investment Plans," *Studies in Personnel Policy, No. 133,* National Industrial Conference Board, 1953.

9. *Elliott Suggestion Service Monthly Bulletin,* Elliott Service Co., 30 North MacQuesten Parkway, Mount Vernon, N.Y., March 1955.

10. See "Getting Better Results from Your Suggestion Plan," *The Management Review,* American Management Association, July 1955.

11. *Mill and Factory,* September 1954. See also *The Management Review,* American Management Association, January 1955, p. 16.

12. A. W. Hendrickson and A. E. Heusser, *Factory Management and Maintenance,* May 1945.

13. *Industrial Relations Programs in Small Plants,* National Industrial Conference Board, Inc., New York, 1929, pp. 39 ff.

PROJECTS

1. Assume that you are the executive given the task of instituting a profit-sharing plan in your plant. What principles of worker psychology would you give special thought? How would you proceed?

2. Assume that you have been given the same kind of task for instituting an employee stock ownership plan. What factors would you consider in organizing the plan? In what

ways does the plan of procedure for instituting a stock ownership plan differ from that for a profit-sharing plan?

3. In what ways would you vitalize a suggestion system already functioning, theoretically at least, in an industrial plant? What would be your steps of procedure? State in one sentence the personnel psychology that you are employing in each step.

4. Compile a list of industrial relations services a company can give its employees at a nominal cost. Ask several workers to check those which they think they would like and those they would not care for. Do workers seem to agree as a whole or are individual differences pronounced?

5. Examine the magazines in your library and list those which have regular departments that treat industrial relations problems. Examples of such magazines are *Business Week, Dun's Review and Modern Industry,* and the *United States News and World Report.*

COLLATERAL READINGS

Blum, Milton L., *Industrial Psychology and Its Social Foundations*, Harper & Brothers, New York, 1949, Chapter 14.

How to Organize a Suggestion System, National Association of Suggestion Systems, Chicago.

Mills, C. Wright, *The New Men of Power*, Harcourt, Brace and Company, New York, 1948.

Seinworth, Herman W., *Getting Results from Suggestion Plans*, McGraw-Hill Book Company, Inc., New York, 1947.

Smith, Henry Clay, *Psychology of Industrial Behavior*, McGraw-Hill Book Company, Inc., New York, 1955, Chapter 11.

Suggestion Plans for Employees, Policyholders Service Bureau, Metropolitan Life Insurance Company, New York, 1948.

CHAPTER TWENTY-FIVE

Organized labor

American workers strike more often and lose more man-days of work than those of any other country. Of the 28 leading industrial nations in the free world, the United States, with only one-fourth of the number of workers, loses at least half of the number of man-days of work lost through strikes. In the last eight years, it has stood first five times in the number of man-days lost per thousand workers, and second three times.[1]

Labor unions have so many psychological aspects that any attempt to discuss them is likely to become a description of human nature itself. Examples of good and bad unionism are as plentiful as the examples of good and bad psychological adjustments by individuals. Some labor union leaders have been indicted and convicted of racketeering; others have made splendid contributions to human welfare.

Few workers join unions because of coercion. Generally, the things that workers want are not different from those to which employers, professional men, and everybody else aspires. Security, opportunity, an improved standard of living, and recognition are universal ambitions. The American labor movement has been motivated through lack of satisfaction of these ambitions, or because it was feared by the working man that once he achieved them, they could not be held.

Even the workers who will not join unions are not without desire for security, opportunity, an improved standard of living, and recognition. But they either have resigned themselves to the belief that these things are unattainable or have concluded that some other method for getting them is more feasible. These men believe that their employer's good will and good sense will provide as much security and recognition for them as they could get through the unions. They may prefer to rely on their own individual efforts; or they may feel that only far-reaching political and economic change could effect any real alteration in their circumstances.[2]

Furthermore, unions are joined because they render business services to employees. As stated by *Business Week:*

Unions exhibit a diversity of forms and functions, but fundamentally, they are all business organizations. They are established to provide a service and

495

they market that service to a special group of customers. The union enterprise is cooperatively owned by its members, and income of the enterprise is used primarily to extend the service it provides. Its slogans may be idealistic, and the preamble to its constitution visionary, but there is no "pie in the sky" utopianism about a union's routine or objectives.[3]

For collective bargaining between unions and management in most plants, large or small, the business agent of the national or international organization negotiates the contract. He renders a business service to the members. He works full time at this, negotiates day in and day out, and is usually of an alert, aggressive character. Business agents of this caliber receive salaries that compare favorably with the salaries of company executives.[4]

Insecurity as a motivating factor

The individual's need for security is recognized as a motivating influence in many industrial situations, particularly in partially explaining the typical union member's loyalty to his union during strike or stress periods. "Security" is a term of many meanings. As a motive, it may refer to the individual's persistent tendency to seek security because of insecurity developed during childhood as when, for example, his parents quarreled and his child world appeared to him to be terribly insecure. It may also refer to the adult's needs for social acceptance by peers such as his fellow workers.

An especially important manner in which the security motive functions in industry today grows out of the typical American worker's economic situation. Most workers make an income that is adequate for their needs *so long as they are employed.* If the income ceases, however, they are likely to be in difficulty in maintaining their standard of living or in meeting installment payments on the mortgage, automobile, appliances, or new furniture. Only a small percentage of salaried and wage-earner workers have fi-

nancial resources that would enable them to live for more than a few months in accordance with their established standard of living. The employer cannot, in many cases, be looked upon as a reliable source of steady income. His markets fluctuate because of conditions beyond his control. He must hire and discharge in accordance with his sales and financial resources. Since the employer cannot always be depended upon, the worker naturally turns to the union as a "service" which protects his work interests. The union rather than the employer becomes a symbol of security and in case of a conflict between the employer and the union, the worker typically remains loyal to the union. In spite of costly strikes, the union seems to offer more security than the employer.

Too many personnel people mistake this feeling of insecurity and the measures adopted by workers and their unions to offset it as merely an unreasonable attempt on the part of the workers to get "something for nothing." They should put themselves in the place of the worker confronted with this insecurity. If our workers trade their American heritage of individual freedom for the socialist mess of pottage, it will be because they are panicked into acceptance from a fear of unemployment with its breadlines, indignity to themselves and their families. Freedom becomes an empty and hollow-sounding word when it means merely freedom to starve or beg. Instead of opposing reasonable demands for and measures guaranteeing a maximum of security, management should exert every effort to give as much security as possible. Instead of instinctively and stubbornly opposing, for instance, the guaranteed annual wage, management should cooperate with its workers in studying the problem jointly to see whether or not it is possible in that particular industry and plant.

Management in the past has too often been put on the defensive by not anticipating legitimate demands of its workers. It has been made seemingly to oppose social progress by not cooperating with its workers in providing as much security as possible. It is put in a very bad light when unions make even very reasonable demands and companies fight them. Employers could win much good will if they seriously and earnestly backed and promoted measures which would give the worker greater security rather than be forced to do so by union leaders.[5]

To the worker, the labor movement is an instrument for enhancing the individual dignity of the man who works with his hands. When a worker's dignity is offended and when his human qualities fail to be recognized, then his resentment is likely to manifest itself in numerous, often irrational, complaints and grievances expressed through wildcat strikes, slowdowns, and other forms of hostility. The workers may hit at union leadership and management alike.[6]

The workers' participation in union affairs

Leonard R. Sayles and George Strauss have reported findings from a series of interviews with union members. They found that the members' participation in day-to-day union activities contrasted sharply with their loyalty to the union in strikes and in NLRB elections. Also, even though they exhibit strong loyalty toward their union as an institution they frequently criticize the union's officials.

The interviews indicated that the average member is convinced he needs his union for protection against arbitrary management action and for obtaining economic security. Union members expressed their need for the union: "Without a union we would be lost; the company could really take advantage of us." Members will endure privations to win strikes. The typical member will remain loyal during a strike even though he is subjected to tremendous pressures—seeing his children hungry, losing his wife's sympathy, and living with an openly hostile community.

At the same time that he demonstrates unswerving loyalty in regard to the union's economic functions, he is apathetic toward the union's internal activities. For example, attendance at regular meetings of large industrial unions averages 2 per cent to 8 per cent of the total membership, but attendance at meetings for a strike vote or contract ne-

gotiation ranges from 40 per cent to 80 per cent.

Many workers do not seek or accept union offices. Reasons given are "All those meetings to go to," "No time with the family," "Always some guy after something he doesn't deserve," and so on.

The average member apparently feels that no one would accept a union office unless he "can get something out of it for himself," either in terms of a better job, improved seniority position, helping out a friend, or in terms of personal power. Particularly in a larger plant, malicious rumors circulate from department to department to the effect that the union has "sold out" or that the officers are incompetent or greedy. . . .

This suspicion is accentuated by the fact that the ideology of a union is equalitarian. In most local meetings it is customary to refer to other members as "brother"; officers regularly use the term in everyday conversation. Nevertheless, the union in itself creates a hierarchy of officers, a system of inequality; so, in a sense, the officers are forced to violate their own moral code—and the rank and file are quick to seize on this as an opportunity to vent their own aggressions. Thus, one member said:

"Every time you elect someone, he stops being one of you and starts throwing his weight around. That's the way people are—but I wouldn't take a union office."

Such deep-felt attitudes cannot be hidden from the officers, who respond with feelings of martyrdom and self-importance. Their complaints often run in these terms:

"Look what I've done for the boys, all the help I've given them. I never get a cent of pay —I never get a word of thanks. After all I've done, I just don't understand how they can say things like that."

Indeed, we observed some executive board meetings which broke down into general "crying sessions"—the leaders exchanging stories about the rank-and-file abuse they had taken, talking about "protection" from it, and of course ending up by doing little or nothing about it. . . .

Normally rank-and-file members are not willing to devote much of their time to the union's internal political activities. This is in sharp contrast to the active members. For the inactive members, the union is a formal institution; for the active members it is an informal, social group as well—attending meetings, working on grievances together, and all the rest being important sources of nonmaterial satisfaction.

For a small group, the union is a way of life; for the majority, it is but a method of representation, although a very important one. For the leaders, the union has become an end in itself; for the rank and file, it is but a means to an end, a way of gaining greater security on the job, *not a great social movement.*[7]

The fact that a union gives its members certain business services partially explains why members do not leave a union even though they know that certain influential officers of the union may have had criminal records and are currently using for their own benefit funds that belong to the union treasury. Also, the fact that a worker joins a union does not mean that he is therefore anticompany. The employer may still be able to gain the good will and cooperation of many of his employees who belong to a union. In some cases, the union employees are "loyal" to the employer and the employer is "loyal" to the union.

Unions have also contributed toward easing some employers' burdens. For example, unions are likely to call the management's attention to rates of pay and other conditions that hinder production. Workmen are more apt to speak their minds freely when they know they have the union to defend their rights. Foremen of unionized plants also must improve their skills in handling their men. Foremen cannot take out grouches on men who are unionized. Recognition of the union tends to clear the atmosphere for the employees and enable them to express their grievances. On the other hand, many unions also act as a kind of wedge between the management and the men, thus preventing management and men from ever understanding each other or cooperating wholeheartedly.

Remsen J. Cole and Associates conducted a questionnaire among employees of a number of Philadelphia companies to find out whether employees are chiefly *for labor organizations* or merely *against management.* The results indicated that the workers probably were against management rather than for labor organizations.[8] This suggests that managements have a heavy psychological responsibility toward their employees.

Publications intended for management often emphasize strategies in dealing with union negotiations rather than techniques for bringing about constructive relations and understanding. Some of the more intelligent leaders in employee relations, however, appreciate their responsibility to workers and the community.

Fred Rudge, consultant in management-employee relations, has described management's failures and opportunities in published reports to industry. One of his reports is condensed as follows:

Most managements fail to see that the power behind the unions lies in the faith and support of its members. They do not see that these union members can, when sufficiently irate, demand an accounting of their leaders' actions or their union's activities on big economic issues.

Certainly, management has a good case of economics to present to the workers. But it does little or nothing to counteract union attacks on its policies. It does not clearly point out its many achievements. Worse, many managements do nothing to identify company interests with employee interests. It is only natural then that the worker will seek the "truth" from his union, which makes a conscious and strong effort to give him status.

Some of the more progressive companies have gone ahead and tried to work out some answers to these employer-employee misunderstandings.

Their findings point out the need for more studies to reveal the real issues, gripes and sources of dissatisfaction that harass the workers. They have discovered, also, the importance of more conferences participated in by all levels of management. Interest in these findings, of course, is the need for clear, well-established channels of communication between management and worker.[9]

In certain unionized industries, the unions have established impressive records of cooperation with managements. Some of the best examples of union-management cooperation have occurred where companies were faced with bankruptcy and unions were faced with loss of jobs. In addition to economic adversity, union recognition with a long history of collective bargaining, strength of the union, integrity of intelligent union officials, and genuine sympathy on the part of management have also been important factors in union-management cooperation.

Dual loyalties

In many cases, both company and union are in competition for the loyalties of the worker. Some people imagine that the worker's dual allegiance to company and union is impossible. In some companies, the workers are split into two sharply defined groups: one, pro-management and anti-union, the other, pro-union and anti-management.

Investigations indicate, however, that in a unionized plant both labor and management can have the allegiance of the worker. As long as these demands are not contradictory, the worker can live up to the expectations of both company and union. He can have dual allegiance and be thought of as loyal by both parties, for he is meeting their requirements.

Theodore V. Purcell conducted a study of a unionized Swift plant from 1949 to 1952 to find out whether the employees' attitudes were favorable or unfavorable toward the company and the union.[10] His findings show that most of the workers had a dual allegiance:

	Per cent
Unfavorable to both company and union ..	0.
Neutral to both	0.5
Favorable to one & unfavorable to other ..	13.
Favorable to one & neutral to other	13.
Positively favorable to both	73.
Stewards with dual allegiance	88.
Foremen with dual allegiance	57.

In general, the majority of workers in a company find that they can favor and support both the company and the union. They can do this in spite of the fact that they often disagree with spokesmen of both management and labor. The workers do not feel that conflict is inevitable, or that they must accept one group and reject the other. Many accept the state of dual allegiance.[11]

Some unions and companies have cooperated in developing programs of education for workers. Such attempts, when sincerely and objectively conducted, are likely to result in long-term improvements in industrial relations.

The few examples, so favorable to the unions, should not cause one to assume that strikes have been eliminated from industries which have had a long experience with unionism. Strikes continue with great frequency in some highly unionized industries.[12] However, the strike records of individual industries vary so greatly that the results of unionization in specific industries are likely to depend upon factors other than extensive unionism. Unionism may become popular in a specific industry because, for example, employees resent certain policies of a particular management. They may be reacting to emotional stress.

Why workers strike

When an industrial conflict reaches the strike stage, everyone loses, especially if the strike is one of long duration. The employer loses in sales and maintenance costs. The customers and stockholders lose. The employees, in particular, lose wages and savings that may require years of labor to recoup.

Labor union leaders claim that they do not want strikes and blame pigheaded industrialists for causing them. Industrialists claim that they do not want strikes and blame the irrationality of power-seeking union leaders. Both the labor leader and the industrialist claim that the other fears and hates him without just cause. Rumors and suspicions flourish. Grievances flare into strikes, slowdowns, and work stoppages.

Studies of groups under stress

The factors in industrial relations that lead to strikes are difficult to analyze scientifically because of the numerous influences and unrecognized variables at work. A strike does not occur because of a few influences. Only the precipitating influences are revealed by most investigations of strikes. The predisposing influences are usually overlooked. Group dynamics and the ways that people react to stress should be studied to discover more comprehensive factors than are revealed by the published reports of strikes. A riotous strike is an act of aggression under stress. A few significant studies have been made of the ways in which people tend to act under stress. For example, a study of lynchings indicated that when the price of cotton went down in fourteen states, the number of lynchings went up.[13] Race riots and similar forms of aggressive expression have been investigated and found to involve strong fears, frustrations, and stress.[14]

One of the best studies of group dynamics and reactions to stress under real-life conditions was made at the Colorado River Relocation Center at Poston, Arizona, during World War II. This was one of the ten relocation centers to which West Coast Japanese-Americans were removed for security reasons after the United States became involved in the war.

The research activity was jointly sponsored by the Navy, the Office of Indian Affairs, and the War Relocation Authority. Its purposes were to advise administrative officers at Poston and to make observations and analyses that might aid in the solution of other administrative problems elsewhere.

Under the guidance of the administration representing the U.S. Government, the evacuees set up their own community government and social structure, and established such public services as stores, schools,

Photograph, by courtesy of Scripps-Howard Newspapers

churches, police and fire departments, a judicial commission, and a newspaper. Thus, except for the fact that Poston's inhabitants were being more or less forcibly detained in the area, ordinary community and group interactions were simulated.

A comprehensive report of this outstanding study was written by Alexander H. Leighton, who listed the following specific types of stress as disturbing to the emotions and thoughts of the individual:

a. Threats to life and health;
b. Discomfort from pain, heat, cold, dampness, fatigue, and poor food;
c. Loss of means of subsistence, whether in the form of money, jobs, business or property;
d. Deprivation of sexual satisfaction;
e. Enforced idleness;
f. Restriction of movement;
g. Isolation;
h. Threats to children, family members, and friends;
i. Rejection, dislike, and ridicule from other people;
j. Capricious and unpredictable behavior on the part of those in authority upon whom one's welfare depends.[15]

Leighton has given many examples of the ways that people react to stress, exemplified by the members of Poston. A few of his findings are briefly summarized:

Cooperation, withdrawal, and aggressiveness are three universal kinds of behavior with which individuals react to authority when subjected to forces of stress that are disturbing to the emotions and thoughts of the individual.

These reactions are particularly common in minorities, and it is often possible "to divide a community roughly into three parts in terms of those who show predominately cooperation, withdrawal, or aggression in relation to the majority group." These divisions of reaction to stress may be counted upon in any subjugated people.

As has often been noted in life, it is aggressive action that gets results. For example, it was not the people who quietly accepted poor food in the relocation centers who secured its improvement, but those who aggressively went about trying to get better food, by writing to high officials.

Aggression, arising from disturbed emotions and thoughts, may stimulate the individual to take decisive actions that will free him from the forces causing the disturbed emotions and thoughts; and it may lead to confused and violent action, wholly inappropriate to the circumstances of the individual.

At first aggressive attitudes were not obvious, but gradually they came out into the open through complaints and demands, disregard of regulations, refusal to work, and so forth. These tendencies finally flowered into a strike.

Three factors "contributed to the rise of aggressive expressions and acts." The first: "A reduction in fear of the Administration and a realization that the aggressive individual could hide in the mass of the people who made up the Center. Another was the continuation without relief of most forms of stress, with an increase in some of them. The third was the fact that because of frustrations and uncertainties, attempts at cooperation continued to be more immediately punishing than rewarding in many instances."

Leighton states that coercion, if employed in sufficient strength, could have prevented some of the demonstrations of aggression, but that this would have retarded cooperation and so have been more costly. The aggressiveness that arose was controlled and directed so that much of it served a useful purpose, not only by altering conditions that gave rise to the gripes, but also by relieving emotional feelings about the conditions.

Some confused and ill-advised aggressions occurred, naturally, and these worsened conditions rather than bettered them. Examples: attacking each other, unreasonable demands, and delinquency.

A few of Leighton's recommendations to administrators and others who deal with people who react aggressively to stresses are the following:

1. In a disturbed community look for all the specific and all the general types of stress, not one or a few; note which are actually present and try to estimate their intensity.

2. Never underestimate the deleterious force of circumstances which foster repeated *frustration, incompatible desires* and *uncertainty.*

3. Never dismiss complaints as trivial; they may be only "gripes," but they may also be clear warnings of imminent trouble and one cannot tell which it is without investigation.

4. Keep in mind that the strength of an administration rests largely on its ability to meet the needs of people; that relief from the various types of stress comprises a major set of needs; and that complaints are clues to needs.

5. Bear in mind that all three of the principal social reactions of individuals to stress (cooperation, withdrawal and aggression), have both advantages, and disadvantages from the point of view of those in authority.

6. Cultivate cooperation, but not extremes of compliance and dependence; there are "yes-men" in all races and creeds and they are usually poor assistants.

7. Regard extremes of withdrawal, apathy, and indifference as bad signs, but accept mass inertia as characteristic of people and learn to rely on its stability.

Consider aggression as a human reaction to circumstances; not merely as innate cussedness or the work of evil men, or a racial peculiarity.

9. Recognize rumors, suspicions, scapegoat tendencies, gang activities, and crime increase as symptoms of aggression arising out of stress.

10. Try to guide and control aggression, but do not try to stamp it out; in most instances one cannot destroy it and even if he could, he would lose a force that might be of much value. It is the horse with spirit that is balking.

11. Remember that it is a common failing of adminstrators to refuse mild requests that they can and should grant, while yielding later to aggressive demand that forces itself on their attention; such behavior encourages the destructive aspects of aggression.

12. Capitalize on the feelings of relief and cooperativeness that are likely to occur after an outburst of aggression; do not set the clock back by an ill-placed act of punishment which rouses new aggressions and controls nothing.[16]

The investigator of strikes who will read Leighton's report will gain a better understanding of group dynamics that lead to strikes in industry.

Of course studies of violent aggressions that develop from frustration and fear do not reveal the basic causes of many strikes and labor union activities of today. Additional questions, such as the following, need to be asked:

1. To what extent are seekers of power in conflict? Either management or labor union leaders or both may be seeking greater economic power in order to maintain or to strengthen their position in the economic life. Sometimes the worker is exploited for the benefit of power-seekers, as reported by Arthur O. England on his return from a study of industrial relations practices in various Mid-West plants:

The average worker is a sympathetic sort of a fellow who is ruled generally by his emotions rather than by logical thinking and reasoning. Sometimes this sympathetic fellow gets taken for a ride. Surrounding us are people who desire power. Their desire for power is a personal one. We have seen how these power boys have "rifled" their way to the top. They may have to distort the facts a little. They may appeal to our needs, those needs reflecting our weaknesses, those areas where doubts can creep in.

These leaders are smart, for their own good, because they understand a fundamental fact about human nature. It's easier to make people unhappy than to make them happy. It's easier to put people on the defensive than to strengthen their prestige. It's like the old story about the mother trying to put her two children to bed. The vociferous neighbor brings them candy and tells them stories. "Why go to bed? Stay up and play like the rest of the kids. Here, have ten pieces of candy. Candy never hurt any youngster. Your mother," the intruder goes on, "must be an old witch to make you go to bed so early and not let you eat all the candy you want." Well? Our mother is truly put on the defensive now. How can she regain the respect and confidence she needs to rear her children properly? The American worker has been kept up long past his bed time. We can't blame him for being a sympathetic individual—that's a rather general American feeling—but he has been the subject of some pretty bad guidance. Too much candy and too little sleep have made a pretty sick fellow out of him.

It's easy to see why a successful concern has to stand for more than a square deal. In addition to its products it must also produce good citizens out of its employees.[17]

2. What stage has been reached in the development of employer-union relations? The life history of most old well-established employer-union relations usually has three stages: (*a*) The *organizational* stage, when the union tries to get a foothold in the company. The employer resists and the union intensifies the fight. The union leaders are of necessity very aggressive and belligerent; (*b*) The *cold neutrality* stage, when the union has won recognition and the employer acts in accordance with the requirements of the contract; (*c*) The *established* stage, when the union and the employer have learned to live and work together in a more or less cooperative manner. The leadership of the union has changed from the hard-boiled fighting variety to a more cooperative type. However, completely genuine cooperation between union and employer is rare, regardless of the stage of stability attained by the union.

An analysis of labor events today indicates that many unions are moving toward the third or established stage. One investigator believed that the following trends are discernible:

(1) a determination on the part of union organizations to participate more fully in the socioeconomic and political life of the country;

(2) unionized efforts to make the guaranteed annual wage a reality in the great industries;

(3) some union recognition of the fact that bigger production means more profits, and should portend a greater share of the returns from such production in form of higher wages and benefits. . . .

(4) the beginning of a trend toward the lessening of the social distinction existing between management and unions through the creation of better understanding between the leaders involved.[18]

These trends should be checked at intervals in the future to see if they continue or waver.

3. Are the labor union leaders trying merely to increase their share of the "economic pie," or are they trying to enlarge the pie? If the returns from a business enterprise may be considered a pie, there are two ways for a union to get more pie. One way is to fight for as big a piece as can be obtained. Another way is to increase the size of the pie through greater worker productivity. The former method is called collective bargaining; the latter, union-management cooperation. Economically, wage increases tend merely to distribute rather than create property.

Are the policies and practices of the union designed to make work and cause featherbedding in order to please members, or are they designed to stimulate members to produce more in a cooperative relationship?

4. Are conflicting ideologies influencing the employer-union relations? So many examples of such conflict have occurred in recent years that only one need be mentioned here. A comparative study was made of two Pacific Coast industries: the pulp and paper industry and stevedoring. These two industries had contrasting records. The former enjoyed industrial peace; the latter suffered from a continuous record of conflict. On the basis of his findings, the investigator of the two groups made several generalizations, one of which concerned ideology:

Where employers and union representatives hold irreconcilable differences in economic belief, and where the union representatives have not only been thoroughly indoctrinated with left wing philosophy, but where this philosophy has been the touchstone of union action, hope for enduring industrial peace is illusory, and conflict, whether open or concealed, pervades and dominates the employer-employee relationship.

Officers of the Longshoremen's Union have assumed since 1934 that the purpose of collective bargaining is not to establish a system of industrial jurisprudence, but rather that it is a device through which, under the cloak of an agreement, unremitting if undeclared warfare can be carried on against the employers. Since any procedure, no matter how devious, has been considered as legitimate under conditions of war, it was this philosophy which dominated the position of the union's representatives. They have looked on the employers not as a necessary and desirable component in a joint industrial effort, but as an inescapable evil. Co-operation and collaboration have been to them unthinkable and basically undesirable. Consequently, the written word, whether it be the language of a collective bargaining agreement or an arbitrator's award, was scrutinized with the objective of finding some way to torture its plain intent and meaning to the advantage of the union, rather than as a rule to be observed and followed. This is definitely the approach of the ideological unionist.[19]

5. Are the policies of the unions and of management based on a desire to strengthen the personality of the individual worker or merely to cater to his weaknesses? Labor unions, in addition to being service organizations are also political organizations. A union politician is, in effect, constantly running for office. Such an objective on his part will naturally cause him to cater to the weaknesses and prejudices of the workers. He will have little interest in policies that strengthen either the worker's personality or the company's economic position.

Achieving peace with the union

The National Planning Association made a seven-year study of labor-management relations under collective bargaining. The study was made in order to learn the reasons behind successful union relations among thirty companies of varied size and in different industries. The study indicated clearly that industrial peace benefits all concerned.

The report revealed no new or magic formula for achieving industrial peace. The investigations did indicate, however, that ". . . if they really try hard enough, management and unions—two historically hostile groups—can co-exist on a basis of reasonable equality in an enterprise, with each retaining its institutional sovereignty."

The main reasons for peaceful relations among the companies investigated are both procedural and psychological. The psycho-

logical similarities are difficult to define, but they are fundamental to good relations. For example, when feelings of "good will" and "mutual trust" were common to both sides, relations were better. And, when both sides acted with good will, they found it beneficial to their interests.

As for procedures, the study found that most successful collective bargaining sessions were carried on without the aid of lawyers or other outside agencies. If both sides have a mutual desire to reach agreement and both sides are frank, their negotiations are likely to be effective especially when the representatives of each group have the authority to make decisions on the spot.

To get labor and management cooperating together in a true spirit of collective bargaining requires more than a set of rules. But if the study proves anything, it is that industrial peace *can* be achieved.[20]

Conflicts between the company and the union can, to some extent, be anticipated. Saul Silverstein, President of the Rogers Corporation, a small manufacturer of paper and related items, decided to try a better way to bargain with his union. Instead of the usual once-a-year negotiating of the contract, the union and management meet once a month and negotiate piecemeal what needs negotiating. As Mr. Silverstein stated:

Long-term agreements can be merely a neat way for management to kid itself into thinking that it can escape continuous human contacts. If you insist upon living up to the letter of a contract with a customer or a supplier, regardless of changed conditions, you may put the customer out of business. Trying to put human relations on the shelf this way may put you out of business in terms of getting your money's worth out of workers living under long-term agreements.

Instead of putting on a show of many horrible scenes once each year, we work at it each month in our regular labor-management meetings. The minutes of these meetings are called "memoranda of understanding" and become, after ten months, the basis of the next annual agreement, to be worked out finally in the last two meetings. In effect, we write a 12-chapter book in single monthly installments.[21]

Of course there is no one cause or cure for labor conflict. The causes are many and the remedies vary with each situation. A common ingredient in those programs that have proved successful is a constructive attitude on the part of management. The importance of this factor has been described by a consulting psychologist on the basis of his experiences in industry:

A single minded concentration on things by management with less regard for humanitarian considerations has probably contributed largely to the industrial development of this country. . . . Whether the growth and increase in efficiency has also sometimes been at the cost of human well being is a debatable question. . . . The major problem facing industry if it is to enjoy labor peace and the benefits of good employee morale is a twofold one: First, it must stimulate a higher degree of empathy in its supervisors and executives to improve their immediate handling of their inter-personal relationships. Secondly, it must arouse management to a clearer awareness of the part that its own attitudes play in clouding and biasing its analysis of the labor relations problems with which it is faced.

To achieve this, it must recognize that the initiative for improvement in this area must come principally from management itself, first because empathy is one of the prime requisites for success as a supervisor or executive, and secondly, because neither the mass of workers nor their union representatives generally have any reason to be aware that there may be an element of the illogic in their attitudes and beliefs.

The key to the resolution of these attitudinal conflicts lies, therefore, in the ability and willingness of those who determine company policy to try objectively and without passion to see both sides of the problem which faces them. Initiative must come from management, for only management is in a position to correct many of the conditions which create or aggravate employee ill-will and feed the fires of their hostility toward itself and what it stands for. . . .

The need for empathy must be of constant concern to management at all levels. Top management must look at itself objectively and appraise its own capacity for empathy.[22]

Some employers are honestly trying to build more responsibility and maturity among the union representatives with whom they deal. Methods used are the following:

First, the employer gives full recognition to the union's collective bargaining status. He wants the union to know that he fully accepts the union as the spokesman and voice of the employees on matters of wages, hours, and working conditions.

Second, the employer does not compete with the union for the loyalty of its employees. As previously stated, employees can be loyal to both the employer and the union for certain relationships.

Third, the employer separates the areas of conflict from the many nonconflicting interests between management and labor. In some relationships such as contract negotiations, grievance procedure, and arbitration, the interests of the company and the union are frequently at cross purposes. In others, there is little or no conflict of interests as in suggestion committees, safety programs, good housekeeping, social and sports activities, annual picnics, and open-house affairs.

Fourth, the employer works with rather than around the union in the field of employee communications. He does not try to out-maneuver the union in getting a message across to employees. He works out with the union an agreement on channels of communication.

Fifth, he recognizes that the union is a political organization and that at times union officials will do certain things simply because it is politically expedient for them.

Sixth, he is firm when necessary. Most unions have far more respect for a company that has analyzed the facts, has all the pertinent information at hand, and will say when the time comes, "Based on all the facts, this, gentlemen, is the best we can do." Until management reaches the point where the union knows that management means just exactly what it says, the union cannot be blamed for trying to put on one more bite and then another and another.[23]

Many employers assume that unions are here to stay and that their objective should be to maintain a balance of power as has been stated by one experienced investigator:

We must face the fact that labor peace in the sense of absolute freedom from conflict is neither possible nor desirable. The answer lies in keeping the conflict within reasonable bounds. This is best accomplished by maintaining a balance of power between management and the union. This can be done if the business is headed by strong and emotionally healthy men who are capable of participative leadership. If any lesson stands out from the experience of the last 50 years, it is that labor problems require the same executive strength and competence as do all other aspects of the business, and are not susceptible to any special "quick tricks" or "gimmicks."[24]

Acknowledgments and References

1. Sidney Lens in *Harvard Business Review*, March–April, 1956.

2. For further information see "Management Looks at the Labor Problem," *Business Week*, Sept. 26, 1952, p. 70.

3. *Loc. cit.*

4. For further information, see *The Management Review*, American Management Association, January 1955, p. 61.

5. Father Edward S. Keller, CSC., "What Makes People Do the Things They Do?" *Personnel Series, No. 155*, American Management Association, 1954, p. 43.

6. See William C. Menninger and Harry Levinson in *Personnel*, American Management Association, September 1955, p. 96.

7. Leonard R. Sayles and George Strauss, "What the Worker Really Thinks of His Union," *Harvard Business Review*, May–June 1953.

8. From "Employee-Employer Relations," a survey of employee opinions conducted in Philadelphia by Remsen J. Cole and Associates, 1940.

9. Fred Rudge, *Management and People*, February 1949.

10. Theodore V. Purcell, "Dual Allegiance to Company and Union—Packinghouse Workers. A Swift–UPWA Study in a Crisis Situation, 1949–1952," *Personnel Psychology*, Spring 1954.

11. See Ross Stagner, "Dual Allegiance as a Problem in Modern Society," *Personnel Psychology*, Spring 1954.

12. John I. Griffin, "Conclusions from Strikes—A Study in Quantitative Economics," *Studies in History, Economics, and Public Law, No. 451*, Columbia University Press, New York, 1939.

13. John Dollard *et al.*, *Frustration and Aggression*, Yale University Press, New Haven, 1943.

14. Alfred McClung Lee and Norman Daymond Humphrey, *Race Riot*, Dryden Press, Inc., New York, 1943.

15. This material is condensed from *The Governing of Man*, by Alexander H. Leighton, Princeton University Press, Princeton, N.J., 1945.

16. *Loc. cit.*

17. Arthur O. England, "An Evaluation of the Personnel Practices in Midwest Plants," *Industrial Relations*, April 1947, p. 37.

18. Melvin J. Vincent, "Labor Under Review: 1953," *Sociology and Social Research*, July–August 1954.

19. Paul Eliel, "Industrial Peace and Conflict: A Study of Two Pacific Coast Industries," *Industrial and Labor Relations Review*, Vol. 2, No. 4 (July 1949), pp. 495–496.

20. For further information, see "The Difference That Isn't There," *Business Week*, Jan. 9, 1954.

21. Lawrence Stessin, "Labor Relations, Bargaining on the Installment Plan," *Forbes Magazine*, August 1, 1954.

22. Robert N. McMurry, "Empathy: Management's Greatest Need," *Advanced Management*, July 1953, pp. 6–11.

23. Adapted from an address by Herbert O. Eby (Labor Relations Director, Pittsburgh Plate Glass Co.) before the California Personnel Management Association. See *The Management Review*, January 1955, p. 38.

24. Robert N. McMurry, "War and Peace in Labor Relations," *Harvard Business Review*, November–December 1955.

PROJECTS

1. Collect newspaper accounts of recent strikes and list the grievances and demands of the strikers. Analyze them. What additional factors of importance did you note?

2. Obtain reports from several magazines concerning one important strike. Compare the several reports for bias. After reading the reports, write your own summary of the issues involved in the strike. Show your summary to several critics, asking them whether they detect indications of bias in your summary.

3. Obtain the copies of official publications of several unions. How do they differ from employee magazines published by employers?

4. Interview some ardent labor union members who are quite vocal in expressing their advocacy of unionism. What adjustment influences, Chapters 2–6, do you detect in their motivation?

COLLATERAL READINGS

Blum, Milton L., *Industrial Psychology and Its Social Foundations,* Harper & Brothers, New York, 1949, Chapter 14.

Harrell, Thomas Willard, *Industrial Psychology,* Rinehart & Company, Inc., New York, 1949, Chapter 15.

Kornhauser, Arthur, Robert Dubin and Arthur M. Ross, *Industrial Conflict,* McGraw-Hill Book Company, Inc., New York, 1954.

Smith, Henry Clay, *Psychology of Industrial Behavior,* McGraw-Hill Book Company, Inc., New York, 1955, Chapter 12.

Stagner, Ross, *The Psychology of Industrial Conflict,* John Wiley and Sons, Inc., New York, 1956, Chapters 11–15.

CHAPTER TWENTY-SIX

Significant trends and cross currents for leadership in industrial relations

One of the defects of the intellectualist conception of progress is its assumption that social change has always been uniform and rectilinear. If we accepted this mode of thought, we should have to doubt whether there has been such a thing as general progress. The line of social movement has been, on the contrary, uneven, jerky, mixed. Few movements have been uniform, and none has been universal in time or place. The human world in its total history and in any particular age or country has exhibited such spasmodic variations and such endless contradictions that almost any general assertion about it can be controverted by specific evidence. Man's experience is like the life of a forest, where all the processes of birth, growth, decay, and death are going on at once. Every age shows highly developed societies and institutions existing alongside of some that are just emerging and others that are passing into oblivion. Within any complex group will be found classes of every type, the extremes being as alien in character as if they belonged to different periods or remote regions.[1]

The study of human relations in industry involves vastly more than observations about the in-plant conditions. The dynamic social and economic forces of the outside community and the world beyond cannot be walled off from the employees within.

The need for a broad frame of reference

The influences among employees at work within a plant are likely to be closely related to outside movements, such as the battle for power on the part of those having opposing political ideologies. Employees in a plant may be pawns or active participants in conflicts between leaders of opposing forces in their drives for greater power in the control of industry. Leaders in several fields are constantly advancing claims that their programs would enhance the well-being of employees and other members of the public.

508

Unfortunately, the relations between the in-plant and the outside social and political movements are seldom given more than casual attention by personnel executives and other members of managements. They limit their investigations to such areas as those of the typical morale survey which deals with working conditions, wages, supervision, and recreation within the plant. Questions are seldom asked about the outside social and political processes and pressures that affect the employee. One reason, of course, for omitting such questions is the fact that American business executives recognize that the employee's political, economic, and religious ideas are under his own control and that the employer should not inquire about them.

And yet as Kornhauser has ably stated:

. . . the investigator can understand and interpret the local morale picture only if he is fully alive to the vastly significant influences which lie entirely outside the company—social and economic conditions in the community and in the world at large. In truth, the specific morale situation can be genuinely understood only if it is seen against the whole background of modern industrial developments and current social disorganization.* The unrest of sweepers in the punch press department is in no small measure the unrest of men and women everywhere in the present-day world. Generalizations about the importance or unimportance of wages, or advancement, or job security, or personal treatment, are shallow and misleading except as they reflect an appreciation of the social-historical changes affecting industry and working people. What do men desire and expect of life in our democracy—and at particular times and places and in particular socio-economic situations—and how far do their desires meet with gratifications or deprivations, and what substitute and balancing satisfactions are provided? The investigator must ask himself questions as broad as these if he is to move toward true and meaningful answers to the specific problems of interpreting morale and unrest in particular worker groups. . . .

. . . valid conclusions in this matter are like complex clinical judgments, aided by whatever scientific evidence is turned up, but necessarily reaching far beyond such data. In the forming of these complex judgments, conceptual guideposts are sorely needed—psychological formulations about motivations and adjustments which will serve to organize thought and inquiry. The development and improvement of these interpretative constructions, through industrial studies as well as by all other means, may prove to be the most valuable contribution psychologists can make in this field. Even in practical research for management purposes, evidence bearing on the complex social-psychological dynamics of the employment relations may provide more important and more enlightening guidance than conclusions about the relative importance of specific factors like wages or supervision. These latter conclusions are inevitably grave oversimplications which are as often misleading as helpful.[2]

Kornhauser concludes that morale surveys as now conducted are too remote from the "larger context of big business, big unions, and their struggles for security, power and advantage. Cooperation and participation may appear to be neat solutions while employees are weak and leaderless—or when the employer is the underdog; glowing conclusions, however, had better be postponed until the implications are examined under more typical circumstances and over longer periods. We can be seriously misled by especially favorable 'pretty' cases."

Other social scientists and philosophers who view the current scene have stressed the need for a study of the broad background of industrial relations. One, for example, who has been active in promoting better industrial relations in this country, stated:

I am going to suggest that the problem of industrial relations must be seen against a larger background than is generally the case. I am going to suggest that it cannot be understood, much less satisfactorily solved, apart from the larger problem of our modern economic system, which in turn is only part of the still larger problem of contemporary civilization. If we are living through one of those great cataclysms in his-

---

* This approach is well represented in Elton Mayo, *The Human Problems of an Industrial Civilization,* The Macmillan Company, New York, 1933. See also G. Briefs, *The Proletariat: A Challenge to Western Civilization,* McGraw-Hill Book Company, Inc., New York, 1937.

A six-year-old gets a look into the future as he peers at the model of the atomic reactor that will power the nuclear power plant General Electric Company will build in the Chicago area for Commonwealth Edison Company. —Photograph Courtesy of the General Electric Company.

A version of the Telkes solar oven was built by Stanford Research Institute after a design by and under the supervision of Dr. Maria Telkes (center of group) of New York University's College of Engineering and consultant on solar energy research to SRI. The cooker was designed to provide experimental low-cost cooking facilities for locations where fuel is scarce. The solar cooker reaches and maintains temperatures up to 400° F and can be used for practical cooking purposes on days of strong sunlight. —Courtesy of Stanford Research Institute, Menlo Park, California.

The product potential of atomic fission and the use of solar radiation is enormous. Automation will help us to put these potentials into products and services that benefit all people. This new technology will, of course, have some important psychological impacts that merit study.

tory which signify the end of one historical epoch and the beginning of another, as a good many thoughtful people believe, then it would be foolish to separate the problem of industrial relations from the other problems of which it is a part, and attempt to solve it in splendid isolation.[3]

TRENDS TO BE OBSERVED IN INDUSTRY

At the turn of the twentieth century, the village carpenter might build an entire house. If he wished, he could also build the furniture and all the equipment in the home, with the exception of items such as the metal products for heating. Since that time, hundreds of companies and thousands of workers are now involved in what was formerly a one-man job. Since each of these can spe-

cialize on a single product or activity, there can be greater proficiency and hence a lower cost for the ultimate consumer. As a result, the carpenter's grandchildren of today have a much higher standard of living, shorter hours of work, and better education.

In the first half of the twentieth century, America developed the greatest industrial age that the world has ever known. Our technology was applied to making and selling more products, better products, products at lower prices, and to giving the customer some value that he wanted. Technology, efficiently utilized by modern management, made possible much greater production with fewer workers.

What are the most likely influences and the directions in the technology of the second half of this century? How will human beings be affected? Answers to questions such as these can be deduced from sciences and from the influences that already affect us. One of these sciences is cybernetics.

Cybernetics is the scientific study of those methods of control and communication which are common to living organisms and machines, especially as applied to the analysis of operations of machines such as digital and other computers, the so-called "brain machines." Cybernetics is derived from a Greek word meaning "steersman."

We have read about guided missiles that automatically make adjustments for variations in the speed of the projectile, wind direction, wind resistance, temperature and, most important of all, *select* the target that is to be hit! We have read about electronic "brain systems," located in a building in New York City, that, even though they are a thousand miles away from a pipeline, automatically open and close valves of the pipes that transport 26 different products which are drawn from storage plants along the pipeline, hundreds of miles in length.

Cybernetics as a science is likely to have a greater effect on our lives during the next 50 years than will the physics that may eventually give us ample and cheap atomic energy. Thus far, cybernetics has had its most prominent applications to the development of computing machines that reel off in 4 hours a 7-day job of preparing a payroll, or do a 3-week production-planning chore in 20 minutes. Everyone who reads newspapers and magazines has learned of machines that can multiply 42 nineteen-digit numbers per second. We have heard about Univac, the Remington Rand, Manchly Division, electronic computer, which among other things enables statisticians to forecast in a few seconds the results of voting in national elections—computations that formerly required many hours. Computations such as these, useful as they may be for actual work, inventory control, production, and marketing, have a significance far greater

than computational only. When a computing machine, capable of making lightning calculations, is teamed up with a feedback system that monitors an automatic process, the potentials for future production and our living standards become vast indeed. They bring about a new kind of automation in industry.

Automation in industry means automatic handling of materials and parts as they go through the production process. To some extent, automation has been used in industry for many years. The current development of this trend, however, which makes use of feedback or self-correcting controls, is a new kind of technology for production.

In the old technology, machines in factories were arranged in an order that would give continuous operation. Machines were used that performed several operations in accordance with a predetermined set of controls. The machines had no "brains" in the sense that they could "store" data and use them later in making computations and "decisions." In the new automation, machines not only perform a sequence of logical operations but they also correct errors that occur in the course of their own operations, and they can choose, according to built-in criteria, between several predetermined plans of action. The idea of feedback is further explained by the following quotation:

But in the long run the new technology of the electronics engineer will have a far greater effect on machine-tool design and on the construction of plant and equipment, and thus a far greater meaning for the businessman, than any of the more spectacular mechanized operations that have so far been installed in our plants and offices. In that fact lies the real significance of automation.

Since the concept of feedback, which lies at the heart of the new technology, is so important, businessmen need to understand it.

Actually the concept is quite simple. In systems employing the feedback principle, the operation of the control device is a function of actual performance rather than of expected performance. For example, if a machining time of 2½ minutes does not produce the desired result, a machine making use of feedback control can automatically allow more turning time rather than stop after a predetermined cycling time.

When such feedback devices are tied together—in what is often called a servomechanism—the result is a closed-loop system of controls. Thus, although certain forms of automatic operation are possible without making use of the feedback concept, it is feedback that makes it possible to construct a complex machine that is self-correcting.

It was the military demands of World War II that gave the greatest impetus to the use of the feedback concept to make closed-loop control systems, as well as to the development of the high-speed computing devices. The speed and maneuverability of aircraft made traditional gunlaying techniques obsolete. In order to meet the pressing military requirements, highly trained scientists went to work on the problem of designing and constructing automatic position-control systems. Out of this work came not only our modern gun directors but a substantial body of new technical knowledge. And on the basis of this knowledge electronic control systems can now be devised for the performance of a great variety of industrial tasks.

That these advances would have considerable industrial importance was recognized from the beginning by virtually everyone familiar with the military's work in this field. But neither the potential benefits nor the problems involved in achieving them have been made clear to the businessman. In fact, from the businessman's point of view, exactly the wrong things have been emphasized.[4]

The theory of feedback came from observations of human beings and animals. The living body makes compensations or corrections in movements in any activity from catching a ball to driving an automobile. That these same adjustments can be built into machines was demonstrated by James Watt's flyball governor, in which over-speeding is translated by means of centrifugal force into a retarding effect upon the throttle of the machine. One writer has said: "The first Industrial Revolution substituted the machine for the common functions of the human arm. The second Industrial Revolution will substitute the machine for the common functions of the human mind."

Instruments for automatic controls and

corrections are coming into use throughout industry. Automation is growing by leaps and bounds. In the 15 years after 1939, industry's spending on instruments expanded twice as fast as on other capital investment. At that time, 5 per cent of the nation's plants were involved in instrumentation programs; 15 years later, about 20 per cent of plants were involved in various kinds of instrumentation projects. As early as 1953, the Ford Motor Company had made a 24-minute motion picture on automation and its beneficent effects on workers.

To many workers who do not understand its potential benefits, "automation" suggests a new kind of machines, quite different from those of the past and so superior to man himself that, ultimately, they may rise like Frankenstein's monster to destroy us all. The word alone is enough to conjure up visions of a wholly automatic factory where machines with superbrains will grind out products 168 hours a week, without any human makers or attendants whatever!

Automation has become a kind of modern bogey-man that frightens many uninformed workers. The Public Opinion Index, for example, took a poll among more than a thousand factory workers, and asked them two questions: First, did they favor the use of new and "improved" machines? They did, by about three to one. Then they were asked how they felt about more automation. They opposed that, three to two![5]

Actually, automation is only another step in the man's quest for a richer, fuller life. Experience shows that only through the widest possible use of new and better machines can we hope to achieve the fullest measure of employment and an ever improving standard of living. This improved standard of living has taken place in our foods as well as in our gadgets as indicated by a recent United States Department of Agriculture report:

Consumers spent an average of $406 per person for food in 1955. . . . This represented 25 per cent of disposable income. However, the same quantity and types of food and services as those purchased during the prewar 1935–39 period would have cost only $266, or 16 per cent of consumer income. Consumers bought more food, more expensive food, more meals in restaurants, and more of other marketing services than in the prewar period.[6]

The effect of automation on the total number employed

Obviously, any improvement in production techniques is bound to cause dislocations for workers. They must have to change from one job to another, sometimes from one location to another. But when we consider the picture as a whole, we note that from 1939 through 1953, the population in the United States increased 22 per cent. The total number of jobs, however, grew by 35 per cent. In the field of manufacturing itself, where automation has advanced most rapidly, employment went up 73 per cent, or more than three times as fast as the population. Production of the new automatic machines is, itself, an expanding industry, employing many more people than in 1939.

One outstanding example of automation that we have seen in our lifetime is the dial telephone. We would naturally assume that it must have thrown thousands of telephone operators out of work; and some of the current propaganda on the subject would seem to confirm that assumption. Yet the latest Federal census, taken in 1950, showed that the number of telephone operators in this country had increased by 79 per cent in the previous ten years. And still the telephone companies keep on advertising for more employees.

Effect of automation on the type of employment

One of the major criticisms of modern mass production techniques is their effects on the assembly line worker. The typical assembly line is characterized as robbing the worker of pride in his work and weighing him down with frustrations.

A Yale Technology Project, for example, undertook to study the relationship between technology and human relations in a few industrial plants in the United States, with particular reference to attitudes and behavior of workers in mass-production industries. For years, there has been a great deal of speculation about the effects of highly repetitive and routinized tasks on workers. Robert H. Guest, Institute of Human Relations, Yale University, has described the findings, in part, as follows:

> Of all occupations in modern industry none has aroused such controversial comment as has that of the assembly worker, and especially the auto assembly worker on the "final line." The extraordinary ingenuity that has gone into the construction of automobile assembly lines, their perfected synchronization, the "all but human" or "more than human" character of the machines, the miracle of a car rolling off the conveyor each minute under its own power—all this has caught and held the world's imagination for a quarter of a century. On the other hand, the extreme subdivision of labor (the man who puts a nut on a bolt is the symbol) conjoined with the "endlessly moving belt" has made the assembly line the classic symbol of the subjection of man to the machine in our industrial age.[7]

The number of Americans who work on a typical assembly line is difficult to estimate. One investigator, however, analyzed the available statistics and estimated the number as three million or one out of twenty-one members of our total labor force.

> These three million workers represent a great diversity of people, including happy workmen. They include very few robots, for the machine by its very nature demands a multiplication of skills.
>
> The three million figure covers both workers on the assembly lines and all other mass production jobs where the work tends to be repetitive and broken down into simple, constituent motions. It includes many a worker, like the repair man on the auto assembly lines, who is a proud and highly skilled technician, and the utility man who fills in at so many spots and seldom does the same job two days running.
>
> It includes some who work alone and more

AUTOMATION   CREATES   JOBS

There is new and reassuring information for those who fear that "automation"—the control of machines by machines—will mean fewer job opportunities. It comes from a special survey of 1,574 companies in metalworking industries recently completed by **American Machinist**, a McGraw-Hill publication. More than one-fifth of the companies reported that they already have automatic loading, transfer or assembly machinery in operation. In these companies as a whole there has been a net increase in total employment since this machinery was installed.

According to the **American Machinist** survey, of these companies with actual experience in automation

> 26% reported increases in employment averaging 21%
>
> 51% reported no change in total employment
>
> 23% reported decreases in employment averaging 16%

More Jobs for the Skilled

Of greater significance, however, is the response by 40% of these companies that they required more skilled maintenance men and by 21% of the companies that they had increased their engineering staffs. This indicates that automation is strengthening a trend already evident in the United States, a trend of expanding opportunity for those with industrial and professional skills and, relatively, of contracting opportunity for the unskilled.

The following chart shows how strong this trend has been over the past 25 years and how strong it may be expected to be over the next 15 years.

There has been a sharp decline in the percentage of unskilled workers in the nation's

—From the Department of Economics, McGraw-Hill Publishing Company, Inc.

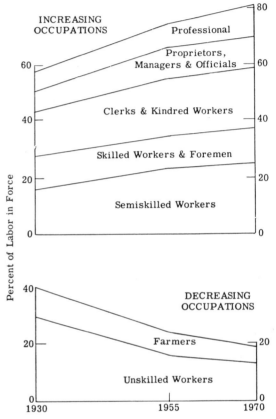

labor force and a corresponding increase in the percentage of those with varying degrees of skill.

It is possible, of course, to cite cases of individuals and groups that do not conform to the charted trends. Farmers, for example, are becoming at the same time more skilled and less numerous. But this does not upset the broad proposition that opportunities are increasing for those who have skills.

Power and Production

Much of the basic explanation for the relative expansion of opportunities for those with industrial and professional skills lies in the increasing use of power-driven machin-

FOR WORKERS WITH SKILLS

	1930	1955	1970
Electrical energy (billion kwh)	52	212	400
Industrial production (1947-49 = 100)	49	135	203
Production manhours (billions)	16.1	27	28.4

*Excludes power used in aluminum and magnesium reduction, both very heavy power users.

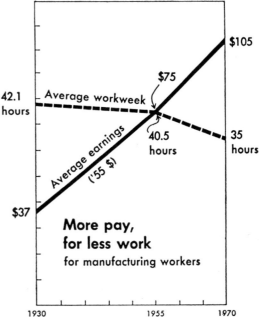

More pay, for less work for manufacturing workers

ery. This has made possible a vastly greater increase in manufacturing production than in the manhours of human labor devoted to it. The [above] chart shows the relative increases in electrical energy and manhours of labor used in manufacturing since 1930 and the rise in industrial production.

Power-driven machines have reduced the amount of human energy required for physical labor, but they have increased the need for skillful handling and maintenance. As the **American Machinist** survey demonstrates, the same is true of automatically controlled machinery.

Higher Wages, More Leisure

The rising average wage of American industrial workers and the decline in hours per week that they must work reflect directly the extent to which the increase in industrial production has outstripped the manhours devoted to it. The final chart shows the increase in weekly wages (in dollars of constant purchasing power) and the decrease in the average workweek in manufacturing since 1930. It also shows the changes that may come in the next 15 years if present trends continue.

There are some who would slow what an earlier editorial in this series characterized as "the continuing process of taking dull and laborious work off the backs and minds of men and transferring it to machines operating in large batteries under automatic control." In doing so they might make the world safer for those with no skill. The far more constructive course is to welcome the expanding opportunities now being provided and be sure that the nation's young people, who are now starting another school year, are prepared to take advantage of them.

who work in teams and talk "all the time and have a lot of fun," as a fellow in Plant X observed. It includes another man at the same Plant X who explained, "I like the routine. You get in the swing of it."[8]

Despite the fact that certain workers appear to like assembly line work, we must recognize that many psychological problems arise from its use in industry. Thus far, no easy answers have been found. Fortunately, however, some investigators who have studied the probable long-term effects of automation think that automation will gradually eliminate the need for, or at least decrease the number of, assembly line workers.

Until recently, the speed of the machine operator limited the speed of production. Now, by means of automation, we have eliminated the operator and the only limit on speed of production becomes the machine itself.

With automation, more and more workers are employed outside the production process. They are maintenance men, salesmen to sell and distribute finished products, and market researchers to think up new things for the machines to make. Few wield tools or operate machines. They rarely touch the product itself.

Demands that technological changes are about to make on business managers

The new technology requires a tremendous increase in the number of trained and educated people in business. In the past, we attempted to multiply first man's physical strength and then his skill. Now we are augmenting man's control over his economic environment by means of machines that multiply his mind-power.

The highly trained, highly educated employees whom we shall need increasingly in the business world will have to work by using their own judgment and their own knowledge. They must be able to live and work in a psychological climate where they give their best voluntarily. They must be

guided by objectives and leadership which they understand and accept. Thus, the new technology involves new basic understanding and competence in the management of working people. Employment, of course, will have to be made as stable as possible.

The new technology necessitates the making of decisions for longer futures than the ones for which we have to make plans and decisions now. Hence, management men will need much better methods for making long-range decisions than we now possess. Our tools of economic analysis will have to go beyond the attempt to read the business cycle to which so many managers and economists confine themselves today.

Obviously, the needs for developing men for management will become even greater than now.[9]

Individuals in a plant, because they will be few in number but important in function, will gain new status.

In the future, because there will be fewer workers, companies will be able to provide more benefits, give employees individual attention, understand their problems more fully than is possible now. But unlike today, it won't take large staffs to accomplish it.

Progress. This will do much toward bringing about the talked of, but little realized, democratic industrial society. Workers will be more highly trained and educated. Their knowledge of industrial processes will be broader.

On the other side of the coin, however, because workers will be more skilled, they will demand more information. At Monsanto Chemical Co.'s plastics division in Springfield, Mass., for instance, management constantly finds in its surveys that the group that insists it isn't being told enough by plant officials is the highly skilled work force. It isn't because these people aren't given the same information as other workers, but because they are more interested in all phases of the business.

In the light of all this, what can we tell about the sort of manager that tomorrow's industry will require?

Many look upon the advance of technology as reason to assume the engineers and technical people will take over at the top. But the reverse is probably more likely to occur. Technicians there will have to be, but the top managers will have to know less about technology—depending

Sacred or Scared?

—by F. F. Bradshaw. Reprinted by permission from **Advanced Management**, Society for the Advancement of Management, Inc., October 1955.

It took man approximately 2,000,000 years to really begin using fire—20,000 to begin firing-up the steam engine—200 years more to build the modern factory—20 years to get fission, fusion, electronics and computers—and a second industrial revolution! Thus does the rate of technological change accelerate by geometrical ratio. When a people's social progress falls behind the progress in technology, the results make history.

The European with geometry and firearms put the Indian with arithmetic and bow and arrow on the reservation. Today Indians learn geometry and calculus but too late to recapture their continent. Until the old generations died out (or were killed off) they could not master the new technologies.

In 1905 over 250,000 young Chinese took the annual examination for government positions. The exams consisted in reciting verbatim the eleven "Sacred Classics" of Chinese literature (some several thousand years old) and writing "original" poems not distinguishable in form or content from those in the classics. Thus were chosen the government executives to manage China in a twentieth century world. This "management development" plan was followed by revolution, beheadings, collapse, torture, firing squads, and "brainwashings."

Thus does history punish a social leadership when education "preserves" a culture instead of "managing" power. This mid-century is another historic testing time for social leadership of our age.

Today in America we are dedicated to freedom. Freedom means decentralization of authority so that individuals, companies, and communities can exercise initiative, make choices and be the source of their own activity. This decentralization of initiative requires decentralizing wisdom and technical know-how. Unless individuals, companies, and communities understand the modern tools and processes they are as helpless today as were the Indians who faced our ancestors with bow and arrow. They are as doomed in the days ahead as was the Chinese student of the Classics that were no longer "sacred."

Technological change can transform classics from *sacred* to *scared*. In this dynamic—nay, electronic—era our "way of life" will triumph not by being "preserved," "pickled," or "embalmed" but by being *transformed* and *grown*. This task requires initiative not just in a few centers but everywhere.

"Cultural lag" from center to border must be cut from thirty years to five. Managers who merely follow and not lead must either be "shot" or retired, or developed. The only American way is development and there is no development in the last analysis but self-development.

Every Chapter of S.A.M. must see to it that in their own communities management does not stand pat, imitate, drift, die-back, or die-off. They must be helped to manage and to advance the technology of their companies and communities.

Mr. Khrushchev is quoted as saying that communist Russia does not need war. She can win the peace, says he, by out-producing capitalism in scientists, in technology, in producers and in products.

The Society for Advancement of Management accepts Mr. Khrushchev's challenge and summons seven thousand "Paul Reveres" in sixty chapters—to spring, not to arms, but to *free* work and decentralized *leadership*.

It may even be difficult to train such men in big companies. Some look ahead to the day when top management will be culled from the on the specialists to provide them with correct information—and more about finances, sales, accounting.

ranks of small businesses where the individual will continue to have the opportunity to learn and use a variety of skills.

But however the management man of the future is trained he will be a specialist in his own right. The professional manager, trained to tap the brains of the specialists, will become a reality.[10]

Will the mobility of labor continue to improve?

The machine now performs much of the work formerly done by men and by animals. At the same time, the individual worker has been enabled to earn more necessities and material comforts. The so-called necessities of today were the luxuries of our grandparents and our parents. A large percentage of people in our country are able to have in the home such necessities as central heating systems, bathrooms, electric lights, radios, telephones, piped gas for cooking, and electrical refrigerators. A pound of good automobile costs less than a pound of butter. In the rear of nearly every home is a garage that houses a car. Outside of the home run miles of smooth highway for recreation and travel, which broaden one's vision and increase one's knowledge.

Provincialism has been decreased through our economic products. Superstitions have been removed from the minds of many people who otherwise would be living in a state of intellectual semidarkness. Our machine age has greatly increased the total fund of information distributed in the home daily through the newspaper, the magazine, the radio, and the telephone.

Today, the masses also participate in the affairs of life far more than the peoples of any previous generations. Years ago most people had to amuse themselves in the home or with their immediate neighbors. The form of living was more or less similar to that which we can still find in the mountains of West Virginia and Tennessee.

The machine age has been an important factor in giving the individual citizen more prompt and accurate information about the affairs of the world and his community than he was previously able to acquire with years of effort. One well-edited newspaper will give the ordinary citizen of today a greater variety of, and more accurate, information than months of effort could have given him previously. Similarly, the devices provided by modern business, such as the automobile, the radio, television, the newspaper, the motion picture theater, the library, and the short working day, allow the present-day worker to express himself more adequately than workers under former economic systems. Today's worker has risen above his environment far more than the primitive man or the pioneer.

Modern technology has given the American worker a rich supply of material comforts, too numerous to list here. But it has also contributed to his feeling that he is not in control of his own destiny. He is caught up in currents of forces which he cannot understand. Furthermore, technology has committed us to an economy of ever expanding production and constant growth. Competition forces the employer to seek new and better ways for getting along with fewer employees. This development benefits customers, but it also may occasionally compel displaced employees to find and adjust themselves to new jobs.

Today, three out of four persons who work for a living are on someone else's payroll. Employees outnumber stockholders about four to one. The opportunity to go into business for one's self has changed, as pointed out by W. Lloyd Warner and Burleigh B. Gardner:

I had the opportunity of studying the development of a strike in a community in New England where there had not been strikes before and where there had been no union organization. During the course of our study, two things happened. The strike was won by the workers and, during it, all the factories in the town in this particular industry went completely union.

When we examined why these events took place, a number of things soon became apparent. Among the variety of reasons given to explain these two results, one essential factor stood out far above the others—the old skill hierarchy for the advancement of workers was gone. The routes of mobility were closed. The route for "getting places" was no longer there for those who worked in the factories. It was not difficult to organize the workers' discontent and focus it against management, for the aspirations of these men not only for themselves but for their families were no longer invested in the open system of equal opportunity once provided by free enterprise but in the closed world of union organization.[11]

When those who compete for the prizes of life find that the rules of the game have been changed and social mobility no longer operates to permit those who strive to advance, then the systems of free enterprise and equal opportunity are doubted and the common people seek other ways to get what they want. To be more concrete, when large numbers of talented young men and women try to acquire the skills and knowledge thought necessary for advancement and, through no fault of their own, either fail to get them or fail to be rewarded when they do, they necessarily lose faith. Since many people in our civilization pay only lip service to the creed of success and make little effort to advance themselves, these people, too, blame the system rather than their own lack of initiative.

You must keep open the channels of mobility, so that no man can say, "Because I was born on the wrong side of the tracks, there is no use struggling here. You have to come from college before you get anywhere in this place."

The recruiting of college graduates to bring broader education and abilities into the organization has its points, but once it becomes the sole avenue of progress you build apathy and frustration at the lower levels. So open it up. See that the good men in your organization are found and give them a chance to use what they have.[12]

The growth of technology has affected the channels for advancement of the worker. The employee who does not have the mental capacity or motivation to train himself for technical work, such as engineering, is apt to turn to the labor union for the satisfaction of his aspirations. At the same time, however, he expects his children to get a higher education. This fact is evident from a survey of 1,500 representative wage earner families. These families are distributed throughout the United States in accordance with employment concentration. Factors such as age and union membership have proper representation. See Table 26-1 for the distributions, by age and region, of mothers who expect that at least one of their children will attend college.

The fact that so many parents expect young people to go to college should intensify the industrial leader's interest in opening and keeping open the channels for personal advancement.

TABLE 26-1

DO YOU HOPE OR EXPECT THAT AT LEAST ONE OF YOUR CHILDREN WILL ATTEND COLLEGE?

		BY AGE				*BY REGION*		
	TOTAL	17–29	30–44	45 AND OVER	EAST	MID-WEST	SOUTH	FAR WEST
Yes	75.7	81.1	73.3	68.1	70.6	79.7	67.5	85.2
No	8.0	2.8	9.6	21.3	8.8	7.6	11.4	3.4
Don't know	16.3	16.1	17.1	10.6	20.6	12.7	21.1	11.4

Of the small proportion who do not expect or hope for one of their children to go to college, the chief reason is the expense. About one in five state that the child or children do not care for school, while a few others mention that the children are planning to go to work. Only one mother in the entire Forum mentioned as an objection the fact that it meant a child's going away from home.

This report of the Wage Earner Forum typifies again one of the basic things which has made America. In no other country in the world would there be the expectation on the part of so many wage earner parents that their children would and should go to college—nor would it eventuate in anything like the proportion which it does here.

From Everett R. Smith, "The American Goal—College," *The Wage Earner Forum,* sponsored by Macfadden Publications, Inc., July 15, 1949, p. 5.

SOCIAL AND POLITICAL TRENDS

The significance of the right to own property

One of the oldest acts for getting applause is for the politician to beat his breast and proclaim that he is for human rights and against property rights. Actually, the right to acquire and own property is one of our most precious human rights. In countries where the rights of property ownership have been thoroughly abolished, the elementary safeguards for the liberty and dignity of the individual have been most cruelly violated. The tyranny that takes away a man's land, savings, business, or home will also take away his life and liberty if it suits those in the positions of the tyrannical power. The rights of property and freedom of speech and press are closely related. As the economist Friedrich Hayek says in his analysis of the trends of our time in *The Road to Serfdom:*

What our generation has forgotten is that the system of private property is the most important guaranty of freedom, not only for those who own property, but scarcely less for those who do not. It is only because the control of the means of production is divided among many people acting independently that nobody has complete power over us, that we are individuals who can decide what to do with ourselves.[13]

Theorists, such as the communist, socialist, or collectivist who oppose private property, argue that the farms and factories belong to the workers. The latter are supposed to be happier when the state owns all means of production. (Actually, the feeling of ownership under such conditions is likely to depend upon the propaganda fed the workers or on the extent of their active participation in the productive enterprise.) This argument is too similar to the fallacious claim that when American workers own stock in the company where they are employed, they will then think of themselves as owners.

In 1948 a satirical story leaked out of Czechoslovakia concerning an American who visited a Czech nationalized factory. This American noticed a few automobiles near the entrance. He was told that the factory belonged to the workers and that the automobiles belonged to the bosses. Later, a Czech visited an American factory and noticed the rows of thousands of automobiles parked at the plant. He learned that the factory belonged to the bosses but that the automobiles belonged to the workers. Certainly, state ownership is no assurance of a high standard of living for the workers.

There are many reasons for the high standard of living in America in comparison with other countries of the world. One is that the United States of America was founded by a Christian people. The Christian virtues shaped the laws and confirmed the moral values of our industrial practices and legislation. Under them, private enterprise became effective.

Of course our ample supply of natural resources provided one essential ingredient for the production of real wealth. But the catalyst in the process was private enterprise. Other nations have had just as great natural resources as the United States but have done little with them. A few nations, too, such as Switzerland, had relatively limited natural resources but have developed them through private enterprise.

Ideological conflict between democracy and totalitarianism

Many people, in their desire to improve their status and to progress, are willing to turn to a totalitarian or similar system in order to get more enjoyments for themselves. Many are willing to forego liberty for themselves and others if the denial of liberty promises more material comforts and the satisfaction of seeing members of the privileged classes put into a position of inferiority.

Furthermore, certain poorly adjusted individuals have tendencies which are more easily satisfied by a totalitarian form of government than by a democracy. They are so

"Abstract Thinking," a lithograph by Mabel Dwight. Any socio-economic planning must take into consideration the kind of abstract thinking depicted above, as well as that of members of other intellectual strata.

Reproduced by courtesy of the artist and the Weyhe Galleries, 794 Lexington Avenue, New York.

emotionally insecure or lacking in direct-attack adjustments that they prefer to let a stronger person "take over" for them. The titles "Fuehrer" and "Duce" both mean "leader."

A democratic form of organization dramatically fails to give its members what the psychiatrist usually terms "belongingness." A protecting envelopment which absolute monarchies or totalitarian forms provide for the individual is lacking here. In a democracy one speaks of a brother-brother relationship instead of a parent-child relationship. Moreover, the parent gives to the child a certain frame of reference, a certain setting for his life (which we term "belongingness") which is of great value to him quite regardless of the actual acts of that parent (with the exception of the act of rejection).

Democracy replaces the damaging nature of this failure only in the fullest possible development of family life. . . .

This presents the second danger—the individual's fear of change. Perhaps this resentment against growth, this fear of change, is so fundamental a human trait that we cannot hope to alter it. The solution which some 85 out of each 100 adults have for any social problem is to get

back to an earlier arrangement or adjustment. So timorous a state of affairs can at least be measurably modified in the upbringing of young children. The search for new objectives and methods just because they are new will lead only to disaster. . . .[14]

Why some persons turn to a totalitarian system

Many persons imagine that the individual's search for new objectives and methods stems entirely from pathetic economic conditions. Low economic status does not, however, seem to explain the origin or the motivating influence of social revolutionary tensions with us. Such tensions and motivations are more likely to have their origins in personal problems that have little or no relation to low income. This fact is proved by the presence of very high-income individuals among radicals such as Communist fellow-travelers. In the late 1940's, for example, a study was made of members of organizations that were clearly Communist fronts, many of them labeled subversive by the Department of Justice. For purposes of identification, anyone who was a member of at least twenty such fronts was considered a fellow-traveler. Of the leading one hundred fellow-travelers at the time of the study, six were millionaires.[15]

Every individual, regardless of his income, must make his own adjustments to his personal problems. Some well-to-do sons and daughters of high-income executives, well-educated individuals, and members of every social class suffer from frustration and project their frustrations against the existing economic or political system. The aggressions that arise from frustration are found among persons of all conditions and in all ages and nations. Such frustrated persons are, of course, apt to seek and find satisfying companionship among others having the same psychological motivations. They join organizations dedicated to the overthrow of the existing order. They sacrifice their own easy life and work hard in order to satisfy the inner urges arising from their maladjustments.

Frustration-motivated behavior in social revolution

As explained by Norman R. F. Maier, frustration-instigated behavior and attitudes appear to be stubborn and unadaptive. Aggression is frequently a by-product of frustration. It tends to be directed at what appears to be the frustrating agent and is often destructive in nature. If what appears to be a frustrating situation is not acted upon, tensions accumulate. They must be relieved by some means.

An example of how frustration affects group behavior is to be observed in a study of Germany before World War II. After losing World War I, she experienced a long period of deprivation crowned by the worldwide depression of the thirties. Hitler increased the Germans' sense of frustration by reminding them continuously of what World War I had done to them. He even

added factors to increase their sense of frustration. So great were the Germans' tensions that they had to be relieved by aggression. Hitler channelized the aggression by pointing to Jews, Communism, imperialism, and so forth.

He focalized the aggressive action to meet the demands of the time. Frustrated individuals are easily organized and unified, although frustration itself contains none of the properties making for unification. Rather this unity must be imposed from without and leadership is, therefore, essential. By synchronizing the aggression the leader can give the movement its force.[16]

The power of the group as a whole is enhanced because each person within the group gains ever increasing strength and confidence from common action. In addition, an in-group, composed of those most outstandingly aggressive, may be formed. Its activities may motivate still greater displays of aggressiveness by the other members of the in-group and at the same time keep non-in-group members at a highly aggressive pitch.

The structure of social organization based on frustration and aggression is simple. It is organized around a leader who is all-important. He is the unifying influence, and it is he who determines the nature of the aggressive pattern. However, all the group members play an important role, because members tend to imitate aggressive actions of their colleagues, and as long as aggression is being demonstrated, the group remains cohesive. When aggression ceases, the group disintegrates. In order to be successful, the leader of a frustrated group must direct aggression in a forceful manner.

The movement, however, is not only strong because of the united action of the individuals. Each individual gains further strength and confidence because of common action. Doubts or alternative acts seldom come to the individual's attention, so choice behavior is at a minimum . . .

The psychological structure of social organization based upon frustration and aggression is necessarily primitive in nature. The group is organized around a leader who supplies the unifying stimulus. It is he who determines the nature of the aggressive pattern. The aggressive actions of part of the individuals in the group may influence those of others. Here imitations may play a part and exert an added unifying factor . . . As long as the aggression is in progress the group is held together. When the aggression ceases, the group disintegrates.

In order to be successful, the leader of the frustrated group must direct aggression in a forceful manner.

If the aggressive action leads to frustration, he may not only lose power, but the new frustrations may be directed against him. To remain in power, he must continue to direct successful aggression since the alternative is disorganization. In a state of disorganization revolution or a redirected aggression from another source is a strong possibility.

1. No great or effective movement is possible unless it rests primarily upon previous frustration. Suffering thus seems to be a prerequisite to reform. Leadership can achieve its greatest heights as well as its greatest depths when it organizes frustrated individuals.

2. . . . Socialism seems to be a movement organized around a goal and [therefore] it has been a movement without great vigor. Communism contains the feature of frustration and it has been a much more vital movement. It follows that an analysis of the membership would show the former to contain a high percentage of idealists and rational individuals, whereas the Communist membership would show a large percentage of frustrated individuals.

3. People are more easily organized around what they do not want than around what they do want. What people positively desire is always in the nature of a goal. What people do not desire may be a negative goal (or the less desirable of two alternatives) and hence the opposite of positive goals; but it may also be something which either has frustrated them, or represents a substitute aggressive possibility for frustrations produced in other manners. It is the aspect of frustration which gives people's dislikes a unifying character.

4. Nations are more effective in waging wars than in constructing a peace program. Waging war involves frustration whereas peace is a goal. . . .

5. To be effective propaganda must take into account the nature of the group it will influence. Obviously goals and appeals to reason will not stop a movement built on aggression . . . Propaganda, however, serves an important purpose in initiating and maintaining aggressive movements. Its character must serve to increase frustration and direct aggression. Logic is not essential.

In goal-motivated societies the propaganda is more of the educational type. It emphasizes the goals to be attained and may attempt to create needs. It will contain statements of facts and appear logical.[17]

When, for some reason, it is desired to create an aggressive attitude in a large group of people, it is important to create in them the experience of many and continued frustrations. In national groups high taxes, personal restrictions, and sacrifices will increase frustration to such an extent that it may be readily channeled in any direction decided upon by leaders. It is essential, in such cases, that each person in the group be given a part to play so that he will identify himself with the group and thus contribute to group unity and action.

Propaganda as a factor in individual insecurity

At least part of the bewilderment being experienced by members of our society at this time is caused by the innumerable ideas and theories being disseminated. From many sides and sources the individual is exhorted to do this or that to improve his own lot or that of his fellow men. Panaceas for any societal ailment, organic or functional, bombard us. Much of this propaganda sounds plausible, yet the over-all effect is confusing.

Although propaganda is as old as recorded history, it has become increasingly complex with the improvement of communications facilities. Newspapers, radios, and magazines blanket the United States. What is said or done anywhere in the world is relayed within hours to anyone who cares to know. Whether the individual realizes it or not, he is continually being showered with propaganda. Some of it is intentional. Some is unintentional. Intentional propaganda emanates from a source that is well aware of what it is promulgating. Unintentional propaganda emanates from sources that pass along what they have heard or what they believe in without intentionally trying to "convert" anyone. Under this heading almost anyone might be classified at some time. But when we speak of propaganda, we will exclude this type for the sake of convenience.

Propaganda attempts to teach people certain attitudes through the use of words and symbols. Education is also concerned with a similar task, but there is a distinction between the two. Propagandists disseminate only those ideas or facts that promote the cause they promulgate. Educators, on the other hand, attempt to present as many sides of a question as are, in their opinion, pertinent. They invite critical thinking; propagandists do not.

Doob defines propaganda as "the attempt to affect the personalties and to control the behavior of individuals toward ends considered unscientific or of doubtful value in a society at a particular time." He defines education as "the imparting of knowledge or skill considered to be scientific or to have survival value in a society at a particular time." Naturally, that which is considered scientific or necessary to survival varies from time to time, and from culture to culture, but the values are agreed upon by the majority in a particular society, and teaching that perpetuates those values is educational.[18] By these definitions, therefore, propaganda is the antithesis of education. It is not considered to be scientific or to have survival value in a particular society.

We are apt to pin the "propaganda" label on symbols which anger us, or with which we disagree, or which come from people we dislike. We dismiss a pamphlet or speech or book or paper by declaring, "It's only propaganda." Despite the fact that propaganda helps to create public opinion, and public opinion helps to create propaganda, people in our society like to believe that the opinions they hold are their own, arrived at without pressure and through careful appraisal of *facts*. Even in wartime the American people want no traffic with propaganda, so during World War II the U. S. Government cooperated in preserving the fiction. Euphemisms employed for various agencies that handled propaganda were: Office of Facts and Figures, Office of Government Reports, Office of the Coordinator of Information, Office of the Coordinator of Inter-American Affairs, Office of War Information, Psychological Warfare Branch (or Division), and so on.[19] Each branch of the service also had its own public relations program.

Propagandists and their propaganda, however, will be with us as long as the world's affairs remain improvable. Almost everyone is affected by propaganda through the intentional or unintentional slant of publications, radio programs, movies, and the ideas or principles, formulated or unformulated, of people in public life, neighbors, churches, clubs, organizations, and others. Some people are interested in the study of its nature. Doob mentions two groups who are so interested. One group is composed of propagandists who want to learn more effective ways of operating; the other group is interested in learning how and why propaganda affects people.[20] Students usually are interested because they realize that it is one of the important influences that mold people's minds, and thus society. Propaganda attempts to shape new attitudes. These attitudes, the propagandist hopes, will motivate his audience to act in a certain way. The ultimate aim of propaganda is action, so the propagandist tries to tie his story to human emotions and to the great drives of the individual. If these drives are behind the individual's attitude he will be impelled to act, and the propaganda will have been successful.

The most outstanding weapon of the propagandist is his constant use of "either-or" terminology: *our* side is "good," "honest," "respectable," "virtuous," "idealistic," and so on; *their* side is "bad," "corrupt," "evil," "sinister." In times of war, *we* are human, just; *they* are inhuman, bestial, and hence must be destroyed.

The propagandist speaks in "polar terms," that is, in opposites. He almost never admits that there is any blemish on his side or any virtue on the other side. This gives him great control, because when people are convinced of the unquestioned rightness of their side and the undoubted wrongness of their opponents, they will enter a conflict willingly. This tendency to polarize gives propaganda a bad connotation. Though statements may be perfectly accurate, they are "slanted" through the omission of all reference to the undesirable aspects of one side or to the desirable aspects of the other side.

There is no scientifically recognized way of analyzing a piece of propaganda as there is of analyzing a chemical compound. However, the Institute for Propaganda Analysis identified seven principal categories into which the techniques of the propagandist fell. These are:

Name calling—giving an idea a bad label—is used to make us reject and condemn the idea without examining the evidence.

Glittering generality—associating something with a "virtue word"—is used to make us accept and approve the thing without examining the evidence.

Transfer carries the authority, sanction, and prestige of something respected and revered over to something else in order to make the latter acceptable; or it carries authority, sanction, and disapproval to cause us to reject and disapprove something the propagandist would have us reject and disapprove.

Testimonial consists in having some respected or hated person say that a given idea or program or product or person is good or bad.

Plain folks is the method by which a speaker attempts to convince his audience that he and his ideas are good because they are "of the people," the "plain folks."

Card stacking involves the selection and use of facts or falsehoods, illustrations or distractions, and logical or illogical statements in order to give the best or worst possible case for an idea, program, person, or product.

Band wagon has as its theme: "Everybody —at least all of *us*—is doing it"; with it the propagandist attempts to convince us that all members of a group to which we belong are accepting his program and that we *must therefore* follow our crowd and "jump on the bandwagon."[21]

Communists have had wide experience with propaganda and have used virtually every trick in the propagandists' repertory. To create confusion and disorder is one of their most reliable techniques. By filtering into such organizations as labor unions and achieving positions of leadership and power (as Communists are ordered to do), they gain an ideal opportunity to create the desired disorder. With this feat accomplished, they insidiously spread their doctrine. They have used the seven devices outlined above in speech and print. They have fostered "in-group" feeling by using banners and buttons, pageants, parades, and rallies. They have used concealed and revealed propaganda, suppression and indoctrination, direct and counter propaganda, a variety of stimuli, repetition, variation, slanting, distortion, urgency, and other devices. Such a wide variety of stimuli cause many intellectual and emotional responses, which are then put to use in the movement.

Revolutionary tactics are carefully planned to give followers emotional satisfactions. An explanation is given by Lasswell and Blumenstock of the ways in which propaganda incited action, devotion, and loyalty to a revolutionary movement in Chicago from 1930 to 1935.[22] The same psychological factors would presumably operate at any time, in any place, in connection with a revolutionary movement.

Lasswell and Blumenstock state that the fundamental task of revolutionary propaganda is to split the conscience against itself, making two disparate entities opposed to one another. Symbols are used to release emotions such as assertiveness, weakness, guilt, and love.

Assertiveness may be aroused and redirected against the established social order by depicting it as deprivational. Thus blame for the fact that a person does not have all he would like is attributed to an outside person or group, not the self. Since factors in the environment are blamed, hostility commonly results and is projected on the world. To utilize this emotion, Communists provide funnels through which it may be channelized to achieve some of their aims. Minor demands are made in an industry, for example. Foremen, employers, and conservative labor leaders are sometimes selected as the enemy in an attack. If a minor victory or concession is won, it serves as an "illusion of victory" and gives a feeling of strength to the attacker. It provides a reason for the individual to think of the environment as weak rather than of himself as weak. When this feeling is experienced by all the members of the "in-group," they may go on to aim at bigger and better targets. The sense of guilt which quite often arises because impulses and wishes are opposed to the established order is also projected against the environment, facilitating the release of aggression against it.

The need for love, one of the basic drives of men, is intensified when the individual is insecure, and because individuals engaged in revolutionary activities are apt to be insecure, the need is great. To satisfy it, love objects are necessary. They are furnished by leaders and heroes of the movement, dead or alive. Optimistic symbols of the future, such as "when *we* have proved *our* strength," serve the same purpose and are part of Communistic technique.

There are, no doubt, individual differences in a person's readiness to believe propaganda. Theoretically, the fellow who is content with his role, is well taken care of physically, is not in a state of fear, and is in complete accord with the aims and ideology of the forces of his nation will not be sensitized to the content of psychological warfare. On the other hand, the person who is at the opposite poles of these characteristics may be so ready to surrender or to show signs of defecting to the other side, that he does not need the propaganda.

In order to test the relative importance of various attitudes and experience in determining the attitudes of the prisoners of war, standardized interviews on several hundred North Korean and Chinese prisoners were carried out. The object was to find out whether the propaganda they heard had any effect on their willingness to surrender. The study confirmed the already existing belief about psychological warfare: namely, that propaganda has a nudging or precipitating effect on behavior. It is secondary to the more physical and material aspects of warfare. Men react to psychological warfare differently depending on their morale and experiences.[23]

Are we entering a new era?

Now that the atomic age is here, many leaders are trying to foresee its significance in relation to human welfare. Thus far, much of its psychological influence seems to have been in the direction of increasing the feeling of insecurity for the individual. A current writer, a science authority for a great newspaper, in his interpretation to readers of a mass-circulation magazine regarding the future significance of atomic energy, pointed out that "if we have peace, we can have paradise; if we have war, we could face doomsday." He also closed his article with the following historical anecdote:

Eighty years ago the Goncourt brothers, after attending a dinner with the leading literary and scientific minds of Paris, made a strange entry in their journal. It reported that scientists were predicting that one hundred years from then (April 7, 1869) man would have solved the secret of the atom and would even be able to "create life in competition with God." To this, the Goncourt brothers added:

"We raised no objection. But we have the feeling that when this time comes in science, God with his white beard will come down to earth, swinging a bunch of keys, and will say to humanity, the way they say at five o'clock at the salon, 'Closing time, gentlemen!'"

Is it "closing time?" Can it be that we have come all the way to the very gates of the Promised Land only to end in a great cloud of atomic dust? At the present stage of world affairs one can only pray that man be preserved for a nobler destiny.[24]

Some writers on the histories of civilizations go so far as to wonder whether our whole Western civilization may be in process of extinction in the ways of the Aztecs and the Incas, the Summerians and the Hittites, and some fifteen others that have existed and perished since the dawn of known history. Are we about to suffer an inexorable doom, one we cannot avert or modify? The historian Toynbee gives us a guardedly hopeful answer:

Our present situation is formidable indeed. A survey of the historical landscape in the light of our existing knowledge shows that, up to date, history has repeated itself about twenty times in producing human societies of the species to which our Western society belongs, and it also shows that, with the possible exception of our own, all these representatives of the species of society called civilizations are already dead or moribund. . . .

There is nothing to prevent our Western civilization from following historical precedents, if it chooses, by committing social suicide. But we are not doomed to make history repeat itself; it is open to us through our own efforts, to give history, in our case some new and unprecedented turn. As human beings, we are endowed with this freedom of choice, and we cannot shuffle off our responsibility upon the shoulders of God or nature. We must shoulder it ourselves. It is up to us.[25]

Suggestions for the person who wants to be aware of the trends of our time

The alert individual will study trends and conditions that affect him. He wants to be an intelligent participant in his changing world. He cannot hope to steer the world to suit himself, but he can become well-adjusted to his part of the world. As previously stated, the best insurance for the individual who seeks the resources whereby he may enjoy life is not wealth or power or fame, but adaptability. Adaptability to meet changing conditions is one outstanding requirement for happy living in this age.

No one can hope to turn earth into heaven. Utopia would be boring if it could be found. Oppressions and injustices have always been a part of life and they will probably continue to be with us. However, being a victim of an oppressive or painful condition is not so oppressive or painful if one can feel himself a worthy participant in the changing order. To lose in a game that one does not understand—in which someone else seems to take all—is far more trying than to take part in a game in which all players know the rules and enjoy the game. The road to inner security for the individual of today is not through a search for abundance by means of politico-economic systems or through provision of abundance by others, but through intelligent participation in the affairs that concern him. That, incidentally, is one reason why many students are in college, even though they do not realize it.

To summarize, the person who wishes to participate intelligently in our social evolution can do so by the application of certain criteria to particular situations as they arise. In the exercise of his critical evaluation, he may ask questions such as the following:

1. What kinds of people, from the standpoint of adjustment, are having the most important influences on our social evolution? Are they the happy, able, well-adjusted personality types or the unhappy, weak, and maladjusted kind who attempt to dominate our order in order to satisfy their frustrations?

2. To what extent do increased government services and expenses, because of increased responsibility assumed by government for the welfare of the individual citizen, cause further psychological problems for the individual?

3. To what extent does a political program or economic plan fortify the positions of those who seek power for the sake of

furthering their own power rather than as service to the general population?

4. To what extent do increased percentages of our citizenry prefer to give up freedom in order to have more unearned welfare aids?

5. To what extent are the potential contributions of individual initiative hindered because of red tape, bureaucracy, and centralized authority without compensating effects from the centralization of power?

6. To what extent are the methods of propaganda being used to cover up deficiencies and to keep the established political party in power?

7. To what extent are incomes of the very able lowered to the levels of unskilled labor in order that the masses may be pleased? If that is being done, how are persons of superior abilities to be stimulated to produce to their capacities?

8. To what extent do those persons who want to keep things as they are, or to return to times as they once were, represent refusals to adjust to inevitable changes? Do such individuals try to foresee what *will be* as distinct from what they think *ought* to be? To what extent do leaders strive for what ought to be rather than accept the expedient?

9. To what extent is our evolution in the direction of a strengthening of character and personality of the individuals who belong to important interest groups, such as those in the ranks of labor, management, students, government workers, and others? This question of positive value adjustments on the part of the individual is basic to all others in our evolution.

Security comes from within; not from without

Most members of the general population cannot be expected to develop any sustaining economic philosophy that will help them endure the rigors of a depression or rapid change, but intelligent persons can

do so. Individual adjustments, attitudes, and beliefs are basic. How shall we approach their development?

Religious training offers an example for us. It may be defined either as a set of beliefs that are to be accepted or as a number of attitudes of faith and a certain aspiration that is to be achieved. Similarly, the individual's adjustment to different problems of life, social evolution, and the economic cycle may be presented in either of these two ways. That is, we may indoctrinate youth and have him believe in an all-wise planner: socialism, communism, some kind of dictatorship, or some other economic creed. Or we may stimulate each person to learn, evaluate, and adjust to the situation in which he finds himself, gaining his satisfactions from living in a world that he enjoys because of its challenges. True security, like happiness, cannot be achieved as an end. It is the by-product of activity directed toward the solving of problems and the interpretation of human experience.

American education has not been directed toward the emotional development of individuals who can stand the strains of inevitable changes. Many theorists and educators merely rant at our problems of unemployment, new machines for living, and the trends in our time. Many demand an economic panacea which, at best, would bring with it new problems, or would be out of tune with life as human beings live it. Certainly no economic or political system will ever remove our problems. Life is a series of changes, and stresses are absolutely certain to arise.

The intelligent person need not wait for a new economic or political system to solve his problems. He can begin at once to develop himself in dealing with the problems within and about himself. Psychologically, the habits of direct attack are the individual's best insurance for meeting the low periods of the business cycle and dealing with the changing conditions around him. Education through the psychological and social

There is no Magic Wand

LET'S not fool ourselves—the future of this country is entirely dependent on how much it is willing to produce at a low enough cost to meet world competition. *Your* future depends on exactly the same thing. All the doles, social security promises, soak-the-rich ideas and ham-and-eggs-every-Thursday plans in the world can't change that fact, for the simple reason that there is no place for the money to come from except *production.*

The 30-hour-week cry, and "more money for less work", and all such plans—if they reduce production—are crude and cruel falsehoods. The less you and I produce, the less there is to divide between us—how can you escape that fundamental truth?

That doesn't mean longer and longer hours, harder and harder labor—not at all. It means an honest day's work and taking full advantage of the modern tools that let you produce more and better work. The more you produce *efficiently* in a normal day, the lower the cost of your product. The lower its cost, the more people who can afford it. The more people who can afford it, the more people who will buy it. The more people who buy it, the more money you can make, and the more secure your job.

That is true and practical social security. We who can produce the machines and you who can use them efficiently are the *only* ones who can make it work.

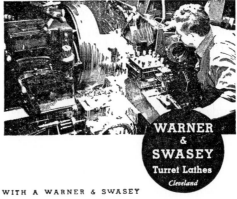

WARNER & SWASEY
Turret Lathes
Cleveland

YOU CAN TURN IT BETTER. FASTER. FOR LESS . . WITH A WARNER & SWASEY

---

sciences will play a larger role in serving the typical citizen. Psychology particularly has limited most of its efforts to pure science. This was necessary for a foundation. Now, however, we should see more applications of its principles.

Putting responsibility for contributions to our evolution into the hands of the psycholo-

trends that affect work life

POSSIBLE ADJUSTMENTS OF THE EMPLOYER
TO OUR CHANGING ORDER

Direct approaches:

Improves service to customers.

Allocates profits to research on new products.

Adopts sense of trusteeship regarding his wealth.

Gives employees greater participation in business.

Develops employees for their advancement vocationally.

Sets up plans to meet employees' needs in depression, such as guaranteed income plans.

Positive substitute activities:

Develops easier products or surer services of little risk.

Habitually retrenches.

Puts available money into a farm rather than a business.

Negative substitute activities:

Blames his troubles on effects of a political party's actions.

Hopes to return to good old days.

Berates modern generation.

Seeks aid from government.

Sells the business and lives on the income.

gist, social scientist, and the individual himself must be supplemented by developing the leadership of intelligent industrialists. Personnel men and other members of management must do a better job.

Suggestions for the leader in industry

One of the easiest ways to solve the individual employee's problem of adjusting to his feelings of insecurity in an insecure world is to provide him with a great political "father." For the emotionally insecure worker in industry, adjustment to the uncertainties of life is not answered by policies and programs of liberalism, collectivism, capitalism, rightism, or leftism. He prefers a great leader on whom he can rely, someone to whom he can give his trust and in whose ability to solve everything that is wrong he can place his faith. The worker would like to have someone be to him a symbol of strength. When such a leader is absent from the political scene, the insecure or immature worker worries and turns to something or someone else.

A few industrialists have played the role

of a strong father, sincerely in most cases, for the benefit of their employees. Industrial democracy, however, is not enhanced by encouraging such forms of identification and dependence. Most industrial leaders disdain such a role because they know that each man should develop himself by learning to depend upon his own inner strengths. Psychological strength on the part of the employee is encouraged when the employer manages his business on the basis of the following policies:

1. *Fulfill the functions of a true trustee.* The employer who honestly believes that any wealth, profit, property, and superior intelligence that he has are to be used as a trusteeship for his employees as well as his stockholders will have few labor troubles. Many employers now practice the role of trustee in regard to the stockholder's money but fail to do so in regard to the employee's interests.

2. *Give employees a real sense of participation in the business.* They are anxious to feel that they "belong." They can take the harsh impacts on their lives more easily if

trends that affect work life

POSSIBLE ADJUSTMENTS OF THE EMPLOYEE TO OUR CHANGING ORDER

Direct approaches:

Improves his abilities by extra training.

Improves his efforts to serve employer and the customers.

Adjusts his expenditures so as to save for emergency.

Improves his understanding of the changing order.

Negative substitute activities:

Blames a company, institution or person for his troubles.

Becomes a radical.

Tries to reform world all by himself.

Seeks aid from government.

"Lives off" relatives or wife.

Positive substitute activities:

Takes a job that is below his capacity in a more stable company, such as a public utility or food concern.

Buys a farm as a protection to his income; not because of a real interest in farming.

Develops a side-line business to the extent of neglecting his main line of work.

they have so intimate an acquaintance with the problems of the employer that they feel themselves a member of the team. Bitterness and recourse to false political promises by employees are often the result of neglectful treatment by employers.

3. *Give systematic training to foremen and supervisors* so that they can put enlightened policies into effect with the employee at the work bench and the desk. Most foremen are too remote from top management. Members of top management and foremen will have to associate with one another so frequently that foremen will know the philosophy of top management and spontaneously pass it on to employees in daily contacts with them.

4. *Keep open the channels and chances for advancement.* The number of executives in business who have interviews with their employees for the purpose of helping each employee to develop himself is small indeed. In fact, such executives are exceedingly rare. Moreover, when an executive does have a talk with an employee regarding his future development, the executive practically never clinches his counsel. The employee usually

leaves with a vague or generalized set of platitudes which are of little practical value. The one thing which must be done to vitalize the interview is to help the employee to outline a definite development program so that he will know just what he should do in order to merit promotion.

5. *Plan and work toward greater economic security for employees.* A few companies have developed guaranteed employ-

> *Private Enterprise*
>
> The power to choose the work I do;
> To grow and have the larger view;
> To know and feel that I am free;
> To stand erect, not bow the knee;
> To be no chattel of the state;
> To be the master of my fate;
> To dare to risk, to lose, to win;
> To make my own career begin;
> To serve the world in my own way;
> To gain in wisdom, day by day;
> With hope and zest to climb, to rise—
> I call that private enterprise.
>
> —Herbert Casson, *The Clarkson Letter,* Clarkson College of Technology, January-February 1948.

ment plans for their employees, but only a few. More employers must strive to provide for income assurance to employees during depressions, old age, and the times when skills are voided because of technological advancement.

6. *Show employees that competitive industry serves customers.* The employee must be helped to discover that his freedom of choice as a customer in the market place includes rights and satisfactions greater than security alone. In fact, when Karl Marx insisted that production should be for the social good and not for profit, he could not foresee the day when employers would give a large part of their effort to just that—serving the people, the customers, and doing it under the competition of business rivals rather than under the inefficiencies of bureaucracy.

Acknowledgments and References

1. Ulysses G. Weatherly, *Social Progress*, J. B. Lippincott Company, Philadelphia, 1926, pp. 157–158.

2. Arthur Kornhauser, "Psychological Studies of Employee Attitudes," *Journal of Consulting Psychology*, May–June 1944, pp. 127–143. See also *Personnel*, American Management Association, November 1944, pp. 170–189.

3. Benjamin L. Masse, "Industrial Relations and Social Change," *Personnel Series*, Number 106, American Management Association, New York, 1947, p. 9.

4. John Diebold, "Automation—the New Technology," *Harvard Business Review*, November–December 1953.

5. From an address by Benjamin F. Fairless before the Greater Johnstown, Pa. Chamber of Commerce. See *The Management Review*, American Management Association, April 1955, pp. 210–212.

6. "The Marketing and Transportation Situation," United States Department of Agriculture, Agricultural Marketing Service, Release April 26, 1956.

7. "Men and Machines—An Assembly-Line Worker Looks at His Job," Robert H. Guest, Institute of Human Relations, Yale University. Adapted from an address at the McGill University Industrial Relations Centre, Montreal. The work on which this paper is based is under the general direction of Charles R. Walker, Director of Research in Technology and Industrial Relations, Yale University. See *Personnel*, American Management Association, May 1955.

8. See William Alvadore Buck, "Mass Production—Boon or Bondage?" *Challenge Magazine*, a publication of New York University, New York.

9. For further information, see H. W. Prentis, Jr., "Industrial Progress of the Future," *The Management Review*, American Management Association, January 1955, pp. 2, 3.

10. "Tomorrow's Management—What Kind of Companies Will We Have . . . What Ideas Will It Take to Run Them . . . What Kind of Men Will Run Them . . . in 1980," *Business Week*, August 15, 1953.

11. W. Lloyd Warner, "Individual Opportunity—A Challenge to the Free Enterprise System," *Personnel Series*, Number 127, American Management Association, New York, 1949, p. 8.

12. Burleigh B. Gardner, "Conserving and Developing Our Human Resources," *Personnel Series*, Number 127, American Management Association, New York, 1949, p. 12.

13. Frederick Hayek, *The Road to Serfdom*, The University of Chicago Press, Chicago, 1944, pp. 103–104.

14. James S. Plant, "Objectives for Children in a Democratic Society," *The Annals of the American Academy of Political and Social Science*, November 1940.

15. Sidney Hook, "The Fellow-Traveler: A Study in Psychology," *The New York Times Magazine*, April 17, 1949.

16. Norman R. F. Maier, "The Role of Frustration in Social Movements," *Psychological Review*, American Psychological Association, Inc., Vol. 49 (1942), pp. 586–599.

17. *Loc. cit.*

18. Leonard W. Doob, *Public Opinion and Propaganda*, Henry Holt and Company, New York, 1948, pp. 237–240.

19. *Ibid.*, p. 232.

20. *Ibid.*, p. 255.

21. A. M. Lee and E. B. Lee, *The Fine Art of Propaganda*, Institute for Propaganda Analysis, Harcourt, Brace and Company, New York, 1939, pp. 23–24.

22. Harold D. Lasswell and Dorothy Blumenstock, *World Revolutionary Propaganda*, Alfred A. Knopf, Inc., New York, 1939, pp. 142–164.

23. Thomas G. Andrews, Denzel D. Smith, Lessing A. Kahn, "An Empirical Analysis of the Effectiveness of Psychological Warfare, *Journal of Applied Psychology*, August 1954, pp. 240–244.

24. William L. Laurence, "Paradise or Doomsday?" *Woman's Home Companion*, Vol. 75 (May 1948), pp. 32–33.

25. Arnold J. Toynbee, *Civilization on Trial*, copyright 1948 by Oxford University Press, Inc.

PROJECTS

1. Keep a record for a few weeks of predicted trends or events forecast by bulletins offering such service, or similar pages in such magazines as *Newsweek* and the *United States News*. Evaluate the results in terms of their accuracy and their exclusive nature.

2. Theodore Roosevelt, in Chicago, April 10, 1899, said: "I wish to preach not the doctrine of ignoble ease but the doctrine of the strenuous life." Can you name any tendencies in recent American life, such as in legislation, where the doctrine seemed to be directed toward ignoble ease?

3. Interview several executives in regard to the probable adoption of automation in their industries. What limitations and advantages do they foresee in regard to the effects on employees, customers, and society?

4. Prepare an inventory of the specific individual differences in people that might play important roles in adjustments to social and economic conditions.

5. Collect published photographs of a famous person whom some people like and others dislike. Separate those poses which present him in a favorable light from those that show him to a disadvantage. List the differentiating elements between the two sets. Suggest how propagandists might use each set of pictures.

6. Make a list of the nationalities often used in the drama or the movies to typify shrewdness, cunning, laziness, suavity, excitability, and other qualities. Suggest possible reasons for each stereotype.

7. Name some of the interest groups in your community. To what extent has each been successful? Which appear to serve the interests of the community as well as their own interest?

8. Study possible changes that might be made in our educational system for a better development of young people to adjust themselves to a changing world.

9. Examine a number of recent proposals for economic planning or control. Give your opinion of the possible consequences if each were to be adopted.

COLLATERAL READINGS

"Automation, A Report to the UAW-CIO Economic and Collective Bargaining Conference," November 12–13, 1954.

"Automation—Special Report to Readers," *Business Week*, October 1, 1955.

Bellows, Roger M., *Psychology of Personnel in Business and Industry*, Prentice-Hall, Inc., Englewood Cliffs, N.J., 1954, Chapter 12.

Ghiselli, Edwin E. and Clarence W. Brown, *Personnel and Industrial Psychology*, McGraw-Hill Book Company, Inc., New York, 1955, Chapter 15.

Grabbe, E. M., "Machines as Decision-Makers: Computers and Automation," Seminar on New Ideas and Methods, Carnegie Institute of Technology, March 1955.

"How a Computer Takes Over," *Business Week*, July 24, 1954.

King, Gilbert, "Photographic Memory," *Control Engineering*, Vol. 2, No. 7, 1954.

Kornhauser, Arthur, Robert Dubin and Arthur M. Ross, *Industrial Conflict*, McGraw-Hill Book Company, Inc., New York, 1954, Part 5.

Prentis, H. W. Jr., "Industrial Progress of the Future," *The Management Review*, American Management Association, January, 1955.

Smith, Henry Clay, *Psychology of Industrial Behavior*, McGraw-Hill Book Company, Inc., New York, 1955, Chapter 1.

Vannah, W. E. and L. E. Slater, *Instrumentation and Control, Pulsebeat of Industry*, McGraw-Hill Book Company, Inc., New York, 1955.

CHAPTER TWENTY-SEVEN

Markets–psychological factors and techniques of studying consumers

A successful merchandiser stated several effective appeals in the following maxims: "Any physical fact, like increasing fatness or the phases of the moon, is much more interesting to any woman than such outside activities as city planning, national politics, or the Bi-Centenary of George Washington; A man customer never grows up, and will spend twice as much time choosing a trout fly as a stair carpet or a refrigerator; People are steadfastly unwilling to skimp on things they buy for their own children. To make sure of a sellout, at least 25 per cent of the merchandise must be in doubtful taste; and no advertisement, no matter how lavish, will persuade people to buy what they don't want."[1]

Those who are aware of the trends in our time recognize that we are in the midst of a revolution. Automation is upon us. The product potentials in modern science and technology are very great but they will be of little value unless people can be stimulated to want and use them. An "automated business" makes not only forceful demands on management and employees, but also requires greater ability from those who market its products. More goods must be sold. Furthermore, automation requires that production be fairly constant, or at least move within a fairly narrow range, over long periods of time.

The burden of these developments will fall increasingly on the people in the distribution of goods—marketing. Hence, the need for marketing knowledge and competence will increase tremendously. This means that we shall have to train more men who can discover new markets, men whose psychological training will be especially helpful in learning about the customer's concepts of what he believes to be of value in his purchases. There will be increased need for men who can analyze an old product in terms of consumer needs and men who can develop new products that will satisfy unrecognized needs of consumers.

Those who distribute goods work in the dynamic area of ideas

The student who chooses some phase of distribution such as advertising or selling as a career should look upon it as more than a way of earning a living. His work should have social values which he regards as important. Only if he can see it as a vital factor in an economic system which maintains the political freedom of the individual and leads to higher levels of spiritual as well as material living will it merit his respect.

The success of our economic system can be measured quantitatively by the volume of goods we produce and consume, but we must not forget that this progress in material things rests upon a sound socio-economic basis. Admittedly, many of those engaged in marketing lose sight of the larger social values of their tasks and become preoccupied with the details of day-to-day transactions. This has led some observers to conclude that *all* Americans are completely materialistic. As one European critic expressed it, "The United States is the only nation in history that went from barbarism to decadence without attaining maturity." It is encouraging to note, however, that the intelligent, responsible leaders in American industry are displaying an increasing awareness of their role in the social and cultural development of our nation. They recognize that ideas, not material things, will really direct the course of our future progress.

American businessmen learned more clearly the dynamic influences of ideas when several thousand hand-picked experts from abroad toured the United States after 1949 to find out what underlies America's high productivity. They were organized into some 200 "productivity teams" under the Marshall Plan, financed mostly by funds provided by the European governments themselves. Most of them stayed long enough—some as long as nine months—to get more than a tourist's view.

These visitors discovered our *attitude to-ward the market.* Before they arrived here, they thought that the major factor in our distributive system was the continental span of our market. They discovered, however, that it is not in width but in depth that the American market differs basically from European concepts and business practice—a qualitative rather than a quantitative difference. "That the American is rich beyond our wildest dreams we knew in Europe," they said, "but that 'wealth' here is not just an economic term but a social one, that it means that there are the same things for the rich and for the poor, this none of us understood—and it is much more important."[2]

In America, unrelenting pressures are constantly exerted on our marketing system. These pressures are usually attributed to our rapid technological developments, ample natural resources, a large land area, and a growing population. These and other factors do play a part, but a basic influence can also be attributed to our striving for a higher standard of living for all members of our population.

As an observant marketer of England stated:

If I were to summarize my impressions of American marketing in one word, that word would be "dynamic." The dynamic nature of American marketing is nowhere more clearly illustrated than in your obsolescence policy. This, it seems to me, is not merely a policy but also a philosophy. There is a driving force in your system which makes it imperative that [this year's] model—whether it be an automobile, a radio, a razor, or a fountain pen—shall immediately render [last year's] version out-of-date.[3]

It is important that employees and other members of our public should learn to appreciate advertising and selling as of positive value to the citizen rather than as clever methods of extracting dollars from obstinate prospects.

In most companies, factory workers imagine that they have no common bond with the work of the salesmen, and the salesmen fail to recognize their relations to the fac-

Sales promotion and advertising can be justified economically and socially as exemplified in this history of Kleenex:

It was offered to the public for the first time in 1924 as a cold-cream remover under the brand name Kleenex. Six years later these disposable tissues were featured as having a second major purpose—as handkerchiefs. Sales doubled, and the next year they redoubled. The public went for Kleenex tissues for handkerchiefs because they were cheap, sanitary, and saved laundry.

As sales went up costs were reduced—and price to the consumer went down. It dropped from 65¢ in 1924 to 50¢ to 35¢ in 1932. Six months later it was down to 25¢ for a box of 200 larger, softer sheets. And here's something particularly worthy of notice—the Kleenex of 1932 was a softer, stronger tissue than the original product and it came in a handy serv-a-tissue package.

Ten years from the date Kleenex was launched nationally, the consumer could buy the large carton of 500 tissues for 41¢ or the regular 200-sheet package for 18¢. Again the sales doubled, and once more the price was cut to 13¢—two for 25¢.

The price shown for 1953 is 17½¢ per box which was a suggested price. Actually in a good many outlets such as supermarkets, the package was sold at a considerably lower price.

It is also interesting to note that in spite of increased costs and the substantially lower buying power of the dollar in 1953 prices were still lower than they were in 1947.

Through the advertised brand name Kleenex the public was educated to the advantage of these sanitary, convenient tissues. Consumer response made possible mass production, which, in turn, made for lower price to the consumer.

—From "Notes on the Progress of Brand Names Research Foundation," **Sales Management,** March 1, 1945, p. 74, for history previous to 1945. See also, Harry W. Hepner, **Modern Marketing: Dynamics and Management,** New York, McGraw-Hill Book Company, Inc., 1955, p. 187.

tory workers. Actually, both are members of the same team and each should respect and help the other. Both should seek to understand how advertising and selling contribute to a higher standard of living.

A leading advertising man, Kenneth Goode, said: "The best modern advertising does not try to sell. It aims to help people buy intelligently." Furthermore, the alert business enterpriser seeks to offer, not only what people want, but also something even better than what they thought they wanted. The successful editorship of Edward Bok is an excellent example:

One of Edward Bok's first acts as editor was to offer a series of prizes for the best answers to three questions he put to his readers: what in the magazine did they like least and why; and what omitted feature or department would they like to see installed? Thousands of answers came, and these the editor personally read carefully and classified. Then he gave his readers' suggestions back to them in articles and departments, but never on the level suggested by them. He gave them the subjects they asked for, but invariably on a slightly higher plane, and each year he raised the standard a notch. He always kept "a huckleberry or two" ahead of his readers. His psychology was simple: come down to the level which the public sets and it will leave you the moment you do it. It always expects of its leaders that they should keep a notch above or a step ahead. The American public always wants something a little better than it asks for, and the successful man, in catering to it, is he who follows this golden rule.[4]

The businessman who expects to become successful must offer a better product or service than his competitors. The superiority of his offering may be in the form of lower cost, more attractive packaging, or greater convenience than the duplicate product or service offered by less successful competitors. The American standard of living has risen partially because enterprisers have outbid each other in catering to the consumer, not at the consumer's immediate level of taste but at slightly higher quality levels, at lower cost, or with greater convenience. The marketer seeks to know the consumers' present preferences, habits, and tendencies in order that he may enable them to take the next step in the direction of a higher standard of living.

Of course, businessmen do not look upon themselves as reformers or improvers of mankind. The objective of their efforts is profits, but the system of competitive enterprise with the rewards of profit for the better enterprisers results in a gradual rise in buying tastes and material conditions of the consumers. Admittedly, consumers often do not know what they want even when they are asked. The enterpriser studies their present preferences and buying practices and offers many new products, a few of which are liked by consumers. When many consumers like the new products, the business prospers. When offerings happen to miss the consumers' wants and result in losses to the enterpriser, we do not have a profit system but a profit-and-loss system.

Identifying the market

To most people, "mass distribution" implies that modern marketing is done in a generalized sort of way. Actually, the modern marketer selects definite targets for his advertising and selling. A "market" is usually defined as a group of buyers, actual or prospective, for a product or service.[5] Factors frequently considered in defining a consumer market are income, age, family status, and financial outlook regarding income in the future. See Table 27-1 as an example of the kinds of data that are considered in selling household appliances. At the time of the study, the market might well have been defined as consisting of those households having an income of $5,000–$7,449, the housewife between 35 and 54 years of age, with

TABLE 27-1

WHICH CUSTOMERS ARE LIKELY TO GO FOR INNOVATIONS IN HOUSEHOLD APPLIANCES?

By Income Group		By Family Status	
Under $3,000	6%	Single	8%
$3,000–$4,999	23%	Married, no children	20%
$5,000–$7,449	39%	Married, children	69%
$7,500 plus	30%	Other	3%
No response	2%		

By Age Group		By Financial Outlook	
18–34 years	28%	Income up, expect rise	27%
35–54	58%	Income steady, expect rise	23%
55–64	10%	Income steady, no change expected	19%
65 and over	3%	Income up, no change expected	8%
No response	1%	No response	8%

From "How Consumers Take to Newness," *Business Week*, September 24, 1955, p. 41. Data: *University of Michigan Survey Research Center.*

children, and a financial outlook of income steady or up with a rise expected.

Men who are responsible for developing and defining markets and setting up marketing programs watch long-term trends in the changing world of consumer wants and preferences. Trends that currently are of special interest to those in distribution are the following:

MARKETS THAT RESULT FROM THE USE OF LEISURE TIME. As automation increases our productivity, the benefits appear not only in more goods and services but also increased leisure time. The average number of hours worked per week in 1930 was 47.2; in 1940, 43.0; and in 1950, 40.8. The forecast for 1960 is 37.7, and by 1980 the 30-hour week should be attained. These figures include agricul-

TABLE 27-2

MEASURING THE

FINANCIAL OUTLOOK OF CONSUMERS

One of the most valuable barometers of how consumers are sizing up their own situation is the University of Michigan's Survey Research Center studies. The 1956 Survey of Consumer Finances, conducted in cooperation with the Board of Governors of the Federal Reserve System, showed that more people felt they were better off financially than in the previous year. Most of them felt that their prospects would continue to be bright for another year. About the same proportions of people were planning for new houses, cars and home appliances as in the year before.

One question was: "Now, considering the country as a whole, do you think that during the next twelve months we will have good times or bad times, or what?" Here are the comparative percentages on answers to this question for each of three years:

Year:	Good times expected	Fair times	Bad times	Uncertain or not ascertained
1956	64%	5%	9%	22%
1955	59	5	12	24
1954	43	8	25	24

Sources: *Surveys of Consumer Finances*, Board of Governors of the Federal Reserve System, Washington, D.C., for years mentioned in table above.

tural work. For nonagricultural workers the prediction for 1960 is 35 hours.

When people have extra leisure time, marketing men try to help them utilize it through the purchase of more products and services.

A generation ago, economists and moralists worried a great deal about what people would do with the increased leisure time that would come from shorter working hours. Businessmen looked upon leisure time only in terms of lost man-hours, reduced production, higher costs, and a lower standard of living. Moralists, too, assumed that idleness would produce only dissipation and more alcoholic stupors. Actually, the per capita consumption of alcoholic beverages has decreased. Per capita whisky consumption declined from about 1.8 wine gallons in 1917 to 1.2 gallons in 1953.[6]

The average American now has some 125 days a year away from his work-bench or desk. He has a two-day weekend, two or three weeks' vacation with pay, 10-to 30-minute coffee breaks morning and afternoon, and early retirement on pension. This means that he spends a lot of time and money on travel, TV viewing, reading, church functions, gardening, do-it-yourself activities, and other amusements.

Nor has the industrial productivity of the people of the United States resulted in their use of extra time on vacuous spectator amusements, as was once predicted by educators. Instead, research shows that they have decreased their recreational expenditures for spectator amusements and increased individual recreation activities.[7]

THE DO-IT-YOURSELF MARKET.[8] Several important changes in American life have stimulated the do-it-yourself market. The old-fashioned handyman in the community who worked for $1 an hour is no longer available. The $75-a-week office worker cannot afford the $150-a-week carpenter or paperhanger.

Investigations by psychologically minded

researchers, however, indicate that the force behind the do-it-yourself movement is not so much a desire to save money as "an accumulation of intense resentment" on the part of the homeowner against the often dictatorial union repairman.[9] Most analysts of the movement think that it has grown out of such influences in modern life as the available leisure time from long weekends and the natural desire to do and see what has been accomplished. This last-mentioned desire has been accentuated as a result of our industrial specialization whereby few workers in a factory or office see the completed articles or services they are helping to make or provide.

THE DIETETIC MARKET. America's millions of dieters have established a trend of major significance to many marketers. For some, it has increased sales; for others, decreased them. Current evidence of the wide interest in diets and dietetic foods can be observed in our modern supermarkets. Dietetic foods are now displayed by approximately 90 per cent of supermarkets. Most of the foods offered are of the low-calorie kind to control overweight and diabetes; some are of the low-sodium variety to control certain disorders of the heart and kidneys; and a few are of the hypoallergenic variety to control food allergies and sensitiveness. Examples are soybean flour, gelatin, eggless cake mix, nonnutritive sweeteners, salt-free canned soups, evaporated goat milk, dry milk, water-packed fruits, sugar-free juices, low calorie soft drinks, saccharin, and so on.

Today, the emphasis on "fitting into last year's suit" is becoming a major business influence in the marketing of many foods. Millions fighting the "battle of the bulge" provide business for the modern marketer. They consume protein bread, nonfat dry milk, oilless salad dressings, sugarless soft drinks, water-packed fruits, and nonnutritive sweeteners. In other fields, too, the dieters are providing a market; they join gym classes, buy bathroom scales, and purchase massage machines as well as many other "reducing" gadgets. Clubs are formed for the purpose of mass weight reduction.

Health authorities support the fact that obesity is one of America's health problems. In addition to those interested in streamlining themselves, there are the diabetics and low-sodium users. Business firms have, as a result, introduced new products suited to these special requirements, and called attention continuously, through advertising, to what is available.

MARKETS IN TERMS OF GEOGRAPHICAL AREAS. In some geographical areas, climatic conditions, customs, and traditions are so well known that extensive research is not necessary to appreciate their influence in sales differences. Hard- and soft-water conditions have a recognized direct bearing on sales for coffee, tea, soap, and detergents as well as on water softeners.

The U.S. Department of Agriculture conducts numerous surveys on what people eat and wear. Lemons, for example, are used for different purposes in certain areas. In Los Angeles they are most widely used as hair rinses, bleaches, and cathartics. In the South, only 10 per cent of the users squeeze lemons on fish but 30 per cent of those on the Pacific Coast do. Lemon pies are made by 44 per cent of the housewives of cities and by 65 per cent in the country. A Boston housewife rarely admits to buying a box of cranberries on impulse. Topeka housewives buy twice as many cranberries on impulse.[10]

U.S.A. stands for the United—not Uniform—States of America. Its more than 3,000 counties differ widely in purchase of certain products: bottled drinks, fishing equipment, clothing, and so on. Tastes in entertainment vary with the area. Some cities have few or no night clubs. An artistic moving picture will have its art values stressed in a city such as Kansas City and its sex angles in Chicago. "Likes and dislikes in movies are more a question of small-town vs. large-town or

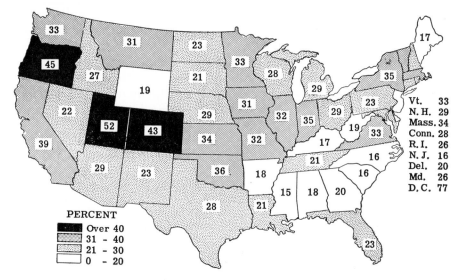

Vt.	33
N. H.	29
Mass.	34
Conn.	28
R. I.	26
N. J.	16
Del.	20
Md.	26
D. C.	77

PERCENT

■ Over 40
▨ 31 – 40
▨ 21 – 30
□ 0 – 20

Many consumer wants and preferences vary with geographical areas. Proportions in college student distributions do also. The proportions of college-age young people who attend college, as shown on this map for 1949–50, range from 15 per cent in Mississippi to 52 per cent in Utah. The numbers on the map exclude summer school and special students. Source: **The Impending Tidal Wave of Students,** A Report of the Committee on Special Projects, The American Association of Collegiate Registrars and Admissions Officers, 1954.

downtown vs. neighborhood audiences than anything else. Small-town audiences want Westerns, comedy and action pictures. Heavy dramas make their big money in the metropolitan centers. Message pictures go well in urban centers and die in small towns."[11]

The differences and similarities in purchasing preferences of regional, state, county, and city areas are so numerous that each marketer finds it necessary to analyze and be guided by them. Sears, Roebuck and Co., for example, has found these differences and similarities so important that their general catalog is printed in 11 different editions to fit the conditions of the sections where their 11 major distributing centers are located.

Some marketing targets are selected by means of consumer surveys; others by the study of trends in consumer behavior. The main principle for the student to appreciate is that if marketing is to be effective, it must be directed toward a market that has been identified before the advertising and selling are planned. Consumer habits and preferences must be analyzed by means of appropriate techniques.

Among psychologists, the best known organization making consumer studies is The Psychological Corporation. However, many advertising agencies and manufacturers have trained psychologists on the staff or in charge of consumer study programs. Many of our corporations have found the services of psychologists very helpful in conducting consumer research.

Marketing men constantly seek to learn what consumers want and to compete with other purveyors of products so as to lower prices and to raise the standard of living. General Motors Corporation, for example, has sent out over thirty million questionnaires since 1933. Most of these have dealt with the design or improvement of automotive products and services. Recipients of the questionnaires have been asked to indicate their preferences for such features as the location of spare wheels and types of upholstery fabrics.

METHODS OF OBTAINING CONSUMER RESEARCH DATA

Several methods of securing consumer research data are in common use. The method varies with the need. A specific problem may demand a special type of laboratory, test campaign, questionnaire, analysis of company records, or field survey. Applied psychologists are interested particularly in the questionnaire and the interview as used in surveys. We shall discuss briefly construction of questionnaires and methods of securing data through field investigators or interviewers.

The free-association or "open-end interview" approach to the consumer

When the consumer researcher wishes to formulate a questionnaire, he does not begin by writing a list of questions which he himself considers appropriate. For him to do so would be to require consumer respondents to think in *his* rather than *their* terms. He wants the respondents' minds to function in terms of their patterns of behavior; not his. One approach to the collection of ideas from typical consumers is to ask them to give their own free associations, to let their minds run freely, and to have them express their thoughts spontaneously about the given topic or product. For example, a manufacturer of toothpaste wished to devise a questionnaire to discover the satisfactions and wants of consumers in regard to the use of toothpaste. An interviewer called on typical users and said: "I am making a study of a product with which you are acquainted and I would like to ask questions about it, but I do not know what people really think about it. When I give you the name of the product, will you kindly tell me whatever comes into your mind. Tell me what you think, no matter how trivial it may seem. The word is 'toothpaste.' Now let your mind run." Sample responses were the following:

1. "I use X brand toothpaste, not because of the radio program or any other type of advertising but because of its taste. It has been proved that toothpaste is of little value, but I'll continue to use it because I like its taste and refreshing feeling in my mouth."
2. "I like the fresh, tangy taste of toothpaste within my mouth."
3. "There's a fresh taste left in my mouth after using it. Much ballyhoo about their qualities. Little real value in the power of destruction of germs. The taste of mint is often too strong."
4. "There are many toothpastes on the market, but I think salt can be used to good advantage. We like the taste of the toothpastes and they are convenient. One of the greatest inventions of the modern era."
5. "Toothpaste and dentifrices have made the appearance of the present generation much improved over those who came before us. It removes dirt and food from between the teeth and has lessened decay. Thus, we have less tooth ailments and other ailments caused by faulty teeth. Has done away with bad breath to a great extent."
6. "Much ado about nothing. All toothpastes are basically the same with different flavoring. The best dentifrice is plain salt or a plain powder that is not tasty. Various companies pick on minor differences to fool the public."
7. "You can pay anywhere from five cents to a dollar for toothpaste. Every toothpaste company is trying to cut the other one's neck. Advertising appeals come in two classes: Be mouth-happy and remove that white film from your teeth."
8. "I can't start to class unless my teeth feel clean whether they are or not."
9. "X Brand is like a dishrag in your mouth."
10. "X Brand is like a mouth full of soap suds."

At first thought, one might think that the nonguided comments of consumers would be difficult to classify and arrange into any logical order. Actually, their comments can be classified very quickly, simply by underlining favorable statements with a red pencil

SUMMARY OF FREE ASSOCIATIONS OF
FIFTY MEN

Reasons for Preferences for Certain Toothpastes:	*Per Cent*
1. "I like a certain toothpaste because the radio programs are good"	14.0
2. "Toothpastes refresh the mouth"	12.0
3. "I use the toothpaste I do because I like the taste"	10.0
4. "It sweetens the breath"	4.0
5. "It's convenient when you're in a hurry"	2.0
6. "The appearance of the teeth is improved"	2.0
7. "It lessens tooth ailments"	2.0
8. "My teeth feel better when using it"	2.0

Reasons for Disliking Certain Toothpastes:	
1. "Advertisers make claims for their products which are impossible"	18.0
2. "Toothpaste is made cheap and sold at a high price"	10.0
3. "Salt and soda are not so expensive and are better for the teeth"	10.0
4. "Some toothpastes are injurious"	6.0
5. "All toothpastes are basically the same with different flavoring"	4.0
6. "I don't like the taste"	4.0
7. "I dislike colored pastes"	2.0

and unfavorable with blue. Each statement can be further classified as shown in the partial tabulation in Table 27-3 of the responses of fifty men to the word "toothpaste."

The major value of the free-association technique is that it reveals what consumers think when they deal with the given product or its class as they use it, shop for it in a retail store, or discuss it with their friends. Any questionnaire made up without resort to free association or a substitute simply funnels the consumer's thinking through unnatural channels. Many a questionnaire has resulted in pages of statistical tables that showed only what people thought while they were thinking in terms of the consumer analyst's patterns, not what people think when they behave in their own unguided manner.

Furthermore, an additional value of the free-association technique, or so-called "open-end interview," is the richness of its yield for advertising ideas. The advertising man who has fifty typical consumers prac-

tice free association concerning his product is almost certain to obtain a supply of ideas for advertising it. He will feel no need for thumbing through magazines to look for themes or ideas that he might use in advertising his own product.

The first few questions used in any questionnaire should be interesting to the respondent. They should establish rapport, put him into a mood favorable to the answering of the main questions of the survey. "Icebreaker" questions are developed most easily when the consumer analyst has learned from free-association techniques how consumers think about the topic of study.

The mailed questionnaire

Many questionnaires in the past have been phrased in such general and vague terms that the person answering them may, while he is answering the questions, feel that his answers are going to be useless, because he is not sure that he understands the questions in the same way that others understand them. Frequently, too, the answering of a questionnaire has involved a great deal of time and expense. In spite of the fact that some persons dislike the questionnaire, it is still widely used and will continue to be used. Fortunately, the phrasers of questionnaires are learning how to make them attractive, inviting, and reliable. The chief psychological factors in securing a high percentage of replies to mailed questionnaires are:

1. The questionnaire should have an attractive physical appearance.
2. The recipient should be made to feel that the questionnaire is worth while.
3. Compensate the answerer for his trouble.
4. For some studies the identity of the real sender should be hidden.
5. The questionnaire should be given a preliminary test on a small group before it is tried on the larger group.
6. Make the questions easy and, if possible, interesting to answer.

Two young members of GM's customer research staff survey some 11,000 questionnaires that were received in the mail in one day after they had been answered by motorists. Between 15 and 20 surveys are made each year by the organization.

1. *The physical appearance of the questionnaire.*—A concern which sells by direct mail would not think of sending out a letter set in solid, monotonous type. The direct-mail expert makes careful tests of returns with regard to copy, color of paper, quality of paper, postage, day of week mailed, and other pertinent factors. It is necessary, therefore, to prepare the physical appearance of the questionnaire with consideration of the same factors used in direct mail. The questionnaire can be illustrated with human-interest pictures that explain its purpose and enable the answerer to state his experience or wants with pleasure as well as ease. Pictures on mailed questionnaires increase the returns greatly. Color illustrations and attractive appearance are essential to large returns in direct mail. They are just as essential to returns in questionnaires.

2. *The addressee should be made to feel that the questionnaire is worth while.*—The person who is asked to answer a questionnaire usually feels that he would be doing the sender a great favor by taking the time to answer the questions. In order to obtain answers, therefore, it is well to make the answerer feel that he is doing himself a favor. Most questionnaires introduce the request for answering as this one did: "We are compiling some data giving us statistics on our business and we would like you to fill in the inclosed questionnaire and return it to us in the inclosed stamped envelope."

Contrast that with this concern, which was trying to get the attitude of their 3,000 dealers toward them as jobbers:

Did you ever get mad at us?!! Perhaps we were at fault in some of your dealings with us. We are doing some housecleaning of our own minds and methods of doing business. Our friends and our enemies can help us improve our service to them by being frank with us. Please check over the following list and make any comments that you wish. We'll appreciate it and thank you in advance.

One jobber received 500 replies from 3,000 dealers by use of a similar request. The replies were followed up by the management through the salesmen.

The appeals which succeed in direct-mail advertising often succeed in questionnaires. One concern phrased its questionnaire to give the impression that a very charming woman was asking a very small favor. The letter gave the reader the impression that her employer had made a wager that the readers would not answer her questionnaire and she was trying to convince him that the recipients were really interested in helping those who wish to improve their methods of work.

When the questionnaire is sent to a specific group, such as kindergarten teachers, accountants, or shoe merchants, it is often possible to appeal to them by offering them a copy of the data when it has been compiled. In that case it is well to specify the date when the report will be completed and available. A request card for the report should be attached to the questionnaire to enable the person who answers the questionnaire to realize that he may have a free copy of the report.

If the copy of the report has no appeal, it is possible to increase the answers by offering a small gift for answering the questionnaire and returning it by a definite date.

3. *Better results may be obtained if the true identity of the sender is hidden.*—Magazine publishers occasionally wish to make an impartial investigation of their readers' preferences. In some cases the candid answers of the person who fills in the questionnaire may reflect against the publisher who sent the questionnaire. In cases where honest answers might offend the sender, it is well to give the recipient the impression that the investigation is being conducted by an accounting firm or by a statistical concern.

Much depends upon the purpose of the questionnaire. If it is to learn about the complaints of the customers, for example, the true identity must be stated.

4. *Decide upon the type or class of people that you wish to reach.*—In certain situations, it is easy to limit the sending of the questionnaire to the desired group. When a company wishes to get customers' reactions and the company has a complete list of customers, the problem of finding the right group is answered. When the reactions of the general public are desired, it is well to find out which segment of the public is to be reached.

When it is important to know what types of people answer the questionnaire, it is well to insert questions that will enable the investigators to tabulate the answers according to groups, such as occupation, education, sex, or age.

5. *Give the proposed questionnaire a preliminary trial on a test group.*—Again the principles of direct mail should be used with the questionnaire. The direct-mail specialist does not use a letter on a large group of prospects until he has tested it on a small group. He finds that he must do this even though he is absolutely certain that he has a good letter. Experience has taught him that it is dangerous to spend large sums of money until he has determined the percentage and quality of returns.

Questions which are quite clear to the researcher may be ambiguous, vague, impertinent, or unnecessary to a large number of strangers. Only a trial survey can determine the probable value of the mailing. In making the trial survey, it is well to have interviewers present the questionnaire to individuals in person and then note their remarks and questions as a guide to revision.

Phrasing the questions

No one enjoys attempting to answer a question that he does not understand. The more certain the reader is that he understands the question, the more willingly he will answer it. For this reason, questions of opinion rather than concrete facts are inhibiting to the answerer of a questionnaire. Questions such as, "Why did you buy a Blank auto?" "What is your opinion regarding our powdered milk?" or, "How would you advise us to change our displays?" are not clear and definite to the consumer, and he cannot answer them correctly. Answers to this type of question, however, may give a copywriter a great many suggestions for new copy in advertisements.

Questions, to be understandable, should be phrased in the vernacular. The academic phrasing, "What dentifrice do you customarily employ?" will puzzle more people than "What do you use to clean your teeth with?"

A more involved question, of a type difficult for anyone to answer, was used in a survey of automobile travel: "From March 1, 1956 to March 1, 1957 please classify out-of-town journeys of some length (round trips of 70 miles or more) made by automobile whether in your own car or in a car belonging to someone else."

People should not be asked to make complicated computations in their recall of purchases or habits. If a man is asked: "How often in the course of a month do you change to a new razor blade?" he must make a bothersome computation. It is better to ask, "How many shaves do you get from a razor blade?"

To achieve certainty of understanding, it is well to have the questions relate to matters of fact rather than opinion, and to give all the possible types of answers after each question. Giving the correct answer will then be easy—it merely requires a checkmark, and compensates for any vagueness in the phrasing of the question.

Questions should be stated positively rather than negatively. For example, it is better to say, "Have you bought any Blank soap this week? Yes—, No—, than to say,

"Have you not bought any Blank soap this week? Yes—, No—."

Negative and positive phrasings were used in a nationwide survey with the question: "Do you think that advertising is *less* (*more*) truthful today than it was a year or two ago?" Each of the two phrasings was used for 3,200 individuals, and was asked of every second person. It was found that 56.5 per cent answered *No* to the *less* phrasing. But the fact that one is not justified in assuming, on the basis of the foregoing, that people therefore think advertising is *more* truthful is indicated by the answers to the positive phrasing, which were only 46.7 per cent affirmative. Also, the *Don't know* answers for the second form of the question were 22.1 per cent, compared with 18.8 per cent for the first form.[12]

The same investigators also found that the words used in expressing alternatives will influence the results obtained. In two surveys, one month apart, the following were asked of comparable samples of 7,867 persons in each of the samples.

Form A—*"Which of these companies do you think well of generally, which not so well?"* (Company name given and response recorded.)

Form B—*"Do you think favorably or unfavorably of the following companies?"* (Company name given and response recorded.)

Essentially these questions are similar, except for the change from *well* and *not so well* to *favorably* and *unfavorably*.

	RESPONSES	
	Form A	Form B
Company	Well	Favorably
	%	%
A	79.4	67.6
B	58.3	46.9
C	52.3	46.8
D	85.5	74.1
E	72.4	62.1

It can be said that the term *favorably* was apparently interpreted as being a more extreme alternative and therefore received fewer responses than the term *well*.[13]

Questions which involve the prestige or personal integrity of the person answering them, such as, "How much did you pay for your last hat?" "Do you do your own washing?" "How often do you take a bath?" do not elicit accurate results. When it is necessary to ask questions which involve the personal affairs of the individual, the questionnaire must come from a third disinterested party or from someone who is able to assure the person that the answers will be kept confidential and used in a legitimate manner.

"It's a survey man asking what programs we watch. What are some real highbrow programs?"
Reproduced by permission of Chicago Tribune—New York News Syndicate, Inc.

Obviously, leading questions should be avoided. However, many questions that do not appear to be leading tend to encourage respondents to answer unduly favorably. "What brands of the following foods do you use?" suggests the use of all the foods listed. This question is improved somewhat when phrased, "If you bought any of the following foods in the last three months, state the brand you bought last." Overstatements are especially encouraged when this type of question is phrased, "What brands of the following toilet requisites do you buy?" And most students would be encouraged to

say *Yes* if asked, "If Dad were to buy a new car, would he be influenced by your choice?"

One concern made its mailed questionnaire attractive to housewives by writing an interesting short story, in pamphlet form, describing the problems of a housewife. The story also set forth her methods of work. The housewife recipient was asked to check the method that she herself used under those conditions, and in this way the manufacturer learned the conditions and methods under which women used his product.

Respondents should be invited to give their comments in addition to their check marks. The comments are likely to reveal the feeling tones and manner of thinking more helpfully than the tabulated check marks.

The personal interview as a source of consumer research data

Sometimes the questionnaire does not elicit the desired data when mailed. It may then be necessary to obtain the information by means of interviewers. If a study were to be made of the reactions of vegetable hucksters, factory workers, or shoe shiners, the results of a mailed questionnaire would be inadequate. When necessary to secure answers to a large number of questions, the interview may be the best method of getting representative answers. Sometimes the same people who will not answer a list of questions by mail will do so when called upon personally.

For research problems that cannot be studied through mailed questionnaires, personal interviews must be obtained. An example of this is the advertiser who wishes to find out which of three proposed headlines, illustrations, or layouts is the best. If the researcher were to hand copies of the three advertisements, identical in every respect except the factor under investigation, to fifty buyers, and ask each buyer of the commodity to state which of the three advertisements was the best, many of the fifty persons would cease to be consumers of the product advertised and become advertising critics. Their reactions would be artificial. By means of interviews, it is possible to plan a technique which will lessen the artificiality of the judgments.

If a study is to be made of three different kinds of copy, three advertisements can be prepared which are identical in all respects except for the copy. Ten other advertisements of different products can be mounted on cardboard. When the investigator calls on typical buyers of the product to obtain their reactions, he may fumble in his brief case for the ten advertisements and "accidentally" pull out the three advertisements and hand them to the prospect with a passing remark such as, "Do you care to look at these while I prepare my ten advertisements for your opinion?" In a few seconds he arranges the ten advertisements and the prospect lays aside the three important advertisements. After a five-minute discussion of the ten advertisements, the interviewer replaces in his brief case the ten advertisements, and then, *incidentally*, asks the prospect about the copy of the three layouts he saw in the early part of the interview. The reactions of the prospect will then approximate those which he would have if he saw the advertisements in a periodical where they would have to compete with many other interests.

If the field interview is used, it is usually necessary to choose and standardize the questions just as carefully as for a mailed form. The interviewers must be instructed also as to how they are to present the questions. They must be trained so that they do not put the answers into the mouths of the informants. When persons are interviewed who are not accustomed to supplying information to oral questions, the interviewer should be trained not to write down the answers in their presence. They may dislike the idea of having someone write down their statements as they make them. In some cases the investigator can be taught to mem-

orize the questions and then informally write the answers on the margin of a newspaper and copy them later.

Interviewer from the Survey Research Center of the Institute for Social Research, University of Michigan, getting survey data from a consumer. Field reports such as these are basic to the planning of programs in modern marketing.

The research interviewer should have some qualities of salesmanship. However, salesmen are not, as a rule, competent to do field work of a research nature. Salesmen are trained to influence the answers of the person interviewed. They are apt to see only those factors of the situation that agree with their own prejudices. They are promoters rather than analysts.

MOTIVATION RESEARCH IN MARKETING

Motivation research tries to discover the relations between overt behavior on the part of people in the market and the underlying inner mental processes such as drives, desires, emotions, impulses, attitudes, avoidances, and preferences. It digs beneath the surface of behavior by indirect methods in order to uncover those motivations of which the individual is wholly unaware or only

8

partially aware. It is person-centered. Most readers are acquainted with some of the techniques used, such as the projective tests —word associations, picture associations, the Rorschach ink-blot test, and the depth interview. Many of the researchers in this field have had training in psychoanalysis.

Psychoanalysis and motivation research are, however, not synonymous. The purposes of the two are different. Motivation research also is more varied in its approaches as to why people behave than psychoanalysis alone. When approaches from the social sciences are used—sociology, cultural anthropology, psychology, social psychology, psychiatry, and psychoanalysis—they are often grouped under the heading of motivation research whenever the areas of their efforts are planned as aids to advertising and selling, particularly the selection of appeals. The social sciences are basic in learning about motives in the market place, hence some investigators prefer to use other terms, such as "Behavioral Science Research" or "Motivation Analysis."

Quantitative research long since has provided the marketer with statistics concerning the numbers of people who buy a product, the approximate percentages that buy the major brands, the ages and incomes of the consumers, and the geographical areas where they live. The modern marketer wants to know more: why some people buy and others do not. If he knows that, he can define his market more precisely and use more effective appeals in his advertising and selling.

Need for motivation analysis

Each researcher who has done an appreciable number of studies of consumer behavior has run into statistics that simply did not jibe with the known facts. In one study, for example, a carefully surveyed sample of consumers were asked whether they preferred to drink the light or the regular type of a certain brand of beverage. A ratio of

3 to 1 stated their preference for the light brew. The actual facts, however, were that the regular outsold the light by a 9 to 1 ratio! Apparently the people questioned answered according to their feeling as to what discriminating people drank.[14]

The inadequacy of direct questioning was also demonstrated when people who were interviewed in the course of a survey were asked the question, "Do you borrow money from a personal-loan company?" All of those interviewed answered "No." This answer was given even though all those interviewed were listed in the records of a local loan company as having recently borrowed money! Similar untruthful answers are given when people are asked about the magazines they read. The answers, if taken at face value, would lead one to believe that the *Atlantic Monthly* has six times its actual circulation, while the pulp magazines, printed by the millions, have negligible appeal. The desire not to appear "low-brow" clearly influences the answers given to this type of question.[15]

CANDY. William A. Yoell made a study for M & M candy and found that candy for some persons is "associated with accomplishment of a job that the person who ate the candy considered disagreeable. The candy was a sort of reward or compensation for doing a tough job. Accordingly, M & M switched its advertising theme in two test markets (Boston and Detroit) from 'Smooth, rich, creamy coated chocolate—everybody likes 'em,' to 'Make that tough job seem easier—you deserve M & M candy.'"[16] A noticeable increase in sales of M & M candy was reported to have followed the change in advertising themes in the test markets.

POWER SHOVEL. A business paper advertisement for this product carried an illustration of a huge machine that lifted an immense load of rock. The machine and its load were far more conspicuous than the operator.

Motivation studies indicated that operators felt hostile toward a machine that made
them look insignificant. The feeling was
corrected by means of a photograph taken
inside the cab, looking over the operator's
shoulder. The advertisement then gave the
operator the feeling that he was in complete
control of the machine, easing the operator's
hostility.[17]

INSTANT COFFEE. A classic example of
the way projective methods were applied to
a marketing problem has been reported for
instant coffee. Powdered instant coffee was
on the market, in some form or other, long
before World War II. Yet for many years
women did not use it to an appreciable extent. Then Mason Haire of the University of
California decided to discover possible motivational influences.

First, he questioned a group of women as
to why they did not use the powdered coffee,
and found that they all agreed upon not liking the taste of it. This seemed a stereotyped answer to Haire, as he doubted that
the taste was that unpleasant to everyone.
Thus, he looked for a more significant answer and tried the following experiment:
Two shopping lists were drawn up which
differed in only the fifth item:

List A

1½ lb. hamburger
2 loaves Wonder bread
Bunch of carrots
1 can Rumford's baking powder
Nescafé instant coffee
2 can Del Monte peaches
5 lb. potatoes

List B

1½ lb. hamburger
2 loaves Wonder bread
Bunch of carrots
1 can Rumford's baking powder
Maxwell House coffee, drip grind
2 cans Del Monte peaches
5 lb. potatoes

List A was given to a group of 50 women
and List B to another group of 50. He then
asked each of the women to describe the
type of women who would go to the store
with such a list. Actually neither list could
possibly give any clue to the personality of
the shopper. In order to comply with Haire's
request, each woman had to project her own
feelings into a word picture.

The results were surprising: 48 per cent
of the women with List A pictured a lazy
woman who does not plan her purchases
well, 12 per cent tagged her as a spendthrift,
and 16 per cent declared she wasn't a good
wife.

Of the women using List B, only 4 per
cent indicated laziness; 12 per cent mentioned bad planning, and none pictured the
shopper as a spendthrift or bad wife.

This seems to indicate rather clearly that
some women did not use powdered coffee
because using it would give them a picture
of themselves that they did not like.[18]

The methods used in motivation research
are not ordinarily a part of the repertoire of
the typical marketing man—he turns to specialists trained in psychology for services in
this area of investigation.[19]

Many psychologists are interested in the
unconscious aspects of human behavior.
There are, broadly speaking, three areas or
levels of motivation:

1. The rational, self-knowing area in
which one is aware of what motivated his
action and is *able and willing to tell why.*
Example:

A man has been looking for a certain kind
of shirt, one that he can wash easily when
on trips away from home. It must be quick-
drying and have no-ironing features. When
he happens to see an advertisement for a
Dacron shirt that offers the desired features,
he is motivated to buy it. Ordinary questioning elicits the information needed to prepare advertising that triggers the purchase
act.

2. The rational area in which one is aware
of what motivated his action and is *able but
unwilling to tell why.* Example:

A man buys a home in an expensive neighborhood because, as he says, "It's a better investment." Actually, he realizes that he wants to become a member of a better social set.

The *Chicago Tribune* Research Department also found that most women do not get overly excited about a hosiery advertisement that displays only stockings or legs. Instead, a hosiery manufacturer should depict a smartly dressed woman wearing hose and being admired by others. He should try to create an image of beauty for the woman as a person.

3. The complex hidden area in which one is not aware of what motivated his behavior and really *cannot fully tell why.*[20] Examples: the morbid gambler's unconscious wish to lose as self-punishment for certain unconscious aggressions or the housewife's bargain hunting as a need to outsmart others and to express aggression toward a mother substitute.

Much of our everyday behavior involves more than one type of motivation. When areas 2 and 3 are especially pertinent to the person's behavior to be studied, special procedures are necessary. These procedures to explore motivation have been known and used for a long time.

To explore areas 2 and 3, procedures such as the depth interview have been brought over from clinical psychology where they have been used for many years.

The depth interview

Motives in buying are very difficult to uncover by direct questioning. When housewives, for example, are asked why they buy a certain brand of a household utility, most of them may mention its high quality. When, however, they are encouraged to discuss the product without prompting or suggestion of answers, they may reveal that the real reason for purchase is the economy, because of assured long life of the article. People are apt to rationalize when casually interviewed about their buying.

The *depth interview* is one of the newer methods of motivational research used by a few large advertisers and agencies. A depth interview is a three-hour detailed case study of the steps and reasons involved in a consumer's behavior. It is an attempt to get better answers than the usual surface responses, such as, "I like Blank's chocolate pudding because it's chocolate," or, "I like it because I like it." The person who is interviewed by the depth technique is stimulated to talk, to reveal his basic attitudes, opinions, and reasons. Only psychologically trained interviewers can use this technique.

Ernest Dichter, a Viennese psychologist, has been a pioneer in the development of depth interviewing. Some of his procedures and findings are partially explained in the following excerpts from an article about his studies for *Time* magazine and the Chrysler Corporation:

The customer's inner needs. The psychologist can be helpful in finding out the needs and innermost wishes the consumer expects to see fulfilled by a type of product. This is what might be called the functional approach.

In a study the author recently completed for *Time* magazine, direct questioning about why people read *Time* evoked such answers as "It condenses the news for me," or "It is written in a brilliant style," or other similar quality descriptions of the magazine. In the functional research approach, however, we are not so much interested in finding out what people think about the magazine, or what they think they think about it, as we are in finding out what the magazine actually *does* for them. In the case of *Time*, this approach showed that one of the major functions of the magazine was to provide what the psychologists call "ego-benefits." That is, it bolstered up the readers, because it made them *feel* like busy executives whose position demanded that they be well informed but whose schedule was so crowded that they needed to get their news quickly. As one reader actually said in response to deeper questioning: "When I read *Time*, I like myself." Such a statement is quite different from a descriptive remark about the product itself; it depicts a real psychological effect produced on the reader.

Now such a functional finding permits action on the part of the publisher. For example, if he knows that some of his readers are looking for such ego-benefits, then he can make use of this knowledge. The more *Time* offers those readers the opportunity to experience this kind of feeling by the way the magazine is written and edited, the better they like the magazine and the more they are inclined to buy further copies at the newsstand or to renew their subscriptions. Furthermore it can be decided, and actually has been, to make a specific appeal to this feeling in *Time's* circulation promotion efforts, where a fraction of a percentage point improvement in the rate of returns will add up to a substantial dollars-and-cents savings.

It is worth noting, too, that in this way *Time* introduces an important new aspect into the whole field of education. For hundreds and possibly thousands of years our good-intentioned educators have attempted to convince us that it is not an easy job to increase our knowledge. *Time* encourages and produces the opposite conviction. While the academic archeologist tells you that it takes scores of years to know the field, *Time* promises you a workable knowledge after only a comparatively few pages of reading.

For the Chrysler Corporation the application of modern functional research operated in the following way. The objective of the executives concerned was to use advertising to get more people to switch from other makes of cars to Chrysler cars. To do this they needed to know why about 75% of all car buyers purchase the same make of car year after year; they wanted to change that habit. Direct questioning uncovered the apparent reason: rational satisfaction with the quality of the previously owned car. The obvious advertising approach, dealing with such surface rationalization, would have been to stress the fact that the new make of car was startlingly different and better, that it was time to get rid of the old car with all its repair bills and troubles.

From the point of view of the psychological findings this was exactly the opposite of the correct approach. A psychological survey revealed that the real reasons for the high percentage of repeat purchases were based on unconscious fear of automobiles as dangerous, powerful instruments, taking the form of fear of the unfamiliarity of a new make of car, fear of disloyalty to the old car which had demonstrated its safety, emotional attachment to the old car, and similar factors. Instead of talking down the old car, the advertiser needed to compliment the prospective customer on his friendship and loyalty to the presently owned car and to promise him that the new car would permit him to

feel the old familiarity within a few hours. The Chrysler executives decided to use this approach in all their advertising and to include it in their sales training courses. The result was a 100% rise in the Starch rating of Chrysler and Plymouth advertisements and a substantial increase in sales.

For the same reasons, the salesmen's usual habit of kicking the tires of old cars brought for trade-in was found to be psychologically detrimental to the transaction. Controlled tests showed that customers actually accepted lower trade-ins when the old car was complimented —"It's easy to see this car was well taken care of"—than when it was deprecated. Thus, functional research reveals the deeper-lying, real motivations for buying behavior and permits correct, effective sales methods to be substituted for others that are often dangerously wrong business-wise.[21]

In another report on his study done for Chrysler Corporation, Dichter stated that no matter how many direct questions the interviewer asked in a "formal" interview, he never got beyond such superficial motives as satisfaction with the previous car, better trade-in allowance, and so forth. The use of depth interviewing and motivational research brought forth truly basic reasons from the interview, such as dread of change, nostalgia, and the like. In explaining the need for the use of special techniques in learning motivations of the consumer, Dichter stated:

. . . whenever we are dealing with motivations in research, we have to employ methods different from the ones used when a simple factual statement of *quantitative* relationship is required. Why should this be so when we are studying such seemingly simple problems as why Mr. Smith bought one brand of dental cream rather than another, or why women listen to certain types of radio programs?

The answer lies in the nature and the mechanisms of human motivations. Motivations are of such a different nature from our other research objectives that the usual research tools no longer suffice. One might well ask, at this point, what is it about motivations that makes them the subject of an almost separate branch of research requiring special tools? I should therefore like to turn now to a discussion of those aspects of motivation which make this necessary.

To begin with, *motivations are dynamic.* If I wanted to find out why Mr. Smith is wearing a blue suit today, the answer most likely would not be a single reason or even a list of reasons. When he opened the closet this morning, the blue suit was hanging nearest him and so he decided to put it on. Then, however, he remembered that he didn't have any tie his wife liked to go with it, and so he selected the brown suit. When he looked this over, he discovered that his wife still had not sewn on the missing button. Annoyed by his wife's neglect, he spitefully reached for the blue suit again. While he was putting on the blue suit, it occurred to him that his decision was a good one after all because he had not been wearing this suit for a long time.

Let us not go any further. This relatively simple example shows us how unsatisfactory any single statement of motivation may be. When questioned for the motivations of his choice, all Mr. Smith may have told us, was that he saw the blue suit first. This despite the complicated dynamics of the true motivation. We can understand, therefore, that a direct questionnaire technique will rarely be adequate for the registration of dynamic motivational mechanisms . . .

. . . a respondent is frequently unaware of his motivations. Dr. Maslow, in a recent study, "A Theory of Human Motivation," says the following about unconscious motivations:

"Everyday conscious desires are to be regarded as symptoms, as surface indicators of more basic needs. If we were to take these superficial desires at their face values, we would find ourselves in a state of complete confusion, since we would be dealing seriously with symptoms rather than with what lay behind the symptoms."

This is extremely important as far as our methodological discussion is concerned. We must be able to distinguish between conscious and *unconscious motivations.* Depth psychology teaches us that unconscious reasons are usually more basic and powerful than the conscious ones. Obviously, a direct question runs no chance of success in uncovering unconscious motivations.[22]

Dichter uncovered some especially important findings regarding the purchase of automobiles. He found that only 2 per cent of car buyers buy convertibles. This 2 per cent figure, however, did not indicate the true importance of convertibles in car buying. When he counted the number of people who stopped in front of showrooms with convertibles in the window and compared the figure with the number who stopped in front of showrooms without convertibles, he found that the convertible was far more important than indicated by the 2 per cent sales figure. Investigation showed that the convertible is a symbol of eternal youth, coveted and dreamed about by almost every car buyer, but seldom actually bought. Convertibles are psychological lures to attract people to showrooms and to increase the attention value of advertisements.[23]

Psychologists realize that motives are difficult to uncover, but Lazarsfeld has shown that they can be uncovered, to some extent, by questionnaire procedures. Helpful answers to "why" can be obtained by asking a series of related questions that reveal aspects of motivation:

A question such as, Why did you change to this dentrifice? will elicit some such response as "I like it," a meaningless phrase. Other respondents may say, "My dentist recommended it to me," while still others report "It cleans teeth better than my former tooth paste." Obviously, then, the question must be rather specific in order to elicit comparable responses. Consider, for example, the following series of questions . . .

What brand of tooth paste did you buy last?
How long have you been using this brand?
What brand did you use before this?

In what respects do you think your present dentifrice is better than the kind you were using?

What was your principal objection to the brand you used before?

These questions elicited specific and meaningful reasons to explain behavior changes.[24]

Sometimes the best answers to "why" can be obtained by asking a series of questions that begin with the words "what" and "when" and "how." Respondents who are unable or unwilling to answer "why" are able and willing to give valid answers when the indirect approach is employed.

Room in a Range Design Forum, planned to resolve new product line specifications through the use of full scale mock-ups depicting design alternatives. By isolating the product feature at issue, in this case the interior cooking possibilities, conflicts in consumer preferences (e.g. with previously expressed surface burner arangement preferencs) were realistically resolved.

To ensure realistic expressions of consumer preferences, new design possibilities were graphically related to actual food mixing needs in this section of a design forum which was directed toward resolving the specifications for a new electric mixer.

Nowland and Company, of Greenwich, Connecticut, has pioneered in the use of full-scale mock-ups to ensure realistic expressions of consumer preferences in the resolution of new product specifications. Their experience has been that this approach is particularly effective when each product feature at issue is isolated for respondent evaluation.

The special contribution of motivation research

Motivation research is usually considered as qualitative rather than quantitative. It deals with why; not *how many?* Its findings must be verified by means of quantitative studies which answer the question as to how many persons behave in terms of specific motivations. A given trigger to action may be present, but whether it is potent with many or few consumers must be answered by conventional procedures such as questionnaires and field interviews, statistically treated. Motivation research does not involve any new techniques for the psychologist nor are its findings alone sufficient for controlling a marketing program. Its findings are, however, very valuable for the improvement of marketing programs. Influences in buying and new markets are revealed. New courses of marketing action are charted, particularly for advertising. Currently, motivation research is growing because it adds a source of new insight for marketing.

Good consumer research is creative

Experts in consumer research need so much statistical ability that they are apt to become engrossed in research techniques and lose sight of the creative aspect of their work. Business executives, particularly those in charge of advertising and selling, do not as a rule think in refined statistical terms. They are essentially promoters and innovators. They utilize the benefits of research, and they utilize its benefits most effectively when field research is an integral phase of their business philosophy. This attitude is fully expressed in the following admonition:

Remember that field research is essentially creative. Its value will be nil to a concern afflicted with complacency. If management's objective for its advertising is merely to ride the Babson sales curve, keep its name before the trade and "build good will and prestige," then it should not use field research. But if a company is progressive and alert, it can use field research profitably, for the research can help to create advertising that will increase sales and reduce unit sales costs.

All too often a business loses sight of the end purpose of its activities—a service to the customer which represents a sound value to him. There is a tendency to feel that service to the customers is the special and exclusive province of sales and service departments. This may explain why we find credit departments which bite the customer; why we find design engineers who concentrate all their efforts on making a better gadget which may or may not be acceptable to the customer; why we find advertising that takes into consideration not what the customer wants to know, but what the advertiser thinks he should know.

Therefore, step number one in any consideration of field research is accepting the fact that every activity the company engages in is on behalf of the customer. This holds true of design, purchasing, distribution, sales, service, promotion, advertising, financing, administration, credit, etc. . . .

To sum up, it may be said that field research answers three questions:

1. What should your advertising say? Obviously, your advertising is most effective when it gives customers information that is pertinent to the selection, application and maintenance of your product. . . .

2. Where to say it? Advertising won't help much if it is directed to the wrong people. One field investigation disclosed that a certain company's direct-mail literature was being sent to purchasing agents, who had no voice whatsoever in the selection of the product. It was learned that production engineers were the real behind-the-scenes authority on purchases. The mailing list was completely revised and made really effective. Field research can indicate to whom to say it as well as what to say.

3. Why? Unless you know why a customer thinks or believes the way he does, there probably isn't much you can do about it. . . .

Also, field research can give you freedom from doubt—doubt that appropriations are spent most effectively—doubt in the minds of management as to whether advertising is justified—doubt of the advisability of spending x dollars or y dollars. Field research answers the *why's* of management about advertising expenditures. It provides a sound sales reason why you say what you say and where you say it.[25]

Acknowledgments and References

1. Abbott Kimball, Inc., *Advertising and Selling*, August 4, 1932, pp. 42–43.

2. See Peter F. Drucker in *Nation's Business*, April 1952, pp. 34 f.

3. Stuart G. Waterhouse, "An Englishman Looks at American Marketing and Distribution Policies," *The Journal of Marketing*, January 1948.

4. Edward W. Bok, *The Americanization of Edward Bok*, Charles Scribner's Sons, New York, 1920, p. 164.

5. For a more detailed definition, see *The Journal of Marketing*, October 1948, p. 209.

6. See "The Leisured Masses," *Business Week*, September 12, 1953.

7. For data concerning the shifts in the ways our recreational activities have changed, 1929 versus 1952, see *Business Week*, September 12, 1953, p. 143. Also reported in Harry Walker Hepner, *Modern Marketing: Dynamics and Management*, McGraw-Hill Book Co., Inc., 1955, p. 31.

8. Sometimes the synonym "Build It Yourself" is used; however, this is a copyrighted term, owned by the Easi-Bild Pattern Co., division of Pattern Publishing Co., Pleasantville, N.Y.

9. Survey by Politz Research, Inc., reported in "Do-It-Yourself: The Greatest Market Development Since Self-Service," *Tide*, October 10, 1953.

10. See Jerome Shoenfeld, "Washington Has Answers for You," *Sales Management*, April 15, 1955.

11. Statement of Nathan Cohen, Associate Editor of *Boxoffice*, reported in *Printers' Ink*, August 12, 1949, p. 54.

12. Sidney Roslow, Wallace H. Wulfeck, and Philip G. Corby, "Consumer and Opinion Research: Experimental Studies on the Form of the Question," *The Journal of Applied Psychology*, Vol. XXIV, No. 3 (June 1940), pp. 334–346.

13. Elmer Wheeler, "The First Ten Seconds: The Crucial Turning Point of the Sales Talk," *Sales Management*, November 15, 1937, p. 49.

14. See James K. Blake, "Consumer Motivation Research," *Dun's Review and Modern Industry,* July 1954.

15. See Louis Cheskin and L. B. Ward, "Indirect Approach to Market Reactions," *Harvard Business Review,* September 1948.

16. William A. Yoell, "Make Your Advertising Themes Match Consumer Behavior," *Printers' Ink,* March 21, 1952.

17. See *Tide,* May 21, 1955, p. 25.

18. Mason Haire, "Projective Techniques in Marketing Research," *The Journal of Marketing,* April 1950.

19. An excellent understandable summary of these and other methods, written for the advertising or marketing man, is George Horsley Smith, *Motivation Research in Advertising and Marketing,* McGraw-Hill Book Company, Inc., 1954.

20. See Daniel Starch, "What Is New about Motivation Research?" *Printers' Ink,* August 19, 1955, p. 39.

21. Ernest Dichter, "Psychology in Market Research," *Harvard Business Review,* Summer 1947, pp. 434–435.

22. Ernest Dichter, "Depth Interviewing," a talk given at Market Research Council, October 15, 1943.

23. *Tide,* July 26, 1946, p. 58. See also Ernest Dichter, *The Psychology of Everyday Living,* Barnes & Noble, Inc., New York, 1947, p. 86.

24. Paul Lazarsfeld, *The Technique of Marketing Research,* McGraw-Hill Book Company, Inc., New York, 1937, pp. 62–91.

25. Charles S. Wilkinson, "The Why and How of Field Research," *Printers' Ink,* July 13, 1945, pp. 28, 36.

PROJECTS

1. Choose any common product on the market today and compose questions which might be used in a free-association interview to determine consumer opinion and the extent of use by the consumer. Contrast an inhibiting question with one easily answered. To what other psychological principles would you give consideration?

2. Obtain a mail-order catalog of a number of years ago and list articles that are no longer on the market or which have been radically changed. Check those which were fads and suggest reasons why the others have disappeared or have been greatly altered.

3. Select a number of articles in popular use today but which you think may no longer be on the market 10 years from now. Present reasons for your selection and indicate what type of article may replace them. How could the manufacturers of the products adjust themselves to the change?

4. Look up the ratings of a number of products in both Consumers Union and Comsumers' Research reports in your library. To what extent do the ratings of the two organizations agree?

5. Leaf through three distinctly different types of magazines, noticing the advertisements. Do the advertisements seem to be designed to appeal to the particular class of readers of that magazine? Why? Why not? Select some good and some poor examples from each of the three mediums.

6. Obtain a copy of a mail questionnaire and analyze it from the viewpoint of the principles discussed in this chapter. Rewrite it if you believe it can be made more effective.

7. Outline the steps you would take in conducting a field survey to determine the potential market for a new type of electric toaster.

COLLATERAL READINGS

Blankenship, Albert B., *How to Conduct Consumer and Opinion Research,* Harper & Brothers, New York, 1946.

Criteria for Marketing and Advertising Research, New York: Advertising Research Foundation, 1953.

Editors of "Fortune," *Why Do People Buy?* New York: McGraw-Hill Book Company, Inc., 1953, Chapter 1.

Hepner, Harry Walker, *Modern Advertising*, McGraw-Hill Book Company, New York, 1956, Chapters 1–5 and 18.

Luck, David J., and Hugh G. Wales, *Marketing Research*, Englewood Cliffs, N.J.: Prentice-Hall, Inc., 1952.

Parten, Mildred, *Surveys, Polls and Samples*, New York, Harper & Brothers, 1950.

Smith, Henry Clay, *Psychology of Industrial Behavior*, McGraw-Hill Book Company, Inc., New York, 1955, Chapter 17.

Vaile, Roland S., E. T. Grether, and Reavis Cox, *Marketing in the American Economy*, The Ronald Press Company, New York, 1952, Part 1.

CHAPTER TWENTY-EIGHT

Advertising: the appeal and its use; measuring the effectiveness of the advertisement

Successful research in appraising advertising must depend upon a method rather than upon the judgment of an individual expert. Unless his system or method yields the same results in the hands of others, the system is unreliable. This means that anyone who seeks to learn a system of appraisal should choose one that depends upon observable factors, recognizable to anyone, rather than upon the opinions of a clever critic.

Advertising is so big a field that this chapter can present only selected aspects of special interest to the psychologist. One of these is the appeal.

THE APPEAL

Researchers in advertising who have made studies of the relative importance of various factors such as long copy versus short copy, big pictures or little pictures or no pictures at all, charts and diagrams as an accompaniment of other pictures or used alone, and testimonial versus reason-why copy seem to agree that none of them is so important as the *appeal* or *theme*. The appeal is the dominant idea which is supposed to arouse a dormant desire in the mind of the prospect and stimulate him to purchase the product. The appeal is far more important than type face, illustration, or headline.

One would expect the theme or appeal to be the one great influence in causing us to be affected by the advertisement. Hand a page of closely typewritten material, haphazardly arranged, to a group of people and ask them to look it over. If the names of the readers are among the words on the list, it is easier for them to find their own names than to find the names of strangers. Twenty-eight adults were used in such an experiment to find out how long it would take each person to find his name on a page of closely typewritten material. Each person's name appeared five times in the copy. An examiner timed the subject with a stop-watch while the subject looked for and underlined his own name five times. Then the subject or person who had found his own name was asked to find the name of a stranger in the same copy. The stranger's name also appeared in five places in the copy and had to be underlined five times. Accurate records were kept for each name, and it was found that the average length of time required for each of twenty-eight persons to find his own name was 72.6 seconds. For these persons to find the names of strangers required 103.7 seconds, or 43 per cent longer.

A theme or appeal in advertising is any idea used by an advertiser when he seeks to influence people of the particular class who are logical prospects for his product or service. The advertiser does not seek to reach everyone with his message. Even though the advertiser sells a so-called mass product such as soap or food, he has narrowed his choice of appeals to the particular class or classes of people who are apt to buy his soap or food. The advertiser thinks of his advertising appeal as a selective device which is designed to be attractive to his prospects; not to all persons. He has defined his market by means of motivation research or the use of some other technique such as the analysis of sales records, coupon returns, questionnaires, or interviews with consumers.

Prospects are usually analyzed and classified on the basis of two general approaches:

1. The *appeals* effective in stimulating the logical prospects.

2. The *media* that will convey the chosen appeals to the prospects and do so profitably. Examples of advertising media are newspapers, magazines, radio, television, direct mail, book matches, displays, and others.

Once the advertising man has learned the characteristics of his logical prospects—their sex, age, income, geographical location, or

An example of an effective appeal. This headline was first used by its author, Jack Cornelius, of Batten, Barton, Durstine & Osborn, for a Community Chest campaign in 1936. It has been a perennial favorite in later campaigns.

other classification—he can easily select his media accordingly. Almost every modern publisher of a periodical, manager of a television station or network, and head of an outdoor posting concern can supply printed data that describe the readers or listeners of his particular medium. By means of such printed data, the advertising man can easily decide which medium or media are most likely to reach the specific classes of prospects whom he wishes to reach. Once he has collected the data necessary for the intelligent selection of media, he also has much information available for making a choice of effective appeals.

How the appeal affects the reader

Psychologically, an appeal is a very complex set of influences in the life of a reader or hearer of advertising. A prospect's

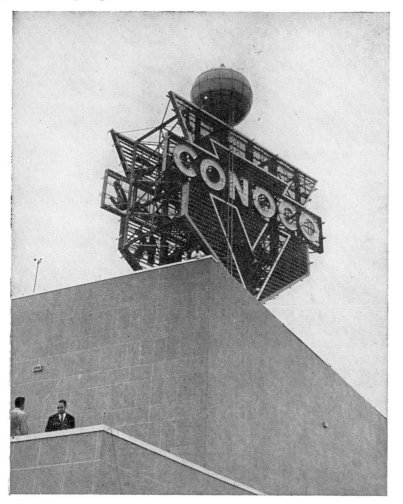

A great deal of modern advertising is designed to have consumers associate pleasant feeling tones with the advertiser's product. Here is a well-planned example. When the Continental Oil Company built a new office building in Houston, a psychologist of the company was asked about the design of a spectacular for the top of the building. He agreed that the name and emblem as rotating signs on the city skyline would attract some attention but would be ineffective unless an additional associative factor were added. He recommended the addition of a weather ball, called the "Sky-High Weather Eye."

The Sky-High Weather Eye has been advertised to the people of the area as reporting United States Weather Bureau forecasts through the use of a color code: Red means Warmer, White means Cooler, Green means No Change in Temperature, and Blinking (any of the three colors) means Rain. The Weather Eye's morning report shows the Weather Bureau forecast for the day up to 5 p.m. After 5 p.m., the Weather Eye's color report indicates the Weather Bureau's forecast for the next day.

The Weather Eye is 15 feet in diameter and has a surface area of 708 square feet. It reports Weather Bureau forecasts from a perch approximately 400 feet above downtown Houston, higher than any building in the vicinity.

In this case, an interest in something important to the individual (the weather) is tied in with something of importance to the advertiser (the Conoco emblem and name). Thus, as the individual looks daily to see what the weather is to be, he also receives a quick flash of the name of the company, the outline of the emblem, and, consciously or unconsciously, is left with an impression that the company is serving the community.

—Courtesy of Melvin S. Hattwick, Continental Oil Company.

actions are greatly influenced by his own inner needs and desires, particularly in the promise of satisfaction of his needs. An analysis of the reader's mental activity when he sees an advertisement would reveal the memories that it arouses, the pleasant and unpleasant feelings, associations, and thoughts of the possibility of satisfaction. Depth interviews uncover numerous unsuspected psychological responses on the part of the reader, responses that are difficult to measure by ordinary questioning. Dichter, for example, found in a study in the field of deodorants that:

. . . The appeal of social acceptance and safety is valid only for a small group of women. A much greater proportion considered such goals as much too far removed. What interested them more than anything else was to be able to like themselves, to feel clean, to consider themselves smart beauty technicians.

Very often in determining advertising campaigns, the advertiser makes the mistake of thinking that death, romance, fear or hope are valid and powerful appeals. This is a lay view of psychological facts. Actually the fear of being embarrassed or of having to consider oneself a failure far outweighs the power of such grandiose concepts as romance, love, death or happiness.

It can be shown again and again that the pure recital of technical claims about a product leaves the reader cold and does not arouse the emotions necessary to make him change to a new product. When buying cigarettes, the smoker is actually afraid to try a new brand. He does not want to give up the known security of his present brand, even though he may find fault with it, for the unknown, although possibly greater enjoyment of the new brand. Therefore to urge him to try brand X because it is different from anything he has ever tasted is a wrong and dangerous appeal.

Not every research method is capable of clarifying the real goals of an advertising campaign. In functional psychological research we distinguish between symptoms expressing the superficial rational explanations of an action and the real, deeper reasons which form the emotional basis of such actions, and are connected with the functional role a product plays in the user's life . . .

Every time a reader views an advertisement three successive steps are set in motion: (*a*) an attempt to get into the advertisement, (*b*) a registering of the psychological effects and (*c*) a registering of the commercial effects of the advertisement.

a) *Ways of getting into the advertisement.* A reader viewing an advertisement for the first time tries to enter it by various means. Either he abandons the attempt after a few seconds of casual observation, or he is caught by the adtisement.

Among the various processes which help him into an advertisement are these: identifying, being curious, arguing, accepting, rejecting, excluding, memorizing, dissecting, assembling, and emotionalizing—feeling pity, hatred, love, sympathy, and so forth.

The channels enabling the reader to enter the advertisement can be grouped into two large classifications: emotional and intellectual forms of immediate reactions.

An emotional entrance would be signified by: "I'm glad they're not talking about me," or "I hate that darn stuff."

That an intellectual process has taken place would be indicated by the exclamation: "Gee, that's an interesting story!" or, "I'm curious to find out what this machine does."

b) *Ways of registering the psychological effects of an advertisement.* An advertisement may leave the reader with any of a number of possible gratifications: "I feel relieved," "I've learned something new," "I feel sure of myself," "My curiosity has been satisfied," or "It makes me feel that I'm smart." . . .

What might be considered a well-planned advertisement can have negative psychological effects if one is not conscious of the mechanisms stimulated by it. This was the case in a study for a well-known reducing remedy. Although women accepted the desirability of slimness, they rejected the advertisement and the product. Investigation showed that the stout women featured in the "before" half of the "before and after" routine were too extreme to be accepted by the readers. Their reaction to the picture was, "That's not me," and "I don't look that bad." The effectiveness of the ad was lost because of this psychological blunder.

c) *Ways of registering the commercial effects of an advertisement.* The real commercial effects of an advertisement are difficult to ascertain solely in terms of actual sales. . . .

The only real test of an advertisement's effectiveness is a knowledge of the thoughts, associations, and mental images produced in the reader. In concrete terms each purchasing act is really the result of a mental rehearsal for buying. A shoe advertisement, for example, is successful if at some point the reader reacts with the thought, "I imagine myself trying on the shoes." Similarly, an airline advertisement produced a desirable commercial effect because it provoked such associations as "I'm daydreaming. I visualize myself sitting in a plane and I'm proud of myself," or "I see myself getting into a plane."

In other words, the closer any advertisement comes to producing thoughts which have the appearance of a purchasing act or which rehearse use of the product, the higher the commercial value of the effect of the advertisement. . . .

An advertising program, brilliantly conceived and executed from a technical viewpoint, may miss completely if it neglects to control the psychological effects. The intangible implications of an advertisement often are more significant than its actual content. No item of merchandise is ever sold unless a psychological need exists which it satisfies. In other words, the actual merchandise is secondary. Advertising's goal has to be the mobilization and manipulation of human needs as they exist in the customer.[1]

Appeals that have been found effective

The experienced advertising man who plans a campaign looks for the dominant idea that will appeal to the consumer classes whom he can reach by means of media available to him. He wants to find out what can be said that will answer the needs of prospects. When we study the progression of appeals of advertisements and sales talks, we find important changes made to increase their effectiveness. Let us note a few examples.

1. In the past, manufacturers of shoes assumed that readers of their advertising were most interested in style, price, construction of shoe, details about fancy punching, and so on. However, one shoe manufacturer conducted a survey of 5,000 men and found that when they were asked what they liked about the shoes they were wearing, 42 per cent replied "fit and feel" or some equivalent; 32 per cent said "wear and tear"; 16 per cent said "style and looks"; 9 per cent said "price and value." The manufacturer changed his advertising accordingly, using themes such as "Walk-Fitted," and benefited by the change.[2]

2. One candy manufacturer found that when he advertised the quality of his candy and made reference to its excellence he did not sell so much as when he changed his appeal to that of buying his brand as a gift. He discovered that the bulk of his business came from men who buy candy to take home to their wives and daughters and from young men who buy it for girls. Price as an appeal was not so important a consideration as the appropriateness of the article for gift purposes.

3. The maker of a game, well-known to the public, devoted his sales and advertising messages to the story of the pleasure his game would yield to the family circle. His advertisements usually pictured father and mother and the two children playing the game with happy smiles on their faces. His appeal for years was: "For Enjoyment." Then, upon consulting a marketing specialist, the appeal was changed: "To Be Popular." With this appeal the players were pictured in a home which was the rendezvous of delighted friends. The response to the advertising doubled in sixty days and the sales of the game tripled.

4. A certain insurance company found that in the advertising of accident insurance the note of protection to loved ones was not nearly so effective as some other appeals, such as the low price of the insurance of this sort. The best-paying advertisement they had was one headed "Three Cents a Day," which explained how many thousands of dollars of protection this small expenditure would bring.

5. One of the most interesting records of appeal effectiveness has occurred in the advertising of "Dr. Eliot's Five-Foot Shelf of Books." Charles W. Eliot, president emeritus of Harvard University, made a famous remark in 1909 to the effect that an individual could acquire the equivalent of a liberal education by devoting fifteen minutes every day to the study of great literature. Since that time, the P. F. Collier & Son Corporation has sold more than 500,000 sets of the Eliot-chosen books.

The basic appeal in the advertising always has been to "get ahead"—to grow. The self-improvement theme has been supplemented with appeals to the reader's desires for self-confidence. One insertion, captioned "How to get rid of an inferiority complex," has been used with success for more than twenty years.

Another successful theme, on a slightly different note, was, "Like a conquering army these books have marched triumphant through the centuries," accompanied by an illustration of a medieval army. Introduced in 1925, this insertion was used until some time in 1936. Copy with a bargain appeal, describing the cost per volume of the Harvard Classics as one-third the price of popular fiction, was instituted some time ago and continues in use.

Long reason-why copy, seeking prompt return of a coupon, has always prevailed, and experiments with more emphasis on an artistic layout and less copy have proved that such an approach carries little weight with the reader who seeks to improve himself.

Seriousness is the key. From its inception, advertising of the Five-Foot Shelf represents the efforts of a conservative and serious salesman. Carefully abjuring flippancy, it has employed a wide variety of sales approaches, always characterized by a note of sincerity and earnestness. The man who feels himself inferior to his fellows evidently does not take it lightly, and is deadly serious when he decides to improve himself.

As described by W. W. Beardsley, advertising manager of Collier books for the past 12 years, "People don't go in for education with a fillip. The luxury type of advertising doesn't sell books."

One innovation introduced by Mr. Beardsley is an illustration picturing the 50 books piled on end instead of on a shelf. The illustration borders the copy on one side and has produced good results.[3]

These five examples from literature in the field of advertising illustrate the reason why advertisers and salesmen seek the one keynote that will touch off the spark of interest in the prospect. The history of advertising reveals many examples of appeals, both ineffective and effective ones. Until recently, psychologists often analyzed instincts as possible sources of effective appeals. Today

we no longer study lists of instincts and reflexes in the quest for effective appeals, because instincts and reflexes usually have been analyzed by means of armchair or laboratory methods only. The modern marketing analyst does not bother with such obsolete approaches to the choice of appeal. He uses more recent and better research techniques, such as analysis of readership surveys:

TABLE 28-1

HOW READERSHIP OF NEWSPAPER ADVERTISEMENTS VARIES BY COPY APPEAL

Copy Appeals	Average Readers-per-Dollar		
Ads featuring a USER benefit:	Men	Women	Total
Popularity and prestige	57	146	203
Style and beauty	24	135	159
Comfort	71	78	149
Health	39	105	144
Ads featuring a PRODUCT advantage:			
Proved successful	52	110	162
Safe	58	80	138
Dependable	62	74	136
Efficient	39	91	130
Convenient	39	91	130
Economical	47	74	121

All evaluations are expressed as average readers per dollar spent for advertising space. These are computed from three factors:

1. The *per cent of readers* interviewed who said they saw or read any portion of the ad (called "Any this Ad" in the Studies).

2. The *line rate* of the newspaper in which the advertisement appeared.

3. The Audit Bureau of Circulations statement of *circulation* at the time of the study.

Line rates and readers per copy differ from one newspaper to another. Therefore it is not permissible to compare readers per dollar of *single* ads in different newspapers.

However, in relative comparisons of *large numbers* of ads, as in these Batten, Barton, Durstine and Osborn, Inc., analyses, these differences tend to average out, and "Average readers per dollar" becomes a valid yardstick, readily understood, easily visualized, and with emphasis where it should be.

Data were obtained from a recent study by the copy research department of Batten, Barton, Durstine & Osborn, Inc., entitled *How Newspaper Advertisements Can Get Extra Readers per Dollar,* a cross analysis of the readership of 3,745 national advertisements reported by "The Continuing Study of Newspaper Reading," a project of the Advertising Research Foundation.

Field surveys of readership

The method of measuring the effectiveness of advertisements by means of field surveys of readership has many minor modifications, but it usually means that an interviewer calls at the homes or offices of a representative sampling of persons. The interviewer asks the interviewee whether he has read a certain issue of a periodical. If the answer is "Yes," the interviewer produces an unmarked copy of the periodical, explains the purpose of his investigation, and asks: "Won't you kindly tell me what you have read as I turn these pages?" The interviewer usually marks the advertisements noted or observed, headlines read, and amount of copy read. Sometimes the name of the advertiser or the product is masked (painted out) and then the interviewer inquires whether the interviewee can identify the product or name of the advertiser. Readership reports often present their findings by giving percentages of readers who (*a*) noted or observed the advertisements, (*b*) read the headline, (*c*) read most of the copy, and (*d*) *identified* the name of the product or advertiser when names were masked.

THE USE OF THE APPEAL IN AN ADVERTISEMENT

The advertiser who knows the important characteristics of consumers that are associated with the buying of his product also selects a basic advertising idea to advertise the product. The product is analyzed for ideas that will cause people to buy it, but these ideas must be presented in some attention-getting, attractive manner. The basic advertising idea is the "vehicle" that holds the reader's interest and is repeated in many advertisements, as is explained by a successful teacher of advertising.

An advertising idea is usually a "vehicle"—it may be a special format (a strip, a cartoon, a unique arrangement of pictures and text), or it may be an advertising character (the Borden cow family, Spry's Aunt Jenny, American Mutual's Mr. Friendly, Philip Morris's page boy, Bon Ami's chick) or a string of testimonialiers (Pond's engaged girls, Lux's movie stars). It may be a special kind of art work (DeBeers' high art paintings, Wyeth's historical series, Cannon's pop-eyed girl).

Such ideas generally depend for their effectiveness upon their distinction (degree of unusualness) and their manner of use. Their creation is an important part of the copywriter's function. You can't write copy until you have *some kind* of idea, even though it be only a conventional one. You can't write a headline or picture captions until you know what parts of your sales idea the other elements of your advertisement will tell.

So, in preparing yourself for a copy job, study ideas. Learn to distinguish between basic sales ideas and vehicular advertising ideas.[4]

The format or kind of advertisement

When an advertising man has studied the needs of representative consumers, decided upon the central theme or appeal appropriate to the campaign, and chosen the vehicular idea, he begins to visualize specific advertisements. He decides whether he shall use as the format a comic strip, picture-and-caption, humor panel, poster, or other variety of advertisement. The most common formats or kinds of advertisements used in magazines are the following:

1. *Conventional:* The illustration is a dominant part of the layout, copy is directly under the illustration, and the headline is usually placed directly under the illustration, above the copy.

2. *Picture-and-caption (news photograph and caption):* A format that duplicates the newspaper picture pages that have large pictures with explanatory captions, the caption usually being placed beneath the picture. In the conventional layout, the picture occupies about one half (or less) of the area of the advertisement. In the picture-

and-caption advertisement, the illustration occupies most of the area of the whole advertisement.

3. *Editorial:* The text is dominant; pictures, if any, are of minor importance; artistic quality of the layout is incidental, because the aim is the attainment of a readable page or advertisement.

4. *Eccentric:* Design dominates the format, as exemplified in some of the futuristic and abstract forms of art.

5. *Comic strip:* Duplicates the newspaper comic strip; pictures are in cartoon style, copy usually in balloons leading from the mouth of the speaker; each picture is a part of a series of related pictures; and text and pictures tell a story by means of fictitious characters and a simple plot.

6. *Humor panel:* Main illustration pictures a humorous situation; humor is usually exaggerated; the selling argument is obviously farfetched and likely to entertain rather than convince the reader.

7. *Oddities:* Repeats the Ripley oddities technique.

8. *Newspaper columnist:* Like the oddities technique, the newspaper columnist technique, such as that used for Aunt Het— Poor Pa, is duplicated for advertising purposes.

Obviously, the format of any given advertisement may be in typical or mixed form, but one of the more common forms is likely to be discernible in the plan of the advertisement.

Researchers in advertising are constantly analyzing the effects on readership of all the objective factors, such as the format. A statistical analysis of 4,241 national advertisements in newspapers, made by the copy research department of Batten, Barton, Durstine and Osborn, Inc., indicated that one of the most useful findings from the Continuing Study of Newspaper Reading is that advertisements which are modeled after editorial formats of current popularity get extra readers per dollar for the advertiser:

		Average number of readers per dollar spent for advertising	
Technique and number of ads			
	MEN	WOMEN	TOTAL
Conventional	3,800	64	85	149
Horizontal comic strips	62	338	361	699
Humor panels	84	321	316	637
News pictures and caption	50	138	146	284
Columnist style	105	76	158	234
Comic strips (vertical or square) ...	121	76	96	172
"Believe It or Not"	19	82	61	143

Less than 15 per cent of the total number of national advertisements followed a format of the editorial feature variety (all above except "Conventional"), but they got up to five times as many readers per dollar as the advertisements that followed the traditional pattern of picture-headline-text-and-logotype.[5]

When Harold J. Rudolph made a statistical analysis of the Daniel Starch readership figures for 2,500 half-and full-page advertisements in *The Saturday Evening Post,* he found that the "comic strip" format on the average did not get quite as much attention as conventional advertisements, but was especially effective in getting thorough readership:

This is to be expected because of the inability of "strip" ads to make use of those elements of high impact value such as large illustrations and generous use of white space.

But second, this survey clearly indicates that "comic-strip" advertisements possess a significant advantage over conventional advertisements in thorough readership. *On the average, "comic-strip" advertisements are read thoroughly by almost twice as many people as conventional advertisements,* and the "comic-strip" ads are actually twice as good for thorough readership as they are for partial readership. The "comic-strip" format, therefore, may be looked upon not as a device for getting attention but as a means of stepping up the thorough reading of the advertiser's message.[6]

Sometimes a change in layout technique will activate an advertisement that has elements proved right by tests but lethargic in effect. Walter H. Weintz, copy director of

VanSant, Dugdale & Company, reported an example:

I recently tried to revise a mail-order advertisement that did not pull satisfactorily. The ad had a good, tested headline and body copy with illustrations that had been successful sales makers in other ads for the same client. But this ad flopped.

I knew the headline, copy, and illustrations were all effective. But they were put together in a very conventional manner — headline at top, a solid block of body copy, illustrations at one side, coupon at the bottom. In terms of layout and typography, it was *just another ad.*

Accordingly we did the ad over, consciously making use of a simple readership-getting device: breaking up the bulk of the body copy into short captions which were placed under the illustrations. This device changed the ad from one composed of a block of copy with incidental illustrations to one made up of a number of illustrations with explanatory copy. Let me emphasize that headline, copy, and illustrations remained the same—only the manner of presenting them was changed, and in a way intended to increase readership. In its new format the ad proved successful.[7]

The illustration

In most cases, the noteworthy part of the advertisement is the illustration. Most people are pictorially minded. Picture shows are far more attractive than lectures. Pictures were our first written language. They attract and hold attention more readily than cold words. One of the most common problems of the advertiser who uses an illustration is its relevancy to the product advertised. A picture of a beautiful woman on a calendar attracts attention to the calendar, but it may not attract attention to the product.

Mark Wiseman studied many readership reports, covering thousands of advertisements, and listed the kinds of pictures most interesting to men and to women. At the head of the list for men was "men" and at the head of the list for women was "women." A part of his explanation follows:

The reason is not that each sex is not interested in pictures of the other but that the sex of the sole or dominant figure in a picture is a symbolic selector: a signal to the reader that the advertisement is directed to one sex and not the other. Men are rarely interested in an advertisement which they think is meant for women, and vice versa, although a larger proportion of women will observe and read a man's advertisement than the other way around. If you use the wrong sex in a picture, you risk missing or misleading your audience.

In a women's advertisement don't use pictures of combat or adventure; don't use diagrams unless they are very simple and easy to understand; don't use sports scenes unless the chief figure is a woman; don't use mechanical equipment unless you show it in use by a woman or in relation to a woman's job; don't use animals which women might fear or dislike.

The kinds of pictures most interesting to women are those containing domestic scenes, foods in full color, babies or small children, women's apparel, decorative details (room furniture, floor coverings, table settings, boudoir accessories). If you use a picture of a woman, give her an interesting coiffure, one or more pieces of jewelry, an unusual dress, and a background — women love details. Be sparing of cartoons—if you use them, be sure they are easy to "get" and do not ridicule women. If you use before-and-after pictures (before using and after using), make them credible—don't let them arouse suspicion that they are faked or doctored.[8]

Data concerning interests in pictures fluctuates from year to year, depending upon the topics of current interest to the public. In wartime, for example, pictures of pretty girls are of less interest than army and aviation subjects. Human interest and crime pictures get high attention at all times and from both sexes.

Harold J. Rudolph's statistical analysis of readership figures for 2,500 half- and full-page advertisements in *The Saturday Evening Post* indicated that the most effective type of picture for attention value is the one that depicts what might happen to the reader if he fails to use the advertiser's product. This type of picture gives considerable emphasis to the reader's problems, and problem-solution advertisements tend to have high attention value.[9] Experimental investigation has indicated that an effective way to depict the reader's situation is to emphasize his need or want.

In Rudolph's study (see Table 28-2), he found that the second most effective type of picture for stopping power is the testimonial or statement of an actual user. People like to see pictures of other people whom they know, even though the acquaintance is through the moving picture, television, or radio. For example, experiments on the stopping power of various types of window displays indicated that having pictures of well-known television personalities increased considerably the stopping power of the displays.

TABLE 28-2

Type of Picture	Index of Attention	Per Cent Loss of Readers
Results of use	96.9	20.0
Product	101.7	22.3
Irrelevant	102.8	11.1
Product in use	106.4	21.3
Testimonial	110.0	11.9
Result of nonuse	122.7	11.4

In studying these data, it is of interest first of all to observe that the type of illustration affects the performance of an advertisement in two ways, namely, in attention and in readership of the copy. Moreover, a picture that is a good stopper may not necessarily be effective in inducing readership of the copy.

In some respects the figures showing the relative loss of readers resulting from various types of pictures are especially significant. These figures show that the greatest loss of readers occurs in the case of an illustration of the product or package and of the product in use. The irrelevant illustration, on the other hand, has the lowest reader loss of any type of illustration shown. This is evidence of the power of irrelevant illustrations to rouse curiosity and carry a high proportion of the audience into the copy. Both the testimonial and the negative type of illustration also show low reader loss, which in turn indicates a high degree of interest in the picture.

From Harold J. Rudolph, *Attention and Interest Factors in Advertising*, Printers Ink Business Bookshelf, Funk and Wagnalls Company in association with Printers' Ink Publishing Company, Inc., New York, 1947, pp. 68 ff.

People enjoy both the real and the ideal. Readers of advertisements prefer to see a product in pleasant surroundings, appropriate to the theme of the advertisement. Generally, people like to imagine themselves in ideal rather than realistic situations. In a study of readers' habits in reading women's magazines, it was found that women preferred to read two kinds of magazine articles: those that dealt with specific household tasks in terms of "how to do it" and those that presented colorful idealistic home settings, the more highly imaginative the better for reader interest.

Of course the type of art work and subject used in an illustration is greatly influenced by the product advertised and the purpose of the advertisement. A product such as linoleum or a carpet requires illustrations that are attractive and in color.

Copy

As previously stated, the dominant factor in successful advertising is not the layout, illustration, color, or size of the advertisement, but the character of the copy itself. The success of an advertisement is determined by the manner in which its central theme or idea identifies the product with some current desire, irritation, problem, or habit on the part of a portion of the buying public. "Stop those runs in stockings," for example, identified Lux soap with current irritations toward runs in stockings.[10]

Copywriting is an art, and, like most arts, its effects depend upon the creative skill of the artist. Furthermore, an art has few invariable rules. However, we can note the findings of some of the most significant researches on copy. One finding from several studies in regard to copy indicates that effective copy is informative.

Charles M. Edwards, Jr., made a seven-year study of the advertising of 72 retail stores. A total of 671 factors, including the kind of advertisement, sales results, weather, media, layout, illustration, headline, price, and copy were considered. The characteristics of successful low-cost advertisements were contrasted with unsuccessful high-cost advertisements. Edwards stated his most significant conclusions, in part, as follows:

When we summarized the findings in each of our studies, we learned that no technique had always succeeded and no technique had always failed. We did discover conclusively, however, *that certain techniques invariably succeed more often than they fail, while certain other techniques invariably fail more often than they succeed.* For example, we learned that an advertisement's chance for success invariably increases as the number of *pertinent* merchandise facts included in the advertisement increases. The more you tell the more you sell!

One store discovered, for instance, the following relationships between the number of merchandise facts included in its advertisements and the sales results of the advertisements.

Of all the store's advertisements that included

4 or more merchandise facts, 44.2% succeeded.
5 or more merchandise facts, 49.6% succeeded.
6 or more merchandise facts, 57.7% succeeded.
7 or more merchandise facts, 60.0% succeeded.
8 or more merchandise facts, 66.7% succeeded.

The necessity of including all the pertinent merchandise facts does not mean, of course, that the mere cramming of all conceivable facts into an advertisement assures the success of the ad. It does mean that an imperative condition for the fullest success of an ad is the inclusion of all the essential merchandise facts—facts that the customer needs or wishes to know about a particular article before she can or will buy it. Actually the *character* of the facts included is more important than the *number* of facts. Whenever a store omits from its advertisements any essential merchandise facts, it instantly reduces sales response.

	Per Cent of Ads That Failed
Facts about appearance omitted (designs, colors, etc.)	60.1
Facts about composition omitted (materials, parts or pieces, etc.)	58.0
Facts about construction omitted (construction, workmanship, etc.)	56.5
Facts about serviceability omitted (uses, benefits of use, etc.)	56.1

Not only must an advertisement contain all the essential facts, it must also present the facts in a definite sequence. It must draw readers through the selling message from the point that interests them (the advantages that they may realize through the use of the merchandise) to the point that interests the store (the completion of the sale). It seems a little incongruous to urge customers to buy the merchandise before telling them the satisfactions that they will derive from possession of the merchandise. . . .

After the advertiser has conveyed his selling message to the customer in an interesting and organized manner, he must not sign off until he has urged or invited the customer, directly or indirectly, to take some specified buying action. The evidence proves conclusively that he can increase sales results appreciably by incorporating into his advertisement one or more of a score of devices for prompting immediate buying action. This conclusion is borne out by the typical findings in a large Eastern store. In this store our analyses disclosed that 65.2 per cent of all the ads that included a direct or an indirect urge to action were successful while only 34.8 per cent were unsuccessful. . . .

As you might expect, our summaries indicate that many factors affect the productivity of an advertisement. We found, however, through our analyses in stores of all types and sizes, that in the advertising of every organization a relatively few factors stand out head and shoulders above all the rest. In each store a few factors are so basically important that their use invariably exerts a marked influence on sales results. Accordingly, for each organization we have aided in developing a check list of the objective elements that are essential to that store's advertising. Although a few of the minor elements vary slightly from store to store, several of the major elements are so universally important that they inevitably recur in all stores' check lists. Accordingly, we have been able to compile a composite check list of the elements that are applicable in all stores.[11]

Daniel Starch found evidence about the importance of copy being informative when he analyzed 583 advertisements from 16 issues from the *Woman's Home Companion,* January 1945 to April 1946. He classified the advertisements into the six groups shown in Table 28-3 and found the number of buyers per dollar of advertising cost as shown in the

Starch Buyometer reports. The tabulation showed that advertisements which were above average in both information and reader interest (Group 1) had three times as great sales power as advertisements that were below average in both informative and reader interest (Group 7).

In the case of some products, such as cosmetics or cigarettes, among which differences between brands are subtle or difficult to state in factual terms, copy technicians rely chiefly on reader interest. High reader interest may go a long way to offset absence of information. However, it does not follow that proper mingling of information and reader interest would not be a more pertinent sales combination than reliance chiefly on reader interest. . . .

It is not easy to understand why copy writers often lean so heavily upon hokum in their writing when they can as easily include useful information. This is something of an overstatement, of course, because it is not entirely an effortless matter to include useful information. The latter may require making a study of the characteristics of the product, learning how it is grown or fabricated, and some inquiry into how the product is used by customers or how it might better be used. So perhaps there is merely laziness on the part of copy writers who eschew information for words, who bridge lapses in their knowledge with nicely turned phrases.

Perhaps they are not lazy but believe that it is better to be smart than soberly helpful. This point of view is hard for many of us to understand, but it is common enough, and it is a point of view that does more harm to the advertising business than any other single fac-

tor. It tends to emphasize superficiality, when information and the sound use of it are of paramount importance.[12]

In another study, Starch analyzed the copy treatment of the 50 least-read and 50 most-read advertisements:

After fifteen years of measuring the readership of magazine advertisements, during which period some 2 million interviews were conducted, I have concluded that the observation of advertising by magazine readers during these years increased 18 per cent and thorough readership of advertisements has increased 24 per cent. By "thorough readership" I mean the reading of half or more of the text matter of an advertisement.

The possible explanation for these increases is that during this period advertising technicians have learned how to prepare better, more readable advertisements. Individual advertising agencies with whom I have had business contact over these years tell me that by paying particular attention to developing readership for their advertisements, they have increased it for some of their clients by as much as 100 to 150 per cent. . . .

In order to examine the principles which are used to produce more readable advertisements, I selected 100 advertisements from our readership records. Fifty of them had been read most thoroughly by the largest number of people.

The most-read advertisements had been read by as many as 30 to 35 per cent of the persons interviewed. This is a very high percentage, since these advertisements contained as many as 400 to 500 words and some more than 1,000. Which is a good deal to read when it is considered that the average one-page magazine advertisement contains approximately 250

TABLE 28-3

INFORMATION AND READER INTEREST IN RELATION TO SALES POWER OF 583 ADVERTISEMENTS

Groups	Number of Ads	Buyers per Dollar	Sales Performance Index
1. Above average in both information and reader interest	113	5.80	163
2. Above average in information but average in reader interest	203	4.92	138
3. Above average in information but below average in reader interest	35	3.38	95
4. Average for all advertisements	583	3.56	100
5. Below average in information but above average in reader interest	30	3.83	107
6. Below average in information but average in reader interest	119	2.83	79
7. Below average in both information and reader interest	34	2.00	56

From Daniel Starch, "Informative Ads Outsell Others by 3 to 1," *Advertising and Selling*, December 1946. See also *The Journal of Marketing*, April 1947, p. 409.

words. The high percentage of readership is also remarkable in view of the fact that the average one-page four-colored advertisement receives thorough readership by 7 per cent of the persons interviewed.

At the other extreme, the 50 least-read advertisements had been read half or more each by only 1 to 2 per cent of the persons questioned.

An analysis of these 100 advertisements from the standpoint of copy treatment revealed that they fell into five general groups. Based upon copy approach, the subjects begin:

1. *People.* In these advertisements people were the center of the illustration and text matter. Usually these persons were doing something or saying something. They were of three different types. There were living persons, often well-known, such as Gary Cooper and Henry Ford. There were fictitious persons such as Little Lulu and Charlie McCarthy. Then there were persons with or without names but representing types, such as a father and son or a family group.

2. *"How to" do things.* These advertisements told readers how to lay out a modern kitchen, launder silks, use tape, prepare certain recipes, or do other useful things.

3. *Striking events, facts, or statements.* Examples are "More Thousands Will Go to Rio by Clipper" and "4,300,000 Jobs to Do Today."

4. *Broad, general assertions.* Examples are "Tavern Wax for Longer Lasting Lustre" and "Ozite Makes Rugs Look Lovelier, More Cheerful."

5. *Product.* These advertisements made no use of persons or their actions. Examples are advertisements that merely show a picture of the package or product, such as a cake of Fels Naptha soap in the wrapper with a headline "The Inside Story" or a large picture of a Van Heusen shirt and collar with a headline "Choose a Name You Can Trust."

Classifying these 100 advertisements in this manner, I derived the following results:

Type of Copy Treatment	50 Read Most	50 Read Least
Advertisements about people ...	29	10
"How to" advertisements	15	2
Striking events, facts, or statements	6	2
Broad, general assertions	0	4
Advertisements about product as such	0	32

Of the 50 advertisements read most, 58 per cent were about people in action, whereas among the advertisements least read, only 20 per cent were about people and in several of these cases the people were not in action. In this successful group none dealt merely with the product as such, without the use of people in action, whereas among the 50 least read, two-thirds were of this variety.

In other words, the two groups of advertisements were exactly reversed in respect to their use of people in action and their dealing with the inert product as such.[13]

MEASURING THE EFFECTIVENESS OF AN ADVERTISEMENT

When Kenneth Goode taught classes in advertising at Columbia University, he showed the students copies of eleven pairs of advertisements whose effectiveness was known from actual use. Each member of the class decided which advertisement of each pair was the better one. The results were almost a matter of chance. Later, he changed his procedure with some classes by first giving them only two guiding principles for evaluating the effectiveness of advertisements:

"Don't tell people how good you made your goods. Tell them how good your goods make them!"

"If your promise of a direct personal benefit as direct reward for your reader's response comes later than the first subheading of your top title, maybe it will come too late!". . .

With these two vital fundamentals, that class thereafter not only voted wrong on fewer advertisements, but fewer members voted wrong. Thus advantaged, in fact, instead of following earlier Columbia classes placing correctly any six or seven advertisements out of 11, it got all 11 right but two![14]

Psychologists and other researchers are seeking better methods of predicting the probable effectiveness of a proposed advertisement. Years ago, they conducted experiments with students as subjects in the laboratories. The results of such experiments had little or no value because laboratory situations did not approximate real life situations.

Most measurement studies of advertising

effectiveness are made after the advertisement has been published or broadcast. However, some important research has been done on predicting results before publication.

The consumer jury or panel ratings

To improve his judgment, almost every advertising man shows sketches of proposed advertisements to the consumers whom he meets. However, when representative consumers are systematically interviewed and shown proposed advertisements, more reliable ratings are obtained. Investigators interview and obtain reactions of selected individuals who are typical buyers of the product. Calls are made at the homes or offices of consumers, who are asked which of two or more advertisements they consider most effective in inducing them to buy the product. Sometimes the proposed advertisements contain only certain constituent elements, so that direct comparisons can be made regarding headline, layout, or some other important factor.

Consumers are interviewed and asked to rank two or more advertisements, as in the following example:

We are making an investigation to see what kinds of advertisements people are interested in. Here are six rough sketches of oil-burner advertisements. Which one of them would be most likely to interest YOU? Look through them and put that one on top. Which would be next? Put that one second. Then arrange the others in the order in which they appeal to you so that finally you have the best on top and the poorest at the bottom. Thank you.

Two advertisements at a time may be compared, each pair shown to exactly the same number of typical prospective customers of the same income classes. Results may be analyzed by social class, size of community, and any other influence that previous consumer studies have revealed as significant. Random samplings are dangerous.

The method may be applied to dealers as well as consumers. Of course, opinions of dealers may differ considerably from those of the consumers of the product.

Many of the consumer-opinion studies have given results remarkably consistent with over-the-counter sales. Results have shown that preliminary advertisements can be ranked correctly as to their later effectiveness.

One of the best studies of the value of the consumer jury test was made under the direction of Neil H. Borden and Osgood S. Lovekin. Seventeen series of advertisements, each series published with a coupon-return provision, were tested for reliability:

The series were submitted to groups ranging from 60 to 120 individuals, the standard of ranking expressed in two questions: (1) "If you were turning the pages of a magazine, which of these advertisements would be most likely to attract your attention?" (2) "Suppose you were going to reply to the offer, which one of these advertisements would be most likely to influence you to do so?" Emphasis in each case was placed on personal, individual answers, not estimates of public effect.

Possibility of chance in a consumer reaction was eliminated by choosing advertisements which showed decided differences in effectiveness, measured by mathematical formula. Similar precision was used to rank the significance of the final response.

Of the 17 series tested, only one was marked by direct contradiction of known results by consumer opinion on both questions. Disagreement occurred in one of the questions for two cases, yet for the remaining fifteen instances, consumer rankings and business rankings from inquiry returns corresponded directly. This correspondence was by a majority proportion in each of the 15, though in some cases, the investigators' reports points out, the majority was insufficient to inspire confidence in their reliability.

Five important conclusions which Borden and Lovekin believe justified by the study are the following:

1. The consumer-opinion method can be depended upon to give correct ranking of effectiveness of advertisements if properly conducted.

2. Conversely, blind use of the method, without appreciation of its limitations, might

give misleading evidence regarding effectiveness of advertisements.

3. Among the more important requirements in using the method is that of securing an audience really interested in the product advertised if a dependable ranking of the advertisements carrying different appeals is to be had.

4. This indicates an important limitation in the use of the method; it should not be applied to products other than those having fairly general use or interest unless an effective and economical way of reaching a jury really interested in the product can be devised.

5. If the differences in the advertisements to be ranked relate not to differences in appeal but to such variables as illustration, arrangement of mass, type, and spacing, then dependable results in ranking probably can be secured whether the jury is actively interested in the product or not.[15]

Prompted-recognition surveys of readership

The prompted-recognition, or aided-recall, method of studying advertisements has been used for many years by Daniel Starch and Staff, which has made available to agencies and others, the tabulated results of various studies of advertisement readership.

The procedure is simple. Readers of a medium are interviewed and asked several questions, such as, "Did you see this ad?" "What product is advertised?" "Did you read the headline?" "Did you read the copy?" "How much of the copy did you read?"

Since 1939, Starch surveys have given the results of the aided-recall test for all advertising of one column or larger, appearing in leading magazines.

From results obtained in the field surveys, the Starch organization compiles for advertisers and advertising agencies the "Advertising Rating Service." Starch supplies percentages of visibility and readership of individual advertisements, includes computed costs per person for visibility and readership, and provides percentages of readership of the component parts of each advertisement.

The prompted-recognition method has certain limitations. For example, some media are read for their news columns; others are only skimmed for personals. The thoroughness of reading varies considerably for different magazines and newspapers of the same general class of publications.

For most national advertisers, it is more economical to buy the Starch reports than to attempt a checkup of readership independently. Obviously, these reports are more in the nature of an audit of what has already been done than a guide to what should be done with a given advertisement, which is often the advertiser's practical need. Furthermore, a measure of general reader interest may have little value for the advertising of a product that interests only a definite small class of consumers or the advertiser who seeks direct action from his copy.

Predicting effectiveness of advertisements previous to extensive use

The marketing expert who believes that he can analyze an advertisement and predict by his subjective analysis the public's response to that advertisement is a dangerous man. His estimate may be worth more than that of the girl at the switchboard in the office, but he is likely to be sadly mistaken if he continues to make predictions based on subjective analysis only.

Consumers' receptiveness to each advertisement of a series can be predicted by means of balanced schedules in daily newspapers or other inexpensive media. For example, some advertisers select six typical cities and run six different advertisements for one week in each city. The advertisements are so arranged that every one of them is run in each of the six orders. For example, the six cities may be designated by letters *A, B, C, D, E,* and *F*. The advertisements may be designated as 1, 2, 3, 4,

READING CORNER WITH WALL SECTIONS CUT

This situational technique was used in in a study of interviewing methods in reader research. Forty-eight women were asked to participate in what appeared to be a study of reading fatigue. Each woman's eyes were tested before and after she had spent one hour and thirty minutes sitting in the chair, reading an advance copy of the **Ladies' Home Journal.** The observers at B and C were hidden from the view of the woman reader by means of a one-way-vision screen. The observers recorded their observations as to what the reader saw or read in the magazine. From 1 to 14 days later, trained field interviewers called at the homes of the 48 women and asked each what she had "seen," "read some of," or "read all of" in the copy of the magazine used in the laboratory. A comparison of the data obtained from the field interviewers with those of the observers in the laboratory showed a remarkably close agreement. See Herbert C. Ludeke and Ruth A. Inglis, of the Curtis Publishing Company, "A Technique for Validating Interviewing Methods in Reader Research," **Sociometry,** Vol. V, No. 2 (1942).

A-Subject

B-Observer

C-Observer

5, and 6. A schedule of the test campaign might be arranged as follows:

A	B	C	D	E	F
1	2	3	4	5	6
2	3	4	5	6	1
3	4	5	6	1	2
4	5	6	1	2	3
5	6	1	2	3	4
6	1	2	3	4	5

This kind of test prevents misjudgments because of unusual news events, weather, or the cumulative effects of preceding adver-

tisements. Such a six-weeks' method involves a great deal of time and it may be expensive, but it is a fairly safe way to predict the public's reaction to the advertisements proposed for use in an advertising campaign.

Split-run tests

When several advertisements are to be tested in order to predict their relative ef-

WHICH AD PULLED THE BETTER? The two advertisements, used by Funk & Wagnalls Company to sell the Language Phone Method, were split-run tested in the **New York Sunday News.** One produced almost 20 per cent more returns than the other. Study both advertisements carefully and then turn to the Appendix, page 628, for the answer. For a complete report of this split-run test, see "The Pay-Off," **Advertising Age,** April 22, 1946, the source of this information.

fectiveness, the conditions under which they are to be tested should be as nearly identical as possible. The split-run test supplies these conditions.

The split-run test means that the publisher of the magazine or newspaper arranges the printing of the copies into two or more divisions. For example, an advertiser may want to know which one of three advertisements, *A, B,* or *C* is the most effective in drawing inquiries. To answer the question, the publisher does the printing so that one third of the copies have advertisement *A,* the second third have *B,* and the last third have *C.* In the printing plant where the three streams of copies meet, a workman or a mechanical device alternates the copies of the several streams. This means that the three advertisements are of the same size,

have the same position, appear on the same day, are read by the same classes of readers, and advertise the same product under directly comparable conditions. Any one factor such as the headline may be changed in order to test its several variations.

Scores of newspapers and magazine publishers are now equipped for and willing to help an advertiser make split-run tests. Alert advertisers have used this device to discover the most effective appeals, headlines, copy, illustrations, coupons, and other factors. The procedure is far more accurate in its predictions than the older laboratory method in which people are asked what they like or think they like.

The split-run method is one of the most scientific tests available to the advertiser but it also has certain limitations. For example, some advertising campaigns must be planned to gradually build up a reputation for an article, a purpose for which the split-run test is not especially applicable. Also, split-run tests can be misleading when the circulation given each advertisement is not large enough to produce volumes of inquiries that are statistically significant.

Split-run tests are more significant for the measuring of effectiveness of different appeals than for determining the most effective presentation of one appeal. A whole series of split-run tests on the presentation of a chosen appeal may reveal which presentation is best, but the best presentation may not sell the goods at a profit.

The split-run test has not displaced all other methods of testing. Certain other techniques still have special values.

Measurements of television and radio advertising

Television and radio are more recent media than the newspaper or magazine, but they have been subjected to closer analysis than any other media. One reason for these extensive studies is the intangible nature of broadcast advertising. When an advertiser buys space in a periodical or on a billboard, he can look at his message whenever he feels so inclined. But when he buys air time, he knows only that his message has been sent out into time-space, and he wonders who heard it. Accordingly, radio stations and market researchers have sought to supply data concerning circulation or listenership.

Automatic recorders have been developed by several inventors. The recorders are attached to radios and record every turn of the tuning dial on a moving tape. Comparison of the tape with broadcasting schedules shows which programs were listened to and how long. The "audimeter," sponsored by the A. C. Nielsen Company, is an example of the recorder.

Until recently the recording device had to be attached to the radio set, but Nielsen has developed a new super-Audimeter which can do its work while stowed in the closet or under the bed. The meter is plugged in only to the electric light wire, over which a signal is passed from a special oscillator attached to the set. The signal, recorded on 16-millimeter film, is constant and shows in coded form whether the set is on or off and to what station it is tuned, if any. Each roll of Audimeter film will record simultaneously the tuning record of four different sets in the home.

Every two weeks the Nielsen home office mails a new magazine or film cartridge to the 1,500 sample homes. As an incentive to the housewife to uphold her end of the deal, two shiny quarters jump out when she inserts the new cartridge in the Audimeter and removes the old one, which is mailed to Nielsen for tabulation. When she pulls out the old cartridge, a buzzer keeps sounding off until she inserts the new one.

One value of the audimeter is in the fact that some programs get 67 per cent of their audiences in nontelephone homes, whereas others get only 35 per cent from the same class of homes. Early reports from the use of the Nielsen automatic recorder indicated that nontelephone homes listen an average of 44 per cent more than do telephone homes. The records also showed that listeners do not turn on the radio and let it blare for hours, regardless of station or program, as some critics of radio have suggested. Audimeters show that 56 per cent of all listening periods are of no more than 15 minutes' duration without switching of stations, the average of all listening periods being about 28 minutes.[16]

The *Program Analyzer* is a mechanical device developed in 1937 by Frank Stanton and Paul Lazarsfeld to make qualitative analyses of listeners' reactions to parts of radio programs. The 10 or 100 persons whose reactions to a program are being analyzed sit in a room where the Program Analyzer has

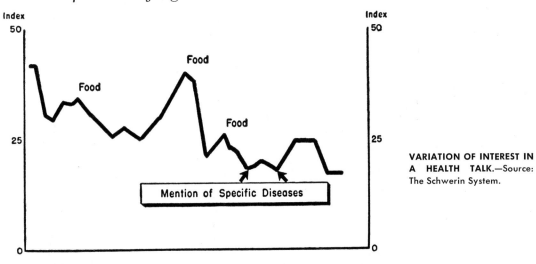

VARIATION OF INTEREST IN A HEALTH TALK.—Source: The Schwerin System.

been installed. Each person holds in his hand two electric push buttons that are connected by wire with the machine. Impulses from the buttons are recorded on revolving rolls of graph paper. Pressure on the green button is registered as favorable reaction and means, "I want to hear more of that kind of material." Pressure on the red button means, "I don't want to hear more of that kind," and is registered as unfavorable. If the respondent is indifferent, he presses neither button.

The program analyzer is used to pretest programs in various stages of production, to discover weak spots in a program, and to measure the effectiveness of appeals. In actual practice, findings from the analyzer are supplemented with further information gathered in oral interviews and through questionnaires.

In New York City, Schwerin Research Corporation is prominent among the companies engaged in research to gauge program appeal. Schwerin tries out programs on a preselected audience and records their reactions. For participation in the test, each person receives some small gift or favor.

In the studio, the audience fills out an amplifying questionnaire and the transcribed show begins. At various "reaction points" during the broadcast the audience is asked to mark at the proper place on a sheet of paper whether they think that part of the show is "good," "fair," or "poor."

Listeners are questioned again after the program, and the results of the entire test are tabulated. Schwerin's client then receives a "profile" of the total reaction to the program; this consists of a graph showing audience acceptance of the show, minute by minute. When desired, "profiles" of reactions by specific age, sex, income, or educational groups are made separately.

Horace Schwerin has described a number of case histories that were affected by the findings from analyses of the programs. One of these was a daytime talk series by a man who discussed health, diet, and the preparation of foods. (See figure on this page.) Listeners sent in letters asking for information or telling how successful certain of the program's recommendations had been. Adult women comprised 70 per cent of the audience, adult men 30 per cent. The sales results, garnered over a period of years, were excellent. When the listeners discovered that the authority substantiated their existing opinions, they, perhaps unconsciously, began to cultivate a respectful, almost hero-worshipping attitude.

This series was subjected to studio testing, with three major findings:

To laymen of advertising, the Milliken Visa Fabrics advertisement may appear to be especially effective. A Gallup and Robinson impact study, however, showed that it was ineffective. Its relative ineffectiveness is indicated by data from the Gallup and Robinson special scoring sytem for "Comparative Proved Name Registration." Comparable figures for proved name registration for the Milliken advertisement were: men,—1; women, 5; but for the Hart Schaffner & Marx advertisement they were decidedly better: men, 25; women, 11. Source: Data courtesy of Gallup and Robinson, Inc., Princeton, N.J.

HOW TO RELAX WITHOUT WRINKLING

Viracle tropical stays cool, crisp and creased on muggiest days

HART SCHAFFNER & MARX

1. Listeners felt the program personality spoke too casually, informally; it spoiled the picture they were constantly building of him as a dignified authority.

2. The level of interest was more stable than for most programs; listeners either liked or disliked it all the way through.

3. High points of interest always occurred where food was mentioned. Apparently, since food preparation is one of the prob-

lems women meet most frequently, it is of more than usual interest.

As a consequence, the conductor of the program put more emphasis on foods—especially on meal preparation—offered more homely philosophy, and spoke with more dignity. The results were impressive. His weekly fan mail which had averaged thirty-five cards and letters, jumped to a new weekly average of three hundred.[17]

Television commercials can be pretested

Several psychologists have developed methods of pretesting television commercials. The Schwerin Research Corporation,

for example, has experimented with the pretesting of commercials through the use of rough films. Before pretesting was introduced, there was a tendency to plan a television campaign around the safest idea—the one most similar to those which had been successfully used before.

Experiments have proved the advantages of pretesting. A rough commercial can be produced inexpensively and, when pretested, a useful and accurate forecast of its future effectiveness is obtained. Experiments indicate that there is little or no significant difference between the recall ratings obtained from a rough and those obtained from a finished commercial, as indicated by these findings from three studies:

Percentage of Audience Remembering Brand Name and at Least One Sales Point

Commercial A		Commercial B		Commercial C	
ROUGH VERSION	FINISHED VERSION	ROUGH VERSION	FINISHED VERSION	ROUGH VERSION	FINISHED VERSION
59	57	48	48	57	59

From Horace S. Schwerin, "How Pretests Help to Create Better TV Commercials," *Printers' Ink*, June 5, 1953, Copyright, 1953, by Printers' Ink Publishing Company, Inc., New York.

Gallup and Robinson, Inc., impact technique

Of the psychologists who have made notable contributions to measuring the effects of advertising, Gallup and Robinson are outstanding. They, for example, developed the *impact technique*. This procedure enables researchers to determine objectively what consumers get out of advertisements. The impact method can be applied to any medium: television, radio, newspapers, magazines, and billboards.

In an impact test for a magazine advertisement, the reader is required to recall an advertisement and "play back" the selling message with the magazine closed. A playback is simply the verbatim report, in the respondent's own words, of everything he or she can remember about a particular adver-

tisement. The playback is the end result of a series of probing questions about the advertisement.

Readers have difficulty in playing back an advertisement which has made no impression upon them. If the advertisement actually has made a memorable impression on a person, then within a limited period after exposure he can recall the advertisement and play back its message. In the case of some advertisements, over 40 per cent of the readers of a magazine have been able to prove that they have seen the advertisement —and this with the magazine closed. In addition they have been able to play back the message the advertiser told in his copy. No differences have been found among various educational groups in the ability to recall and play back a copy story. Readers with only a grade-school education play back as many advertisements as those with a college education.

The procedure as applied to newspaper advertisements has been described as follows:

All interviews are conducted within 24 hours after the test issue is delivered, thus avoiding confusion with ads appearing in the next day's issue. Respondents have no advance notice that they will be interviewed and they do not see a copy of the newspaper during the Impact interview.

Interviewing procedure is as follows:

1. Interviewers find qualified readers of "today's newspaper"; that is, readers who can prove that they read the issue by describing a story, article, cartoon, ad, or other item without reference to the paper at the time of interview.

2. The interviewer hands the respondent several cards containing the names of major advertisers in the issue and asks him to call out the names of any ads he thinks he remembers seeing.

3. After recording the names of all ads the respondent thinks he saw, the interviewer goes back and asks a series of depth questions about each ad mentioned. Questions include what the ad looked like, what it said, and whether it created any urge to buy, with appropriate probes.

4. After taking down verbatim all the information the respondent can give on each ad, the interviewer asks a series of detailed copy questions about specific test ads.

These questions are often phrased to get at understandability, believability or more detailed impressions. They normally are designed with reference to the test ads only.[18]

Gallup-Robinson researches indicate that the flow of ideas is greatest when communication is rewarding to the reader or viewer, when statements or claims are validated, and when the reader or viewer is not required to perform mental work, like figuring out what analogies or coined phrases mean.

Gallup has reported that effective advertising is that which uses "not words or phrases, but ideas. Ideas distinguish more than anything else the advertising that penetrates from that which does not get into the minds of people who read or hear it. Boast copy is of little value. Believable proof copy is the kind that sticks with people. Demonstrations are especially effective... The gimmick-y ads usually don't work. Gimmicks tend to get in the way of idea expression."[19]

Impact studies are forcing a new conception of advertising effectiveness—effectiveness which places emphasis upon ideas as opposed to advertising gadgetry.

Bodily reactions as indicators of responsiveness to advertisements

Psychologists have, from time to time, experimented with mechanical devices as a means toward measuring responses to advertising. If such a machine could be found, it should give us more nearly valid measurements than the present ones that depend upon the respondent's introspective impressions. One of these devices has been the psychogalvanometer.

The *psychogalvanometric* method has been used to pre-test radio programs and periodical advertisements. When advertisements are being tested for consumer reactions, electrodes are fastened to the hands and arms of those who are to view (or listen) to a series of advertisements. Each person's total response to a given advertisement is manifested through nerve impulses that are transmitted to the skin surface. The electrodes pick up these impulses and they are recorded on a tape. Gordon Eckstrand and A. R. Gilliland have shown that, under properly controlled conditions, it is possible to predict by this method the extent to which some advertisements will be effective in producing sales.[20]

Psychological studies of the electrical resistances of the human body have been made since 1880. The evidence shows that the autonomic nervous system is in activity all the time and that it responds to very small stimuli; that, as in the case of the lie detector, certain stimuli produce certain bodily reactions which it is almost impossible for the individual to prevent; and that the functioning of the human sweat glands is closely associated with bodily resistance or tension.

Improved galvanometers measure the most minute change in the functioning of the human sweat glands. By exposing subjects to external stimuli—copy, advertisements, packages, odors, sounds, or anything else—the effect of these stimuli upon the subject may be measured. The device indicates whether or not an advertisement or a radio program "aroused" minute changes in the functioning of the human sweat glands. By exposing subjects to external stimuli—copy, advertisements, packages, odors, sounds, or anything else—the effect of these stimuli upon the subject may be meas-

ured. The device indicates whether or not an advertisement or a radio program "aroused" the subject to a marked degree. Unfortunately for the purposes of advertising, the "machine" cannot indicate the direction of the "arousal": toward or away from the purchase of the product. Any findings obtained from such a machine must be combined with other types of testing.

Obviously, the problem of measuring the effectiveness of advertising has not as yet been solved, but psychologists are constantly improving old techniques and developing new ones.

Acknowledgments and References

1. Ernest Dichter, "A Psychological View of Advertising Effectiveness," *The Journal of Marketing,* July 1949.

2. Richard Giles, "Bostonian Shoe Advertising Is Revolutionized after Survey Among 5,000 Men," *Printers' Ink,* September 22, 1939.

3. Judith Cortada, "The Five-Foot Shelf: Lesson in Merchandising," *Advertising Age,* March 31, 1941.

4. Mark Wiseman, "Ideas," *Advertising and Selling,* September 1945.

5. "BBDO Has IBM Cards on Thousands of National Ads, Covered 247 Ways," *Advertising Age,* June 23, 1952.

6. Harold J. Rudolph, *Attention and Interest Factors in Advertising,* a Printers' Ink Bookshelf Volume published by Funk & Wagnalls Company, New York, 1947, p. 20.

7. Walter H. Weintz, "There *Is* a Relation between Readership and Sales," *Printers' Ink,* May 9, 1947, p. 34.

8. Mark Wiseman, "Illustrations: 1," *Advertising and Selling,* February 1947, pp. 74, 76.

9. E. K. Strong, Jr., and J. E. Loveless, "Want and Solution Advertisements," *Journal of Applied Psychology,* American Psychological Association, Inc., Vol. 10, pp. 346–366; Vol. 11, pp. 8–24. See also Harold E. Burtt, *Psychology of Advertising,* Houghton Mifflin Company, Boston, 1938, pp. 106 ff.

10. Henry C. Link, "Finds Four-Fifths of Ads Usually Fail to Click," *Sales Management,* February 1, 1933.

11. Charles M. Edwards, Jr., "Pretesting of Advertising: a Prerequisite for Profits," *Advertising and Selling,* June 1945, pp. 73, 74, 153.

12. Daniel Starch, "Informative Ads Outsell Others by 3 to 1," *Advertising and Selling,* December 1946. See also *The Journal of Marketing,* April 1947, p. 409.

13. Daniel Starch, "Why Readership of Ads Has Increased 24%," *Advertising and Selling,* August 1946, p. 47.

14. *Advertising and Selling,* October 1948, p. 123.

15. "Reliability Tests for Consumer Opinion," *Advertising and Selling,* June 6, 1935, originally reported by Graduate School of Business Administration, Harvard University.

16. "Audimeter," *Business Week,* October 21, 1939, p. 34; taken from *The Nielsen Researcher,* house organ of A. C. Nielsen Company. See also *Advertising Age,* October 16, 1939, p. 16.

17. Charles Hull Wolfe, *Modern Radio Advertising,* Funk & Wagnalls Company in association with Printers' Ink Publishing Company, Inc., New York, 1949, pp. 203, 205.

18. For further information, see "Gallup Tells What Makes a Good Ad on TV or in Print," *Printers' Ink,* November 6, 1953, and cover story, *Tide,* August 15, 1952. The interview procedure described above is quoted from a circular, *Impact Tests of Newspaper Advertising,* Gallup and Robinson, Inc., Princeton, N.J.

19. See "Gallup Tells What Makes a Good Ad on TV or in Print," *Printers' Ink,* November 6, 1953.

20. Gordon Eckstrand and A. R. Gilliland, "The Psychogalvanometric Method for Measuring the Effectiveness of Advertising," *Journal of Applied Psychology,* American Psychological Association, Inc., Vol. 32 (August 1948), pp. 415–425.

PROJECTS

1. Alexander Hamilton Institute ran advertisements with the following headings:
   a. "Those Who Shy at Unpleasant Facts Should Not Read This Page."
   b. "Men Who Are Satisfied to Wait Ten Years for Success Will Find Nothing Interesting on This Page."
   c. "Afraid to Face the Facts—Then Don't Read This Page."
   d. "Men Who Know It All Are Not Invited to Read This Page."
   One of these pulled marvelous results. Select the one that pulled best. See Appendix, page 628, for answer.

2. One of the country's most successful teachers of dancing says that he does not sell people *dance study.* He sells them what dancing will do for them, such as bring them popularity, health, charm, relaxation, or other benefits. A lawyer, for example, who buys the lessons does not "take lessons"; he relaxes. Apply this principle to the advertising of a canned food, an automobile, a bank account, or a radio.

3. James W. Young has built a business of selling men's ties through the use of split-run tests in *Sunset* magazine. For example, he tried three different headlines: (a) HAND WOVEN by the mountain people of New Mexico, (b) SHABBY HUSBAND made over — by my hand-woven ties, and (c) HUSBANDS LOVE my hand-woven ties (and you). The first outpulled the others by a wide margin. Why?

4. A split-run test in *The New York Times Magazine* for the sale of a popular-audience book tried two different appeals in the headline. The headline "How to win friends and influence people" produced twice as many sales as "How to ruin your marriage in the quickest possible way." Why?

5. One advertising man claimed that an advertisement is like a pretty girl—the more she only partly reveals her charms, the more interesting she becomes. Study advertisements which have been written to induce readers to ask for more information. Give examples of the copy that has been written for that purpose.

6. Find an opportunity to observe one or more persons while they are listening to the radio for at least four different programs. What do you notice about their attention to the radio broadcast every minute while you are observing? What do they do when the commercial comes on? Are they more attentive to musical, announcer-read, or drama-type commercials?

7. As an advertising man in a large manufacturing concern, you are asked by your employer to design a coupon to be used with the product which will draw responses from a large number of users and will stimulate sales of the product. Design such a coupon and point out the characteristics of it which justify your opinion that it will fulfill your employer's request.

COLLATERAL READINGS

Dichter, Ernest, "A Psychological View of Advertising Effectiveness," *The Journal of Marketing,* July, 1949.

Haire, Mason, "Projective Techniques in Marketing Research," *The Journal of Marketing,* April, 1950.

Lucas, Darrell B., and S. H. Britt, *Advertising Psychology and Research,* McGraw-Hill Book Company, Inc., New York, 1950, Chap. 5.

Martineau, Pierre, "It's Time to Research the Consumer," *Harvard Business Review,* July–August, 1955.

"Not the Thinking You'd Expect," *Business Week,* Nov. 6, 1954.

Shepard, Mills, "What Is the Formula for an Effective Advertisement?" *Advertising Agency,* April, 1952.

Vicary, James M., "Free Association Tests Can Help Advertisers," *Printers' Ink,* Sept. 3, 1948.

Wulfeck, J. W., and E. M. Bennett, *The Language of Dynamic Psychology as Related to Motivation Research,* McGraw-Hill Book Company, Inc., New York, 1954.

CHAPTER TWENTY-NINE

Salesmanship that serves consumers

People do not buy what they really need merely because they need it. They must be sold. For example, in 1797, American farmers made their plows out of crooked tree-forks. The implement was so crude that it only scratched the soil and required a small herd of steers to drag it over the ground. In that year, Charles Newbold patented a metal plow that would turn the soil in neat, smooth furrows. The operation of the plow required only one man and two oxen. Newbold showed farmers fields of splendid grain for which his metal plows had turned the sod, but the farmers still believed that iron plows would poison the soil and produce only weeds. Years of salesmanship were necessary before farmers could be induced to use the better implement. People must be taught not only the psychological arts but also the use of available resources for material living.

Salesmanship, at its best, renders a service to consumers. It breaks us away from our ruts in living and induces us to adopt the new and better devices that modern technology has made available to us.

The best selling is helpful selling. The way to sell is to serve as shown in the example that follows:

The career of Gerald M. Loeb, partner in E. F. Hutton & Company, New York, is not a dramatic one. It is a repetitious tale of building brick by brick. It is a story of personal devotion to an austere, back-breaking schedule in Wall Street. Loeb rises so early that by the time he reaches Schrafft's at 31 Broadway, where for 20 years he has breakfasted at precisely 7:30 A.M., he has already read all the morning newspapers from beginning to end. By the time the Stock Exchange opens at 10 A.M., Loeb has spent two hours at his desk digesting the bulletins on late developments flashed him by branch offices and correspondents all over the globe. He maintains a very heavy correspondence with corporation officials, makes many personal calls on business leaders, and keeps almost as well posted on developments in a number of industries as do many insiders. . . .

As an ambitious young man from San Francisco in E. F. Hutton's New York statistical department, Loeb soon set himself apart from the statisticians who stayed statisticians. They never got any order-giving clients, according to Loeb, "because their approach was academic. 'What do you think of General Motors?'

THE MAN WHO MADE THE
BEST MOUSETRAP WAITS
FOR THE WORLD TO MAKE
A BEATEN PATH TO HIS
DOOR

Cartoon by Nate Collier. Reproduced by special permission from **The Saturday Evening Post**, copyright, 1924, by The Curtis Publishing Company.

someone would ask them. 'It's a good company,' they would answer. That was the end of the discussion. I would answer the question with some others. 'Why do you want to know? Do you own General Motors stock? Do you plan buying it? What else do you own? Have you other motor stock? How much of your capital is invested?' And then they would get a reply that applied to them personally on what they should do and whether I thought General Motors at the price and as things appeared in the market was going up or going down. Such personal attention made another customer every time."

From management's point of view, there are important implications in the moral of this story. Management's challenge is to educate its salesmen to such a belief in the product or service that they can confidently orient their appoach and thinking to developing the *customer's* interest in the product—not breaking his resistance with "high-pressure" selling. Put in another way, it is making the prospect want to buy, not "selling" him. As Loeb expressed his own attitude, "I don't sell. People buy from me."[1]

Willard M. Thompson has reported a department store research study of how expert salespeople sell. Recordings were made of the ways a panel of 50 expert salespeople actually sell. Their techniques were analyzed. As a result, an important definition of personal selling emerged:

Personal selling in stores is not entirely focused, as current definitions imply, upon the objective of helping customers buy. It also serves the broader purpose of helping customers obtain maximum personal satisfaction for money spent.[2]

Training salesmen in the permissive-type techniques

The standardized or "canned" sales talk can be taught to salesmen by drilling them until they perform it satisfactorily. This kind of selling is not at all appropriate for low-pressure selling in which the prospect and the salesman communicate with each other.

In this kind of high-level salesmanship, it is necessary to learn to sense the customer's needs and wants. The salesman must not only be able to communicate his ideas and proposals to the prospect, but he must also develop the ability to understand what the prospect is attempting, explicitly and implicitly, to communicate to him. To perform effectively in this kind of two-way communication in face-to-face situations, the salesman needs a basic concept, a frame of reference, about human behavior. The adjustment concept as described in Chapters 2–8, or some equally helpful frame of reference, is essential. The skillfull use of such a concept must, of course, be developed through years of experience in much the same manner as it is developed by the skilled clinician.

Rules for the salesman's behavior have little value for low-pressure selling. The development of psychological insight is far more valuable. John M. Frey has described the needs and methods of training salesmen in this kind of effective communication, in part, as follows:

What should a salesman understand about the communication process that will help his selling efforts? He should understand what the process of communication entails; the complex social context in which it occurs; the difficulties that are likely to arise; the difference between statements of feeling and statements of content; the context in which words are spoken. Further, he should be aware that different people are bringing to each situation different assumptions, perceptions, and feelings based on their personal experience and "self" concept; that these assumptions, perceptions, and feelings are constantly interacting with his own, that he is intellectually, emotionally, and very personally involved in most situations; that recognition and acceptance of responsibility for this involvement are vital. . . . sales trainers could well borrow a concept from the field of supervisory training:

"We have to stop telling supervisors how they should behave and what their attitudes

should be. . . . Let us remember that our new objective is to assist people in learning from their own experience. We are no longer trying to change them; we are giving them the opportunity to change themselves, if they wish, by reflecting upon and re-evaluating their own experiences. . . . We are not interpreting their own experience *for them;* we are not telling them *our* personal experience. Instead, *we are allowing them to examine* and *re-evaluate their own experience."*[3]

Working within such a conceptual scheme, Roethlisberger proposes three ways in which the trainer can facilitate the process of self-learning: (1) helping people to recognize the attitudes they bring to experience; (2) helping people to ask better questions of experience; and (3) providing them with a useful way of thinking about matters of human behavior so that they can make better observations about themselves and their relations to others. . . .

Role-Playing

The most promising approach, I believe, centers around the use of role-playing. This is essentially a self-explanatory term. In sales training role-playing puts one man acting as a buyer, another as a salesman. Many variations are possible. For instance, the "buyer" can be told to act as he himself personally feels. Or he can be given a few basic "facts" about himself, or even a relatively complete characterization to portray. As for the "salesman," he can be given many, few, or no facts about the "buyer." Each instructor will naturally want to adopt the particular variation that suits his own personal preference and situation.

To illustrate what a company can do with role-playing, here is the experience of a firm employing a fairly large salesforce in a highly competitive industry:

In the beginning the salesmen—particularly the older, more experienced ones—were skeptical of the value of this role-playing. Agreement was finally reached, however, to experiment with the plan on an informal basis in one department. At first the salesman acting the part of the "buyer" played the role as he himself felt. The acting was somewhat stilted. The players were rather embarrassed, and a number of jokes and humorous comments were made. The ensuing discussions were restrained and brief.

But soon the atmosphere changed. The initial embarrassment was gone. The participating salesmen began to get deeply involved in what they were doing. So did the observing salesmen. The formal discussions waxed hot and heavy, continuing in informal groups for days afterward. One salesman suggested acting out the part of a real buyer whom he had recently come in contact with. This was done, and it worked out very well.

At times the discussions wandered. At times they got out of hand. But for the most part they were remarkably beneficial. The salesmen gradually became more consciously aware of the assumptions, perceptions, and feelings that they were bringing to a particular situation, and of how these feelings and attitudes were inextricably interwoven into their relationship with a buyer. They also became more perceptive of the feelings and emotions of a buyer. And they began to recognize the nature—and consequences—of the term "involvement."

In the particular situation of the company making this experiment the problem of price negotiation has continually loomed large. Quite naturally, therefore, the bargaining process arose in almost every role-playing situation. Initially, the natural tendency of the discussions was to focus on the "best" method of bargaining with a buyer—a natural error in this day of "how-to-sell" books. Consequently, a strong effort was made to guide the discussions away from a "right-wrong" basis to a "what happened" basis, which was found to be far more profitable.

In general, then, it would seem that role-playing can be used with considerable success. One great advantage of the method is that it forces learning by doing—practicing—rather than just talking. The men cannot say, for instance, that they should be tactful; they must *be* tactful. Role-playing allows the players (and observers) to learn from their own experience, in a sheltered atmosphere. Because the men are not "playing for keeps," they are free to experiment. At the same time, role-playing gets the players close enough to an actual situation so that they become excited and concerned about it.

Note that, in addition, role-playing is relatively practical. In contrast to the case method of instruction, it does not require prior preparation on the part of the salesmen, nor does it require the development of case materials.[4]

Of course this kind of superior salesmanship is applicable only to salesmen of high intelligence. Most salesmanship training must be given to typical rather than exceptionally able men and deal with the more simple aspects of the sales situation.

Training in selling is beneficial to all personality types

The need for careful selection and training of salesmen is indicated by the oft-repeated statement of sales managers that "the top quarter of the average sales force sells three-fourths of the total volume." The editors of *Sales Management* asked several hundred subscribers regarding the truth of this statement and the answers were as follows:

In 8% of the companies, the top quarter sold 71 to 80% of total volume.

In 35% of the companies, the top quarter sold 51 to 70% of total volume.

In 29% of the companies, the top quarter sold 41 to 50% of total volume.

In 28% of the companies, the top quarter sold 30 to 40% of total volume.[5]

Considerable statistical evidence is now available which indicates that sales results depend primarily on the selling methods used rather than on the personality type only. Field studies of the selling methods used by individual salesmen have been made by a number of organizations. C. Y. Belnap, of Trade-Ways, Inc., has furnished the following example of the close relation between selling methods and sales volume:

The salesmen in this case are food jobbers' men: driver salesmen operating in representative cities, towns, and rural areas throughout the United States.

After eliminating the factors of geographic differences, of city, town, and rural differences, and of store differences on the routes studied, there remained only two other factors which could account for the wide variations in sales as between the men. These two factors were variations either in the personalities of the salesmen themselves or in the methods they were using.

The experienced observers making the survey reported that as regards personality, the salesmen seemed to divide about equally into four groups:

1. Men whose personalities appeared "negative, colorless, weak, drab."
2. Men described as "quiet, serious, steady, plodding."
3. Men described as "genial, cordial, familiar, easy-going, back-slapping."
4. Men described as "aggressive, energetic, breezy, decisive, high pressurer."

As this type of sales operation is a routine daily grind, you'd suppose the men in the second group—the serious, steady, plodding type—would be the fellows who make the most sales. But they weren't. All four groups were getting just about the same average order per stop. But the individuals making up each group differed widely among themselves in volume of sales. So the methods which the men were using were checked against their orders to see whether it was differences *in what they did* which accounted for the differences in *how much they sold.*

Regardless of their personality rating, men who started their calls by making a physical count of the dealer's stock of the sixteen products in the line they handled averaged orders two and one-half times as large as the orders obtained by the men who didn't make this their first step.

Again, the men who discussed the week's special offer with the dealer *before* trying for the regular order, averaged 27 per cent more per call than the men who wrote up the regular order first and then brought up the subject of the special.

Or take a third method. Only 15 per cent of the men suggested to the dealer what quantities of each item he should buy, but they averaged orders 300 per cent larger than the orders of the men who let the dealer himself suggest what he needed.

To be sure, this is only one sales operation. But it illustrates the point: that it's not so much the men themselves as it's the methods they use, which determine their sales volume.[6]

These and several other analyses of how salesmen spend their time and what they actually do in the presence of prospects have put a new emphasis on the development of effective methods regardless of the kind of personality that uses the methods. Also, observations of 4,000 cases in department stores throughout the country brought out the fact that on only 16 per cent of the cases observed was there any actual showing of merchandise by the sales people; 53 per cent did not use suggestive selling with regard to merchandise in their own departments, and only 2 per cent suggested merchandise in other departments.[7]

Anyone who wants to conduct an experiment on the power of suggestion can do so. As an example, the old story of the sergeant and the apricots is repeated here:

The young sergeant was passing out apricots in small paper dishes to the chow line. He decided to experiment. He asked the next few men as they came by: "You don't want any apricots, do you?" And 90 per cent of them said: "No."

To the question, "You *do* want apricots, don't you?" approximately 50 per cent answered: "Yes, I'll take some."

The sergeant then started asking: "One dish of apricots or two?" And despite the fact that soldiers don't like army apricots, 40 per cent took two dishes, and 50 per cent took one.
—*Connecticut Mutual Topics.*

Formulas for selling

E. St. Elmo Lewis in 1898 formulated the slogan, "Attract attention, maintain interest, create desire." Later he added a fourth point, "Get action." Numerous additions and substitutions have been made to this theory of selling, such as "Gain confidence" and "Give satisfaction."

Strong has formulated a theory of selling in terms of "Want, solution, action, and satisfaction."[8] This formula, like its predecessors, also deals largely with mental states; it directs the attention and efforts toward what goes on in the prospect's mind. Some sales managers who have trained salesmen claim that it is very difficult and decidedly confusing for a salesman to focus attention upon what the prospect is thinking. An easier and more effective method is to train the salesman to think of what he himself does rather than what may be happening in the mind of his prospect. The mental states of the prospect cannot be ignored, but *the emphasis should be upon what the salesman does and the objective factors of the selling act.* The salesman should think in terms of:

1. *The prospect as an individual*—his education, health, business affiliations, and so on.

2. *The situation of the prospect*—his problems, financial status, and other objective characteristics relevant to the purchase of the salesman's product.

3. *The methods or acts in the sales canvas* —the time of day he calls, the methods of demonstrating, the words he speaks, the number of calls, the method of closing the sales talk, and other controllable acts on the part of the salesman.

When, for example, a leading nursery management studied the records of interviews with farmers and other prospects for fruit trees and berry plants, the carrying of the brief case proved to be an important factor in the selling:

	Per Cent of Interviews Producing Orders	Average Order	Sales per Interview
When brief case was carried	86	$39	$34
When it wasn't carried	45	28	11

This management also found that it was helpful for the salesman to introduce himself on a first call on a home owner:

> In the first calls that began in this way, the salespeople got permission to prepare plans 86% of the time.
> In the first calls that did not begin in this way, they got permission only 33% of the time.[9]

Obviously, such simple but very important acts can be taught salesmen.

Directing the sales talk toward the prospect's problem

The dominant attitude of the true salesman is that of the man who wishes to render service. Many men do not want to sell a prospect unless that prospect really needs the article under consideration. Some concerns are even changing the title of salesman to "serviceman," or, in the case of those who sell to dealers, "merchandise counselors." This attitude toward the prospect is expressed in the frequent mention of the "'You' viewpoint," "Prospect analysis," or the "Objective attitude." Selling has become a matter of "combing" the prospect's situation and then capitalizing that part of the situation which can be made more satisfying.

The best salesmen study the prospect, capitalize the immediate situation, and then arouse in the mind of the prospect a feeling of want. The prospect must be made to feel that his present situation could be better or more profitable. A man may wear the same suit for a year, but he may not have any sense of want for a new suit until his wife mentions his shabbiness so often that he wants a new suit. The *need* may be present; but, until that need is transformed into a *want*, it might as well not exist so far as the salesman is concerned. The salesman must induce in the prospect a feeling of inadequacy, a *felt need*. This feeling of a need or a conscious want takes place as soon as the salesman demonstrates his article in such a way that it fits into the prospect's problems. The suggested purchase becomes an answer or a solution to a want. In a few cases the salesman finds it an easy matter to fit his product or service into the wants of the prospect, as in the case of the fire insurance salesman who finds that his prospects want fire insurance right after a big fire in the community. At such times, they have a felt need or a conscious want. However, it is usually necessary for the salesman to arouse the want or to connect his product with some present want.

The salesman who sells books for school children does not create a new want on the part of the mother, but he associates his books with the "want" for her child's success. The automobile salesman does not create new wants, but associates the new big car with the prospect's present want of social prestige. He shows the prospect how he can have his want satisfied *now*. The skillful salesman is adept in the art of presenting means to *immediate* satisfactions.

To do this, the salesman does not emphasize the product itself but describes the product as an *end*. The product is not even the means to the desired end. The salesman gives a vivid description of the product so that the prospect pictures himself as enjoying those delights which the product gives. The automobile salesman does not say: "When you have this car, it will give your wife a lot of pleasure," but, "When you have this big car, your wife and your friends will realize that it is worthy of a man of your caliber."

It often happens that the inventor of a machine is unable to sell it. The technical expert knows so much about it that he describes the machine. The salesman describes not only the things that the machine does but also the satisfactions and pleasures that it gives. He describes not just the means to the end but the end in its most pleasant aspects. The dealer is given attractive descriptions of the profits to be made from handling the product rather than a description of the product itself.

Some salesmen who sell to dealers think that they are giving the dealer service when they arrange his stock for him, sweep the store, wait on customers, or wash the windows. These acts are not rendering a service based on the goods the salesman sells. They are merely a method of approach to put the dealer in a receptive state regarding the salesman's commodities. The approach may be made from any one of several angles.

The approach

Tricky approaches are popular with a few salesmen. They refuse to discuss their proposition with anyone except the "big boss," because they are calling on a "personal matter." The "personal matter" approach is an exceedingly weak and stereo-

typed start for an interview. It is a deceitful method of getting into an office, because any official can be made to leave a meeting of his board of directors if his secretary tells him that a man wants to see him about the "accident" his son just had.

Generally, investigators of selling techniques believe that *the first 10 seconds before a customer are especially important.* First impressions are likely to last throughout the sales interview.

Salesmen are advised to cultivate a voice that reflects pleasant feelings and helps the customer to have a pleasant participating experience during the interview.

The rule in this connection is, *Keep the voice up on the last syllable.*

An *up*-rising voice holds attention. A dying-out voice loses attention.

Macy's in New York conducted an experiment on this point and found that when sales-people greeted customers with "Good Morn*ing*"—keeping their voices up on the last syllable—there was a marked warming up of customers and an increase in sales tickets.[10]

One firm whose canvassers found it difficult to gain admission to the homes of wealthy women instructed them to wear a hat and carry a cane and light-colored kid gloves. The maids and butlers then assumed that the canvasser was making a social call and readily admitted him. And a woman who sold books hired a big car and a liveried chauffeur. Thereafter she had no difficulty in gaining admission to the homes of the well-to-do. Of course, simpler schemes are used, such as leaving a certificate for a small gift one day and presenting the gift the next day. This device has been worked successfully, but it is of doubtful value in the long run, unless the companies promoting it can train their salesmen to use it skillfully.

Elmer Wheeler has conducted many researches regarding ten-second sales messages or "Tested Selling Sentences." He adapted his technique to Johns-Manville salesmen's needs in making an effective approach to arousing interest in home improvements on the part of housewives:

Johns-Manville realized the importance of the first ten seconds. In a study of the psychological factors surrounding the sale of home improvements and to introduce the new Housing Guild plan, we watched J-M salesmen approach doors. We studied their opening words and their approaching techniques. Our observations again proved that what was said and done during the first ten seconds either got them past the door, or failed.

One salesman would approach the door and say: "I'm from Johns-Manville. Would you be interested in knowing about the new Housing Guild plan of improving your home at a cost similar to the down payments made for your radio and refrigerator?"

The answer was usually "No." Desire had not been aroused. Curiosity not piqued. Several different and shorter approaches were tested. Finally, this "Tested Selling Sentence" and the "Tested Technique" were evolved:

The salesman approached the door. He rang the bell, stepped back slightly, and when the woman came to the door he held a booklet toward her and said:

"This is *your free* copy of *101 Ways to Improve Your Home.*"

As she unhooked the screen door, or opened the door wider, to reach out and receive the booklet, the salesman would quickly open the booklet to a page and say:

"Here is a kitchen *before* remodeling, and here is one *afterwards.*"

The woman was, naturally, interested in seeing how other women were remodeling their kitchens. Her interest was aroused in ten short seconds.[11]

Salesmen often try to find out a prospect's hobby before they call. This kind of interest in a prospect's affairs is legitimate if the salesman does not try to bluff. His interest in the prospect's hobby should be that of a learner. He can have a genuine desire to learn something about the hobby, but if he exhibits an artificial interest merely to make a sale, he is likely to make himself ridiculous. The salesman should mention the hobbies of the prospect in such a way that the prospect is pleased with himself because the salesman is willing to listen to his exploits. Sincerity is always important for the salesman, but it is especially important when hobbies are discussed.

Furthermore, the prospect approached by the salesman should be a live prospect at the time of the call. Studies of automobile selling, for example, indicate that typical motorists who buy new cars gather information and think about cars for about two months before they purchase.[12] During the "period of gestation" the prospective buyer gathers information and makes up his mind as to which cars he should look at before buying. In many cases he wants more information than is given in automobile advertising. At the same time, he is often reluctant to ask for such information because he does not wish to be subjected to "sales pressure." If a salesman can bring to his attention some new type of information that is sufficiently attractive to overcome his reluctance, and get him to say who he is before he becomes exposed to competitive solicitation—then the salesman has a far better chance of selling him.

The demonstration and sales talk

When the salesman enters the presence of the prospect, he is apt to say: "I am Mr. So-and-so and I represent the Blank Company. I would like to show you one of our new grommets." This kind of opening is stereotyped and bores the prospect unless he happens to be in a receptive mood. Some of the best salesmen omit introductory remarks and plunge at once into the demonstration. The various types of demonstration may be classified as follows:

1. SAMPLE IN THE SALESMAN'S HAND. In this common type of demonstration, the salesman shows the device to the prospect. He shows what it does and how it operates. The prospect looks on and shows interest, asks questions, or gives evidence of boredom.

The buyer makes up his mind in advance. "The typical motorist is in the buying mood only about 2 months out of every 3 or 4 years." During the "period of gestation" the prospective buyer gathers information and makes up his mind as to which cars he should look at before buying. In many cases he wants more information than is given in automobile advertising. At the same time, he is often reluctant to ask for such information because he does not wish to be subjected to "sales pressure." If the manufacturer can bring to his attention some new type of information that is sufficiently attractive to overcome his reluctance, and get him to tell who he is before he becomes exposed to competitive solicitation—then the salesman has a far better chance of selling him.—From "27 Suggestions for Locating Prospects," C. R. Report No. 3606, General Motors Corporation, Detroit, Mich.

2. SAMPLE IN THE PROSPECT'S HAND. The salesman hands the device immediately to the prospect. It is so placed that the prospect is compelled to touch, taste, smell, hear, see, or manipulate the article. If the article is novel in appearance, the prospect may be eager to observe or to try it. This method has been used with success in selling pianos and washing machines. The salesman delivers the article to the home, and the prospect accustoms herself to the use of it.

3. THIS-IS-WHAT-YOU-ARE-LOSING METHOD. The salesman tries to show the prospect what a man in his position is actually losing in convenience or in dollars and cents. He takes out a pencil and a pad and asks the prospect just enough simple and generally known facts about his business to enable the salesman to compute the prospect's daily, monthly, or yearly loss. Some salesmen actually use a new shiny silver dollar or a crisp ten-dollar bill to dramatize the loss. One salesman had a printer make some blank checks with the name of the bank as "The Bank of Lost Money." To the prospect he handed a check for the amount that was

being lost annually through failure to use his product.

4. THIS DEVICE WILL ENABLE YOU TO DO MORE OR BE MORE. The salesman does not dwell on the old situation or the present situation, but proceeds at once to the future situation—the prospect's. He shows how much money the dealer can make if he stocks these goods.

5. THE COMPARISON METHOD. This method combines 3 and 4. The salesman does not emphasize the commodity itself but shows the prospect his present situation and then shows him how much better the new or other device would be for his needs. This does not mean that the salesman should knock his competitor's product or give the prospect the impression that he must be a "boob" because he is not using his article. If tactfully done, even the correspondence school salesman can make the prospect feel, without embarrassment, that he could be using his evenings to better advantage and obtain more money and prestige if he were to change his present status. The salesman should always be careful to avoid statements

that might make the prospect feel that the salesman considers him unfortunate or ignorant just because they have never met before.

6. THE MOVING PICTURE AND GRAPHIC CHART METHODS. It is often difficult for the salesman to demonstrate the service or article with the service or article itself, so he must depend upon some graphic means to enable the prospect to realize his present situation and to visualize the best possible situation. The film method of demonstration is one of the very best methods, because the prospect can really see the benefits claimed for the product instead of attempting to visualize them. The moving picture machine is a means of demonstration that should be used more frequently. The chief objection to most of the films seems to be that they deal with the manufacturer's problems rather than with the customer's problems.

7. THE STUNT METHOD. The stunt is the favorite form of demonstration to the beginner in selling. It has its place in the sales interview, but it often directs the prospect's attention to the stunt as a stunt rather than to the article as a solution of the prospect's problems. Any dealer can crowd the sidewalk with people by putting a stunt in the window, but the store management does not want everybody to stop. Only the worthwhile prospects should be attracted to the window. The circus sideshow barker wants to attract everyone to his entertainment, and the stunt is legitimate advertising for him; but the salesman cannot depend upon a stunt to do his selling. The stunt may be made an attention-getter, but it should be relevant to one strong talking point.

The sales talk

The first rule of the successful sales talk is that it must deal with the prospect's situation and be directed toward a more satisfied, more contented, or more effective prospect-situation. The talk that starts nowhere and gets nowhere seldom leads to a sale. Even though a salesman dislikes the "canned" sales talk, he should have certain definite goals in each talk. Far more sales have been lost through lack of a planned sales talk than because of having the talk too highly standardized.

One "quota-beating" salesman who sells a specialty tells his prospect that he has planned his sales talk so that he, the prospect, will be able to see clearly what his machine can do and that the prospect can judge for himself as to whether the machine will make money for him. Then he hands the prospect a small printed card, saying: "This card has listed on it the six most common questions which my prospects ask or want to ask while I demonstrate this machine. If I do not make myself clear on some point, check that question. Of course, if you think of a point not on the card, be sure to ask that." A significant part of this scheme is the fact that the salesman has omitted from the card the most common question asked by the prospects and which every prospect is almost sure to ask. When the prospect raises that question, the salesman acts as though the prospect has thought of something no one ever before thought of. He scratches his head, then answers the point, and compliments the prospect's ingenuity; but at the same time the acceptance of that point practically commits the prospect to the purchase of the machine. The above method can be adapted to almost any product or service sold today.

A major fault of some salesmen is to talk in abstract terms. They discuss *quality* in a general way. The word "quality" and similar terms should never be used. Quality should be described by actual examples of what a user did with this machine under certain trying conditions. The salesmen of a paper company, selling paper towels, do not talk about superior absorbency. They take two inkwells having the same amount of ink in them and stick their own towel into one inkwell and a towel of another brand into the other inkwell. After a few seconds, the difference in their absorbent qualities can be seen by the prospect.

Advertisers long ago learned that people do not read advertisements that are full of abstract ideas. They want pictures that illustrate a concrete and definite situation. All abstractions such as *best, strongest, newest, value, service,* and *most economical* should be avoided; the talking point should be stated in terms of the concrete with actual instances of how that characteristic has been proved by other users.

The use of definite terms in the sales talk does not necessitate boresome technical descriptions of how the product is made, the kind of raw materials used, or the way it is sold. When technicalities are used, they should be related to the prospect's problems. The reason for a detailed description of a gear in a machine should be stated to the prospect to convince him that, while a specific part has been giving trouble in some machines of other makes, it cannot cause difficulties in this brand. The prospect wants definite facts that he can grasp.

Goodall Company, manufacturer of Palm Beach suits, operated a retail laboratory and experimented with various sales approaches to customers. The company found that when salesmen addressed customers with a time-honored bromide, such as, "Can I help you?" 7 per cent bought. When salesmen used the system of letting the customers alone until they asked for help, 12 per cent bought. But when the salesmen greeted customers with specific comments about the merchandise, such as, "This will be this year's most popular tan," 25 per cent bought.[13]

The sales talk should be definite in its mental imagery, but it should also have human interest. Cold, intellectual appeals are not so stimulating to action as are appeals that arouse the warmer emotions. The prospect wants to hear a story. He likes to have a lump in his throat and a tear in his eye. He wants to hear about people and things that make him smile, that cause him to love more devotedly, to sacrifice a little, and to dream new dreams. The prospect wants to take sides with what he believes to be right. It is necessary to invest the sales talk with an emotional tone. As the old banker said to a young salesman: "If you are trying to sell the services of a bank, show the prospect the pictures of your officers. Describe the little human-interest aspects of their work. Tell how one of those officers helped a man to pull out of a bad situation and achieve business success. Don't talk the usual talk about the financial strength of the bank."

Answering objections

The true salesman hopes that the prospect will raise objections before he buys. The objection offers the salesman an opportunity to demonstrate his product. One of the best salesmen in the country always has a pang of regret when the prospect indicates that he is sold and wants to sign on the dotted line. This salesman enjoys selling: the meeting of minds, the fencing-like encounter, the parries, the thrusts, and losing or gaining a new friend. He sells because he loves the game of selling.

Objections are a natural part of the process of selling. The prospect seldom welcomes the salesman with open arms. Can we blame the prospect? If we try to analyze the various ideas in the prospect's mind, we can understand why he does not, as a rule, want to see another salesman. The reason is that the salesman interrupts the prospect's *ongoing activity.* Even a newborn baby objects to having its activity thwarted or retarded. Hold a baby with his arms tight against his body and he will soon show his anger in no uncertain manner. When the salesman comes to see a prospect, he interrupts the flow of ideas and activities of the prospect. The worthwhile prospect is always busy doing something else, mentally or physically. The most natural response of the prospect to the salesman is that he does not need or does not want what the salesman has to offer. The salesman must, first of all, get the prospect into a new line of thought, and, if the salesman has planned his demonstration and sales talk in the right manner, the sale should follow as a matter of course. The live prospect will make some objections in order to clarify his ideas and to ascertain whether he really understands what the salesman has just told him.

When the prospect says, "I am not interested," the salesman can say: "I know that you are not interested, Mr. Prospect. That's why I called. You have never used this device and Mr. Blake of the Samson Company thought I ought to show it to you." The salesman who can smile and accept the objection with nonchalance will be able to go ahead with the demonstration. The objections of most dealers to buying because conditions are bad can be answered with definite, prepared figures to show the dealer that business will continue regardless of conditions. Certain professional and other people who are not affected by the current conditions are always buying. The bank clearings of the city may show that they are greater than last year in that town. Ask the dealer to look out on the street and see the cars that are going up and down. People are still wearing clothes and eating.

To answer objections, the salesman should be able to show facts and figures that have been collected by a disinterested person. If the buyer does not believe that the salesman's shirts do not fade, the salesman should show the results of tests conducted under conditions that will satisfy the prospect. The shirt that went through the tests should be handed to the prospect for inspection. The salesman often depends upon his wits and bullying to answer objections, when the objections could be answered far more easily by just a tested sample, a page of charts, or a testimonial letter.

"The price is too high" is one of the arguments which should be answered in a straightforward manner rather than by evasion or humor. If the price objection is evaded, the customer may not mention it again but may refuse to buy. After all, the customer should know why the price asked is fair. A direct answer to the price objection is the dramatized form of answer. A salesman of washing machines capitalizes the high price of his machine by demonstrating the machine with money in his hand. Every time he points out a strong feature of his machine, he places a dollar bill or a quarter on that part of the machine. When he gets through he adds up the amount of money and shows the prospect that the price asked is fair in comparison to the value.

If the prospect has been sold during the sales talk, neither price nor any other objection will prevent the sale. The prospect may raise the question of price, but he may do it because he really desires to have ample justification for the price. The salesman who is unduly price-conscious has never been convinced that the product is worth the price asked. If his standard of living has been on a scale below that of the price level of the article he is selling, it will be necessary for the sales manager to re-educate the salesman.

When the prospect wants a handy excuse for not buying, he objects to the price. Only one other excuse is more common: *I'll see you next time.* If the dealer presents this excuse, it simply means that the salesman has not done a good job of convincing him that he can make money with the line. The salesman can answer: "Of course, I'll see you next time, but that will not be for three months. In the meantime, according to my quota, 4,600 people are going to buy this article in this county. They will pay the dealers who sell them a gross profit of $2,300. You will want to be one of the dealers to have your share in the profits."

The salesman should not have the impression that it is well to "annihilate" the prospect when he makes an objection. To knock the prospect's objection too hard causes him to lose his self-respect. When an objection is stated, the salesman should restate the objection briefly and fairly; then the prospect knows that his objection is appreciated. Pay the prospect a compliment when he raises a threadbare objection—act as if it were an unheard-of objection and answer it—not too quickly but satisfactorily to the prospect's sense of worthwhileness.

The answering of objections should never degenerate into an argument. The salesman may be able to win the argument; but, if he does, he loses his sale. As soon as the discussion between salesman and prospect tends toward the argumentative type, the salesman should use humor. In fact, since most salesmen do not take the trouble to prepare evidence that will meet objections, they should at least collect a set of anecdotes that will answer the most frequent objections.

The art of getting the order on the order book

The psychological moment to close has received much attention in sales discussions. As a matter of fact, there are few true psychological moments when the prospect wishes to order and the salesman catches the prospect off his guard for the order. Orders that must be "caught on the fly" are often countermanded. The salesman should not pounce upon the prospect for the order. If the salesman has studied the needs of the prospect and is anxious to render a real service, the order will follow of its own accord.

It is true, however, that some prospects find it difficult to make a decision and the salesman must help them to decide. A few salesmen claim that they can recognize the moment when the prospect is ready to decide. They note whether the prospect leans forward, toward the salesman, and toys with the sample. One salesman even claimed that a prospect once told him that he did not

want the article under discussion but the salesman said: "Your lips tell me that you do not want the article and yet your body tells me that you do, because you leaned toward me when you said that you could not buy it now." The prospect admitted that he wanted the article, but that he had an inhibiting objection which he hesitated to mention. When the objection was stated and answered, the prospect bought. In the best sales canvasses, the salesman and the prospect get into the same mood or attitude, into a mental state of mutuality of interest, so that the salesman does not view the prospect as a mere plaything but as a fellow businessman whose interests are complementary to his own.

The salesman may help the prospect to make a decision by arranging the situation so that he need decide only a minor point. The experienced life insurance salesman does not, as a rule, ask the prospect whether he does or does not want his policy. Rather, he asks him: "Will it be convenient for you to have our medical examiner call at your home on Tuesday evening and give you the health examination?" If the prospect indicates that that time is satisfactory, he has also indicated incidentally that he will take the insurance. The jobber salesman often does the same when he asks about the method of shipment or the date of delivery, the salesman naming a plan that he knows will be satisfactory to the customer.

Some salesmen apply this "minor-decision" method too frequently, when they get into the habit of asking for a trial order. The trial order of a half-dozen lot is easily asked for and easily given. But a trial order simply means that the sale was not completed. The customer still has many mental reservations, or he would give a worthwhile order. Of course, the trial order may be used as a starting point and the amount can be stepped up to a profitable figure.

The prospect will find it easier to buy if the salesman has succeeded in getting him to say "Yes" several times during the interview. The prospect who is in a hostile or negative attitude is hard to persuade, whereas the agreeing prospect is in a mood for further action. The unskillful salesman who tries to have his prospects "Yes" themselves into an order is likely to lose his grip on the situation. This method can be used only by those who are unusually adept at controlling the sales situation. The salesman can concentrate on the one point which appeared to appeal most to the prospect. Automobile salesmen know that the points about a car that appeal to those who know cars are not the points that appeal to prospects. The salesmen tend to be interested in the mechanical qualities of the car, whereas many prospects are interested in the accessories, such as the cigar lighter and the vanity case. The real estate salesmen know that building construction does not interest the modern housewife nearly so much as the design of the fireplace and the arrangement of the cupboards in the kitchen. It is legitimate, therefore, to emphasize those factors that appeal most to the prospect in hand.

Each prospect varies in his susceptibility to assistance in making the decision to buy. Some prospects sell themselves. Others must be pushed and tugged at. Still others need a simple sales technique to do the thing they want to do but cannot, because the habit of turning down all salesmen is too strong to allow them to lift themselves out of the channels of indecision.

Aggressive selling produces more orders than easy-going salesmanship. The man who has lived among farmers knows the pleasure they get from chatting with strangers. It is often assumed that a sort of easy-going, chatty sales canvass is necessary when selling to farmers. A sales manager who traveled with a sales crew that sold a five-dollar product to farmers found that the salesmen who used the most aggressive and shortest canvass had the biggest sales record. The salesmen who spent not more than ten minutes with any farmer made the greatest

number of sales. Action begets action. The most common methods of stimulating prospects to act are:

1. An aggressive, definite sales canvass.
2. The use of a minor decision, which makes it easy to buy without a big decision.
3. Getting the prospect into an agreeable and agreeing mood.
4. Showing the prospect that he can purchase with ease right now.
5. Showing him the danger of delay, such as "A coming change in price," "Temporary trial offer," "Only one to a customer," "You are now losing $50 per month by not having it," or "The continued inconvenience should be ended now."

Appealing to his emotions: "Prove that you are a man of decision," "Sign now and surprise the children," "This is worthy of a businessman of your prestige."

Failure to get the order

Salesmen are often asked how many calls they are willing to make on a prospect before dropping him. The correct answer may be one or a dozen. Some of the largest accounts that business firms have are the result of ten or more calls. One thousand retailers kept accurate check for six months to learn how many calls salesmen made on them before giving up the job as hopeless. Here is the surprising result of that check-up:

48.2 per cent made 1 call and quit.
24.4 per cent made 2 calls and quit.
14.7 per cent made 3 calls and quit.
12.7 per cent made 4 calls and quit.

Yet it was discovered that 60 per cent of their merchandise was bought by these dealers at the fifth call or after.[14]

Only careful research can reveal the extent to which persistence in selling is profitable. Trade-Ways, Inc., has published results of one study on "What Price Persistence?"

Persistence is a virtue—but sometimes it's costly in selling. Here are some striking facts from a recent study of the work of a force of industrial salesmen.

	Per Cent of Time	*Per Cent of Sales Volume*
Calls on active customers	19	80
1st and 2nd calls on *new* prospects	25	17
Follow-up calls on *old* prospects	37 ⎱ 44%	2 ⎱ 3%
Calls on former customers	7 ⎰	1 ⎰

Forty-four per cent of the actual selling time, to get 3% of the business.[15]
From *Profit-Makers*, issued by Trade-Ways, Inc., New York. Also reported in *Printers' Ink*, April 19, 1940, p. 92.

Persistence is as essential in selling today as it ever was. But mere persistence may be only boresome to the prospect and fatiguing to the salesman. Persistence means more than footwork. It means headwork as well. Selling hard requires more than merely trying hard to sell. When the salesman finds that he cannot get an order, he should close his sample case without insisting upon an order, but he should prepare the way for his next call by saying: "I am sorry that I don't have a sample of our Palate brand of food with me. I shall ask the house to mail you a sample for your wife and when I call again in four weeks, you can tell me how you like it." Before the salesman makes his next call, he should write a friendly letter to the prospect and explain the profit or value of his article.

The salesman should, during the interview, have learned one subject that interests the prospect. He can bring the prospect a newspaper clipping, a photograph, a book, or any other article or idea that will interest him. Each call means that the salesman must present something new and worthy of the prospect's consideration. The turn-down should not actually take place. The good salesman does not allow it. No interview, when it ends, should give the salesman a sense of relief. It should simply pave the way for another interview when new ideas may be presented in a new way with more attractive applications.

The basis of success in salesmanship is skill in human relations

This skill usually originates in early childhood; that fact explains why many sales managers think that good salesmen are born that way. The adjustments which lead to human-relations skills begin so early that observers imagine that the skill is hereditary or some accident of birth.

Potential sales ability on the part of some boys can be observed in many typical American families at, let us say, the evening meal. Father comes home tired and eats in silence. Mother is busy serving the dinner. The children eat in silence or amuse themselves by picking on each other. But sometimes in such a family one boy cheerfully talks about the happenings of the day. He enjoys his sports. He likes to talk about his experiences and his friends. The others listen occasionally. Gradually he acquires skill in making others listen to him and respect his statements. In later adulthood, selling is a natural vocation for him, and his sales manager is likely to speak of him as a "born salesman."

Many college graduates drift into selling, especially those who find that their education has not trained them for any specific vocation. They drift into selling by force of circumstance rather than from a spontaneous or intelligent choice. Such men are almost certain to fail as salesmen unless they go through the usual psychological steps which enable a person to enjoy selling. These steps are likely to involve one or more of the following:

1. An intellectual conviction that selling is a socially valuable vocation.

2. An emotional experience which makes selling an important vocation.

3. A series of adjustment habits which lead to satisfaction from dealing with peo-

ple, as exhibited by the typical extravert.

Thus far, the lessons from the school of experience rather than the laboratory have been used as a guide in learning salesmanship. It is true that some laboratory experiments have been conducted for the development of methods to measure the relative effectiveness of elements composing a sales interview, but very few applications of these methods have been applied to actual sales situations.[15] The experimental laboratory study has the serious disadvantage of artificiality. Even though selling cannot be studied as an exact science it can be learned as a worthy art. Our appreciation of its worth will increase as we recognize its contributions to our social and economic well-being.

Acknowledgments and References

1. J. M. Hickerson, "Successful Sales Techniques," *Harvard Business Review,* September–October, 1952.

2. Willard M. Thompson, "How Expert Salespeople Sell," *Journal of Retailing,* Fall 1955, p. 150.

3. See F. J. Roethlisberger, "Training Supervisors in Human Relations," *Harvard Business Review,* September 1951, p. 51.

4. John M. Frey, "Missing Ingredient in Sales Training . . . for Today's Competitive Market," *Harvard Business Review,* November–December 1955, pp. 126–132.

5. "Marketing Pictograph," *Sales Management,* May 15, 1940.

6. Corning White, "The Mathematics of Salesmanship," *Printers' Ink Monthly,* August 1940, p. 34.

7. *Retailing,* April 30, 1934. See also *Domestic Commerce,* June 10, 1934, p. 158.

8. Edward K. Strong, Jr., *Psychology of Selling and Advertising,* McGraw-Hill Book Company, Inc., 1925, Chapter XXII.

9. *Salesmaker No. 1,* C. W. Stuart & Company, Inc., Newark, N.Y., 1945.

10. J. N. Bauman, "How the Professional Salesman Makes His Approach," *Sales Management,* June 15, 1955, p. 58.

11. Elmer Wheeler, "The First Ten Seconds: The Crucial Turning Point of the Sales Talk," *Sales Management,* November 15, 1937, p. 49.

12. From "27 Suggestions for Locating Prospects," *C. R. Report,* No. 3606, General Motors Corporation, Detroit, Michigan.

13. *Business Week,* May 25, 1940, p. 45.

14. *Sales Management,* January 1, 1938, p. 18.

15. Fred McKinney, "An Empirical Method of Analyzing a Sales Interview," *Journal of Applied Psychology,* Vol. XXI (1937), p. 280.

PROJECTS

1. Have a friend coöperate with you in practicing dealer sales situations. He is the prospective buyer and you are attempting to sell him certain articles. Have your friend include the following objections as well as others he may think of:

    a. I want the exclusive agency.
    b. I never had a call for it.
    c. I'm all stocked up now. Got too much of your stuff on the shelf.
    d. I'm too busy to talk to you now.
    e. I'm satisfied with the house I buy from now.
    f. You come to see me only when you can't sell Jones, up on the corner.

    After you have met your friend's objections, discuss with him the best methods of answering them.

2. List some of the expressions, methods, or mannerisms that irritate you when used by a salesman. Find out from others whether these are personal prejudices of your own or are general. Work out specific corrections for each item you have noted.

3. List the kinds of information a salesman should gather concerning a prospect before calling on him. Give possible sources where the information might be obtained.

4. Salesmen frequently carry a sample or some related object to show to the prospect while

making the sales talk. Think of interesting and original related objects that might be used in selling the following:

a. Lawnmowers.
b. Office furniture.
c. Home insulation.
d. Fire insurance.
e. Coal.
f. Advertising space in a local paper.
g. Safety equipment for a factory.
h. Vacation trip by airplane.

Tell how and when you would use the related object in your sales talk.

5. Clip several magazine advertisements of articles you believe you could sell quite successfully. Analyze all the reasons for your choice. Do the same for an article you think you could not sell. Analyze your reasons from the standpoint of your own likes and dislikes, your personality, the qualities of the article, the nature of the market, and other possible factors. Which factors seem to be the most important?

6. Outline a program whereby a salesman might utilize to the fullest extent the manufacturer's advertising of his product over the radio, in periodicals and newspapers, and on outdoor posters. Illustrate specifically how each of these aids could be tied into the sales talk for a product such as a vacuum sweeper.

7. Read in trade papers about concerns that have done outstanding work in sales-training schools. Analyze the ideas gathered and present them in a letter of application to one of the companies, explaining to the company addressed why you chose the company as your preferred employer.

8. A woman went into a ready-to-wear store to buy a blouse. The sales girl showed her blouses in three different price ranges and then held up the most expensive one and said, "I'd like to see you buy this one."

    Was this a good reason for the prospect to buy? What might the sales clerk say that would be more appropriate?

9. The story has been told of the animal painter, De Auber, that, having painted a picture, he rubbed raw meat over the representation of a rabbit in the foreground. His reason was that a Mrs. Blank, a prospect for the purchase of the picture, was coming to see the picture. He assumed that when her pet poodle smelled the rabbit and got excited about it, the woman would buy the picture.

    The woman came to see the picture, the poodle smelled of the rabbit and got excited, and the woman bought at the artist's price!

    Was this ethical selling on the part of the artist?

COLLATERAL READINGS

Brewster, Ray C., "More Psychology in Selling," *Harvard Business Review,* July–August, 1953, pp. 91–99.

Davis, James H., *Increasing Wholesale Drug Salesmen's Effectiveness,* Ohio State University, Bureau of Business Research, Columbus, 1948.

Frey, John M., "Missing Ingredient in Sales Training . . . for Today's Competitive Market," *Harvard Business Review,* November–December, 1955, pp. 126–132.

Kirkpatrick, Charles A., *Salesmanship: Helping Prospects Buy,* South-Western Publishing Company, Cincinnati, 1951.

Strand, Carl B., *Salesmanship for Vocational and Personal Use,* Gregg Publishing Division, McGraw-Hill Book Company, Inc., New York, 1949.

Thompson, Willard M., "How Expert Salespeople Sell," *Journal of Retailing,* Fall 1955.

CHAPTER THIRTY

How to read reports of psychological researches

Not the truth in anyone's actual or supposed possession, but the sincere effort he has exerted to master the truth, makes the worth of the man. For not through the possession but through the pursuit of truth comes that widening of a man's powers by which alone is achieved his ever-growing perfection. Possession makes one stagnant, lazy, proud. If God held shut in His right hand the whole of truth, and in His left had only ever-active striving after truth with the certainty of ever and always erring, and He said to me, "Choose!" I should humbly reach toward His left hand, saying, "Father, give me this! The pure truth is indeed for Thee alone!"—Lessing, *Eine Duplik*[1]

The difference between scientific research as "lived" by the pure scientist and as viewed by the layman may be illustrated by an incident in the life of the great scientist Faraday. He gave a lecture in the Royal Institution in London before a group of celebrities of the day. He brought a magnet close to a coil of wire. An electric current was produced.

After the demonstration a lady asked him, "Professor Faraday, even if the effect you explained is obtained, what is the use of it?"

Faraday replied, "Madam, will you tell me the use of a newborn child?"

The pure scientist conducts his experiments without regard for their practical or commercial value. Eventually some of the experiments may have practical value, but the scientist seeks truth mainly. Louis Agassiz, Lord Kelvin, Oersted, and others made their great discoveries without thought of personal gain. Some of their apparently useless discoveries have led to very valuable results for modern civilization.

The value of research in technical matters is now generally accepted, and it is probable that research in the human-relations problems of our economic life will make unusual strides in this and the next generation. As has often been stated, the keynote of the twentieth century will be hu-

Administration offices in Center for Advanced Study in the Behavioral Sciences, Stanford, California. The "students," called Fellows, come from the faculties of other universities.

View of part of the library of the Center. In addition to the library of the Center, the Stanford University and other libraries are available to the Fellows.

One of the fifty offices for the use of the Fellows.

Main meeting room.

One of the important developments in American scientific work is that single sciences are no longer expected to explain many of the events in human behavior. Interdisciplinary approaches are being used more and more each year. The members of several sciences come together for the study of important behavioral problems and principles.

An example of this trend is indicated by the opening on September 20, 1954, of the Center for Advanced Study in the Behavioral Sciences. The director, Ralph W. Tyler, explained the purpose of the new foundation as follows:

"The behavioral sciences have come to a stage of development calling for more—and more effective—communication between specialists. The Center is designed to provide a working atmosphere where this communication can take place. It is an opportunity for a selected number of university faculty members concerned with the study of human behavior to come together in one place in order to help one another gain new skills and insights and to work upon common problems in addition to their individual specialties."

The Center is an independent and non-profit corporation located at Stanford, California. It selects its fellows each year from the large and growing list of nominations submitted by university representatives. A grant from the Ford Foundation established the Center for a five-year period, ending August 31, 1959.

man engineering. Occasionally, political and international disruptions appear to make this prediction incorrect, but such disruptions are only temporary.

The practical man finds himself in many situations where it is difficult for him to utilize scientific research. Lack of time often compels him to make a quick decision. Sometimes business expediency does not permit changes wrought by science. A company may have established a reputation for a certain product or service and it would be difficult to make a change, even though scientific studies indicate that a change to a better product might be made. Moreover, the present "laws" of commerce are not nearly so exact and fixed as the laws of physics and chemistry.

In spite of the many difficulties in the way of predicting and stimulating human behavior in business, psychological research has become a recognized phase of modern economic life. The student who becomes a businessman learns that if he wishes to market a new product, he must do more than try it out in his wife's kitchen, ask the opinions of his friends, or consult his salesmen. He finds that his own company's records and past statistics of monthly reports do not enable him to predict the public's reception of a new idea or invention. Snap judgments and empirical rules may lead him astray. But even the best feasible research study is none too reliable.

Professional research organizations

In one issue of a trade journal, ten professional research organizations were advertised. Some of them have been in existence for years. Others seem to advertise once or twice and then disappear. The ability and reliability of these research organizations must be rated in the same manner that we rate individuals. A few individuals are competent for a specific task, but there are many who are not. The executive who hires a professional research worker or research organization should be acquainted with research principles if he wishes to secure competent service. Otherwise he may be handed a voluminous report that looks impressive but is filled with fallacious conclusions. Statistics are often helpful, but they also can be very dangerous. The reader should at least know the essential terms and methods which are common to research reports in the field of analyzing and controlling human behavior.

Starting important researches

When an executive or a group of executives decides that a research shall be made of some problem or problems, certain questions should be asked and answered in advance. These are:

1. JUST WHAT IS THE PROBLEM? What is it that is to be learned? How shall the problem be stated, in order that the persons making the research may keep it clearly in mind? Shall the research be limited to a single specific problem or shall the investigation have a broad and generalized scope?

2. WHO SHALL PERFORM THE RESEARCH? In many cases the executives decide that some accountant or statistician now in the company can do the work. Such an attempt to save money is conjectural. The findings of a single research may be used to modify a company's production schedule for a year and may involve thousands of dollars. It does not pay to take chances. Only a few large concerns have a staff of researchers who are qualified to conduct a psychological investigation. The fact that an engineer knows calculus and can plot nice curves does not mean that he is qualified to make a market investigation or standardize psychological tests for employment. Trained and experienced workers are just as important in psychological research as in other branches of industry.

3. WHAT SHALL BE THE METHOD OF SECURING THE DATA? Shall the company start a research department with laboratories of its own; shall field investigators be used; shall the data be secured by questionnaire; shall a test campaign be conducted; and so on? Can the necessary data be secured? Are the facts now available in the company's records? Is it possible to obtain the facts?

4. DO THE EXECUTIVES HAVE A FAIR ATTITUDE TOWARD THE RESEARCH? Are they seeking to obtain data to prove a present theory, or are facts wanted regardless of their pleasantness or unpleasantness? Are the executives future-minded or past-minded? Is the

research for the purpose of finding out "why the horse was stolen" or to prevent the stealing of horses in the future?

5. HOW MUCH TIME SHALL BE ALLOWED FOR THE INVESTIGATION? Does the company expect the researchers to achieve functions of the administrative executive, or is the research to present facts for the guidance of the executives? One sales manager hired a research man to make a consumer analysis. He agreed to expect his report at the end of three months. However, at the end of two weeks he began to write letters to the researcher, asking him why the sales had not increased in the territory where the analysis was being made. When a company starts a business research department of its own, definite results of proved commercial value should not be expected for one or two years. Furthermore, some of the executives of companies having sales researchers are inclined to expect the sales research department to act as a sales promotion department. If research is to fulfill its function of making discoveries of value to the business, it must be allowed sufficient time and remain advisory and independent of immediate problems of showing a profit on the balance sheet.

Points to look for when analyzing a research report

When any statistical report is analyzed, it is necessary to look for fallacies regardless of the ability or reputation of the author. Administrators must operate on the plan of delegating functions and responsibilities to others. When an executive selects the most competent researcher he can find and gives him a research problem, he tends to assume that whatever the statistician says must be true. However, the reader of the statistics must be alert to detect and question discrepancies. It is impossible for the executive or the student to know all or most of the errors in statistics or logic that may occur, but some of the more common ones can be pointed out.

1. IS THE UNIT OF MEASUREMENT SOUND? In statistics, the units of measurement are the bricks from which the whole statistical structure is built. The units of measurement may be individuals, foot-pounds, wages, accidents, or businessmen, but the unit must be sound in its entity. One sales manager asked his salesmen to predict the condition of business for the next month. Each salesman was to state whether he expected to have an increase in sales over the preceding month. Approximately 80 per cent of the weekly reports of the sales force were optimistic. They were of the type: "Conditions here look very good for next month. I expect to sell more than I did this month." At the end of the month for which the sales had been predicted, less than 10 per cent of the salesmen had had an increase in sales, and the total volume of business for the sales force was 15 per cent below that of the preceding month. The reason for the unreliability of the investigation was that the salesmen knew that the sales manager usually expected optimistic reports and they sent in the expected viewpoint lest they appear to be alibi-artists and expecters of failure. The prediction could not be reliable because the units of measurement, statements by individual salesmen, were unreliable.

2. ARE THE DATA IN THE REPORT AUTHENTIC? Occasionally statistics are quoted by bankers, salesmen, publishers, and others, and it is impossible to find anyone to substantiate the figures. A notable example is the oft-quoted figures regarding the incomes of men who begin their vocational life at the age of 20. At the age of 45, 16 per cent are supposed to be dead; 65 per cent self-supporting; 15 per cent dependent, wholly or in part; and only 4 per cent are supposed to have accumulated anything and kept it. When they are 65 years of age, 85 per cent of the men still living are quoted as dependent on children, relatives, or charity.

An attempt has been made to find the original source of these figures but has met with no success. The life insurance companies that were consulted said that they had seen the figures and their salesmen had used them, but the originator was not known. So far as they know, no one really knows what the correct figures are.

3. ARE SINGLE CAUSES INTERPRETED TO GIVE RISE TO SINGLE EFFECTS OR EVENTS? In human relationships, effects are seldom brought about by single events or causes. The "new American tempo" is not the effect of one cause, such as the development of the physical sciences. Increases in crime cannot be attributed solely to a change in religious devotion or divorce. Labor unrest is not caused alone by universal education. Psychological abnormalities cannot be attributed solely to a thwarting of the sex impulse or to heredity. Increases and decreases in sales cannot be attributed to the lone influence of the new sales manager. Decreased labor turnover cannot be interpreted as wholly the result of a newly organized personnel department or of profit sharing.

The veteran advertising manager of an ice-cream company "showed" how his advertising efforts had increased the per capita consumption of ice cream in his territory. He should also have mentioned as factors of influence: improved quality of the product, pure food laws, greater number of retail outlets, lower cost of production, and greater competence of company management.

4. ARE GRAPHIC CURVES OF INCREASE AND DECREASE COMPARED WITH BASIC CURVES OF INCREASE AND DECREASE? Frequently they are not. This kind of error is common in reports of individual executives to the management. The sales manager may show that sales have increased 20 per cent each year over the preceding year for the past five years. He should also show how much the industry as a whole has increased during that period. The employment manager may show that labor turnover has decreased each year for the past three years. He should also

compare his curve of decrease with the employment situation of the community.

5. ARE THE GRAPHS IN THE REPORT PROPERLY CONSTRUCTED? The person who wishes to understand statistical reports needs an understanding of some of the more common principles of graphic charting.

If the statistician wishes to construct a simple line curve to show the amount of building construction in a certain city over a given period of years, it is possible to construct the graph so that a small or a great increase or decrease may appear to have taken place. This may be done regardless of the actual facts in the situation. The curve can be made to appear unstable and to have fluctuated violently, or to have fluctuated little and to have great stability. The construction and type of graph is often determined by the impression that the statistician wishes to make on his readers. One of the best statistical devices for comparative data is the index number.

Table 30-1 illustrates three possible sets of index numbers, or series of simple relatives, which might be constructed from the *actual* sales data in the first column.

The method is simply to divide each year's sales by the sales in the base period which one may think best. The base periods here used are (1) the year 1943, (2) the year 1956, and (3) the yearly average for the five years 1952–1956, inclusive.

What practical purpose is accomplished by the use of these index numbers? Examination of the data for the two variables—sales of the company and of the whole industry—is much easier when the data are in the form of index numbers. The two columns headed "Actual Sales" are much harder to compare than the three index-number arrangements for the same data.

When a base period has been chosen suitable to whatever purpose the analyst may have in mind, the curves are readily brought into each other's neighborhood by the index-number method. Then it is easy to answer such questions as: How does the long-time growth of our company show up in comparison with our industry as a whole? . How much more, or less, did a boom or depression affect us than it did the industry generally? How does our recent position compare with that of the industry?

The index number is not the only method of analysis which can be used on occasions to answer such questions as these; but it is one of the most effective, and, when properly understood and applied, one of the easiest. Some statisticians prefer to use the semi-logarithmic charts.

Graphs are the quickest, clearest, and most condensed method of conveying valuable information to the reader, but he should realize their potency for misinformation as well as for administrative guidance.

6. IS THE NUMBER OF UNITS STUDIED SUFFICIENTLY LARGE TO REPRESENT THE GROUP FAIRLY? It is obvious that if we wish to study any single human trait, such as the general intelligence of salesmen, it is necessary to test the intelligence of a large typical group of salesmen. If we were to draw conclusions

from the measurements of only ten salesmen, we should be very liable to fall into error. Psychometrists have developed several formulas which show the required size of the group, or, in some cases, the unreliability of the conclusions drawn from a group of a given size. We shall leave these more complicated formulas to the statisticians, but the layman can approximate a decision from two simple questions:

Do the measures extend over the entire *range* for the group in question? An example is that of the study of intelligence of college students. If we were to measure the intelligence of only those students who fail in college or those who graduate with honors, we should not be testing a representative sampling of the factor under study. Tests would have to be made of those who fail, those who do passing work, those who do average work, those who are slightly above the average, and those who are the best—all in their proper proportions.

The next question is: How *many* students must we have on each part of the entire scale? We can answer this by noting whether the number of cases measured distribute themselves according to the normal

TABLE 30–1

SHOWING ACTUAL SALES BY YEARS AND INDEX NUMBERS THEREOF

| Year | Actual Sales (thousands of tons) | | Index Numbers | | | | | |
| | | | On 1943 Base as 100 | | On 1956 Base as 100 | | On 1952–56 Base as 100 | |
	XYZ CO.	ENTIRE INDUSTRY	XYZ CO.	ENTIRE INDUSTRY	XYZ CO.	ENTIRE INDUSTRY	XYZ CO.	ENTIRE INDUSTRY
1943	5.2	31,300	100.0	100.0	36.4	70.8	50.3	73.8
1944	4.0	23,513	76.9	75.1	28.0	53.2	38.7	55.4
1945	6.3	32,151	120.2	102.7	43.7	72.7	44.4	75.8
1946	7.9	42,773	151.9	136.7	55.2	96.8	76.4	100.8
1947	8.5	45,060	163.5	144.0	59.4	101.9	82.2	106.2
1948	8.0	44,462	153.8	142.1	55.9	100.6	77.4	104.8
1949	7.0	34,671	134.6	110.8	49.0	78.4	67.7	81.7
1950	8.4	42,132	161.5	134.6	58.7	95.3	81.2	99.3
1951	3.6	19,783	69.2	63.2	25.2	44.7	34.8	46.6
1952	9.0	44,943	173.1	143.6	62.9	101.7	87.0	105.9
1953	7.3	37,932	140.4	121.2	51.0	85.8	70.6	89.4
1954	11.5	45,394	221.2	145.0	80.4	102.7	111.7	107.0
1955	15.8	48,294	303.8	154.3	110.5	109.2	152.8	113.8
1956	14.3	44,214	275.0	141.3	100.0	100.0	138.3	104.2

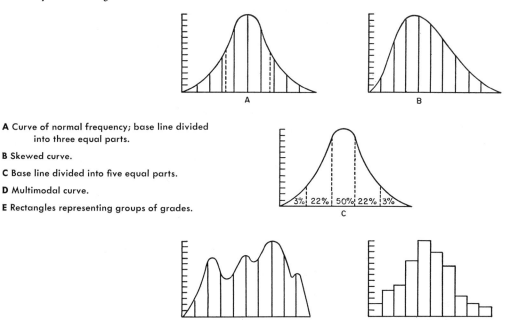

A Curve of normal frequency; base line divided
   into three equal parts.

B Skewed curve.

C Base line divided into five equal parts.

D Multimodal curve.

E Rectangles representing groups of grades.

frequency (normal probability) curve. When the base line of the theoretical probability curve has been divided into five equal parts and vertical lines have been erected at the dividing points, five areas result, which include the following percentages, reading from left to right: 3, 22, 50, 22, 3. This bell-shaped curve seems to apply to many living characteristics. It has even been found that when the number of hairs on the left hind legs of a large number of bees are counted, the frequency curve has this bell-shape. Because of this universality of distribution of human traits, many schools and colleges grade their students in conformity with this curve.

When an insufficient number of cases have been studied, the frequency curve may be skewed or multi-modal in form. This discussion applies only to human traits or reactions found in a representative number of nonselected persons. That is, if we wish to test the intelligence of only the best 10 per cent of salesmen in one company, the normal frequency curve would not result. But if we were to test the best 10 per cent of all salesmen in a thousand companies, the

plotted results would probably follow the normal curve.

7. HAVE THE DATA FOR A GROUP BEEN CHECKED BY CONTROL GROUPS? When a group of persons are experimented upon in the laboratory to determine the effects of smoking, caffeine, scolding, praise, music, lighting, or a system of wage payment, it is also necessary to measure the same or similar reactions of another group of persons who are not affected by the same stimuli. One investigator experimented upon the effects of periodicity of women in the performing of certain mental functions. A control group of men was used because obviously they could not be affected by the same organic condition. It was found that the men had more fluctuations which could be looked upon as cyclical for twenty-eight-day periods than the women! If the control group of men had not been used, it is probable that the data of the women only would have given quite another impression.

Sometimes experimenters try a new method of sales management or lighting or wage payment and find that the production figures go up the next month. These stimuli do cause changes in production, but it is well to check the new plan by allowing certain groups to work under the old system so that the one factor which is blamed or praised for the change may really be known beyond any chance factors that may be bringing about the change. In the experiments on the effects of drugs, it is absolutely essential to have control groups because of the effect of suggestion. It is also essential in proving the effects of new methods of motivating or training employees.

8. DO THE CONCLUSIONS AND SUGGESTIONS HARMONIZE WITH GENERAL EXPERIENCE AND THE JUDGMENT OF PERSONS EXPERIENCED IN THE FIELD STUDIED? Because of the opportunities for misinterpretation of statistics, it is well to compare the findings with empiri-

---

A Brief Check List for Evaluating Scientific Articles

1. The analysis of the purpose of the article:
   — is the purpose clearly stated?
   — will the purpose be supported or refuted by the kind of data collected?
   — is sufficient account taken of previous studies in this particular field?

2. The analysis of the design of the sampling procedure of the experiment involved:
   — is the design of the experiment so formulated that it will give an adequate answer to the purpose of the experiment?
   — how are the subjects selected: from the total population, a restricted population, or other?
   — is the number of subjects adequate to take care of the purpose of the experiment satisfactorily?
   — are there proper and adequate controls (e.g., have controls been properly equated with experimental group)?

3. Analysis of the procedure of the scientific article:
   — are the procedures so described that any other experimenter could duplicate the experiment to check the findings?
   — are the data systematically collected and presented?

4. Analysis of the results:
   — are results correctly and clearly presented?
   — are the units of measurement sound?
   — are graphs properly drawn?
   — are tables properly constructed?
   — are statistical procedures essentially sound?
   — are the proper tests of significance made, such as critical ratio, *et al.*?
   — do the verbal statements agree with the quantitative and tabular data?

5. Analysis of conclusions:
   — are the conclusions warranted by the data presented?
   — are significant trends recognized?
   — are the limitations of the experiment recognized?

For a more thorough discussion of analyzing scientific articles see John E. Anderson, "Methods of Child Psychology," in Leonard Carmichael, *Manual of Child Psychology*, John Wiley and Sons, New York 1946, pp. 1–42; and Dael Wolfle, Rensis Likert, Donald G. Marquis, and Robert R. Sears. "Standards for Appraising Psychological Research," *The American Psychologist*, No. 4 (1949), pp. 320–328.

cal conclusions. The man who has had years of experience in any field is likely to know many facts and principles that cannot be revealed by laboratory experiments.

It should be kept in mind at all times that laboratory experiments in human reactions usually deal with one factor or one set of factors only. An experiment may be sound so far as it goes, but *psychological laboratory conditions seldom approximate actual conditions.* Some important human reactions cannot be subjected to experiment. Several psychologists have attempted to measure the reactions of persons when in love, angry, fearful, or sexually excited; but it has been very difficult to achieve genuine mental states in the laboratory. All psychological laboratory experiments should be looked upon as laboratory experiments which may or may not carry over into actual life and business.

If the investigation does not agree with the past experience of those who are conversant with the empirical facts, then it may be necessary to repeat parts of the research. On the other hand, if the study does indicate that it would be advisable, all things considered, to make certain changes, the research will have been a waste of time and money unless the changes are made.

Conclusion

The research "tools" presented in this chapter are not comprehensive, but the discussion is an attempt to stimulate certain types of students to go on and acquire further skills in measuring human reactions.

Acknowledgments and References

1. As quoted in Zechariah Chafee, *The Inquiring Mind,* Harcourt, Brace and Company, New York, 1928.

PROJECTS

1. Examine a standard book on the construction and interpretation of graphs and charts and list some of the common errors and fallacies in this field. Find a graph or chart that misrepresents the data on which it is based and reconstruct it so that it presents a true picture.

2. A doctor made the following statement: "I had all the nicotine removed from a cigarette, making a solution out of it. I injected half the quantity into a frog with the effect that the frog died almost instantly. The rest was administered to another frog with like effect. Both frogs were grown and of average size. The conclusion is evident that a single cigarette contains enough poison to kill two frogs."

   Is this a valid argument to prove the harmfulness of cigarette smoking? What would be the effect of taking the white of an egg and injecting a part of it into the human bloodstream? (For guidance in obtaining the answer, look up the chemical nature of rattlesnake venom.)

3. In reading a research report, how can one detect whether the writer tried to prove a point or merely to present the facts that he happened to find? What are the distinguishing characteristics of reports that *defend a position* compared with those that *try to promote an idea?*

4. In a discussion group of thirty industrial executives, the leader of the group was opposed to a bonus for the foreman of a gang of seven workers. Three of the members of the group had had experience with bonuses for the foreman of small units of production. These three men were heartily in favor of a bonus for the foreman as well as the workers. The leader of the discussion group then asked the members of the group to vote for or against a foreman's bonus. The three who had had experience with such a situation voted in favor of the bonus; the remaining members of the group who had had no such experience opposed it.

   How can the voting of these executives be explained?

5. Statistically, is the difference between two and three the same as the difference between ten and eleven? If 10 men can build a house in 100 days, can 1,000 men build the house in one day?

6. Discuss statistical data of business which are often compared but which really are not comparable, such as bond prices during the Civil War and World War II or wages in London and in Chicago. Is homogeneity in comparisons of psychological data possible?

7. Distinguish between immediate or superficial causes and remote or fundamental causes. How does this apply to retail costs? To unemployment? To sales records?

COLLATERAL READINGS

Bellows, Roger M., *Psychology of Personnel in Business and Industry,* Prentice-Hall, Inc., New York, 1954, Chapter 3.

Burtt, Harold E., *Applied Psychology,* Prentice-Hall, Inc., New York, 1948, Appendices I and II, pp. 803–812.

Ghiselli, Edwin E., and Clarence W. Brown, *Personnel and Industrial Psychology,* McGraw-Hill Book Company, Inc., New York, 1955, Chapter 1.

Harrell, Thomas Willard, *Industrial Psychology,* Rinehart & Company, Inc., New York, 1949, Chapter 3.

Hartley, Eugene L., Herbert G. Birch, and Ruth E. Hartley, *Outside Readings in Psychology,* Thomas Y. Crowell Company, New York, 1950, Chapters 1 and 2.

Smith, Henry Clay, *Psychology of Industrial Behavior,* McGraw-Hill Book Company, Inc., New York, 1955, Chapters 13 and 18.

APPENDIX

Social knowledge test

Each question has several possible answers. Underline the one answer that is correct or the most nearly correct, and put its letter in the parentheses at the end of the dotted line. Do not omit any question, even if you must guess.

1. "Come off the oil" means:
   (a) that your wallet is empty (b) to stop bragging (c) you look like a gigolo (d) you've got dandruff ... ( )
2. "Skid Row" refers to:
   (a) a London street (b) a term used in ice-hockey (c) the lowest level of the underworld (d) a snowy road .... ( )
3. The term "to fade" is used in:
   (a) dice (b) golf (c) dress designing (d) billiards .... ( )
4. "Snafu" is:
   (a) a Hollywood actor (b) a term meaning scram (c) a term meaning easy going (d) a term meaning difficulties in progress .... ( )
5. A "queer" is:
   (a) a stool pigeon (b) a storybook fairy (c) an insane person (d) a homosexual .... ( )
6. A "pug" is:
   (a) a bulldog (b) an English tavern (c) a strong cigar (d) a prize fighter ( )
7. A "frog" is:
   (a) a railroad worker (b) a prostitute (c) a thief (d) a Frenchman .. ( )
8. "To give the bird" is to:
   (a) heckle (b) give a dinner party (c) double-cross (d) pay tuition .. ( )
9. "Scuttlebutt" refers to:
   (a) rumors (b) bet (c) used cigarette (d) a whistle .... ( )

10. "Two-fingers" refers to:
    (a) a brand of candy bar (b) a sign to obtain someone's attention (c) a symbol of secrecy (d) a measure used by bartenders .... ( )
11. The term "soup" is slang for:
    (a) nitroglycerine (b) jail (c) freighter (d) poison .... ( )
12. An "uncle" is:
    (a) a jockey (b) a hockey goalie (c) a gambler (d) a pawnbroker .. ( )
13. A "hot rod" is:
    (a) a hot spoon (b) a fat fisherman (c) a fast auto (d) a lucky gambler ( )
14. "Red-eye" is a term for:
    (a) strong arms (b) bookies (c) pink lady beverage (d) cheap whiskey .. ( )
15. A "necktie party" is:
    (a) for girls only (b) for men only (c) a hanging (d) a high school dance .... ( )
16. The figures on the opposite sides of a die of dice always add up to:
    (a) 4 (b) 6 (c) 7 (d) 11 .... ( )
17. A "cat" is:
    (a) a game of casino (b) a poker hand (c) a dead beat (d) a sharp character .... ( )
18. "Heaven-beck" refers to:
    (a) a bird of paradise (b) an angel (c) a minister (d) a chicken coop ( )
19. "Little joe" is a term used in:
    (a) golf (b) cards (c) dice (d) horse racing .... ( )

20. "Foo-foo" is:
(a) perfume (b) ketchup (c) a dog-biscuit (d) a rattle .... ( )
21. A "beezer" refers to:
(a) a dagger (b) a stiff test (c) nose (d) magazine .... ( )
22. A "foul ball" is:
(a) a vexatious person (b) an army officer (c) a rum drink (d) a cop .. ( )
23. A "skin slammer" refers to:
(a) a doctor (b) adhesive tape (c) a drummer (d) a politician .... ( )
24. A "cokey" is:
(a) a horse (b) a bad mistake (c) a drug addict (d) an imbecile.. ( )
25. A "deep-sea chef" is:
(a) a fisherman (b) a lover of sea-food (c) a dishwasher (d) a man who prepares tabasco sauce ...... ( )
26. A "quail" is:
(a) a dog (b) a truant boy (c) a woman (d) a foreigner .... ( )
27. A "snow bird" is:
(a) a dope addict (b) a nude painting (c) a race horse (d) a night club .... ( )
28. The term "shiv" refers to:
(a) a bad cold (b) a delirium (c) a chaplain (d) a knife .... ( )
29. A "chucker" is a name for:
(a) chuck wood (b) a baseball pitcher (c) a braggart (d) an ex-travagant person .... ( )
30. A "daisy cutter" is:
(a) a farm implement (b) a milli-ner (c) a low ball (d) a rustic ... ( )
31. "Boondocks" refers to:
(a) a country shack (b) a back-woods location (c) a small canoe (d) a hound .... ( )
32. To "highball" is to:
(a) stagger (b) tip-toe (c) dance (d) go at top speed .... ( )
33. "Little Phoebe" is:
(a) a stolen purse (b) a dice term (c) a deputy sheriff (d) a baby's doll .... ( )
34. An "eightball" is:
(a) a poor loser (b) an incompe-tent person (c) a team mascot (d) a good sport .... ( )
35. A "sun-pecked jay" is:
(a) a bird (b) a rustic, city person (c) an informer (d) a bird food .. ( )
36. In the language of sports, a "screw-armer" is:
(a) a southpaw (b) a right-hander

(c) a man who fixes roller skates (d) a water boy .... ( )
37. "Dominie" is a term referred to when speaking of:
(a) a game (b) a priest (c) sugar (d) profanity .... ( )
38. "Annie Oakley" refers to:
(a) a free pass (b) an English ac-tress (c) Tom Oakley's wife (d) a machine gun .... ( )
39. The "black gang" refers to:
(a) slaves (b) spiritualists (c) a secret society (d) machinists in the Navy .... ( )
40. A "job robber" is:
(a) a foreman (b) a bookie (c) an overzealous piece worker (d) a stool pigeon .... ( )
41. "To lower the boom" means:
(a) to hit somebody (b) to anchor (c) to be inebriated (d) to bluff .. ( )
42. "Joe" refers to:
(a) a man (b) the mouth (c) dope (d) a cup of coffee .... ( )
43. "Yack" means:
(a) to talk seldom (b) a stupid per-son (c) a criminal (d) a billy-goat .... ( )
44. A "bim" is:
(a) a jitterbug (b) a plastic record (c) a convict (d) a tough girl ... ( )
45. A "chippy" is:
(a) a billiard ball (b) a girl (c) a small ship (d) a score of three in dice .... ( )
46. A "gibroni" is:
(a) a crying doll (b) a jerk (c) a pilot (d) a chef .... ( )
47. To "lose one's marbles" means to:
(a) lose money (b) be a simpleton (c) be drunk (d) lose a job ..... ( )
48. A "bindle stiff" is:
(a) a flower (b) a college professor (c) a tramp (d) a dead crook .... ( )
49. A "thornback" is:
(a) a rose bush (b) a spinster (c) a bank-teller's window (d) a fish ... ( )
50. A "gapper" is:
(a) an addict in need of dope (b) a ditch digger (c) a consumptive (d) a fishing rod .... ( )
51. In a game of dice the "odds" are the same for making the number four as for making the number:
(a) 8 (b) 6 (c) 10 (d) 7 ...... ( )

52. "Land grabbers" are:
(a) chains (b) shoes (c) animals
(d) farmers .... ( )
53. A "whey belly" is:
(a) a fat man (b) a bald man (c) a
starved cat (d) a poor horse ..... ( )
54. A "geek" is:
(a) a clown (b) the wildman in the
circus sideshow (c) a bookie (d) a
ham .... ( )
55. A "pad" is:
(a) a tiger (b) a one-room apartment (c) a bald man (d) a stone.. ( )
56. The expression "croaker" refers to:
(a) morticians (b) bootleggers (c)
doctors (d) preachers .... ( )
57. A "flunkie" is:
(a) a dope addict (b) a goal in ice
hockey (c) a brain who wears glasses (d) a cringing person .... ( )
58. A "ridgerunner" is:
(a) a southern hillbilly (b) a mountain climber (c) a ski instructor
(d) a forester .... ( )
59. "Run-em" is a term used in:
(a) horseracing (b) casino (c) poker (d) bridge .... ( )
60. A "round heel" is:
(a) a politician (b) a poor prize
fighter (c) an alcoholic (d) a salesman .... ( )
61. A "vegetable" is:
(a) a fruit (b) a helpless patient
(c) a worm (d) a stag party .... ( )
62. "Slum" has reference to:
(a) a boarding house (b) meat stew
(c) prison clothes (d) beer ...... ( )
63. The term "down and go" is used in:
(a) Air Force (b) racing (c) football (d) cards .... ( )

64. "Flat ball" refers to:
(a) baseball (b) bowling (c) football (d) golf .... ( )
65. A "tout" is a person who:
(a) never bets (b) is a tightwad
(c) is often seen at the race tracks
(d) wears zoot suits .... ( )
66. "Travelers" are:
(a) nervous twitches (b) head lice
(c) crutches (d) tears in stockings ( )
67. A "hood" is:
(a) a woman's head gear (b) a
criminal (c) a fence (d) a pot ... ( )
68. A "chit" is:
(a) a young girl (b) a receipt (c)
a bill (d) a small black bird ..... ( )
69. "Red lead" refers to:
(a) hot steel (b) whiskey (c) a
bullet (d) ketchup .... ( )
70. When one is a "shiny-back" it
means that he belongs to:
(a) a football team (b) an orchestra (c) a baseball team (d) a bald
men's club .... ( )
71. A "twist" is:
(a) a woman (b) a tennis racket
(c) a prison trusty (d) a formal
dance .... ( )
72. A "hussle" is:
(a) a fishing rod (b) an attorney
(c) a bothersome situation (d) a
beer party .... ( )
73. A "binte" is:
(a) an isolated cottage (b) an overcoat (c) a humorous book (d) an
unwieldy crow-bar .... ( )
74. A "dizzy stick" is:
(a) a pogostick (b) a clarinet (c) a
drummer (d) a cigarette .... ( )
75. A "night line" is:
(a) a policeman's beat (b) a sheik's
conversation (c) a fishing device
(d) a rendezvous .... ( )

II. KNOWLEDGE OF THE UPPER SOCIAL STRATA

Encircle "T" if the statement is true; "F" if it is false.

1. Table service is usually placed
with the oyster fork at the outer
edge, so that one uses the silver
from the outside toward the plate T F
2. Replies to all invitations may be
typewritten or engraved .... T F
3. Children should remain seated
when being introduced .... T F
4. When shopping, it is not good
etiquette to thank the salesman .. T F
5. Informal invitations should be written by the lady herself in the first
person .... T F
6. The person who calls on the telephone should be the one who ter-
minates the conversation .... T F

7. On the whole, for engaged couples it is in good taste to show signs of affection in public .... T F

8. Manners do not change much fundamentally; only in outward manifestations .... T F

9. After one has finished eating, the fork should be laid on the plate with the tines upward .... T F

10. Letters of condolence should be sent on black-edged paper ...... T F

11. At a concert it is customary to applaud the performance between the various movements of a symphony .... T F

12. A man should not ask a young lady for a date in the presence of others .... T F

13. If an inexperienced servant blunders, you should pretend, if you can, not to know it .... T F

14. "Double-redouble" is descriptive of a phrase of contract bridge ...... T F

15. A woman should not permit a new chance acquaintance to pay for her meals in the train .... T F

16. When a newcomer is introduced to the members of a group, his name must be repeated to each member of the group .... T F

17. When serving a meal, all drinks should be served on the right ... T F

18. When a servant at a door says "Not at home," this phrase means that the lady of the house is not at home to visitors; it is a more polite expression than "Not receiving" because it leaves the pleasant uncertainty that it is quite possible she really is out .... T F

19. A "bread and butter" letter is written to your hostess thanking her for a pleasant weekend .... T F

20. If a clergyman is present at a dinner party, in a home, he should be asked to say grace .... T F

21. At informal dinners, people do not usually go in to dinner arm in arm .... T F

22. A navy blue or black suit will not do in place of a cutaway at a very small or country wedding .... T F

23. The time limit for occupancy of a hotel room is usually between three and six P.M. of the following day .... T F

24. The expression "Meet so-and-so" is

permitted in society .... T F

25. Pink and blue stationery are in especially good taste .... T F

26. Etiquette concerning the armed services makes it necessary to introduce a rear admiral, for example, as admiral .... T F

27. It is never proper for a man to look over a restaurant bill before paying it when he has people dining with him .... T F

28. Formal invitations are written in the third person .... T F

29. When one is introducing a friend to another friend, the younger person is presented to the older person .... T F

30. A person is stymied in golf when he cannot putt directly because of interference from another ball .... T F

31. A full dress suit does not require a shirt with a stiff front .... T F

32. A man sitting next to a strange woman in a theater should assist her when she wishes to take off her coat .... T F

33. When registering at a hotel, it is proper to sign, "Mr. John Doe and Wife" .... T F

34. In a restaurant, a woman waits until she is seated before removing her coat .... T F

35. It is not necessary to answer informal invitations .... T F

36. Any guest who is older than the guest of honor may leave before he, or she, does .... T F

37. It is correct for an unmarried woman to ask the gentleman she knows best to act as host when giving a dinner .... T F

38. In good society, ladies do not kiss each other when they meet either at parties or in public .... T F

39. The proper way for a bachelor to entertain a debutante is to ask her to tea or to the theater .... T F

40. The butler is the most important servant in every big establishment .... T F

41. A very smart invitation to a wedding ceremony is one that has a raised margin formed by a plate mark .... T F

42. In a Pullman car, a woman may dress in her own berth or in the dressing room .... T F

43. Appropriate dressing plus good taste is all that is necessary for good attire .... T F
44. Chukker is a period of play in a polo game .... T F
45. The phrase table d'hôte on a menu means a fixed price for a meal, regardless of how much or how little of it one orders .... T F
46. One should wipe one's mouth before drinking any water .... T F
47. Wedding announcements are invitations to attend the ceremony .. T F
48. An unmarried woman signs her name "Alice Burt" rather than "Miss Alice Burt" .... T F
49. It is snobbish not to adopt the customs of the community of which one has become a member ..... T F
50. When casual acquaintances meet, the man should be the first to speak to the woman .... T F
51. It is not wise to tip the head waiter even if special attention is desired, as it is the head waiter's duty to give special attentions .... T F
52. Ladies always wear gloves to formal dinners and take them off at the table, putting them in their laps .... T F
53. It is correct for a man to shake hands with his gloves on if they cannot be removed quickly ..... T F
54. It is permissible to drink bouillon by lifting the cup, as one would drink tea .... T F
55. The engagement ring may be worn in public before the betrothal is announced .... T F
56. Red wine is preferable to white wine with fish courses .... T F
57. It is not correct for the hostess to be served first .... T F
58. The term "My dear" in correspondence is more formal than "Dear".. T F
59. A young man may continually go to see a young girl even if she shows him scant attention or even if she indicates that she is not interested .... T F

60. One should congratulate a woman on her engagement .... T F
61. A man raises his hat when giving directions to a strange woman on the street .... T F
62. A woman never rises to an introduction .... T F
63. When an engagement is broken, gifts, letters, etc., are returned ... T F
64. When paying your respects to the bride and groom, it is proper to offer them both congratulations ... T F
65. The invitation to the church ceremony always requests the honor and never the honour of your presence .... T F
66. The fundamental difference between a ball and a dance is that people of all ages are asked to a ball, while only those of approximately the same age are asked to a dance .... T F
67. The word "ball" is never used except in an invitation to an affair that is public .... T F
68. In hotels, "European Plan" means that meals are included in the rate charge .... T F
69. When entering a room with a guest the hostess goes first only when the guest is a stranger in the house ... T F
70. When a man is walking with two women on the street, he should walk between them .... T F
71. When first names are to be written on a card, the husband's name is written first .... T F
72. If the maid offers to do some extra work while you are a guest at the home in which she is employed, it is not necessary that you tip her .. T F
73. Antibes is a summer resort on the French Riviera .... T F
74. As long as the audience enjoys it, a person who talks well should be encouraged to monopolize the conversation .... T F
75. The bride should always carry flowers at a formal wedding .... T F

KEY TO SOCIAL KNOWLEDGE TEST

I. Knowledge of the Lower Social Strata

1. (b) to stop bragging
2. (c) the lowest level of the underworld
3. (a) dice
4. (d) term meaning difficulties in progress
5. (d) homosexual
6. (d) prize fighter

7. (d) Frenchman
8. (a) heckle
9. (a) rumors
10. (d) a measure used by bartenders
11. (a) nitroglycerine
12. (d) pawnbroker
13. (c) a fast auto
14. (d) cheap whiskey
15. (c) a hanging
16. (c) 7
17. (d) sharp character
18. (c) a minister
19. (c) dice
20. (a) perfume
21. (c) nose
22. (a) a vexatious person
23. (c) a drummer
24. (c) drug addict
25. (c) a dishwasher
26. (c) woman
27. (a) dope addict
28. (d) knife
29. (b) a baseball pitcher
30. (c) low ball
31. (b) a backwoods location
32. (d) go at top speed
33. (b) dice term
34. (b) an incompetent person
35. (b) a rustic, city person
36. (a) southpaw
37. (b) priest
38. (a) a free pass
39. (d) machinists in the Navy
40. (c) an overzealous piece worker
41. (a) to hit somebody

42. (d) a cup of coffee
43. (b) a stupid person
44. (d) tough girl
45. (b) girl
46. (b) a jerk
47. (b) be a simpleton
48. (c) tramp
49. (b) spinster
50. (a) an addict in need of dope
51. (c) 10
52. (b) shoes
53. (d) a poor horse
54. (b) the wild man in the circus sideshow
55. (b) one-room apartment
56. (c) doctors
57. (d) cringing person
58. (a) southern hillbilly
59. (c) poker
60. (b) poor prize fighter
61. (b) helpless patient
62. (b) meat stew
63. (d) cards
64. (b) bowling
65. (c) is often seen at the race tracks
66. (b) head lice
67. (b) a criminal
68. (b) receipt
69. (d) ketchup
70. (b) an orchestra
71. (a) woman
72. (c) a bothersome situation
73. (b) overcoat
74. (d) cigarette
75. (c) fishing device

II. Knowledge of the Upper Social Strata

1. True
2. False
3. False
4. False
5. True
6. True
7. False
8. True
9. True
10. False
11. False
12. True
13. True
14. True
15. True
16. False
17. True
18. True
19. True
20. True
21. True
22. False
23. True
24. False
25. False
26. True
27. False
28. True
29. True
30. True
31. False
32. False
33. False
34. True
35. False
36. False
37. True
38. True
39. True
40. True
41. True
42. True
43. True
44. True
45. True
46. True
47. False
48. True
49. True
50. False
51. False
52. True
53. True
54. True
55. False
56. False
57. True
58. True
59. False
60. False
61. True
62. False
63. True
64. False
65. False
66. True
67. True
68. False
69. True
70. False
71. False
72. False
73. True
74. True
75. False

NORMS

Rank for College Students	For Lower Social Strata		For Upper Social Strata	
	RAW SCORE OR NUMBER RIGHT		RAW SCORE OR NUMBER RIGHT	
	Men	Women	Men	Women
Highest fifth	58–75	45–75	56–75	60–75
Second fifth	53–57	38–44	51–55	55–59
Middle fifth	49–52	31–37	48–50	52–54
Fourth fifth	42–48	23–30	45–47	47–51
Lowest fifth	0–41	0–22	0–44	0–46

The most helpful interpretation of the scores on the "Social Knowledge Tests" is to score both the Lower and Upper Social Strata sections and note the difference or similarity between the two rankings, connecting them by a line, as in these four examples:

Quintile on Lower	Quintile on Upper	Quintile on Lower	Quintile on Upper
5———————5		5	5
4	4	4	4
3	3	3	3
2	2	2	2
1	1	1————————1	

Quintile on Lower	Quintile on Upper	Quintile on Lower	Quintile on Upper
5	5	5	5
4	4	4	4
3	3	3	3
2	2	2	2
1	1	1	1

A test of personality maturity

A person may have high abstract intelligence and still lack personality maturity. He may be bright in the study of certain books, but he may never have studied the kinds of books or had the experiences that are necessary to make him a well-adjusted, mature adult.

Maturity is, after all, not a matter of age. Some young people are relatively mature, and some old people are still children in their points of view and attitudes toward important aspects of life. In Chapter 9 we described the way in which the following personality-maturity test was developed. Apply the questions to yourself and refer to the key on pages 621 and 622 for the proper scoring. Then consult the table at the end of the key, entitled "What Your Score Means."

PERSONALITY-MATURITY TEST.* Check **one** and only **one** of the possible answers to each question.

1. The manner in which my employers or teachers have treated me is that they
   - ☐ a. always tried to make my life miserable by constant nagging.
   - ☐ b. had a tendency to criticize me whenever they could.
   - ☐ c. were indifferent to me so long as I conformed with their regulations or performed work satisfactorily.
   - ☐ d. helped me in my work a great deal.
   - ☐ e. helped me and praised me for my conscientiousness.
   - ☐ f. condemned me when at fault and praised me when I deserved it.

2. When taking part in card games or athletic contests where my side or I fail to win, I usually react to the defeat
   - ☐ a. by studying possible reasons for the defeat in order to improve my skill.
   - ☐ b. by admiration of the perfection of the other person's skill.
   - ☐ c. by feeling inferior to the other person.
   - ☐ d. by feeling that, at any rate, I'm superior in other things.
   - ☐ e. by realizing the relative unimportance of defeat or victory in such games and promptly forgetting the defeat.

   - ☐ f. by thinking the other fellow got the breaks that time; maybe I will next time.

3. When forced to give up a plan or ambition such as to go to college, to make a fortune, to marry a certain person, etc., I find that I
   - ☐ a. am sure that I shall be unhappy for the rest of my life.
   - ☐ b. have so many interests that I soon have something to take its place.
   - ☐ c. am determined to get it at any cost if it takes the rest of my life.
   - ☐ d. am sure that God's will is for the best.
   - ☐ e. try to reconcile myself to the loss and make the best of it.
   - ☐ f. figure that's my luck and I shouldn't have hoped for anything in the first place.
   - ☐ g. never had a plan or ambition of vital importance that I had to give up.
   - ☐ h. am unhappy for some time but get over it.

4. The extent to which people seem to like me is
   - ☐ a. either very much or not at all.
   - ☐ b. people like me a little but not enough to have me for their best friend.

---

* From *Finding Yourself in Your Work* by Harry Walker Hepner. Copyright, 1937, by D. Appleton-Century Company, Inc. Copyright, 1931, 1932, by The Psychological Corporation.

☐ *c.* everyone seems to like me at first meeting.

☐ *d.* people like me only if they know me very well.

☐ *e.* no one likes me.

☐ *f.* many people like me to some extent.

☐ *g.* I cannot tell.

☐ *h.* people like me if I can do them a favor.

☐ *i.* people like me at first but later they change their opinion.

5. My tendency to call the attention of others to my failures, defeats, or inabilities is

☐ *a.* I always tell people about them whenever they seem interested.

☐ *b.* I tell people about my failures only when it's incidental to the conversation.

☐ *c.* I very seldom mention my defeats to anyone to avoid seeking sympathy.

☐ *d.* I never mention my defeats; people think I'm either looking for sympathy or admitting my inferiority.

6. People whose opinions differ from mine

☐ *a.* are unsocial and peculiar.

☐ *b.* are egotistical.

☐ *c.* are in need of more training.

☐ *d.* are justified in having their own opinions.

☐ *e.* simply differ from me in background.

☐ *f.* are in need of more years of experience.

☐ *g.* are usually superior to me in intelligence.

☐ *h.* are more informed on the particular subject.

7. The kind of opponent I prefer in a game or contest is one who is

☐ *a.* a master and my superior, because I have a greater chance of improving my skill.

☐ *b.* somewhat superior, because it makes the contest more stimulating to me.

☐ *c.* an equal, since we both do our best and have an equal chance to win.

☐ *d.* an inferior whom I know I can beat. (Then I feel I'm superior in one thing at least.)

☐ *e.* a good sport, regardless of his skill.

8. Life, for me, is worth while in the extent to which I have the privilege of living in a political, social, and economic world that

☐ *a.* is on a simpler scale than this present organized society.

☐ *b.* would remain as it is now.

☐ *c.* is orderly and seemingly logical in its changes for the better.

☐ *d.* is in a state of change where I can utilize its changing requirements for my own development and the satisfactions of others.

☐ *e.* is constantly changing.

☐ *f.* is considerably improved over this world.

9. My tendency to argue with my associates is

☐ *a.* I'm always ready for a good, hot argument.

☐ *b.* I usually argue if I'm at all interested.

☐ *c.* I seldom argue with anyone; I prefer an intellectual argument with myself.

☐ *d.* I dislike to get into arguments and avoid them as much as possible.

☐ *e.* I hate arguments.

☐ *f.* I argue only in a free-for-all discussion.

☐ *g.* I like to test the other person's knowledge.

10. When a person not in my family criticizes me, my usual reaction is to

☐ *a.* analyze the critic as to why he criticized me.

☐ *b.* ask him for the reason of the criticism.

☐ *c.* say nothing and forget about it.

☐ *d.* criticize him when I get the chance.

☐ *e.* defend myself verbally if I think I am right.

☐ *f.* say nothing but hold a grudge against him.

11. In order to succeed in a vocation, family influence, "pull," or "drag" is

☐ *a.* always harmful. Eventually it will be difficult for the benefited person to face future problems without his usual "drag."

☐ *b.* usually harmful rather than helpful.

☐ *c.* helpful only in getting started in one's vocation.

☐ *d.* helpful at times but not necessary.

☐ *e.* always helpful but not necessary.

☐ *f.* necessary in order to achieve prominence.

□ *g.* always helpful and always necessary.

12. I believe that the extent to which an individual can learn to enjoy life nobly depends upon

□ *a.* the way in which he responds to his environment (assuming that the environment is reasonably good) and uses it to develop his natural abilities.

□ *b.* the way in which he responds to an environment that has many facilities for his development.

□ *c.* the way in which he utilizes his environment, even though the facilities of that environment are poor.

13. My reaction to the thought of my own death is to

□ *a.* greatly abhor the thought.

□ *b.* dislike the thought but do not express my feeling.

□ *c.* take it for granted as an eventual inevitability and not think about it often.

□ *d.* frequently speculate about it, wishing that I had the nerve to become experimental.

□ *e.* secretly wish that I were dead but not often say it to others.

□ *f.* openly wish that I were dead.

□ *g.* never give it a thought.

14. The extent to which I try to make a favorable impression on other people is to

□ *a.* make definite plans and devote much time to it.

□ *b.* seldom plan to do so in advance but if the opportunity arises try to make a good impression.

□ *c.* devote a slight amount of time to it.

□ *d.* dislike the practice in others and never do it myself.

15. When confronted by an unusual problem in work or study

□ *a.* I never hesitate to seek help from someone who knows more about it.

□ *b.* I usually ask some close friend to help me.

□ *c.* I very seldom bother anyone enough to ask him to help me.

□ *d.* I usually ask a friend if I am sure he knows more about it.

□ *e.* I make every effort to solve it before asking anyone for help.

16. Life, for me, is worth while to the extent to which I have the privilege of living among friends and relatives who are

□ *a.* more congenial than the present ones.

□ *b.* stimulating intellectually.

□ *c.* I need more friends and relatives than I now have in order to be happy.

□ *d.* the ones I now have are sufficient to stimulate me satisfyingly.

□ *e.* they are unnecessary for my happiness.

□ *f.* interested in the things that interest me, common interests.

17. When a member of my family criticizes me severely or nags me, my usual reaction is to

□ *a.* resent it but say nothing.

□ *b.* keep peace in the family by agreeing with the other person and flattering him.

□ *c.* say nothing but try to get even later.

□ *d.* maintain my self-respect by arguing back.

□ *e.* try to understand the reason why the other person is criticizing or nagging me.

□ *f.* get angry and argue.

18. My feeling about calling the attention of others to my activities, abilities, or achievements is

□ *a.* I seek the attention of others and do it deliberately.

□ *b.* I seek the attention of others but do not do it obviously.

□ *c.* I like the attention of others but do not solicit it.

□ *d.* I hate to call attention to myself in any way and always avoid speaking about myself.

19. The importance of my personal appearance to me is

□ *a.* very great; I spend much time in studying and improving it.

□ *b.* moderate, and I devote only a small amount of time to it.

□ *c.* so slight that I spend only enough time at it to keep from looking conspicuous.

□ *d.* of little or no interest to me.

□ *e.* very important to me, but I spend only a moderate amount of time on it.

20. I find enjoyment in the companionship and friendship of
   - ☐ *a.* members of the opposite sex; they understand me better.
   - ☐ *b.* people who are congenial to me regardless of their sex.
   - ☐ *c.* members of my own sex because I get along with them better.
   - ☐ *d.* I do not feel the need of companionship or friendship with anyone of either sex.

21. The way in which I react to religion is
   - ☐ *a.* that I do not personally need any religion but think that it is necessary for most people.
   - ☐ *b.* I read about and observe various religions and eventually may decide upon one for myself.
   - ☐ *c.* I am inventing a religion of my own which I hope will some day be satisfactory for me.
   - ☐ *d.* I now have a religion which satisfies me.
   - ☐ *e.* the religion of my parents is most satisfactory to me.
   - ☐ *f.* the religion of my parents is not satisfactory but I accept it.
   - ☐ *g.* that religion is very burdensome to me but necessary.

22. The extent to which I study and read about social or economic changes in other countries of the world is
   - ☐ *a.* I am not interested in conditions in other parts of the world.
   - ☐ *b.* I am too busy solving my own problems to think about those in other parts of the world.
   - ☐ *c.* I am trying to locate accurate information about conditions there.
   - ☐ *d.* I am more interested in conditions in other parts of the world than in those here.
   - ☐ *e.* I should like nothing better than to study and read about conditions in other parts of the world.
   - ☐ *f.* I am interested in studying conditions in other parts of the world in order to make comparisons with my own part of the world.

23. When forced to speak in public, I find that
   - ☐ *a.* it is extremely difficult and causes me embarrassment or stuttering.
   - ☐ *b.* it is difficult, but I can manage it without much evidence of embarrassment.
   - ☐ *c.* It is a challenge to my self-respect so that I do it without flinching.
   - ☐ *d.* I can usually speak without much effort.
   - ☐ *e.* I always enjoy speaking to an audience.
   - ☐ *f.* it is very difficult unless I am sure of the friendliness of the audience.

24. The extent to which I study or read about social, political, or economic changes in my own country is
   - ☐ *a.* I read much relative to them.
   - ☐ *b.* I read only those things I'm especially interested in.
   - ☐ *c.* I read them only when there's nothing else to read or when I have to.
   - ☐ *d.* I read them incidentally as I read the newspapers and periodicals.
   - ☐ *e.* I read them only enough to be able to discuss them intelligently.

25. My reaction to seeing news items published about myself is
   - ☐ *a.* I enjoy seeing them and often show them to my friends.
   - ☐ *b.* I rather like to see my name in print, but it's not very important to me.
   - ☐ *c.* seeing my name in print is of no interest to me at all.
   - ☐ *d.* seeing my name in print amuses or disgusts me.
   - ☐ *e.* I am proud to show people my name in print if the item isn't derogatory.
   - ☐ *f.* I intensely dislike to see my name in print.

26. My attitude toward omens, premonitions, etc., is that
   - ☐ *a.* in my life I have known them to indicate almost without exception success or failure of some activity.
   - ☐ *b.* they usually predict the success or failure of some activity.
   - ☐ *c.* I can't decide whether it is chance or whether they actually do predict.
   - ☐ *d.* I don't believe they ever predict anything for anyone.
   - ☐ *e.* I realize they are false but find myself heeding them.

27. The extent of my activity in group or social meetings is
   - ☐ *a.* I always try to lead in the discussions.
   - ☐ *b.* I take part in the discussions only if I know something about the subject.

□ c. I do not take part in the discussions unless I am positive of the worth and truth of what I am saying.

□ d. I never take part in the discussion because I very much dislike talking in a group.

□ e. I take part to keep things moving but not to lead.

28. The extent to which I visit fortune-tellers is

□ a. I consult them only when confronted with a serious dilemma and can't decide what to do.

□ b. I visit them sometimes when friends I know are going to do so.

□ c. I only consult them when I wish to see if I can discover the techniques used.

□ d. I never go to a fortune-teller; I think they're fakes.

□ e. I go there for entertainment.

29. The extent to which I take financial risks is

□ a. I take many serious risks because if I win I win a great deal.

□ b. I take serious risks only when the balance is in my favor.

□ c. I take no serious risks; the losses would overwhelm me if I didn't win.

□ d. I take a few minor chances since I wouldn't be greatly injured should I lose.

□ e. I take no chances of any kind; I prefer to be safe where I am now.

30. When emotional problems or difficulties confront me

□ a. I enjoy them because I love to overcome them; they stimulate me.

□ b. they don't interest me particularly; I'm used to them.

□ c. they are just another obstacle in my path which temporarily impedes me.

□ d. I have no emotional problems or difficulties.

□ e. I stick them out although they wear me down.

31. In regard to nature, I believe that

□ a. nature is intrinsically good; if I could be in complete harmony with nature I could avoid all evil.

□ b. nature is essentially good, but it must be subject to control by man.

□ c. nature is evil; if it could be completely subjugated we could eliminate all vice.

□ d. only a few things in nature are innately bad, but they do not cause us great worry now that science has shown us that even innate mechanisms can be used advantageously.

□ e. nature is neither good nor bad; it simply offers material with possibilities and limitations for the individual's development.

32. My attitude toward the world in general is that

□ a. it is filled with evil; the faster I can escape it the better off I shall be.

□ b. it has a great many temptations so that it is difficult for anyone to remain good.

□ c. the world is an interesting panorama; I am interested in utilizing my time in investigating it.

□ d. the world is good if people would live lives of worth and true goodness.

□ e. I live only once, so I intend to enjoy it instead of trying to explain it.

□ f. I am a part of the world, whether good or evil, so I intend to live to the fullest extent of my capabilities.

33. Assuming that everyone wants enough money to satisfy his needs for food, clothing, and shelter, I also want more money

□ a. so that I can have a better house, larger car, more beautiful clothes, etc.

□ b. to carry out plans that I would like to put into effect, such as improving my business or professional ability.

□ c. I don't want any more money.

□ d. to be able to share it with others.

□ e. I don't want any more money because I think it destroys more happiness than it creates.

□ f. I want enough money so that I can do as I please.

34. When I read the daily papers, my attitude toward items relating to my vocation (managing a home is considered a vocation) is

□ a. I always read items relating to my vocation.

□ b. I read only those items that especially interest me.

□ c. I very seldom read anything about my vocation; I have enough of that all day long.

□ d. I never read anything about it. I hate it.

KEY TO PERSONALITY-MATURITY TEST

Subtract total minus score from total plus score.

1. (a) −3
   (b) −2
   (c) +4
   (d) 0
   (e) −1
   (f) +6

2. (a) +4
   (b) 0
   (c) −3
   (d) −3
   (e) +8
   (f) −4

3. (a) −3
   (b) +10
   (c) 0
   (d) −5
   (e) +2
   (f) −3
   (g) +6
   (h) 0

4. (a) 0
   (b) −3
   (c) 0
   (d) 0
   (e) 0
   (f) +8
   (g) −2
   (h) −2
   (i) 0

5. (a) −3
   (b) +8
   (c) +2
   (d) −1

6. (a) −2
   (b) 0
   (c) −3
   (d) +8
   (e) +4
   (f) −2
   (g) −1
   (h) −1

7. (a) −2
   (b) +6
   (c) 0
   (d) −5
   (e) +8

8. (a) 0
   (b) −5
   (c) +6
   (d) +6
   (e) +2
   (f) −3

9. (a) −2
   (b) +8
   (c) 0
   (d) 0
   (e) −4
   (f) 0
   (g) 0

10. (a) +8
    (b) +6
    (c) −3
    (d) −2
    (e) +4
    (f) −4

11. (a) −2
    (b) 0
    (c) +8
    (d) +8
    (e) 0
    (f) −4
    (g) −4

12. (a) −1
    (b) −2
    (c) +8

13. (a) −2
    (b) −3
    (c) +10
    (d) −1
    (e) −2
    (f) −3
    (g) −1

14. (a) −1
    (b) +8
    (c) −2
    (d) −2

15. (a) +6
    (b) −3
    (c) 0
    (d) 0
    (e) +2

16. (a) −4
    (b) +8
    (c) −2
    (d) 0
    (e) −4
    (f) +4

17. (a) 0
    (b) −3
    (c) −3
    (d) +2
    (e) +8
    (f) −2

18. (a) −1
    (b) −4
    (c) +8
    (d) 0

19. (a) −2
    (b) +4
    (c) 0
    (d) −3
    (e) +4

20. (a) −3
    (b) +8
    (c) −3
    (d) −3

21. (a) −2
    (b) +6
    (c) +4
    (d) +8
    (e) −2
    (f) −3
    (g) −3

22. (a) −5
    (b) 0
    (c) +6
    (d) −2
    (e) 0
    (f) +8

23. (a) −4
    (b) +6
    (c) 0
    (d) +4
    (e) +2
    (f) 0

24. (a) +6
    (b) 0
    (c) −4
    (d) 0
    (e) +4

25. (a) −3
    (b) +8
    (c) 0
    (d) 0
    (e) −2
    (f) −3

26. (a) −5
    (b) −4
    (c) −3
    (d) +10
    (e) −4

27. (a) +4
    (b) +6
    (c) 0
    (d) −4
    (e) 0

28. (a) −4
    (b) −3
    (c) −3
    (d) +10
    (e) 0

29. (a) 0
    (b) +6
    (c) 0
    (d) +8
    (e) −4

30. (a) 0
    (b) +4
    (c) +6
    (d) 0
    (e) −1

31. (a) −4
    (b) −4
    (c) −3
    (d) 0
    (e) +10

32. (a) −3
    (b) −3
    (c) +6
    (d) 0
    (e) −2
    (f) +10

33. (a) −2
    (b) +8
    (c) −2
    (d) 0
    (e) −2
    (f) 0

34. (a) +4
    (b) +4
    (c) −3
    (d) −4

WHAT YOUR SCORE MEANS

Score	
0–99	Below average for people of the general population
100	Average for people of the general population
101–248	Above average for people of general population
162	Average for college students

Executive reaction pattern test

Underline the term or degree which most adequately describes your likes, beliefs, record, and so on. Do not try to think of what you would or should do, but answer according to what you have done.

1. Number of meetings of a technical nature or of trade associations attended—local organizations as well as national or state:
   - ☐ *a.* Ten or more per year.
   - ☐ *b.* From 5 to 10.
   - ☐ *c.* From 1 to 5.
   - ☐ *d.* Few or none.
   - ☐ *e.* None.

2. Activity in trade or technical association meetings:
   - ☐ *a.* Took very active part as a leader.
   - ☐ *b.* Frequently took part in discussions.
   - ☐ *c.* Occasionally asked questions.
   - ☐ *d.* Rarely took part.
   - ☐ *e.* Never took part.

3. Time devoted to personal appearance:
   - ☐ *a.* Large amount.
   - ☐ *b.* Considerable amount.
   - ☐ *c.* Moderate amount.
   - ☐ *d.* Few minutes a day.
   - ☐ *e.* Neglect it.

4. Amount of study given to subjects related to my business since leaving school:
   - ☐ *a.* Spent all available time on such subjects.
   - ☐ *b.* Studied business subjects frequently.
   - ☐ *c.* Occasionally spent time in study of my business.
   - ☐ *d.* Seldom gave any.
   - ☐ *e.* Never gave any.

5. When I have read the daily papers, I have read items relating to business:
   - ☐ *a.* Almost exclusively.
   - ☐ *b.* Much of the time.
   - ☐ *c.* Frequently.
   - ☐ *d.* Occasionally.
   - ☐ *e.* Never, except by accident.

6. My record of leadership in my youth:
   - ☐ *a.* Frequently organized games, teams, or clubs.
   - ☐ *b.* A leader in activities.
   - ☐ *c.* Little marked leadership.
   - ☐ *d.* Willing to follow other leaders.
   - ☐ *e.* Disregarded playmates.

7. I actually associated with men whose ability was:
   - ☐ *a.* Much greater than mine.
   - ☐ *b.* Somewhat greater.
   - ☐ *c.* About the same.
   - ☐ *d.* Slightly less than my own.
   - ☐ *e.* Considerably less.

8. When I was not busy taking recreation or taking care of routine matters and had some time for thinking along any line, I devised new methods, plans, or systems. The percentage of such available time devoted to improvements was from:
   - ☐ *a.* 75–100 per cent
   - ☐ *b.* 50–75 " "
   - ☐ *c.* 25–50 " "
   - ☐ *d.* 5–25 " "
   - ☐ *e.* 2–5 " "
   - ☐ *f.* 0–2 " "

9. My thinking of improvements dealt with problems relating to (underline as many as apply):
   - ☐ *a.* Organization of company as a whole.
   - ☐ *b.* Organization of work within one department.
   - ☐ *c.* Organization of work between departments.
   - ☐ *d.* Stimulating employees.
   - ☐ *e.* Cutting costs.
   - ☐ *f.* Increasing sales.
   - ☐ *g.* Better service to customers.
   - ☐ *h.* New mechanical inventions.
   - ☐ *i.* Better financing.
   - ☐ *j.* Helping society in general.

10. My family influence has:
    - ☐ *a.* Greatly stimulated me to do my best.
    - ☐ *b.* Stimulated me slightly.
    - ☐ *c.* Had no effect—good or bad.
    - ☐ *d.* Had slightly negative effect.
    - ☐ *e.* Had pronouncedly negative effect.

11. A rival or rivals:
- ☐ a. Stimulated me strongly and I tried to beat them.
- ☐ b. Stimulated me slightly.
- ☐ c. Did not affect me at all.
- ☐ d. Discouraged me slightly.
- ☐ e. Discouraged me greatly.

12. I met my financial obligations:
- ☐ a. Always promptly.
- ☐ b. Fairly promptly.
- ☐ c. As best I could.
- ☐ d. Sometimes with failure.
- ☐ e. Sometimes with neglect.

13. In times of failure or discouragement:
- ☐ a. I persisted.
- ☐ b. I persisted to a limited extent.
- ☐ c. I thought of ways out of the difficulties and applied them to the problems.
- ☐ d. I thought of remedies but did not apply them.
- ☐ e. I just quit and regretted that I was not trained to solve them.

14. My energy supply:
- ☐ a. Compels me to keep busy at all times.
- ☐ b. Is plentiful.
- ☐ c. Is enough to meet my needs.
- ☐ d. Is small and I force myself to keep going.
- ☐ e. Prevents my attaining many possibilities.

15. My attitude toward risks:
- ☐ a. I took many serious business risks.
- ☐ b. I took a few serious business risks.
- ☐ c. I took no serious risks.
- ☐ d. I took a few minor chances.
- ☐ e. I took no serious or minor chances.

16. The extent to which I tried to make a favorable impression on important persons:
- ☐ a. I made definite plans and devoted much time to impressing the right persons.
- ☐ b. I devoted a slight amount of time to making a good impression.
- ☐ c. I seldom planned to do so in advance, but, if opportunity arose, I tried to make a good impression.
- ☐ d. I never noticed such opportunities.
- ☐ e. I disliked the practice in others and never indulged myself.

17. Problems or difficulties around me:
- ☐ a. Stimulated me greatly.

- ☐ b. Stimulated me mildly.
- ☐ c. Had no effect.
- ☐ d. Caused slight discouragement.
- ☐ e. Caused pronounced discouragement.

18. Criticisms from others regarding my work have:
- ☐ a. Greatly stimulated me to do better.
- ☐ b. Slightly stimulated me to do better.
- ☐ c. Had no effect.
- ☐ d. Worried me.
- ☐ e. Caused resentment.

19. Anticipating problems before they arose:
- ☐ a. Gave them much thought.
- ☐ b. Gave them some thought.
- ☐ c. Planned to meet present problems only.
- ☐ d. Let all problems take care of themselves.
- ☐ e. Passed them on to experts.

20. When conversing with superiors:
- ☐ a. I felt at ease and talked freely.
- ☐ b. I talked freely, but was not at perfect ease.
- ☐ c. I talked fairly freely, but was ill at ease.
- ☐ d. I talked little, because I was ill at ease.
- ☐ e. I felt inferior and said nothing.

21. When conversing with inferiors:
- ☐ a. I tried to make them feel at ease.
- ☐ b. I let them talk.
- ☐ c. I talked more than they.
- ☐ d. I monopolized the conversation.
- ☐ e. I tried to make them feel inferior.
- ☐ f. I did not think of any differences between us.

22. In group discussions:
- ☐ a. I said nothing.
- ☐ b. I spoke occasionally.
- ☐ c. I spoke when I had something worth saying.
- ☐ d. I dominated the conversation.

23. The amount of time I devoted to work has been:
- ☐ a. Far too much to enjoy life fully.
- ☐ b. About the right amount.
- ☐ c. Too much.
- ☐ d. Too little.
- ☐ e. Decidedly too little.

24. Ability to influence others:
- ☐ a. I could influence large numbers of persons.

☐ *b.* I could influence small numbers of persons.
☐ *c.* I could influence some individuals.
☐ *d.* I could influence those who were under obligations to me.
☐ *e.* Had difficulty in influencing anyone.
☐ *f.* Don't know—I never tried.

25. The number of technical or trade journals I read fairly regularly:
☐ *a.* 5 or more.
☐ *b.* 3 to 5.
☐ *c.* 2 or 3.
☐ *d.* 1 or 2.
☐ *e.* None.

26. My interest in my past work has been:
☐ *a.* Very great and enjoyable.
☐ *b.* Usually enjoyable.
☐ *c.* Slightly enjoyable.

☐ *d.* Little or none.
☐ *e.* Mostly negative.

27. The number of my friends who would help me in putting across a really good idea:
☐ *a.* A great many—50 or more.
☐ *b.* Many—10 to 50.
☐ *c.* Few—5 to 10.
☐ *d.* Very few—1 to 5.
☐ *e.* None.

28. The extent to which I have gone out of my way to help others:
☐ *a.* Often inconvenienced myself.
☐ *b.* Occasionally inconvenienced myself.
☐ *c.* Seldom inconvenienced myself.
☐ *d.* Never inconvenienced myself.
☐ *e.* Believed in taking care of myself and in letting others do the same.

KEY TO THE EXECUTIVE REACTION PATTERN TEST

1. (a) +10	2. (a) +6	3. (a) 0	4. (a) +3
(b) +2	(b) +4	(b) +2	(b) 0
(c) −3	(c) −6	(c) −5	(c) −1
(d) −5	(d) −2	(d) −2	(d) −8
(e) −5	(e) −6	(e) −3	(e) −8

5. (a) +6	6. (a) 0	7. (a) +1	8. (a) +6
(b) +2	(b) +3	(b) +3	(b) +5
(c) 0	(c) 0	(c) −5	(c) 0
(d) −6	(d) −5	(d) 0	(d) −1
(e) −8	(e) 0	(e) 0	(e) −5
			(f) −5

*9. (a) +2	10. (a) +2	11. (a) +3	12. (a) +4
(b) 0	(b) −5	(b) −1	(b) −4
(c) +2	(c) −3	(c) −2	(c) −5
(d) +2	(d) +3	(d) 0	(d) −5
(e) 0	(e) −3	(e) −5	(e) −5
(f) 0			
(g) 0			
(h) +2			
(i) +2			
(j) +2			

13. (a) +4	14. (a) +5	15. (a) +5	16. (a) −6
(b) −3	(b) +2	(b) 0	(b) +2
(c) −3	(c) −2	(c) −2	(c) +1
(d) 0	(d) 0	(d) −3	(d) 0
(e) 0	(e) 0	(e) −5	(e) 0

17.		18.		19.		20.	
(a)	+4	(a)	+2	(a)	+4	(a)	+4
(b)	−2	(b)	−2	(b)	0	(b)	−2
(c)	−5	(c)	0	(c)	−3	(c)	−4
(d)	−5	(d)	−4	(d)	−4	(d)	−4
(e)	−5	(e)	+4	(e)	+5	(e)	−4

21.		22.		23.		24.	
(a)	+3	(a)	−5	(a)	−2	(a)	+4
(b)	+6	(b)	−5	(b)	+6	(b)	+2
(c)	−3	(c)	+5	(c)	0	(c)	−1
(d)	−3	(d)	+5	(d)	−2	(d)	−4
(e)	−3			(e)	−2	(e)	−4
(f)	−3					(f)	−4

25.		26.		27.		28.	
(a)	+10	(a)	+5	(a)	+10	(a)	+4
(b)	+5	(b)	−3	(b)	0	(b)	−4
(c)	0	(c)	0	(c)	−4	(c)	−4
(d)	−4	(d)	−6	(d)	0	(d)	−4
(e)	+2	(e)	−6	(e)	0	(e)	−4

* Number 9 should also be scored on the total number of items underlined. If only one or two items are underlined, give no extra credit. If three or more items are underlined, give a plus score equal to the total number of items underlined. Example: if the five items *c, d, h, i, j* are underlined, each item having a + 2 score, the total score for question No. 9 would be 10 + 5, or 15.

Assign plus and minus values to your own answers according to the above key. Add all the values having a plus sign. Add all those having a minus sign. Then add the two sums algebraically. Find the position of your final score in one of the six grades in the extreme left-hand column of the probability table. Read to the right and the per cent figures will indicate, statistically, the percentage of businessmen who made the same score in the test.

Example: Of the businessmen who made a score of minus 40 to minus 120, 100 per cent were in the lower-most category of business position; of those who made a score of plus 81 and above, 14 per cent were in the middle, 29 per cent in the upper middle, and 57 per cent in the uppermost classification of position held in business.

PROBABILITY TABLE SHOWING THE RELATION BETWEEN SCORES IN EXECUTIVE REACTION PATTERN TEST AND CLASSIFICATION OF POSITION IN BUSINESS

Score in Test	Lower-most	Lower middle	Middle	Upper-middle	Upper-most
+ 81 and up	...	...	14%	29%	57%
+ 51 to + 80	...	13%	22%	22%	43%
+ 21 to + 50	7%	30%	33%	21%	9%
− 9 to + 20	15%	39%	34%	9%	3%
− 10 to − 39	59%	18%	18%	5%	...
− 40 to − 121	100%	...	...	...	...
Mean	− 23.1	+ 14.8	+ 23.0	+ 40.5	+ 62.9
Median	− 25.0	+ 13.5	+ 26.0	+ 41.0	+ 66.0

Answers to tests in text

INTERPRETATION OF ANSWERS TO PRE-MARITAL TEST—"Am I Well-Balanced?" (page 260)

The first 10 questions should be answered *yes*, the last 10, *no*. If you answered 15 or more correctly, you would appear emotionally well-balanced and in that respect likely to be happy in marriage. A score of 10 or less suggests that you may not yet be ready to assume the responsibilities of marriage.

On the basis of rating scales, using extremes (quintiles), the validity of this test is about .40. Copyright of test and scoring by Clifford R. Adams, Associate Professor of Psychology, Pennsylvania State University.

WHICH ONE WOULD YOU HIRE? Answers to quiz on pages 286, 287

Here is the actual sales ranking of the salesmen whose records are given. How right were you?

1st: Former doctor	5th: Veteran
2nd: Rose from ranks	6th: Former failure
3rd: Old-timer	7th: Had own business
4th: Smooth operator	8th: Social register

The results of a study of the reliability of judgments of intelligence from photographs are reported in the *Journal of Abnormal and Social Psychology*, July 1939. Care was taken in this experiment to use a large number of photographs and a group of "judges" accustomed to sizing up people on relatively short notice.

Photographs of the "passport" type were taken of 150 first-year male college students, all of whom were taken in the same position, at the same distance from the camera and facing it squarely. The intelligence of the subjects was estimated by the Thurstone Intelligence Test IV given by a person experienced in testing. The raw scores were found to range from 35 to 150.

Subsequently the photographs, numbered for identification purposes, were given to a group of ten experienced personnel managers and social workers with careful instructions to classify them, according to the subject's intelligence, into eight groups, ranging from *lowest* to *highest*.

It was found that all the judges estimated intelligence with an approximately equal degree of inaccuracy; the pooled estimates of the judges had an equally low correlation with intelligence ($.07 \pm .055$); and the judges were no more accurate in estimating extremes of intelligence than they were in estimating average or near-average levels.

ANSWER TO FIVE-CIRCLE CHARACTER TEST (page 322)

If you have a plus score on any one trial, the probabilities are very great that you "peeped."

ANSWERS TO SAFETY VIOLATIONS PICTURE PUZZLE (page 386)

In the drawing which depicts a scene in a bottling house operation, there are shown thirty-four distinct unsafe practices or conditions, as follows:

1. Man in foreground is removing foreign body from another's eye with dirty handkerchief instead of using proper first-aid facilities.
2. Man is smoking in room where alcoholic beverages are being bottled and near can of gasoline.
3. Welder does not have electric arc covered and is welding near can of gasoline.
4. Welder has sharp protruding tools in his pocket.
5. Welder has sleeves rolled up while welding.
6. Welder's pliers, chisel, and so on, are lying in aisleway.
7. Cable from welding machine is stretched across aisle.
8. Girl on bottling line has long flowing hair, uncovered. It may get caught in the moving machinery.
9. Same girl is wearing loose bracelets on arm.
10. She is also wearing shoes with high heels.
11. Stool on which she is sitting has broken back-rest and braces.
12. Man at capper has grip around bottle and might be cut if the bottle broke.
13. There is no guard on capper, and operator is not wearing goggles.
14. There is no guard on filler pump belt.

15. Man is oiling moving machinery.
16. Same man has waste rag hanging from pocket, where it might get caught in moving machinery.
17. Same man has loose sleeves that might get caught in moving machinery.
18. Man carrying cartons has them stacked so high he can not see in front of him.
19. Same man has hole in sole of shoe.
20. Man in right background is climbing over power conveyor.
21. Girl at left is running.
22. Man is carrying ladder in a hazardous manner and not looking where he is going.
23. Fire extinguisher is blocked by cases.
24. Hand truck is in middle of floor.
25. Ladder on which man is working is set up incorrectly.
26. There is broken glass in back door.
27. Cartons are thrown across aisle.
28. Bucket is set in aisle.
29. Section of pipe is lying in aisleway.
30. Labels are scattered on floor.
31. Broken bottles are on floor.
32. Lid is off sewer along bottling line.
33. Bottle caps are scattered on floor.
34. There are no sprinklers in building.

Answer to Test on page 573

Copy A, "Today Not Tomorrow," outpulled Copy B, "It's Fun . . . ," by 19.7 per cent.

Answer to Project Question 1, page 581

Heading d, "Men Who Know It All Are Not Invited to Read This Page."

Author Index

629

Subject Index